American Poets, 1880-1945
Third Series
Part 2: N-Z

Dictionary of Literary Biography

Documentary Series

Yearbooks

Dictionary of Literary Biography • Volume Fifty-four

American Poets, 1880-1945
Third Series
Part 2: N-Z

Edited by
Peter Quartermain
University of British Columbia

A Bruccoli Clark Book
Gale Research Company • Book Tower • Detroit, Michigan 48226

1987

Advisory Board for
DICTIONARY OF LITERARY BIOGRAPHY

William Stanley Braithwaite, Introduction to *Anthology of Magazine Verse for 1913* (1913) (pp. 605-607) reprinted by permission of William Stanley Braithwaite, Jr., the Estate of William Stanley Braithwaite.

Amy Lowell, Preface to *Some Imagist Poets* (1915) (pp. 610-611) reprinted by permission of G. d'Andelot Belin and Brinton P. Roberts, Trustees under the Will of Amy Lowell.

Harriet Monroe, Introduction to *The New Poetry: An Anthology* (1917) (pp. 615-618) reprinted by permission of Marguerite F. Fetcher, the Estate of Harriet Monroe.

Louis Untermeyer, Introduction to *Modern American Poetry: An Introduction* (1919) (pp. 624-625) reprinted by permission of Norma A. Untermeyer, the Estate of Louis Untermeyer.

James Weldon Johnson, Preface to *The Book of American Negro Poetry* (1922) (pp. 628-641) and Preface to the Revised Edition (1931) (pp. 641-643), copyright 1922, 1931 by Harcourt Brace Jovanovich, Inc.; renewed 1950 by Grace Johnson, 1959 by Mrs. Grace Nail Johnson. Reprinted by permission of the publisher.

Countee Cullen, Foreword to *Caroling Dusk: An Anthology of Verse by Negro Poets* (1927) (pp. 646-647). Copyright © 1927 by Harper & Row, Publishers, Inc. Renewed 1955 by Ida M. Cullen. Reprinted by permission of Harper & Row, Publishers, Inc.

Donald Davidson, Foreword to *Fugitives: An Anthology of Verse* (1928) (pp. 650-651) reprinted by permission of Mary Davidson Bell, the Estate of Donald Davidson.

Ezra Pound, Preface to *Active Anthology* (1933) (pp. 653-658), from Ezra Pound, *Selected Prose, 1909-1965*. Copyright © 1973 by the Estate of Ezra Pound.

James Laughlin IV, Preface to *New Directions in Prose and Poetry* (1936) (pp. 660-662). Copyright © 1936 by New Directions.

Oscar Williams, Introduction to *A Little Treasury of Modern Poetry, English & American* (1946) (pp. 664-672). Copyright 1946 Charles Scribner's Sons; copyright renewed. Reprinted by permission of Charles Scribner's Sons.

Library of Congress Cataloging-in-Publication Data

American poets, 1880-1945, third series.

(Dictionary of literary biography; v. 54)
"A Bruccoli Clark book."
Includes index.
1. American poetry—20th century—History and criticism. 2. American poetry—19th century—History and criticism. 3. American poetry—Bio-bibliography. 4. Poets, American—Biography—Dictionaries. I. Quartermain, Peter. II. Series.
PS324.A44 1987 811'.52'09 [B] 86-19562
ISBN 0-8103-1732-X

Contents

Contents

American Poets, 1880-1945
Third Series
Part 2: N-Z

Dictionary of Literary Biography

John G. Neihardt
(8 January 1881-4 November 1973)

Alexander Globe
University of British Columbia

BOOKS: *The Divine Enchantment: A Mystical Poem* (New York: J. T. White, 1900);

The Wind God's Wooing (Bancroft, Nebr.: Blade, 1904);

The Lonesome Trail (New York & London: John Lane, 1907);

A Bundle of Myrrh (New York: Outing, 1907);

Man-Song (New York: Kennerley, 1909);

The River and I (New York & London: Putnam's, 1910);

The Dawn-Builder (New York & London: Kennerley, 1911);

The Stranger at the Gate (New York: Kennerley, 1912);

Life's Lure (New York & London: Kennerley, 1914);

The Song of Hugh Glass (New York: Macmillan, 1915);

The Quest (New York: Macmillan, 1916);

The Song of Three Friends (New York: Macmillan, 1919);

The Splendid Wayfaring: The Story of the Exploits and Adventures of Jedediah Smith and his Comrades, the Ashley-Henry Men, Discoverers and Explorers of the Great Central Route from the Missouri River to the Pacific Ocean, 1822-1831 (New York: Macmillan, 1920);

Two Mothers (New York: Macmillan, 1921);

The Laureate Address of John G. Neihardt upon Official Notification of his Choice as Poet Laureate of Nebraska (Chicago: Book Fellows, 1921);

The Song of the Indian Wars (New York: Macmillan, 1925);

Poetic Values: Their Reality and Our Need of Them (New York: Macmillan, 1925);

Indian Tales and Others (New York: Macmillan, 1926);

Collected Poems, 2 volumes (New York: Macmillan, 1926); volume 1 republished as *Lyric and Dramatic Poems* (Lincoln: University of Nebraska Press, 1965);

Black Elk Speaks, Being the Life Story of a Holy Man of the Ogalala Sioux, As Told to John G. Neihardt (New York: Morrow, 1932);

The Song of the Messiah (New York: Macmillan, 1935);

The Song of Jed Smith (New York: Macmillan, 1941);

A Cycle of the West: The Song of Three Friends, The Song of Hugh Glass, The Song of Jed Smith, The Song of the Indian Wars, The Song of the Messiah (New York: Macmillan, 1949); republished as *The Mountain Men* [first three poems] (Lincoln: University of Nebraska Press, 1971); and *The Twilight of the Sioux* [last two poems] (Lincoln: University of Nebraska Press, 1971);

When the Tree Flowered: An Authentic Tale of the Old Sioux World (New York: Macmillan, 1951); republished as *Eagle Voice: An Authentic Tale of the Sioux Indians* (London: Melrose, 1953);

All Is But a Beginning: Youth Remembered, 1881-1901 (New York: Harcourt Brace Jovanovich, 1972);

Luminous Sanity: Literary Criticism Written by John G. Neihardt, edited by John Thomas Richards (Cape Girardeau, Mo.: Concordia, 1973);

Patterns and Coincidences: A Sequel to All Is But a Beginning (Columbia: University of Missouri Press, 1978).

RECORDINGS: *A Cycle of the West—The Song of Three Friends* (Orpheus Records, MC-1001, 1957);

Lyrics of John G. Neihardt (Orpheus Records, MC-1002, 1957);

Lecture on ESP (Oregon, Wisc.: New Frontiers Center, 1966);

The Wonder of It All (Lincoln, Neb.: Thompson Co. & Roto Records, RC-1004, 1970);

Flaming Rainbow: Reflections and Recollections of an Epic Poet (United Artists Records, UA-LA-157-L3, 1973);

John G. Neihardt Reads from his Cycle of the West and Selected Poems (Caedmon Records, CDL5 1665, 1981).

OTHER: *The Poet's Pack,* edited by Neihardt (Chicago: Book Fellows, 1921).

John Neihardt's reputation rests on five historical epics begun in 1912, completed in 1941, and collected in the 656-page volume, *A Cycle of the West* (1949). The heroes are the white trappers who opened the Rocky Mountains to fur trading, the explorers who pushed overland to California, and the Indian populations decimated by white settlement on the plains of Montana and Wyoming. Neihardt used historical situations to explore archetypal human passions such as loyalty and betrayal, love and lust, courage and cowardice, pride in cultural values, and the will to survive. Each hero is tested in a crisis whose outcome has profound moral consequences, revealing human compassion and fortitude, or betraying bestial self-interest. The often powerful epics avoid narrow didacticism, but their aesthetic values remain firmly entrenched in nineteenth-century modes of thought. While this trait ensured Neihardt an early and apparently lasting popularity in the Midwest, it raises problems about his place in the relativistic sophistications of twentieth-century literature. His completed cycle seems like a throwback when it is compared with modernist poetry published within the same decade, works such as T. S. Eliot's *Four Quartets* (1936-1942) and Wallace Stevens's *Notes toward a Supreme Fiction* (1942).

Neihardt was born on 8 January 1881 near Sharpsburg, Illinois, to indigent parents descended from Pennsylvania German and Irish stock. Although uneducated, his father, Nicholas Neihardt, passed on his love of reading everything from Darwin to modern poets; the son was named John Greenleaf after Whittier. To emphasize his German roots John later adopted the middle name Gneisenau, after the Prussian field marshall August Graf Neithardt von Gneisenau (1760-1831), who helped defeat Napoleon at Waterloo. Within a decade, Neihardt's father abandoned the family. Used to adversity, his mother, Alice Culler Neihardt (who had decorated log-cabin homes with curtains made of newspapers and a carpet cut from a wagon cover, then decorated with walnut-stain patterns), moved the family to frontier country in Wayne, Nebraska. Suffering a fever during 1892, Neihardt received a vocation to write poetry in a shaman-style dream where he found himself flying through space. Shortly afterward, his poem "Ambition" appeared in the *Bloomington Eye.* In 1893 the precocious twelve-year-old Neihardt entered the Nebraska Normal School at Wayne, paying his way by ringing the bell every half hour. Outstripping his classmates, he undertook a special additional program in classics, learning Greek and graduating at age sixteen in 1897 with a Bachelor of Science degree. During the next year he began his first long poem, *The Divine Enchantment,* a romantic treatment of the visions sent by the Hindu deity Vishnu to the virgin Devanaguy. Despite her imprisonment by the tyrant Kansa, she bears Cristna (Krishna), the incarnation of Vishnu. Published at Neihardt's own expense in 1900, the book did not sell a single copy. The poet became so disenchanted with it that he bought back and burned every copy that he could find. In another equally rare, early book, *The Wind God's Wooing* (1904), the Greek fisherman Glaucus finds himself transformed into a minor sea deity who lures women to their deaths at sea.

Neihardt served his poetic apprenticeship, like most of his life, in financial privation, working at numerous odd jobs and moving regularly. In 1900, for example, he resettled with his mother at Bancroft, Nebraska, near an Omaha Indian reserve whose natives honored him with the title Little Bull Buffalo. By 1915, when *The Song of Hugh Glass*, the first song in *A Cycle of the West*, was published, Neihardt had essayed a wide range of genres: journalism for midwestern newspapers; literary reviews for the *New York Times*; the nonfiction book *The River and I* (1910); numerous short stories, some collected in *The Lonesome Trail* (1907); two novels, *The Dawn-Builder* (1911) and *Life's Lure* (1914); four closet dramas, of which *The Death of Agrippina* (1911) and *Eight Hundred Rubles* (1913) were later published as *Two Mothers* (1921); and five volumes of poetry, *The Divine Enchantment* (1900), *The Wind God's Wooing* (1904), *A Bundle of Myrrh, Man-Song* (1909), and *The Stranger at the Gate* (1912).

The early verse evoked praise: in a short essay on contemporary American poets published in the October 1912 issue of *Poetry Review*, Harriet Monroe ranked Neihardt with Ezra Pound, though her review of *The Quest* in the March 1917 issue of *Poetry* censured his "old-fashioned" diction and " 'masterful male' attitude." *A Bundle of Myrrh* drew its title from the Song of Solomon 1.13—"A bundle of myrrh is my well-beloved unto me; he shall lie all night betwixt my breasts"—a reference to the book's then-daring mixture of biblical allusion and sensuality. From a more recent perspective, there is too little sophistication in these self-indulgent adolescent outpourings. The male dominates, the woman submits. In "The Witless Musician," the poet exclaims, "I am a musician for the first time!/ I have found an instrument to play upon!/She is my violin—she is my harp!" The volume attracted Mona Martinsen (1884-1958), whose mother from Indiana had wed a wealthy German with important American financial interests. A sculptor who had studied in New York and in Paris under Rodin, she was elated by Neihardt's lyrics and wrote to him. The ensuing courtship by mail ended with her trav-

eling to Omaha and marrying Neihardt on 29 November 1908, the day after she arrived. The marriage, which produced four children, survived until her death fifty years later. Neihardt's second volume of lyrics, *Man-Song*, has a bas-relief cover designed by his wife. In 1912, a year after the republication of *A Bundle of Myrrh* by New York publisher Mitchell Kennerley, *The Stranger at the Gate*, subtitled *A Lyric Sequence Celebrating the Mystery of Birth*, was dedicated to Enid, the couple's first child. Sugary sentimentalities stand awkwardly beside masculine clamor. Toward the end of the volume, the baby arrives with military "Triumph": "Up through the Gates of Birth—/The Victor comes! The Victor comes!" The popularity of these three volumes led to a collected edition of his lyrics, *The Quest* (1916).

By 1912 Neihardt had realized the limitations of his early work. His short fiction, for which magazine editors hounded him, taught him how to organize narratives; his exercises in poetic drama taught him how confrontations reveal character; and his association with Indians and interest in western history released him from the prison of self. From 1913 to 1941 Neihardt was engrossed in writing the five songs of *A Cycle of the West*. To support a growing family, he would work until he had saved enough money to devote a few uninterrupted years to his epics and a series of related prose works. From 1912 to 1920 Neihardt spent three days a week writing and editing a literary page for the *Minneapolis Journal*. He worked full time as literary editor at the prestigious *St. Louis Post-Dispatch* during 1926-1930 and again in 1936-1938. He also served as associate editor of the *Mark Twain Quarterly* from its first issue in 1936 until 1954. Still, his creative energies were devoted to reading for his epics, searching through archives, interviewing survivors of various battles, and visiting the scenes of events to assure geographical, botanical, and meteorological authenticity. In 1915 he began the lucrative speaking tours that attracted large, enthusiastic audiences, including people who did not normally read poetry. Farmers would regularly burst into laughter or tears. His ninety-minute appearance on the Dick Cavett television show of 27 April 1971 brought more viewer response than any other guest the host could remember.

The subjects for Neihardt's *A Cycle of the West* were first sketched in prose books. *The River and I*, the account of a 2,000-mile canoe journey down the Missouri River, was commissioned by *Outing* magazine in 1908, serialized in four installments in *Putnam's* magazine from December 1909 to March

MAN-SONG CONTD.

One notices also that he has a special affection for 'lust' and 'cosmic', as Shelley for 'liquid'.

While the tone is sufficiently sexual, there is nothing regrettable, or pornographic in Mrs Churton Braby's sense of the word. A metaphor is sometimes a little nude, however, as in The Fugitive Glory, when the rejected Satyra, foretelling the aging and inwardness of her rival, says

Naked she stands - this thing that seemed a nymph,

All dew and moonlight! Nature! See the hag!

Fetid - a strutting womb - a suck-device -

The italics are Mr Neihardt's, but I endorse them. It is a powerful passage, however. As an almost irrelevant detail, one may note that when Satyra asks "Do Storms send up their cards?", she is using a phrase rather too modern for her classical name.

The book will be judged largely by the two drama-poems, and will possibly be less popular with some readers, who prefer a collection of shorter verses - each complete and concise, a distilled essence of passion ... that could be detached, for example, and sent to a friend as a memento of a mood. Few in these simple days really read tragedies, though they may chatter of old legends. Yet The Passing of the Lion is more than merely creditable. It has an ancient Athenian mould, but the real story is universal: the wavering between heroism and her-ism, between

2

Page from reader Arthur Hooley's report to publisher Mitchell Kennerley about Neihardt's second collection of poetry (courtesy of Vassar College Library)

1910, then published in book form in 1910. The experience provided Neihardt with invaluable first-hand experience of adventures similar to those of the trappers and mountain men he celebrated in *The Song of Hugh Glass* (1915) and *The Song of Three Friends* (1919). His school text, *The Splendid Wayfaring* (1920), a biography of Jedediah Smith, provided the basis for *The Song of Jed Smith* (1941). For the two epics on the Indian battles, *The Song of the Indian Wars* (1925) and *The Song of the Messiah* (1935), invaluable background was supplied by *Black Elk Speaks* (1932), with its reminiscence of the Ghost Dance movement of 1889-1890. Earning him the name Flaming Rainbow from Black Elk himself, this work attracted the active interest of Carl Jung and anthropologists.

The poems were composed in an order different from that in which they are collected in *A Cycle of the West. The Song of Hugh Glass*, written between October 1913 and June 1915, was, by 1942, reprinted four times singly, eight times with *The Song of Three Friends,* and also in the *Collected Poems.* Its success prompted the University of Nebraska to award him an honorary Litt.D. in 1917, at the ceremony where Willa Cather was similarly honored. Standing first in the completed *A Cycle of the West, The Song of Three Friends* was written next, between February 1916 and September 1918. For this book Neihardt shared with Gladys Cromwell the Poetry Society of America prize for the best volume of poetry published in 1919. A year later, enthusiasts in Wayne, Nebraska, founded a Neihardt Club and started a newsletter titled *Goldenrod.* In 1921 the Nebraska legislature passed a bill proclaiming him Poet Laureate of Nebraska and the Prairies; Neihardt responded with a *Laureate Address* (1921). The University of Nebraska created a nonteaching chair for him in 1923, for which he prepared the 1925 lectures published under the title *Poetic Values,* which Edmund Wilson called "very earnest and well informed" in a brief review for the *New Republic* (17 November 1926).

The fourth work in *A Cycle of the West, The Song of the Indian Wars,* was composed in 1921-1924 and published in 1925. A year later followed the *Collected Poems,* a republication of *The Quest, Two Mothers, The Song of Three Friends,* and *The Song of Hugh Glass.* Expectations for these books ran high: the Pulitzer brothers, Ralph and Joseph, Jr., prepared a party at the *St. Louis Post-Dispatch* to celebrate his winning the 1927 Pulitzer Prize for poetry. They were dumbfounded when the award went instead to the now-forgotten New York socialite Leonora Speyer for *Fiddler's Farewell;* Wil-

liam Rose Benét expressed his shock publicly in the *Saturday Review of Literature* (14 May 1927): "If [Neihardt] is not a poet in line for the Pulitzer Award, there is no such poet in our States." Though Neihardt accepted the news stoically enough, commenting that he had not expected to win, the disappointment caused a six-year hiatus in his work on *A Cycle of the West.* The first part of *The Song of the Messiah,* the fifth song in the complete cycle, had been finished in 1925-1926, but the rest of the poem was not taken up until 1932-1935. When it was published in 1935, Benét again expressed his firm conviction that Neihardt's achievement deserved a Pulitzer Prize (*Saturday Review,* 7 December 1935). That award eluded him, but he did win the 1936 Annual Poetry Prize given by the Friends of American Writers Society and the Golden Scroll Medal of the National Poetry Council to add to an honorary degree granted by Creighton University in 1929. *The Song of Jed Smith,* placed third in the completed cycle, was finished in 1941. Eight years later, in 1949, Neihardt was offered his first long-term job, as poet in residence and lecturer in English literature at the University of Missouri at Concordia. An extremely popular teacher, he remained there until 1961, the year in which the first Sunday of August was proclaimed annual Niehardt Day by the governor of Nebraska.

In *The Song of Three Friends,* two fur trappers die because of their desire for the same woman, an Indian girl who chooses Will Carpenter over Mike Fink, a character based on the American folk hero of the same name. Fink's jealously is compounded by wounded pride, as he must suffer not only the loss of a woman and of his self-esteem in a small community but also the humiliation of defeat by Carpenter at cards and in a fist fight. The third friend, Frank Talbeau, finally convinces the two to restore their friendship through their old custom of shooting a cup of whiskey from each other's head. The toss of a coin gives Fink the first shot, which kills Carpenter, apparently by accident. Fink's eventual taunt that the shooting was deliberate leads Talbeau to chase him into the wilderness at gunpoint, with neither arms nor water, to "think of all the wrong you've done!" Talbeau later relents, realizing that he has wrongly assumed the role of God. After a frantic search, he finds his friend dead from thirst, the corpse's eyes plucked clean by carrion crows.

In *The Song of Hugh Glass* Glass, an old trader, is revitalized by a handsome young man, the golden-haired Jamie, whom he saved during an Indian raid, at the cost of a wound to his leg. Al-

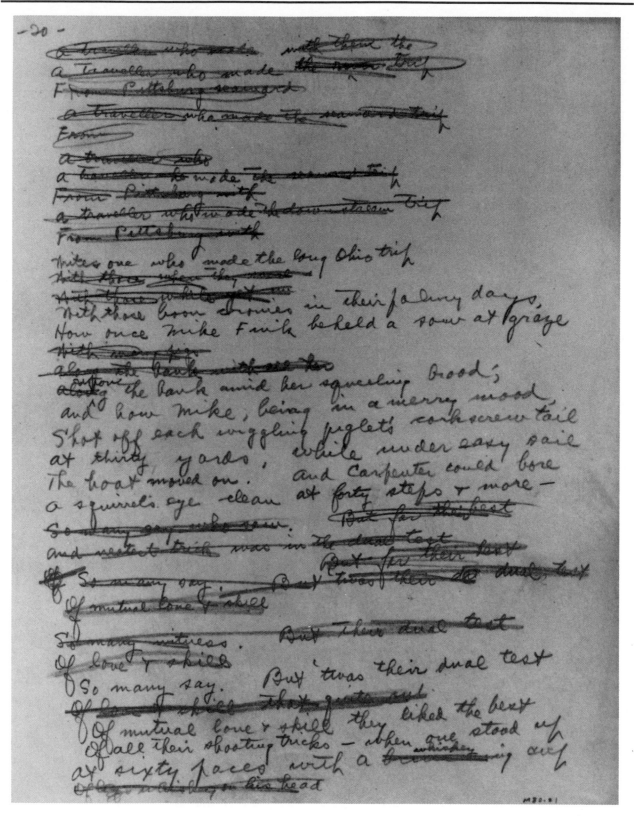

Pages from the first draft for The Song of Three Friends *(by permission of Hilda N. Petri, Trustee for the John G. Neihardt Trust; courtesy of Joint Collection, Western Historical Manuscript Collection, University of Missouri, Columbia, and State Historical Society of Missouri Manuscripts)*

-71-

Set brimming for a target on his head
~~and felt unmoved the~~
And felt the gusty passing of the lead,
Hot from the other's rifle, lift his hair.
And ever was the tincup smitten fair
~~Frets like drink~~
~~Twas more a rite of friendly that~~
~~To this it seemed~~
~~Twas a rite of love there for a while~~
~~To justify the faith much in each~~
By each to prove the faith of each anew:
For 'twas a rite of love between the two
And not a mere capricious feat of skill.
~~Aw hell, let's find a spot the whiskey, Bill~~
~~So Mike would end a wrangle~~
"Och, sure and can ye shoot the whiskey, Bill?"
So Mike would end a wrangle. "Damn it, Fink, (Come on)
Jets abore a pair of cups & have a drink!"
~~So Carpenter would~~
So Carpenter would stop a row grown stale.
And neither feared that either love ~~would~~ could fail
Or either skill might falter.

                     Thus appear
The doughty three who held each other dear
For qualities they best could comprehend. (395)

John G. Neihardt in the study at his house in Branson, Missouri, early 1930s (by permission of Hilda N. Petri, Trustee for the John G. Neihardt Trust)

though Jamie nurses Glass back to health, he is later persuaded by the self-serving Jules LeBon to abandon Glass to die after he has been badly mauled by a bear. Glass survives and, though left without supplies and crippled by a mutilated leg, he crawls a hundred miles overland to safety. Pitted like unaccommodated Lear against the unrelenting forces of nature and the psychological corrosion of memories of Jamie, Glass is at first bent on revenge, but he eventually realizes that his condition is mirrored by a larger tragedy. From a bluff he observes the fateful migration of the Ree, who are being driven west by Indian enemies and white encroachments. He now sees that the will for individual and community survival runs against all odds. After a twenty-five-mile trek, Glass finds Jamie, ironically blinded by the rifle that had earlier been stolen from Glass. In place of the destructive vengefulness in *The Song of Three Friends*, love impels forgiveness at the end of *The Song of Hugh Glass*.

The Song of Jed Smith focuses on the forging of the first overland trail to California—from Great

Salt Lake, along the Colorado River and through the Mojave Desert to San Diego in 1825, then back across the Sierra Nevada and the Great Salt Desert to a rendezvous at the southern end of Bear Lake in 1827. Smith's exploits are reported at secondhand by three former companions, whose earthiness contrasts with Smith's religious fervor, which interprets every drop of water as an answer to prayer. Although Neihardt intended Smith as the most enlightened of the white heroes in *A Cycle of the West,* Smith's singleminded assault on the deserts, which claim thirty-two of the company's fifty horses, is too relentless to sustain interest. He struggles merely against natural obstacles. Human difficulties, such as his hostile reception by Spanish authorities in California, are ignored. Unfortunately, Neihardt did not complete a poem on white settlement of the West: in 1922 he wrote to a friend that he was planning "The Song of the Mormons" to celebrate the struggles of white families opening up new lands. However, in the completed cycle, the reader is awkwardly thrown from the age of itinerant trappers in the 1820s to the armed confrontations between settlers and Indians forty years later.

The last two poems depict the breakup of Plains Indian culture. *The Song of the Indian Wars* begins with the crisis felt by the Indians as "The driving breed, the takers of the world," invade the plains. To capitalize on the Montana gold rush of 1862, the whites ask for permission to strike a road through Indian territory, following the Bozeman Trail, first traveled in 1863 by John M. Bozeman. Troubled by the whites' previous duplicity, the Sioux leaders Red Cloud and Sitting Bull resist selling their land, which they consider their mother, for a few beads and blankets. After the logs to build Fort Phil Kearney have been hauled in, the Indians attack, slaughtering all the whites to a man at the Fetterman Massacre of 1866. In answer to the building of the Union Pacific (in 1865-1869) and the destruction of Crazy Horse's village by an army ambush, Indian forces under Crazy Horse and Sitting Bull massacre General Custer and his company of 400 men at the Little Bighorn (Montana, 1876). But howitzers and gunboats eventually subdue the resistance. Family by family the Indians are forced to surrender so that their children will not starve; Crazy Horse, brought to a fort where he expects to talk with a white commander, is killed in a scuffle while being led to jail (1877). Crazy Horse's dying words, the end stops emphasizing his sense of dignity, sum up the tragedy of the North American Indian:

> That country was my own.
> I only wanted to be let alone.
> I did not want to see my people die.
> They say I murdered Long Hair and they lie.
> His soldiers came to kill us and they died.

The Song of the Messiah reaches on a dozen years to the mission of the Paiute Indian Wovoka and the catastrophe of Wounded Knee. The poem opens in a wasteland of starving Indians and sick cattle. The natives believe that they are being punished for giving their land away. In the spring of 1889 Wovoka, rumored to have come back from the dead, preaches his vision of a future restoration of plenty for the Indians on lands purged of white men. (For a shrewd anthropological study of this and similar movements, see Kenelm Burridge, *New Heaven, New Earth,* 1969.) Red Cloud, now an old man, endorses the call for faith, which is celebrated in "The Dance." Sitting Bull joins the general expectation but soon warns the people that they have overliteralized the message. As white soldiers mobilize and Indians arm, the prophet promises that enemy guns will have no power over believers. Sitting Bull is shot and Indian resistance collapses in the brutal slaughter of Wounded Knee in South Dakota on 29 December 1890. The work ends with Sitanka, inspired by a vision of coexistence, about to call out "my brother" to the soldier who kills him.

In an age increasingly dominated by imagism, Eliot's objective classicism, and the New Critical attention to verbal detail, Neihardt's poetic remained unabashedly romantic. In *Poetic Values: Their Reality and Our Need of Them* (1925), he insists that all great art begins as a sudden revelation of a "mood" which the artist then tries to reproduce in his chosen medium. The result "is a sense of exaltation, of expanded awareness, and the loss of one's habitual self." In this inspirational moment, "areas of hitherto hidden meaning are illumined as in a dream . . . , revealed as in a vision." As a consequence, he adds, "Art blends, by imperceptible degrees, into Ethics; while in the realm of its origin it is obviously one process with essential Religion . . . , with a passionate desire to understand larger and larger relations, and, so far as these may be ascertained, to be lost in them." In contrast to the "analytical tendency of our time, [which] has resulted in a vast accumulation of facts that are to the livable truth as broken pieces of glass are to a window pane," art gives "an impression of permanence" allowing us to "live humanly." His emphasis on the moral and spiritual aspects of art led him to play down verbal texture. For Neihardt poetry's "characteristic processes are concerned, not with words, but with images; not with logic, but with analogies, images being linked together in chains of meaning by virtue of likeness."

Neihardt's practice of composition reflects these views. He would read over the previous day's work to evoke the mood, then draft and complete a block of new lines each day, with few or no later revisions. Indeed, his forte was to evoke moods rather than create a language that has the proverbial quality of great literature. His reverence for the antique led to a conservative attitude toward language: "Anyone who truly loves poetry has noted that a great line or passage seems old," he noted in *Poetic Values.* Consequently, archaisms and classical allusions abound in the earliest poems of *A Cycle of the West.* For example, in *The Song of Hugh Glass,* as a flock of birds rise out of the trees at the approach of horses and warriors, the narrator asks, "What augury in orniscopic words/Did yon swart

Enid Neihardt, Nick Black Elk, Ben Black Elk, Standing Bear, and John G. Neihardt (by permission of Hilda N. Petri, Trustee for the John G. Neihardt Trust)

sibyls on the morning scrawl?" As years of writing passed, the earthy colloquialisms of the trappers and the dignified metaphorical speech of the Indians enlivened the verbal texture of the poems. Neihardt eventually worked his rhymed couplets into a tough, masculine prosody with ample enjambment, final punctuation at the caesura, and end stops after the first line to prevent sing-song regularity.

The genre that galvanized his literary responses was the most popular nineteenth-century form—melodrama. Melodramatic characters need not be stereotype robots (as Dickens proves), and ironies can be created by juxtaposition. But in melodrama there is no question of moral ambiguity. As James L. Smith (*Melodrama*, 1973) and D. Grimsted (*Melodrama Unveiled*, 1968) have explained, characters in melodrama respond to situations as heroes or villains. The action-filled plots may have suspenseful interruptions, yet they have none of the perturbations of modern narratives. In the American metamorphosis, the western adventurer pits himself against the forces of nature or the Indian; the early-nineteenth-century noble

savage tends to become the brutal warrior once his lands are threatened by white settlement; pathetic fallacy dominates the settings; nature can crush the hero, but just as often it is the one force that civilizes him; urbanization and domesticity are seen as failings (hence Neihardt's intuitive abandonment of "The Song of the Mormons"); women usually present temptations that destroy the social fabric; and the language leans toward archaic, "poeticized" expression. Neihardt's attraction to the form may well have been cemented through his friendship with Vachel Streamer, an actor who had worked under Edwin Booth. Neihardt stayed with Streamer at the Players Club in New York for several weeks early in 1907. An abortive offer that year to stage one of his short stories, "The Discarded Fetish," spurred him to try his hand at four short verse dramas. While in New York, he could have seen Ibsen's *Hedda Gabler* and *The Doll's House* or Shaw's *Captain Brassbound's Conversion*, but Neihardt's *The Death of Agrippina* (1911) and *Eight Hundred Rubles* (1913) resemble the melodramas that were then playing in New York during his visit—for example, David Belasco's *Girl of the*

Golden West and the Hippodrome extravaganza of "OVER 600 PEOPLE . . . ON THE STAGE AT ONE TIME WHEN THE SIOUX INDIANS ATTACK THE STAGE COACH!"—or the melodramatic spectacles that appeared in the next decade on the silver screen, such as D. W. Griffith's *The Birth of a Nation* (1915). Although Neihardt wrote about the modern movements heralded in 1913 by Pound's first imagist manifesto ("A Few Don'ts by an Imagiste," in the March issue of *Poetry*) and the Armory Show (which opened in New York the previous month), he resisted the new art as degrading. Instead he preferred the spiritual enlightenment of figures such as Jedediah Smith, Black Elk, or Wovoka, as heralded by his vision in 1892 and continued in his parapsychic experiments of the 1960s and 1970s.

The archetypal struggles depicted in *A Cycle of the West* are often gripping, and richer on second reading. Time and again the temporal and spatial transitions, essential mileposts in a long narrative, capture the scenic grandeur of the American West

John G. Neihardt holding Black Elk's drum in the library of his house in Columbia, Missouri, circa 1958-1959 (by permission of Hilda N. Petri, Trustee for the John G. Neihardt Trust)

as effectively as any photograph by Ansel Adams: "The sunset reared a luminous phantom spire/ That, crumbling, sifted ashes down the sky" (from *The Song of Hugh Glass*). But the epics are not likely to be rescued from critical obscurity, undeserved as it may be in the case of *The Song of Hugh Glass* and *The Song of the Messiah*. As with most works of its length and nature, paraphrase, brief quotation, or anthologization cannot convey the cumulative power of *A Cycle of the West,* and the pressure on university curriculums prevents the study of many 600-page poems, particularly of one in a nineteenth-century genre that has fallen into a critical limbo. The narratives are too straightforwardly chronological, without any of the complex dislocations of twentieth-century plots that might make them more popular in academic circles. The nineteenth-century assurance in the recoverability of historical truth sits uneasily with current views. What ambiguities or ironies exist in the poems usually result more from the juxtaposition of scenes or characters (as in Griffith's films) than from a critical examination of motives or a masterful command of language. Finally, because the poems are set in wilderness contexts, there are none of the ambiguities inherent in city life. Neihardt's epics sing out of tune with the urban cultures where most poetry is now read.

Bibliography:

John Thomas Richards, *Rawhide Laureate, John G. Neihardt: A Selected, Annotated Bibliography* (Metuchen, N.J.: Scarecrow Press, 1983).

Biographies:

Julius T. House, *John G. Neihardt, Man and Poet* (Wayne, Nebr.: Jones, 1920); republished in *Luminous Sanity: Literary Criticism Written by John G. Neihardt,* edited by John Thomas Richards (Cape Girardeau, Mo.: Concordia, 1973);

Lucile F. Aly, *John G. Neihardt: A Critical Biography* (Amsterdam: Rodopi, 1977).

References:

John Thomas Richards, *SORRAT: The History of the Neihardt Psychokinesis Experiments, 1961-1981* (Metuchen, N.J.: Scarecrow Press, 1982);

Blair Whitney, *John G. Neihardt* (Boston: Twayne, 1976).

Papers:

The largest Neihardt collection, among the Western Historical Manuscript Collection in the Elmer

Ellis Library of the University of Missouri at Columbia, comprises 558 letters, documents, and literary items, including drafts for *A Cycle of the West* and for *Black Elk Speaks*. This collection also includes fifty-seven tape cassettes and seven videotapes of Neihardt reading and lecturing. Manuscripts of one or two of his poems, often presentation copies, may be found in the special collections of the John Hay Library at Brown University, the Poetry Collection at the State University of New York at Buffalo, the Henry M. Seymour Library at Knox College (which also has more than one hundred Neihardt letters), the special collections of the Fred Lewis Pattee Library at Pennsylvania State University, the Humanities Research Center of the University of Texas at Austin, and the special collections of the University of Virginia. Other collections of papers are noted by J. T. Richards in *Rawhide Laureate*.

Lizette Woodworth Reese
(9 January 1856-17 December 1935)

Harriette Cuttino Buchanan
Appalachian State University

BOOKS: *A Branch of May: Poems* (Baltimore: Cushings & Bailey, 1887);

A Handful of Lavender (Boston & New York: Houghton, Mifflin, 1891);

A Quiet Road (Boston & New York: Houghton, Mifflin, 1896);

A Wayside Lute (Portland, Maine: Thomas B. Mosher, 1909);

Spicewood (Baltimore: Norman, Remington, 1920);

Wild Cherry (Baltimore: Norman, Remington, 1923);

The Selected Poems (New York: Doran, 1926; London: Longmans, 1927);

Little Henrietta (New York: Doran, 1927);

Lizette Woodworth Reese, edited by Hughes Mearns (New York: Simon & Schuster, 1928);

A Victorian Village: Reminiscences of Other Days (New York: Farrar & Rinehart, 1929);

White April, and Other Poems (New York: Farrar & Rinehart, 1930);

The York Road (New York: Farrar & Rinehart, 1931);

Pastures and Other Poems (New York: Farrar & Rinehart, 1933);

The Old House in the Country (New York: Farrar & Rinehart, 1936);

Worleys (New York: Farrar & Rinehart, 1936).

Lizette Woodworth Reese's name is unfamiliar to most modern readers of poetry; yet she continues to be included in standard reference works

Lizette Woodworth Reese

about American poetry and southern literature because of her significance in literary history. At the turn of the century, a time when American literature was largely devoted to faint imitations of worn-out Victorian forms, Reese was writing and publishing poetry that was uniquely fresh and straightforward in its presentation of the verities of life. While written in strictly traditional poetic forms, her verse creates a personal world, with its own system of images and symbols, that foreshadows the development of much of modern poetry. In this way, she stands as an important transitional figure between nineteenth- and twentieth-century poets.

Reese was born in the village of Huntingdon (now Waverly), a suburb of Baltimore, Maryland, to David and Louisa Sophia Gabler Reese. One of four daughters, Lizette Reese had a twin sister, Sophia Louisa. She spent most of her childhood and began her teaching career in Waverly, and spiritually and literally she never was far removed from this village, the subject matter of her writing. Reese's formal education went only as far as the public schools of Baltimore would take her, but her real education came from her extensive reading in the classics of English literature. Here she found the forms she emulated and confirmation of the moral values that she consistently upheld. In 1873 Reese began her teaching career by accepting a post at Saint John's Parish School, an Episcopal school in Waverly. Three years later, she began teaching in the Baltimore public school system, where she came to be much admired and respected, both for her teaching ability and for her poetic work.

Ever since she had been able to write, Reese had been composing poetry, but her real career as a poet began with the writing and publication of "The Deserted House" shortly after she began teaching. Reese's story about the development of this poem is significant because it describes the process of creation for all of her work. Each day as she walked to Saint John's School, Reese passed an old deserted house, which reminded her of Alfred Tennyson's "The Moated Grange." Drawing on both the real stimulus and its literary analog, Reese wrote "The Deserted House," in which the house she describes is neither the house she saw every day nor the house in Tennyson's poem, but it shares with both a sense of "silence and solitude." With the encouragement of her friend Mrs. Laura DeValin, Reese personally presented the poem to William Hand Browne, editor of the *Southern Magazine,* where it was published in June of 1874. Reese's literary career was thus launched by a poem

Sophia Louisa and Lizette Woodworth Reese, circa 1864 (courtesy of the Clifton Waller Barrett Library, University of Virginia)

that, while its style lacks the polish she later developed, embodies a theme and a use of language that are maintained throughout her work.

The theme of "The Deserted House" is the enduring beauty of nature despite the decay of man-made things and the peace that surrounds an isolated, deserted spot. These themes and the poem's verse form are conventional, but the language and imagery are unusual. Eschewing trite and "poetic" language, Reese describes the house in detail with simple, straightforward language. She personifies natural elements in such descriptions as "melancholy flowers," "lone/And wild-mouthed herbs," "desolate green grasses," and

> Old lichened faces, overspun
> With silver spider-threads—they wear
> A silence sad to look upon.

The favorable reception of this poem encouraged Reese to continue polishing for publication the poems that she wrote in her meager spare time. Many of the poems in her first volume, and in subsequent volumes, first saw print in magazines such as the *Atlantic Monthly,* the *Bookman, Harper's Monthly, Scribner's,* and the *Smart Set.*

Thirteen years after the appearance of "The Deserted House," Reese published her first book, *A Branch of May* (1887), a collection of thirty-three poems. Using her own money and funds raised from 100 friends who subscribed seventy-five cents each, Reese had the Baltimore firm of Cushings and Bailey print 300 copies of the book (at a total cost of ninety-two dollars). In addition to the copies she distributed to subscribers, Reese sent some twenty-odd copies to the leading literary figures of the time, including Thomas Wentworth Higginson, William Dean Howells, and Edmund Clarence Stedman, all of whom received it favorably. With Stedman, Reese began a correspondence and friendship that she cherished. Visiting often in his home, she became acquainted with many of the literati who helped influence her career.

Although there are only thirty-three poems in *A Branch of May,* the range of forms and subject matter is representative of Reese's work as a whole. Reese preferred the shorter lyric forms of couplet, quatrain, sonnet, and ballad or song. The twin couplets "Doubt" and "Truth" reveal an incisiveness and an impatience with sentimentality that are characteristic of Reese's work. The confusions of "Doubt"—"Creeds grow so thick along the way,/ Their boughs hide God; I cannot pray"—are balanced by "Truth"—"The old faiths light their candles all about./But burly Truth comes by and blows them out." With their simple language, these couplets demonstrate the strengths of the images that Reese creates by describing inanimate objects or subjective qualities as animate entities.

Reese's experiments with various verse forms in *A Branch of May* include her only attempt at the dramatic monologue. Reflecting the influence of Robert Browning (whose poetry she did not like as well as his wife's), "The Death Potion" tells, with marvelous irony, of a woman's desire to poison her rival. A chant overheard from the church across the way "(*Hear, Lord Jesus!*)" provides ironic counterpoint to the woman's plotting and self-justification about the death potion. This poem and the epigram that prefaces the volume—"Another rhymer? quoth the World./Faith, these folks be mad!"—reveal Reese's ironic turn of mind, but irony was a mode that she chose not to develop in poetry, preferring instead the nature lyric and straightforward presentations of conventional, universal truths.

One of Reese's favorite forms, and the one in which she excelled, was the sonnet. While she experimented with all types of the sonnet, she, on the whole, followed the advice of Thomas Bailey Aldrich who "wrote to me that he considered the Shakespearean form of the sonnet the weaker one, because of the last two lines, which, to his thinking, spoiled the music of the other twelve." One variation of the sonnet uniquely her own is the beautifully evocative "Mid-March" that after an initial ten-line stanza rhymed *abab cdcd ee* ends with a quatrain:

> The days go out with shouting; nights are loud;
> Wild, warring shapes the wood lifts in the cold;
> The moon's a sword of keen, barbaric gold,
> Plunged to the hilt into a pitch black cloud.

For the most part, however, Reese's many sonnets are variations of the Italian form.

In addition to being a fine example of Reese's use of the sonnet, "Mid-March" embodies one of her dominant themes, the beauty and grandeur of nature, especially in the spring or the fall—the seasons of change. The lyric "Sweet Weather" also expresses this theme:

> Now blow the daffodils on slender stalks,
> Small keen quick flames that leap up in the mold,
> And run along the dripping garden-walks:
> Swallows come whirring back to chimneys old.
> Blown by the wind, the pear-tree's flakes of snow
> Lie heaped in the thick grasses of the lane;
> And all the sweetness of the Long Ago
> Sounds in that song the thrush sends through the rain.

In lines such as "A shred of gold upon the grasses tall,/A butterfly is hanging dead," another nature lyric, "After the Rain," combines image and rhythm into a texture similar to that later sought by the imagist poets. Many of the longer lyrics of *A Branch of May*—including "A Spinning Song," "A Song," "The Singer," and "The Dead Ship: A Keltic Legend"—reflect the ballad tradition of the English literature that Reese loved and the folk traditions of the Maryland of her childhood.

Reese's second volume of poetry, *A Handful of Lavender* (1891), published by Houghton, Mifflin, includes all the poems from *A Branch of May* as well as forty-three new ones. While some of the new poems continue to treat the themes of nature and love, *A Handful of Lavender* contains a greater number in which the subject matter reveals Reese's debt to her wide reading. "Love, Weeping, Laid This Song," subtitled "On a Copy of the Iliad Found

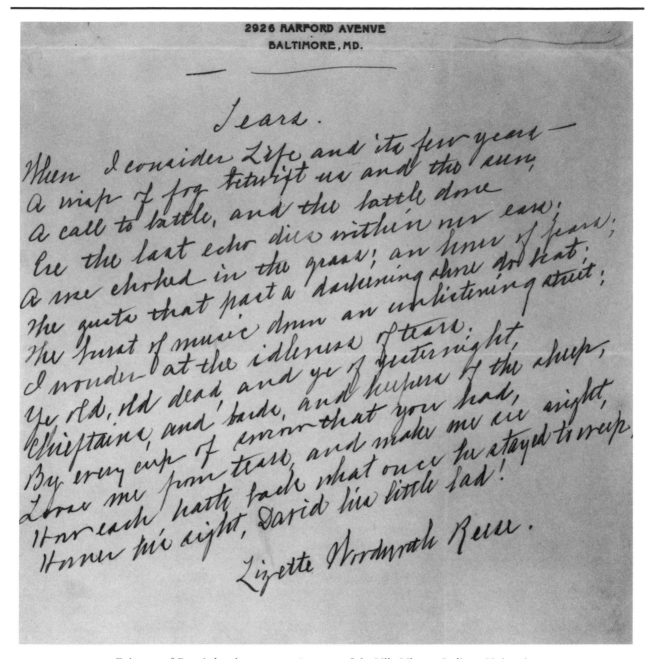

Fair copy of Reese's best-known poem (courtesy of the Lilly Library, Indiana University)

With the Mummy of a Young Girl," wonders at the power of Homer's epic, as vivid in the modern world as it was in ancient Egypt: "For us, as once for her, in that old dusk,/Troy trembles like a reed before the blast!" "For a Flyleaf of Herrick's Poems" and "The Garden at Bemerton," subtitled "For a Flyleaf of Herbert's Poems," are nature poems expressing Reese's admiration of those poets. With "The Hawthorn Tree in York Lane" and "April Weather," Reese strikes chords that re-verberate through all of her poetry and prose. In "The Hawthorn Tree in York Lane," the particular tree outside Reese's grandfather's home on the York Road in Waverly becomes symbolic of all blooming trees, which remind people of spring and youth and romance; the lane also becomes universalized, evoking especially those of the countryside described by the English poets whom Reese loved. In "April Weather" springtime is symbolic of rebirth, both in nature and in the human spirit.

Reese's later work continues such symbolism, but April also becomes associated, rather frighteningly, with eternity.

There are oblique references in Reese's poetry to a brief and disappointing romance. The final poem in *A Handful of Lavender,* the sonnet "Compensation," provides the most concrete evidence about this romance. Here she indicates her will to forget the lover.

> All day I bar you from my slightest thought;
> Make myself clear of you or any mark
> Of our wrecked dawn and the uprising lark;
> Am stern and strong, and do the thing I ought.

Compensation comes in dreams of the lover that she has by night, a dream lover perhaps more satisfying than the real one, who would come between her and her stern sense of Victorian duty.

The publication of *A Quiet Road* (1896) marks the end of the first stage of Reese's career. In ad-

Lizette Woodworth Reese (courtesy of the Clifton Waller Barrett Library, University of Virginia)

dition to the nature poems and to the poems celebrating literary subjects and authors, there are poems in which a new note of sadness and loss appears. "In Time of Grief " is reminiscent of Emily Dickinson's poetry, poetry Reese came to know only after her own, similar patterns of imagery had been established.

> Dark, thinned, beside the wall of stone,
> The box dripped in the air;
> Its odor through my house was blown
> Into the chamber there.
>
> Remote and yet distinct the scent,
> The sole thing of the kind,
> As though one spoke a word half meant
> That left a sting behind.
>
> I knew not Grief would go from me,
> And naught of it be plain,
> Except how keen the box can be
> After a fall of rain.

Another theme in this volume that appears for the first time in Reese's poetry is the richness of Death, which is welcomed in a manner reminiscent of Dickinson, as in the final two lines of "Growth": "Old Age holds more than I shall need,/Death more than I can spend." The quatrain "Reserve" expresses a thought that is clearly part of Reese's poetic creed:

> Keep back the one word more,
>   Nor give of your whole store;
> For, it may be, in Art's sole hour of need,
>   Lacking that word, you shall be poor indeed.

Reese's reserve as a poet is apparent in the brevity of her poems and in the care with which she weighed and polished each word. She once said, "composition for me was a most difficult task. My thought was quick, the picture in my mind clear, but the expression slow in coming; it was always a hard process to make my words as vital and as distinct as my thoughts and my pictures were."

Reese's first three volumes of poetry firmly established her reputation in American and English literary circles. On the basis of these three volumes Jessie B. Rittenhouse made the critical assessment that did much to establish that reputation. In *The Younger American Poets* (1904) Rittenhouse praised Reese's "swift-conceiving fancy that turns into poetry the near-by thing that many overlook." She urged readers to go to Reese "for truth, truth that has become personal through experience; go to her for beauty, uplift, and refreshment, and above all for the recovery of the departed mood."

With her reputation firmly established, Reese chose to refrain from book publication for thirteen years, accounting for her silence by saying, "I had nothing to say, except at long intervals, and therefore did not try to say it." During this period of relative silence, Reese did, however, continue to publish occasionally in magazines. In November 1899, Reese published the sonnet "Tears," her best-known and most frequently anthologized poem, in *Scribner's* magazine. While the theme is conventional—the idleness of the tears shed over one brief life in light of the greater reality of eternity—the images and language are arresting. Life becomes: "A wisp of fog betwixt us and the sun," "A rose choked in the grass, an hour of fears," "The burst of music down an unlistening street." The popularity this sonnet enjoyed rests on its certain confirmation of conventional morality in simple, but striking, language.

When Reese once more produced a book of poetry, it was *A Wayside Lute* (1909), published by Thomas B. Mosher, who also acquired the rights to Reese's earlier works and republished them in limited editions during the eleven-year gap between the first edition of *A Wayside Lute* and the appearance of *Spicewood* in 1920. Reese later acknowledged that she owed "Mr. Mosher much in the way of gratitude for keeping my name and work before a too-easily forgetful audience." *A Wayside Lute* is dedicated to the memory of Edmund Clarence Stedman and the grief expressed in the last two lines of the dedicatory poem echo throughout the volume: "Hearts, how bare the dark, the light,/Since he is not here!" The opening poem, "To-Day," Reese's longest single poem (128 lines), ponders the nature and wonder of life, the mystery of faith, and the function of art. While the narrative thread of the poem is weak, the images of life and art, especially of song, are strong. The singer makes his song, and as he plays:

> The oldest things of all,
> Go gleaming past, and as they go, they cry—
> Love, Longing, Tears, and gray Remembering;
> A foot, a voice, a face!—
> And there, in some dim place,
> The little honey-colored flowers of spring.

Using an image that she repeated frequently, Reese closed the poem by stating that "Each day is but a pool within the grass,/.../Where earth and heaven do meet as in a glass." The function of art is a new

theme in this volume, and Reese's didactic view about that function is made clear in the closing lines of the sonnet "To Art": "Cry through the dark, and drive the world to light;/Strike at the heart of time, and rouse the years." The final poem in the volume, "In Memoriam," is an extraordinarily laconic example of Reese's reserve and later was to serve as the epitaph on her tombstone.

> The long day sped;
> A roof; a bed;
> No years;
> No tears.

During the eleven years between *A Wayside Lute* and *Spicewood*, Reese's mother, one of the central figures in her life, died. *Spicewood*, dedicated to her mother, contains many poems that once again deal with grief and the longing for the return of hope. The tone of these poems, however, is now less detached and more passionately personal than in Reese's earlier work. In the sonnet "The Common Lot" the speaker expresses the inconsolable grief of recent hurt by comparing her sense of insignificance to the bustle of ongoing life and of spring. "Out in the spring my jonquils blow again,/ . . . But I would die, I am so hurt, so hurt!" In yet another sonnet, "Arraignment," Life is addressed and condemned: "You poured my dreams like water on the ground:/I think it would be best if I were dead." In addition to the more personal voice that speaks in *Spicewood*, there are more references to the village of Huntingdon and to the Old York Road.

After a teaching career of forty-five years, Reese retired in 1921 and was able to devote more time to writing. The year 1923 saw the publication of her sixth volume of verse, *Wild Cherry*, and saw the dedication, at Western High School where she had taught, of a bronze commemorative plaque inscribed with the sonnet "Tears." With characteristic self-effacement, Reese commented that the plaque did not recognize her work in particular but was an "acknowledgment and recognition of the fine art of poetry."

After the intensely personal poems of *Spicewood*, *Wild Cherry* returns to a more remote tone. Several poems continue to be based on Reese's response to English literature, especially that of the renaissance, or to the beauties of nature, but the dominant theme is grief and the difference that a personal awareness of death makes to life. In "White Flags" Reese ponders the effect of baring the garden of white irises in order to dress a grave:

I knew before that they were white,
In April by a wall,
A dozen or more. That people died
I did not know at all.

Along with the more detached attitude toward grief, the poems of *Wild Cherry* reflect a coming to terms with the life that continues after the death of a loved one. The narrator of the sonnet "Our Common Hoard" relates anecdotes and happenings that she wishes she could share with a dead woman, but instead of feeling pain about her absence she finds a sense of continuity in memory. "That still we share, as each with each, is plain,/. . . Since loveliness is left, then so is she!" The consolation of the loveliness of memory and of nature became a dominant theme in the remainder of Reese's poetry.

The Selected Poems (1926) draws largely from the first four volumes of Reese's poetry and includes thirty-three verses previously unpublished in book form. These new poems continue the poet's struggle to deal with death and with the emptiness that death visits on the living. Several times in these poems the rending of a personality or of dreams is presented in the arresting metaphor of the deliberate tearing up of a flower. "To Life" entreats life not to "Unpetal the flower of me,/And cast it to the gust." In "Questioning" the poet asks, "Can one tear dreams in two, as though each were/A flower to unpetal?" The dominant theme remains, however, the consolation of spring and renewal, even if tinged with sad memory. In "In Winter" the poet responds to winter with "I dig amongst the roots of life" searching for the promise of spring which will bring "New loveliness for house, for field,/And with it the ghost of the old."

In the next year, Reese published *Little Henrietta* (1927), a narrative poem commemorating the death, when they were both small children, of Reese's cousin Henrietta Matilda. Although Reese called it "my first long poem," *Little Henrietta* is not one sustained poem but is rather a series of thirty-nine short poems linked by the single narrative thread. *Little Henrietta* is the only unrhymed poetry that Reese ever wrote. Although it is unrhymed, the meter is regular; each poem is a ten-line stanza in which the sixth line, in trimeter or tetrameter, violates the iambic-pentameter norm. Reese had been working on these verses intermittently for some time before she felt compelled to pull together her feelings about her grief: "I tried to trace the beginnings and the loneliness of grief in a normal human being, who, overwhelmed at first, and

rebellious at heart, eventually accepts the bitter experience, and in faith and trust, awaits an everlasting restoration." While the subject of this poem is highly emotional, Reese, as usual, avoids sentimentality. Instead she tells a genuinely touching story of what Henrietta's life and death meant to her family. As in her other poetry, Reese makes use of significant detail to depict both the immediacy of personal reality and the universality of the experience. One such detail is the child's rag doll, Blimbo, which figures in poems ten, eleven, and twenty-one. In the first of these poems Blimbo is brought to comfort Henrietta at bedtime; in the next her importance to Henrietta is explained: "And she who had no mother of her own,/Made herself double parent to poor Blim." Finally in poem twenty-one, "Poor staring Blimbo lay upon the floor," a poignant reminder of the dead child whose toys the living cannot yet bear to put away. Eventually the pain lessens, and in spontaneous response to nature there is a renewal of joy.

Out of the common recompense of life,
By littles we began
To measure loss by gain; and wrecks by ports;
And darks by lamps; a beggar's sack by gold.
That we had loved we knew; now were we sure,
That having loved, we had not lost at all.

Little Henrietta ends with the affirmation that pain and grief are part of a divine plan for life:

What have we kept of all?—
That Love, being lit of God, fails not or ends:
That years are but His way to make us climb;
And tears His way to make us understand.

The sentiment and faith expressed here resonate throughout Reese's next work, a volume of prose reminiscence.

A Victorian Village: Reminiscences of Other Days (1929) draws from Reese's memories of her childhood on the Old York Road in Waverly and provides what she considers the important facts of her teaching and writing careers. Describing Waverly and the Victorian attitudes that shaped her life, Reese lovingly looks backward to "the age of faith. We were as sure of God as we were of the sun." Later she notes, "Life at that time was an unhurried and secure affair." *A Victorian Village* places Reese's poetry in the context of her life.

Continuing the more prolific writing of her retirement, Reese published another volume of poetry, *White April, and Other Poems*, in 1930. The

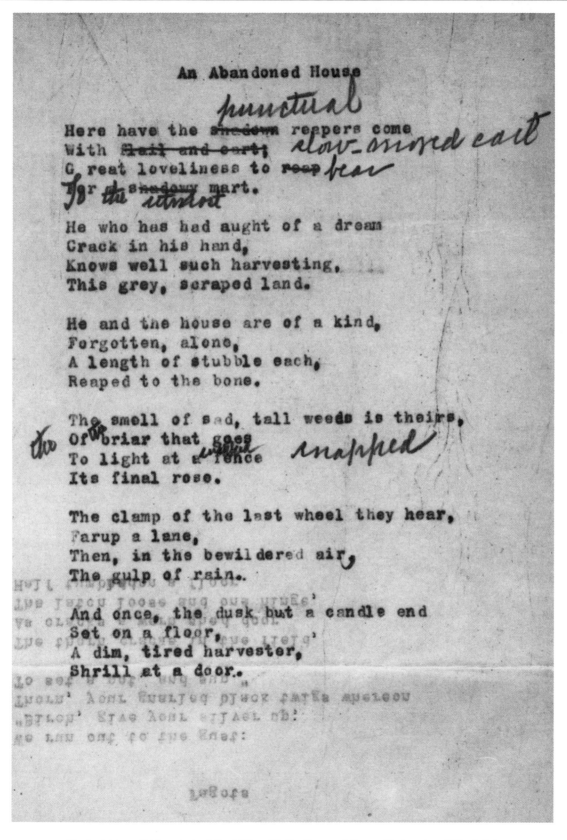

An Abandoned House

punctual

Here have the ~~sundown~~ reapers come
With ~~flail and cart;~~ *slow-moved cart*
Great loveliness to ~~reap~~ *bear*
~~For a shadowy~~ mart.
For the utmost

He who has had aught of a dream
Crack in his hand,
Knows well such harvesting,
This grey, scraped land.

He and the house are of a kind,
Forgotten, alone,
A length of stubble each,
Reaped to the bone.

the
The smell of sad, tall weeds is theirs,
Of briar that ~~goes~~ *snapped*
To light at ~~a fence~~
Its final rose.

The clamp of the last wheel they hear,
Far up a lane,
Then, in the bewildered air,
The gulp of rain.

And once, the dusk but a candle end
Set on a floor,
A dim, tired harvester,
Shrill at a door.

Revised typescript (courtesy of the Clifton Waller Barrett Library, University of Virginia) poems in this volume reflect more strongly the quiet acceptance of death as a part of life that was reached at the end of *Little Henrietta*. The sonnet "Comfort" reiterates "Grief may be swift; swifter is loveliness" and concludes: "You stumble from your tears, to reach at last,/A door, and an imperishable roof." The title of the volume reflects the private symbolism in which Reese developed about the whiteness of the flowers, shrubs, and trees that bloom in April. The emotion attached to this symbolism is not merely joy at the renewal of spring, it is something more powerful and frightening. In the title poem, the beauty of an orchard in spring overwhelms the poet as drowning in a pool might: "I clutch, I gasp, and all at once each spring/That I have known comes sharply to my mind."

The poet struggles with the ambivalent emotions that spring arouses and "Dripping with April, April to the heart,/I run back to the house, and bolt the door!" This sense of the awesome power of spring is underscored by the final sonnet in *White April*, "The White Fury of the Spring," in which the April whiteness and weather combine into a fearsome storm that the poet feels will invade the house "And drag me out to the white fury there." Poems such as "Shepherding" and "Plowing" anticipate the pastoral tone of Reese's later poetry.

In 1931 Reese published *The York Road*, a miscellany of autobiographical reminiscences, short stories, and fictional character sketches, some of which had been published previously in magazines. In one of these, Reese makes an analogy about the effect of the constant retelling of memories that aptly describes what has happened over the course of her work: "A stone passing from hand to hand, and taking on a consistent polish, it becomes smoother and rounder under the continuous telling."

The primarily pastoral poems of the final volume of poetry published in Reese's lifetime, *Pastures and Other Poems* (1933), exhibit much of this kind of smoothness and roundness. In the title poem, pastures, sheep, and the shepherd represent the world, its people, and God. In *Pastures* Reese draws into herself, exploring fewer themes and employing fewer verse forms than before. Her principal themes are the bounty and beauty of nature, death, and the loss of loved ones. God and the comforts of religion are more visible, implicit in the pasture/shepherd poems and explicit in several others, as in the quatrain "Sacrament":

Each thing is dual; hence our help in need;
Bread turns to flesh and wine to blood;
An oaken switch may set a mob at bay;
Or a rose buy a rood.

Except for a few quatrains, Reese limits her forms here to the comfortable balladlike lyrics for which she was best loved and to the sonnet in which she excelled.

At the time of her death in 1935, Reese was polishing *The Old House in the Country* (1936), a rhymed narrative poem patterned after *Little Henrietta*, and was beginning a fictionalized account of her early life, the extant fragment of which was published as *Worleys* (1936). In an introduction to *Worleys*, Reese's publisher John Farrar commended Reese's ability to create art from her memories and provided an amusing anecdote that illustrates Reese's reserved personality. According to Farrar, whenever he asked her when her next volume of poetry could be expected, Reese would answer that she was currently working on a mystery story and had, in fact, completed several chapters. Then, unheralded, a new volume of poems would appear. "Of this mythical mystery story we heard much for several years. . . . Yet I am inclined to think her own production of one was some kind of private joke, since we have been unable to find among the manuscripts she left a scrap of anything that remotely resembles even the first paragraph of such a novel." This subterfuge seems characteristic of a woman who polished and crafted her work carefully before she felt ready to share it with the public.

In a career that spanned more than sixty years, Reese's poetic voice was clear and unwavering. Although the range in content and form of her songs was narrow, she explored and crafted thoroughly and beautifully within that range. At the height of her reputation, in the first quarter of the twentieth century, critics cited her mastery of lyric forms and of the sonnet. Later she was viewed as an influential transition figure between the artificial conventionality of the Victorian poets and the daring poetic explorations of the moderns. Currently, she is recognized primarily for her historical significance, although many of her poems deserve renewed attention. The poems most appealing to modern tastes are not those for which she was best loved and which were most frequently anthologized at the first part of this century. Reese's work, however, is most rewarding when it is read as a whole. Her careful craftsmanship, her record of a developing personality, and her evolving personal symbolism cast a spell that grows stronger as the reader moves from volume to volume.

References:
Horace Gregory and Marya Zaturenska, "Lizette Reese," in their *A History of American Poetry* (New York: Harcourt, Brace, 1942), pp. 79-83;

H. George Hahn, "Twilight Reflections: The Hold of Victorian Baltimore on Lizette Woodworth Reese and H. L. Mencken," *Maryland Historian,* 11 (1980): 29-38;

R. P. Harriss, "April Weather: The Poetry of Lizette Woodworth Reese," *South Atlantic Quarterly,* 29 (April 1930): 200-207;

Carlin T. Kindilien, "The Village World of Lizette Woodworth Reese," *South Atlantic Quarterly,* 56 (January 1957): 91-104;

L. Ruth Murray Klein, "Lizette Woodworth Reese, A Biography," Ph.D. dissertation, University of Pennsylvania, 1943;

H. L. Mencken, "In Praise of a Poet," *Smart Set,* 31 (May 1910): 153-155;

W. Gordon Milne, "Lizette Reese Revisited," *Susquehanna University Studies,* 8 (June 1969): 207-212;

Robert D. Rhode, "Lizette W. Reese: 'Fair White Gospeler,' " *Personalist,* 31 (1950): 390-398;

Jessie B. Rittenhouse, "Lizette Woodworth Reese," in her *The Younger American Poets* (Boston: Little, Brown, 1904), pp. 27-45.

Papers:
The bulk of Reese's papers are at the Clifton Waller Barrett Library at the University of Virginia. The Enoch Pratt Free Library in Baltimore also has a collection of papers placed there by the Lizette Woodworth Reese Memorial Society and by Warren Wilmer Brown, her literary executor.

Lola Ridge
(12 December 1873-19 May 1941)

Peter Quartermain
University of British Columbia

BOOKS: *The Ghetto, and Other Poems* (New York: Huebsch, 1918);

Sun-Up, and Other Poems (New York: Huebsch, 1920);

Red Flag (New York: Viking, 1927);

Firehead (New York: Payson & Clarke, 1929);

Dance of Fire (New York: Smith & Haas, 1935).

PERIODICAL PUBLICATIONS: "The Georgians At Home," *New Republic,* 17 (11 January 1919): 316-317;

"Kreymborg's Marionettes," *Dial,* 66 (11 January 1919): 29-31;

"Salt Water," *New Masses,* 3 (September 1927): 27.

In *The Never-Ending Wrong* (1977) Katherine Anne Porter tells of the "enormous" crowd assembled outside Charlestown Prison, in Boston, on the evening of 22 August 1927. Anarchists Nicola Sacco and Bartolomeo Vanzetti were to be executed at midnight for a murder that many believed they

did not commit, and the police, on horseback, sought to keep the crowd clear of the center of the square. "They galloped about, bearing down upon anybody who ventured out beyond the edge of the crowd. . . . Most of the people moved back passively before the police, almost as if they ignored their presence; yet there were faces fixed in agonized disbelief, their eyes followed the rushing horses as if this was not a sight they had expected to see in their lives. One tall, thin figure of a woman stepped out alone, a good distance into the empty square, and when the police came down at her and the horse's hoofs beat over her head, she did not move, but stood with her shoulders slightly bowed, entirely still. The charge was repeated again and again, but she was not to be driven away. A man near me said in horror, suddenly recognizing her, 'That's Lola Ridge!' "

Lola Ridge (as she came to call herself) was more an emotional than an intellectual revolutionary, and she was a political revolutionary years be-

Lola Ridge

fore the fashion for communism or class-consciousness or sympathy and activity for the pro-letariat took hold of American writers and intellectuals in the 1930s; her book *Red Flag* was published in 1927, well before the Crash. Romantic, idealistic, and astonishingly intense, her personality and her powerful sympathy for the poor gave her, in the 1920s, considerable fame as a writer and as a revolutionary and considerable success as a shaker and mover (she kept Alfred Kreymborg's important little magazine *Others* alive when Kreymborg was ready to give it up). Kreymborg, who deeply admired her, wrote of "the flame that carried her, . . . the frailest of humans physically and the poorest financially." In the 5 June 1927 issue of the *New York Times Book Review* an anonymous reviewer called her "the woman on the spiritual barricade fighting with her pen against tyranny," and the readers of that journal would have known what was meant. Emanuel Carnevali wrote to Kay Boyle from Italy in 1924 that "she is a woman suffering, but suffering with the snarl of a lioness and not with any self-pity. Her poetry is intensely vivid, and she herself, both in her poems and in her life, is a lioness flinging herself madly against the walls of the ugly city." He also called her "one of the most beautiful signs we have of women's emancipation." As Kay Boyle reflected,

looking back in 1951, Lola Ridge's commitment to the arts and to the working class was "so dramatized that people felt the necessity of either defending or abusing her whenever her name came up." She was, as Horace Gregory remarked, a legend in her own life; she was the nearest prototype in her time of the proletarian poet of class conflict, voicing social protest or revolutionary idealism. Necessarily, perhaps, her work suffers from the faults endemic to writing which is devoted to persuading the reader or declaiming Truth, and which avoids the "literary."

Lola Ridge—who was christened Rose Emily Ridge and who, as a child, liked to be called Rose Delores—was the only surviving child of Joseph Henry and Emma Reilly Ridge. She was born in Dublin, Ireland, on 12 December 1873. Her mother had a married sister in New Zealand, and in 1887 when the child was thirteen Emma Ridge immigrated to New Zealand, taking her daughter with her: they may, some time during the next few years, have lived for a time in Australia. In 1895 when she was twenty-one, Rose Emily Ridge married Peter Webster, manager of a gold mine in New Zealand. The marriage was not a success, and she moved to Sydney, New South Wales, where she went to Trinity College and where she studied painting with Julian Rossi Ashton at the Académie Julienne. Although her ambition was to be a painter, she seems to have spent much of her time writing poems, many of which she destroyed (to her later chagrin) when, after her mother's death, she immigrated to the United States. Some of her early poems are preserved in the Mitchell Library in Sydney.

When she arrived in San Francisco in 1907 she was thirty-three years old, with a failed marriage behind her; yet she was idealistic and hopeful, making a new beginning. Presenting herself as an Australian poet and painter, she called herself Lola Ridge and claimed to have been born in 1883—a pretense to youth which led her later friends and acquaintances to think she was more ill than she was (in 1929 she contracted pulmonary tuberculosis, and she was—perhaps because of her poverty—frequently ill) and to exclaim over her fragile and worn appearance (Harry Salpeter called her "blood-drained, ravaged by illness"; Kay Boyle says she was "fragile enough to be blown away like a leaf"). In its obituary the *New York Times* said she was fifty-seven rather than sixty-seven when she died in 1941. For her new beginnings she invented a romantic idealized version of herself: she made herself up.

In California she sold her first poems to be published in North America to the *Overland Monthly,* which in its March 1908 issue identified her as "a young Australian poet and artist, who is not without fame in her own land" and promised to print "several pieces of verse from her pen . . . from time to time." In introducing "The 'Te Kapiti Extended,'" a comic colloquial monologue more or less in the manner of Robert Service, the magazine called her style "breezily strong, and, in her sentimental moods, appealingly beautiful." In June it published "Under Song: The Song of the Bush," an undistinguished sentimental mood piece. By the time the poem appeared, Lola Ridge had left California for New York.

In Greenwich Village, where she settled, she turned to writing for a living and spent something like the next three years composing advertising copy and writing fiction for popular magazines. As she herself said, she eventually stopped "because I found I would have to do so if I wished to survive as an artist": the work she was doing for the magazines was acutely at odds with her deeply felt and increasingly radical social convictions. As early as April 1909 she published, in Emma Goldman's radical monthly *Mother Earth,* "The Martyrs of Hell," which begins:

> Not your martyrs anointed of heaven
>   The ages are red where they trod;
> But the hunted—the world's bitter leaven,
>   Who smote at your imbecile God;

collected in *The Ghetto, and Other Poems* (1918) as "A Toast," the poem is indeed different in sentiment from "Under Song" of less than a year before:

> The mystical, the strong
>   Deep-throated Bush
>   Is humming in the hush
> Low bars of song:
> Far singing in the trees
>   In tongues unknown—
>   A reminiscent tone
>   On minor keys.

Emma Goldman published only one other poem by Ridge, "Freedom," in June 1911, and in the years immediately following Lola Ridge made her living as a factory worker, an artists' model, an illustrator, and an organizer of educational groups. It was during these years, at a meeting of the Ferrer Association (named for Francisco Ferrer, Spanish martyr to the radical cause), that she met David

Lawson, who became her second husband on 22 October 1919. She lived ascetically, and the reputation she acquired of having chosen deliberately to lead a life of poverty is probably accurate: even in the days of comparative prosperity following the publication of *The Ghetto, and Other Poems,* she lived in what Horace Gregory described as a "large, barely furnished, wind-swept, cold water loft . . . in downtown Manhattan." In her dedication to the cause of the downtrodden and to the cause of the new literature, she was wholehearted, selfless, and completely without pretense. William Carlos Williams, who seems to have found her tiresome, called

Title page for Ridge's first book, which Alfred Kreymborg called "the most uncompromising excoriation I've ever seen between two American bookboards" (courtesy of the Lilly Library, Indiana University)

her "that Vestal of the Arts, a devout believer in the humanity of letters" and exclaimed impatiently, "she made a religion of it."

Living in the Lower East Side, then absenting herself from New York City for perhaps as much as five years in the mid 1910s, and publishing nothing for several years, Lola Ridge caught the public eye when, in its 13 April 1918 issue, the *New Republic* devoted three pages to "The Ghetto," a sequence of poems which she later revised and which form part of the longer sequence of the same name in *The Ghetto, and Other Poems,* published late in the same year. She gained immediate recognition. In his review of the book for the *New Republic* (16 November 1918), Francis Hackett voiced the general opinion when he called "The Ghetto" the "most vivid and sensitive and lovely embodiment that exists in American literature of that many-sided transplantation of Jewish city-dwellers which vulgarity dismisses with a laugh or a jeer." In his review for *Poetry* (March 1919) Kreymborg called "The Ghetto" "a magnificent pageant of the Jewish race in nine chapters"; the book as a whole, he said, was "the most uncompromising excoriation I've ever seen between two American bookboards" of "average American gentlefolk who are so content with conditions as they are that they never disturb themselves." Technically, the poems are forceful rather than polished; they rely a great deal on rhetoric. As most critics noticed—and Conrad Aiken most clearly articulated in a review for the *Dial* (25 January 1919)—the poems are more like preliminary sketches than like thought-through conceptions and have "the extravagances of the brilliant but somewhat too abounding amateur." Lola Ridge's great gift, which persists through all her writing, is that of vivid metaphor—and in "The Ghetto" such metaphors abound: "The street crawls undulant,/Like a river addled/With its hot tide of flesh/That ever thickens," and some sketches are quite effective, rhetorical though they are:

> What if a rigid arm and stuffed blue shape,
> Backed by a nickel star
> Does prod him on,
> Taking his proud patience for humility . . .
> All gutters are as one
> To that old race that has been thrust
> From off the curbstones of the world . . .
> And he smiles with the pale irony
> Of one who holds
> The wisdom of the Talmud stored away
> In his mind's lavender.

With the publication of *The Ghetto, and Other Poems* her poetry began to appear in established magazines such as the *Dial,* the *Literary Digest,* and *Poetry* as well as in the *New Republic.* Part of her success had undoubtedly to do with the shock value of her materials, such as the Negro baby thrown into a burning house by white women during the East St. Louis race riots, an event which informs the ironic "Lullaby," which critics singled out for praise. Kreymborg, an old friend, singled out "The Song of Iron," though it is one of the weaker poems in the book.

When the *Others* movement was in its heyday, members of the group met regularly, most often

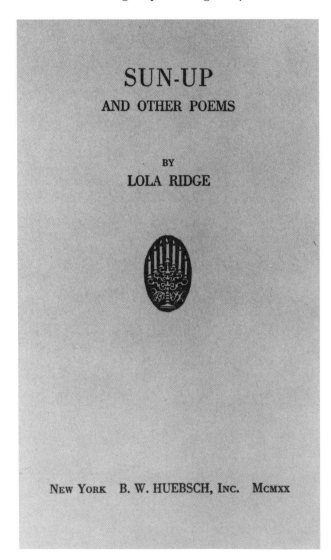

Title page for Ridge's second book, which contains personal lyrics as well as public poems addressed to anarchists Emma Goldman and Alexander Berkman (courtesy of the Lilly Library, Indiana University)

at Kreymborg's or at Lola Ridge's. In 1919, when Kreymborg "was positive the venture had outlived its usefulness," Lola "kept the movement going by giving a party nearly every time she sold a poem or an article, . . . in her dark room on Fifteenth Street." There would gather such people as Aiken, Williams, Marianne Moore, Orrick Johns, Waldo Frank, Emanuel Carnevali. It was at her home that Kreymborg met Edwin Arlington Robinson, and Williams met Robert McAlmon. In February 1919, when her poems were appearing in *Others* and she was an associate editor of the magazine, she was in Chicago reading and lecturing for The Others Lecture Bureau.

While *Sun-Up, and Other Poems* (1920) contains public poems in the vein of those in *The Ghetto, and Other Poems* or even of those in *Mother Earth* a decade before, it also includes many more personal lyrics. The title poem is a sequence drawing on her childhood: as Elaine Sproat observes in her biographical sketch of Ridge for *American Women Writers* (1981), "its flashing pictures resemble those of the Imagists; psychologically, it shares ground with the experiments of James Joyce." Some of the short poems, such as "Thaw" ("Blow through me, wind,/ As you blow through apple blossoms"), start off as though she had been reading H. D.'s (Hilda Doolittle's) "Heat." The public poems, addressed to her anarchist friends Emma Goldman and Alexander Berkman, satirize "all the policemen like fat blue mullet" or announce that the poet's function is "kindling the slow fire" in the exploited workers' hearts. Generally, the public poems are a little more strident than those in *The Ghetto, and Other Poems*, and it was with the personal poems in mind that Herbert Gorman pronounced, in the *New York Times Book Review* (9 January 1921), that with *Sun-Up, and Other Poems* Lola Ridge "takes a foremost place among American women writing poetry."

Her association with *Others* (which ceased publication in 1919) and with Harold Loeb (whose Sunwise Turn Bookshop she had frequently visited) led to her appointment, in February 1922, as American editor of *Broom*, which Loeb edited from Rome. The job included living quarters at the office, which occupied the basement in the home of Marjorie Content (Loeb's estranged wife) at 3 East Ninth Street, and a salary which Loeb described as "barely enough to live on." Ridge accepted only on condition that she be listed in *Broom* as American editor and that (as she wrote Loeb) "all American Mss, drawings, too, . . . come to this office." She moved into her new living quarters, with her husband, on 1 March. One of her first acts as American editor was to write to Loeb suggesting "an occasional all-American number which could present an unbroken contour of American art to Europe and . . . give you a chance to take a few weeks' rest on the other side"; one such number did appear, in January 1923. But there were difficulties.

One of Ridge's jobs was to run a small *Broom* salon, at which (in Kay Boyle's words) "the flesh and its appetites, and the accoutrements of material poverty, were set aside. . . . Every Thursday afternoon, and perhaps one evening in the month, Lola held open house. She and her husband were poorer than church mice, and this basement . . . was their church." Here, "hungry, ill, and fragile," she would, with the help of Kay Boyle, or even Oscar Williams, feed tea, cake, and encouragement to such visitors as John Dos Passos, Elinor Wylie, Jean Toomer, Edwin Arlington Robinson, Monroe Wheeler, Marianne Moore, and Louis Ginsberg— and she gathered materials for *Broom*.

Matthew Josephson, who was generally unsympathetic toward Lola Ridge, in his memoir, *Life Among the Surrealists* (1962), said that her position as American editor "was difficult at best. She was supposed to be in charge of the New York office, gathering and selecting copy and sending it on to us with her recommendations. . . . It made her unhappy when most of the writers she recommended were rejected by the editors in Europe. Harold Loeb had not accorded her a free hand, although she had gathered most of the materials that made up the January 1923 issue." That issue published work by Kenneth Burke, Jean Toomer, Hart Crane, Marianne Moore, Malcolm Cowley, and William Carlos Williams (the first installment of what would become Williams's *In The American Grain*), all gathered by Lola Ridge—and a poem by Gertrude Stein. Ridge had devoted herself utterly to promoting *Broom* in the face of great difficulties, refusing at times even to draw her salary. As American editor she had protested the inclusion of Stein in the issue for June 1922 (which had gone to press shortly after she took office), though it was the final installment of her series "If You Had Three Husbands": "Gertrude Stein . . . is mostly blah! blah! . . . In a few years her work will be on the rubbish heap with the rest of the literary tinsel that has fluttered its little day and grown too shabby even for the columns of the daily." On hearing Loeb's decision to include Stein's short piece "Wear" in the January 1923 issue she cabled, 15 November 1922: "Resign on inclusion of Gertrude Stein in American Number."

The disagreement, however, was deeper than simply a quarrel over Stein: it was a profound difference of literary taste and judgment. Under Loeb's editorship with the assistance of Matthew Josephson *Broom* had become a distinctly modernist, avant-garde, and Dadaist magazine, embracing as one of its tenets the notion (as Josephson put it in *Broom*, June 1922) that "The machine is our magnificent slave, our fraternal genius. We are . . . friend to the skyscraper and to the subterranean railroad as well." Such a view was completely alien to Lola Ridge, to whom the machine was simply the instrument by which the wealthy capitalist exploited and oppressed the worker: the machine belonged in art only as an object of hatred and scorn. Nevertheless, her resignation could not go into effect immediately, and while awaiting her replacement she still worked—as Loeb said, looking back in 1951, "energetically, with and without pay, with and without assistants." Visiting New York in Jan-

uary 1923 Loeb found Lola Ridge "ill and tired, . . . waiting for someone to supplant her." When Loeb gave up the editorship of *Broom* in 1923 (the March issue was his last, and it went to press before January; the magazine had a brief revival in New York, from August 1923 to January 1924, under Josephson), Ridge stayed on in the basement at East Ninth Street, rent free, with her husband. When in the spring she met Josephson, she asked him for his definition of poetry and offered her own: "My idea of the poem is a snowflake sparkling and melting in the sun." The real disagreement between Lola Ridge and the editors of *Broom* is that she was not by temperament a modernist at all and that she in fact resisted the modern; idealistic, sentimental, and politically a revolutionary, she preferred Kreymborg (whom Loeb had found too conservative as coeditor of *Broom*) to Stein; she wanted to open the pages of *Broom* to Evelyn Scott ("She is perhaps the most brilliant critic in America") while

Edna St. Vincent Millay and Lola Ridge being arrested for picketing against the executions of Nicola Sacco and Bartolomeo Vanzetti, August 1927, and title page (courtesy of the Lilly Library, Indiana University) for the long poem Ridge wrote in response to the executions

Loeb opened them to Stravinsky, Pirandello, Picasso; she saw poetry either as a medium for political protest (she denied that it was propaganda) or as an aesthetic, remote, otherworldly object.

This attitude hardened over the next few years, and her remaining three books increasingly exhibit an aesthetic conservatism, a drift toward the abstract and symbolic and toward the mystical or spiritual. She maintained her connections with radical causes—even though increasing ill health led her further and further into the life of a semi-invalid. On its foundation in 1926 *New Masses* made her a contributing editor, and she published both verse and prose in its pages. *Red Flag* (1927) includes poems saluting the Russian Revolution, commemorating martyrs of other struggles, and offering rebels like Spartacus as models. As Allen Guttman remarks, her lines on Alexander Kerensky suggest "her own fascination with the contrast between weakness and strength"; weak herself (she was, in 1927, fifty-three years old, constantly undernourished, more or less constantly ill), she described Kerensky as the "flower the storm spewed white and broken out of its red path." Most of the poems in the book are personal, however: lyrics celebrating or recording spiritual beauty; sonnets on her contemporaries. The public poems tend to be the exclusive domain of her loose free verse, and in the personal poems she moves more and more toward traditional forms and structures and toward a stylized "poetic" diction.

In 1927 she was particularly active in the picketing, marches, and rallies protesting the execution of Sacco and Vanzetti. On 10 August she was arrested (along with Edna St. Vincent Millay, Katherine Anne Porter, and others) and on her release continued to protest the execution, which took place at midnight, 22 August 1927. Her poem "Three Men Die," which first appeared in the Spring 1931 issue of the *Left* (and is the most successful poem of her last book, *Dance of Fire*, 1935), is her clearest statement in verse on that event, but on 1 September 1927, after two nights without sleep, she began a short, intense lyric which, within the week, became the complete plan (save the final section) of *Firehead* (1929), her response to the Sacco and Vanzetti affair. It was not until in 1929 when she went to Yaddo, the artists' colony on the Trask estate at Saratoga Springs, New York, that she was able to complete this work; she did so in two-and-a-half months. Some 200 pages long, *Firehead* (published in December 1929) recounts the story of the Crucifixion from various points of view (including those of the two Marys, Judas, and Pe-

Lola Ridge, 1935 (photograph by Marjorie Content; courtesy of the Lilly Library, Indiana University)

ter) in nine sections. It was acclaimed as her masterpiece. Stephen Vincent Benét was quoted in the *New York Times* (21 May 1941) as saying that it showed the unmistakable sign of genius and that "I know nothing like it in American letters." Writing in the *Saturday Review* (28 December 1929), Louis Untermeyer called it a noble failure: "If all of *Firehead* attained the level of its second half, Lola Ridge's new work would be . . . one of the most impressive creations of any American poet." The major flaws in the work are the clutter of vivid detail which obscures the main thrust of the movement, an abstract and incompletely formulated mysticism or spirituality which makes for prolixity, and a fondness for archaic diction and inversions. William Rose Benét's judgment in his obituary for Ridge (*Saturday Review*, 31 May 1941) that *Firehead* "will stand as one of the most remarkable long poems written by man or woman in our time" has not lasted through the intervening years, though some passages, especially in the second half, are notable.

In 1930 she paid a second visit to Yaddo, where she outlined an ambitious poem cycle, "Lightwheel," which would include *Firehead* and

LOLA RIDGE

DANCE

OF

FIRE

NEW YORK : NINETEEN THIRTY-FIVE

HARRISON SMITH AND ROBERT HAAS

Title page for Ridge's last book, which is based on her belief that "we are living in a dynasty of fire" (courtesy of the Lilly Library, Indiana University)

five other books (set in ancient Babylon, renaissance Florence, Mexico under Cortez and Montezuma, the French Revolution, and postwar Manhattan). In 1931 she traveled to the Middle East and in 1935-1937 (on a 1935 Guggenheim Fellowship) to Mexico to research this project, but it grew little beyond its outline. Her last book, *Dance of Fire* (1935), was not on the whole successful. The most interesting of the poems in the book (besides "Three Men Die") is the sequence of twenty-eight sonnets, "Via Ignis," though their intensity is dissipated by abstractions:

> This is to bear, with cleavage and in pain
> Adhesions wrenched at, and to suffer thrust;
> This is to feel the slip of the earth's crust
> And rage of forces, ages overlain.

"It is difficult to discover why," Hildegarde Flanner observed in a review for *Poetry* (October 1935), "she lapses into archaisms of speech and with no more

reason discards them." Overall, *Dance of Fire* explores Lola Ridge's lifelong preoccupation with fire as a symbol of spirit, of the transcendence of suffering, of the exaltation of spirit. "I feel we are living in a dynasty of fire," she wrote in her preface to the book; "We are still in the midst of the fire dance; the flame that breaks down, fuses and forms, is still burning nakedly in humanity. And unlike the stars which move in perfect harmony in the great design, we rush to impact on our courses. But man is no mere puppet of destiny, and he alone can extricate himself from chaos. We may come forth, for a period, into the time of light." The late poems, on the whole, are rendered elusive if not inaccessible by a private diction of extreme abstractness and hence imprecise suggestiveness. The substance of the poetry remains amorphous.

On 19 May 1941 she died at her home, 111 Montague Street, Brooklyn, aged sixty-seven. In her memory S. A. DeWitt established, in *Poetry*, the Lola Ridge Memorial Award, which was discontinued after 1950. In 1923 she had won *Poetry*'s Guarantor's Prize, and in 1935 and 1936 she received the Shelley Memorial Award. When, in an essay on Kreymborg in 1919, she commented that Whitman "was concerned only with the broad and common currents of existence—whatever surrounded and included the life of crowds—and like most democrats he was unaware of nuances," she was also (unwittingly) describing herself. A political radical of left-wing persuasion, though unlike most American left-wing writers she had firsthand knowledge of working-class life, she was enamored of large abstractions like "the triumph of the working class," and her literary career, which moves from the romanticized realism of *The Ghetto, and Other Poems* to the mannered symbolism of *Dance of Fire*, is coherent in its predilections, in its strengths and weaknesses. It is not untypical of "proletarian" American writers. Her work displays little or no interest in puns, wordplay, syntactic play, rhythmic subtlety: her cadenced verse is loose and relies on image and simile—and on "poeticisms." In her public poetry she is too often intent on the rhetoric of exhortation or denunciation, in her personal, on the private, symbolic, and abstract. Her best work is in *The Ghetto* and *Sun-Up*, but there are good poems scattered through her works. There is no biography, and she has been the subject of no critical study, which is to our loss—as is the lack of a volume of selected poems, to say nothing of her absence from anthologies. Like many others of her generation—such as Skipwith Cannell, Donald Evans, Alanson Hartpence, Orrick Johns, and Billy

Saphier the machinist poet—she was not an impressive poet, but she has nevertheless been unduly neglected.

References:
Horace Gregory and Marya Zaturenska, *A History of American Poetry, 1900-1940* (New York: Harcourt, Brace, 1946);
Matthew Josephson, *Life Among the Surrealists: A Memoir* (New York: Holt, Rinehart & Winston, 1962);
Alfred Kreymborg, *Our Singing Strength: A History of American Poetry* (New York: Coward-McCann, 1929);
Kreymborg, *Troubadour: An American Autobiography* (New York: Boni & Liveright, 1925);
Harold A. Loeb, *The Way It Was* (New York: Criterion, 1959);
Robert McAlmon, *Being Geniuses Together 1920-1930*, revised, with supplementary chapters, by Kay Boyle (Garden City: Doubleday, 1968);
Katherine Anne Porter, *The Never-Ending Wrong* (Boston: Little, Brown, 1977);
William Carlos Williams, *The Autobiography of William Carlos Williams* (New York: New Directions, 1951).

Papers:
Lola Ridge's papers in public collections are few and scattered. There is a handful of letters at Yale University and at the University of Texas at Austin. The Mitchell Library, Sydney, Australia, has manuscripts of some very early poems.

Elizabeth Madox Roberts
(30 October 1881-13 March 1941)

Anne E. Rowe
Florida State University

See also the Roberts entry in *DLB 9, American Novelists, 1910-1945.*

BOOKS: *In the Great Steep's Garden* (Colorado Springs: Goudy-Simmons, 1915);
Under the Tree (New York: Huebsch, 1922; London: Cape, 1928; enlarged edition, New York: Viking, 1930);
The Time of Man (New York: Viking, 1926; London: Cape, 1927);
My Heart and My Flesh (New York: Viking, 1927; London: Cape, 1928);
Jingling in the Wind (New York: Viking, 1928; London: Cape, 1929);
The Great Meadow (New York: Viking, 1930; London: Cape, 1930);
A Buried Treasure (New York: Viking, 1931; London: Cape, 1932);
The Haunted Mirror (New York: Viking, 1932; London: Cape, 1933);
He Sent Forth a Raven (New York: Viking, 1935; London: Cape, 1935);
Black is My True Love's Hair (New York: Viking, 1938; London: Hale, 1939);
Song in the Meadow (New York: Viking, 1940);
Not by Strange Gods (New York: Viking, 1941).

According to one of her biographers, Elizabeth Madox Roberts, upon seeing a portrait of Elizabeth Barrett Browning captioned "Poet," declared at the tender age of eight that she too wished to be a poet. Her childhood resolution was fulfilled. Although she is remembered today more for her fiction than her poetry, she published during her lifetime a small but generally excellent body of poetry.

Most of Roberts's life was spent in Kentucky, a fact which had a major influence on her writing. She was born in 1881 in Perryville, Kentucky, but her family moved in 1884 to nearby Springfield, another rural community which would become the basis for many of the small towns depicted in her poetry and fiction. Roberts's parents, Simpson and Mary Elizabeth Brent Roberts, were influential in a variety of ways for the aspiring writer. Her father was never successful financially; he ran a store and worked on various engineering projects in the area. The family's mild poverty led Elizabeth to make up a family, the Wilsons, whose affluence counterpointed the Robertses' wants. The imaginary family was a forerunner of some of the characters Roberts would later create in her fiction and poetry. Equally important for Roberts's development were the

Elizabeth Madox Roberts

hours her father spent telling his children tales and legends. The elder Roberts had lost many of his books in a fire, and his daughter later remembered that she grew up with "phantom books" as her father recollected them and retold their stories to his children. One other significant family influence was the fact that Roberts's mother's ancestors were among pioneers who followed after Daniel Boone into the Kentucky wilderness. Roberts re-created these larger-than-life pioneers, especially Boone, in her work, most notably in her novel *The Great Meadow* (1930).

Roberts's early education was at a private academy, Professor Grant's school, in Springfield. After she had completed schooling there, her family sent her to board with relatives in Covington, Kentucky, where she attended high school. In 1900 she entered the State College of Kentucky (later the University of Kentucky) but because of ill health and financial problems was forced to withdraw after a year.

Returning home to Springfield, she opened a private school. She also taught in a Sunday school as well. She spent the years between 1901 and 1914 teaching in Springfield and other nearby communities. She made visits to relatives in Colorado, and in 1914 she stayed there for a year or so. The Colorado experience led to the publication of her first volume of poetry, *In the Great Steep's Garden* (1915). The following year Roberts enrolled again at the University of Kentucky, where she spent a year. The poetry she wrote during this period was highly praised by Prof. James Noe, who recommended Roberts to Prof. Robert Morss Lovett at the University of Chicago.

Encouraged by this enthusiastic response to her work, Roberts in 1917, at the age of thirty-six, registered as a freshman at the University of Chicago. The Chicago years were crucial to her development as a poet. Before, she had worked in relative isolation; here she became a part of a literary group which included Yvor Winters and Glenway Westcott. She met regularly with this group, exchanged criticism and ideas with them, and worked hard at developing her poetic style. She was encouraged by the editor of *Poetry* magazine, Harriet Monroe, who accepted some of her poems, and she won the Fiske Poetry Prize in 1922.

Having earned a Ph.B. in 1921, at the age of forty, Roberts had at last completed her university degree and, perhaps more important, prepared herself for a writing career which would continue for the next twenty-one years. In both her fiction and poetry Roberts explored similar themes: the relationship between internal perception and external experience (drawn from her study of the philosophy of George Berkeley); the influence of the rural setting (modeled on her native Kentucky) on the rhythms of life; and, most important, the phenomenon of the passage of time from one generation to the next.

Roberts's work in fiction has received considerably more critical attention than her poetry. Although the quality of her seven novels and two collections of short stories is varied, several of her novels are first-rate, especially *The Time of Man* (1926) and *The Great Meadow* (1930). Both of these novels (the first dealing with the growth of Ellen Chesser from childhood into a mature woman and the second chronicling the life of Diony Hall, who was among the pioneers following after Daniel Boone into the Kentucky wilderness) are notable for their skillful portrayal of these women's inner lives and their responses to the rural world of which they are a part.

Critics often describe Roberts's fiction as "poetic prose." Her poetry is not so much a departure from her fiction as a complement to it. Roberts wrote and published poetry throughout her writing career, and she seemed equally comfortable in either genre.

Roberts's first volume of poetry, *In the Great Steep's Garden* (1915), is largely apprentice work. A Colorado friend, Kenneth Hartley, had photographed a number of mountain flowers, and for each of his photos Roberts wrote a short poem. This privately printed collection of seven photos and seven poems has received scant critical attention, and it is far less important than Roberts's next two volumes of poetry.

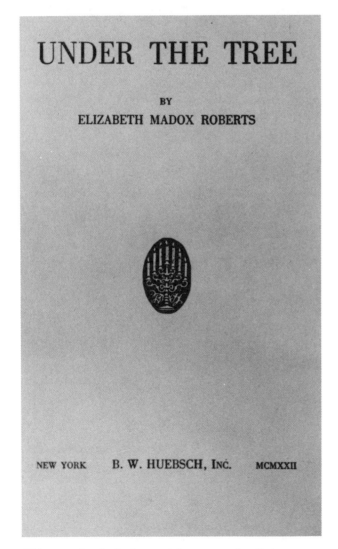

Title page for the book containing poems that Roberts wrote while she was a student at the University of Chicago (courtesy of the Lilly Library, Indiana University)

Many of the poems in *Under the Tree* (1922) were written in Chicago or grew out of her experiences there. Harry Modean Campbell and Ruel E. Foster have quoted Roberts as saying that in her poetry she aimed "to make clear [the] obscure relations in the worlds and systems of things and ideas," to keep "close to my own experience . . . in Kentucky," and to use "child speech and child psychology for my images." Most of the poems in this volume are written from the point of view of a child and the setting is usually small town life.

In their brief section on Roberts's poetry, Campbell and Foster cite "August Night" as a typical Roberts poem. It opens with a specific localized scene, offers a childlike perception of it, and concludes with a penetrating observation:

> We had to wait for the heat to pass,
> And I was lying on the grass,
>
> While Mother sat outside the door,
> And I saw how many stars there were
> ....
> So many of them and so small,
> Suppose I cannot know them all.

Although the poems collected in *Under the Tree* can appeal to both the child and the adult reader, they have been republished most often in anthologies for children. Conventional in rhyme and meter, they are nevertheless remarkable for the way in which Roberts uses simple images to lead the reader to contemplate complex issues.

More experimental in form and more varied in subject matter are the poems collected in Roberts's final volume of poetry, *Song in the Meadow* (1940). The influence of Gerard Manley Hopkins, whose work Roberts read in the 1930s, is evident in these poems as Roberts experiments in free verse, sprung rhythm, and less-conventional rhyme schemes. The point of view in these poems is no longer limited to that of the child, and Roberts broadens her range from the contemplation of simple physical objects to considerations of legend and the past as well as contemporary social issues.

Song in the Meadow is divided into three sections. "Maidens and Lovers," the first section, continues some of the themes of *Under the Tree*, as "Evening Song," in which the speaker muses over the relationship of the outside world and the inner life, explaining that in her sleep she winds her senses "in a little ball," which she goes on to describe as "a lonely ball" and "a lonely mesh." Then, "I fold

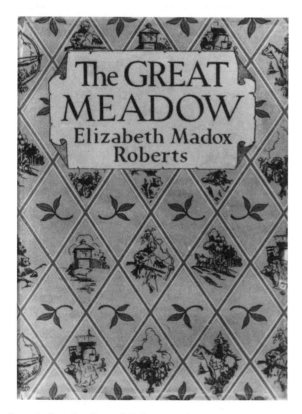

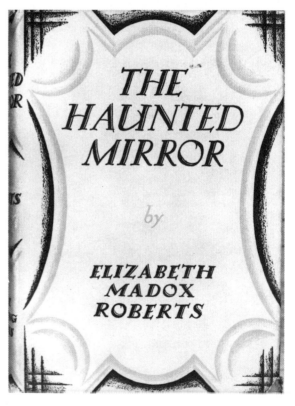

Dust jackets for four of Roberts's volumes of fiction, the genre in which she earned her literary reputation (courtesy of the Lilly Library, Indiana University)

it over with my dream,/And wind it round and round with flesh."

The second section, "The World and the Earth," includes poems dealing with contemporary social themes. "Man Intolerant" treats war and ends on a note of despair: "Man," says Roberts, is "set adrift on a deep that can never be sounded,/And hurls without compass and grace/Toward the last holocaust, the infinite merciless first-last unknowing abyss." As evidenced by these lines, some of the poems in this section are much darker than her earlier ones.

In part three, "Legends," Roberts draws on national legends and the ancient stories of fairy tales. "Cinderella's Song" is a fanciful contrast to the poems in the preceding section:

> On, little cat beside my stool,
> My tabby cat, my ashy one,
> I'll tell you something in your ear,
> It's I can put the slipper on.

In this poem Cinderella says that she can wait for her beloved, thus aligning herself with many of Roberts's heroines (such as Diony Hall of *The Great Meadow*) who play the traditional woman's role of patient waiting.

Elizabeth Roberts came late to her work as a serious writer of fiction and poetry and left a modest number of poems (including some which have not been published). Her poetry, which is really an extension of the lyrical quality of all her writing, has earned for her a small but secure niche in the history of American poetry.

References:

Harry Modean Campbell and Ruel E. Foster, *Elizabeth Madox Roberts: American Novelist* (Norman: University of Oklahoma Press, 1956);

Frederick P. W. McDowell, *Elizabeth Madox Roberts* (New York: Twayne, 1963);

Earl H. Rovit, *Herald to Chaos: The Novels of Elizabeth Madox Roberts* (Lexington: University of Kentucky Press, 1960);

Robert Penn Warren, "Elizabeth Madox Roberts: Life Is From Within," *Saturday Review*, 46 (2 March 1963): 20-21, 38.

Papers:

The largest collection of Roberts's papers is at the Library of Congress.

Edwin Arlington Robinson

Nancy Carol Joyner
Western Carolina University

BIRTH: Head Tide, Maine, 22 December 1869, to Edward and Mary Palmer Robinson.

EDUCATION: Harvard University, 1891-1893.

AWARDS AND HONORS: Pulitzer Prize for *Collected Poems,* 1922; D.Litt., Yale University, 1922; Levinson Prize (*Poetry* magazine), 1923; Pulitzer Prize for *The Man Who Died Twice,* 1925; D.Litt., Bowdoin College, 1925; Pulitzer Prize for *Tristram,* 1928; Gold Medal, National Institute and American Academy of Arts and Letters, 1929.

DEATH: New York, New York, 6 April 1935.

SELECTED BOOKS: *The Torrent and The Night Before* (Cambridge: Privately printed, 1896);
The Children of the Night (Boston: Richard G. Badger, 1897);
Captain Craig (Boston & New York: Houghton, Mifflin, 1902; London: A. P. Watt, 1902; enlarged edition, New York: Macmillan, 1915);
The Town Down the River (New York: Scribners, 1910);
Van Zorn (New York: Macmillan, 1914);
The Porcupine (New York: Macmillan, 1915);
The Man Against the Sky (New York: Macmillan, 1916);
Merlin (New York: Macmillan, 1917);
Lancelot (New York: Thomas Seltzer, 1920);
The Three Taverns (New York: Macmillan, 1920);
Avon's Harvest (New York: Macmillan, 1921);
Collected Poems (New York: Macmillan, 1921; London: Cecil Palmer, 1922);
Roman Bartholow (New York: Macmillan, 1923; London: Cecil Palmer, 1923);
The Man Who Died Twice (New York: Macmillan, 1924; London: Cecil Palmer, 1924);
Dionysus in Doubt (New York: Macmillan, 1925);
Tristram (New York: Macmillan, 1927; London: Gollancz, 1928);
Collected Poems, 5 volumes (Cambridge, Mass.: Dunster House, 1927);
Sonnets, 1889-1917 (New York: Crosby Gaige, 1928);

Fortunatus (Reno: Slide Mountain Press, 1928);
Modred (New York, New Haven & Princeton: Brick Row Bookshop, 1929);
Cavender's House (New York: Macmillan, 1929; London: Hogarth Press, 1930);
Collected Poems (New York: Macmillan, 1930);
The Glory of the Nightingales (New York: Macmillan, 1930);
Selected Poems (New York: Macmillan, 1931);
Matthias at the Door (New York: Macmillan, 1931);

Photograph by Pirie MacDonald

Nicodemus (New York: Macmillan, 1932);
Talifer (New York: Macmillan, 1933);
Amaranth (New York: Macmillan, 1934);
King Jasper (New York: Macmillan, 1935);
Collected Poems (New York: Macmillan, 1937);
Selected Early Poems and Letters, edited by Charles T.
    Davis (New York: Holt, Rinehart & Winston,
    1960);
Uncollected Poems and Prose, edited by Richard Cary
    (Waterville, Maine: Colby College Press,
    1975).

One of the most prolific major American poets of the twentieth century, Edwin Arlington Robinson is, ironically, best remembered for only a handful of short poems. Aside from a few that he complained were "pickled in anthological brine"—"Richard Cory," "Miniver Cheevy," and "Mr. Flood's Party"—most of his work is not widely known. The 1,500-page collected edition of his work (1937) contains the twenty volumes of poetry published during his lifetime, including the thirteen long narratives which critics have ignored or denigrated but which he regarded as among his best work. Indeed, the long poems that occupied his energies during the last dozen years of his life were not designed for popular appeal, and his stubborn insistence on traditional forms at a time of extraordinary technical experimentation led to the critical attitude that his work is anachronistic, a throwback to the nineteenth-century triumphs of Robert Browning, Alfred Tennyson, and Matthew Arnold. Such a view and the concomitant lack of interest in his work is unfortunate, for Robinson was a true innovator within the constraints of the traditional forms; his attitude, tone, and eclectic subject matter genuinely anticipate the main thrust of twentieth-century American poetry. As Robert Frost, in his introduction to *King Jasper,* put it, Robinson was "content with the old-fashioned way to be new."

In an age when other prominent poets were engaged in many other pursuits, Robinson stood alone in his unmitigated devotion to writing poetry. T. S. Eliot with his career in publishing, William Carlos Williams with his medical practice, Wallace Stevens with his executive position in an insurance company, and Frost, seemingly the most "professional" poet, with his teaching jobs and his speaking tours—all had other interests and accomplishments. Robinson, on the other hand, did virtually nothing in his life save write poetry: he neither married nor traveled; he neither taught nor gave public readings; he neither had professional prep-

aration nor any extended occupation other than the writing of poetry. On the occasion of his fiftieth birthday he was treated to an encomium in the *New York Times Book Review* (21 December 1919), which published comments by sixteen writers, including this statement from Amy Lowell: "Edwin Arlington Robinson is poetry. I can think of no other living writer who has so consistently dedicated his life to his work." Hermann Hagedorn used as the epigraph for the first and still the most valuable biography this quotation from Robinson:

> In the great shuffle of transmitted characteristics, traits, abilities, aptitudes, the man who fixes on something definite in life that he must do, at the expense of everything else, if necessary, has presumably got something that, for him, should be recognized as the Inner Fire. For him, that is the Gleam, the Vision and the Word! He'd better follow it. The greatest adventure he'll ever have on this side is following where it leads.

The expense of Robinson's single-mindedness was virtually everything else in life that people strive for, but it eventually won for him both fortune and fame, as well as a firm position in literary history as America's first important poet of the twentieth century.

The time and place of Robinson's birth contributed both positively and negatively to that position. Born in the tiny hamlet of Head Tide, Maine, and growing up in the somewhat larger town of Gardiner, he lived in a remote corner of the nation that was nevertheless relatively close to the cultural center, Boston. Also, he had the advantage of a neighborhood that helped to cultivate his literary interests at an early age. Born in 1869, at the threshold of the gilded age, when the industrial revolution was making an irreversible impact on his surroundings, he was deeply aware of and later recorded the dichotomy of material wealth versus emotional and spiritual health as values in his society. Robinson reached his majority in 1890, that decade notorious in American literary history because of its poetic aridity. When he published his first volume in 1896, he could admire no living American poet, much less enjoy membership in a literary community.

Robinson's immediate family also helped and hindered him. Both of his parents, Edward and Mary Elizabeth Palmer Robinson, were of old New England stock, although his mother's family was the more illustrious as well as the more thoroughly

The Robinson family home in Gardiner, Maine (courtesy of Edwin Arlington Robinson's Heirs)

traditional in that she had bona fide Puritan ancestors. It is often noted that Robinson is related on the distaff side to Anne Bradstreet, the first genuine American poet. The stronger influence in Robinson's home was his father, Edward, an eminently practical man of Scotch-Irish descent, who had a strong sense of civic responsibility and sufficient business acumen to retire from his mercantile business with a fortune of $80,000, in 1870, at fifty-one. It was then that he moved his family from Head Tide to Gardiner, where his three sons could receive a better education. Edward Robinson had nothing against education so long as it enabled a person to improve his financial opportunities. He sent his studious eldest son, Dean, to medical school but prevented his continuing in medical research; he groomed his affable middle son, Herman, to take up the family business ventures, principally land speculation; and he advised his youngest, Edwin, called Win, to follow the scientific (or non-college-preparatory) track in high school, although he did send him, eventually and somewhat grudgingly, to Harvard as a special student. Although business success was Edward Robinson's chief goal, he was not without cultural interests. He often

spent his evenings singing with the others around the family piano or reading excerpts from William Cullen Bryant's *Library of Poetry and Song.* It has been said that memories of childhood constitute a writer's capital. Robinson's memories are generally those of an upper-middle-class, rural, Calvinistic upbringing in which the arts were part of his home environment but secondary to an emphasis on the practical necessities of earning a living. He both represented and rebelled against that background.

Robinson's only published autobiographical account is a magazine piece, "The First Seven Years," which appeared in the December 1930 issue of *Colophon* and is now included in *Uncollected Poems and Prose* (1975). In it he pointed out his early enthusiasm for poetry and his parents' lack of awareness that that interest was developing into a serious career goal. He acknowledged the influence of his neighbor, Dr. Alanson T. Schumann, an amateur versifier who encouraged metrical exercises for Robinson during his high school years. He reported that when he was seventeen he "became violently excited over the structure and music of English blank verse" and made several metrical translations from Cicero, Vergil, and Sophocles.

He went on to say, "It must have been about the year 1889 when I realized finally . . . that I was doomed, or elected, or sentenced for life, to the writing of poetry." The seven years to which the title refers is the period between that realization and the publication of his first book in 1896. In that period he published a few poems in the local newspaper, the *Harvard Advocate,* and in two or three magazines. He also noted that he collected a pile of rejection slips "that must have been one of the largest and most comprehensive in literary history." Eventually he decided to publish his poems on his own and paid fifty-two dollars to the Riverside Press in Cambridge to print 312 copies of a forty-four-page pamphlet "named, rather arbitrarily, from the first and last poem: *The Torrent and The Night Before.*" With that pamphlet Robinson's poetic career was launched.

Ever the restrained New Englander, Robinson did not record the dismal family circumstances of those first seven years. His brother Dean, thwarted in his ambition to become a pathologist and, by dosing himself for facial neuralgia, acquired a drug habit that lost him his medical practice and led to his eventual suicide. His brother Herman met Win's putative fiancée, Emma Shepherd, and

married her. Win managed to go to Harvard for two years partially because he needed medical treatment in Boston for his lifelong difficulties with one ear. His father died of a stroke in 1892. Much of the family fortune was lost during the recession of 1893. Finally, in 1896, his mother died of black diptheria, a disease so contagious that the undertaker would not set foot in the house and her sons were required to make the burial preparations themselves. A few weeks after his mother's death Robinson received in the mail the surprise he had planned for her—the copies of his first book. He did not open the package for a day, he reported to his friend Harry Smith, and when he did the books "looked so small and devilish blue" they made him sick, but, he went on, "now I am feeling better and beginning to foster my same old ridiculous notion that they may amount to something some day." They have.

The forty-six poems in *The Torrent and The Night Before* present an impressive variety in theme, subject matter, and technique. Consistent with his future practice, all the poems are in rhymed or blank verse. (All his life Robinson strenuously objected to free verse, replying once when asked if he wrote it, "No, I write badly enough as it is.")

The poet's parents, Edward and Mary Palmer Robinson (courtesy of Edwin Arlington Robinson's Heirs)

The poet in 1888, the year he graduated from high school

The deceptive simplicity of the words tends to obscure the artistry of the work, with the commonplace scene of the octet transfigured into a striking metaphor in the sestet, where the tone, subject matter, theme, diction, and technical mastery are all quintessentially Robinsonian. The combination of the realistic, narrative mode and the more romantic, expository mode is deftly indicated by the switch from first person narration to the generalized address at the end. These two forms are not always in the same poem, but the combination of narrative and expository writing is perhaps Robinson's most characteristic trait. The undeniably gloomy "message," or theme, of the poem, couched as it is in a deliberate matter-of-fact and unpreten-

Edwin Arlington Robinson, 1896 (photograph in chiaroscuro by William E. Butler, courtesy of Special Collections, Colby College, Waterville, Maine). Robinson commented about this photograph: "I have a look that might lead one to think that I had just eaten the lining out of my own coffin, but that is the fault of an uncomfortable feel somewhere in my spinal column."

These early poems, however, are distinguished from his later practice in that there are more examples of elaborate verse forms: villanelles and ballades appear along with the more conventional quatrains and the form of which he was to become a modern master, the sonnet. One of the sonnets is "The Clerks," the poem whose rejection by the editor of the *New York Sun* Robinson cited as the final impetus for him to publish his own book. It is in many ways representative of his early work:

I did not think that I should find them there
When I came back again; but there they stood,
As in the days they dreamed of when young blood
Was in their cheeks and women called them fair.
Be sure, they met me with an ancient air,—
And yes, there was a shop-worn brotherhood
About them; but the men were just as good,
And just as human as they ever were.

And you that ache so much to be sublime,
And you that feed yourselves with your descent,
What comes of all your visions and your fears?
Poets and kings are but the clerks of Time,
Tiering the same dull webs of discontent,
Clipping the same sad alnage of the years.

tious tone is also typical. The self-consciousness of the climactic line, "Poets and kings are but the clerks of Time," however, is indicative of Robinson's earliest work.

Charles T. Davis, in his introduction to *Selected Early Poems and Letters* (1960), says, "The odd fact about Robinson is that he began, in a sense, as a mature poet, almost immediately conscious of his artistic goals and aware of his own powers and weaknesses." This notion has become a critical commonplace, with some validity. His first brief character sketch of the sort that are now called his Tilbury poems is placed second in *The Torrent and The Night Before:* "Aaron Stark," the miser with "eyes like little dollars in the dark." And the name Tilbury is first mentioned in this volume in "John Evereldown," a dialogue between a man and his wife. Two of his best-known poems, "Credo" and "Luke Havergal," appear in this volume, along with several others that are highly regarded. Nevertheless, this earliest collection also contains poems that may legitimately be considered juvenilia, and, while it would be difficult to consider these efforts derivative, some do indicate a dependence on earlier poets that does not appear in Robinson's more mature work. In fact, more individual poems from this volume than any other were omitted from the first *Collected Poems* (1921). To say that Robinson was at the height of his powers in 1896 implies that no development occurred in the remaining forty years of his career. Such a claim is a distinct disservice to the poet and his art.

When Robinson received his packet of pamphlets in December 1896, he literally gave them away, both to local acquaintances and, more important, to editors of journals and to writers who he thought might be sympathetic to his work. Richard Cary, former curator of the Robinson collection at Colby College, included in *Early Reception of Edwin Arlington Robinson* (1974) nineteen reviews from journals which received the volume and named twenty-five other recipients—such as Robert Bridges, Thomas Hardy, and Algernon Charles Swinburne—who did not respond publicly to the book. The nineteen reviews are, if somewhat tentative, generally favorable, since editors rarely take up valuable space by panning an unsolicited, privately printed book of poems. Many of them were noncommittal notices that quoted a sample poem, but some were quite extensive, the most thorough and thoughtful one being that of William Peterfield Trent, in the April 1897 issue of the *Sewanee Review*. Trent suspected that the writer was young and noted some poems that seemed derivative, but he

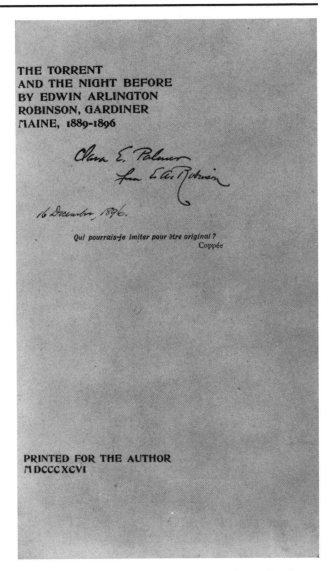

Title page for Robinson's first book (courtesy of the Lilly Library, Indiana University). When reviewer Harry Thurston Peck accused the poet of depicting the world as a "prison-house," Robinson denied the charge, saying instead that it was "a kind of spiritual kindergarten, where millions of bewildered infants are trying to spell God with the wrong blocks."

also offered the book "some ungrudging praise."

The most noteworthy review of *The Torrent and The Night Before* was that of Harry Thurston Peck, published in the February 1897 issue of the *Bookman*. Peck found many of the poems too somber for his liking and said that Robinson's "humour is of a grim sort, and the world is not beautiful to him, but a prison-house." In response to that comment Robinson wrote a letter of rebuttal, published in the March 1897 *Bookman*, which has become as well known a critical statement as he was ever to

Front cover for Robinson's second book (courtesy of the Lilly Library, Indiana University). As Allen Tate remarked half a century later, the volume was "little noticed at the time but one which marks the beginning of a new era in American poetry."

make: "I am sorry that I have painted myself in such lugubrious colours. The world is not a prison house, but a kind of spiritual kindergarten, where millions of bewildered infants are trying to spell God with the wrong blocks."

Certainly Robinson was anything but pessimistic regarding his career during this period. As his letters indicate, he was buoyed by the critical success of *The Torrent and The Night Before* and had a second manuscript ready within months of his first publication. A vanity press in Boston, Richard G. Badger and Company, solicited his business and promised promotion and distribution as well as an attractive product, all advantages over the situation of the book he had printed privately. Although Robinson was unable to pay the costs of vanity publishing, he accepted the offer of his friend William

Butler to do so. Using a vanity press rather than the "respectable publisher" for which he had originally looked also gave Robinson the advantage of speed. Almost exactly one year after his first book appeared, *The Children of the Night* was printed attractively in two formats, a 500-copy trade edition bound in light tan cloth with a red and green art nouveau design, as well as a 50-copy limited edition printed on vellum. The book was designed and marketed for the Christmas trade, and the strategy was successful: 300 copies had been sold by January.

Included in *The Children of the Night* are forty-four of the forty-six poems published the previous year as well as forty-three additional poems. The new poems are in much the same vein as the earlier ones, but there are some important additions. One has become Robinson's best-known poem, "Richard Cory," notable for its contrast between the aloofness of the eponymous character and the down-to-earth quality of the unusual narrator who speaks in the first person plural, "We people on the pavement"; the effectiveness of the surprise ending in which the sensational event is related in understated diction; and the consistent image pattern of royalty. Also added are twenty-seven "Octaves," an eight-line, blank verse form, usually written as one sentence, that Robinson claimed was more difficult to write than the sonnet. The octaves are somewhat somber philosophical speculations or pronouncements whose generalizations are given force by a striking image or an unusual choice of words. "Octave XVII," for example, uses a quite ordinary travel metaphor but concludes with a startling oxymoron:

> We lack the courage to be where we are:—
> We love too much to travel on old roads,
> To triumph on old fields; we love too much
> To consecrate the magic mix of dead things,
> And yieldingly to linger by long walls
> Of ruin, where the ruinous moonlight
> That sheds a lying glory on old stones
> Befriends us with a wizard's enmity.

Reviews of *The Children of the Night* were mixed, with some critics providing only lukewarm notices, apparently because of the vanity imprint. With a few exceptions the notices were extremely brief and in local newspapers rather than in journals with national circulations. But the prestigious Thomas Wentworth Higginson, writing for the *Nation* in June 1898, found that the poet "does his work deftly and thoroughly." Allen Tate, in an essay collected in his *On the Limits of Poetry* (1948), called this book "little noticed at the time but one which marks the beginning of a new era in American poetry."

Until 1897 Robinson lived in his childhood home in Gardiner, sharing the house, after his parents died, with his two brothers, Herman's wife, Emma, and his three nieces. According to one biographer, Chard Powers Smith, he left the house in the fall of 1897 after a dispute with Herman over Emma, a triangular situation that Smith maintains is the biographical impetus for the predominance of triangular love affairs in Robinson's poetry. In November of 1897 Robinson "discovered" New York, sharing an apartment with a friend and encountering a cosmopolitan society he had not known theretofore. One of his new acquaintances was the erudite derelict Alfred H. Louis, an English Jew with a checkered legal and literary career, a pianist, philosopher, and impromptu orator who had no visible means of support. Louis became the prototype for the title character in Robinson's long poem "Captain Craig."

Emma Shepherd Robinson, wife of the poet's brother Herman (courtesy of Edwin Arlington Robinson's Heirs)

The story of the difficulties attendant upon the publication of "Captain Craig" is symptomatic of Robinson's early struggle for recognition. In the spring of 1900 he wrote a friend that he had finished the work and was satisfied with it, but that he might not be so pleased after it came back from "six or seven publishers." The comment proved prophetic, for the poem was examined by five publishing houses before it was finally accepted. For three months the manuscript languished in a Boston brothel, having been left there by a reader for Small, Maynard and Company and the thoughtful lady of the house having kept it until the client returned. Robinson almost despaired of ever getting "Captain Craig" into print and wrote a group of shorter poems to be published under the title "Isaac and Archibald." Eventually, however, two of his friends, by agreeing to contribute to the publication costs of the long poem, persuaded Houghton, Mifflin to publish the volume under its imprint. In 1902 *Captain Craig*, a volume comprised of the title poem and fifteen shorter poems, finally appeared.

Originally, "Captain Craig" was just over 2,000 lines long, the first of the long narratives that were to dominate his poetry in the last half of his career. In the first of the three sections of the poem, the narrator and his drinking cronies in Tilbury Town meet Captain Craig and presumably save him from starvation. A confessed failure, the captain is unable even to beg:

> There was a time
> When he had fancied, if worst came to worst
> And he could work no more, that he might beg
> Nor be the less for it; but when it came
> To practice he found out that he had not
> The genius.

He has a large capacity for conversation, however, and the narrator is fascinated. When the narrator leaves to go on a six-month trip, the captain writes him voluminous letters, which the narrator saves "for the jokes." Among the jokes are frequent classical and literary allusions, reminiscences of old acquaintances, the recounting of dreams, criticism of poetry, and comments of a vaguely philosophical sort. The third section recounts the narrator's return to Tilbury and the death of the captain, who bequeaths to his benefactors "God's universe and yours." In the funeral procession the Tilbury band "Blared indiscreetly the Dead March in Saul."

As in all of Robinson's long poems, unity in "Captain Craig" is achieved through theme rather

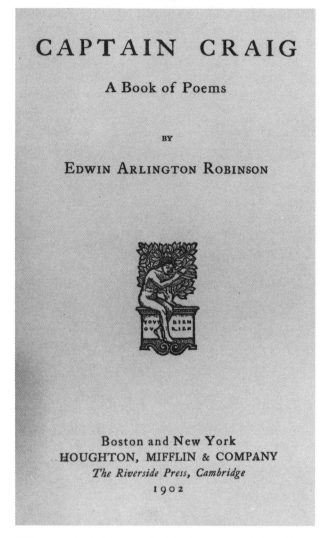

CAPTAIN CRAIG

A Book of Poems

BY

EDWIN ARLINGTON ROBINSON

Boston and New York
HOUGHTON, MIFFLIN & COMPANY
The Riverside Press, Cambridge
1902

Title page for Robinson's third book (courtesy of the Lilly Library, Indiana University). The long title poem was rejected by five publishers—including one whose reader mislaid it in a brothel for three months—before Houghton, Mifflin agreed to publish it along with fifteen shorter poems.

than structure, with the personality of the Captain far more significant than the action described. In his first speech to his group of admirers he makes what may be considered a thesis statement:

> "You are the resurrection and the life"
> He said, "and I the hymn the Brahmin sings;
> O Fuscus! and w'll go no more a-roving."

This quotation is a pastiche of references to the Bible, Emerson, Horace, and Byron, the juxtaposition of which creates an extraordinarily dense texture and anticipates the early work of T. S. Eliot.

It is an illustration of the complexity of this fine poem.

The critics were not kind to *Captain Craig*. Praise was reserved for some of the short poems included in the volume, such as "Isaac and Archibald," "The Klondike," and "Sainte-Nitouche." "Captain Craig" was either ignored, noted as a difficult and puzzling poem, or derogated. Bliss Carman in the December 1902 *Reader* called it "worse than Browning . . . a mistake rather than a failure." And in the March 1903 *Critic* Clinton Scollard suggested that "the volume might have been vastly improved from an artistic standpoint had the author so willed it." According to the biographers, especially Emery Neff, Robinson realized that he was taking a risk in writing so experimental a poem as "Captain Craig," but when the critics did not respond as he had hoped, he was devastated.

The poor critical response to *Captain Craig* is sometimes cited as the reason for the eight-year lapse in Robinson's creative efforts, but other reasons may account for his period of diminished activity. For long periods between 1898 and 1905 he was nearly destitute, living for the most part in a tiny room in a fourth-floor, walk-up apartment house in New York. He held intermittent jobs: as office assistant at Harvard for six months in 1899, as an advertising editor in Boston for two months in 1905, and most notoriously, as time-checker for the construction of the IRT Subway in New York for nine months in 1903-1904. Also, he began to drink heavily; frequenting bars was not only a way to forget his troubles but also a way to get a free lunch, since dispensers of liquor were required by law to provide food with the drink. During this period he came perilously close to falling into permanent dissolution, as both his brothers had done. His whimsical "Miniver Cheevy," the poem about the malcontent modern who yearned for the past glories of the chivalric age and who, finally, "coughed, and called it fate,/And kept on drinking," is presumably a comic self-portrait.

It was President Theodore Roosevelt who almost single-handedly pulled Robinson out of the gutter. In 1904 his son, Kermit, brought home a copy of *The Children of the Night*. Roosevelt read it, voiced his approval sufficiently for Charles Scribner's Sons to republish it in 1905, and wrote a review for the *Outlook* in which is included the statement "I am not sure I understand 'Luke Havergal'; but I am entirely sure that I like it." He also granted Robinson a sinecure in the New York Customs House, a post he held from June 1905 until Roosevelt stepped down from office in 1909.

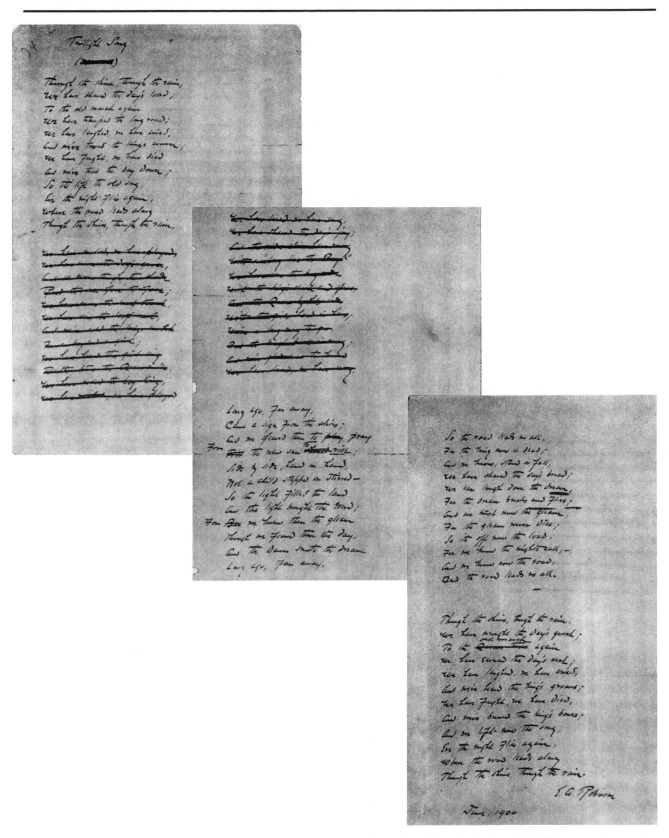

Manuscript for a poem published in Captain Craig. *Robinson considered discarding the poem until William Vaughn Moody suggested that he delete the second and third stanzas. Robinson complied "with joy" (by permission of Edwin Arlington Robinson's Heirs; courtesy of the Watkinson Library, Trinity College, Hartford).*

THE TOWN DOWN THE RIVER

A BOOK OF POEMS

BY

EDWIN ARLINGTON ROBINSON

NEW YORK
CHARLES SCRIBNER'S SONS
1910

Title page for Robinson's fourth book, dedicated to President Theodore Roosevelt, who had almost single-handedly established Robinson's reputation as a poet (courtesy of the Lilly Library, Indiana University)

The $2,000 he received annually for his non-demanding job gave Robinson financial security, but it had a debilitating effect on his writing. He published a few poems in magazines and worked on a new interest, the writing of drama, but he produced no new volume of poetry until after he had resigned his post. In 1910 he at last discharged the debt he felt he owed the former president by producing *The Town Down the River,* named for New York and dedicated to his most prestigious sponsor, Roosevelt.

The Town Down the River is a collection of thirty-three short poems, similar in form to *The Children of the Night* but differing from those in the earlier volume in the predominance of objective, psychological portraits. Some are portraits of public figures: poems to Lincoln and Roosevelt begin

and end the volume, and in the middle is a lengthy dramatic monologue, "The Island," spoken by Napoleon on St. Helena. The most prominent theme in the book is one that has come to be associated with all of Robinson's work, private failure. "Clavering," for example, is one of a group of interrelated poems having to do with a circle of friends. It begins,

> I say no more for Clavering
>   Than I should say of him who fails
> To bring his wounded vessel home
>   When reft of rudder and of sails.

"Miniver Cheevy" appears in this volume, as does the only slightly lesser-known "How Annandale Went Out," the dramatic monologue in sonnet form that deals with euthanasia and probably is based on the suicide of his brother Dean. Other themes represented in this volume are satires on the writing of poetry, "Momus" and "Shadrach O'Leary," and elegiac verse, notably "Leonora" and "For a Dead Lady," whose final stanza is surely an example of what Robinson called "unmistakable" poetry:

> The beauty, shattered by the laws
> That have creation in their keeping,
> No longer trembles in applause,
> Or over children that are sleeping;
> And we who delve in beauty's lore
> Know all that we have known before
> Of what inexorable cause
> Makes Time so vicious in his reaping.

The variety of topics and the artistic control demonstrated in this volume indicate a marked step in Robinson's poetic development.

The Town Down the River received more reviews than any of the preceding volumes. None was negative, but most were only mildly approbative. Joyce Kilmer's review-essay in the *New York Times Book Review* (8 September 1912) is important, however, because it is an overview of Robinson's work. His reputation was growing in England as well as the United States. One of the most interesting opinions was voiced in a *Boston Sunday Post* interview (2 March 1913) with British poet Alfred Noyes. When asked about current American poets, Noyes told the reporters that Robinson was the second-best poet writing in America. (Noyes's nomination for the foremost Yankee poet was somebody named Brian Hooker.)

Ever since Robinson had moved from Gardiner, he had lived in a variety of furnished rooms

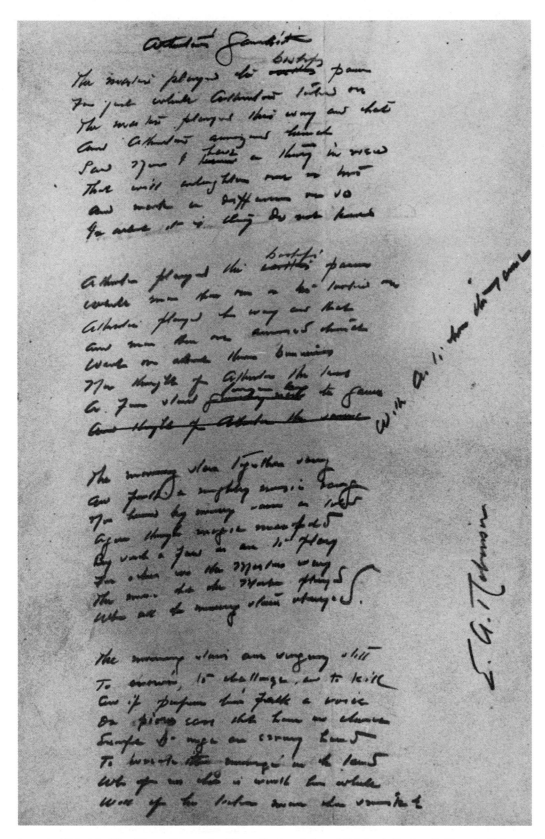

Draft for a poem published in The Town Down the River *(by permission of Edwin Arlington Robinson's Heirs; courtesy of the Watkinson Library, Trinity College, Hartford)*

or made extended visits to friends. In 1911 Hermann Hagedorn persuaded him to try summering at a place where a small group of artists lived and worked, the MacDowell Colony in Peterborough, New Hampshire. In 1911 Robinson reluctantly accepted the invitation, bringing with him a telegram to show as an excuse to leave before the season was over in case he did not find the situation to his liking. The reverse was true, however; he found the place so congenial to his work that he returned to Peterborough every summer until his death, and one of his rare prose pieces is an encomium to the MacDowell Colony entitled "The Peterborough Idea."

Although Robinson had begun to acquire a reputation as a poet, he was still in need of an adequate income, and for a few years he tried his hand at fiction and drama. The fiction has not survived, but two plays, *Van Zorn* (1914) and *The Porcupine* (1915), were brought out by Macmillan after Scribners refused them. The plays were neither popular nor critical successes, but by accepting them, as well as bringing out a new edition of *Captain Craig* in 1915, Macmillan was able to publish his next volume of poetry, the one which established Robinson as a major poet.

The Man Against the Sky, published in 1916, marks the midpoint of Robinson's publishing career and is his most-important single volume. Of the twenty-six poems included, fourteen had received prior magazine publication, and almost all of them are representative of Robinson's mature work. Among the most noteworthy are "Flammonde," the brief reworking of "Captain Craig" which opens the volume; "Cassandra," an attack on American capitalism; "Ben Jonson Entertains a Man from Stratford," a lengthy dramatic monologue in which Johnson reminisces about his friend Shakespeare; and the title poem, which describes a variety of ontological stances. Robinson maintained that "The Man Against the Sky" was the most succinct statement of his philosophy, but it is a somewhat unsatisfactory meditation emphasizing transcendental idealism in negative terms. (The final line of the poem, "Where all who know may drown," has frequently been misinterpreted as a straightforward statement; Robinson insisted that it was meant to be ironic.) Four of the eleven short poems which Yvor Winters called Robinson's greatest are in this volume: "Hillcrest," "Veteran Sirens," "The Poor Relation," and "Eros Turannos." Louis O. Coxe has persuasively argued that "Eros Turannos" is archetypically Robinsonian.

The immediate critical response to *The Man Against the Sky* was overwhelmingly positive. Amy Lowell's enthusiastic review for the *New Republic* (27 May 1916) was republished as the first chapter in her *Tendencies in Modern American Poetry* (1917), the first book of criticism which included a serious discussion of Robinson. Harriet Monroe sanctified him through a strong review in *Poetry* magazine (April 1916). And William Stanley Braithwaite, long a Robinson champion, proclaimed in the *Boston Evening Transcript* (26 February 1916) that "In this man American poetry has its deepest vision, its most enduring utterance." Richard Cary has pointed out that the wide critical acceptance of Robinson after 1916 indicates a change in critical taste rather than a substantive change in Robinson's method or manner. With *The Man Against the Sky*, Robinson arrived.

One year later, in 1917, Robinson published the first of his single, book-length poems, *Merlin*, a 2,500-line blank verse narrative which retells that part of the Arthurian legend involving Merlin's relationship with Arthur and with Vivian. Robinson presents Merlin realistically, as a prophet without magical powers, whose personal interests are in conflict with his public responsibilities as adviser to the king. It was intended to provide a symbolic commentary on World War I.

The critics who had found *The Man Against the Sky* so appealing were dismayed by the new direction Robinson had taken. Harriet Monroe wondered in *Poetry* (July 1917) why Robinson had bothered to use so threadbare a subject as the Arthurian romances, and Odell Shepard in the *Dial* (11 October 1917) objected to the Jamesian quality of the writing. Later critics have given only faint praise to the poem.

While Robinson was preparing *Merlin* for the publishers, he was already working on its sequel, *Lancelot*. Because Macmillan had lost money on *Merlin*, it refused to publish the second Arthurian poem, necessitating the finding of a new publisher. Eventually Samuel Roth, an editor for the Thomas Seltzer Publishing Company, agreed to take it, and the book appeared under the Seltzer imprint in 1920. It was the last time Macmillan was to refuse a Robinson manuscript.

In contrast to their reactions to *Merlin*, critics applauded *Lancelot*, some insisting it was better than *Merlin*, some ignoring the earlier poem altogether. Most later critics have paid little attention to the volume, although Chard Powers Smith, who quoted *Lancelot* in the title for his critical biography of Robinson, *Where the Light Falls* (1965), claims that

Edwin Arlington Robinson at the MacDowell Colony in Peterborough, Vermont (courtesy of the Watkinson Library, Trinity College, Hartford)

Robinson included this drawing in a 1914 letter to Edith Brower. As his letter explains, he was dismayed over the mixed reviews and widespread misinterpretations of his play Van Zorn, *which he had spent eight years writing (by permission of Edwin Arlington Robinson's Heirs; courtesy of Special Collections, Colby College, Waterville, Maine).*

Robinson's response to Harriet Monroe's "poet's circular" requesting submissions for her new magazine, Poetry *(by permission of Edwin Arlington Robinson's Heirs; courtesy of the University of Chicago Library, Department of Special Collections,* Poetry Magazine *Records, 1912-1936, Box 38, Folder 33)*

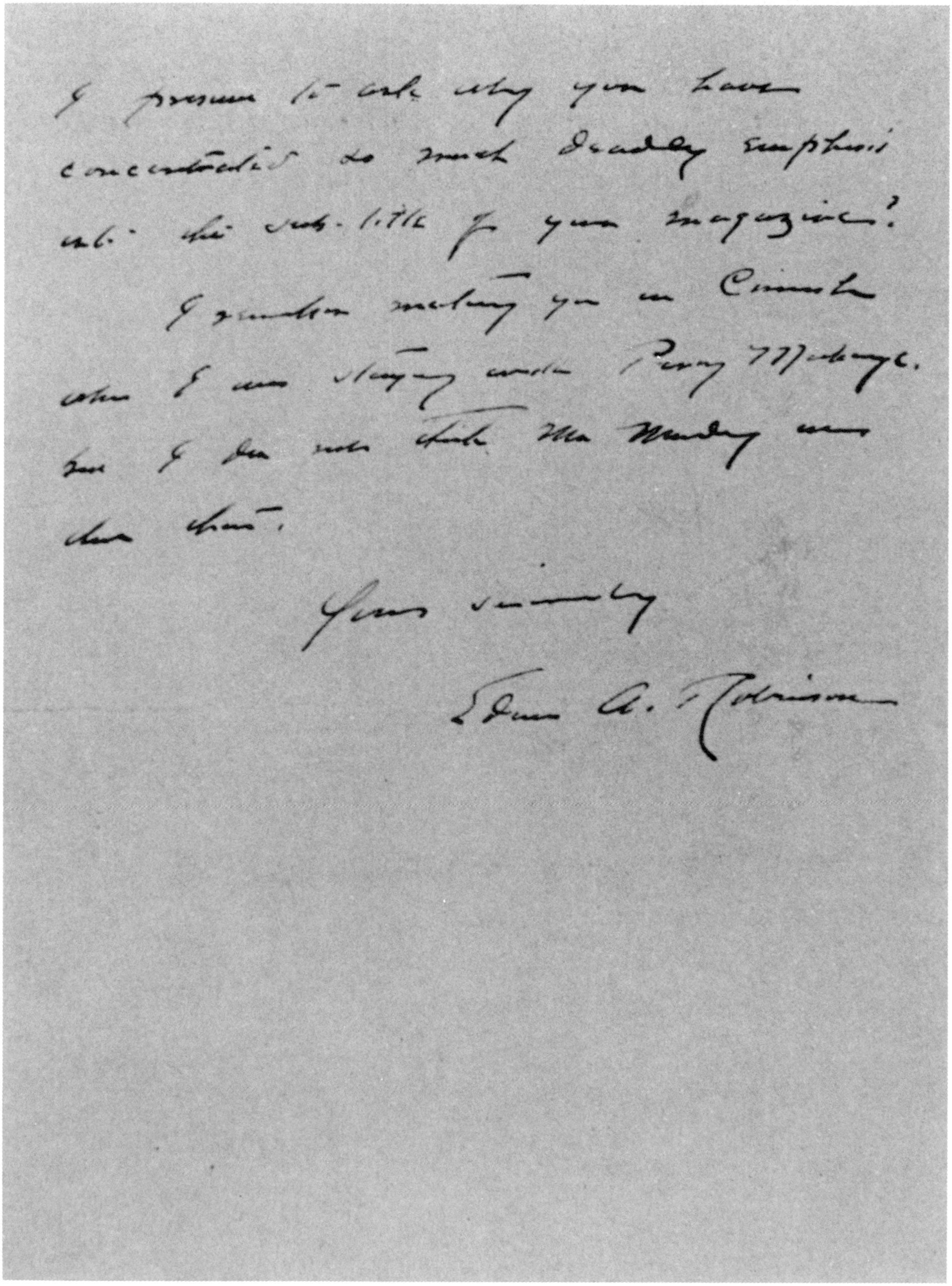

I presume to ask why you have concentrated so much deadly emphasis on the sub-title of your magazine?

I remember meeting you in Cornish when I was staying with Percy MacKaye, but I do not think Mr. Moody was there then.

Yours sincerely

Edwin A. Robinson

Merlin and *Lancelot* should be considered a single entity representing Robinson's most important work, both in conception and in autobiographical significance.

In 1920 Robinson also published a substantial collection of short and medium-length poems, *The Three Taverns.* Among the twenty-nine poems are sonnets and short, rhymed narratives, the most notable being "The Mill," an often-anthologized piece which conveys to the careful reader the story of a double suicide. The most distinctive quality of this collection, however, is the abundance of biblical references and subjects: the title poem is a dramatic monologue spoken by Paul just before he gets to Rome, and the concluding one, "Lazarus," is principally a blank-verse conversation among Lazarus, Mary, and Martha. Other medium-length poems such as "Tasker Norcross," a Tilbury poem, deal with fictional characters and with characters from American history, as in "John Brown," which concludes with the line that is inscribed on a plaque on Robinson's studio at the MacDowell Colony: "I shall have more to say when I am dead." Reviewers generally wrote favorable notices of *The Three Taverns;* later critics have almost entirely ignored it.

Actually, during the early 1920s reviewers barely had time to review one volume before another appeared. In 1921 Robinson published two more volumes. *Avon's Harvest* is a book-length poem that deals with a macabre situation: Avon believes himself to be haunted annually by the ghost of an old school enemy who had been drowned when the *Titanic* sank; the morning after he relates his story he is found dead, and the narrator says, "He died, you know, because he was afraid." Reviews were scanty but positive. Although John Farrar in the *Bookman* (May 1921) called it "a dime novel in verse," he approved of it. An interesting piece of scholarship is "A Note on 'Avon's Harvest,' " by David Brown in *American Literature* in 1933, in which he explains that substantial revisions in the poem were made after reviewers misinterpreted it.

Robinson had a chance to publish a revised version of *Avon's Harvest* that same year, for his first *Collected Poems* also appeared in 1921. "Captain Craig" was the one other poem that underwent extensive revisions. In *Collected Poems* some forty-three poems were dropped from *The Children of the Night* (including the title poem), and fourteen previously uncollected poems were added at the end of the volume. Otherwise, the title *Collected Poems* means what it says: it is a collection of the poetry which had appeared in nine previous volumes. One curiosity of *Collected Poems* is that the volumes are not presented in chronological order. *The Man Against the Sky* (1916), his biggest critical success, comes first. Thereafter the volumes are arranged so that the book-length poems are interspersed among the volumes of short pieces.

Among the new poems in *Collected Poems* are three of his best known: "Mr. Flood's Party," "The Tree in Pamela's Garden," and "Rembrandt to Rembrandt." These three represent Robinson's work at the height of his powers: "Mr. Flood's Party," the rhymed narrative dealing with a lonely but valiant old man, is one of the best of the Tilbury poems. "A Tree in Pamela's Garden" is one of the cryptic, perfectly constructed sonnets which demonstrates Robinson's ability to empathize with women, and "Rembrandt to Rembrandt," whose subject is a historical figure and whose theme is a meditation on aesthetic theory, closes *Collected Poems* and is one of Robinson's most celebrated blank verse poems of medium length. The 592-page volume indicated to those who had been unaware of Robinson the extent of his achievement, and reviewers were duly impressed. In the following year this volume earned for Robinson the first Pulitzer Prize ever awarded for poetry.

The publication of *Roman Bartholow* in 1923 marks the beginning of Robinson's later phase, that

Edwin Arlington Robinson (courtesy of the Watkinson Library, Trinity College, Hartford)

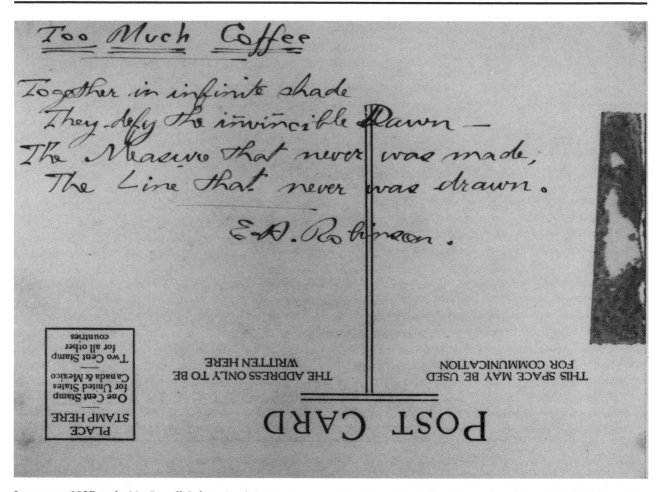

In summer 1927 at the MacDowell Colony, Louis Untermeyer remembered later, "There had been a long night of elevated discussion which turned out to be more spirituous than spiritual." The next day Robinson slid this postcard over the door of Untermeyer's cottage (by permission of Edwin Arlington Robinson's Heirs; courtesy of the Lilly Library, Indiana University).

period in which he wrote hurriedly and concentrated on book-length narratives almost to the exclusion of other forms. In the last fourteen years of his life he published eleven books, nine of them single poems. *Roman Bartholow,* with more than 4,000 lines, is second only to *Tristram* in length and presents the sort of domestic situation that was to intrigue Robinson in his later years. The title character, recuperating from an illness, is visited by his old friend, Penn-Raven. Bartholow's wife, Gabrielle, realizing that Penn-Raven is the more attractive of the two men, commits suicide. The triangular relationship is then discussed at length by the two remaining principals and an outside observer, Umfraville. The poem is flawed by lack of clarity in characterization and a plethora of unrelated images. It is perhaps Robinson's least successful poem, and both reviewers and later critics have written predominantly negative assessments.

The Man Who Died Twice, published in 1924, is different from its immediate predecessor in almost every respect and won for Robinson his second Pulitzer Prize. Here the narrator finds Fernando Nash beating a drum for the Salvation Army. Nash had once been a good musician and a promising composer, but his career has been cut short by debauchery. One night he hallucinates a symphony performed by rats in his room and shortly thereafter imagines his own magnum opus. He is unable to complete it, however, before his physical collapse, and when he recuperates he is spiritually regenerated and resigned to spend the rest of his days as a street musician. This poem is a variation on the theme of "Captain Craig," although the grotesque imagery is more controlled than in the earlier poem. The combination of down-to-earth diction, classical allusion, and understated humor contributes to its success. Occasionally excerpts from this poem are anthologized, a measure of its acceptance among scholars.

In 1923 Robinson had made his one trip abroad, spending six weeks in England. An impetus for his making the trip at that time was his dismay at the passage of the Eighteenth Amendment. He observed in a letter to Witter Bynner that prohibition should be placed along with free verse and motion pictures as a "triumvirate from hell." He reported having a good time in London and Oxford, but he cut short his trip so he could spend two months at Peterborough, where he began to work on a book of short poems. The result was *Dionysus in Doubt,* published in 1925. The title poem and "Demos and Dionysus" are propagandistic poems decrying the curtailment of individual freedom through the imposition of behavioral standards. Also included are eighteen sonnets, notably "The Sheaves" and "Karma," as well as two poems of medium length, "Genevieve and Alexandra" and "Mortmain." Reviewers generally preferred any of the other poems to the Dionysus ones, objecting to their didacticism.

Robinson's single popular triumph, *Tristram,* appeared in 1927. His longest poem and reminis-

Edwin Arlington Robinson (courtesy of the Watkinson Library, Trinity College, Hartford)

cent of his previous treatment of the Arthurian legends, it received elaborate praise and sold 57,000 copies in the first year. Robinson's lifetime appreciation of opera, especially those of Richard Wagner, perhaps contributed to his interest in the topic. As he had done with his earlier Arthurian poems, he made his characters' actions realistic rather than the result of their having drunk a magic potion. The poem is tied together with carefully unified imagery, and the portrait of Isolt, looking out over the sea after hearing of Tristram's death, is justly celebrated:

> And white birds everywhere, flying, and flying;
> Alone with her white face and her gray eyes,
> She watched them there till even her thoughts were white,
> And there was nothing alive but white birds flying,
> Flying, and always flying, and still flying,
> And the white sunlight flashing on the sea.

For the only time in his life Robinson was lionized: he agreed to attend a dramatic reading of the poem in New York and allowed a reception to be given for him after it. The royalties made him financially secure at last, and the book earned him his third Pulitzer Prize. Although Robinson was to write seven more volumes, he experienced his final triumph with *Tristram.*

Cavender's House (1929), *The Glory of the Nightingales* (1930), and *Matthias at the Door* (1931) are all reworkings of earlier themes. *Cavender's House* is similar to *Avon's Harvest* in that Cavender speaks with a ghost, in this case the wife he has murdered after he suspected her of infidelity. The other two long poems are principally variations on the theme examined earlier in *Roman Bartholow*—domestic tragedies dealing with flawed friendships, unfaithful wives, and suicides. These later poems are, however, more carefully composed than the earlier ones. Although critics treated them with respect, they almost always compared them to *Tristram* and found them wanting.

Nicodemus, a volume of ten medium-length poems, appeared in 1932. Nine of the ten are character sketches of biblical, historical, or Tilbury figures. Most often noted by the reviewers were "The March of the Cameron Men," "Ponce de Leon," and the title poem. "Annandale Again," the third poem Robinson wrote on the character of Annandale, summarizes his much earlier poem "The Book of Annandale."

With *Talifer* (1933) Robinson attempted a new mode of writing—a domestic comedy rather than

My life was rather mixed up during these years

Was there any reason, (other than Horace's advice to poets) that eight years should have elapsed between Captain Craig and this book ?

———   ———   ———   ———

In Miniver Cheevy there is the line:

'He dreamed of Thebes and Camelot
    And Priam's neighbors.'

I believe this casual reference is your first Arthurian mention. How long before Merlin did the idea of extended treatment of the legends occur to you.

No connection

You characterize Tristram as:

Tristram the loud-accredited strong warrior,
Tristram the loved of women, the harp-player
Tristram the learned Nimrod among hunters ————

an excellent and adequate picture of the Tristram of tradition. But then you leave out, almost entirely, those sides of his character mentioned in the first and last lines.

I have often wondered why you did not treat more fully his youth –– was it because of limitations of space, or because Malory had already treated those phases

For the first reason there is, to my mind, no excuse –– the only flaw I can see in Tristram is that it is too short.

I omitted most J. Malory's details, and, in spite of your complaint, still think the poem long enough. But why do not you disagree with me –

E. A. R.

Robinson's handwritten responses to typed questions about (top) The Town Down the River *and (bottom)* Tristram *(by permission of Edwin Arlington Robinson's Heirs; courtesy of the Lilly Library, Indiana University)*

a tragedy. Instead of his usual triangular situation, this poem involves two women and two men who change partners. After an unsuccessful marriage to the intellectual Karen, Talifer weds the more pliant Althea. Talifer's friend, Dr. Quick, then takes Karen as his wife, but he soon leaves her to her books in Oxford and returns to admire the success of Talifer's second marriage. Karen perhaps represents Robinson's opinion of independent women. Most of the reviewers did not like the poem and politely said so. Richard Crowder, however, has written an article in the *Personalist* (January 1962) reassessing the poem and suggesting an allegorical interpretation.

Allegorical interpretations of Robinson's last two poems, *Amaranth* (1934) and *King Jasper* (1935), are inevitable. *Amaranth* is cast in the form of a dream, in which Fargo, a former painter who is now a pumpmaker, visits the "wrong world" guided by his host, Amaranth, "the flower that never fades." The people they meet are primarily failed artists or writers who, when they look into Amaranth's eyes, can see the truth about themselves. Several casually commit suicide, actions which do not detract from the grotesque comedy of the piece. Reactions to his poem were mixed, though many critics greeted it enthusiastically, and several later critics, such as Floyd Stovall in his *American Idealism* (1943) and Dolores Brien in *Research Studies* (June 1968), have presented various interpretations of this ironic and ambiguous poem.

In January 1935 Robinson was diagnosed as having an inoperable cancer. During his stay in the hospital he read galley proofs of his final poem, *King Jasper*, completing the corrections only hours before he sank into his final coma. *King Jasper* is a complex, highly symbolic work which is an appropriate culmination of Robinson's career, for it combines the themes of personal failure, artistic endeavor, materialism, and the inevitability of change. It deals with Jasper and his family—his wife, Honoria; his son, Jasper, Jr.; his son's wife, Zoë; and Jasper's old enemies, a father and son both named Hebron. Jasper's empire comes crashing down on him, but Zoë, so named because she represents the life force, prevails. The same sort of dreams and grotesque images Robinson had used in earlier works appear in this poem, as well as lengthy conversations attempting to analyze motivations. Although the poem is set in modern times, it has a vaguely Arthurian air about it. It has been interpreted as a commentary on American politics as well as a philosophical construct. Although the poem is not entirely successful because

it tries to do too many things, it is nevertheless a fitting conclusion to the Robinson canon. Published posthumously, the book was introduced by a now well-known essay by Robert Frost, who wrote in glowing terms of his contemporary and chief rival, commenting particularly on Robinson's profundity, humor, and technical skill. It is a Robinsonian irony that Frost does not mention the poem he set out to introduce.

Magazines and newspapers throughout the country took elaborate notice of Robinson's death, reminding their readers that he had been considered America's foremost poet for nearly twenty years and praising his industry, integrity, and devotion to his art. During his lifetime Robinson suffered the extremes of obscurity and fame, but Robinson the poet maintained a steadfast course in spite of both of those encumbrances. He often said that a poet cannot be definitely placed until he has been dead half a century. While he is no longer considered the brightest star in the poetic firmament, part of his work remains among the greatest American poetry.

In an interview with Joyce Kilmer (*New York Times Magazine*, 9 April 1916) Robinson once defined poetry as "a language which tells us, through a more or less emotional experience, something that cannot be said. All real poetry, great or small, does this. And it seems to me that poetry has two characteristics. One is that it is, after all, undefinable. The other is that it is eventually unmistakable." With his metrical control, precise diction, and keen observation of human triumphs and frailties, Robinson's poetry remains unmistakable.

Letters:

Selected Letters, edited by Ridgely Torrence (New York: Macmillan, 1940);

Untriangulated Stars: Letters to Harry de Forest Smith 1890-1905, edited by Denham Sutcliffe (Cambridge: Harvard University Press, 1947);

Edwin Arlington Robinson's Letters to Edith Brower, edited by Richard Cary (Cambridge: Harvard University Press, 1968).

Bibliographies:

Charles Beecher Hogan, *A Bibliography of Edwin Arlington Robinson* (New Haven: Yale University Press, 1936);

William White, *Edwin Arlington Robinson: A Supplementary Bibliography* (Kent, Ohio: Kent State University Press, 1971);

Nancy Carol Joyner, *Edwin Arlington Robinson: A Reference Guide* (Boston: G. K. Hall, 1978).

Biographies:

Hermann Hagedorn, *Edwin Arlington Robinson: A Biography* (New York: Macmillan, 1936);

Rollo Walter Brown, *Next Door to a Poet* (New York: Appleton-Century, 1937);

Emery Neff, *Edwin Arlington Robinson* (New York: Sloane, 1948);

Chard Powers Smith, *Where the Light Falls: A Portrait of Edwin Arlington Robinson* (New York: Macmillan, 1965);

Louis O. Coxe, *Edwin Arlington Robinson: The Life of Poetry* (New York: Pegasus, 1969).

References:

Wallace L. Anderson, *Edwin Arlington Robinson: A Critical Introduction* (Boston: Houghton Mifflin, 1967);

Ellsworth Barnard, *Edwin Arlington Robinson: A Critical Study* (New York: Macmillan, 1952);

Barnard, ed., *Edwin Arlington Robinson: Centenary Essays* (Athens: University of Georgia Press, 1969);

David Brown, "A Note on 'Avon's Harvest,'" *American Literature,* 11 (November 1933): 343-349;

Richard Cary, ed., *Appreciation of Edwin Arlington Robinson: Twenty-Eight Interpretive Essays* (Waterville, Maine: Colby College Press, 1969);

Cary, ed., *Early Reception of Edwin Arlington Robinson: The First Twenty Years* (Waterville, Maine: Colby College Press, 1974);

Charles Cestre, *An Introduction to Edwin Arlington Robinson* (New York: Macmillan, 1930);

Richard Crowder, "Redemption for the Man of Iron," *Personalist,* 43 (January 1962): 46-56;

James Dickey, Introduction to *Selected Poems,* by Robinson, edited by Morton Dauwen Zabel (New York: Macmillan, 1965);

Edwin S. Fussell, *Edwin Arlington Robinson: The Literary Background of a Traditional Poet* (Berkeley: University of California Press, 1954);

Nancy Joyner, "Robinson's Poets," *Colby Library Quarterly,* 9 (March 1972): 441-455;

Estelle Kaplan, *Philosophy in the Poetry of Edwin Arlington Robinson* (New York: Columbia University Press, 1940);

Amy Lowell, *Tendencies in Modern American Poetry* (New York: Macmillan, 1917), pp. 3-75;

David Perkins, *A History of Modern Poetry from the 1890s to the High Modernist Mode* (Cambridge & London: Harvard University Press, 1976), pp. 119-131;

William Ronald Robinson, *Edwin Arlington Robinson: A Poetry of the Act* (Cleveland: Western Reserve University Press, 1967);

Floyd Stovall, *American Idealism* (Norman: University of Oklahoma Press, 1943), pp. 169-177;

Lawrance Thompson, Introduction and notes to *Tilbury Town: Selected Poems,* by Robinson (New York: Macmillan, 1953);

Hyatt H. Waggoner, *American Poets: From the Puritans to the Present* (Boston: Houghton Mifflin, 1968), pp. 262-292;

Yvor Winters, *Edwin Arlington Robinson* (Norfolk, Conn.: New Directions, 1946).

Papers:

Substantial holdings of Robinson papers are in the Colby College Library, the Houghton Library at Harvard University, the New York Public Library, and the Library of Congress.

Carl Sandburg

Penelope Niven
Earlham College

BIRTH: Galesburg, Illinois, 6 January 1878, to August and Clara Mathilda Anderson Sandburg.

EDUCATION: Lombard University, 1898-1902.

MARRIAGE: 15 June 1908 to Lilian Steichen; children: Margaret, Janet, Helga.

AWARDS AND HONORS: Levinson Prize (*Poetry* magazine), 1914; Poetry Society of America Awards, 1919, 1921; Phi Beta Kappa Poet, Harvard University, 1928; Litt.D., Lombard College, 1928; Litt.D., Knox College, 1928; Litt.D., Northwestern University, 1931; elected to the National Institute of Arts and Letters, 1933; Friends of Literature Award, 1934; Pulitzer Prize for *Abraham Lincoln: The War Years*, 1940; elected to the American Academy of Arts and Letters, 1940; special diploma, Lincoln Memorial University, 1940; Litt.D., Lafayette College, 1940; Litt.D., Wesleyan University, 1940; Litt.D., Yale University, 1940; Litt.D., Harvard University, 1940; Litt.D., Syracuse University, 1941; Litt.D., Dartmouth College, 1941; LL.D., Rollins College, 1941; Phi Beta Kappa Poet, College of William and Mary, 1943; LL.D., Augustana College, 1948; honorary Ph.D., Upsala College, 1950; Pulitzer Prize for *Complete Poems*, 1951; National Institute and American Academy of Arts and Letters Gold Medal, 1952; Commanders Cup of the Order of the North Star (Sweden), 1953; Poetry Society of America Gold Medal, 1953; Tamiment Institute Award, 1953; LL.D., University of Illinois, 1953; New York Civil War Round Table Silver Medal, 1954; Boston Arts Festival Poetry Prize, 1955; Litt.D., University of North Carolina, 1955; Award of Merit, University of Louisville, 1955; humanities award, Albert Einstein College of Medicine, 1956; named honorary ambassador for North Carolina, 1958; Lincoln Day speaker, U.S. Congress, 1959; Litt.D., Upsala College, 1959; Litteris et Artibus medal from King Gustav VI of Sweden, 1959; Roanoke-Chowan Poetry Cup for *Harvest Poems*, 1960; named poet laureate of Illinois, 1962; Presidential Medal of Freedom, 1964.

DEATH: Flat Rock, North Carolina, 22 July 1967.

SELECTED BOOKS: *In Reckless Ecstasy*, as Charles A. Sandburg (Galesburg, Ill.: Asgard Press, 1904);

Incidentals, as Charles Sandburg (Galesburg, Ill.: Asgard Press, 1907);

The Plaint of a Rose, as Charles Sandburg (Galesburg, Ill.: Asgard Press, 1908);

Joseffy, as Charles Sandburg (Galesburg, Ill.: Asgard Press, 1910);

Chicago Poems (New York: Holt, 1916);

Cornhuskers (New York: Holt, 1918);

Carl Sandburg, 1926 (courtesy of the Carl Sandburg Collection, University of Illinois Library at Urbana-Champaign)

The poet's parents, August and Clara Mathilda Anderson Sandburg

The Chicago Race Riots, July, 1919 (New York: Harcourt, Brace & Howe, 1919);

Smoke and Steel (New York: Harcourt, Brace & Howe, 1920);

Slabs of the Sunburnt West (New York: Harcourt, Brace, 1922);

Rootabaga Stories (New York: Harcourt, Brace, 1922);

Rootabaga Pigeons (New York: Harcourt, Brace, 1923);

Abraham Lincoln: The Prairie Years, 2 volumes (New York: Harcourt, Brace, 1926); republished in part as *Abe Lincoln Grows Up* (New York: Harcourt, Brace, 1928);

Selected Poems, edited by Rebecca West (London: Cape, 1926; New York: Harcourt, Brace, 1926);

Carl Sandburg, edited by Hughes Mearns (New York: Simon & Schuster, 1926);

Good Morning, America (New York: Harcourt, Brace, 1928);

Steichen, The Photographer (New York: Harcourt, Brace, 1929);

Potato Face (New York: Harcourt, Brace, 1930);

Early Moon (New York: Harcourt, Brace, 1930);

Mary Lincoln: Wife and Widow, by Sandburg and Paul Angle (New York: Harcourt, Brace, 1932);

The People, Yes (New York: Harcourt, Brace, 1936);

Abraham Lincoln: The War Years, 4 volumes (New York: Harcourt, Brace, 1939);

Storm Over the Land: A Profile of the Civil War Taken Mainly from Abraham Lincoln: The War Years (New York: Harcourt, Brace, 1942; London: Cape, 1943);

Home Front Memo (New York: Harcourt, Brace, 1943);

The Photographs of Abraham Lincoln, by Sandburg and Frederick Hill Meserve (New York: Harcourt, Brace, 1944);

Remembrance Rock (New York: Harcourt, Brace, 1948);

Lincoln Collector: The Story of Oliver R. Barrett's Great Private Collection (New York: Harcourt, Brace, 1949);

Complete Poems (New York: Harcourt, Brace, 1950; revised and expanded edition, New York: Harcourt Brace Jovanovich, 1970);

Always the Young Strangers (New York: Harcourt, Brace, 1953); republished in part as *Prairie-Town Boy* (New York: Harcourt, Brace, 1955);

The Sandburg Range (New York: Harcourt, Brace, 1957);

Harvest Poems, 1910-1960 (New York: Harcourt, Brace, 1960);

Wind Song (New York: Harcourt, Brace, 1960);

Honey and Salt (New York: Harcourt, Brace & World, 1963);

The Wedding Procession of the Rag Doll and the Broom Handle and Who Was in It (New York: Harcourt, Brace & World, 1967);

Breathing Tokens, edited by Margaret Sandburg (New York: Harcourt Brace Jovanovich, 1978);

Ever the Winds of Chance, edited by Margaret Sandburg and George Hendrick (Urbana-Champaign: University of Illinois Press, 1983).

OTHER: *The American Songbag,* edited, with introduction and notes, by Sandburg (New York: Harcourt, Brace, 1927);

Edward Steichen, comp., *The Family of Man,* prologue by Sandburg (New York: Published for the Museum of Modern Art by the Maco Magazine Corp., 1955).

American poet and biographer Carl Sandburg sketched a revealing portrait of himself in the preface to his *Complete Poems* (1950): "there was a puzzlement," he said, "as to whether I was a poet, a biographer, a wandering troubadour with a guitar, a midwest Hans Christian Andersen, or a historian of current events. . . ." He was seventy-two in 1950 and "still studying verbs and the mystery of how they connect nouns. . . . I have forgotten the meaning of twenty or thirty of my poems written thirty or forty years ago. I still favor several simple poems published long ago which continue to have an appeal for simple people."

Sandburg wrote a landmark six-volume biography of Abraham Lincoln. A consummate platform performer, he roamed the United States for nearly a half century, guitar in hand, collecting and singing American folk songs. For his own children and children everywhere he wrote *Rootabaga Stories* (1922) and *Rootabaga Pigeons* (1923), some of the first authentic American fairy tales. He was a journalist by trade; his newspaper reportage and commentary documented labor, racial, and economic strife and other key events of his times. But Carl Sandburg was first and foremost a poet, writing poems about America in the American idiom for the American people. The titles of his volumes of poetry testify to his major themes: *Chicago Poems* (1916), *Cornhuskers* (1918), *Smoke and Steel* (1920), *Good Morning, America* (1928), *The People, Yes* (1936).

Louis Untermeyer described Sandburg in

Carl Sandburg, 1893 (courtesy of the Carl Sandburg Collection, University of Illinois Library at Urbana-Champaign)

1923 as the "emotional democrat" of American poetry, the "laureate of industrial America." Harriet Monroe, founder and first editor of *Poetry: A Magazine of Verse*, gave Sandburg's poetry its first serious audience in 1914. She believed that this son of Swedish immigrants was particularly suited to write about the "incomplete, but urgent and hopeful" American democracy. She wrote in *Poets and Their Art* (1926) that Sandburg was bent on the business, "in the deepest sense a poet's business, of seeing our national life in the large—its beauty and glory, its baseness and shame."

Sandburg's vision of the American experience was shaped in the American Midwest during the complicated events which brought the nineteenth century to a close. His parents were Swedish immigrants who met in Illinois, where they had settled in search of a share of American democracy and prosperity. August Sandburg helped to build the first cross-continental railroad, and in the twentieth century his son Carl was an honored guest on the first cross-continental jet flight. August Sandburg was a blacksmith's helper for the Chicago Burlington and Quincy Railroad in Galesburg, Illinois, when his son was born on 6 January 1878 in a small cottage a few steps away from the roundhouse and railroad yards. Carl August Sandburg was the second child and first son of the hardworking Sandburgs. He grew up speaking Swedish and English, and, eager to be assimilated into American society, he Americanized his name. In 1884 or 1885, "somewhere in the first year or two of school," he began to call himself Charles rather than the Swedish Carl because he had "a feeling the name Carl would mean one more Poor Swede Boy while the name Charles filled the mouth and had 'em guessing."

There were seven children in the Sandburg family, and the two youngest sons died of diphtheria on the same day in 1892. Charles Sandburg had to leave school at age thirteen to work at a variety of odd jobs to supplement the family income. As a teenager he was restless and impulsive, hungry for experience in the world beyond the staid, introverted prairie town which had always been his home. At age eighteen, he borrowed his father's railroad pass and had his first look at Chicago, the city of his destiny. In 1897 Sandburg joined the corps of more than 60,000 hoboes who found the American railroads an exhilarating if illicit free ride from one corner of the United States to another. For three and a half months of his nineteenth year he traveled through Iowa, Missouri, Kansas, Nebraska, and Colorado, working

Carl Sandburg at Lombard College (courtesy of the Carl Sandburg Collection, University of Illinois Library at Urbana-Champaign)

on farms, steamboats, and railroads, blacking stoves, washing dishes, and listening to the American vernacular, the idiom which would permeate his poetry.

The journey left Sandburg with a permanent wanderlust. He volunteered for service in the Spanish-American War in 1898 and served in Puerto Rico from July until late August. As a veteran, he received free tuition for a year at Lombard College in Galesburg and enrolled there in October 1898. He was offered a conditional appointment to the U.S. Military Academy at West Point, New York, on the basis of his Spanish-American War service, but in June 1899 he failed entrance examinations in arithmetic and grammar. He returned to Lombard, where he studied until May of 1902, when he left college without enough credits for graduation.

At Lombard, he encountered the first catalyst for his poetry, Prof. Philip Green Wright, econo-

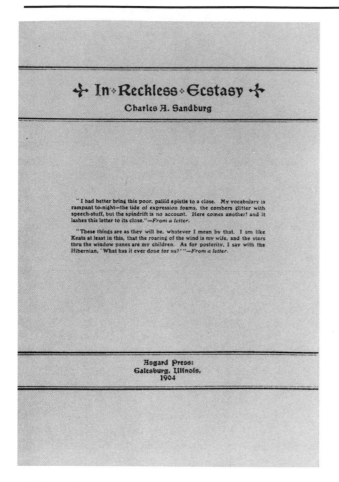

+ In · Reckless · Ecstasy +
Charles A. Sandburg

"I had better bring this poor, pallid epistle to a close. My vocabulary is rampant to-night—the tide of expression foams, the combers glitter with speech-stuff, but the spindrift is no account. Here comes another! and it lashes this letter to its close."—*From a letter.*

"These things are as they will be, whatever I mean by that. I am like Keats at least in this, that the roaring of the wind is my wife, and the stars thru the window panes are my children. As for posterity, I say with the Hibernian, 'What has it ever done for us?'"—*From a letter.*

Asgard Press:
Galesburg, Illinois,
1904

Title page for Sandburg's first book, printed by one of the poet's professors, Philip Green Wright, on the small handpress in Wright's basement

mist, scholar, and poet. Wright fostered Sandburg's interest in writing and published the young poet's first small books at his Asgard Press, which he modeled after William Morris's Kelmscott Press and its offspring, Elbert Hubbard's Roycroft Press. On the small handpress in the basement of his Galesburg home, Wright set the type for Charles A. Sandburg's *In Reckless Ecstasy* (1904), *Incidentals* (1907), *The Plaint of a Rose* (1908), and *Joseffy* (1910). The last book was commissioned by Joseffy, a magician, musician, inventor, and wanderer, who wanted an "appreciation" to promote his lyceum appearances. The three other early works, slim booklets which are now rare collectors' items, contain Sandburg's juvenilia, which he viewed in retrospect as "many odd pieces . . . not worth later reprint." They record the tentative and conventionally modeled lyrics of a young poet deeply influenced by Villon, Browning, Kipling, Emerson, and Whitman, as well as idealistic aphorisms in the style of Elbert Hub-

bard. These early writings are foretokens of the major themes of Sandburg's later poetry, as well of the idealism which led him to become an activist and organizer for the Social Democratic party in Wisconsin from 1907 until 1912.

By the time he was thirty Sandburg had tried a variety of jobs, often supporting himself as an itinerant salesman of Underwood and Underwood stereopticon equipment and pictures. He tried to establish himself as a Lyceum and Chautauqua lecturer, published occasional poems, and worked for a variety of periodicals. In 1908 he married Lilian Steichen, sister of photographer Edward Steichen, who had already achieved some international success with his artistic photographs. Lilian Steichen was a beautiful Phi Beta Kappa graduate of the University of Chicago, a schoolteacher, and an active Socialist. Sandburg said later that the three chief influences in his life were Philip Green Wright, Edward Steichen, and Lilian Steichen Sandburg, his wife for fifty-nine years. He called her Paula, and she urged him to return to his christened name Carl, to affirm his Swedish roots. She also urged him to concentrate on his poetry, and her steady faith in his work undergirded his long struggle to find his own poetic style and a serious audience for his poetry.

From 1910 until 1912 Carl and Paula Sandburg lived in Milwaukee, where Sandburg was instrumental in the Milwaukee Socialists' unprecedented political victory in 1910. When Emil Seidel was elected Milwaukee's first Socialist mayor in that year, Sandburg, then thirty-two, was appointed his secretary. Sandburg left city hall in 1911 to write for Victor Berger's *Social Democratic Herald* in Milwaukee. In June 1911 the Sandburgs' first child, Margaret, was born. A second daughter died at birth in 1913; Janet was born in 1916, and Helga was born in 1918. In 1912 the Sandburgs moved to Chicago, where Sandburg joined the staff of the Socialist *Chicago Evening World,* which had expanded in the wake of a pressman's strike that closed most other Chicago newspapers. Once the strike was settled, the *World* went out of business, and Sandburg found work with small periodicals such as the business magazine *System* and *Day Book,* an adless daily newspaper owned by W. E. Scripps. He contributed occasional articles to the *International Socialist Review,* often using the pseudonym Jack Phillips. Sandburg struggled to find an outlet for his poetry and enough income to support his young family. His fortunes turned in 1914 when Harriet Monroe of *Poetry* published six of his radical, muscular poems in the March issue of her forward-looking journal. This first significant recognition of his work brought him into a Chicago literary circle which included Edgar Lee Masters, Theodore Dreiser, Vachel Lindsay, Emanuel Carnevali, Alice Corbin Henderson, Floyd Dell, and others. His poetry also came to the attention of Ezra Pound, who was the magazine's foreign editor. Masters and Dreiser encouraged Sandburg to construct his first book of poetry, and Henderson, then assistant editor of *Poetry,* brought the collection to the attention of Alfred Harcourt, a young editor at Henry Holt and Company, who risked his own job to persuade the firm to publish Sandburg's *Chicago Poems* in 1916.

Carl Sandburg found his subject in the American people and the American landscape; he found his voice, after a long, lonely search and struggle, in the vivid, candid economy of the American vernacular. He worked his way to a rugged, individual free-verse style which spoke clearly, directly, and often crudely to the audience which was also his subject. His poetry celebrated and consoled people in their environments—the crush of the city, the enduring solace of the prairie. In his work for the *Day Book,* the *Chicago Daily News,* and the News-

paper Enterprise Association (NEA), Sandburg had become a skilled investigative reporter with passionate social concerns. He covered war, racial strife, lynchings, mob violence, and the inequities of the industrial society, such as child labor, and disease and injury induced in the workplace. These concerns were transmuted into poetry. *Chicago Poems* offered bold, realistic portraits of working men, women, and children; of the "inexplicable fate" of the vulnerable and struggling human victims of war, progress, business. "Great men, pageants of war and labor, soldiers and workers, mothers lifting their children—these all I touched, and felt the solemn thrill of them," Sandburg wrote in "Masses." "And then one day I got a true look at the Poor, millions of the Poor,/patient and toiling; more patient than crags, tides, and stars; in-numer-/able, patient as the darkness of night—and all broken, humble ruins of nations."

Sandburg's themes in *Chicago Poems* reflect his Socialistic idealism and pragmatism, but they also contain a wider humanism, a profound affirmation of the common man, the common destiny, the common tragedies and joys of life. Just as Sandburg's subject matter transcended that of conventional po-

Emil Seidel, the first Socialist mayor of Milwaukee, and his secretary, Carl Sandburg (photograph by Harry L. Taylor)

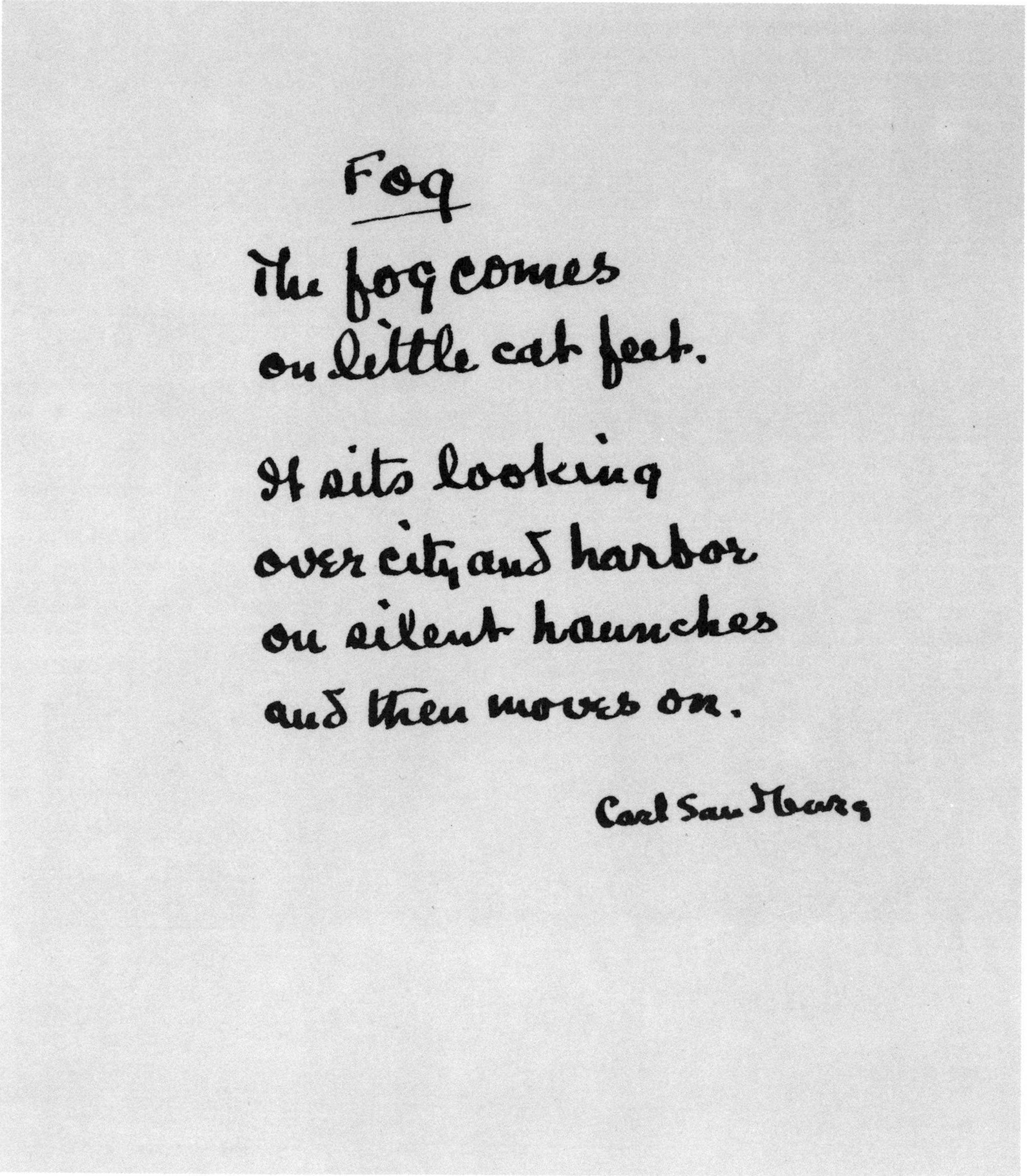

Fog

The fog comes
on little cat feet.

It sits looking
over city and harbor
on silent haunches
and then moves on.

Carl Sandburg

Manuscripts for two poems collected in Chicago Poems *(by permission of Maurice Greenbaum, Trustee for the Estate of Carl Sandburg; "Fog" courtesy of the Carl Sandburg Collection, University of Illinois Library at Urbana-Champaign; "Kin" courtesy of the Lilly Library, Indiana University)*

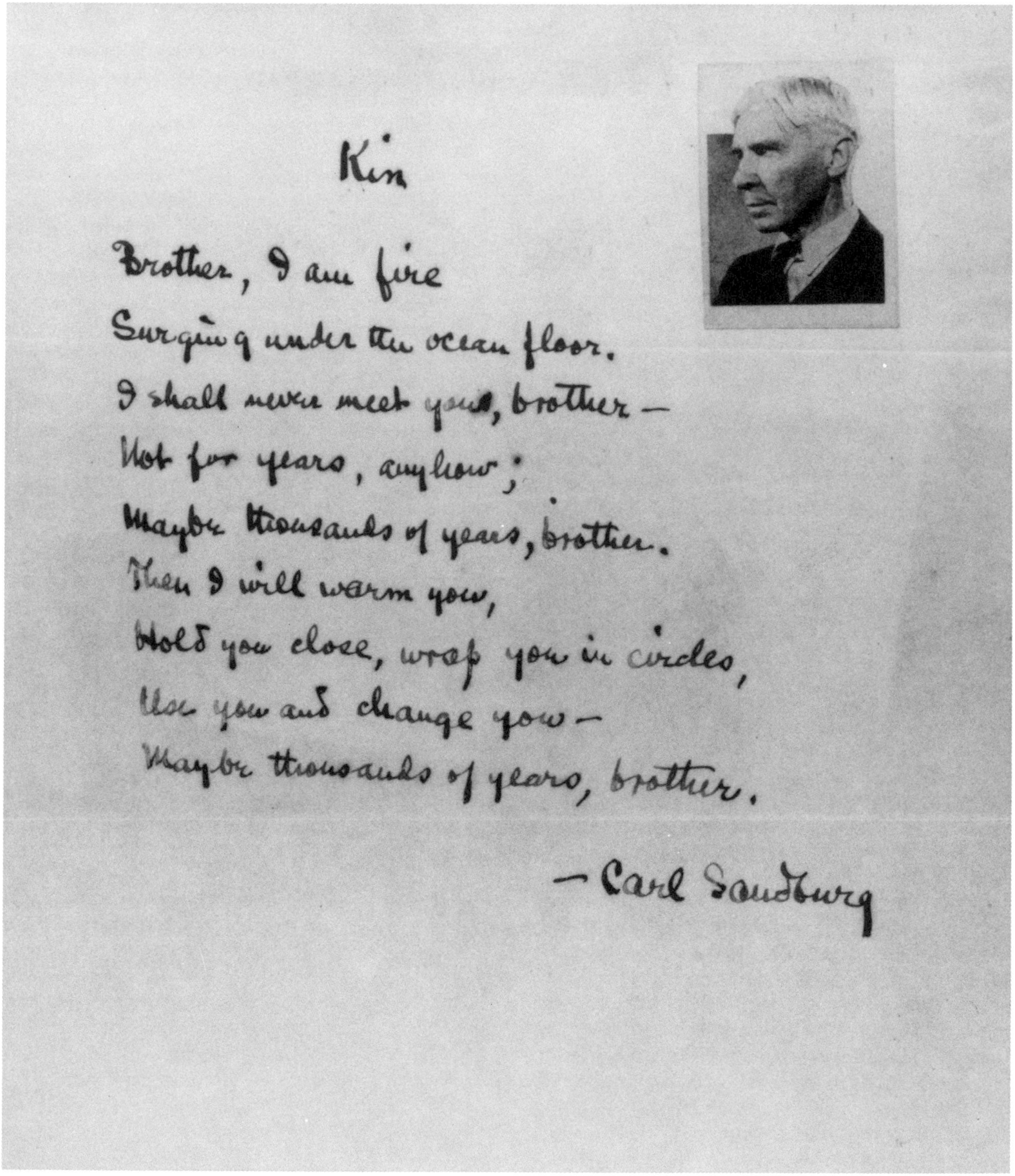

Kin

Brother, I am fire
Surging under the ocean floor.
I shall never meet you, brother —
Not for years, anyhow;
Maybe thousands of years, brother.
Then I will warm you,
Hold you close, wrap you in circles,
Use you and change you —
Maybe thousands of years, brother.

— Carl Sandburg

etry, his free verse form was unique, original, and controversial. Some critics found his forms "shapeless" and questioned whether Sandburg's work was poetry at all. In her *Tendencies in Modern American Poetry* (1917), Sandburg's respected friend and colleague Amy Lowell called him a lyric poet but stated that "the lyricist in him has a hard time to make itself heard above the brawling of the marketplace." She praised Sandburg's virility and tenderness, his originality and strength, and ratified his importance as a democratic poet. But she objected to the propagandistic overtones she perceived in Sandburg's poetry. In June 1917 Sandburg wrote to Lowell in his own defense that his aim was not to advance social theories, but "to sing, blab, chortle, yodel, like people, and people in the sense of human beings subtracted from formal doctrines."

The reviews for *Chicago Poems* were predictably disparate in their assessment of what the reviewer for the *American Library Association Booklist* (October 1916) called Sandburg's "tradition-shattering poetry," but the criticism which caused him long hours of reflection was Lowell's view that there was too much propaganda in his work. He continued as a journalist, joining the *Chicago Daily News* in 1917 as a labor reporter and editorial writer, but he was a poet by vocation. His newspaper job exposed him to the issues and conflicts of his time. The grim realism of labor conflict, racial strife, and mob violence in Chicago and the growing chaos of World War I led Sandburg to a growing cynicism and pessimism. He struggled for an equilibrium which would help him avoid the confusion of poetic theme and propaganda of action. But Sandburg was becoming the poet of democracy, and he believed that the poet had a public duty to speak to his times.

Cornhuskers (1918) is a celebration of the prairie, the agrarian life, the people living it. The volume includes some revealing autobiographical poems, many gentle, lyrical evocations of his family life, and poignant portraits of American working men and women reminiscent of *Chicago Poems*. The strength of *Cornhuskers* rests in its remarkable war poems. In the concluding section, "Shenandoah," Sandburg sketches with a deceptively gentle irony the phantoms of soldiers who died in past battles of earlier wars. He concludes with a forceful and bitter attack on modern warmongers who use the lives and deaths of "A Million Young Workmen, 1915":

> The kings are grinning, the kaiser and the czar— they
> are alive riding in leather-seated motor cars, and
> they have their women and roses for ease, and they
> eat fresh poached eggs for breakfast, new butter
> on toast, sitting in tall water-tight houses reading
> the news of war.
> I dreamed a million ghosts of the young workmen
> rose in their shirts all soaked in crimson . . . and
> yelled:
> God damn the grinning kings, God damn the kaiser
> and the czar.

Critical reception for *Cornhuskers* was mixed, ranging from the view that Sandburg was in the front rank of American poets to the opinion that his outspoken idealism prevented him from being a poet at all. Some reviewers described him as the first American poet of his generation, revealing the "vitality and strength of the English tongue as it was in its beginnings" (*Review of Reviews*, January 1919), while others, such as the *New York Times* reviewer, commented on the melancholy mood of the book, attributing it to "the racial soberness of the Scandinavian" (12 January 1919).

By the time the book appeared in October 1918, Sandburg was in Stockholm, Sweden, for his first closeup view of his parents' homeland, as well as for a brief view of World War I. He stayed on after the November Armistice to continue his work as Eastern European correspondent for the Newspaper Enterprise Association and became entangled with wartime bureaucracy when he brought back to the United States a trunk full of Russian literature and propaganda and some funds intended for the Finnish People's Republic Movement in New York. His good intentions validated, Sandburg was not charged with any violations of the Trading with the Enemy Act, but he was sobered and distressed by the questioning of his loyalty as an American citizen. Back at work at the *Chicago Daily News,* he covered a range of postwar issues, as well as the ongoing racial and labor conflict in Chicago. He was assigned to investigate the background of racial tensions in the city during the summer of 1919, and his thoughtful series of articles proved tragically prophetic when the Chicago Race riots erupted in late July. Alfred Harcourt gathered Sandburg's columns into a book entitled *The Chicago Race Riots, July, 1919* (1919).

Once again, Sandburg transmuted the harsh reality of his times into poetry, and the emerging volume, *Smoke and Steel* (1920), was dedicated to his brother-in-law, Edward Steichen. As in preceding volumes, Sandburg vividly depicts the daily toil of the working man and woman, "the people who must sing or die." The smoke of spring fields, au-

Carl Sandburg, 1927 (photograph by Wilt Crowell; courtesy of the Carl Sandburg Collection, University of Illinois Library at Urbana-Champaign)

tumn leaves, steel mills, and battleship funnels is the emblem and extension of "the blood of a man," the life force which undergirds the industrial society and the larger human brotherhood: "Deep down are the cinders we came from—/You and I and our heads of smoke," he wrote in the title poem. Sandburg's American landscape broadens in *Smoke and Steel* from Chicago and the prairie to specific scenes in places such as Gary, Indiana; Omaha; Cleveland; Kalamazoo; Far Rockaway; the Blue Ridge; the Potomac; New York. In all of these places Sandburg found a common theme, the struggle of the common man, the quest of the "finders in the dark." "I hear America, I hear, *what* do I hear?," he wrote in "The Sins of Kalamazoo."

Sandburg's voyage to Sweden and his perspective of World War I are transcribed in the poems in two sections of *Smoke and Steel* titled "Pass-

ports" and "Playthings of the Wind." Harsh depictions of human cruelty (a lynching is graphically described in "Man, the Man-Hunter," for instance) are juxtaposed to the gentle, often joyous lyricism of poems about Paula Sandburg, family, home, the beauty of nature.

Smoke and Steel is a strong but uneven work, and it elicited contradictory critical views. In a review for the 15 January 1920 issue of the *New Republic* Louis Untermeyer hailed the book as "an epic of modern industrialism and a mighty paean to modern beauty" and named Sandburg and Robert Frost as America's two major living poets. Other critics charged that Sandburg had no sense of the past or vision of the future and that he had begun to produce an undiscriminating quantity of work, often imitating himself in the process. In the 9 December 1920 issue of the London *Times* a reviewer mused that Sandburg's poems were true to a certain kind of life and that they were undoubtedly American, but questioned whether Sandburg's work constituted "a high and right art."

The negative appraisals were overshadowed for Sandburg by the welcome acclaim of his friend Amy Lowell. "Reading these poems gives me more of a patriotic emotion than ever 'The Star-spangled Banner' has been able to do," she wrote in the *New York Times* (24 October 1920). "This is America and Mr. Sandburg loves her so much that suddenly we realize how much we love her, too." Earlier lectures about propagandistic poetry aside, Lowell forecast that posterity would rank Sandburg "high on the ladder of poetic achievement."

In 1921 Sandburg was forty-three years old, comfortably employed by Victor Lawson and Henry Justin Smith at the *Chicago Daily News,* and a poet whose three books had earned him a widening reputation and prestigious awards—including the Poetry Society of America Award, which he shared with Margaret Widdemer in 1919, and the Poetry Society of America Annual Book Award, which he shared with Stephen Vincent Benét in 1921. He lived with his wife and three small daughters in Elmhurst, Illinois, and traveled with increasing frequency on the college lecture circuit, reading his poetry and playing and singing American folk songs from his flourishing collection. His growing disillusionment with "the imbecility of a frightened world" was intensified by deep personal sorrow and anxiety at the discovery that his eldest child, Margaret, suffered from nocturnal epilepsy, an illness for which there was no effective treatment in 1921. Sandburg heightened his lecture activity to supplement his income so that Margaret could have every possible medical treatment for her mystifying illness, and he began to work in earnest on the *Rootabaga Stories* (1922), a charming, whimsical series of fables invented for his own children. A sequel, *Rootabaga Pigeons,* appeared in 1923.

He managed amid family stress to produce his fourth book of poetry, a slim volume entitled *Slabs of the Sunburnt West* (1922), dedicated to his youngest child, Helga. The book begins with a muted portrait of Chicago, "The Windy City," a catalogue of the city's monotony and vitality, its weather and its people. "And So Today," an extended eulogy to an unknown soldier, brings a certain closure to the war poems of this period of the poet's life. There are poems to well-known subjects—including sculptor Constantin Brancusi, Charlie Chaplin, and Robert Frost. The title poem uses the vehicle of the journey of an overland pas-

senger train to unite the past and present members of the great "procession" of "wonderful hungry people" who created the American nation. For the first time, Sandburg made extended use of the catalogue, the repetitive accrual of images in parallel forms and the quotation of American slang and platitudes.

These devices irritated some critics, who found Sandburg's work incoherent and his vocabulary dated. "Slang is last night's toadstool growth," Clement Wood wrote in the *Nation* (26 July 1922), warning that Sandburg wrote in "unfamiliar rhythms, and a vocabulary that tomorrow will speak only to the archaeologist." But other critics admired Sandburg's virility and originality, his mellower, more musical tone and his cogent style. Malcolm Cowley pointed out in the *Dial* (November 1922) that Sandburg's use of parallel constructions and repetition yielded verse which "is highly organized," producing effects "as complex and difficult sometimes as those of Swinburne's most intricate ballades. . . ." The *New York Times* reviewer warned that Sandburg "is already in danger of becoming the Professional Chanter of Virility" (4 July

Sandburg and his grandchildren, Karlen Paula and John Carl, 1945 (photograph by John R. Whiting; courtesy of the Carl Sandburg Collection, University of Illinois Library at Urbana-Champaign)

Connemara, the house in Flat Rock, North Carolina, that the Sandburgs bought in 1945 (photograph by June Glenn, Jr.)

1922), but on one point reviewers and Sandburg's large audience of readers agreed: he was a completely American poet, the Poet of the People.

Slabs of the Sunburnt West made frequent use of prose structures at a time when Sandburg was discovering an interesting fact of literary economics: prose paid better than poetry. His *Rootabaga Stories* were so successful that Alfred Harcourt proposed that Sandburg follow his longtime wish to write a juvenile biography of Abraham Lincoln. From the disillusioning realities of the world he had documented so long in poetry, journalism, and political speeches, Sandburg turned to the refuge of history and legend. He began to immerse himself in Lincoln research and in American folklore and folk music. For the next seventeen years, in the prime of his creative life, Sandburg focused on one central, overriding subject: Abraham Lincoln.

He took "occasional detours" for poetry, producing two significant volumes, *Good Morning, America* in 1928 and *The People, Yes* in 1936. But the poet who had shown the American people the reality of their language and their lives in his innovative verse forms began the long work of presenting to them the higher reality of their mythology and legends in the tragic folk hero Lincoln and in *The American Songbag*, an anthology of American folk music that he edited in 1927.

The title poem of *Good Morning, America*, composed and delivered as the Phi Beta Kappa Poem at Harvard University in 1925, was Sandburg's strongest affirmation yet of "the little two-legged joker . . . Man." The collection begins with thirty-eight "Tentative (First Model) Definitions of Poetry" and moves—with a panoramic sweep reflecting Sandburg's departure from realism—into mythology, legend, history, and a universal humanism. Sandburg converts an informed view of history, the product of his mounting Lincoln research, into poetic subject matter. His extended catalogue of proverbs and folk idioms foreshadows the content of *The People, Yes* as it dramatizes "the short miserable pilgrimage of mankind."

Sandburg's two-volume *Abraham Lincoln: The Prairie Years* brought him new celebrity and financial stability in 1926. *The American Songbag*, warmly received and reviewed in 1927, testified not only to Sandburg's versatility but to his comprehensive interest in documenting the American experience. If the Poet of the People needed further ratification of his place as a popular American literary figure, *Good Morning, America* received such an endorsement from the majority of critics. Sandburg was compared to Whitman, praised for his humor, his vision, the rhythms of his verse. Some critics, such as Perry Hutchison, chided that Sandburg demonstrated no real growth as a poet, that he had "sat too long at the feet of Walt Whitman" (*New York Times*, 21 October 1928). But the consensus was that "sunburned Carl Sandburg, in love with the earth,"

Carl Sandburg, 1948 (photograph by June Glenn, Jr.; courtesy of the Carl Sandburg Collection, University of Illinois Library at Urbana-Champaign)

as Leon Whipple called him in *Survey* (1 November 1928), had found the subject and the style vigorous and free enough for "a Continental plateau and the Great Divide. . . ."

In the early 1930s Sandburg formed a life-long friendship with Archibald MacLeish, and the men carried on an introspective dialogue about the obligations of the poet to speak to the issues of his times. The Depression years provoked in Sandburg a profound desire to console "the people of the earth, the family of man," to lift the hopes of the people who, "In the darkness with a great bundle of grief," marched "in tune and step/with constellations of universal law." Sandburg relinquished his *Chicago Daily News* job in 1932 to devote his full time to writing biography and poetry; he began to take a "detour" from work on the last stages of *Abraham Lincoln: The War Years* to write a long, innovative poem based in part on the lessons he had learned from Lincoln and American history. *The People, Yes* (1936), an epic prose-poem, is in many ways the culmination of Sandburg's work as a poet. He crafted it over an eight-year period, fusing the American vernacular with the details of history and contemporary events. Sandburg's immersion in the Lincoln era had given him an informed sense of history, and he saw striking parallels between Lincoln's time and the Depression years. Believing that economic inequity lay at the root of all social injustice, from labor conflict to racial and civil strife, he responded to the economic and social upheavals of the 1930s with *The People, Yes,* his testament to the seekers and the strugglers, the people who were the counterparts of his own immigrant parents. "Man is a long time coming," Sandburg concluded in the final, one hundred and seventh, stanza of the poem. "Man will yet win./Brother may yet line up with brother."

The critics looked for coherence and could not find it, sought structure and could not find that, and wondered anew if the Poet of the People could in fact write poetry at all. But there was generous praise for Sandburg's vision of the American people as heroic, for his lusty humor and vivid irony, for his success in rendering "the authentic accents of his brother." Sandburg's readers embraced the book and wrote to him in legions to thank him for it. He took all responses in stride. He had written the poem he wanted to write, and he called it the "best memorandum I could file for the present stress."

In 1940 Sandburg won the Pulitzer Prize for the four-volume *Abraham Lincoln: The War Years,*

Frank Lloyd Wright, Alistair Cooke, and Carl Sandburg appearing on The Chicago Dynamic Hour *(WTTW, Chicago), 1957 (courtesy of the Carl Sandburg Collection, University of Illinois Library at Urbana-Champaign)*

published in 1939. *The People, Yes* was his last major book of poetry. During the decade of the 1940s Sandburg lectured widely, wrote occasional poetry, involved himself actively in the war effort, and worked as a syndicated columnist. A collection of his newspaper columns and radio broadcasts was published as *Home Front Memo* (1943), along with the text and photographs from *Road to Victory*, a patriotic exhibit which he and his brother-in-law, Edward Steichen, had created for the Museum of Modern Art in 1942.

Sandburg and MacLeish were critical of writers who remained detached from the national emergency of World War II, and Sandburg cautioned that "A writer's silence on living issues can in itself constitute a propaganda of conduct leading toward the deterioration or death of freedom."

Sandburg's commitment to speak to the issues of his times, his passion for American history, and his desire to try writing in every genre led him to sign a contract on 11 September 1943 to write an epic historical novel that Metro-Goldwyn-Mayer Studios could make into what the studio hoped would be a popular wartime film. Sandburg was an innovator, seldom afraid to risk new ventures; thus he set out in 1943, at age sixty-five, to write his first and only novel, *Remembrance Rock*. It was finally completed and published in 1948, but the film version was never made.

Sandburg had tried almost every genre by the time he won the Pulitzer Prize for poetry in 1951 for his *Complete Poems* (1950). In *Always the Young Strangers* (1953) he recorded the first twenty years of his life. Sandburg enjoyed the height of his ce-

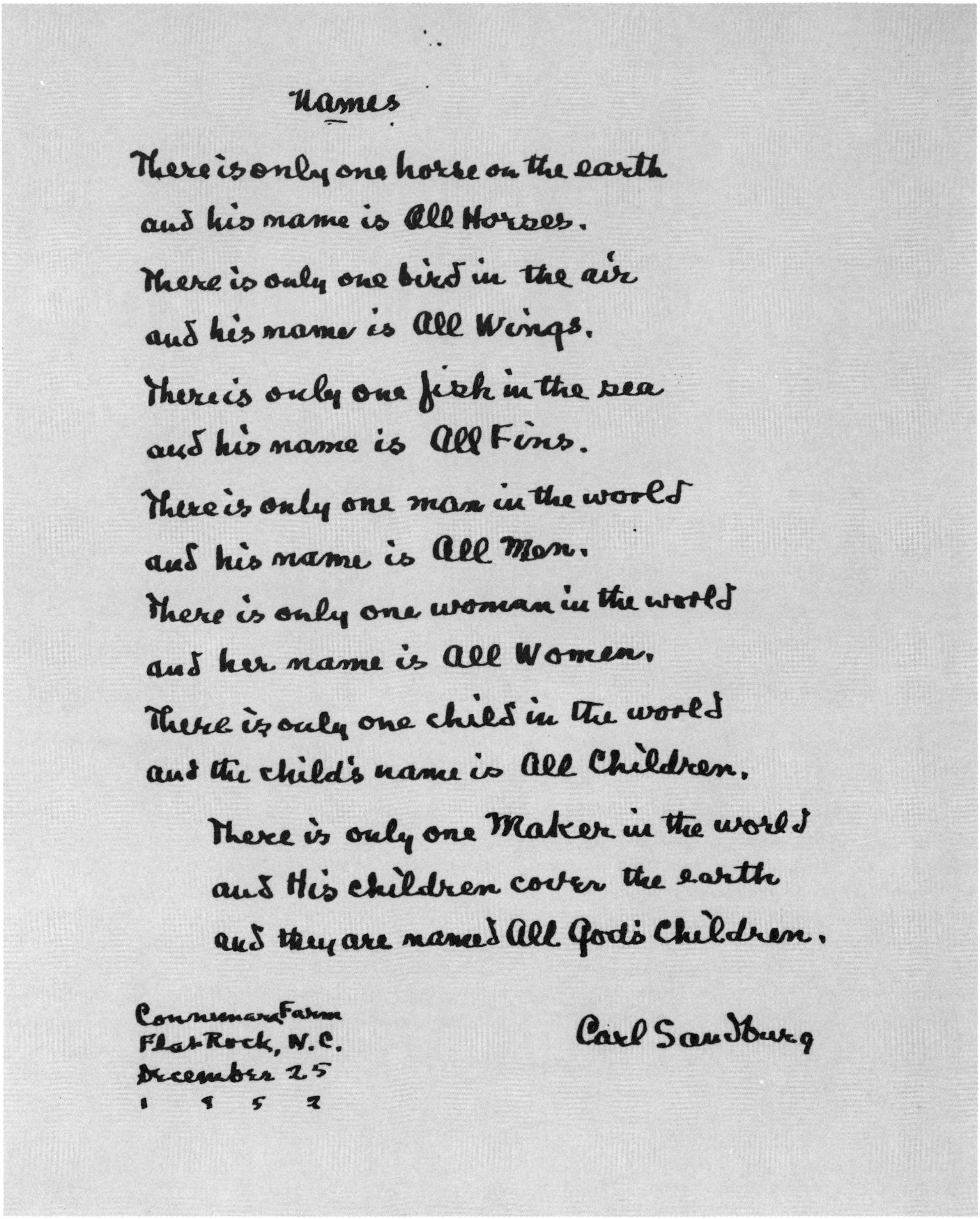

Names

There is only one horse on the earth
and his name is All Horses.
There is only one bird in the air
and his name is All Wings.
There is only one fish in the sea
and his name is All Fins.
There is only one man in the world
and his name is All Men.
There is only one woman in the world
and her name is All Women.
There is only one child in the world
and the child's name is All Children.

There is only one Maker in the world
and His children cover the earth
and they are named All God's Children.

Connemara Farm
Flat Rock, N.C.
December 25
1 9 5 2

Carl Sandburg

Manuscript for a poem that was published in part in the prologue to The Family of Man *and collected in its entirety in* Wind Song *(by permission of Maurice Greenbaum, Trustee for the Estate of Carl Sandburg; courtesy of the Carl Sandburg Collection, University of Illinois Library at Urbana-Champaign)* lebrity in the 1950s, traveling widely as an increasingly visible public figure. He was a natural for the new medium of television, and his familiar face, with high cheekbones framed by the sweep of white hair, was photographed and recognized across the nation he celebrated throughout his life and work. In 1959 Sandburg and Edward Steichen traveled to the Soviet Union with *The Family of Man,* an exhibition of photographs and text which they had jointly arranged as a celebration of humanity. Sandburg made his second and final trip to Sweden at the end of that journey.

Sandburg wrote, traveled, and entertained audiences as long as he had the strength to do so. He went to Hollywood in 1960 to spend a year and a half as creative consultant to George Stevens and his film *The Greatest Story Ever Told.* The octogenarian Sandburg had by the 1960s become known as a legend in his time. "A legend in our time," he often exclaimed. "Jesus, it could be worse."

"Being a poet is a damn dangerous business," Sandburg observed at his eighty-fifth birthday dinner in 1963, on the event of the publication of his final book of poetry, *Honey and Salt.* The volume is notable for its variety, but its quality is uneven. Some of the poems are sentimental caricatures of his early work, but many of them reveal powers which had stayed and grown. *Honey and Salt* is a summation of Sandburg's life and work weighted with reflections on the passage of time, the waning of physical and creative powers, the perdurability of the physical universe, and the transitory nature of human life. *Honey and Salt* contains whimsy and pain, sentimentality and strength, and Sandburg's enduring idealism, memory, and hope, as well as his rudimentary affirmation of the bonds of universal life and the family of man.

The Sandburgs left the midwestern heartland in 1945, moving to the mountains of North Carolina in search of more solitude and space for the family and Paula Sandburg's thriving herd of championship dairy goats. They settled at Connemara, a 245-acre estate in Flat Rock, North Carolina. Carl Sandburg died there in the hush of the mountain summer on 22 July 1967 at age eighty-nine. His wife, Paula, survived him, along with daughters Margaret, Janet, and Helga, and Helga's children, John Carl and Karlen Paula, who as teenagers had legally taken their grandmother's maiden name, Steichen. At the simple funeral ceremony in a nearby chapel, Edward Steichen placed a pine bough on Sandburg's coffin, in memory of their years of fellowship.

Unlike American writers whose families had long been American citizens, Sandburg felt no compulsion to serve a literary apprenticeship abroad. While others found stimulation and sustenance in Paris, London, or Rome, Sandburg turned to Milwaukee and Chicago. Sandburg's immigrant father never learned to write the language his son used to explore, describe, interpret, and celebrate the American experience. August and Clara Sandburg were strangers to the American prairie and the robust complexity of the city Carl Sandburg sought to interpret for them and others like them. Witnessing the obstacles thrust before the modest hopes of simple working people such as his parents, he became the passionate champion for people who did not have the words or power to speak for themselves. During the turbulent events of nearly a century of American life, Sandburg sought to articulate and affirm the hopes of the average American citizen. "There are poets of streets and struggles, of dust and combat, of violence wanton or justified, of plain folk living close to a hard earth," Sandburg wrote in "Notes for a Preface" in

Carl and Paula Sandburg on the porch at Connemara, late 1950s (photograph by June Glenn, Jr.)

Manuscript for a poem collected in Harvest Poems *(by permission of Maurice Greenbaum, Trustee for the Estate of Carl Sandburg; courtesy of the Lilly Library, Indiana University)*

Carl Sandburg, Librarian of Congress L. Quincy Mumford, and Robert Frost in Washington, D.C., 1960 (courtesy of the Library of Congress)

his *Complete Poems.* He was convinced that "When men lose their poetic feeling for ordinary life, and cannot write poetry of ordinary things, their exalted poetry is likely to lose its strength of exaltation."

Sandburg found his subject and his themes in ordinary life. He viewed himself as "one more seeker" in the long procession of humanity. His celebration of the durable human spirit transcends time or place. This uniquely American poet found in the American experience symbols for the universal human experience. "The people take the earth/as a tomb of rest and a cradle of hope," he wrote in *The People, Yes.* "Who else speaks for the Family of Man?/They are in tune and step/with constellations of universal law."

Carl Sandburg spoke for the Family of Man in bold new forms and subjects. Twentieth-century critics have seriously underestimated his influence in legitimizing and popularizing the free-verse form in American literature. Sandburg was often his own best critic; he anticipated that some of his work would later be judged as dated and obsolete. If some of his poems seemed "to be not for this hour," he suggested, they could be "passed by as annals, chronicles or punctuation points of a vanished period." He was a conscientious public poet

whose work, to be comprehended fully, must be read within the context of his times.

Yet as the spokesman for the great human family, Carl Sandburg, biographer, historian, troubadour, and poet, speaks to any period, any place.

Letters:

The Letters of Carl Sandburg, edited by Herbert Mitgang (New York: Harcourt, Brace & World, 1968);

Carl Sandburg, Philip Green Wright, and the Asgard Press, 1900-1910, compiled by Joan St. C. Crane (Charlottesville: University of Virginia Press, 1975).

Biographies:

Karl Detzer, *Carl Sandburg: A Study in Personality and Background* (New York: Harcourt, Brace, 1941);

Harry Golden, *Carl Sandburg* (Chicago: World, 1961);

Joseph Haas and Gene Lovitz, *Carl Sandburg: A Pictorial Biography* (New York: Putnam's, 1967);

Paula Steichen, *My Connemara* (New York: Harcourt, Brace & World, 1969);

North Callahan, *Carl Sandburg: Lincoln of Our Literature* (New York: New York University Press, 1970);

Helga Sandburg, *A Great and Glorious Romance* (New York: Harcourt Brace Jovanovich, 1978);

Paula Steichen, "Hyacinths and Biscuits," in *Carl Sandburg Home Handbook 117* (Washington, D.C.: National Park Service, 1982).

References:

Gay Wilson Allen, *Carl Sandburg, Pamphlets on American Writers*, No. 101 (Minneapolis: University of Minnesota Press, 1972);

Norman Corwin, *The World of Carl Sandburg: A Stage Presentation* (New York: Harcourt, Brace, 1960);

Richard Crowder, *Carl Sandburg* (New York: Twayne, 1964);

Hazel Durnell, *The America of Carl Sandburg* (Seattle: University of Washington Press, 1965);

Harry Hansen, *Midwest Portraits* (New York: Harcourt, Brace, 1923);

Amy Lowell, *Tendencies in Modern American Poetry* (New York: Macmillan, 1917), pp. 139-232;

Harriet Monroe, *A Poet's Life* (New York: Macmillan, 1938);

Monroe, *Poets and Their Art* (New York: Macmillan, 1926), pp. 29-38;

Edward Steichen, ed., *Sandburg: Photographers View Carl Sandburg* (New York: Harcourt, Brace & World, 1966);

Louis Untermeyer, *American Poetry Since 1900* (New York: Holt, 1923);

Untermeyer, *Modern American Poetry* (New York: Harcourt, Brace, 1936);

Mark Van Doren, *Carl Sandburg, With a Bibliography of Sandburg Materials in the Collections of the Library of Congress* (Washington, D.C.: Library of Congress, 1969).

Papers:

The principal repository of Carl Sandburg's papers and books is the Carl Sandburg Collection of the University of Illinois Library at Urbana-Champaign, which also includes an extensive photographic and tape archive, particularly the Carl Sandburg Oral History Collection, compiled by Penelope Niven. In addition, more than 10,000 of Sandburg's books and many of his papers are housed at Connemara, the Carl Sandburg Home, a National Historic Site and National Park in Flat Rock, North Carolina. A smaller collection of memorabilia and some early editions of his work may be seen at the Carl Sandburg Birthplace in Galesburg, Illinois.

George Santayana

(16 December 1863-26 September 1952)

William G. Holzberger

Bucknell University

BOOKS: *Lines on Leaving the Bedford St. Schoolhouse* (Boston: Privately printed, 1880);

Sonnets and Other Verses (Cambridge, Mass. & Chicago: Stone & Kimball, 1894; revised and enlarged edition, New York: Stone & Kimball, 1896);

The Sense of Beauty: Being the Outlines of Aesthetic Theory (New York: Scribners, 1896; London: A. & C. Black, 1896);

Platonism in the Italian Poets (Buffalo: Paul's Press, 1896);

Lucifer: A Theological Tragedy (Chicago & New York: H. S. Stone, 1899); revised as *Lucifer; Or, The Heavenly Truce: A Theological Tragedy* (Cambridge, Mass.: Dunster House, 1924);

Interpretations of Poetry and Religion (New York: Scribners, 1900; London: A. & C. Black, 1900);

A Hermit of Carmel And Other Poems (New York: Scribners, 1901; London: Johnson, 1902);

The Life of Reason; Or, The Phases of Human Progress: Introduction and Reason in Common Sense (New York: Scribners, 1905; London: Constable, 1905);

The Life of Reason; Or, The Phases of Human Progress: Reason in Society (New York: Scribners, 1905; London: Constable, 1905);

The Life of Reason; Or, The Phases of Human Progress: Reason in Religion (New York: Scribners, 1905; London: Constable, 1905);

The Life of Reason; Or, The Phases of Human Progress: Reason in Art (New York: Scribners, 1905; London: Constable, 1905);

The Life of Reason; Or, The Phases of Human Progress: Reason in Science (New York: Scribners, 1906; London: Constable, 1906);

Three Philosophical Poets: Lucretius, Dante, and Goethe, Harvard Studies in Comparative Literature, volume 1 (Cambridge: Harvard University, 1910);

Winds of Doctrine: Studies in Contemporary Opinion (London: Dent/New York: Scribners, 1913);

Egotism in German Philosophy (New York: Scribners, 1915; London & Toronto: Dent/New York: Scribners, 1916); republished as *The German Mind: A Philosophical Diagnosis* (New York: Crowell, 1968);

Character and Opinion in the United States: With Reminiscences of William James and Josiah Royce and Academic Life in America (London: Constable, 1920; New York: Scribners, 1920);

Soliloquies in England, and Later Soliloquies (London: Constable, 1922; New York: Scribners, 1922);

Poems, Selected by the Author and Revised (London: Constable, 1922; New York: Scribners, 1923);

George Santayana

Scepticism and Animal Faith: Introduction to a System of Philosophy (London: Constable, 1923; New York: Scribners, 1923);

Dialogues in Limbo (London: Constable, 1925; New York: Scribners, 1926; enlarged edition, New York: Scribners, 1948);

Platonism and the Spiritual Life (London: Constable, 1927; New York: Scribners, 1927);

The Realm of Essence: Book First of Realms of Being (London: Constable, 1927; New York: Scribners, 1927);

The Realm of Matter: Book Second of Realms of Being (London: Constable, 1930; New York: Scribners, 1930);

The Genteel Tradition at Bay (New York: Scribners, 1931);

Some Turns of Thought in Modern Philosophy, Five Essays (Cambridge: Cambridge University Press, 1933; New York: Scribners, 1933);

The Last Puritan: A Memoir in the Form of a Novel (London: Constable, 1935; New York: Scribners, 1936);

Obiter Scripta: Lectures, Essays and Reviews, edited by Justus Buchler and Benjamin Schwartz (London: Constable, 1936; New York: Scribners, 1936);

The Realm of Truth: Book Third of Realms of Being (London: Constable, 1937; New York: Scribners, 1938);

The Realm of Spirit: Book Fourth of Realms of Being (London: Constable, 1940; New York: Scribners, 1940);

The Background of My Life, volume 1 of *Persons and Places* (New York: Scribners, 1944; London: Constable, 1944);

The Middle Span, volume 2 of *Persons and Places* (New York: Scribners, 1945; London: Constable, 1947);

The Idea of Christ in the Gospels; Or, God in Man, A Critical Essay (New York: Scribners, 1946);

Dominations and Powers: Reflections on Liberty, Society, and Government (London: Constable, 1951; New York: Scribners, 1951);

My Host the World, volume 3 of *Persons and Places* (New York: Scribners, 1953; London: Cresset, 1953);

The Poet's Testament: Poems and Two Plays, edited by John Hall Wheelock and Daniel Cory (New York: Scribners, 1953);

The Idler and His Works, and Other Essays, edited by Cory (New York: Braziller, 1957);

George Santayana's America: Essays on Literature and Culture, edited by James Ballowe (Urbana: University of Illinois Press, 1967);

Santayana on America: Essays, Notes, and Letters on American Life, Literature, and Philosophy, edited by Richard C. Lyon (New York: Harcourt, Brace & World, 1968);

Physical Order and Moral Liberty: Previously Unpublished Essays of George Santayana, edited by John and Shirley Lachs (Nashville: Vanderbilt University Press, 1969);

Poems of George Santayana, selected by Robert Hutchinson (New York: Dover, 1970);

Lotze's System of Philosophy, edited by Paul Grimley Kuntz (Bloomington: Indiana University Press, 1971);

The Complete Poems of George Santayana: A Critical Edition, edited by William G. Holzberger (Lewisburg: Bucknell University Press/London: Associated University Presses, 1979).

Collections: *The Works of George Santayana*, Triton Edition, 15 volumes (New York: Scribners, 1936-1940);

Persons and Places: Fragments of Autobiography, edited by William G. Holzberger and Herman J. Saatkamp, Jr., volume 1 of *The Works of George Santayana* (Cambridge: MIT Press, 1986).

OTHER: "My Poetry," in *The Philosophy of George Santayana*, edited by Paul A. Schilpp (Evanston & Chicago: Northwestern University, 1940; revised, 1951), pp. 598-600.

George Santayana is widely regarded as one of the great philosophers and men of letters of our time. A prolific author, he is well known for his many books and scores of articles on philosophy, religion, history, literature, and culture, and for his novel, *The Last Puritan* (1935). But before turning to prose, Santayana was a poet. His earliest efforts in verse were composed while he was at the Boston Latin School in the early 1880s; he also wrote poems during his undergraduate years at Harvard (1882-1886) and while a graduate student in Germany (1886-1888). He continued to produce poetry during the years that he was teaching philosophy at Harvard (1889-1912), until about the turn of the century when his career as a poet came to a halt after his verse drama *Lucifer* (1899) failed to attract critical attention. His last volume of new poetry was *A Hermit of Carmel And Other Poems* (1901). The book entitled *Poems* (1922) is his selection of poems from his earlier books. Except for a few poems written during the later part of his life, Santayana's poetry is a product of his youth and early middle age. His polished prose style, however, is extremely poetic, full of brilliant images and in-

George Santayana, 1886

genious metaphors. In fact, this distinctive poetic style has been the consternation of students of Santayana's technical philosophical system and of other philosophers, who, like Bertrand Russell, have complained that the poetry of Santayana's discourse continually distracts the mind from the logic of his argument.

The concentration of Santayana's poetry within the earlier part of his career, together with the characteristics of that poetry, have placed him among the most important of the American neo-traditionalist poets, specifically within a branch of that school known as the Harvard Poets, a group associated with Harvard University during the last quarter of the nineteenth century and the first decade of the twentieth. Other prominent Harvard Poets were William Vaughn Moody, Hugh Mc-Collough, George Cabot Lodge, and Trumbull

Stickney, all of whom, as Santayana points out, died young. This group of poets, which remains a minor but significant movement in American poetry, immediately preceded the great modernists, T. S. Eliot, Ezra Pound, Robert Frost, William Carlos Williams, and Wallace Stevens, who were to set the tone and style for twentieth-century poetry in English.

George Santayana was born in Madrid on 16 December 1863 to Spanish parents. His mother, Josefina Borrás de Santayana, the widow of an American businessman in Manila, George Sturgis of Boston, separated from her second husband and returned to America with her three Sturgis children when Santayana was five. Three years later, Santayana's father, Agustín Ruiz de Santayana, took him to Boston to live with his mother, two half sisters, and half brother in his mother's house on Beacon Street. His father remained briefly in Boston before returning to Spain for good in 1873. Santayana did not see him again until he was nineteen years old and had completed his first year at Harvard. These early years in America were difficult for the sensitive Spanish boy, whose first American schooling was in Miss Welchman's kindergarten among much younger children and later at a rather rough public elementary school. It was not until he moved to the Boston Public Latin School in the autumn of 1874 that he began to feel more at ease and accepted in his new country. Early removal from his native land to a culture and climate totally foreign to the one into which he had been born and spent the first years of his life seems to have had a permanent effect upon Santayana, making him feel forever the stranger wherever he went, even when he later returned for visits to Spain, where he believed that his "Yankee manners" set him apart. This sense of dislocation probably accounts for the alienation that Santayana claimed always to have felt and that is expressed so frequently in his writings, both verse and prose.

The theme of alienation combines in Santayana's poetry with several other major themes that constitute the intellectual and critical substance of his verse. Disillusionment with Christianity, particularly with the Roman Catholicism to which he had been so aesthetically drawn during his childhood, combines with skepticism and stoic resignation in his first sonnet series. However, his keen interest in and respect for the great religions of history remained with him for the whole of his life, even though he had resigned literal belief in the doctrine of supernaturalism upon which all of them were based. Love and friendship and the intellectual life,

IV

O world, thou choosest not the better part!
It is not wisdom to be only wise
And on the inward vision close the eyes,
But it is wisdom to believe the heart.
Columbus found a world, and had no chart,
Save one that faith deciphered in the skies:
To trust the soul's invincible surmise
Was all his science and his only art.
Our knowledge is a torch of smoky pine
That lights the pathway but a step ahead
Across a void of mystery and dread.
Bid, then, the tender light of faith to shine,
By which alone the human heart is led
Unto the thinking of the thought divine.

1884

Page from Santayana's notebook, circa 1890. This poem was published as the third sonnet in Santayana's first sonnet series (by permission of Mrs. Daniel Cory, the Estate of George Santayana; courtesy of the Poetry Collection, State University of New York at Buffalo).

particularly the life of the wandering student, is a principal theme of his lyric poems and of his youthful letters in verse, written to his friends during his graduate studies in Germany. Other dominant themes of the poems are the historical migration of peoples and cultures (such as that from Spain to the New World) and the spiritual barrenness of modern life as compared with classical Greece and Rome and Europe of the high middle ages. America, with its emphasis upon the acquisition of wealth and its preoccupation with material things, particularly becomes a symbol for the banality of modern existence. This theme is especially evident in Santayana's four Sapphic odes, which, like the sonnets, are among the finest of his poetic productions. All of these poems are characterized by a style and diction redolent of the great English romantics: regular meters and rhyme schemes and the use of an elevated and rather distinctively "literary" diction, including archaisms. These characteristics of the neotraditionalists were generally eschewed by their successors, the moderns.

Nevertheless, some of the great moderns are indebted to Santayana. T. S. Eliot was Santayana's pupil at Harvard, and Eliot's well-known "objective correlative" was borrowed directly (and silently) from Santayana's discussion of the way poets exploit the link between emotions and the objects that arouse them, in chapter ten, "The Elements and Function of Poetry," in *Interpretations of Poetry and Religion* (1900). Wallace Stevens, during his Harvard undergraduate days at the turn of the century, also knew Santayana. The philosopher was sufficiently impressed by "Cathedrals Are Not Built Along the Sea" (1899), a sonnet that Stevens showed him, to respond by composing a sonnet of his own in answer to it, "Cathedrals by the Sea." The philosophical naturalism and skepticism expressed later in Stevens's mature poetry is perfectly consonant with Santayana's philosophical system. Both Wallace Stevens and Robert Lowell—whom Santayana befriended and encouraged at the beginning of Lowell's career in the late 1940s—expressed their regard for Santayana by making him the subject of major poems: Stevens's "To An Old Philosopher in Rome" (1952) and Lowell's "For George Santayana 1863-1952" (1959).

Santayana's own undergraduate years at Harvard were essentially happy ones. He lived simply on an allowance of $750 per year from his mother. Tuition cost $150, and room and board absorbed $250 more. That left about a dollar a day for clothes, books and supplies, car fares, amusements, and other expenses. He managed very well on this

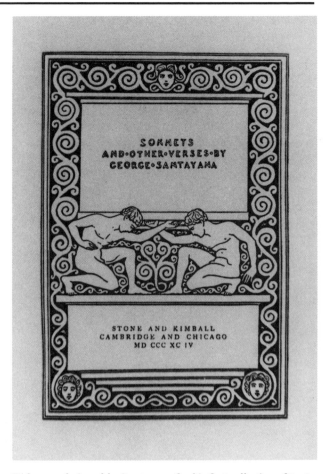

Title page designed by Santayana for his first collection of poetry

modest budget, made friends, drew cartoons for the *Harvard Lampoon,* and served on the editorial board. He belonged to the O.K. (Orthoepy Klub), a college literary society, and became president of the Philosophical Society. Except for some difficulties with mathematics and Greek, Santayana did well in his studies and his A.B. degree was awarded (in absentia) summa cum laude in 1886.

The Harvard bachelor's degree was conferred in absentia because Santayana had already left for graduate study in Europe, where he shared (with Charles Augustus Strong) a fellowship awarded by the Harvard philosophy department. German philosophy in the 1880s was very influential, particularly in the area of the newly developing scientific psychology, and Santayana studied, at Göttingen and Berlin, with several outstanding German theorists. He was not, however, comfortable with the new physiological psychology, and he failed to master German sufficiently to write a doctoral dissertation in that language. After two years' study in Germany, he therefore returned to Amer-

George Santayana, circa 1895 (charcoal portrait by Andreas Martin Andersen)

ica to complete his graduate studies at Harvard. "Lotze's System of Philosophy," which Santayana later described as "my dull thesis on Lotze," was completed in 1889, and he was awarded the doctorate. (This dissertation has been edited by Paul Grimley Kuntz and published in 1971 by the Indiana University Press.) He was also immediately employed by Harvard as an instructor in philosophy and taught there along with his distinguished mentors, William James and Josiah Royce, during the period now referred to as the "golden age" of the Harvard philosophy department. In 1898 Santayana was promoted to the rank of assistant professor, and in 1907, following publication of his monumental five-volume *The Life of Reason* (1905-1906), he was made full professor. He taught regularly at Harvard, spending almost every summer in Europe, until his retirement in 1912 at the age of forty-eight, when he removed to Europe permanently, never returning to the United States.

The *Harvard Monthly*, the college literary magazine which Santayana helped found in 1885, pro-

vided for the first important publication of his poems. Several of Santayana's early sonnets, translations, and lyrics were originally published in the *Monthly*. A sonnet beginning "I would I might forget that I am I" (later to become number seven of the first sonnet series) appeared in the first issue (October 1885), and the magazine continued to provide an outlet for his poetry until 1903.

Sonnets and Other Verses (1894), the first collection of Santayana's poems, is a slim volume, with an attractive title page designed by Santayana himself. It was published by the enterprising firm of Herbert S. Stone and Hannibal Ingalls Kimball, two young Harvard graduates, whose ambition was to publish the Harvard Poets. The first edition consisted of 510 copies, 60 of which were printed in a large-paper format, bound in vellum, and published in slipcases. The book enjoyed a modest local success, and the author began to be fêted by Cambridge and Boston hostesses as an interesting young man of talent. *Sonnets and Other Verses* contains the twenty sonnets of Santayana's first sonnet series, number three of which is the much-anthologized "O world, thou choosest not the better part!" These sonnets record Santayana's abandonment of religious faith: "Slow and reluctant was the long descent,/With many farewell pious looks behind,/And dumb misgivings where the path might wind,/And questionings of nature, as I went" (sonnet two). With the abandonment of religious faith came also a resignation of the normal human ambitions and pursuits. In their place came stoic acceptance of the human condition and the position of the observer rather than of the participant, and these attitudes characterized Santayana's life from about the age of thirty to the end. Sonnet thirteen perfectly expresses this attitude:

Why this proud piety, that dares to pray
For a world wider than the heaven's cope?
Farewell, my burden! No more will I bear
The foolish load of my fond faith's despair,
But trip the idle race with careless feet.

Also included in this first collection are five titled sonnets on various subjects and a group of four sonnets, "To W. P.," an elegy for his young friend Warwick Potter, who had died suddenly in the autumn of 1893, a few months after graduating from Harvard. The death of this young man who, Santayana said, was like a younger brother to him, together with the unsuitable marriage that his beloved elder half-sister Susana had made the previous year to a widower with six children in Spain,

On the Three
Philosophical Poets.

Falling untempered from the ethereal blue,
The light of truth might scorch the eyes, and blind.
Therefore these giant oaks their branches twined
And betwixt earth and heaven the lattice drew
Of their green labyrinth. Rare stars shone through,
Low, large, and mild. The infinite, confined,
Suffered the measure of the pensive mind,
And what the heart contrived it counted true.
Scant is that covert now in the merciless glare,
Stripped all those leafy arches, riven that dome,
Unhappy laggard, he whose nest was there.
Some yet untrodden forest be my home,
Where patient time and woven light and air
And streams a mansion for the soul prepare.

A 1936 version of a sonnet first drafted in 1911. The facsimile reproduced here is the frontispiece to volume six of the Triton Edition of Santayana's works, which includes his essay "Three Philosophical Poets" (by permission of Mrs. Daniel Cory, the Estate of George Santayana).

℅ Brown Shipley & C°
123, Pall Mall, London, S.W. 1

Paris, June 23, 1936

Dear Mr. Wheelock
          In regard to a fancy
title for the limited edition of
my works, would Triton Edition
be at all the sort of thing required?
It seems senseless, but I understand they all do more or less.
What suggested the word to me
is that my windows in Rome
look down on the Fontana del
Tritone and Via del Tritone.
The Triton, by Bernini, is well
known, and might be reproduced
for a frontispiece or paper-cover.
Then there is the association with
Wordsworth's sonnet: "a pagan
suckled in a creed outworn"
and "hear old Triton blow his
wreathèd horn."

Page from a letter from Santayana to Scribners editor John Hall Wheelock concerning the title for Scribners' fifteen-volume collection of Santayana's works (by permission of Mrs. Daniel Cory, the Estate of George Santayana) and in 1893 the death of his father, whom Santayana had loved (whereas he only respected his mother), served to bring about this complete change of heart, resignation, or what Santayana referred to much later in his autobiography by the Greek word *metanoia*.

Santayana's five Sapphic odes are also included in this first edition of *Sonnets and Other Verses*. The odes reiterate and reinforce the themes of the sonnets. Man is a part of Nature, not something separate and distinct, and it is as a child of Nature that man understands himself most truly. The wisest man is one who seeks to understand Nature and live according to her laws. Supernaturalist religions and idealistic philosophies are mere delusions and evasions of reality. The first ode expresses Santayana's dissatisfaction with modern America and commercial civilizations generally:

> What god will choose me from this labouring nation
> To worship him afar, with inward gladness,
> At sunset and at sunrise, in some Persian
>   Garden of roses;
>
>   . . . .
>
> So would I dream awhile, and ease a little
> The soul long stifled and the straitened spirit,
> Tasting new pleasures in a far-off country
>   Sacred to beauty.

The second ode expresses Santayana's contempt for what he saw as the modern preoccupation with material possessions:

> My heart rebels against my generation,
> That talks of freedom and is slave to riches,
> And, toiling 'neath each day's ignoble burden,
>   Boasts of the morrow.
>
>   . . . .
>
> What would you gain, ye seekers, with your striving,
> Or what vast Babel raise you on your shoulders?
> You multiply distresses, and your children
>   Surely will curse you.

This ode ends with the memorable line in which the poet admonishes the reader to "learn to love, in all things mortal, only/What is eternal."

The section "Various Poems" contains five pieces, including one of Santayana's finest lyrics, "Cape Cod":

> The low sandy beach and the thin scrub pine,
> The wide reach of bay and the long sky line,—
>   O, I am far from home!
> The salt, salt smell of the thick sea air,

George Santayana, 1930s

> And the smooth round stones that the ebbtides
>   wear,—
>   When will the good ship come?

In composing "Cape Cod," Santayana was told by fellow Harvard Poet William Vaughn Moody that here he had been truly inspired. Concluding the first edition of *Sonnets and Other Verses* are two dramatic pieces, a fragment of a draft of a play called *The Marriage of Venus*, here simply entitled "Chorus," and a lengthy "Prelude" that was later to become part of the full-length romantic drama *Lucifer: A Theological Tragedy* (1899).

In 1896 Stone and Kimball brought out a slightly revised and somewhat expanded edition of *Sonnets and Other Verses*. The most significant difference is the addition of the thirty poems of the second sonnet series, love sonnets in the Platonic tradition. According to the conventions of the Italian renaissance sonneteers, the passion of the poet for the lady of his heart is eventually transmuted into a selfless adoration of supreme good, and the lady herself is metamorphosed into that highest

Epitaph

O Youth, O Beauty, ye who fed the flame
That here ~~is~~ was quenched, breathe not your lover's name.
He lies not here. Where'er ye dwell anew,
He loves again, he dies again, in you.
~~Gather~~ Pluck the wild rose & weave the laurel crown
To deck your glory, not his false renown.

—

Page from the notebook Santayana titled "Posthumous Poems" and dated 13 October 1943 (by permission of Mrs. Daniel Cory, the Estate of George Santayana; courtesy of the Clifton Waller Barrett Library, University of Virginia) value which is God. Of course in Santayana this Christian Platonism must be taken only metaphorically, and in this way it expresses the philosophical truth that nothing on earth can be lasting; all material existence is perpetually in flux; only the immaterial can endure; only the *essences* of things are immortal. This second sonnet series demonstrates the significance of Plato's idealism in Santayana's otherwise materialistic philosophy.

Though Santayana had many women friends, he never married nor was he ever seriously linked with a woman romantically. There has been much speculation regarding the possible identity of the Dark Lady of Santayana's sonnets, but the poet himself said that there was no single real-life counterpart; he insisted rather that he was simply using a time-honored convention in which to express his feelings and ideas. *Sonnets and Other Verses* was republished in 1906 by Fox, Duffield and Company of New York, with the single omission of "Prelude."

Santayana's last book of new poems, *A Hermit of Carmel And Other Poems* (1901), contains two long verse dramas—the title poem and "The Knight's Return"—together with fifteen poems under the heading "Elegiac and Lyric Poems," three translations from Italian and French poems by Michelangelo, Alfred de Musset, and Théophile Gautier, and ten poems characterized as "Convivial and Occasional Verses." The two dramatic works are of that nineteenth-century genre called "closet drama," plays written to be read rather than staged. They tend to be somewhat melodramatic and heavy-handed. The best poems in this collection are among the "Elegiac and Lyric Poems"; especially impressive and well known are "Sybaris," "Avila" (in which Santayana celebrates the ancient walled city in Castile, where he spent the earliest years of his life), "King's College Chapel," "In Grantchester Meadows," "Before a Statue of Achilles," and "Cathedrals by the Sea."

With the publication of *A Hermit of Carmel And Other Poems* in 1901, Santayana's career as an actively practicing poet came to an end. He felt that the times were not propitious for the writing and publication of poetry because the dominant literary form had become the novel. This perception, combined with the failure of his volumes of verse, his dramatic poems, and his full-length tragedy *Lucifer* (1899) to attract critical acclaim or more than a modest audience, caused Santayana, except for an occasional effusion, to give up poetry and devote himself entirely to the production of prose works. From the turn of the century until his death he produced mainly books of philosophy but in 1935

George Santayana, 1950

published a widely read novel, *The Last Puritan: A Memoir in the Form of a Novel*, which was an almost successful candidate for a Pulitzer Prize for 1936 (the prize was awarded to Margaret Mitchell's *Gone With the Wind*). Near the end of his life he also wrote a three-part autobiography, *Persons and Places*, which comprises *The Background of My Life* (1944), *The Middle Span* (1945), and *My Host the World* (1953).

After 1901 Santayana continued to teach philosophy at Harvard and to write philosophical books, articles, and reviews until, with the death of his mother early in 1912, he came into a modest inheritance that enabled him to resign his professorship. He took up permanent residence in Europe and devoted himself exclusively to writing. *Poems* (1922) contains previously published works, including the two sonnet series, a collection of miscellaneous sonnets, the five Sapphic odes, his "Athletic Ode," and a group of lyrics called "Various Poems," which were taken from *A Hermit of Carmel And Other Poems*. The single previously uncollected poem in this book is "A Minuet on Reaching the Age of Fifty." Santayana's preface for this volume is an important statement of his argument for the continued use of traditional methods and forms in the creation of poetry. "To say that what was good once is good no longer," he wrote, "is to give too much importance to chronology." This short preface, in fact, constitutes a remarkably objective critical essay on Santayana's poetry. *Poems* was republished in the first volume of the Triton Edition of *The Works of George Santayana* (1936-1940).

The years 1922-1940 were devoted to prose works, principally to *Realms of Being* (1927-1940), the four-volume master statement of his philosophical system; but toward the end of his long life, Santayana returned to writing poetry. At the outbreak of World War II he was living in Rome, where, since the 1920s, he had had his principal residence. In the autumn of 1941, toward the end of his seventy-seventh year, Santayana decided that he could no longer look after himself properly while continuing to live in hotels. On 14 October he moved into the convent nursing home in the Via Santo Stefano Rotondo operated by the Blue Sisters of the Little Company of Mary, an order of English nuns. Here he wrote *Persons and Places*. After the war, Santayana began putting into order a collection of early unpublished poems and translations, as well as two early blank-verse plays, *The Marriage of Venus: A Comedy* and *Philosophers at Court*. He made a final fair copy of the poems, entitling them "Posthumous Poems," dated the manuscript Rome, 13 October 1947, and on the first page dedicated the work to his long-time friend and literary secretary Daniel Cory. These poems, together with the two plays, were edited by Cory and John Hall Wheelock of Scribners and published in 1953, a year after Santayana's death, as *The Poet's Testament: Poems and Two Plays*. Most of the poems of this collection were written much earlier in Santayana's career, but it also includes two later ones, written toward the end of his life, "Epitaph" and "The Poet's Testament," an impressive lyric that expresses Santayana's philosophy:

I give back to the earth what the earth gave,
All to the furrow, nothing to the grave.
....
I sang to heaven. My exile made me free,
From world to world, from all worlds carried me.
....
To trembling harmonies of field and cloud,
Of flesh and spirit was my worship vowed.

Until a few weeks before his death, on 26 September 1952, Santayana had been working on an English translation of a long pastoral poem by Lorenzo de' Medici. Called "Ombron and Ambra," it was left not quite finished and some of the manuscript is in rough and unrevised form. This translation, together with some eighty-odd poems and fragments of poems, discovered in manuscript after Santayana's death, were edited and included in *The Complete Poems of George Santayana: A Critical Edition* (1979), the first comprehensive collection of Santayana's verse. That edition also contains a lengthy biographical introduction.

Since his death, Santayana's importance as a philosopher, critic, and man of letters has been increasingly reaffirmed, and numerous books, articles, and doctoral dissertations have been devoted to all aspects of his work. Two full-scale biographies are being written and should be published soon. Together with the general reawakening of scholarly interest in the life and work of George Santayana is a renewal of critical interest in his verse, which because of its beauty, technical mastery (particularly in the sonnets), and philosophical profundity deserves a place of honor among the poetry of the genteel tradition.

Letters:

The Letters of George Santayana, edited by Daniel Cory (New York: Scribners, 1955).

Bibliography:

Herman J. Saatkamp, Jr., and John Jones, *George Santayana: A Bibliographical Checklist* (Bowling Green, Ohio: Philosophical Documentation Center, Bowling Green State University, 1982).

Biographies:

George W. Howgate, *George Santayana* (Philadelphia: University of Pennsylvania Press/London: Oxford University Press, 1938);

Daniel Cory, *Santayana, The Later Years: A Portrait with Letters* (New York: Braziller, 1963);

Willard E. Arnett, *George Santayana* (New York: Washington Square Press, 1968);

Newton Phelps Stallknecht, *George Santayana* (Minneapolis: University of Minnesota Press, 1971).

References:

William Archer, *Poets of the Younger Generation* (London & New York: John Lane/Bodley Head, 1902), pp. 373-384;

Witter Bynner, "Santayana the Poet," *Mark Twain Quarterly,* 5 (Winter-Spring 1942): 2;

Irwin Edman, "Philosopher as Poet," *Journal of Philosophy,* 51 (21 January 1954): 62-64;

Elizabeth Flower and Murray G. Murphey, "George Santayana: The Exile at Home," in their *A History of Philosophy in America* (New York: Capricorn, 1977), pp. 773-807;

Horace Gregory and Marya Zaturenska, *A History of American Poetry, 1900-1940* (New York: Harcourt, Brace, 1942), pp. 67-78;

William G. Holzberger, Introduction to *The Complete Poems of George Santayana: A Critical Edition,* edited by Holzberger (Lewisburg: Bucknell University Press/London: Associated University Presses, 1979), pp. 23-82;

Holzberger, "The Unpublished Poems of George Santayana: Some Critical and Textual Considerations," *Southern Review,* new series 11 (Winter 1975): 139-155;

Lois Hughson, *Thresholds of Reality: George Santayana and Modernist Poetics* (Port Washington: Kennikat Press, 1977);

Muna Lee, "Bronze of Syracuse," *Poetry,* 23 (March 1924): 338-341;

Archibald MacLeish, "Santayana the Poet," in *American Criticism 1926,* edited by William A. Drake (New York: Harcourt, Brace, 1926), pp. 141-146;

Philip Blair Rice, "The Philosopher as Poet and Critic," in *The Philosophy of George Santayana,* edited by Paul A. Schilpp (Evanston & Chicago: Northwestern University, 1940; revised, 1951), pp. 263-291;

Jessie Belle Rittenhouse, *The Younger American Poets* (Boston: Little, Brown, 1904), pp. 94-109;

Louis Untermeyer, *American Poetry Since 1900* (New York: Holt, 1923), pp. 287-290;

Carl Van Doren, *Many Minds* (New York: Knopf, 1924), pp. 83-101;

Bruce Weirick, *From Whitman to Sandburg in American Poetry* (New York: Macmillan, 1924), pp. 124-127;

Douglas Lawson Wilson, "Santayana: The Poet in America," Ph.D. dissertation, University of Pennsylvania, 1964;

Elkin Calhoun Wilson, *Santayana and Keats* (Birmingham, Ala.: Commercial Printing, 1980);

Wilson, *Shakespeare, Santayana, and the Comic* (University: University of Alabama Press, 1973).

Papers:

The Rare Book and Manuscript Library at Columbia University has five notebooks of Santayana's poems, plus individual pieces. The Lockwood Memorial Library at the State University of New York at Buffalo has one notebook containing Santayana's earliest poems. The Clifton Waller Barrett Library at the University of Virginia has the notebook containing Santayana's posthumous poems. The following libraries have individual manuscripts of poems by Santayana: Baker Memorial Library, Dartmouth College; Houghton Library, Harvard University; Lilly Library, Indiana University; Humanities Research Center, University of Texas, Austin; and Yale University Library. Santayana's correspondence with the publishing firms of Stone and Kimball and Charles Scribner's Sons may be found in the Scribner Archives at the Princeton University Library.

Anne Spencer

(6 February 1882-25 July 1975)

Sharon G. Dean
Indiana University

See also the Spencer entry in *DLB 51, Afro-American Writers from the Harlem Renaissance to 1940.*

WORKS: "The Poems," in *Time's Unfading Garden: Anne Spencer's Life and Poetry,* by J. Lee Greene (Baton Rouge & London: Louisiana State University Press, 1977), pp. 175-197.

Hailed by critics as perhaps the most technically sophisticated and modern poet of the Harlem, or New Negro, Renaissance, Anne Spencer, nonetheless, had to struggle against the label of "lady poet" and the call to join the ranks of her poetic sisters of the 1920s and 1930s by giving voice to the "true poetic spirit the lyric cry of Negro womanhood." She remained highly "individualistic," in the words of Sterling Brown, Arthur P. Davis, and Ulysses Lee, the editors of *The Negro Caravan* (1941), and her mentor and friend James Weldon Johnson suggested that her poems were "perhaps too unconventional." Her work was largely unpublished during her lifetime except for some thirty poems that Johnson himself shepherded into print, and it is yet to be collected in a separate volume, although forty-two of the fifty extant poems and fragments have been published as an appendix to J. Lee Greene's 1977 biography. Despite such a small canon, Spencer devoted much of her time to writing: "Writing and reading—it's just what I've been doing all my life. It's a way of talking to yourself about cultures, your people, just like another person . . . you're not only looking, you're seeing," as she stated in the taped diary that she kept from the 1950s until her death.

She was born Annie Bethel Bannister, on a plantation in Henry County, Virginia, the only child of Joel Cephas and Sarah Louise Scales Bannister. Her father was of mixed black, white, and Indian ancestry; her mother was the illegitimate child of a slave woman and a wealthy Virginia aristocrat. Anne Spencer was fond of reminding people that she was born "on R. J. Reynolds' plantation near Martinsville. . . . Sargeant Reynolds is grand, isn't he? And he doesn't even know that he's kin

Anne Spencer, 1945 (courtesy of Chauncey E. Spencer)

to me. My grandmother whose picture is upstairs looks just like one of them." In 1886 Sarah Louise left her husband and moved to Bramwell, West Virginia. Her daughter spent the winter with a family friend in Winston-Salem, North Carolina, before Sarah was able to take her to Bramwell. Even then she found that she was unable to work and care for her daughter at the same time and placed her as a foster child in the home of Mr. and Mrs. William Dixie, one of Bramwell's most prominent black families. Well treated by her mother and the Dixies, she had a happy childhood. With the Dixie children she was taught at home and did not attend school until 1893, when at the age of eleven she was enrolled in the Virginia Seminary and Normal School in Lynchburg, Virginia. By that time her mother had reassumed the surname Scales, and she enrolled her daughter as Annie Bethel Scales. She graduated in 1899, at age seventeen, as valedictorian of her class. On 15 May 1901 she married her school sweetheart, Edward Alexander Spencer. The couple had two daughters and a son. Beginning in 1924 she spent more than twenty years as the librarian at the all-black Dunbar High School in Lynchburg. The school library was a branch of the Jones Memorial Library in Lynchburg, where blacks were not allowed, but Spencer—as an employee—was given borrowing privileges and often subverted the whites-only lending rules by withdrawing books from the Jones Library and making them available for black readers. She also boycotted segregated public transportation, sometimes hitching rides on produce wagons.

In 1919 James Weldon Johnson, who was then working as field secretary for the NAACP, sought out Anne Spencer, who chartered and founded the local chapter of the NAACP. It was also through this contact that arrangements were made for the first publication of her poems and the occasion for Johnson's decision that Annie

Anne Spencer in her wedding dress, 1901 (courtesy of Chauncey E. Spencer)

Scales Spencer should have a pen name. As he informed her in a letter: "I have decided that Anne Spencer is the way in which you should sign—that makes a splendid pen name." Spencer agreed, stating with characteristic self-possession, "I like the pen name—really I like every thing that belongs to me!" Her first published poem, "Before the Feast of Shushan," appeared in the February 1920 issue of *Crisis,* the official organ of the NAACP. Johnson also sent some of her poetry to H. L. Mencken, editor of the *Smart Set,* who offered encouragement and criticism but did not publish any of her poetry. In 1922 five of Spencer's poems appeared in *The Book of American Negro Poetry,* edited by Johnson. His biographical headnote for Spencer's poems initiated the myth of Anne Spencer as the raceless, refined, and atypical black poet. Calling Spencer's work "unique," he praised its "maturity" and its lack of the subjectivity that characterized the poetry of "her predecessors and most of her contemporaries," adding that she employed more "economy of phrase and compression of thought" than other black poets: "At times her lines are so compact that they become almost cryptic, and have to be read more than once before they will yield their meaning and beauty." He also found her unique among the black poets of her time because "practically none of her poetry has been motivated by race." She was then almost forty, and in the succeeding three decades her poems were published in every major anthology of black American poetry as well as in important general anthologies such as Louis Untermeyer's *American Poetry Since 1900* and *The Norton Anthology of Modern Poetry,* in which she was only the second black woman poet to be included.

Another of Johnson's comments—that Spencer "takes great pride and pleasure in the cultivation of her beautiful garden"—may have invited her too easy categorization as another "lady in her garden," but his remark does focus on one of the crucial centers to her life and work, her garden at 1313 Pierce Street and the cottage that her husband, Edward, built there as a retreat for her. Throughout her life she would spend "a working day" in the cottage she called Edankraal—"Ed" for Edward; "an" for Annie; and "kraal" from the African word for place—writing in her notebooks and, beginning in the 1950s, taping a diary. In her notebooks she wrote that her happiness in her retreat gave birth to poetry: "Art—a *substitute* for natural living—can be born either of joy or sorrow; as mother the former is very unlikely."

The largest portion of her poetry is set in a garden, where Spencer found an ideal world that

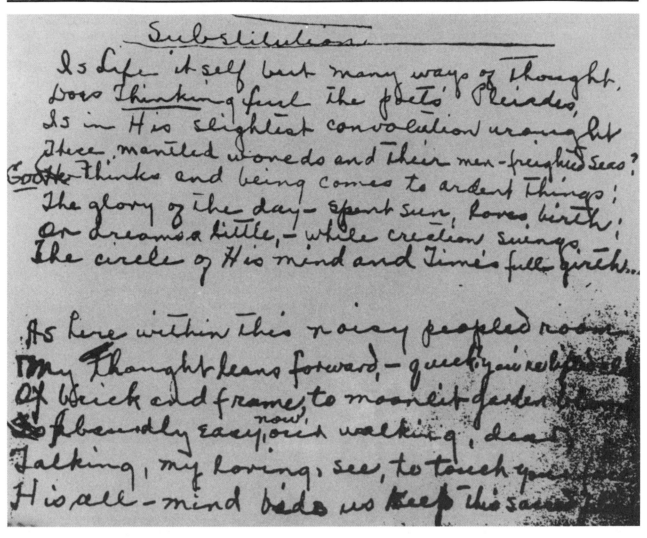

Manuscript for an early version of a poem first published in Countee Cullen's 1927 anthology, Caroling Dusk *(by permission of Chauncey E. Spencer, the Estate of Anne Spencer; courtesy of the Anne Spencer Memorial Foundation, Inc.)*

she set against a more sordid one. One of her earliest and favorite poems—first published in Countee Cullen's *Caroling Dusk* (1927), the definitive anthology of the Harlem Renaissance, and revised in 1973—the sonnet "Substitution" provides a partial explanation of why she wrote. Like many of her poems, this sonnet begins with a question:

> Is Life itself but many ways of thought,
> How real the tropic storm or lambent breeze
> Within the slightest convolution wrought
> Our mantled world and men-freighted seas?

This question has been answered in the affirmative by the end of the poem. Just as "God thinks . . . and being comes to ardent things," the speaker creates her own world: she has power to "substitute" one world for another. She may be in a "noisy peopled room," but her thought can lift her "clear/ Of brick and frame to moonlit garden bloom,—" the ideal landscape of the imagination. Thus, life is indeed "but many ways of thought," in which the garden is very like a sacred poem, and God's "All-Mind bids us keep this sacred place!"

The garden can also be a place of grief, as in "For Jim, Easter Eve," her last published poem, written in 1948 as an elegy for James Weldon Johnson, who had died in an automobile accident ten years earlier. It was published in *The Poetry of the Negro, 1746-1949* (1949), edited by Langston Hughes and Arna Bontemps. The poem begins:

> If ever a garden was a Gethsemane,
> with old tombs set high against

the crumpled olive tree—and lichen,
this, my garden has been to me.
For such as I none other is so sweet:
Lacking old tombs, here stands my grief,
and certainly its ancient tree.

But, as is characteristic in her poems, the thematic movement is from intense grief to final resignation, brought about by the speaker's finding spiritual solace in the peaceful garden: "what is pain but happiness here/amid these green and wordless patterns,—/indefinite texture of blade and leaf://Beauty of an old, old tree,/last comfort in Gethsemane." The poem also demonstrates Spencer's preference for a metered verse (mostly iambic) and her predilection for biblical or mythological allusions.

Spencer's sacred garden is often tinged with mysticism and even a hint of pantheism, as in her often-anthologized "Life-Long, Poor Browning," which was first published in *Caroling Dusk*. Characteristically, the poem relies on ellipses at key points for its effect; it begins with the lament that "Life-long, poor Browning never knew Virginia," and—alluding to his well-known lines "Oh to be in England/Now that April's there"—goes on to suggest that he would have felt differently if he had seen Virginia, for "Heaven's Virginia when the year's at its Spring." Virginia literally becomes heaven in the poem as the speaker describes Browning's presence in the place that he did not know in life: "He's haunting the byways of wine-aired leaven/And throating the notes of the wilding on wing." The poem ends with the suggestion of another mystical presence: "Think you he meets in this tender green sweetness/Shade that was Elizabeth . . . immortal completeness!"

The identification of the garden with immortal love like that attributed to Robert and Elizabeth Barrett Browning appears again in the quiet lyric "He Said," which was unpublished during Spencer's lifetime. The speaker, Edward Spencer, expresses his attitude toward his wife and the garden that symbolized their love. At first identifying her "garden at dusk" as "the soul of love," the poem ends by equating love with the poet as well: "your garden at dusk/Is your soul, My love."

A different lover speaks in "Lines to a Nasturtium (A Lover Muses)," first published in the October 1926 issue of *Palms* and later revised. The poem illustrates the ongoing dialectic in Spencer's poetry (and indeed her life) between the fact and the imagination. The male speaker addresses the nasturtium:

Flame-flower, Day-torch, Mauna Loa,
I saw a daring bee, today, pause, and soar,
    Into your flaming heart;
Then did I hear crisp, crinkled laughter
As the furies after tore him apart?
    A bird, next, small and humming,
Looked into your startled depths and fled. . . .
Surely, some dread sight, and dafter
    Than human eyes as mine can see,
Set the stricken air waves drumming
    In his flight.

He goes on to observe the similarity between the bee's engulfment by the nasturtium and the sense that his lover, with "Motions gracious as reeds by Babylon" and "Hands like, how like, brown lilies sweet," engulfs him, too: "*As once in her fire-lit heart I felt the furies*/Beating, beating."

When Johnson republished "Before the Feast of Shushan" in his 1922 anthology, he remarked that the poem "displays an opulence, the love of which has long been charged against the Negro as

Anne and Edward Spencer, 1938 (courtesy of Chauncey E. Spencer)

Exterior and interior of Edankraal, Spencer's garden retreat at her home in Lynchburg, Virginia (courtesy of Chauncey E. Spencer)

one of his naive and childish traits, but which in art may infuse a much needed color, warmth and spirit of abandon into American poetry." This poem represents her most sustained employment of dramatic monologue to express themes of sexual equality and feminine defiance. Its irony is enhanced by the choice of a male speaker, the Persian King Ahasuerus, sitting in his opulent garden. The poem adapts the Old Testament story of Vashti, the independent-minded Queen of Persia, who in the Book of Esther refuses the king's order to come before him. In Spencer's poem Ahasuerus is disturbed by Vashti's unconventional behavior, her attempt to teach him "a new thing," that love is a sacrament, a sacred communion that he cannot command as he does submission. He does not understand her spiritual view of love, equating it instead with physical passion. He can only point to the maze of differences between the ways men and women love:

> And I am hard to force the petals wide;
> And you are fast to suffer and be sad.
> Is any prophet come to teach a new thing
> Now in a more apt time?
> Have him 'maze how you say love is sacrament;
> How says Vashti, love is both bread and wine;
> How to the altar may not come to break and drink,
> Hulky flesh nor fleshly desire!

Instead of asking Vashti to explain her desires, he asserts his male prerogative, summing up the attitude that intimidates and injures all women:

> I, thy King, teach you and leave you, when I list.
> No woman in all Persia sets out strange action
> To confuse Persia's lord—
> Love is but desire and thy purpose fulfillment;
> I, thy King, so say!

Almost a companion piece to "Before the Feast of Shushan" is "Sybil Warns Her Sister" (later revised and retitled "Letter to My Sister"), which first appeared in Charles S. Johnson's collection *Ebony and Topaz* (1927). The poem further defines what Gloria Hull calls Spencer's sense of "woman-self and a female identity." In speaking of the poem Spencer herself said that although she had no biological sisters, she had spiritual sisters, and it was to these "sisters of the world" that she addressed this warning:

> It is dangerous for a woman to defy the gods;
> To taunt them with the tongue's thin tip,
> Or strut in the weakness of mere humanity,
> Or draw a line daring them to cross;

and it is equally dangerous to "mince timidly." Instead, echoing Emily Dickinson, Spencer counsels her sister to hide her feelings and

> Light no lamp when dark comes down
> Raise no shade for sun;
> Breathless must your breath come through
> If you'd die and dare deny
> The gods their god-like fun.

Spencer's clearest statement of protest against the traditional woman's roles forced upon her appears in an autobiographical headnote that she wrote for Countee Cullen's *Caroling Dusk*: "Mother Nature, February, forty-five years ago forced me on the stage that I, in turn, might assume the role of lonely child, happy wife, perplexed mother—and so far, a twice resentful grandmother. . . . I write about some of the things I love. But I have no civilized articulation for the things I hate. I proudly love being a Negro woman—it's so involved and interesting. *We* are the PROBLEM—the great national game of TABOO."

Despite this strong statement of racial identity, Spencer went on to say that she reacted "to life more as a human being than as a Negro being," and she usually avoided writing the kind of protest poetry popular during the Harlem Renaissance. One of the few poems in which she deals specifically with the plight of black people is "White Things," a poem suggested by an account of the lynching and burning of a pregnant black woman in the South and published in the March 1923 issue of *Crisis*. It is unforgettable for its powerful but controlled rage. The poem begins quietly:

> Most things are colorful things—the sky, earth, and
>   sea.
>   Black men are most men; but the white are free!
> White things are rare things; so rare, so rare
> They stole from out a silvered world—somewhere.

As the poem continues it reverses the traditional connotations of black and white, setting up a fundamental analogy between men of color—both blacks and native Americans—and nature. White things may be "rare" but, the poem implies, they are also aberrations of nature, and whites, "with their wand of power," have blanched the color from "The golden stars with lances fine/The hills all red and darkened pine" in their westward movement to fulfill their sense of manifest destiny. In the second stanza the comparison implied in the

Anne Spencer at age ninety-one, in the living room of her house in Lynchburg (courtesy of Chauncey E. Spencer)

extended metaphor of the first is expressed overtly: whites have "pyred a race of black, black men,/And burned them to ashes white." Yet in asserting their power they discover that the black man's white skull is "a glistening awful thing" and a reminder of a larger and more awful power than theirs. The skull is "a ghoul" that seems to have been made

> In the face of God with all his might,
> And swear by the hell that sired him:
>   "Man-maker, make white!"

"White Things" may be one of Spencer's best poems, and it is also notable because, more than two decades before the publication of Richard Wright's *Black Boy* (1945), it presents a similar depiction of whiteness as a destructive force. This poem is the only one of the poems published in a magazine during Spencer's lifetime that was not published in one of the anthologies that included

Spencer's work. Even though these same collections contain other poems of social protest, it was implied that the anger at the white man expressed in Spencer's poem was too overt.

An example of Spencer's reaction "to life more as a human being than as a Negro being" is "At the Carnival," first published in Johnson's *The Book of American Negro Poetry* and easily her most frequently anthologized poem. Perhaps her most striking poem as well, it is set apart from the rest by its fatalism and its setting in an urban "garden after Eden," a tawdry carnival of grotesques visited by a narrator who

>   came incuriously—
> Set on no diversion save that my mind
> Might safely nurse its brood of misdeeds
> In the presence of a blind crowd.
> The color of life was gray.
> Everywhere the setting seemed right

For my mood!
Here the sausage and garlic booth
Sent unholy incense skyward;
There a quivering female-thing
Gestured assignations, and lied
To call it dancing;
There, too, were games of chance
With chances for none;

but "amid the malodorus/Mechanics of this un-lovely thing" the speaker has encountered the "Gay Little Girl-of-the-Diving-Tank," a high diver who begins to symbolize the possibility of redemption from this sordid life. The speaker recognizes her at "a glance, and what you are/Sits-by-the-fire in my heart./. . ./Guilt pins a fig-leaf; Innocence is its own adorning." This "darling of spirit and form," who is "brave and water-clean," is "Leaven for the heavy ones of earth," and the speaker is convinced that "what makes/the plodder glad is good; and/ Whatever is good is God." Yet by the poem's con-clusion it is clear that although she has given the speaker a moment of hope, the "Girl-of-the-Diving-Tank" cannot redeem this wayward world. It is more likely that her innocence will be sacrificed to it: "Years may seep into your soul/The bacilli of the usual and the expedient." The poem ends with a prayer for her salvation: "I implore Neptune to claim his child to-day!"

"At the Carnival" and "White Things" offer a graphic picture of reality that is unusual in Spen-cer's poetry, which is generally more oblique and less bitter. Spencer credited South African writer Olive Schreiner with having influenced her life and her work more thoroughly than any of the other spokespersons for liberty to whom she felt drawn and about whom she wrote poems: Harriet Beecher Stowe, John Brown, Irish revolutionary Terence MacSwiney, and LeRoi Jones. Like Anne Spencer, Olive Schreiner was self-educated, a passionate reader, a "Free Thinker," and a rationalist. At the end of her life Spencer was writing a long poem, "A Dream of John Brown: On His Return Trip Home." Unfinished at her death and still unpub-lished, the completed portion suggests that the poem would have been an appropriate conclusion to Spencer's struggle for universal justice and her struggle to find beauty even in a hostile world.

Despite her public concerns Spencer was es-sentially a private poet, and "1975," the last poem she completed before she died at ninety-three, em-bodies her retrospective thoughts on her life as poet. Once again set in the garden, the poem in-structs the reader to

Kneel
And the curly worm sentient *now*
Will *light* the word that tells the poet what a poem is.

Biography:
J. Lee Greene, *Time's Unfading Garden: Anne Spen-cer's Life and Poetry* (Baton Rouge & London: Louisiana State University Press, 1977).

References:
Gloria T. Hull, "Afro-American Women Poets: A Bio-Critical Survey," in *Shakespeare's Sisters,* edited by Sandra Gilbert and Susan Gubar (Bloomington: Indiana University Press, 1979), pp. 165-182;

Erlene Stetson, "Anne Spencer," *CLA Journal,* 21 (March 1978): 400-409.

Papers:
The Spencer Family Papers are at the Anne Spen-cer House and Garden Historic Landmark in Lynchburg, Virginia. The holdings include literary documents, photographs, letters, fragments of poems, Spencer's taped diary, a 1959 autobio-graphical sketch presented to her children, and Harlem Renaissance memorabilia.

Gertrude Stein

Meredith Yearsley

See also the Stein entry in *DLB 4, American Writers in Paris, 1920-1939.*

BIRTH: Allegheny, Pennsylvania, 3 February 1874, to Daniel and Amelia Keyser Stein.

EDUCATION: A.B., Harvard University, 1898; Johns Hopkins Medical School, 1897-1901.

AWARD: Médaille de la Réconnaissance Française, 1922.

DEATH: Neuilly-sur-Seine, 27 July 1946.

BOOKS: *Three Lives: Stories of The Good Anna, Melanctha and The Gentle Lena* (New York: Grafton Press, 1909; London: John Lane, Bodley Head/New York: John Lane, 1915);

Portrait of Mabel Dodge at the Villa Curonia (Florence, Italy: Privately printed, 1912);

Tender Buttons: Objects, Food, Rooms (New York: Claire Marie, 1914);

Have They Attacked Mary, He Giggled. (West Chester, Pa.: Printed by Horace F. Temple, 1917);

Geography and Plays (Boston: Four Seas, 1922);

The Making of Americans, Being A History of A Family's Progress (Paris: Contact Editions, 1925; New York: A. & C. Boni, 1926; London: Owen, 1968); abridged as *The Making of Americans, The Hersland Family* (New York: Harcourt, Brace, 1934);

Descriptions of Literature (Englewood, N.J.: George Platt Lynes & Adlai Harbeck, 1926);

Composition as Explanation (London: Leonard & Virginia Woolf at the Hogarth Press, 1926);

A Book Concluding with As a Wife Has a Cow, A Love Story (Paris: Editions de la Galerie Simon, 1926; Barton, Millerton & Berlin: Something Else Press, 1973);

An Elucidation (Paris: transition, 1927);

A Village Are You Ready Yet Not Yet A Play in Four Acts (Paris: Editions de la Galerie Simon, 1928);

Useful Knowledge (New York: Payson & Clarke, 1928; London: John Lane, Bodley Head, 1929);

An Acquaintance with Description (London: Seizin Press, 1929);

Lucy Church Amiably (Paris: Plain Edition, 1930; New York: Something Else Press, 1969);

Dix Portraits, English text with French translations by Georges Hugnet and Virgil Thomson (Paris: Libraire Gallimard, 1930);

Before the Flowers of Friendship Faded Friendship Faded, Written on a Poem by Georges Hugnet (Paris: Plain Edition, 1931);

How to Write (Paris: Plain Edition, 1931; Barton: Something Else Press, 1973);

Operas and Plays (Paris: Plain Edition, 1932);

Gertrude Stein (photograph by Carl Van Vechten, by permission of Joseph Solomon, the Estate of Carl Van Vechten)

Matisse Picasso and Gertrude Stein with Two Shorter Stories (Paris: Plain Edition, 1933; Barton, Berlin & Millerton: Something Else Press, 1972);

The Autobiography of Alice B. Toklas (New York: Harcourt, Brace, 1933; London: John Lane, Bodley Head, 1933);

Four Saints in Three Acts, An Opera To Be Sung (New York: Random House, 1934);

Portraits and Prayers (New York: Random House, 1934);

Lectures in America (New York: Random House, 1935);

Narration: Four Lectures (Chicago: University of Chicago Press, 1935);

The Geographical History of America or The Relation of Human Nature to the Human Mind (New York: Random House, 1936);

Is Dead (N.p.: Joyous Guard Press, 1937);

Everybody's Autobiography (New York: Random House, 1937; London & Toronto: Heinemann, 1938);

A Wedding Bouquet, Ballet Music by Lord Berners, Words By Gertrude Stein (London: J. & W. Chester, 1938);

Picasso [in French] (Paris: Libraire Floury, 1938); translated into English by Alice B. Toklas (London: Batsford, 1938; New York: Scribners/London: Batsford, 1939);

The World is Round (New York: William R. Scott, 1939; London: Batsford, 1939);

Paris France (London: Batsford, 1940; New York: Scribners/London: Batsford, 1940);

What Are Masterpieces (California: Conference Press, 1940; expanded edition, New York, Toronto, London & Tel Aviv: Pitman, 1970);

ida A Novel (New York: Random House, 1941);

Petits Poèmes Pour un Livre de Lecture, French translation by Madame la Baronne d'Aiguy (Charlot, France: Collection Fontaine, 1944); republished in English as *The First Reader & Three Plays* (Dublin & London: Maurice Fridberg, 1946; Boston: Houghton Mifflin, 1948);

Wars I Have Seen (New York: Random House, 1945; enlarged edition, London: Batsford, 1945);

Brewsie and Willie (New York: Random House, 1946);

Selected Writings, edited by Carl Van Vechten (New York: Random House, 1946);

In Savoy, or Yes Is for a Very Young Man (A Play of the Resistance in France) (London: Pushkin, 1946);

Four in America (New Haven: Yale University Press, 1947);

The Mother of Us All, by Stein and Virgil Thomson (New York: Music Press, 1947);

Blood on the Dining Room Floor (Pawlet, Vt.: Banyan Press, 1948);

Two (Hitherto Unpublished) Poems (New York: Gotham Book Mart, 1948);

Last Operas and Plays, edited by Van Vechten (New York & Toronto: Rinehart, 1949);

Things As They Are, A Novel in Three Parts by Gertrude Stein, Written in 1903 but Now Published for the First Time (Pawlet, Vt.: Banyan Press, 1950);

Two: Gertrude Stein and Her Brother and Other Early Portraits [1908-12], volume 1 of *Unpublished Works of Gertrude Stein* (New Haven: Yale University Press/London: Cumberlege, Oxford University Press, 1951);

In a Garden, An Opera in One Act, libretto by Stein, music by Meyer Kupferman (New York: Mercury Music, 1951);

Mrs. Reynolds and Five Earlier Novelettes, volume 2 of *Unpublished Works of Gertrude Stein* (New Haven: Yale University Press/London: Cumberlege, Oxford University Press, 1952);

Bee Time Vine and Other Pieces 1913-1927, volume 3 of *Unpublished Works of Gertrude Stein* (New Haven: Yale University Press/London: Cumberlege, Oxford University Press, 1953);

As Fine As Melanctha (1914-1930), volume 4 of *Unpublished Works of Gertrude Stein* (New Haven: Yale University Press/London: Cumberlege, Oxford University Press, 1954);

Absolutely Bob Brown, Or Bobbed Brown (Pawlet, Vt.: Addison M. Metcalf Collection, 1955);

Painted Lace and Other Pieces 1914-1937, volume 5 of *Unpublished Works of Gertrude Stein* (New Haven: Yale University Press/London: Cumberlege, Oxford University Press, 1955);

Stanzas in Meditation and Other Poems [1929-1933], volume 6 of *Unpublished Works of Gertrude Stein* (New Haven: Yale University Press/London: Cumberlege, Oxford University Press, 1956);

Alphabets & Birthdays, volume 7 of *Unpublished Works of Gertrude Stein* (New Haven: Yale University Press/London: Oxford University Press, 1957);

A Novel of Thank You, volume 8 of *Unpublished Works of Gertrude Stein* (New Haven: Yale University Press, 1958; London: Oxford University Press, 1959);

Gertrude Stein's America, edited by Gilbert A. Harrison (Washington, D.C.: Robert B. Luce, 1965);

Writings and Lectures 1911-1945, edited by Patricia Meyerowitz (London: Owen, 1967); republished as *Look at Me Now and Here I Am: Writing and Lectures, 1909-1945* (Harmondsworth & Baltimore: Penguin, 1971);

Lucretia Borgia, A Play (New York: Albondocani Press, 1968);

Motor Automatism, by Stein and Leon M. Solomons (New York: Phoenix Book Shop, 1969);

Selected Operas and Plays, edited by John Malcolm Brinnin (Pittsburgh: University of Pittsburgh Press, 1970);

Gertrude Stein on Picasso, edited by Edward Burns (New York: Liveright, 1970);

I Am Rose (New York: Mini-Books, 1971);

Fernhurst, Q.E.D., and Other Early Writings (New York: Liveright, 1971; London: Owen, 1971);

A Primer for the Gradual Understanding of Gertrude Stein, edited by Robert Bartlett Haas (Los Angeles: Black Sparrow Press, 1971);

Reflections on the Atomic Bomb, volume 1 of *The Previously Uncollected Writings of Gertrude Stein,* edited by Haas (Los Angeles: Black Sparrow Press, 1973);

Money (Los Angeles: Black Sparrow Press, 1973);

How Writing is Written, volume 2 of *The Previously Uncollected Writings of Gertrude Stein,* edited by Haas (Los Angeles: Black Sparrow Press, 1974);

The Yale Gertrude Stein: Selections (New Haven & London: Yale University Press, 1980).

PERIODICAL PUBLICATIONS: "Normal Motor Automatism," by Stein and Leon M. Solomons, *Psychological Review,* 3 (September 1896): 492-512;

"Cultivated Motor Automatism," *Psychological Review,* 5 (May 1898): 295-306;

"Henri Matisse" and "Pablo Picasso," *Camera Work,* special number (August 1912): 23-25, 29-30;

"From a Play by Gertrude Stein," *New York Sun,* 18 January 1914, VI: 2;

"Aux Galeries Lafayette," *Rogue,* 1 (March 1915): 13-14;

"A League," *Life,* 74 (18 September 1919): 496;

"Two Cubist Poems. The Peace Conference, I and II," *Oxford Magazine,* 38 (7 May 1920): 309;

Review of *Three Stories & Ten Poems* by Ernest Hemingway, *Chicago Tribune,* European edition, 27 November 1923, p. 2;

The Making of Americans, transatlantic review, 1 (April 1924): 127-142; 1 (May 1924): 297-309; 1 (June 1924): 392-405; 2 (July 1924): 27-38; 2 (August 1924): 188-202; 2 (September 1924): 284-294; 2 (October 1924): 405-414; 2 (November 1924): 527-536; 2 (December 1924): 662-670;

"The Life of Juan Gris The Life and Death of Juan Gris," *transition,* no. 4 (July 1927): 160-162;

"Bibliography," *transition,* no. 15 (February 1929): 47-55;

"Genuine Creative Ability," *Creative Art,* 6 (February 1930), supplement: 41;

"Scenery and George Washington," *Hound & Horn,* 5 (July/September 1932): 606-611;

"Basket," *Lion and Crown,* 1 (January 1933): 23-25;

Review of *Roosevelt and His America* by Bernard Faÿ, *Kansas City Star,* 20 January 1934;

"Why Willows," *Literary America.* 1 (July 1934): 19-20;

"Plays and Landscapes," *Saturday Review of Literature,* 11 (10 November 1934): 269-270;

"Completely Gertrude Stein: A Painting Is Painted as a Painting," *Design,* 36 (January 1935): 25, 28;

Review of *Puzzled America* by Sherwood Anderson, *Chicago Daily Tribune,* 4 May 1935, p. 14;

"English and American Language in Literature," *Life and Letters Today,* 13 (September 1935): 19-27;

"A Portrait of the Abdys," *Janus* (May 1936): 15;

Dialogue with Nunez Martinez, *Ken,* 1 (2 June 1938): 103-104;

"The Situation in American Writing" [symposium], *Partisan Review,* 6 (Summer 1939): 40-41;

"Ballade," *Confluences,* 11/12 (July 1942): 11-12;

"Liberation, Glory Be!," *Collier's,* 114 (16 December 1944): 14-15, 61-63; 114 (23 December 1944): 51, 74-76;

"Now We Are Back in Paris," *Compass* (December 1945): 56-60;

"Capital, Capitals," by Stein, with music by Virgil Thomson, *New Music,* 20 (April 1947): 3-34;

"I Like American and American," *'47,* 1 (October 1947): 16-21;

"Jean Atlan: Abstract Painting," *Yale French Studies,* no. 31 (May 1964): 118.

Just as the postimpressionists and cubists made us see paint and then made us see painting, Gertrude Stein made us see words and then made us see writing. Immensely various and wide-ranging, her work amounts to a systematic investigation of the formal elements of language (parts of speech, syntax, phonetics, morphemics, etymology, punctuation) and of literature (narrative, poetry, prose, drama, and genre itself). In the course of these investigations, as Marianne DeKoven has pointed out, Stein reinvented literary signification (in "the most substantial and successful body of experimental writing in English"), creating a language that both disrupts conventional modes of signification and provides alternatives to them: "The modes Stein disrupts are linear, orderly, closed, hierarchical, sensible, coherent, referential, and heavily focused on the signified. The modes she substitutes are incoherent, open-ended, anarchic, irreducibly multiple, often focused on what Roland Barthes calls the 'magic of the signifier.'"

America, Gertrude Stein believed, was the first nation to enter the twentieth century. Although she lived in France for most of her writing life, she was most emphatically an American, and, as she wrote in her 1938 book on her friend Pablo Picasso, she felt completely in tune with "the century where nothing is in agreement, neither the round with the cube, neither the landscape with the houses, neither the large quantity with the small quantity." Again and again, stimulated by her undergraduate training in philosophy and psychology (notably with William James), she asked and investigated deceptively simple questions that reflected key issues of the century: questions to do with being, time, entity, identity, mind, language, and human nature—questions addressed by Alfred North Whitehead (a close friend of Stein's), Bertrand Russell, Martin Heidegger, and Ludwig Wittgenstein. What is knowledge? What is mind? What is human nature? What is poetry? What is prose? What is literature? What is composition?, she asked. What do these *do*? She knew that, even in asking these questions, she was suggesting a new vocabulary of thought. Like Wittgenstein, she realized that she must invent a way of showing what could not be written *about*. Writing *about* things, explaining, was a nineteenth-century way of seeing: in the twentieth century there had to be ways of seeing what seeing itself was. In her work, as in Wittgenstein's thinking, the subject disappears as the telling, the seeing, and the language system itself are placed in the foreground. She investigated in literature what would later be documented by theorists such as Roland Barthes, Marshall McLuhan, and Jacques Derrida.

Stein's writing may be roughly divided into three groups: relatively straightforward narratives—*Three Lives* (1909) and the best-selling memoirs *The Autobiography of Alice B. Toklas* (1933), *Everybody's Autobiography* (1937), and *Wars I Have Seen* (1945); critical and exegetical work—*Composition as Explanation* (1926), *Lectures in America*

(1935), *Narration* (1935), and *What Are Masterpieces* (1940); and works which demolish conventional notions of poetry, prose, and genre—her still lifes, portraits, geographies, plays, novels, operas, series, and philosophical discourses. Most of her writing falls into this third group, and in an important sense she discovered writing qua writing—a poetry of thinking, seeing, and hearing grounded in the activity of language. "Language as a real thing is not imitation either of sounds or colors or emotions it is an intellectual recreation," she wrote in one of her American lectures. "And so for me the problem of poetry was and it began with *Tender Buttons* to constantly realize the thing anything so that I could recreate that thing." She was and is a poet's poet, whose work is a technician's paradise of innovations.

During Stein's lifetime, however, her innovative writing, often the butt of reviewers' parodies, received little recognition or understanding. Her achievement was mostly overshadowed by her celebrated role as American eccentric in Paris and hostess of the popular salons she and her brother Leo Stein held in their Paris studio/apartment at 27, rue de Fleurus, which became a mecca for tourists, writers, and artists. Championing the modern movement, Leo and Gertrude Stein, with their older brother and sister-in-law, Michael and Sarah Stein (who lived nearby on the rue Madame), amassed a major collection of postimpressionist and modernist art—works by Paul Cézanne, Paul Gauguin, Henri de Toulouse-Lautrec, Edouard Manet, Henri Matisse, Pablo Picasso, Pierre Bonnard, Juan Gris, and others. Not only did Gertrude Stein form close relationships with Picasso, Matisse, Georges Braque, Robert Delaunay, and Marie Laurencin, she also became acquainted with such avant-garde writers as Max Jacob and Guillaume Apollinaire, the flamboyant promoter of the cubists. Leo Stein, who at the time of his sister's arrival in Paris in 1903 had decided to devote himself to painting and art criticism, was at first the dominant force in the salons. But when Gertrude Stein wholeheartedly embraced cubism—which Leo Stein could not—it was she who became the driving force, with the able support of her lifelong friend and lover Alice B. Toklas. After Gertrude and Leo had separated in 1913 or 1914 and some of Gertrude Stein's early work (which Leo Stein thought nonsense) had been published, 27, rue de Fleurus became a literary mecca (rivaling Pound's and Joyce's), where Gertrude met and coached such writers as Ernest Hemingway and Sherwood Anderson and began a series of literary friendships that was to include, among others, Bravig Imbs, Edith Sitwell and her brothers, Ford Madox Ford, Robert McAlmon, Scott Fitzgerald, and Natalie Clifford Barney. Visitors also included writers as various as Hilda Doolittle (H.D.), William Carlos Williams, John Dos Passos, Mina Loy, and Djuna Barnes and, significantly, composers—Erik Satie, George Antheil, Aaron Copland, and Virgil Thomson (who appreciated the rhythmical elements of Stein's work, collaborated with her on her operas, and set many of her pieces to music).

Stein's influence is readily discernible in the writing of such major poets as Louis Zukofsky, in, for example, his work with prepositions, in his playful epigrammatic pieces, and in the dense multivalent composition of longer works such as *"A"* (which he began writing in 1927 and completed in 1974) and *80 Flowers* (1978). Robert Duncan's work, *Writing Writing* (1964), *From the Laboratory Notebooks* (1969), and *A Book of Resemblances* (1966; which includes his Stein imitations), also reflects her influence as does the work of such Canadian poets

as Steve McCaffery, George Bowering, and B. P. Nichol and the "concrete" and "sound" poets of the 1960s. Perhaps the most wide-reaching offshoot of Stein's work, however, has occurred in the writing of the so-called $L=A=N=G=U=A=G=E$ poets (Lyn Hejinian, Bruce Andrews, Charles Bernstein, Diane Ward, Bob Perelman, and others) whose work (which appears in little magazines such as $L=A=N=G=U=A=G=E$, *Roof,* and *This*) emerged in the 1970s and 1980s. These writers share with Stein an interest in the surfaces, opacity, and polysemy of language, and, like Stein, they approach writing as universally poetic.

"Why in fact have we not heard more generally from American scholars upon the writings of Miss Stein?," asked William Carlos Williams in an article for the Winter 1930 issue of *Pagany* (which he wrote with the silent collaboration of Zukofsky)—they connected her work with that of Laurence Sterne and Johann Sebastian Bach. Forty years after her death, with the emergence of theories about texts from Roland Barthes and Jacques

Daniel and Amelia Stein (seated at the table) with their five children (left to right): Simon, Gertrude, Michael, Leo, and Bertha (courtesy of the Beinecke Rare Book and Manuscript Library, Yale University)

Derrida, the academic establishment is only beginning to understand her achievement.

On 3 February 1874 Gertrude Stein was born to Amelia Keyser and Daniel Stein in Allegheny, Pennsylvania. She was the youngest of a planned family of five children and was deeply impressed by the fact that she would not have been born at all if two other children had not died in infancy. It was a fact that strengthened her bond with the second youngest of the family, her brother Leo. Being the youngest was a role that suited her, however: "It is better if you are the youngest girl in a family to have a brother two years older," she wrote in *Everybody's Autobiography,* "because that makes everything a pleasure to you, you go everywhere and do everything while he does it all for you and with you which is a pleasant way to have everything happen to you." This pleasant way was to continue for Gertrude for nearly forty years: throughout her childhood, university training, and early career she remained very close to Leo. For the rest of her life, "Baby Woojums"—as she became known to Alice B. Toklas ("Mama Woojums") and close friends— expected and received care and protection from others, even as a Jew in Nazi-occupied France.

In the spring of 1875 the family moved to Vienna, followed by another move to Passy, France, in 1878, as Daniel Stein pursued various business interests. In Europe the family lived a comfortable, prosperous life, full of treats, dancing lessons, and excursions for the children, who in Vienna had a Hungarian governess and a Czech tutor. This early exposure to a mélange of languages (Stein spoke German and French before she spoke English) apparently fascinated Stein even at the time: "Our little Gertie is a little Schnatterer," wrote her Aunt Rachel, who lived with the family in Vienna. "She talks all day long and so plainly. . . . [and] toddles around the whole day & repeats everything that is said and done." Here perhaps were the beginnings of Stein's lasting interest in the habits and forms of language. It was not until 1879 when the family returned to America to live with the Keyser grandparents in Baltimore that Gertrude had her first experience of "proper" English. Even then, most of the English she heard was that of an immigrant family, none of whom spoke the language very well.

In 1880 when Gertrude Stein was six, the family moved to California, where Daniel Stein had invested in the San Francisco street railway. Here they spent a happy first year at Tubb's Hotel in Oakland: "I do love Tubb's hotel very well with Eucalyptus and palms," Stein wrote forty-one years later in "A Sonatina Followed by Another"—eu- calyptus and palms would always mean for her Tubb's Hotel. The following year (1881) the Steins rented a ten-acre farm, the rambling "Old Stratton House," on the eastern outskirts of Oakland. Stein described it in her 1,000-page novel *The Making of Americans:*

> There was, just around the house, a pleasant garden, in front were green lawns not very carefully attended and with large trees in the center whose roots always sucked up for themselves almost all the moisture, water in this dry western country could not be used just to keep things green and pretty and so, often, the grass was very dry in the summer, but it was very pleasant then lying there watching the birds, black in the bright sunlight and sailing, and the firm white summer clouds breaking away from the horizon and slowly moving. It was very wonderful there in the summer with the dry heat, and the sun burning, and the hot earth for sleeping; and then in the winter with the rain, and the north wind blowing that would bend the trees and often break them, and the owls in the wall scaring you with their tumbling.
> . . . .
> In the summer it was good for generous sweating to help the men make the hay into bales for its preserving and it was well for ones growing to eat radishes pulled with the black earth sticking to them and to chew the mustard and find roots with all kinds of funny flavors in them, and to fill ones hat with fruit and sit on the dry ploughed ground and eat and think and sleep and read and dream and never hear them when they would all be calling; and then when the quail came it was fun to go shooting, and then when the wind and the rain and the ground were ready to help seeds in their growing, it was good fun to help plant them, and the wind would be so strong it would blow the leaves and branches of the trees down around them and you could shout and work and get wet and be all soaking and run out full into the strong wind and let it dry you, in between the gusts of rain that left you soaking. It was fun all the things that happened all the year there then.

She led a carefree life, roaming the countryside with Leo, being educated erratically, sometimes with governesses, sometimes at schools (there is no record of her graduation from Oakland High School), developing the habit of doing what she wanted, not what teachers had in mind for her.

Gertrude Stein, circa 1895 (courtesy of the Beinecke Rare Book and Manuscript Library, Yale University)

Holding themselves apart from the rest of the family, Leo and Gertrude reveled in each other's company, reading together Jules Verne, Mark Twain, George Eliot, and all of Shakespeare, as well as science handbooks, encyclopedias, and history. Already they were regularly attending art galleries, theater, and opera.

Family life was easygoing and undisciplined. With Daniel Stein increasingly involved in his job as vice-president of the Omnibus Cable Company, the children were left in the hands of their indulgent mother, whom Gertrude described in *The Making of Americans* as "very loving in her feeling to all of her children, but they had been always . . . after they stopped being very little children, too big for her ever to control them. She could not lead

them nor could she know what they needed inside them." In 1885 Amelia Stein became too weak with illness to manage the large house, and the family moved to a smaller one in Oakland, where the children helped to care for her. She died of cancer in 1888. But the children apparently took her death in stride: "we had all already had the habit of doing without her," Gertrude Stein wrote in *Everybody's Autobiography*.

Three years later (1891) Daniel Stein died, releasing the children from the tyranny of his erratic and domineering ways. Leo and Gertrude Stein, who thought him aggressive and illiterate, had never liked him. For Gertrude Stein, fathers and fathering would remain synonymous with arbitrary authority: "There is too much fathering going on just now and there is no doubt about it fathers are depressing," she later wrote, commenting on the dictatorships and the political atmosphere of the 1930s.

When Michael Stein, the eldest child (then twenty-six), took over the guardianship of the younger children—Simon (twenty-three), Bertha (twenty), Leo (nineteen), and Gertrude (seventeen)—he found his father's finances had deteriorated. "I was most awfully shocked when Mike brought home my father's business books and Leo and I went through them with him," Gertrude wrote later; "There were so many debts it was frightening." But Michael Stein soon became branch manager of the Central Pacific Railway, to whom he sold his father's relatively worthless cable-company holdings, and the five children were provided with enough income to free them from hav-

ing to earn a living. As Gertrude Stein put it, "Mike's own statement was that he knew if it was not done he had us all on his hands because none of us could earn anything . . . to live on and something had to be done." In 1892 the family dispersed, Gertrude and Bertha Stein moving to Baltimore to live with their mother's sister and Leo Stein transferring from the University of California at Berkeley to Harvard. "I left the more or less internal and solitary and concentrated life I led in California and came to Baltimore," Gertrude Stein recalled, "and lived with a lot of my relations and principally with a whole group of very lively little aunts. . . . they did have to say and hear said whatever was said. . . . That inevitably made everything said often. I began then to consciously listen to what anybody was saying and what they did say while they were saying what they were saying." The next

Gertrude Stein at Johns Hopkins University, circa 1897 (courtesy of the Beinecke Rare Book and Manuscript Library, Yale University)

year (1893) Gertrude Stein followed Leo Stein to Harvard, entering Harvard Annex (which was renamed Radcliffe College in 1894).

Like Leo Stein, she studied psychology with William James, who deeply impressed her: "Prof. James . . . is truly a man among men," she wrote in a theme for her English composition teacher, poet William Vaughn Moody—"a scientist of force and originality embodying all that is strongest and worthiest in scientific spirit; a metaphysician skilled in abstract thought, clear and vigorous and yet too great to worship logic as his God, and narrow himself to a belief merely in the reason of man." From James she learned methods of scientific investigation and the value of an open mind ("If you reject anything that is the beginning of the end as an intellectual," she was to recall his saying), both of which informed her appreciation of visual art and her own writings for the rest of her life. Under James's supervision she conducted experiments with automatic writing designed to reveal the character of the subconscious mind in normal subjects. The poetic quality and the repetitiveness of the subjects' writings were immediately recognized by Stein and her co-researcher Leon Solomons (with Solomons she published an article, "Normal Motor Automatism," in 1896, and she published another independently in 1898). James's theories of the human being (people think themselves as thinkers), knowledge (they know things by acquaintance or by knowledge about them), consciousness (they think in a continuously present stream), and identity (they sense identity by recognizing sameness along the continuum of their thoughts and perceptions) are reflected in much of Stein's writing. Particularly in her early creative work—including *Three Lives* (1909), *The Making of Americans* (1925), and "A Long Gay Book" and "Many Many Women" (both in *Matisse Picasso and Gertrude Stein with Two Shorter Stories*, 1933)—she continued exploring things she had studied under James, such as the identity of her characters as it is revealed in unconscious habits and rhythms of speech, the classification of all possible character types, and the problem of laying out as a continuous present knowledge that had accumulated over a period of time. Her investigations of identity led her eventually to a new concept: entity—the memory-free mode of consciousness that occurs in the act of doing anything, when the individual cannot be conscious of his identity.

Although she did not receive her Harvard A.B. until 1898, Gertrude Stein began to study medicine at Johns Hopkins University in the fall

Gertrude Stein in California with her nephew Allan, the son of Michael and Sally Stein (courtesy of the Beinecke Rare Book and Manuscript Library, Yale University)

of 1897 in preparation for a career in psychology. But after failing four courses, she abandoned her medical studies in 1901, except for doing some brain research in 1902. During this time she spent her summers in San Francisco with the Michael Steins and in Europe with Leo Stein (whose trip around the world in 1895 and permanent move away from Baltimore in 1900 very likely made it difficult for Gertrude Stein to stay there). Like Leo Stein, she was more and more attracted to Europe. With him she traveled to Tangier, Granada, and Paris in 1901 and then to Italy and England in 1902 (spending much of her time in London reading English literature in the British Museum).

In the winter of 1903 she began early drafts of *The Making of Americans* while living in New York with Mabel Weeks and several other women. It was here that she wrote "Q.E.D." (published posthumously as *Things As They Are*, 1950, and later in *Fernhurst, Q.E.D., and Other Early Writings*, 1971)—

the story of her painful and traumatic love affair with May Bookstaver during her last years at Johns Hopkins, an affair complicated by Bookstaver's involvement with another woman, Mabel Haynes. During 1904-1905 she re-examined the three-cornered affair in another story, "Fernhurst," based on a scandal at Bryn Mawr. Parts of this story became melded into *The Making of Americans.* Both stories are convoluted and obscure (somewhat in the style of Henry James), a style that disappeared in her next works, *The Making of Americans* and *Three Lives.*

In the fall of 1903 Gertrude Stein left behind her in America the disappointments of her medical studies and her friendships and found herself plunged into the "atmosphere of propaganda," as Leo called the barrage of talk among artists and literati who gathered every Saturday evening at 27, rue de Fleurus in Paris. By the age of thirty, the following year, Gertrude Stein had made up her mind to settle down with Leo Stein in Paris and to devote herself to writing. She wrote of this time in *The Making of Americans:* "It happens often in the twenty-ninth year of a life that all the forces that have been engaged through the years of childhood, adolescence and youth in confused and ferocious combat range themselves in ordered ranks. . . . the straight and narrow gate-way of maturity and life which was all uproar and confusion narrows down to form and purpose and we exchange a great dim possibility for a small hard reality."

Gertrude Stein's exposure to painters and the concepts of interest to visual artists had a profound effect on her writing. During the summer of 1904 with Leo Stein in Fiesole, she saw the Charles Losier collection of Cézannes in Florence and began purchasing paintings. "Everything I have done has been influenced by Flaubert and Cézanne," Stein said in an interview with Robert Haas in 1946 (she translated some Flaubert stories in 1909); "this gave me a new feeling about composition. Up to that time composition had consisted of a central idea, to which everything else was an accompaniment and separate but was not an end in itself, and Cé-

A 1969 photograph of 27, rue de Fleurus in Paris, where Stein lived from 1903 until 1938 (courtesy of Edward M. Burns)

zanne conceived the idea that in composition one thing was as important as another thing. Each part is as important as the whole, and that impressed me enormously, . . . so much that I began to write *Three Lives* under this influence." Stein considered the highly acclaimed "Melanctha" (the second part of *Three Lives*), which recounts the story of a Negro woman, the "quintessence" of "this idea of composition." It was an idea that also helped to shape Stein's other early prose works—*The Making of Americans*, "A Long Gay Book," and "Many Many Women"—works where the reader is often forced away from any sense of larger movement or central idea by detailed and minute repetitions and variations in phrasing.

The Steins' purchase of Matisse's controversial *La Femme au Chapeau* in 1905 led to friendship with the painter and an introduction to Picasso, who soon became a regular at the rue de Fleurus gatherings, bringing with him Max Jacob, Guillaume Apollinaire, Marie Laurencin, and a crowd of other artists, patrons, and critics. Almost immediately, Gertrude and Picasso became friends. Sharing a roughness of manner and childlike enthusiasm, isolated in the world of their creative imaginations by an unfamiliar language, each had begun to sense his own genius. In 1906, although he had not worked from a model for eight years, Picasso asked to paint her portrait. During the ninety sittings their friendship deepened as they talked about theories of composition: "I began to play with words then," Stein told Haas in 1946. "I was a little obsessed by words of equal value. Picasso was painting my portrait at that time, and he and I used to talk this thing over endlessly. At this time he had just begun on cubism. And I felt the thing I got from Cezanne was not the last in composition. . . . I felt . . . I had to recapture the value of the individual word, find out what it meant and act within it." Not long after, she began thinking of this problem in terms of literary portraiture: "I began then to want to make a more complete picture of each word, and that is when the portrait business started." Her investigations and reinvention of portraiture continued alongside other literary interests off and on for the rest of her life. Wendy Steiner suggests this evolved through three phases: the portraits of 1908-1911 are concerned with character types (for example, "Two. Gertrude Stein and Her Brother," "Five or Six Men," "Italians," and "A Kind of Woman"); the portraits of the second phase (1913-1925) are concerned with visual elements and then with "melody" (for example, "Portrait of Mabel Dodge at the Villa Curonia," "Guillaume Apollinaire," and "Susie Asado"); and the portraits of 1926-1946 are concerned with entity, or what Stein called "self-contained movement" (for example, "Jean Cocteau," "Georges Hugnet," and "Bernard Fay"). In "Portraits and Repetitions" (one of the lectures she gave in America during 1934-1935) Gertrude Stein described the evolution of her investigations, explaining that while she was writing *The Making of Americans*, "by listening and talking I conceived at every moment the existence of some one" (stressing the immediacy, continuous present, and nature of seeing and thing seen). She went on,

> it was like a cinema picture made up of succession and each moment having its own emphasis. . . .
>
> Then as I said I had the feeling that something should be included and that something was looking and so concentrating on looking I did the Tender Buttons because it was easier to do objects than people if you were just looking. Then I began to do plays to make the looking have in it an element of moving and during this time I also did portraits that did the same thing. In doing these things I found that I created a melody of words that filled me with a melody that gradually made me do portraits easily by feeling the melody of any one. And this then began to bother me because perhaps I was getting drunk with melody and I do not like to be drunk. . . .
>
> I began again not to let the looking be predominating not to have the listening and talking be predominating but to once more denude all this of anything in order to get back to the essence of the thing contained within itself . . . some portraits . . . I . . . think did do what I was then hoping would be done.
>
> . . . perhaps two that did it the most completely . . . were portraits of Georges Hugnet and Bernard Faÿ.

Like a painter whose works reflect the sequence of discoveries he makes in techniques that will capture perception, techniques that are perceptions in themselves, Stein was embarked on an exploratory reinvention of literary possibility—a "dynamic program of theory, experimentation, discovery and new theory" as Steiner calls it—that was to continue through all her writings. But, like the painters who stimulated her, she found almost no one in the first decades of the century who understood what she was doing. For many years she had only the stead-

Gertrude Stein at 27, rue de Fleurus, circa 1905 (courtesy of Edward M. Burns)

Leo, Gertrude, and Michael Stein, outside 27, rue de Fleurus, circa 1907 (courtesy of Edward M. Burns)

fast support of Alice B. Toklas, who arrived in Paris in 1907 and who was for many years her only audience.

Born into the bohemian middle class in San Francisco, Toklas had become acquainted with the Michael Steins during their various trips there to check on their real estate and business holdings. When she arrived in Paris in the fall of 1907 with her friend Harriet Levy, she immediately contacted the Steins, and, as she noted in *What Is Remembered* (1963), went to meet them—an event she was never to forget: "In the room were Mr. and Mrs. Stein and Gertrude Stein. It was Gertrude Stein who held my complete attention. . . . She was a golden brown presence, burned by the Tuscan sun and with a golden glint in her warm brown hair. She was dressed in a warm brown corduroy suit. She wore a large round coral brooch and when she talked, very little, or laughed, a good deal, I thought her voice came from this brooch. It was unlike anyone else's voice—deep, full velvety like a great contralto's, like two voices. She was large and heavy with delicate small hands and a beautifully modelled and unique head." Later she would recall when they

met Alfred North Whitehead, "He was my third genius for whom the bell rang. The first two had been Gertrude Stein and Picasso."

Toklas herself, Mabel Dodge recalled, "was slight and dark, with beautiful gray eyes hung with black lashes—and she had a drooping, Jewish nose, and her eyelids drooped, and the corners of her red mouth and the lobes of her ears drooped under the black folded Hebraic hair, weighted down, as they were, with long heavy Oriental earrings. . . . Alice wore straight dresses made of Javanese prints. . . . She looked like Leah, out of the Old Testament, in her half-Oriental get-up—her blues and browns and oyster whites—her black hair—her barbaric chains and jewels—and her melancholy nose. Artistic."

With Gertrude Stein, Alice Toklas was immediately caught up in the world of art and artists. She took French lessons from Picasso's mistress Fernande Olivier. At her first salon, she recalled, "The room commenced to be crowded. There were not only French but Russians, a few Americans, Hungarians and Germans. The discussions were lively but not entirely friendly. A very small Russian

Gertrude Stein near Fiesole, Italy, summer 1908 (courtesy of Edward M. Burns)

Alice B. Toklas and Gertrude Stein in Venice, circa 1908 (courtesy of the Beinecke Rare Book and Manuscript Library, Yale University)

girl was holding forth explaining her picture, a nude holding aloft a severed leg. It was the beginning of the Russian horrors." Even more lively was the famous Banquet Rousseau in honor of painter Théodore Rousseau which she attended with Gertrude Stein at Picasso's studio in late summer or autumn 1908. Some thirty guests, including Apollinaire, Braque, Jacques Vaillant, Max Jacob, and Marie Laurencin, drank more and more wine while the ordered dinner did not arrive. Stein and Toklas, who later found that a pet donkey from a neighboring café had eaten the flowers off her hat, were asked but declined to sing American Indian songs. Rousseau was made to play his violin. Apollinaire sang songs and recited poems.

During the summer of 1908 Toklas and Harriet Levy took a villa near the Steins in Fiesole. Back in Paris, Toklas learned to type and began transcribing *The Making of Americans,* taking over as Gertrude Stein's handmaiden from Etta Cone, who had typed *Three Lives* (completed in 1906 but not published until 1909). Already Gertrude and Leo Stein had disagreed about Gertrude Stein's writing and their views on art, and it was clear to Gertrude Stein that she must look elsewhere for sustained emotional support. Sometime late in 1908, she chose a life, as husband and wife, with Alice Toklas, who moved to 27, rue de Fleurus early in 1909. Henceforth Toklas not only looked after the household and typed Stein's manuscripts, she responded to them and encouraged Stein, she read proofs (beginning with those for *Three Lives*), she sought out publishers and saw that manuscripts were safely stored, and she protected Stein from unwanted intrusions. "Fernande was the first wife of a genius I was to sit with," Stein has Toklas recall in *The Autobiography of Alice B. Toklas* (1933), "The geniuses came and talked to Gertrude Stein and the wives sat with me."

Toklas would also figure prominently in Stein's writings, sometimes under her own name, sometimes under pet names, such as "Pussy" or "Ada" (as in the portrait "Ada"), sometimes as the addressee of valentines or love poems, and sometimes as a counterpoint voice in dialogues (for example, in the long poem "Lifting Belly") or in snatches of conversation from daily life.

During the years before World War I, while cubism was reaching its zenith, Stein's inventions in her search for "the value of the individual word" strayed further and further from conventional semantic relations. The referentiality in the 1909 portraits of Matisse and Picasso ("One whom some were certainly following was one who was completely charming") gave way to the opacity and obscurity of the 1912 *Portrait of Mabel Dodge at the Villa Curonia*—"The only reason there is not that pressure is that there is a suggestion. There are many going. A delight is not bent. There had been that little wagon."—and finally exploded into what DeKoven calls the "fecund incoherence," rich in sound, image, and suggestion and dense with open-ended connections, of *Tender Buttons* (1914). Stein also wrote during this time some astonishingly lyrical portraits, notably 'Susie Asado' and 'Preciosilla,' both inspired by flamenco dancing she had seen during her sojourn in Spain in 1912. "The strict discipline that I had given myself," Stein wrote of this work, "the absolute refusal of never using a word that was not an exact word all through the *Tender Buttons* and what I may call the early Spanish and *Geography and Plays* period finally resulted in things like 'Susie Asado' and 'Preciosilla' etc. in an extraordinary melody of words and a melody of excitement in knowing that I had done this thing."

It was while staying with Mabel Dodge at her villa in Florence in the fall of 1912 that Stein had composed her portrait of Dodge, who immediately had 300 copies printed and bound them in Florentine wallpaper. Dodge's distribution of these pamphlets among the literati in New York, along with the appearance of the Matisse and Picasso portraits in the August 1912 issue of Alfred Stieglitz's magazine *Camera Work,* had a marked effect on

Cover for Stein's second book (Sotheby Parke Bernet, sale number 3966). Mabel Dodge, the subject, served as publisher and had the 300 copies bound in various colors and designs of floral wallpaper.

Stein's reputation as a herald of international modernism. Dodge herself wrote an article on Stein for *Arts and Decorations* magazine. After a trip to London in 1913 in search of publishers and the appearance of *Tender Buttons* (published by the poet Donald Evans at his Claire Marie press) in 1914, Stein was regularly courted as an important member of the modernist movement. More and more visitors—including Roger Fry, Wyndham Lewis, Henry Lamb, Augustus John, Jacob Epstein, Nancy Cunard, Lady Ottoline Morrell, Marcel Duchamp, and Francis Picabia—came to the rue de Fleurus Saturday evenings to see Gertrude Stein and the Picassos rather than Leo Stein, who had come to loathe cubism. By the spring of 1914 Gertrude and Leo had divided up the treasures they had collected since their life together in Baltimore in 1897 and parted for good, Leo Stein moving to Florence and Gertrude staying on at 27, rue de Fleurus.

"Poetry," Stein wrote in *Lectures in America*, "is essentially a vocabulary just as prose is essentially not.... a vocabulary entirely based on the noun.... concerned with using with abusing, with losing with wanting, with denying with avoiding with adoring with replacing the noun." The "vocabulary" was not a lexicon of terms but a repertoire of activities. In *Tender Buttons* there began to evolve some of the most revolutionary ideas about poetry yet to emerge in English: "in *Tender Buttons* I was making poetry . . . but in prose I no longer needed the help of nouns and in poetry did I need the help of nouns. Was there not a way of naming things that would not invent names, but mean names without naming them."

Divided into three sections ("Objects," "Food," and "Rooms"), the work presents a series of still lifes with titles such as "A Chair," "A Frightful Release," "Water Raining," "Roastbeef," "Lunch," "End of Summer," and "Way Lay Veg-etable." The subsections, varying from one line to several pages in length, are characterized throughout by great energy and ebullience as unexpected phrases jar and collide, often counterpointing a simple sentence structure that suggests the discourse of reasoned exposition. The pieces are not intended to be imagist, nor are they intended to be translated into one final right meaning. They are instead, as Marjorie Perloff has noted, "constructing a way of happening rather than an account of what has happened, a way of looking rather than a description of how things look." The words enact, are equivalent to, the energy of the thing seen. Thus in "A Box" four-sidedness is reflected in the number of phrases beginning "out of," just as enclosedness is reflected in the grammatical structure

Birth Place of Marechal JOFFRE at Rivesaltes april 1917

Postcard of Alice B. Toklas and Gertrude Stein with "Auntie," the Model T Ford they had converted to a truck so that they could deliver supplies for the American Fund for the French Wounded (courtesy of Edward M. Burns)

of the last clause, which forces the reader back into the sentence to sort out the syntax:

> Out of kindness comes redness and out of rudeness comes rapid same question, out of an eye comes research, out of selection comes painful cattle. So then the order is that a white way of being round is something suggesting a pin and is it disappointing, it is not, it is so rudimentary to be analysed and see a fine substance strangely, it is so earnest to have a green point not to red but to point again.

Other examples of this method include "A Sound"—"Elephant beaten with candy and little pops and chews all bolts and reckless reckless rats, this is this."—"Sugar," which begins, "A violent luck and a whole sample and even then quiet. Water is squeezing, water is almost squeezing on lard. . . ." and "Celery":

> Celery tastes tastes where in curled lashes and little bits and mostly in remains.
>
> A green acre is so selfish and so pure and so enlivened.

Pieces such as these and the rhythmic and evocative "Susie Asado" (in *Geography and Plays*, 1922), Marjorie Perloff has pointed out, must be read as multiple interlocking and open-ended systems in which each element and system is as important as any other. In "Susie Asado" such systems include the sound patterns of flamenco-dance rhythms, the system of erotic suggestions in phrases such as "the wets," the pun on "sweet tea" or "slips slips hers," and the system of effects suggesting something like a Japanese tea ceremony in a garden—"told tray," "sash," "rare bit of trees," and the Japanese sound of the name Susie Asado:

> Sweet sweet sweet sweet sweet tea.
> > Susie Asado.
> Sweet sweet sweet sweet sweet tea.
> > Susie Asado.
> Susie Asado which is a told tray sure.
> A lean on the shoe this means slips slips hers.
> > When the ancient light grey is clean it is yellow, it is a silver seller.
> > This is a please this is a please there are the saids to jelly. These are the wets these say the sets to leave a crown to Incy.
> > Incy is short for incubus.
> > A pot. A pot is a beginning of a rare bit of trees. Trees tremble, the old vats are in

> bobbles, bobbles which shade and shove and render clean, render clean must.
> > Drink pups.
> > Drink pups drink pups lease a sash hold, see it shine and a bobolink has pins. It shows a nail.
> > What is a nail. A nail is unison.
> > Sweet sweet sweet sweet sweet tea.

When war broke out in August 1914, Stein and Toklas were visiting the Whiteheads at their home, Lockridge, in Wiltshire, Stein having just signed a contract with John Lane for the English edition of *Three Lives*. Other guests included Bertrand Russell, George Moore, and Lytton Strachey. What had begun as a weekend visit turned into a six-week sojourn before they went back to Paris in October. Portraits of the guests and snatches of their conversation are captured in Stein's poem "Lockridge" (in *Bee Time Vine*, 1953).

"I very well remember at the beginning of the war being with Picasso on the boulevard Raspail when the first camouflaged truck passed," Stein recalled in *Picasso:*

> It was at night, we had heard of camouflage but we had not yet seen it and Picasso amazed looked at it and then cried out, yes it is we who made it, that is cubism.
> > Really the composition of this war, 1914-1918, was not the composition of all previous wars, the composition was not a composition in which there was one man in the centre surrounded by a lot of other men but a composition that had neither a beginning nor an end, a composition of which one corner was as important as another corner, in fact the composition of cubism.

At first, frightened by the zeppelin raids in 1915, Stein and Toklas fled to Barcelona and then to Palma de Majorca, where they stayed over the winter. But in 1916, encouraged by the outcome of the Battle of Verdun, they returned to Paris and volunteered their services to the American Fund for the French Wounded. Their assignment was to distribute medical supplies, and for this purpose Gertrude purchased and drove "Aunt Pauline" (or "Auntie"), the first of a series of Ford cars that she owned. After the war she bought "Godiva," so named because her dashboard was bare of all accessories. Fords had special significance for Stein because they were repetitions, all modeled on a prototype and manufactured in series, a form which she regarded as particularly modern and which she tried in her own work in pieces such as "Descriptions of Literature," "Lifting Belly," and "Patriarchal Poetry," where a word or phrase ("a book," "lifting belly," and "patriarchal poetry," in these cases) is repeated in a series of forty to a hundred or more varying sentences.

To some extent Stein and Toklas resumed their old life when they returned to Paris in 1916. Picasso was there bringing with him Erik Satie and Jean Cocteau, both of whom became friends of Stein's. But cubism, as an avant-garde art form, was dead (one of its original publicists, Apollinaire, would never recover from war wounds, dying in 1918)—a new art movement, Dada, was on the horizon. Stein's work after 1914 never returned to the cryptic word kaleidoscope of *Tender Buttons*.

Full of the joyfulness of phrases such as "a little lounge a clean piece of murder girder," the short poems of 1913 (collected in *Bee Time Vine*) are similar in their effects to *Tender Buttons*. But many of them reveal new explorations, such as the incorporation into the carefully chosen words of a dramatic format where Stein plays on both the character names and their dialogue, as in these lines from "In":

(I no)   He is says.
           He is says he is. says.
           He is says
           He is says

Gertrude Stein in 1919, seated beneath Pablo Picasso's 1906 portrait of her (courtesy of Edward M. Burns). When Stein's friends had complained that she did not resemble the recently completed portrait, Picasso had replied, "She will."

(B)   Nine Tea
                    Nine tea times.
                    Nine tea times four tea.
                    Nine tea four tea.

By 1914, in pieces such as the long poems "Oval" and "Emp Lace," both in *Bee Time Vine*, Stein was choosing words not so much for their individual dynamism as for their rhythmical effects in repetitions, as, for example, these lines from "Oval":

> Wipe.
> Wipe it.
> Wipe with it.
> With it.
> Wipe.
> Wipe lay it.
> Wipe loan lying.
> Wipe.
> Wipe with.
> Wipe with stretches.

Whereas the *Tender Buttons* poems had been justified at both margins, Stein now began to work in lists, which allowed her to incorporate the dynamic of dramatic dialogue, as, for example, in the long poem "Lifting Belly" (written during 1915, 1916, and 1917 in Majorca, Paris, and in Perignan and Nimes, where she was assigned by the American Fund):

> I do not mention roses.
> Exactly.
> Actually.
> Question and butter.
> I find the butter very good.
> Lifting belly is so kind.
> Lifting belly fattily.

Lists of short sentences were often varied by very long highly rhythmical sentences, as in this sentence from "Emp Lace":

Gertrude Stein at 27, rue de Fleurus, circa 1923 (courtesy of Edward M. Burns)

Cow come out cow come out cow come out come out
cow cow come out come out cow cow come out cow
come out cow come out come out cow come out
cow come out cow come out cow come out cow come
out cow come out cow cow come out cow come out.

The sheer diversity of play in Stein's work during this period (and with much of her work from this point on in her career) defies categorization. DeKoven has labeled this period "Voices and Plays" while Haas has pointed out Stein's interest in both the audible world in general and the movement and relations of things and people in space. But her explorations included the reinvention of genre concepts (for example, by labeling writings "geography" or by making "Sonnets that Please" which seem to be like sonnets but do not look like them) and the challenging of any assumptions about structure that capture her attention (for example, a forty-one-part play, "Counting Her Dresses," in *Geography and Plays*, where each part is divided into two to seven one-line "acts," or a play, "The King or Something," also in *Geography and Plays*, divided into ninety-seven "Pages"). Stein *changed* forever the meaning of terms such as "poem" and "play."

Always sensitive to rhythms in the sounds she heard every day, Stein recreated in the poems, plays, and portraits of this period everything from snatches of conversation, war news, the sound of her car, or machinery in the street to nursery rhymes, aphorisms, and the act of sex. The long poem "A Sonatina Followed By Another" (in *Bee Time Vine*), for example, doodles its way through the rhythms of nursery rhymes: "Come along and sit to me sit with me sit by me, come along and sit with me all the next day too." (echoing "London Bridge is Falling Down"); "I wish I was a fish with a great big tail, a polly wolly doodle a lobster or a whale." (echoing "Patticake"). The title of this poem refers to Stein (who was not a musician) improvising on the piano, and the piece proceeds very much as though someone is trying this or that melody or rhythm and then meandering on to another.

Rather than particular things singled out and intensely seen (as in the still lifes of *Tender Buttons)*, the objects, people, and activities in the work of this period come primarily from Stein's daily life. "Lifting Belly," for instance, with its erotic undercurrent ("Kiss my lips. She did./Kiss my lips again she did."), begins with references to burning olive wood in Majorca, is full of references to Alice Toklas, "Baby" (Gertrude), and objects from their daily life (apricots and decorated candles), and ends with references to Aunt Pauline (her first Ford) and to

Miss Cheatham, someone she knew in Nimes. The phrase "lifting belly," repeated again and again, is not so much defined (it ceases to have any reference at all after the twentieth repetition, a discovery about language we all make as children) as used to pace the flirtatious rhythm in the piece.

Stein was delighted to see the American troops ("doughboys") when they arrived in 1917, having not seen so many Americans together since her last trip to the United States in 1904. Pieces like "Work Again," "Decorations," and "Won" are among the war poems (collected in *Geography and Plays* and *Bee Time Vine*) that refer to them. Another war poem, "Accents in Alsace" (in *Geography and Plays*), begins,

Act I. The Schemils.

Brother brother go away and stay.
Sister mother believe me I say.
They will never get me as I run away.
. . . .

The Schemmels.
Sing so la douse so la dim.
Un deux trois
Can you tell me wha
Is it indeed.

It ends with the lyrical,

Sweeter than water or cream or ice. Sweeter than bells of roses. Sweeter than winter or summer or spring. Sweeter than pretty posies. Sweeter than anything is my queen and loving is her nature.

Stein and Toklas were sent to Alsace in 1918 to help provide relief for civilians. So dedicated to the volunteer effort were they that they sold their last Matisse, the once controversial *La Femme au Chapeau,* in order to take the assignment. At the end of the war the French recognized their services with the Médaille de la Réconnaissance Française.

"If you write not long but practically every day you do get a great deal written," Stein remarked. By 1921 an enormous number of manuscripts had accumulated; only a small portion of them could be included in the collection entitled *Geography and Plays* brought out by the Four Seas Company of Boston in 1922. Many would not be published until after Stein's death, when they appeared in the Yale edition of the unpublished writings, which includes *Bee Time Vine and Other Pieces 1913-1927* (1953), *Painted Lace and Other Pieces*

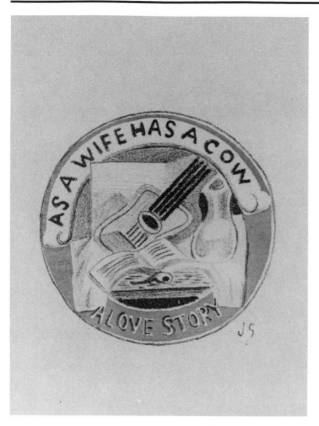

Front cover for A Book Concluding with As a Wife Has a Cow, *in which Stein investigated whether there was any real difference between poetry and prose (Sotheby Parke Bernet, sale number 3966)*

1914-1937 (1955), and *As Fine As Melanctha (1914-1930)* (1954) with five other volumes.

"For me the work of Gertrude Stein consists in a rebuilding, and entire new recasting of life, in the city of words," wrote Sherwood Anderson in his introduction to *Geography and Plays.* "Here is one artist who has been able to accept ridicule, who has even foregone the privilege of . . . wearing the bays of the great poets, to go live among the little housekeeping words, the swaggering bullying street-corner words, the honest working, money-saving words, and all the other forgotten and neglected citizens of the sacred and half forgotten city." Although the book firmly established Stein's reputation in literary circles, its reviews were seldom flattering. Typically she received acclaim and appreciation from writers, such as Mina Loy, while critics and journalists, such as H. L. Mencken, denounced the book as "dreadful stuff, indeed."

The book did not bring the "gloire" Stein had long sought. But this lack was offset somewhat by her being sought out as teacher in the early 1920s

by writers such as Sherwood Anderson and Ernest Hemingway, whose work she profoundly affected. She read all of Hemingway's manuscripts, consoled him in 1922 when his wife left the only manuscripts for all but two of the stories he had written on a train, and encouraged him to have enough confidence in his writing to take a year off from journalism. Eventually Hemingway was able to give her something in return: first he arranged for the serialization of *The Making of Americans* in Ford Madox Ford's *transatlantic review,* and then when the magazine folded before the entire work could be published, he persuaded Robert McAlmon's Contact Editions to publish it in book form in 1925. Akin to Joyce's *Ulysses* (1922) and Proust's *Remembrance of Things Past* (1913-1927) in its encyclopedic nature, this massive work narrates the history of America, of life's passage from birth to death, and of Stein and her family; explores habits of attention and quirks in the movement of thought; and evolves a grammar of continuous present—its publication was something she had long awaited.

In 1922, tired after the preparation of *Geography and Plays,* Toklas and Stein had retired for several months to Saint-Rémy in Provence. "It was during this winter," Stein wrote in *The Autobiography of Alice B. Toklas,* "that Gertrude Stein meditated on the use of grammar, poetical forms and what might be termed landscape plays." The following year (1923) they took their first annual summer in the country around Belley and thus began the Saint-Rémy or romantic/bucolic period in Stein's writing, full of cows, oxen, sheep, birds, streams, brooks, hills, valleys, and meadows. The writing itself sometimes went on outdoors, much in the manner of a painter with his easel, as Virgil Thomson recalled: "The scene took place in a field, its enactors being Gertrude, Alice, and a cow. Alice, by means of a stick, would drive the cow around the field. Then at a sign from Gertrude, the cow would be stopped; and Gertrude would write in her copybook. After a bit she would pick up her folding stool and progress to another spot, whereupon Alice would again start the cow moving around the field till Gertrude signaled she was ready to write again." The shift in her work was reflected by a shift in her interests in art during the 1920s to the nonabstract neoromantic painters: Christian Berard, Pavel Tchelitchew, Leonid Berman, and Francis Rose.

Stein's works of this period include the landscape plays (such as "A Saint in Seven," written in 1922 and published in *Composition as Explanation,* 1926), the long poem "Patriarchal Poetry" (written in 1927 and published in *Bee Time Vine and Other Pieces 1913-1927,* 1953), *A Novel of Thank You* (written in 1925-1926 and published in 1958), *An Acquaintance with Description* (written in 1926 and published in 1929), "As a Wife Has a Cow" (written and published in 1926), and *Lucy Church Amiably* (written in 1927 and published in 1930)—named after a church in the town of Lucey, near Belley—and *Four Saints in Three Acts* (written in 1927 and published in *Operas and Plays,* 1932). There were also shorter pieces about the Saint-Rémy area: "A Comedy Like That," "The Four Regions," and "Capital Capitals" (a conversation among the four capitals, Aix, Arles, Avignon, and Les Beaux, which was set to music by Virgil Thomson and performed in New York in 1929). Stein's "landscape plays" are balanced compositions that have the stasis of a landscape painting but at the same time the activity of things in relation to one another (as in a play). Saints, because they are magical simply by existing, are also landscapes. "In *Four Saints,*" Stein said, "I made the Saints the landscape. All the saints that I made and I made a number of them because after all a great many pieces of things are in a landscape all these saints together made my landscape." By calling her compositions "saints" or "landscapes" Stein invented new ways to think about literature and avoided the worn-out expectations conjured up by words such as "poem" or "novel."

One problem Stein was investigating in this work was whether there was any real difference between poetry and prose. Many of these pieces, though they purported to be novels or prose, are extremely lyrical, as in this sentence from "As a Wife Has a Cow: A Love Story":

> Happening and have it as happening and having it happen as happening and having to have it happen as happening, and my wife has a cow as now, my wife having a cow as now, my wife having a cow as now and having a cow as now and having a cow and having a cow now, my wife has a cow and now. My wife has a cow.

Another example of the lyricism of Stein's work during this period is this passage from "A Saint in Seven":

> In pleading sadness length of sadness in pleading length of sadness and no sorrow. No sorrow and no sadness length of sadness.
> A girl addresses a bountiful supply of seed to feed a chicken. Address a bountiful

supply of trees to shade them. Address a bountiful supply to them.

Lucy Church Amiably, which Stein called "A Novel of romantic beauty and nature and which Looks Like an Engraving," also exhibits this poetic quality:

> Very little daisies and very little bluettes and an artificial bird and a very whited anemone which is allowed and then after it is very well placed by an unexpected invitation to carry a basket by an unexpected invitation to carry a basket back and forth back and forth and a river there is this difference between a river here and a river there.

As in the poetry of *Tender Buttons,* Stein was still concerned with meaning (recreating) things without naming them: "I found in longer things like Operas and Plays and Portraits and Lucy Church Amiably . . . that I could come nearer to avoiding names in recreating something. . . . And here was the question if in poetry one could lose the noun as I had really and truly lost it in prose would there be any difference between poetry and prose. . . . I decided and Lucy Church Amiably had been an attempt to do it, I decided that if one definitely completely replaced the noun by the thing in itself, it was eventually to be poetry and not prose which would have to deal with everything that was not movement in space." She was beginning to discover that all writing that was not newspaper writing was poetry. She was also investigating the simple but profound question: how to write—investigations that culminated in the book by that title published in 1931.

Concurrently she was investigating grammar, trying to create paragraphs or long sentences that had both the "unemotional" balance of a sentence (where unity is based on static syntactic relationships) and the "emotional" movement of a paragraph (based on a series of sentences). Poems of this period, such as "As Eighty" in *Bee Time Vine,* reflect this interest in grammar.

Much of Stein's writing, as DeKoven has pointed out, has been devoted to demolishing and replacing the worn-out conventions and hierarchical orders of discourse invented by patriarchal society. But the long poem "Patriarchal Poetry" is not "about" this concern; rather it places the term "patriarchal poetry" into the multiple suggestive incoherent mode of discourse it is opposed to, where it stands out like a rock, meaning nothing and heard only as a drum beat. " 'Patriarchal Poetry' is

Alice B. Toklas and Gertrude Stein in the Model T Ford that Stein called "Godiva" because it was bare of all accessories, late 1920s
(courtesy of the Beinecke Rare Book and Manuscript Library, Yale University)

not cubistic at all," wrote Virgil Thomson, who knew Stein while she was composing it, "not angular or explosive or in any way visual. It is rounded, romantic, visceral, auditory, vastly structured, developed like a symphony." Beautifully musical, the piece modulates through highly rhythmical interweavings of word motifs often reminiscent of the repeated squeakings and jerkings of a piece of machinery: "Is it best to support Allan Allan will Allan Allan is it best to support Allan Allan will Allan best to support Allan will patriarchal poetry Allan will patriarchal poetry Allan will patriarchal poetry is it best to support Allan. . . ." Its final lines resound with the long drawn-out cadence of the symphonic finale:

Patriarchal poetry has to be which is best for them at three which is best and will be be and why why patriarchal poetry is not to try try twice.

Patriarchal Poetry having patriarchal poetry. Having patriarchal poetry having patriarchal poetry. Having patriarchal poetry. Having patriarchal poetry and twice, patriarchal poetry.

He might have met.

Patriarchal poetry and twice patriarchal poetry.

In 1925 Edith Sitwell, after an unsuccessful attempt to have Hogarth Press publish *The Making of Americans*, realized that Gertrude Stein needed more publicity, and she therefore arranged for

Stein's first lectures, which were given in 1926 at Oxford and Cambridge. For the occasion Stein, by then fifty-two, wrote *Composition as Explanation* (1926), in which she outlined with deceptive simplicity the crucial entanglement of the time at which artistic composition occurs, the composition itself and the composition (that is, make-up) of the artist's generation or historical period. The lectures were a great success and shortly afterward resulted in, among other things, the publication of another collection of pieces: *Useful Knowledge* (1928). Stein was by now regularly published in such magazines as the *Little Review, Vanity Fair,* and *transition.* Her work had appeared through the 1920s in such avant-garde publications as *Broom, This Quarter, Black & Blue Jay, Blues,* and *Pagany.* But her work simply was not getting published quickly enough, and in 1930 Toklas published *Lucy Church Amiably,* the first of the five Plain Editions, printed in monotype on cheap paper and bound with simple covers. Toklas did the distribution herself.

Stein and Toklas were living at this time a pleasantly domestic life of gardening, preserving, and baking cakes (Toklas's specialty) in their summer residence at Bilignin. Basket, the white poodle they had acquired in 1928 (so named because Toklas thought he should "carry a basket of flowers in his mouth"), had made a dog lover of Stein. "I am I because my little dog knows me," she would write in 1935: ones's identity was the self that others knew. The story of how they acquired their summer retreat provides a typical example of Gertrude Stein's childlike egotism and dependence on others to work things out for her. As Toklas recalled later, "one day from the valley below we saw the house at Bilignin and Gertrude said, I will drive you up there and you can go and tell them that we will take their house. I said, But it may not be for rent. She said, The curtains are floating out the windows. Well, I said, I think that proves someone is living there." When they discovered that the lieutenant who lived there had no intention of moving, Stein arranged for him to be promoted so he would be posted elsewhere and have to move. They signed the lease papers in spring 1929, having only seen this seventeenth-century villa from the outside. "Inside," Janet Hobhouse says, "was the furniture of the descendants of Brillat-Savarin himself. Outside was a lovely semi-formal garden, with gravel walks and flower beds. There were little balconies and shutters and a spectacular view of the countryside. It was a perfect home for a woman of letters."

At the end of her second decade in the twentieth century Stein made an important discovery about poetry: "there was something completely contained within itself and being contained within itself . . . moving, not moving in relation to anything not moving in relation to itself but just moving. . . . Well it was an important thing. . . . because it made me realize what poetry really is." The portrait of Bernard Faÿ written in 1929, she felt, was one of the pieces where she achieved this self-contained movement:

> Patience is amiable and amiably.
> What is amiable and amiably.
> Patience is amiable and amiably.
> What is impatience.
> Impatience is amiable and amiably.

The movement here is delightful and quite comic. The first three lines swing along in a carefree forward lilt which is suddenly halted by the opposition in the fourth line. But, like a happy-go-lucky person, who is not long depressed by the perplexities of life, the fifth line picks up the lilt again, swinging the opposition along with it. Perhaps Bernard Faÿ was such a person, but it really does not matter.

The following year, Stein recalled, she began again to worry about the difference between poetry and prose: "As this thing came once more to be a doubt inside me I began to work very hard at poetry. . . . At that time I wrote Before the Flowers of Friendship Faded Friendship Faded and there I went back again to a more or less regular form to see whether inside that regular form I could do what I was sure needed to be done and also to find out if eventually prose and poetry were one or not one."

Before the Flowers of Friendship Faded Friendship Faded (the second Plain Edition, 1931) began as a free translation of Georges Hugnet's poem *Enfances* but quickly became a Steinian étude in which she experimented with conventional poetic rhythms:

> They will be white with which they know they
> see, that darker makes it be a color white for
> me, white is not shown when I am dark in-
> deed with red despair who comes who has
> to care that they will let me a little lie like not
> I like to lie I like to live I like to die I like to
> lie. . . .
> ....

A little lake makes fountains
And fountains have no flow,
And a dove has need of flying
And water can be low[.]

Just as Noam Chomsky would later use nonsense combinations of words to reveal purely syntactic relations in language, Stein used incoherent sentence combinations to reveal the movement of thought and rhythm that occurs in conventional poetry.

Publication plans originally were to print the two poems side by side, presenting the book as a collaboration. But when it came time to go to press Hugnet insisted on treating Stein's work merely as a translation. The two poems were never published together in book form, although they appeared on facing pages in *Pagany* (Winter 1931). Instead Toklas brought out Stein's poem as a Plain Edition, with

a clear message to Hugnet in the title.

Early in the 1930s Stein came to the conclusion that "There could no longer be form to decide anything, narrative that is not newspaper narrative but real narrative must of necessity be told by any one having come to the realization that the noun must be replaced not by inner balance [such as the syntactic balance of sentences] but by the thing in itself and that will eventually lead to everything"— a universal form: writing. "Winning His Way: A Narrative Poem of Poetry," a fifty-six-page poem written in 1931 (published in *Stanzas in Meditation and Other Poems [1929-1933]*, 1956), reflects this concern with the melding of poetry and prose. "The 'story,' as a structure of consecutive happenings to be followed, has been pretty thoroughly destroyed by its explosion or transubstantiation into lyricism," notes Donald Sutherland, "and the

Gertrude Stein with Olga and Pablo Picasso on the terrace at Bilignin, summer 1930 (courtesy of Edward M. Burns)

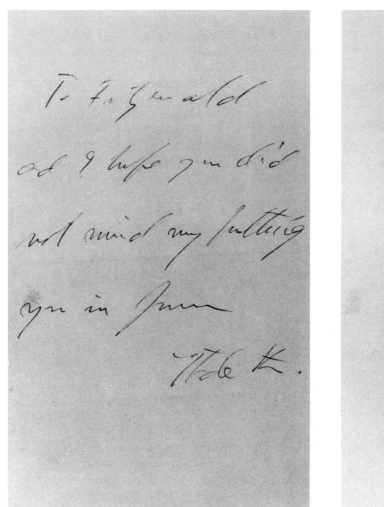
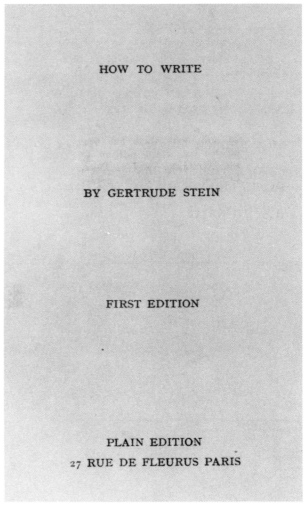

Inscription to F. Scott Fitzgerald and title page (from the collection of Matthew J. Bruccoli). The inscription refers to the line "That is the cruelest thing I ever heard is the favorite phrase of Gilbert."

'narrative' is now almost entirely in the verbal and lyrical events of the poem itself, which moves at an astonishing pace."

> They could. See. Seem. In proportion.
> This. Was. As if. A shock. Of. Then.
> Who. Are hours. With. That. It. Was oftener.
> Thinking. In their heart. Sublime.
> Nicely. Known. Should they. Better. Belie.
> If they ask. Of it. To be better. Soon.

If "Winning His Way" transubstantiates narrative into lyricism, "Stanzas in Meditation" (150 pages long), written in 1932, transubstantiates ideas: "it came to Gertrude Stein," Sutherland points out, that "after all grammar and rhetoric are in themselves actualizations of ideas and the beginning, perhaps, of a conversion of ideas into poetry, since

they are in their way shapes or schemes, aesthetic configurations. . . ." In "Stanzas in Meditation," he adds, "Stein solved the problem of keeping ideas in their primary life, that is of making them events in a subjective continuum of writing. . . . about ideas about writing." Stanza XII is a meditation on the thought configuration suggested by the word "which":

> She was disappointed not alone or only
> Not by what they wish but even by not which
> Or should they silence in convincing
> Made more than they stand for them with which.

Sutherland, who places the poem with Pound's *Cantos* and T. S. Eliot's *Four Quartets* in the "tradition of the long, rambling, discursive poem whose interest and energy are primarily in the movement

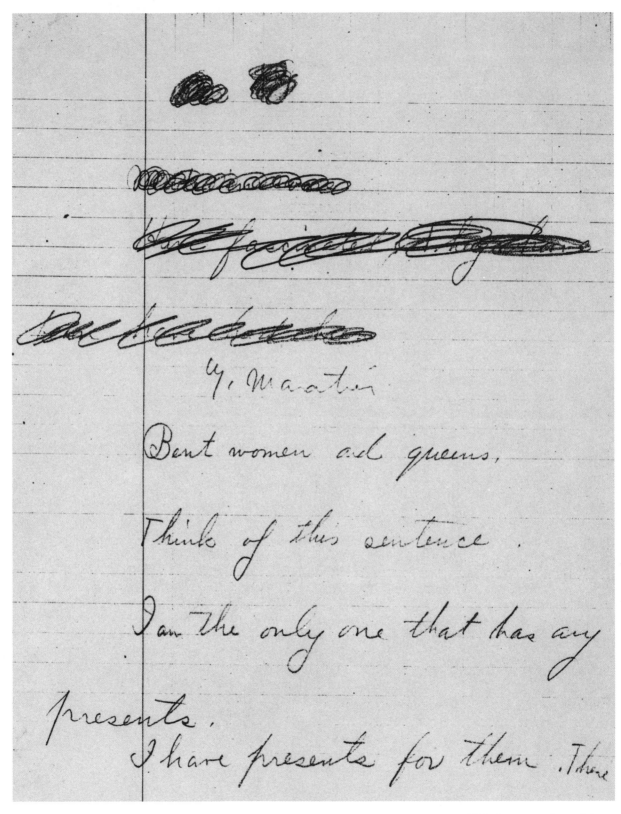

The first two pages of the manuscript for Stein's portrait of Paris art dealer Georges Maratier, published in Portraits and Prayers
(by permission of the Estate of Gertrude Stein; from the collection of Robert A. Wilson)

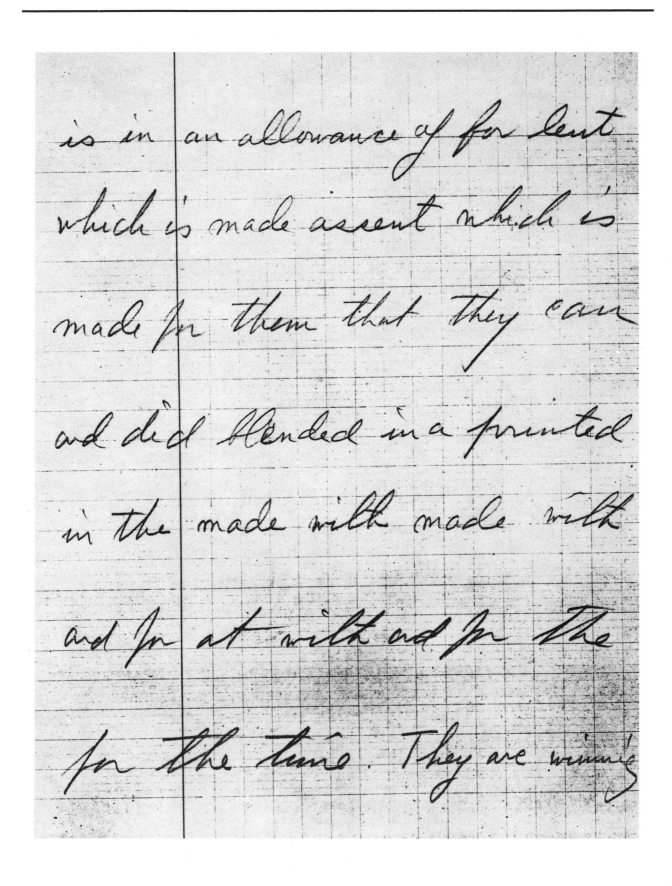

of the poet's mind writing," likens the "tense and elegant behavior of the syntax" to the vibrant line in the drawings of Gabrielle Picabia (a close friend of Stein's) and describes its musicality as "a rhetorical accent rather than a properly temporal element. . . . an intensive, as against a progressive, metric . . . [where] both the temporality and the spatiality . . . are 'ideal'—functions of the sense, of the articulate 'thoughts' succeeding each other in a meditation."

Stein was discovering here what she would later call "entity"—"the moment you are you without the memory of yourself." The writing in "Stanzas in Meditation" not only occurs at such moments but forces the reader into that mode of consciousness. In "Stanzas in Meditation," as Sutherland points out, "The nowness and thisness of a thought, not its connections with past or future thoughts or with an objective context of thoughts, are the conditions of its life, and of thought generally at its most vibrant." In the same way, Stein would argue in "What are Masterpieces," it is entity—the memory-free mode of consciousness—that is crucial to the creative work of the genius or the masterpiece, not "identity"—the self-conscious or audience-oriented mode, structured as it is by the memory of past experiences. In the same vein, Wendy Steiner points out that Stein's late portraits sought "to present the individual as an entity, as a degree, a mode, of movement"—not in relation or comparison to anything else.

Diagramming entity involves diagramming the reader's thought as it is bombarded with juxtapositions of sentences of various rhetorical movements or forces, and the interweaving of phrases that sometimes do and sometimes do not objectivize themselves or particular words. This process is apparent in these selections from "A French Rooster. A History," one of the shorter poems of this period, which was written in 1930 and published in *Stanzas in Meditation:*

II

Pottery needs the damp
It needs noise hardly at all

Virgil Thomson and Gertrude Stein (courtesy of Edward M. Burns)

It is less different from porcelain
It is less well known.

. . . .

XII

Our by relief
In mentioning either
They will generously lead
In patience weather
They will make it be
Relieve their holding
It is in August
That they will be there.

These lines from another 1930 poem, "Abel" (published in *Stanzas in Meditation*), are also an example of Stein's diagramming:

Blame means does it
Halve means like it
Shoulder means hours now
Women mean like it
Who makes their care
To please running with ease[.]

In "Narrative" (also written in 1930 and collected in *Stanzas in Meditation*), as in many other works, Stein asks, What is the entity of the form itself ?:

A narrative now I know what a narrative is,
it is not continuous it must contain that they
wish and are and have been and it is that
they lean in and together.

This is what a narrative is it does not
need to be in remain it is that they include
in conclude in into remain.

Two events in Stein's life during the 1930s helped to highlight for her the issue of identity versus entity. The first was the great success of *The Autobiography of Alice B. Toklas* (1933), which brought her her first income from writing and made her come to terms with for the first time the way an audience changes the writing: "When you are writing before there is an audience anything written is as important as any other thing and you cherish anything and everything that you have written. After audience begins, naturally they create something that is they create you, and so . . . something is more important than another thing, which was not true when you were you that is when you were not you as your little dog knows you." That is to say, the audience tends to make one write out of one's identity rather than one's entity, which results in inferior work.

Stein, who was not really interested in conventional biographical prose writing, had wanted Toklas to write her autobiography for some time. But when Toklas did not get around to it, Stein took the task on herself, perhaps, as Sutherland suggests, as a relief from the intense concentration of writing "Stanzas in Meditation." Since it was written entirely from Toklas's point of view, reproducing very well her clipped, laconic speech, Stein had ample license to build exactly the legend of herself that she chose, only at the end revealing herself as the true author. Some old friends and acquaintances of Stein's, who thought they had been misrepresented, banded together and complained bitterly in "Testimony Against Gertrude Stein," which was published in the February 1935 issue of *transition*. But the public loved the book, in both America and Paris. It was reprinted as a Literary Guild selection in August 1933. "La Gloire," for which she had waited so long, had arrived.

Her agent soon began to pressure her to take advantage of it with a lecture tour, the second event that would bring identity/entity to the fore: as she lectured she heard more and more what the audience heard and was confronted again and again by her identity for them. For some time she resisted the trip, until one of the "doughboys" she had known during World War I, William Rogers (whom she called "Kiddie"), who had since become a reporter, came to Bilignin and persuaded her. A whole boatload of reporters came out to the S.S. *Champlain* to meet her when she arrived in New York on 24 October 1934. "Why don't you write the way you talk?," one asked. "Why don't you read the way I write?," Stein answered. She had a tremendous ability to communicate her intelligence and wit both in lectures and question periods.

While she was lecturing in the East, she took her first airplane trip to Chicago to see *Four Saints in Three Acts*. The production, with music by Virgil Thomson, choreography by Frederick Ashton, and an all black cast, had been extremely popular since its Broadway run, which opened in February. Crisscrossing back and forth to university, college, and cultural group audiences, her five-month tour included Philadelphia, Boston, Chicago (her favorite city, where Robert Hutchins and Mortimer Adler arranged for her to give seminars for the Great Books program at the University of Chicago; her lectures were later published as *Narration*), Baltimore, Charlottesville, New Orleans, Dallas, Austin, Houston, Pasadena, and San Francisco. By the time she returned to Paris on 12 May 1935, she had

Alice B. Toklas and Gertrude Stein, 7 November 1934, before their first airplane flight, from New York to Chicago for that city's opening of Four Saints in Three Acts *(photograph by Carl Van Vechten, by permission of Joseph Solomon, the Estate of Carl Van Vechten; courtesy of the Beinecke Rare Book and Manuscript Library, Yale University)*

become a seasoned air traveler (who saw the lines of Picasso and Braque in the landscape below) and had visited almost every corner of the country. She had had tea at the White House and been entertained royally everywhere she went. And she had acquired a new publisher, Bennett Cerf of Random House, who agreed to publish one book by her each year.

In 1936 she lectured again at Oxford and Cambridge, presenting *What Are Masterpieces,* which examined the relationship of identity/entity to masterpieces and genius. During the trip to America, she had begun contributing pieces to various journals on such subjects as "American Food and American Houses." This "identity" writing for

audiences continued through her last years and included among other things a series of articles on money in 1936, *Everybody's Autobiography* (1937), *Paris France* (1940), "The Winner Loses, A Picture of Occupied France" (*Atlantic Monthly,* November 1940), and *Wars I Have Seen* (1945), for which she kept a journal through World War II.

The "entity" writing in Stein's final years, however, resulted in some of her most philosophical work, including *Four in America* (1947), *The Geographical History of America or The Relation of Human Nature to the Human Mind* (1936), *ida a Novel* (1941), *Brewsie and Willie* (1946), "Dr Faustus Lights the Lights" (in *Last Operas and Plays,* 1949), and *The Mother of Us All* (1947). In *Four in America* she examined the relationship between identity (public role) and entity (independent quality of genius) by placing four "geniuses," Henry James, George Washington, Ulysses S. Grant, and Wilbur Wright, into roles they did not have. In *The Geographical History of America,* she tried to distinguish human mind (entity) from human nature (publicly defined identity). She spent the summer after her American tour at Bilignin mulling over these problems in the company of Thornton Wilder. Artistic endeavor, Stein believed, was a process of discovering what one knows regardless of the interests of any audience. "All the thousands of occasions in the daily life go into our head to form our ideas about these things," she said to Wilder. "Now if we write . . . these things we know flow down our arm and come out on the page. The moment before we wrote them we did not really know we knew them; if they

are in our head in the shape of words then that is all wrong and they will come out dead; but if we did not know we knew them until the moment of writing, then they come to us with a shock of surprise. . . . Now of course there is no audience at that moment. . . . At that moment you are totally alone at this recognition of what you know." Characteristically work of this period proceeds as a series of propositions, queries, conclusions, and meditative games somewhat in the manner of Wittgenstein's *Philosophical Investigations* (1953).

All through the rumblings of war in the late 1930s, Gertrude Stein had firmly believed it would not happen, regarding it mainly as an intrusion upon her work. But, as she had seen change was a principle of art, she came also to accept it as a principle of life. When the landlord terminated the lease for 27, rue de Fleurus in 1938, Stein and

Gertrude Stein in 1937, standing in front of Pablo Picasso's 1906 portrait of her (courtesy of Edward M. Burns)

*Gertrude Stein singing "On the Trail of the Lonesome Pine,"
her favorite song, at Bilignin, summer 1937 (photograph by
W. G. Rogers; courtesy of the Beinecke Rare Book and
Manuscript Library, Yale University)*

expired in 1943. They moved to Le Colombier in nearby Culoz, where in August German officers were billeted, followed by Italian troops in September. Stein and Toklas did not live without anxiety. More than once they set out to leave. But the villagers, who knew exactly who they were and who could easily have denounced them as Jews, loved them, protected them, and encouraged them to stay. The mayor of Culoz, in fact, kept their names off the official records required by the Germans.

Just as Stein had reveled in the company of the "doughboys" in 1917, so also she welcomed the American troops in France in 1944. For her their arrival marked the end of the war. Toklas baked her victory cake; in December they moved back to Paris; and from then until Stein's death in 1946, she surrounded herself with GIs, talking to them, entertaining them wherever she went, and catching the rhythms of their voices in one of her last works, *Brewsie and Willie.*

On 19 July 1946 Gertrude Stein collapsed on her way to stay at a country house lent to her by Bernard Faÿ. She was immediately rushed to the American Hospital at Neuilly, where against medical discretion she ordered that the doctors operate. On 23 July she made her will, providing for Toklas out of the estate, making Toklas and Allan Stein executors, bequeathing her Picasso portrait to the Metropolitan Museum in New York and her unpublished manuscripts to the Yale University Library, and providing Carl Van Vechten, her lifelong friend and supporter, with the funds to publish all of her unpublished work. Then she settled in to wait, heavily sedated and in considerable pain, for the operation on 27 July. She died of inoperable cancer while still under anesthesia. "What is the answer?," she had asked Toklas just before her death. Toklas remained silent. "In that case what is the question?," Stein added.

How do we read this writing, that, along with the work of Alain Robbe-Grillet, Samuel Beckett, John Barth, Donald Barthelme, and William S. Burroughs, questions our defining notions of poetry, narrative, language, writing, literature, and finally the world? Stein might well ask of her critics some forty years after her death: "Why don't you read the way I write?" Very few have dealt with her work as twentieth-century art that, as DeKoven notes, "*must* reflect the . . . fragmented twentieth century reality, with its subjectivist epistemology, its emphasis on nonrational areas of the mind, its notion of consciousness as a chaotic flow of private associations, its vision of events as acausal, of time

Toklas moved happily to 5, rue Christine: "We were tired of the present which also was the past because no servant would stand the kitchen, there was no air in the house, the garage they had built next door had made it uncomfortable." When Basket, who had been painted and photographed almost as much as his mistress, died later that year, Stein and Toklas acquired another white poodle, Basket II. And when war was declared in September 1939, they quickly packed away their belongings in Paris and returned to Bilignin for the winter, where they coped with shortages in a spirit of adventure, chopping wood, making jam, and going on long walks in search of firewood. When they ran out of money, they "ate Cézanne." *Mrs. Reynolds* (1952), a novel Stein began in 1940, is largely an account of the experiences of a woman like herself in occupied France. Eventually they were forced to give up even Bilignin, when the lease as nonlinear, of truth and reality as plural and undetermined. . . . [where] art is no longer seen as primarily representative or mimetic."

Posing a direct challenge to the assumptions of academic literary criticism in general, Stein's work has not lent itself to the hermeneutic and thematic textual explications that have dominated critical approaches in the twentieth century. Commentary has abounded with marginalizing terms such as "hermetic," "difficult," "experimental," and "inaccessible," which do nothing to come to terms with the very real and rich patterns, designs, and demands of Stein's writing. Following Bridgman, a number of critics have focused on erotic readings of Stein's work, applying the label "erotic" to phrases which are simply affectionate and completely ignoring the dense collage of other effects and activities in the writing. Stein's work is full of references to people, places, and objects from her daily life, but biographical approaches, which attempt to attach some extrinsic or objective meaning to it, are a distraction from the aesthetic object of the texts and a denial of their essential multiplicity. Stein herself firmly believed that writing as art had nothing to do with the facts of daily living (identity): though it might contain those facts, its wellspring was located in the part of our beings that is unconscious of daily worries and pleasures (entity). The writing neither invites interpretive criticism, nor does it need it. Almost completely interlocking in its vocabulary, likely at any moment to involve anything from punning transliteration of foreign languages to challenges of the whole gamut of formal assumptions, her work is virtually impossible to generalize about and, as Stein intended, cannot be known or understood through explanation. Rather the writing exemplifies her thought and is emblematic, in its pluridimensionality, of the twentieth century.

The best introduction to Stein's work is her own exegetical and critical writing (*Composition as Explanation, Lectures in America, Narration, What Are Masterpieces*, and *How Writing is Written*) and her interview with Robert Bartlett Haas. The introductions to the Yale editions of unpublished writings, particularly the one to *Stanzas in Meditation* by Donald Sutherland, are valuable—as are the introductions to *The Geographical History of America* and *Four in America* by Thornton Wilder and the introduction to *How to Write* by Patricia Meyerowitz. Haas's *Primer for the Gradual Understanding of Gertrude Stein* provides the most useful general approach to Stein's writing, since it presents the work in Stein's own terminology and in its chronological

sequence as an evolution of investigations.

The emergence of semiotics and critical techniques from the work of Barthes, Derrida, and Kristeva, among others, has resulted in the late 1970s and the 1980s in criticism, notably from Marjorie Perloff and Marianne DeKoven, that begins to come to terms with the great diversity, play, resonance, and perception in Stein's work. But those who characterize her writing as a series of styles do it an injustice, for this approach suggests both the inappropriate distinction between style and content and the inaccurate notion that the work proceeded in a neat orderly progression. Nor is the word "experiment" accurate: "Artists do not experiment," Stein said, "Experiment is what scientists do; they initiate an operation of unknown factors in order to be instructed by its results. An artist puts down

Gertrude Stein at the window of her apartment at 5, rue Christine in Paris, on V-E Day (courtesy of Edward M. Burns)

Alice B. Toklas and Gertrude Stein with their poodle Basket II and some American soldiers in their 5, rue Christine apartment, 1946 (courtesy of Edward M. Burns)

what he knows and at every moment it is what he knows at that moment." We have still to learn to read as Stein wrote.

Always a writer's writer, Stein's influence is still growing. The persistent activity of her artistic vision makes her a major writer of this century, comparable in the magnitude of her perception and achievement to her contemporaries Ezra Pound and James Joyce.

Interview:

Robert Bartlett Haas, "Gertrude Stein Talking: A Transatlantic Interview," *Uclan Review*, 8 (Summer 1962): 3-11; 9 (Spring 1963): 40-48; 9 (Winter 1964): 44-48.

Letters:

Sherwood Anderson/Gertrude Stein Correspondence and Personal Essays, edited by Ray Lewis White (Chapel Hill: University of North Carolina Press, 1972);

Dear Sammy Letters from Gertrude Stein & Alice B. Toklas, edited by Samuel M. Steward (Boston: Houghton Mifflin, 1977).

Bibliographies:

Robert Bartlett Haas and Donald Clifford Gallup, *A Catalogue of the Published and Unpublished Writings of Gertrude Stein* (New Haven: Yale University Library, 1941);

Robert A. Wilson, *Gertrude Stein: A Bibliography* (New York: Phoenix Bookshop, 1974);

Ray Lewis White, *Gertrude Stein and Alice B. Toklas: A Reference Guide* (Boston: G. K. Hall, 1984).

Biographies:

W. G. Rogers, *When this you see remember me: Gertrude Stein in person* (New York & Toronto: Rinehart, 1948);

Elizabeth Sprigge, *Gertrude Stein: Her Life and Work* (New York: Harper, 1957);

John Malcolm Brinnin, *The Third Rose: Gertrude*

Stein and Her World (Boston: Little, Brown, 1959);

Alice B. Toklas, *What Is Remembered* (New York, Chicago & San Francisco: Holt, Rinehart & Winston, 1963);

Four Americans in Paris: The Collections of Gertrude Stein and Her Family (New York: Museum of Modern Art, 1970);

James R. Mellow, *Charmed Circle: Gertrude Stein & Company* (New York & Washington: Praeger, 1974);

Linda Simon, ed., *Gertrude Stein: A Composite Portrait* (New York: Avon, 1974);

Janet Hobhouse, *Everybody Who Was Anybody: A Biography of Gertrude Stein* (New York: Putnam's, 1975).

References:

Richard Bridgman, *Gertrude Stein in Pieces* (New York: Oxford University Press, 1970);

Marianne DeKoven, *A Different Language: Gertrude Stein's Experimental Writing* (Madison: University of Wisconsin Press, 1983);

Donald Gallup, ed., *The Flowers of Friendship: Letters Written to Gertrude Stein* (New York: Knopf, 1953);

William H. Gass, "Gertrude Stein: Her Escape from Protective Language," *Accent,* 18 (Autumn 1958): 233-244;

Robert Bartlett Haas, Introduction to *A Primer for the Gradual Understanding of Gertrude Stein,* edited by Haas (Los Angeles: Black Sparrow Press, 1971);

Mabel Dodge Luhan, *European Experiences,* volume 2 of her *Intimate Memories* (New York: Harcourt, Brace, 1935);

Marjorie Perloff, "Poetry As Word-System: The Art of Gertrude Stein," *American Poetry Review,* 8 (September/October 1979): 33-43;

Wendy Steiner, *Exact Resemblance to Exact Resemblance: The Literary Portraiture of Gertrude Stein* (New Haven: Yale University Press, 1978);

Donald Sutherland, *Gertrude Stein: A Biography of Her Work* (New Haven: Yale University Press, 1951);

Virgil Thomson, *Virgil Thomson* (London: Weidenfeld & Nicolson, 1967);

William Carlos Williams, "The Work of Gertrude Stein," *Pagany,* 1 (Winter 1930): 41-46; collected in *Selected Essays of William Carlos Williams* (New York: Random House, 1954), pp. 113-120.

Papers:

The major repository for Stein materials is the Beinecke Library at Yale University, which has most of Stein's manuscripts, correspondence, and unpublished notebooks. There are also significant collections at the Bancroft Library, University of California at Berkeley, and the University of Texas at Austin.

George Sterling

(1 December 1869-17 November 1926)

Dalton Gross
Southwest Texas State University

BOOKS: *The Testimony of the Suns and Other Poems* (San Francisco: W. E. Wood, 1903; revised edition, San Francisco: A. M. Robertson, 1907);

The Triumph of Bohemia: A Forest Play (San Francisco, 1907?);

A Wine of Wizardry and Other Poems (San Francisco: A. M. Robertson, 1909);

The House of Orchids and Other Poems (San Francisco: A. M. Robertson, 1911);

Beyond the Breakers and Other Poems (San Francisco: A. M. Robertson, 1914);

Ode on the Opening of the Panama-Pacific International Exposition (San Francisco: A. M. Robertson, 1915);

The Evanescent City (San Francisco: A. M. Robertson, 1915);

Yosemite: An Ode (San Francisco: A. M. Robertson, 1916);

The Caged Eagle and Other Poems (San Francisco: A. M. Robertson, 1916);

The Play of Everyman, Based on the Old English Morality Play, New Version, blank-verse version by Sterling and Richard Ordynski, based on the play by Hugo von Hofmannsthal (San Francisco: A. M. Robertson, 1917);

Thirty-Five Sonnets (San Francisco: Book Club of California, 1917);

The Binding of the Beast and Other War Verse (San Francisco: A. M. Robertson, 1917);

Lilith: A Dramatic Poem (San Francisco: A. M. Robertson, 1919; revised edition, New York: Macmillan, 1926);

Rosamund: A Dramatic Poem (San Francisco: A. M. Robertson, 1920);

To a Girl Dancing (San Francisco, 1921);

Sails and Mirage and Other Poems (San Francisco: A. M. Robertson, 1921);

Selected Poems (New York: Holt, 1923);

Truth (Chicago: Bookfellows, 1923; revised edition, San Francisco: Bohemian Club, 1926);

Strange Waters (San Francisco, 1926?);

Robinson Jeffers: The Man and the Artist (New York: Boni & Liveright, 1926);

Five Poems (N.p.: Privately printed, 1927);

Sonnets to Craig (Long Beach, Cal.: Upton Sinclair, 1928);

Poems to Vera (New York: Oxford University Press, 1938);

After Sunset (San Francisco: J. Howell, 1939).

PERIODICAL PUBLICATIONS: "Joaquin Miller," *American Mercury,* 7 (February 1926): 220-229;

"The Shadow Maker" [a biographical sketch of Ambrose Bierce], *American Mercury,* 7 (September 1926): 10-19;

George Sterling (photograph by Arnold Genthe)

"A First-Class Fighting Man," *American Mercury,* 10 (January 1927): 76-80;

"The Testament of an American Schopenhauer: George Sterling's 'Pleasure and Pain!,' " edited by Joseph W. Slade, *Resources for American Literary Study,* 3 (Autumn 1973): 230-248.

George Sterling is nearly forgotten today, but he seemed one of the nation's most promising poets in the years immediately preceding World War I. Although his work is no longer read, Sterling was praised extravagantly in his time by a large number of major authors; Ambrose Bierce, Jack London, Upton Sinclair, and Theodore Dreiser all declared him to be a great poet. These writers all knew Sterling so well that it was hard for them to be objective. Yet their opinions are an accurate reflection of the reputation Sterling once enjoyed in his home state of California. The changes in poetic taste that began in the years preceding World War I destroyed his hopes for national recognition, but he remained popular in San Francisco, where he maintained a sort of local supremacy until his death in 1926.

The qualities that account for Sterling's early successes are the same qualities that made him seem old-fashioned in the 1920s. Sterling employed deliberately archaic, mannered, formally poetic diction, sometimes aiming at a sweeping cosmic portentousness, as in "The Testimony of the Suns," and sometimes at a Wildean jeweled beauty, as in "A Wine of Wizardry," which dazzled readers with its strangeness after Bierce arranged for its publication in *Cosmopolitan* in September 1907. Over the years he refined his poetic approach rather than modifying it. His finest work, the dramatic poem *Lilith* (1919), is vastly superior to his earlier work, but the themes and techniques are essentially the same. When *Lilith* appeared in its final version in 1926, it appealed only to a few conservative critics and to Sterling's California audience.

Although Sterling for a time virtually came to symbolize San Francisco bohemia, he spent his first twenty-one years on the East Coast. He was born in 1869 in Sag Harbor, New York, a wealthy whaling community on eastern Long Island. The eldest son of George Ansel Sterling, a successful doctor, and of the former Mary Parker Havens, whose family had done well in both whaling and banking, Sterling grew up in comfortable circumstances. When he was sixteen, his parents became converts to Roman Catholicism and determined to make priests of their three sons. In 1886 the two older sons were sent to St. Charles College in Ellicot City, Maryland. Sterling did reasonably well during the three years he studied there, but there is little in his later life or poetry to indicate that he was much impressed by his religious training. Perhaps the most lasting influence of St. Charles was the teaching of the poet Father John Bannister Tabb (1845-1909), whose lecture on Keats Sterling still remembered in detail twenty-five years later. After three years, Sterling refused to continue training for the priesthood. His parents then tried to persuade him to become a doctor, but they had no success. In 1890 he was sent to San Francisco to work for his uncle, Frank C. Havens, a real-estate magnate.

It was to be another ten years before Sterling wrote poetry he wished to preserve, but in San Francisco he quickly became part of the city's literary bohemia. Memories of Bret Harte were still fresh; Joaquin Miller, then internationally famous as "the poet of the Sierras," lived nearby in a bizarre rural home he called The Hights; Frank Norris was writing novels; and, most significant for Sterling, Ambrose Bierce was writing stories, poems, and epigrams in addition to working for William Randolph Hearst on the *San Francisco Examiner.* Eventually Sterling met Bierce, whose judgments in poetry he thought nearly infallible.

During these same years Sterling did well working for his uncle, but he remained only an employee, acquiring no wealth of his own. On 7 February 1896 he made an ill-fated marriage to Caroline Rand, whose sister, Lila, was married to Havens. Sterling was a competent businessman rather than an enthusiastic one, and the tensions growing out of his marriage seem to have exacerbated his increasing discontent with his whole way of life—a discontent that manifested itself in expanding interests in poetry and in philandering. By 1905, after considerable local success with his poetry, Sterling had decided to abandon business and move to Carmel. Property he received from Lila Havens provided a small income, and, in theory at least, gardening and hunting would keep expenses down. Sterling was one of the first settlers in what was soon to be a prominent artists' colony.

As Sterling became a serious writer, he fell more and more under the spell of Bierce. Poetry, Bierce believed, should concern itself with "beauty"—not at all with the mundane problems of society and not primarily with the shifting currents of abstract ideas. He despised the realism of William Dean Howells, just as he despised the socialistic tendencies of poets such as Edwin Markham. Bierce, whose own thinking was harshly Spencerian, despised socialists whether they hap-

Joaquin Miller, George Sterling, and Charles Warren Stoddard in Monterey, 1905 (courtesy of the Bancroft Library, University of California, Berkeley)

pened to be writers or not. This attitude was to make some difficulties over the years for Sterling, who considered himself a socialist, but in the early stages of his career he took Bierce's advice about poetry and followed it minutely. Between 1901 and 1907 he kept up a steady correspondence with Bierce, who had moved to Washington, D.C. in late 1899, and his most important poems underwent careful analysis—and a great number of minor revisions—by Bierce. In 1901 Bierce arranged for Sterling's "Memorial Day Ode" to appear in the *San Francisco Examiner*. The early drafts of Sterling's "The Testimony of the Suns," written the next year, convinced Bierce that he had discovered a genius.

"The Testimony of the Suns," a vastly ambitious work, is a poetic expression of the nebular hypothesis, which states that the universe is infinite in both time and space and that stars are constantly being born through a very slow accretion of matter, only to live out their lives and die. To Sterling this concept meant that the immutable laws of the universe are, from a human point of view at least, senseless. The agonizing processes of evolution and development of civilizations are all for nothing. Life in any given solar system must eventually end, and the whole process must be repeated over and over forever. Sterling's work at its best makes the reader feel some of the power and sweep of his theme, but even his strongest effects are marred by excesses of rhetoric. Sterling's poetic technique was to improve over the next twenty years, and his philosophical attitudes were to remain the same. In 1923 he wrote an essay called variously "Life," "Implications of Infinity," and "Pleasure and Pain!" This essay is little more than a prose elaboration of what is implicit in "The Testimony of the Suns."

With the publication of *The Testimony of the Suns and Other Poems* in 1903, Sterling was established locally as a poet. At about the same time he and Jack London began an intense friendship which became legendary on the West Coast. In that same year London's *The Call of the Wild* swept the country. Both Sterling and London were flamboyant public figures, and their chosen roles complemented each other instead of conflicting. London was the raw, vital proletarian who had sailed the seas and prospected for gold in the Klondike. Sterling was the suave, sensitive poet whose profile was always being compared to Dante's. Joseph Noel's *Footloose in Arcadia* (1940) contains a colorful if rather hyperbolic history of their explorations of every variety of San Francisco night life. Soon Sterling was being called "Greek" by his new friend and was calling him "Wolf." Each had the highest regard for the other's work. Sterling served as a model for Mark Hall in London's *The Valley of the Moon* (1913) and, more importantly, for Russ Brissenden, the brilliant, cynical poet in *Martin Eden* (1909).

By 1904 Sterling had completed his second long poem, "A Wine of Wizardry," which Bierce succeeded in placing in *Cosmopolitan* three years later. In one sense this poem was sixty years ahead of its time, for its dissolving imagery is almost certainly psychedelically inspired—probably by the hashish Sterling shared with London. The poem is little more than a series of shifting scenes visited by the personification Fancy after the narrator sips a mysterious wine by the sea. "A Wine of Wizardry" is a phantasmagoria of the supernatural and terrifying, filled with grotesque imagery, violent colors, and roaring sounds. Bierce was especially impressed by the lines "The blue-eyed vampire, sated at her feast,/Smiles bloodily against the leprous moon." When the poem appeared in *Cosmopolitan* in September 1907, Bierce, in the same issue, touted Sterling's new work as "a very great poem" and proclaimed him the greatest living American poet. Other critics, not surprisingly, disagreed, and Bierce demolished them with gusto in the December issue, using the rough-and-ready techniques he had learned in San Francisco journalism. For the first time Sterling was a national celebrity.

Sterling's reputation was always greatest in San Francisco. He remained with the San Francisco publisher A. M. Robertson until Holt brought out his *Selected Poems* in 1923, but after 1907 his poems frequently appeared in national magazines such as *Century* and *Harper's*. In 1912 his "Ode on the Centenary of the Birth of Robert Browing" won one of two second prizes in the *Lyric Year* poetry contest—a contest that is now chiefly remembered because Edna St. Vincent Millay's "Renascence" was relegated to a prizeless fourth place. Yet, as Sterling was eventually forced to realize, it was only in California that he was generally accepted as a great poet.

The years between 1905 and 1914, when Sterling reigned as "King of Carmel," were probably the happiest of his life. In Carmel, amid splendid scenery, he could devote himself to poetry and enjoy the company of novelists Mary Austin, Harry Leon Wilson, James Hopper, and Grace McGowan Cooke. Other residents included photographer Arnold Genthe and painter Xavier Martínez. Among visitors and short-term residents were Witter Bynner, Bliss Carman, William Rose Benét, Upton Sinclair, and Sinclair Lewis. Sterling, a prodigious writer of letters, corresponded voluminously with other authors, many of whom he met at Carmel. Some exchanges, like that with Witter Bynner, continued for little more than a year. Others, like that

Jack London and George Sterling (courtesy of the Bancroft Library, University of California, Berkeley)

Sterling preparing for the production of his play The Triumph of Bohemia *at the Bohemian Club Grove in 1907 (courtesy of the Bancroft Library, University of California, Berkeley)*

with Upton Sinclair, continued throughout Sterling's life and were of major importance to both parties. Sterling rejoiced in Carmel's swimming, hunting, and hiking, and he loved to preside over the evening abalone feasts, where guests improvised verses for "The Abalone Song" while tenderizing their dinners with rocks to the rhythm of the chant. Many of the poems collected in *A Wine of Wizardry and Other Poems* (1909), *The House of Orchids and Other Poems* (1911), and *Beyond the Breakers and Other Poems* (1914) reflect Sterling's fascination with Carmel scenery, but they are not his most impressive work.

By 1914 Sterling was beset by a number of problems which made him decide to leave Carmel. After years of quarreling, he and his wife were

divorced. At the same time the Havens financial empire crumbled, and Sterling, who had always been a heavy drinker, was becoming an alcoholic. Sterling, who had given his wife all his property other than rights to his poetry, rather Quixotically decided to move to New York, where he intended to live very simply on what money he could earn from the sale of his poems. The result was a year of rejection by editors, periods of actual hunger, and finally the humiliating loans of small sums to enable him to return to San Francisco. Sterling, who had not realized how rapidly tastes in poetry were changing, had seriously misjudged his standing as a poet, and he increasingly found himself ignored.

Together

We enter not to happiness through pride,
And though our grief be lonely, still our joy
Another's heart shall foster, not destroy.
Man is not man save she be at his side,
The woman, she whose lamp is truer guide
Than witching moon or cold, estranging
        star —
A beacon where the troubled tempests are,
At midnight and the changing of the tide.

As hand in hand they passed from Paradise —
Our primal parents — so must we return,
The man and woman, ~~hand in hand~~
        equal in their fate,
        ~~once more~~
Whom tears and time have patiently made wise,
O year for which the years forever yearn,
When two, not one, stand at the shining
        Gate
        ~~door~~ !

                                George Sterling

Manuscript (courtesy of the Lilly Library, Indiana University)

Edwin Markham, William Gibbs McAdoo, and George Sterling (photograph by Underwood & Underwood)

The pain and confusion from this failure were compounded by a series of personal losses. The disappearance of Bierce in Mexico in 1914, Jack London's death in 1916, and the suicide of his former wife in 1918 marked the end of his close human contacts. Superficially he was frenetically gregarious, always ready for foot races at dawn after all-night parties; but for all his popularity he was essentially isolated.

One great consolation was that in San Francisco he reigned supreme. When San Francisco held the Panama-Pacific International Exposition in 1915 to celebrate the opening of the Panama Canal, a Gate of the Four Seasons was erected, with the name of a poet on each of the four pillars. Sterling found himself in company with Goethe, Dante, and Shakespeare. (When Harriet Monroe saw the exposition, she was inspired to a savage attack on Sterling in *Poetry*, March 1916.) Sterling enjoyed a free room at San Francisco's Bohemian Club, which he had joined in his days of prosperity, and he was frequently asked to serve as guide and host to visiting literary dignitaries.

The years immediately after his return to San Francisco marked the nadir of Sterling's poetry. Many of the poems in *The Caged Eagle and Other Poems* (1916) and all of the poems in *The Binding of the Beast and Other War Verse* (1917) are war poems. Even good poets have written poems in the heat of war fever which seemed embarrassingly bad once the war fever had passed. For Sterling, who had been hysterically pro-Ally since 1914 and whose natural tendency was toward the rhetorical, the result was disastrous. In 1919, however, Sterling published the first version of *Lilith: A Dramatic Poem*, which may be considered his finest work. This poem was the product of long gestation and careful reworking. References to it appeared in his letters ten years before its publication, and the poem underwent still further revision before the Macmillan edition was published in 1926. Lilith, a hypnotically beautiful servant of the devil, is at once deceiver and bringer of unwelcome truth. In pursuit of her, the medieval hero, Tancred, is tricked into betraying (and made to realize that he is capable of betraying) his father, his friend, and his sweetheart. The entire poem is fraught with moon imagery and contains the mixture of the jeweled and the demonic which Sterling had conjured up (but controlled far less effectively) in "A Wine of Wizardry." The poet, justifiably, seems to have been prouder of *Lilith* than of any of his other work.

Sterling, who had always been generous, was especially helpful to younger writers during the last years of his life. He praised the as yet nearly unknown Robinson Jeffers and provided Carey McWilliams with information for a biography of Ambrose Bierce. With less success, he tried to arrange financial assistance for Michael Gold and access to the New York literary world for Whit Burnett. Perhaps only one writer whom Sterling befriended can legitimately be called his disciple. Clark Ashton Smith's science-fantasy stories reveal the influence of Sterling in style, imagery, subject matter, and philosophical attitude. Ironically, these stories were written after Sterling was dead, and the volumes of Smith's poetry which Sterling praised so highly are now seldom read.

During the 1920s Sterling corresponded frequently with both H. L. Mencken and Theodore Dreiser, and his poems often appeared in Mencken's *Smart Set*. In the last years of his life he turned to prose writing. In Mencken's *American Mercury* he published reminiscences of Ambrose Bierce (September 1926) and Joaquin Miller (February 1926). Increasingly, however, he found himself publishing in poetically conservative small magazines such as *American Parade*. Beset by poverty, alcoholism, and failing health, Sterling took cyanide in his room at the Bohemian Club in 1926. Although he still had fervid admirers at the time of his death, the world had passed him by.

Bibliography:
Cecil Johnson, *A Bibliography of the Writings of George Sterling* (San Francisco: Windsor Press, 1931).

References:
Dalton H. Gross, "George Sterling: King of Carmel," *American Book Collector,* 21 (October 1970): 8-15;

Gross, "The Letters of George Sterling," Ph.D. dissertation, Southern Illinois University, 1968;

Joseph Noel, *Footloose in Arcadia: A Personal Record of Jack London, George Sterling, Ambrose Bierce* (New York: Carrick & Evans, 1940);

Franklin D. Walker, *The Seacoast of Bohemia* (Santa Barbara: Peregrine Smith, 1973).

Papers:
Sterling's papers are widely scattered. The most important collections are at the Henry E. Huntington Library in San Marino, California, which has Sterling's correspondence with Jack London and many miscellaneous manuscripts; the Bancroft Library of the University of California at Berkeley, which has a large collection of Sterling's letters; the Lilly Library of Indiana University, which has letters to Upton Sinclair, to Mary Craig Kimbrough (later Mrs. Upton Sinclair), and many manuscripts; and the Berg Collection of the New York Public Library, which has Sterling's letters to Ambrose Bierce and a number of manuscripts.

Wallace Stevens

Joseph Miller

BIRTH: Reading, Pennsylvania, 2 October 1879, to Garrett Barcalow and Margaretha Catharine Zeller Stevens.

EDUCATION: Harvard College, 1897-1900; LL.B., New York Law School, 1903.

MARRIAGE: 21 September 1909 to Elsie Viola Kachel; daughter: Holly Bright.

AWARDS AND HONORS: Levinson Prize (*Poetry* magazine), 1920; *Nation* Poetry Prize, 1936; elected to the National Institute of Arts and Letters, 1946; Harriet Monroe Poetry Award, 1946; Litt.D., Wesleyan University, 1947; Bollingen Prize in Poetry, 1950; Poetry Society of America Gold Medal, 1951; National Book Award for *The Auroras of Autumn*, 1951; Litt.D., Bard College, 1951; Litt.D., Harvard University, 1951; Litt.D., Mount Holyoke College,

1952; Litt.D., Columbia University, 1952; National Book Award for *The Collected Poems of Wallace Stevens*, 1955; Pulitzer Prize for *The Collected Poems of Wallace Stevens*, 1955; L.H.D., Hartt College of Music (Hartford), 1955; Litt.D., Yale University, 1955.

DEATH: Hartford, Connecticut, 2 August 1955.

BOOKS: *Harmonium* (New York: Knopf, 1923; revised and enlarged, 1931);
Ideas of Order (New York: Alcestis Press, 1935; enlarged edition, New York & London: Knopf, 1936);
Owl's Clover (New York: Alcestis Press, 1936);
The Man with the Blue Guitar & Other Poems (New York & London: Knopf, 1937);
Parts of a World (New York: Knopf, 1942);
Notes toward a Supreme Fiction (Cummington, Mass.: Cummington Press, 1942);
Esthétique du Mal (Cummington, Mass.: Cummington Press, 1945);
Transport to Summer (New York: Knopf, 1947);
Three Academic Pieces: The Realm of Resemblance, Someone Puts a Pineapple Together, Of Ideal Time and Choice (Cummington, Mass.: Cummington Press, 1947);
A Primitive like an Orb (New York: Gotham Book Mart, 1948);
The Auroras of Autumn (New York: Knopf, 1950);
The Relations between Poetry and Painting (New York: Museum of Modern Art, 1951);
The Necessary Angel: Essays on Reality and the Imagination (New York: Knopf, 1951; London: Faber & Faber, 1960);
Selected Poems (London: Fortune Press, 1952);
Selected Poems (London: Faber & Faber, 1953);
Raoul Dufy: A Note (New York: Pierre Berès, 1953);
Mattino Domenicale, English and Italian, with Italian translations by Renato Poggioli (Turin: Guilio Einaudi, 1954);
Thirteen Ways of Looking at a Blackbird (New York: Knopf, 1954);
The Collected Poems of Wallace Stevens (New York: Knopf, 1954; London: Faber & Faber, 1955);
Opus Posthumous, edited by Samuel French Morse (New York: Knopf, 1957; London: Faber & Faber, 1959);
Poems by Wallace Stevens, edited by Morse (New York: Vintage, 1959);
The Palm at the End of the Mind: Selected Poems and a Play by Wallace Stevens, edited by Holly Stevens (New York: Knopf, 1971).

In "Of Modern Poetry," a poem first published in 1942, Wallace Stevens sets forth the dilemma of the poet in the modern world:

> The poem of the mind in the act of finding
> What will suffice. It has not always had
> To find: the scene was set; it repeated what
> Was in the script.
> > Then the theatre was changed
> To something else. Its past was a souvenir.

Until sometime in the eighteenth century, around the time of the French Revolution perhaps, poets lived in a world where the existence of absolute values and of a providential order in the cosmos was all but universally accepted. It was only with the romantics that the individual imagination was invoked as a sanction for the values and order that men needed to live their lives, when the world had ceased to supply such a sanction. Such is the real distinction between the modern poet and his predecessors. In his own life Stevens himself experienced this loss of faith in a providential order; he took up the challenge of the poet in the modern world; and the success he had in "finding what will

Wallace Stevens, 1948 (photograph by Sylvia Salmi; courtesy of the Henry E. Huntington Library and Art Gallery)

suffice," which is considerable, is the measure of his greatness.

Wallace Stevens was born in Reading, Pennsylvania, on 2 October 1879, the second of five children, to Garrett Barcalow Stevens and his wife Margaretha Catharine Zeller, known as Kate. The family were prominent members of the Dutch Reformed church, and the three Stevens boys attended elementary schools run by the Evangelical Lutheran church. There is a photograph, circa 1893, of Wallace Stevens in a cassock and surplice, but before long, presumably during his years at Harvard, he became an agnostic, and such he remained up to the last days of his life. In lieu of faith in a supreme being and a providential order determined from on high, Stevens sought to discover a transcendent beauty and a transcendent wisdom in the world itself by means of a union of the imagination and external reality, in what he called a "Supreme Fiction," which is to be found in poetry. In his "Adagia," a collection of aphorisms on poetry and imagination that was included in *Opus Posthumous* (1957), he wrote "The relation of art to life is of the first importance especially in a skeptical age since, in the absence of a belief in God, the mind turns to its own creations and examines them, not alone from the aesthetic point of view, but for what they reveal, for what they validate and invalidate, for the support they give." One of his late poems, "The Bed of Old John Zeller," contrasts the religion of his grandfather ("the habit of wishing") with Stevens's practice of poetry: "It is easy to wish for another structure/Of ideas and to say as usual that there must be/Other ghostly sequences and, it would be, luminous/Sequences. . . ./It is difficult to evade/That habit of wishing and to accept the structure/Of things as the structure of ideas." This spiritual quest, this difficult, skeptical acceptance of the structure of things as the structure of ideas, is the abiding theme of Wallace Stevens's life and work. It amounts ultimately to nothing less than a rediscovery of a sustaining faith through the imagination.

Garrett Barcalow Stevens was a prominent lawyer in Reading, and the family led a comfortable bourgeois life. Kate Zeller Stevens had been a schoolteacher in Reading before her marriage. Of his home life Wallace Stevens wrote later: "We were all great readers, and the old man used to delight in retiring to the room he called the library on a Sunday afternoon to read a five- or six-hundred page novel. The library was no real institution, you understand; just a room with some books where you could go and be quiet. My mother just kept

house and ran the family. When I was younger I always used to think that I got my practical side from my father, and my imagination from my mother." Holly Stevens, the poet's daughter, recalling her childhood in Hartford, says, "As I grew up our house was quiet too, but Sunday afternoons became devoted to listening to the New York Philharmonic orchestra concerts on the radio, and Saturday afternoons to opera, either on the radio or on records. At other times we read, and my mother 'just kept house' and worked in the garden or played the piano. Like his father before him, mine did not entertain business associates at home." Wallace Stevens was all his life an intensely private man, and this quiet, private, daily life is the subject of such poems as "The House was Quiet and the

The poet's birthplace, 323 North Fifth Street, Reading, Pennsylvania

The poet's parents, Garrett Barcalow and Margaretha Catharine Zeller Stevens (courtesy of the Henry E. Huntington Library and Art Gallery)

The Stevens children: Elizabeth, Garrett Barcalow, Jr., Mary Katharine, Wallace, and John Bergen (courtesy of the Henry E. Huntington Library and Art Gallery)

World was Calm," "Large Red Man Reading," and "A Quiet Normal Life" and is implicit in many others. "Poetry is a response to the daily necessity of getting the world right," he wrote in "Adagia"; and also: "Wine and music are not good until afternoon. But poetry is like prayer in that it is most effective in solitude and in the times of solitude as, for example, in the earliest morning."

Shortly before his thirteenth birthday Stevens was enrolled at Reading Boys' High School, where he followed the classical curriculum, which comprised the study of Greek and Latin languages and history, science, and mathematics, as well as English grammar and composition, and the English and American classics. He was an honor-roll student, a reporter for the student newspaper, and a prize-winning orator. One of his high school classmates later said that "at high school Wallace was a whimsical, unpredictable young enthusiast, who lampooned Dido's tear-stained adventures in the cave, or wrote enigmatic couplets to gazelles."

In September 1897 Wallace Stevens went to Harvard, where he studied for three years as a special student, living at 54 Garden Street in Cambridge, in a rooming house run by three spinster sisters. One of his fellow inhabitants of this rooming house later wrote of him: "I recall especially his bursting out of his room to recite a new combination of words or a new metaphor that he had just invented, and to share his delight which was infectious." Later Stevens wrote that his "first year away from home, in Cambridge, made an enormous difference in everything." For one thing he was writing poetry, and his first known published poem, "Autumn," appeared that year in the Reading Boys' High School magazine the *Red and Black*. He was also studying diligently, primarily languages and literature, and with instructors of a high caliber, such as Charles Townsend Copeland, whom he later counted among his friends, and Barrett Wendell, whose lecture "Elegance" at the Lowell Institute would certainly have interested the young Stevens. And it was at Harvard that he came to know George Santayana, whose aesthetic philosophy was to have a considerable influence upon his own poetic theory.

In his second year at Harvard Stevens began to keep a journal, which, edited with a commentary by his daughter, is now the principal source of information about his early life and thought. In this journal he recorded daily activities, notes on his reading, poems in various stages of revision, and some extensive observations or meditations upon

nature at particular times and places, which read like prose poems and often bear a resemblance to poems he wrote much later in his life. His early poems are more full of echoes of John Keats and Percy Bysshe Shelley than observations of nature, but even when they are sentimental and derivative and sprinkled with archaic poeticisms, they are technically quite accomplished. The first of Stevens's poems to appear in the *Harvard Advocate* was in the 28 November 1898 issue, and it was followed by others over the next two years in that magazine and in the *Harvard Monthly*. In the spring of 1899 he was appointed a staff member and subsequently became a member of the editorial board of the *Harvard Advocate*, for which he wrote stories and sketches as well as poems. A contemporary colleague on the *Advocate* staff has described Stevens the student editor as "a large, handsome, healthy, robust, amiable person, with light curly hair and the most friendly of smiles and dispositions . . . frank and amusing . . . modest, almost diffident, and very tolerant and kindly towards, alike, his col-

Wallace Stevens, circa 1893 (courtesy of Holly Stevens)

The Harvard Advocate *staff for 1899; Stevens is standing at the far right (courtesy of Harvard University Archives).*

leagues and contributors of manuscripts." In the second semester of his third year Stevens was elected president of the *Harvard Advocate* and took on the task of writing editorials on a wide range of campus activities. For the first issue under his direction, dated 10 March 1900, he wrote three editorials, a short story, and a poem. "You see," he said years later in an interview, "I was the editor of the magazine, and often one had to furnish much of the material himself." With such experience behind him it is not surprising that the young poet would try his hand at professional journalism.

Because as a special student he had never worked toward a degree and because his father was paying to keep Wallace's two brothers in university at the same time, Wallace Stevens left Cambridge for New York City in the middle of June 1900. There he applied for jobs at the offices of various newspapers and magazines, wrote some sample articles for the *New York Evening Post,* and at the end of the month accepted a position with the *New York Tribune,* to be paid "according to the space I fill." He filled enough space to make a modest living and even took a cut in pay in October when he

accepted a regular salary of fifteen dollars a week with a promise of an immediate raise for good work. As a reporter he covered the election campaigns and heard William Jennings Bryan deliver four speeches in three hours. But Stevens seems to have been neither greatly inspired by the work nor ambitious for success in the world of newspapers. "My work on the *Tribune* is dull as dull can be," he wrote in his journal (10 November 1900). "I'm too lazy to attempt anything outside—& the fact that I work two days a week . . . spoils whatever laziness hasn't made on her own." This statement does not mean that he wasted his time. He explored New York from top to bottom and made a special point of seeing the beauties of nature in this urban setting: the trees in Washington Square and the sunset over the Palisades. He studied New York like a text and wrote down his observations and reflections: for example, "West street, along the North River, is the most interesting street in the whole city to me. I like to walk up and down and see the stevedores and longshoremen lounging about in the sun. . . . The street is as cosmopolitan and republican as any in the world. It is the only one that

Cathedrals are not built along the sea;
The tender bells would jangle on the hoar
And iron winds; the graceful turrets war
With bitter storms the long night angrily;
And through the precious organ pipes would be
A low and constant murmur of the shore
That down those golden shafts would rudely pour
A mighty and a lasting melody.

And those who knelt within the gilded stalls
Would have vast outlook for their weary eyes;
There, they would see high shadows on the walls
From passing vessels in their fall and rise.
Through gaudy windows there would come too soon
The low and splendid rising of the moon.

Manuscript for a sonnet that, after its appearance in the May 1899 issue of the Harvard Monthly, *provoked Stevens's mentor George Santayana to respond with a sonnet titled "Cathedrals by the Sea" (by permission of the Henry E. Huntington Library and Art Gallery)*

Wallace Stevens, 1900 (photograph by Bachrach; courtesy of the Henry E. Huntington Library and Art Gallery)

leaves the memory full of pictures, of color and movement. Clattering trucks and drays, tinkling and bouncing horse-cars, hundreds of flags at mastheads, glimpses of the water between piers, ticket-brokers & restaurant piled on restaurant." And elsewhere: "New York is so big that a battle might go on at one end, and poets meditate sonnets at another. . . . Ate a big, juicy 'bifstek' chez l'Hotel Martin, ce soir. Mais je ne parle pas au garçon; j'eus trop de peur." Often Stevens spent his mornings reading poetry, and from time to time he wrote a poem himself. He attended concerts and plays as often as he could afford. He saw Sarah Bernhardt in Rostand's *L'Aiglon* and in *Hamlet,* and he went several times to see Ethel Barrymore as Mme. Trentoni in Clyde Fitch's *Captain Jinks of the Horse Marines* and was so charmed by her that he hurriedly wrote out a rough draft of a play to be called "Olivia: A Romantic Comedy."

It did not take long for this carefree way of life to pall. Stevens enjoyed New York—"this elec-

tric town which I adore"—but he also found himself lonely there, often depressed, and frustrated in his ambitions, which were as yet fairly vague. "I should be content to dream along to the end of my life—and opposing moralists be hanged," he had written in his journal while still at Harvard. "At the same time I should be quite as content to work and be practical—but I hate the conflict whether it 'avails' or not. I want my powers to be put to their fullest use—to be exhausted when I am done with them. On the other hand I do not want to have to make a petty struggle for existence—physical or literary. I must try not to be a dilettante—half dream, half deed. I must be all dream or all deed." The greatest influence in Stevens's life in favor of the deed rather than the dream was clearly his father, who since he had left home had been sending him letters full of fatherly advice rather in the style of Lord Chesterfield. In March of 1901, in the middle of writing "Olivia: A Romantic Comedy," Stevens went home to Reading for a brief visit and had "a good long talk with the old man in which he did most of the talking. . . . We talked about the law, which he has been urging me to take up. I hesitated—because this literary life, as it is called, is the one I always had as an ideal & I am not quite ready to give it up because it has not been all that I wanted it to be." A week later he noted in his journal, "I recently wrote to father suggesting that I should resign from the Tribune & spend my time writing. This morning I heard from him &, of course, found my suggestion torn to pieces. If I only had enough money to support myself I am afraid some of his tearing would be in vain. But he seems always to have reason on his side, confound him." He then made inquiries concerning the publishing business as a possible career, only to learn that the positions were chiefly clerical and paid low wages. Wallace Stevens seems to have been a fairly conventional young man, not heedless of his father's prudent advice, without the slightest taste for *la vie de bohème*—that "petty struggle for existence—physical or literary"—and, on 1 October 1901, he entered New York Law School.

Stevens attended New York Law School for the next two academic years, graduating on 10 June 1903. Then he worked for a year as a law clerk for the New York attorney W. G. Peckham, in whose offices he had clerked during his last year in law school and with whom he made an extensive camping trip in the remote Canadian Rockies in the summer of 1903. On 29 June 1904 he was admitted to the bar in New York State and began the long and difficult task of establishing himself as a successful

IX

Sonnet.

Explain my spirit - adding word to word,
As if that exposition gave delight.
Reveal me, lover, to myself more bright.
"You are a twilight, and a twilight bird."

Again! For all the untroubled senses stirred,
Conceived anew, like callow wings in flight,
Bearing desire toward an upper light.
"You are a twilight, and a twilight bird."

Burn in my shadows, Hesperus, my own,
And look upon me with triumphant fire.
Behold, how glorious the dark has grown!
My wings shall beat all night against your breast,
Heavy with music - feel them there aspire
Home to your heart, as to a hidden nest.

Page from a poetry notebook that Stevens kept in 1908 (by permission of the Henry E. Huntington Library and Art Gallery) insurance lawyer. After a short-lived law partnership with Lyman Ward, who had been a special student with Stevens at Harvard, he drifted in and out of three New York law firms before joining the New York branch of the American Bonding Company of Baltimore, the first insurance firm for which he worked, in January of 1908. This position gave Stevens the financial security he needed to propose marriage during the following Christmas holidays to Elsie Viola Kachel, whom he had met in Reading four years earlier. They were married in Reading on 21 September 1909, and the Stevenses lived at 441 West Twenty-first Street in New York for the next seven years. Stevens's father died in 1911, and his mother in 1912. In 1913 he was named a law officer at the New York office of the Fidelity and Deposit Company of Maryland, which had bought the American Bonding Company. The following year he was hired as a resident vice-president at the New York office of the Equitable Surety Company of St. Louis and remained there after the firm merged with the New England Casualty Company of Boston in 1915 to become the New England Equitable Insurance Company. When that company abolished his position in 1916, he joined the home-office staff of the Hartford Accident and Indemnity Company, where he remained to the end of his life, having become a vice-president in 1934. In May of 1916 Wallace and Elsie Stevens moved permanently to Hartford, Connecticut, where their daughter, Holly Bright Stevens, an only child, was born on 10 August 1924. His new position involved a good deal of travel for Stevens, all over the United States and occasionally to Canada, and it was on business that he made the first of several trips to Florida, in 1916.

Had Wallace Stevens been a different sort of person, the foregoing summary could easily be the end of the story. Many another young man has gone into the adult world of business and abandoned his halfhearted literary pretensions as so much youthful folly. Stevens himself gave up writing poetry for some ten years when he entered law school. "A good many years ago," he wrote a friend in 1937, "when I really was a poet in the sense that I was all imagination, and so on, I deliberately gave up writing poetry because, much as I love it, there were too many other things I wanted not to make an effort to have them. I wanted to do everything that one wants to do at that age: live in a village in France, in a hut in Morocco, or in a piano box at Key West. But I didn't like the idea of being bedeviled all the time about money and I didn't for a moment like the idea of poverty, so I went to work

like anybody else and kept at it for a good many years." He did not write any poems during his years as a struggling young lawyer, but it is apparent from Stevens's journal that he never ceased to be a poet "in the sense that I was all imagination," even while he was all business at the same time. For one thing, on his frequent business trips he made extensive notes on the places and people and views of nature that he saw, many of which are suggestive of details to be found in poems he wrote years later.

Furthermore, Stevens did not cut himself off from the literary and artistic community during those years which saw the arrival of international modernism in America, and nowhere was the atmosphere of revolt and experimentation in painting and literature livelier than in New York. He came to know many of the painters and writers who frequented Greenwich Village, among them William Carlos Williams, Marianne Moore, Alfred Kreymborg, and E. E. Cummings, and he took part in their projects and entertainments from time to time. The famous Armory Show of 1913, which introduced the works of the early modern masters to America, created a whirlwind of enthusiasm for new ideas in all the arts and was doubtless the origin of Stevens's lifelong avocation as a connoisseur and collector of pictures. This period also marks the beginning of Stevens's interest in the arts of China and Japan, in which he found the clarity and freshness that stimulated his imagination and heightened his perceptions of familiar things. He often visited the American Art Galleries, where Chinese and Japanese jades and porcelains were exhibited. He wrote: "The sole object of interest for me in such things is their beauty. Cucumber-green, camellia-leaf-green, apple-green etc. moonlight, blue, etc. ox-blood, chicken-blood, cherry, peachblow etc. etc. Oh! and mirror-black."

This orientalism was, in fact, a continuation of the same general enthusiasm for the Orient that had been running in and out of the arts of France and England for more than a hundred years: Chippendale chinoiserie, the exoticism of Eugène Delacroix, and the aestheticism of the French impressionists, of James McNeill Whistler, and of many other artists in the late nineteenth century. The litany of colors that Stevens found in the Oriental jades and porcelains signals his long interest in colors, the names of colors, and color symbolism. His reading in Oriental poetry is reflected in the haikulike stanzas of "Thirteen Ways of Looking at a Blackbird" (first published in the December 1917 issue of *Others*). He responded naturally to the ideas and techniques which the imagists had discovered in Japanese poetry, and the spirit of mild exoticism is never far from Stevens's own poetry, particularly in the early period. He liked the Chinese feeling for landscape—traditional, stylized, symbolic—and one can see, even in the titles, the affinity between many of Stevens's landscape poems—such as "The Evening Bell from a Distant Temple" and "Fine Weather after Storm at a Lonely Mountain Town"—and the seven traditional Chinese landscapes, which are meant to comprehend all landscapes.

Stevens could now see his undergraduate attempts at poetry in perspective, founded as they were upon antiquated English and American poetic models. Suddenly a whole new light was being shed on the art of poetry by the French symbolistes, the impressionist painters, and the arts of China and Japan; and Stevens found his interest in writing poetry revitalized. In August of 1913 he wrote his wife: "I have, in fact, been trying to get together a little collection of verses again; and although they are simple to read, when they're done, it's a deuce of a job (for me) to do them. Keep all this a secret. There is something absurd about all this writing of verses; but the truth is, it elates me and satisfies me to do it."

In 1914 two such collections of his verses appeared in little magazines, Stevens's first published poems since his last undergraduate poems had appeared in the *Harvard Advocate* in 1900. The first of these comprises ten poems published in the *Trend,* eight poems in the September 1914 issue under the title "Carnet de Voyage" and "Two Poems" in the November issue. All but four of these poems definitely date from no later than 1909, and none of them can be considered as anything more than juvenilia. But that same November in Harriet Monroe's *Poetry: A Magazine of Verse* Stevens published another four poems, part of a sequence of eleven poems to be entitled "Phases." These poems were all recent work, based on the theme of the European war. None of these poems was ever reprinted during the poet's lifetime, but they are written in the modern idiom, and it is here that Stevens's mature work, leading up to *Harmonium* (1923), properly begins.

The years 1914 and 1915 saw the beginning of a new period of intense creativity for Stevens as a poet, as if the images, influences, and inchoate ideas of fifteen years suddenly merged and came into focus. Two of Stevens's great early poems, the first of any sustained length, were both published in 1915: "Peter Quince at the Clavier" (*Others,* August 1915) and "Sunday Morning" (*Poetry,* November 1915). With remarkable speed he worked through and resolved a number of problems that his new style posed for him. What seemed to his contemporaries as mere affectation and obscurity

Elsie Stevens in Hartford's Elizabeth Park, circa 1916 (courtesy of Holly Stevens and the Henry E. Huntington Library and Art Gallery)

were for Stevens a way of escaping everything trite and vague that he now saw in the conventional nineteenth-century poetic diction. He sought a position that was both antirationalist and antirhetorical from which to grasp reality, things as they really are, and to put their essence into words. Stevens found inspiration for this effort in Stéphane Mallarmé and the other French symbolistes, and company and encouragement in the imagist movement. Early in 1913 Pound published his anthology *Des Imagistes*, with samples of verse by James Joyce, H. D. (Hilda Doolittle), William Carlos Williams, F. S. Flint, Ford Madox Hueffer, and Amy Lowell among others, and in March of that year, in *Poetry*, Ezra Pound (in an article attributed to F. S. Flint) spelled out three rules for imagists: "1. Direct treatment of the 'thing,' whether subjective or objective. 2. To use absolutely no word that did not contribute to the presentation. 3. As regarding rhythm: to compose in sequence of the musical phrase, not in sequence of a metronome." This movement could not fail to have a strong and lasting influence on Stevens, but it did not take long for him to recognize the banality of mere images and to see the possibilities of such images as symbols of larger things. A good example of Stevens's expanded use of imagism is "Six Significant Landscapes" (first published in *Others*, March 1916). Essentially a sequence of six imagist poems, it incorporates as well Stevens's Orientalism, his color symbolism, his antirationalist posture, and his idea of the imagination, the image-making faculty, as a means of contact with a reality beneath the surface of things. In "Six Significant Landscapes" "significant" is the operative word.

Imagism appealed to the exotic and aesthetic tastes of Stevens, and nowhere is his subtle play of images over the surface of a profound reality more evident than in "Peter Quince at the Clavier," the aesthete's poem *par excellence* and one of Stevens's most beguiling creations. As the title suggests, the mood is comic, Peter Quince being, of course, one of the literal-minded mechanicals in *A Midsummer Night's Dream*. The shape of the poem is that of a piece of baroque music, precisely balanced, decorated with trills and runs and harmonious rhymes, and its images are predominantly those of sound: cymbals, horns, tambourines, sighs, simperings, and other noises. The music of the clavier conjures up the story of Susanna and the Elders, a favorite subject of renaissance and baroque painters, and it is handled with an Oriental refinement of sensuality. The image of Susanna bathing, in her world of innocence and sensuous beauty, is no sooner

evoked than it is shattered, when the "simpering Byzantines" shine the lamp of reason on Susanna and reveal her and her shame. The fourth stanza of the poem is a reflection and recapitulation. The poet reflects that "Beauty is momentary in the mind," like music, "But in the flesh it is immortal"— the reverse of conventional wisdom. Beauty in the mind is a sterile abstraction, a mere image, but when it is embodied in the physical, conjured up by the sounds of the clavier, rousing the lust of the Elders, it then partakes of the eternal cycle of things, like the seasons in nature, and "Susanna's music" survives in her memory, and the memory of her, and "makes a constant sacrament of praise," by being a mysterious ritual of the union of permanence and change and of the spiritual in the physical.

"Susanna's music," physical beauty as a sacrament of praise, as a substitute for the sacraments of religion, inspired Stevens's great poem of the *Götterdämmerung*, "Sunday Morning." While this poem is thoroughly archaic and nostalgic in its style, it departs from the nineteenth-century tradition of poems on faith and doubt in that it sees the modern world's loss of faith in Christianity as no different from the loss of faith in Zeus, neither more nor less certain, neither more nor less calamitous. In his "Adagia" Stevens says, "The death of one god is the death of all." This is not to say that the death of God is not calamitous: it is the very calamitousness that gives "Sunday Morning" its profoundly elegiac tone.

The poem opens with a woman in a peignoir in a vivid scene full of color and light, scent and taste, warmth and freedom, and natural beauty: "Coffee and oranges in a sunny chair,/And the green freedom of a cockatoo/Upon a rug." But the woman cannot accept this beauty, because "she feels the dark/Encroachment of that old catastrophe," which is the old religion, whereby "The pungent oranges and bright, green wings/Seem things in some procession of the dead," because religion posits truth and beauty in the permanence of a supernatural world rather than in the ever-changing, ever-dying natural world where we live.

In stanzas two and three the meditative voice of the poet takes over. In a tentative, questioning way he develops his idea that the woman could find the same divinity within herself, that the things of earth are to be cherished in their state of constant flux, and that the break with the confinements of supernatural religion would be a liberation to her: "These are the measures destined for her soul." He sets Christianity in the larger context of man's history of mythmaking by comparing it to the worship of Jove, which is certainly dead. In the inevitable evolution of things men will see Christianity in the same light, and then earth shall "Seem all of paradise that we shall know."

Stanzas four and five each begin with a statement by the woman, followed by a meditation on the part of the poet as an answer to her. "She says, 'But in contentment I still feel/The need of some imperishable bliss.' " The poet replies directly that "Death is the mother of beauty." The only imperishable bliss is in the cycles of nature, in the woman's memory, and in her desire for a profounder contact with nature. This idea is developed further in stanzas seven and eight: the paradise of religion is seen as a colorless inhuman dream world, where

Elsie and Wallace Stevens, circa 1920 (courtesy of the Henry E. Huntington Library and Art Gallery)

rivers never reach the sea and ripe fruit never falls from the trees. By contrast the earth itself can be a source of bliss to those who recognize its permanence in changefulness, represented by the sun: "Their chant shall be a chant of paradise," and "They shall know well the heavenly fellowship/Of men that perish and of summer morn." Men will find themselves liberated, even glorified, in their new unbelief. As Stevens said in his essay "Two or Three Ideas" (in *The Necessary Angel*, 1951): "in an age of disbelief, when the gods have come to an end, when we think of them as the aesthetic projections of a time that has passed, men turn to a fundamental glory of their own and from that create a style of bearing themselves in reality. They create a new style of a new bearing in a new reality."

In the final stanza of "Sunday Morning" the poet brings the reader back from this tentative myth of an earthly paradise to the uncertain situation of the present. A voice from nowhere enters the poem and tells the woman that "The Tomb in Palestine/Is not the porch of spirits lingering./It is the grave of Jesus, where he lay." This proclamation removes Jesus from the realm of spirits, who do not change, and returns him to the realm of men, who do. It does not deny his immortality so much as to deny his transcendence over the world of change. Now he is as immortal as we are, neither more nor less, a member of "the heavenly fellowship/Of men that perish." And so the poem ends as a kind of hymn to Mutability, to Death as the mystical mother of Beauty.

As A. Walton Litz observes, "Sunday Morning" stands alone, different in both language and mood from the poems around it, like "an orphan in the larger context of *Harmonium*, and in the entire canon of Stevens' poetry," and it "belongs not to a personal tradition but to the major line of meditative religious verse, and we learn to read it by reading traditional English poetry, not by reading Wallace Stevens." Furthermore, he adds, "Sunday Morning" differs markedly from Stevens's later long poems in that he does not attempt to substitute any theory of the imagination or of poetry for the lost certainties of religion, and "by remaining skeptical and open the poem connects with the widest range of our personal and cultural experience." "Sunday Morning" has remained one of Stevens's most popular and widely anthologized poems.

In 1916, when the Stevenses moved to Hartford, Wallace Stevens kept up with his Greenwich Village literary friends, visiting them and attending their parties on his frequent trips to New York. They often found him shy, diffident, or aloof, but

The offices of the Hartford Fire Insurance Company and the Hartford Accident and Indemnity Company moved to this new building in 1921. Stevens's office was on the first floor, to the right of the pillars.

always agreeable and personally formidable, someone to be reckoned with. Even after the publication of his first book, *Harmonium,* in 1923, many literary people did not see Stevens as an outstanding poet but as merely one of many young modernist poets, most of whom are now totally forgotten. Because he was an insurance lawyer and not a professional man of letters, many people considered him a cultured dilettante and not a dedicated poet at all, but nothing could be further from the truth. Between mid 1916 and the end of 1917 he published about a poem a month in various little magazines, and by 1923 he had published nearly a hundred poems in less than ten years.

One of the New York activities that continued to interest Stevens, even after the move to Hartford, was the theater. A "new theater" had sprung up in New York, radically innovative, modernist, symbolist, and avant-garde, inspired by William Butler Yeats, Gordon Craig, and the Japanese Nō theater, among others. Stevens wrote three plays for this new theater. His first, *Three Travellers Watch a Sunrise,* was awarded the Players' Producing Company prize in May of 1916 for the best one-act play in verse and was published in *Poetry* in July of the

same year, but it was not produced until 1920. His two other plays, written for the Wisconsin Players in New York, were each performed only once, in October of 1917. *Carlos among the Candles* was published in *Poetry* the following December, but *Bowl, Cat and Broomstick* was not published in its entirety until 1969, when it appeared in the *Quarterly Review of Literature.* All three plays, being poetic rather than dramatic, were not successful on the stage, and Stevens soon lost interest in writing for the theater. "I gave up writing plays," he wrote years later, "because I had much less interest in dramatic poetry than elegiac poetry." Yet the plays are of interest. They are virtually without characters or action, but they are rich in ritual and symbol and full of witty language and aesthetic posturing. Carlos, the only figure in *Carlos among the Candles,* is "an eccentric pedant of about forty" and clearly an ironic persona for Stevens himself, who was soon to be forty when the play was written. "He speaks in a lively manner," the stage directions prescribe, "but is over-nice in sounding his words." Carlos pirouettes about the stage, flourishing a taper, lighting candles and blowing them out again, and with each candle he comments in an affected way upon the subtle feelings it inspires in him: "It is like ten green sparks of a rocket, oscillating in air," for example; or "It is like the diverging angles that follow nine leaves drifting in water, and that compose themselves brilliantly on the polished surface." Carlos is a dandy and clearly close kin to the excitable and dandified forty-year-old mock hero of "Le Monocle de Mon Oncle," which Stevens wrote the following year and published in the December 1918 issue of *Others*.

In the framework of *Harmonium*, "Le Monocle de Mon Oncle" is the perfect counterpart to "Sunday Morning." They are of roughly the same length, and both are set off in regular numbered stanzas, but, where "Sunday Morning" is an elegiac meditation, "Le Monocle de Mon Oncle" is high comedy. Witty and urbane, elegant and extravagant, it represents the pinnacle of Stevens's poetic virtuosity in his early manner. It is a monologue in the voice of "an eccentric pedant of about forty," a mercurial Pierrot figure, on the theme of love, language, and the "faith of forty." As an example of the influence of Jules Laforgue the poem has often been compared to T. S. Eliot's "The Love Song of J. Alfred Prufrock" (1917), and the hero of Stevens's poem is much like Prufrock but more of a dandy and a poet and less anxious, less downcast and disillusioned. Indeed he seems almost gay compared to Prufrock.

"Le Monocle de Mon Oncle" is a kaleidoscope of ironies and reversals, whimsies and mock sentiments. It teeters coyly between youth and old age, spring and autumn, melodrama and farce, the spiritual and the sexual, the sublime and the ridiculous. It is addressed vaguely to Love, which is everything from the "Mother of Heaven" to the "verve of earth," Eve and Venus, a loved-one or a lover, and, in a more extended sense, love as that saving contact with the reality inherent in things, which Stevens always associated with art and language and the power of the imagination. Language as the vehicle of love is as much the subject of this poem as any kind of attachment of one person for another. Hence the verbal fireworks: "Most venerable heart, the lustiest conceit/Is not too lusty for your broadening./I quiz all sounds, all thoughts, all everything/For the music and manner of the paladins/ To make oblation fit. Where shall I find/Bravura adequate to this great hymn?" The religious language in this stanza and throughout "Le Monocle de Mon Oncle" is never wholly ironic, and the great love in the poem would in a conventionally religious poet be called the love of God. The witty language is reminiscent of the verbal wrestling with

faith and doubt in the religious poetry of the metaphysical poets of the seventeenth century, while the language of "Sunday Morning" is closer to that of William Wordsworth and Matthew Arnold. The poet-voice in "Le Monocle de Mon Oncle" explicitly distinguishes himself from those "fops of fancy" who "in their poems leave/Memorabilia of the mystic spouts,/Spontaneously watering their gritty soils." He says, "I know no magic trees, no balmy boughs,/No silver-ruddy, gold-vermilion fruits." His love, that is, is not to be confused with the mystical madness of William Blake, nor with the fairy supernaturalism of Yeats, nor with the Christianity of Gerard Manley Hopkins. In the final stanza he says he is like a rabbi, a dark rabbi, when young, observing the nature of mankind, and "Like

Wallace Stevens, circa 1922 (courtesy of Holly Stevens and the Henry E. Huntington Library and Art Gallery)

The house at 735 Farmington Avenue in West Hartford, where the Stevenses lived from 1924 to 1932

a rose rabbi, later, I pursued,/And still pursue, the origin and course/Of love, but until now I never knew/That fluttering things have so distinct a shade." "The figure of the rabbi," Stevens wrote later, "has always been an exceedingly attractive one to me because it is the figure of a man devoted in the extreme to scholarship and at the same time to making some use of it for human purposes." While the character in the poem is, as Stevens said he had in mind, "simply a man fairly well along in life, looking back and talking in a more or less personal way about life," this "looking back and talking" is no idle reminiscence but an attempt to make some sense of his experience of forty years, of the new perspective on "the origin and course of love" that approaching age offers, and to make "some use of it for human purposes." The "looking back and talking" is nothing less than poetry, its source and substance; "the poet," Stevens wrote in his "Adagia," "is the priest of the invisible," and "God is a symbol for something that can as well take other forms, as, for example, the form of high poetry." The final stanza of "Le Monocle de Mon Oncle," like the final stanza of "Sunday Morning,"

brings the reader back to the ambiguity and uncertainty of the present situation, and the "fluttering things" which "have so distinct a shade" are not unlike the "casual flocks of pigeons" that "make/Ambiguous undulations as they sink,/Downward to darkness, on extended wings." The stoic resolution of the two poems is the same—that reality is to be found in the changefulness of things—but the tone of the two poems is so different they might almost be seen as mirror images of one another.

If "Sunday Morning" and "Le Monocle de Mon Oncle" are the side panels in the triptych of *Harmonium,* framed by the gilt and gems of the shorter poems, the centerpiece is "The Comedian as the Letter C." This first of Stevens's many long poems he wrote in 1922, at the time he was working with great doubt and dissatisfaction to put together his first volume of poetry, and it is a summary and recapitulation of his poetic career to date, together with a tentative prognosis for the future. He wrote it at about the same time that T. S. Eliot was writing *The Waste Land* (1922), and there are many similarities between the two poems—their autobiographical foundations and their moods of irony, wistfulness, and revulsion—but Stevens's poem is cast in the form of a picaresque narrative in the mock heroic vein, and its hero is himself a comedian.

Crispin as a character had his origins in the commedia del l'arte and made numerous appearances in various guises in the French theater of the seventeenth and eighteenth centuries. He is a valet, a saint, a jack-of-all-trades, a musician, a pedant, a knave, and a notorious poetaster. "The Comedian as the Letter C" is the story of his odyssey from Bordeaux to the Yucatan and eventually to Carolina, where he settles down and raises a family. Subsumed in this narrative are the story of European poetic traditions transplanted in America, the story of Stevens's poetic development up to 1922, and the story of an introspective Everyman in search of some adequate position vis-à-vis the outside world and the life around him. Stevens wrote

later of this poem, "The long and short of it is simply that I deliberately took the sort of life that millions of people live, without embellishing it except by the embellishments in which I was interested at the moment: words and sounds." He also said, "I suppose that I ought to confess that by the letter C I meant the sound of the letter C; what was in my mind was to play on that sound throughout the poem. While the sound of that letter has more or less variety, and includes, for instance, K and S, all its shades may be said to have a comic aspect. Consequently, the letter C is a comedian." Indeed, at a profound level it is language that is the hero of this poem. Much of the comedy of the piece arises from the contrast, as Stevens pointed out, between "the every-day plainness of the central figure and the plush, so to speak, of his stage."

In part one Crispin, an ordinary man and a jumble of conflicting identities that he has received

Wallace and Holly Stevens, circa 1925 (photograph by Katherine Lee Endero; courtesy of the Henry E. Huntington Library and Art Gallery)

from outside himself, like an actor, sets out on a sea voyage in pursuit of an adequate "mythology of self." He leaves behind him the conventional late romantic poetry and thought of the nineteenth century, "that century of wind," "a wordy, watery age," symbolized by the figure of Triton, a myth from which all true belief has vanished, leaving only "memorial gestures." He seeks a substitute myth within himself—"Crispin/became an introspective voyager"—and in the sea he finds a salty, wild, formless, inscrutable reality on which to project his new myth, "the veritable ding an sich, at last." "The last distortion of Romance/Forsook the insatiable egotist," and he finds all his old theatrical ruses "shattered by the large."

In part two Crispin arrives in Yucatan, only to be confronted by "the Maya sonneteers" and their poetic conventions, more inflated and more vulgar than those from which he fled. "But Crispin was too destitute to find/In any commonplace the sought-for aid./He was a man made vivid by the sea." What he does find to his liking in Yucatan, however, is a new material for poetry that is rich and ripe and brightly colored, lavish and extravagant. "The fabulous and its intrinsic verse/Came like two spirits parleying, adorned/In radiance from the Atlantic coign,/For Crispin and his quill to catechize." He lets himself go, to the point where he is in danger of turning Dadaist, of finding "a new reality in parrot-squawks," and he is chastened only by a sudden thunderstorm, which is as frightening as the fauna and flora had been seductive. Here is yet another new experience. Perhaps here is "the span/Of force, the quintessential fact, the note/Of Vulcan, that a valet seeks to own." Crispin is "studious of a self possessing him," like a comedian studying a new role.

Crispin leaves the Yucatan, in part three, to escape the "jostling festival" of the jungle and to seek a new austerity in a northern climate, where "The myrtle, if the myrtle ever bloomed,/Was like a glacial pink upon the air." "How many poems he denied himself/In his observant progress," like Stevens the young man. First he thinks, "Perhaps the Arctic moonlight really gave/The liaison, the blissful liaison,/Between himself and his environment," but directly that seems "Wrong as a divagation to Peking,/To him that postulated as his theme/The vulgar." Then Crispin thinks perhaps it is in the tension between the two elements, reality and the imagination, that the blissful liaison is to be found, and presently he finds himself going up a river in Carolina—a country somewhere between the arctic and the tropics—surrounded by spring and human

activity and "all the arrant stinks/That helped him round his rude aesthetic out."

Beginning with part four the poem falls somewhat in intensity, because the autobiographical allegory comes to an end, and Stevens proceeds to speculate about his own, and Crispin's, future. The poem begins with the note: "man is the intelligence of his soil," but Crispin the romantic has become a realist, having "gripped more closely the essential prose/As being, in a world so falsified,/The one integrity for him, . . ./To which all poems were incident," and so now he turns around and states that "his soil is man's intelligence." Crispin settles down and founds a colony. He expands his new philosophy into the social sphere and establishes a reign of realism, celebrating the trivial and quotidian. But, by expanding his ego into an entire colony, Crispin has become an old windbag. Now his "Commingled souvenirs and prophecies," "These bland excursions into time to come,/Related in Romance to backward flights,/However prodigal, however proud,/Contained in their afflatus the reproach/That first drove Crispin to his wandering." He declares that "All dreams are vexing. Let them be expunged."

In part five Crispin is discontented and rebellious, but ever contemptuous of "fugal requiems," of "a tragedian's testament," of projecting his own fate upon all men, because "For realist, what is is what should be." Enter "his duenna" to the rescue, who, like a fairy godmother, "brought/Her prismy blonde and clapped her in his hands." Now he is married and content, like Candide, to tend his own garden. Exit poetry. The quotidian, he finds, saps the philosopher out of a man, but "For all it takes it gives a humped return,/Exchequering from piebald fiscs unkeyed." This last line was Stevens's own favorite example of C as a comic letter, and it serves equally well as an example of the plush of the stage upstaging Crispin, precisely at the point where he abjures the world of art for the world of facts.

Instead of producing poems Crispin produces daughters, four of them, in part six, where the comedy takes on a riotous and slightly cruel aspect. Crispin, in his "return to social nature," suddenly finds his house overrun by "children nibbling at the sugared void," these "unbraided femes,/Green crammers of the green fruits of the world." There is a decided decline from the first daughter, "His goldenest demoiselle," who seems like an inhabitant "of a country of the capuchins,/So delicately blushed, so humbly eyed," to the fourth, who is "Mere blusteriness that gewgaws jollified,/All din

3

Parfait Martinique: coffee mousse, rum on top, a little cream on top of that.

Literature is the better part of life. To this it seems inevitably necessary to add provided life is the better part of literature.

Thought is an infection. In the case of certain thoughts it becomes an epidemic.

It is life that we are trying to get at in poetry

After one has abandoned a belief in god, poetry is that essence which takes its place as life's redemption.

Art, broadly, is the form of life or the sound or color of life. Considered as form (in the abstract) it is often indistinguishable from life itself.

The poet seems to confer his identity on the reader. It is easiest to recognize this when listening to music — I mean this sense of things: the transference.

Page from one of two notebooks of aphorisms that Stevens called "Adagia" and kept from about 1930 until his death (by permission of the Henry E. Huntington Library and Art Gallery) and gobble, blasphemously pink." When they grow up their love lives look distinctly sordid. Worst of all, one of them becomes "A pearly poetess, peaked for rhapsody." Crispin feels the same ambivalence toward his daughters that he felt toward the tropics. The poem ends at this point, without any resolution, but with a question: considering the daughters as poems, Crispin cannot know whether they are "Seraphic proclamations of the pure/Delivered with a deluging onwardness," or mere "after-shining flicks,/Illuminating, from a fancy gorged/By apparition, plain and common things,/ . . . proving what he proves/Is nothing." What, then, speaking of the relationship between the poet and his poems, "can all this matter since/The relation comes, benignly, to its end?" Perhaps these are understandable sentiments from a middle-aged businessman about to publish his first volume of poetry. The only answer he has to this question, which is not really an answer, is, "So may the relation of each man be clipped." And with that the poem is clipped.

Harmonium was published by Alfred A. Knopf in September of 1923, in an edition of 1,500 copies, and to celebrate the event Stevens took his wife the following month on a cruise to California via Havana and the Panama Canal, returning overland through New Mexico—their first extended vacation since their marriage in 1909. The sea and clouds in the Gulf of Tehuantepec occasioned one of Stevens's most beguiling poems, "Sea Surface Full of Clouds," which was first published in the July 1924 issue of the *Dial.* This poem, lush, meditative, and imagistic, full of color symbolism and ritualized repetition, has an undeniable power of enchantment, but in the final analysis it does not fulfill one's expectations. There is at the heart of the poem a vacuity, as if the poet strove with verbal pyrotechnics to excite an exhausted imagination. After writing it Stevens virtually gave up writing poetry for nearly a decade. His book received very little notice. In 1924 his first and only child was born, and the house grew noisy. "She babbles and plays with her hands and smiles like an angel," he wrote to Harriet Monroe. "Such experiences are a terrible blow to poor literature. And then there's the radio to blame, too." He devoted his energy to his work at the insurance company, and—"haphazard denouement"—he fell out of the habit of writing poetry. He wrote later that "One of the essential conditions to the writing of poetry is impetus. That is the reason for thinking that to be a poet at all one ought to be a poet constantly. . . . Writing poetry is a conscious activity. While poems

may very well occur, they had much better be caused." Stevens found himself in the same dilemma where he had left Crispin, unable to reconcile the world of the imagination to the exigencies of reality, and sapped by the quotidian—"now this thing and now that/Confined him, while it cosseted, condoned." When Knopf proposed a new expanded edition of *Harmonium* in 1931, Stevens had only fourteen poems to add, and all of them, with the exception of "Sea Surface Full of Clouds" and possibly three others, had been written before 1923.

"Thought tends to collect in pools," Stevens wrote in his "Adagia," and "It is not every day that the world arranges itself in a poem." When he did return seriously to writing, sometime in 1933, the new poems witness a remarkable advance in thought and feeling. Gone are the coruscating gauds of *Harmonium,* and in their place is a calmer and surer, if barer, diction. "A change of style is a change of subject," as one of the "Adagia" has it, and with this new diction came a new attitude on the part of the poet in his relationship to the world, to the absence of God and the inevitability of death, a new firmness and resolution, as indicated in the title of his next volume of poems, *Ideas of Order,* which was published in a limited edition by the Alcestis Press in 1935 and, with three new poems, by Knopf the following year.

The tone of the new volume is set by the opening poem in the Knopf edition, "Farewell to Florida," which was in fact the last written, too late to appear in the Alcestis Press edition. The poet renounces the tropical moon: "The moon/Is at the mast-head and the past is dead./Her mind will never speak to me again." He renounces the heat and color of the South, the "coraline sea" and "vivid blooms," to return to the North that is "leafless and lies in a wintry slime/Both of men and clouds. . . . To be free again, to return to the violent mind/ That is their mind, these men, and that will bind/ Me round." It is as if Crispin were once again leaving the squawking parrots and thunderstorms of Yucatan in search of "the blissful liaison,/Between himself and his environment," and "America was always north to him." Wallace Stevens is seeking in the poems of *Ideas of Order* to work beyond the impasse where he left Crispin in Carolina. There is certainly some success in his endeavor, and Stevens's own judgment on the volume was "that *Harmonium* was a better book than *Ideas of Order,* notwithstanding the fact that *Ideas of Order* probably contains a small group of poems better than anything in *Harmonium.*"

The house at 118 Westerly Terrace in Hartford that the Stevenses bought in 1932 (courtesy of Holly Stevens and the Henry E. Huntington Library and Art Gallery)

The poem in *Ideas of Order* most notable for its coldness and bleakness is "Like Decorations in a Nigger Cemetery." The title, Stevens said, "refers to the litter that one usually finds in a nigger cemetery and is a phrase used by Judge Powell last winter in Key West." He wrote in the same letter, to Morton Zabel of *Poetry* magazine: "It is very difficult for me to find the time to write poetry, and most of these have been written on the way to and from the office." The fifty separate parts of this poem are more like fifty individual poems, poetic *pensées*, jottings, images, focused on a central theme and arranged very loosely along the variations of that theme, much as Stevens customarily arranged the poems within any one volume. That theme is the autumn of middle age, the prospect of death, the absence of God, and the increasing chaos of the outside world. The poet insists upon these hard realities but stops short of despair in favor of a salvation to be found in the play between the private imagination and the realities of the present moment. There he finds meaning and order. Stanza three might be taken as a characteristic statement of the theme: "It was when the trees were leafless first in November/And their blackness became apparent, that one first/Knew the eccentric to be the base of design." Some of the stanzas are

more imagistic, more haikulike, than others, but on the whole they are more abstract than similar earlier exercises, such as "Thirteen Ways of Looking at a Blackbird," and some of them are utterly obscure, like the cryptic notes one might write to oneself on the way to the office.

By far the best-known poem in *Ideas of Order* is "The Idea of Order in Key West." It is set once again in Florida, but the tropics now are transformed by a new coolness and clarity. The tone of this poem is elegiac, like that of "Sunday Morning," and the language is simplicity itself. The theme is again the emergence of order out of chaos in the creation of a work of art, as a result of the poetic imagination responding to an outside reality. A girl is walking along the beach, singing of the sea, but she does not express the genius of the sea: "She sang beyond the genius of the sea." The sea is inchoate and inarticulate reality. "It may be that in all her phrases stirred/The grinding water and the gasping wind;/But it was she and not the sea we heard." She masters, orders, and renders meaningful "The meaningless plungings of water and the wind," "And when she sang, the sea,/Whatever self it had, became the self/That was her song, for she was the maker." As a result of hearing the girl's song, the poet and his companion, Ramon Fernandez, are left with a heightened sense of beauty and order in what they see around them. They are inspired by the "Blessed rage for order," which is the impetus behind all art. The poem amounts to no less than an apology for the artifice of art and a justification of Stevens's idea of a romantic realism: an expressiveness not of the physical world but of the imagination in contact with that world, the "blissful liaison." He wrote in his "Adagia" that "Reality is the spirit's true center," and "The ultimate value is reality," while at the same time "Realism is a corruption of reality."

After the publication of *Ideas of Order* Stevens became gradually better known as a poet, but the notices his books received were far from unanimously favorable. Critics such as Stanley Burnshaw and Geoffrey Grigson found much to object to in the dandified virtuosity of *Harmonium* and the serene aestheticism of *Ideas of Order,* in view of the hard realities of a world sunken in depression and threatened by the rise of fascism and the prospects of war. Stevens was shocked and offended by this criticism, feeling that his work spoke as strongly in favor of peace and order in the world as that of the leftist propagandists, and perhaps more eloquently. But the fact cannot be ignored that in the 1930s the Stevenses lived a life that was more than a little remote from poverty and social chaos. In 1932 they bought a very large, new, "colonial" house on a half-acre lot on Westerly Terrace in Hartford, and that same year Stevens could write to a friend that "Generally speaking, there seems to be a feeling in Hartford that things are going to grow better rather than worse." In 1934 he became a vice-president of the Hartford Accident and Indemnity Company, thereby securing firmly his position in the business world. As for his politics very little can be said, as he seems not to have had any strongly held or consistent political views. He was briefly an admirer of Mussolini, as were many other people, and he was by profession a capitalist, but it would be a gross distortion to attribute any fascist sympathies to his life or work. On the contrary, he could only be called a laissez-faire capitalist in the realm of art and the imagination, passionately a champion of individuality, freedom, and spontaneity, and disdainful of ideologies, regimentation, and vulgar materialism. Stevens did not turn a blind eye to the suffering in the world around him, but it cannot be denied that, like many artists, he was more self-absorbed than other men. In his "Adagia" he wrote, "Life is not people and scene but thought and feeling," and "The world is myself. Life is myself." For the Knopf edition of *Ideas of*

Order Stevens confronted his critics directly with a little manifesto on the dust jacket, in which he said, "The book is essentially a book of pure poetry. I believe that, in any society, the poet should be the exponent of the imagination of that society. *Ideas of Order* attempts to illustrate the role of the imagination in life, and particularly the role of the imagination in life at present. The more realistic life may be, the more it needs the stimulus of the imagination." For Stevens pure poetry served a social function by its very purity. In his "Adagia" he wrote: "Poetry is a purging of the world's poverty and change and evil and death. It is a present perfecting, a satisfaction in the irremediable poverty of life." And in "Mozart, 1935" he addressed the poet at the keyboard: "Be thou that wintry sound/ As of the great wind howling,/By which sorrow is released,/Dismissed, absolved/In a starry placating."

But Stevens could not comfortably leave the question there. He seems to have been seriously concerned with the true relationship of a private introspective poet and the world of politics and society, and seriously dismayed by the criticism of himself as an irrelevant aesthete. He set about immediately to write a sequence of five poems on this theme, each of them centered around the image of a statue standing in a public place. The statue functions generally as a symbol for art, "but not specifically a symbol for art," he wrote to Ronald Latimer; "its use has been somewhat broadened and, so far as I have defined it at all, it is a symbol for things as they are." Various characters appear in the poems, and each is defined by his particular relationship to the statue. The first of these poems, "The Old Woman and the Statue," was published in the Summer 1935 issue of the *Southern Review,* and the five together were published as *Owl's Clover* by Latimer's Alcestis Press in August of 1936. They are among the weakest of all Stevens's poems, written as they are in long verse paragraphs, full of loose syntax and flaccid rhetoric, utterly unlike the tight little stanzas in which he excelled. Stevens was immediately dissatisfied with *Owl's Clover* and began at once to cut whole sections out of it before including it the following year in *The Man with the Blue Guitar & Other Poems.* He eliminated it altogether from *The Collected Poems of Wallace Stevens* (1954), and the full Alcestis Press version was republished only in *Opus Posthumous* (1957).

The principal interest *Owl's Clover* has for readers today is as a contrast to "The Man with the Blue Guitar." On the dust jacket of *The Man with the Blue Guitar & Other Poems* Stevens once again

19

ne faut point croire que cette règle ne soit fondée que sur
la fantaisie de ceux qui l'ont faite. Il n'y a que le vrai-
semblable qui touche dans la tragédie".

         Racine, Préface, Bérénice, 1670.

Racine, too, was a tea drinker
         Edward Bunyard, The Epicure's Companion p348

"The aim of the serious dramatist is to invent a situation in which several characters reveal – in a way
which is spontaneous because it is produced by the
situation – the fundamental nature of their being
and their attitude to life. Now the poet is someone
who devotes his life to exactly such a process of
self-revelation as drama attempts to produce in
characters: his poems are speeches from the drama
of the time in which he's living. The dramatist defines in his characters the level at which their
feelings blend into poetry".

         Stephen Spender, Poetry And Expression-
ism. New Statesman & Nation, March 12, 1938

"It is less difficult for the philosopher than
for the artist to be in disagreement with his period.
There is little parallel between the two cases. The
one pours his spirit into a creative work, the other
ponders on the real with the understanding
mind. It is in the first case by depending

*Page from one of two commonplace notebooks that Stevens called "Sur Plusieurs Beaux Sujects" and kept from 1932 until 1953
(by permission of the Henry E. Huntington Library and Art Gallery)*

stated his intentions, this time drawing a distinction between *Owl's Clover* and the new poems: "The effect of *Owl's Clover* is to emphasize the opposition between things as they are and things imagined; in short, to isolate poetry. . . . This group deals with the incessant conjunctions between things as they are and things imagined. Although the blue guitar is a symbol of the imagination, it is used most often simply as a reference to the individuality of the poet, meaning by the poet any man of imagination."

The contrast in style between *Owl's Clover* and "The Man with the Blue Guitar" is even greater than the contrast in theme. "The Man with the Blue Guitar" consists of thirty-three separate exercises, variations on a central theme, written in tetrameter couplets, varying in length from four to eight couplets. The couplets are bright and musical, and the poems together move in a rhythm that is more musical than rhetorical. Within the poems there is a remarkable subtlety and playfulness, reflecting the play between reality and the imagination that Stevens is espousing. Both are "fluttering things" with "so distinct a shade," always changing and renewing one another. In poem thirty-two, for example, the poet says, "Nothing must stand/Between you and the shapes you take/When the crust of shape has been destroyed./You as you are? You are yourself./The blue guitar surprises you." Stevens sought most of all to avoid or to destroy that "crust of shape," whatever makes things static and dull and two-dimensional, be it religious conformity or social engineering or the poetics of literal-minded realism. In his "Adagia" he said, "Life is the elimination of what is dead."

Once Wallace Stevens had returned from the detour of *Owl's Clover* to the central path of his poetry in "The Man with the Blue Guitar," he seems to have discovered anew the "impetus" that is "one of the essential conditions to the writing of poetry," never to lose it again for the rest of his life. Between 1937 and 1942 he wrote all the poems that make up *Parts of a World*, which was published by Knopf in September of 1942, as well as what may be his greatest long poem, *Notes toward a Supreme Fiction*, which was published the following month in a limited edition by the Cummington Press and included five years later in *Transport to Summer* (1947). Many of the poems of this period display an increasing concentration on the theme of Stevens's poetic theory, leading up to the definitive poetic statement of that theory in *Notes toward a Supreme Fiction*. As a prelude to that poem it may be useful first to look briefly at some of Stevens's

prose works, in which he develops some of his ideas about poetry. The most important of his essays were written as public lectures and published in *The Necessary Angel* (1951), and the later lectures together with miscellaneous notes and reviews were included in the *Opus Posthumous* (1957).

The seven essays that Stevens collected in *The Necessary Angel*, which bears the subtitle *Essays on Reality and the Imagination,* were intended, he wrote in the introduction, "to disclose definitions of poetry" and "to be contributions to the theory of poetry and it is this and this alone that binds them together." "Obviously, they are not," he added, "the carefully organized notes of systematic study." Neither the book as a whole nor any of its parts can be understood as a philosophical investigation into metaphysics or aesthetics. On the contrary, the essays are more like prose poems or meditations on the theory of poetry. Most of Stevens's central ideas are to be found here, worked and reworked through an exuberance of images, quotations, and allusions, and served up in a form scarcely more straightforward than in the poems themselves. In "The Noble Rider and the Sound of Words," a lecture written during World War II and delivered in spring 1941, when "the pressure of reality"— that is, "the pressure of an external event or events on the consciousness to the exclusion of any power of contemplation"—was burdensome and the ignobility of so many things was painfully evident, Stevens wrote that nobility "is the imagination pressing back against the pressure of reality. It seems, in the last analysis, to have something to do with our self-preservation; and that, no doubt, is why the expression of it, the sound of its words, helps us to live our lives." "The Figure of the Youth as Virile Poet," a lecture delivered in summer 1943, can be read as a manifesto for the autonomy of the individual imagination as the only saving grace in a world of cold logic and poor facts. In "Three Academic Pieces," published separately in 1947, Stevens argued that the resemblances between things, which are perceived by the imagination, are a significant component of the structure of reality and added, "Poetry is a satisfying of the desire for resemblance. As the mere satisfying of a desire, it is pleasurable. But poetry if it did nothing but satisfy a desire would not rise above the level of many lesser things. Its singularity is that in the act of satisfying the desire for resemblance it touches the sense of reality, it enhances the sense of reality, heightens it, intensifies it. . . . It makes it brilliant." In "Imagination as Value," a lecture delivered in 1948, Stevens wrote: "The imagination is the power

Robert Frost and Wallace Stevens, 1935 (courtesy of the Henry E. Huntington Library and Art Gallery)

of the mind over the possibilities of things; . . . the imagination is the power that enables us to perceive the normal in the abnormal, the opposite of chaos in chaos"; and "the chief problems of any artist, as of any man, are the problems of the normal and . . . he needs, in order to solve them, everything that the imagination has to give." In "The Relations between Poetry and Painting," separately published in 1951, he wrote: "The paramount relation between poetry and painting today, between modern man and modern art is simply this: that in an age in which disbelief is so profoundly prevalent or, if not disbelief, indifference to questions of belief, poetry and painting, and the arts in general, are, in their measure, a compensation for what has been lost." He wrote in his "Adagia," "After one has abandoned a belief in God, poetry is that essence which takes its place as life's redemption." Few poets can ever have taken poetry so seriously. It is this faith in poetry, the embodiment of the imagination, as a means of salvation in a fallen world that informs *Notes toward a Supreme Fiction* and all of Stevens's subsequent poems.

Notes toward a Supreme Fiction is, like most of Stevens's long poems, a sequence of interrelated short poems, a perfect union of his lyric gift and his powers of sustained thought and feeling. It is a philosophical meditation somewhat in the manner of Wordsworth's *The Prelude* (1850), "a philosophical Poem, containing views of Man, Nature, and Society," as Wordsworth put it, and the views that Stevens's poem expresses on the equal and inseparable validity of objective reality and the individual imagination are surprisingly close to those developed originally by Wordsworth and Coleridge, who first established the position of the poet in an unstable and hostile world. In a 1940 letter Stevens wrote: "If one no longer believes in God (as truth), it is not possible merely to disbelieve; it becomes necessary to believe in something else. Logically, I ought to believe in essential imagination, but that has its difficulties. It is easier to believe in a thing created by the imagination." In "Asides on the Oboe," he added, "I say that one's final belief must be in a fiction. I think that the history of belief will show that it has always been in a fiction. Yet

Elsie and Wallace Stevens, circa 1938 (courtesy of Holly Stevens)

the statement seems a negation, or, rather, a paradox." That paradox is summed up in one of his "Adagia": "The final belief is to believe in a fiction, which you know to be a fiction, there being nothing else. The exquisite truth is to know that it is a fiction and that you believe in it willingly." This exquisite truth proceeds from the marriage of reality and the imagination, and such is the central theme of *Notes toward a Supreme Fiction.*

The long poem consists of thirty shorter poems, three sets of ten, plus a short prologue and a coda. The first section, "It Must Be Abstract," emphasizes the poet's belief that the supreme fiction is less a substitution of poetry for religion than a dissolution of the distinction between the two. It is not a new cultus, because it is abstract, that is, utterly mysterious, defying definition. Only a fiction that cannot be contained will continue to satisfy the powers of men's minds. In the second section, "It Must Change," Stevens returns to the theme of "Sunday Morning," that the vision of a

changeless reality is insipid, that poetry must "give a sense of the freshness or vividness of life." Poem eight, one of the wedding poems, says: "Then Ozymandias said the spouse, the bride/Is never naked. A fictive covering/Weaves always glistening from the heart and mind." Likewise Stevens takes his readers back to the dazzling language of *Harmonium* in this section to give them a taste of the volatility and playfulness in his philosophical argument, "To compound the imagination's Latin with/The lingua franca et jocundissima." In the third section, "It Must Give Pleasure," Stevens develops one of his deepest convictions, that "the purpose of poetry is to contribute to man's happiness," and be "a present perfecting, a satisfaction in the irremediable poverty of life." Pleasure, peace, order, and beauty are all attributes of the supreme fiction. It is important to remember, as is clear from the coda, that *Notes toward a Supreme Fiction* is a war poem, perhaps the greatest poem to come out of World War II. The pursuit of a supreme fiction is anything but an exercise in idle aestheticism. "It is a war that never ends," Stevens says; it is the pursuit of a sustaining faith: "How gladly with proper words the soldier dies,/If he must, or lives on the bread of faithful speech." It is the function of the poet to supply the "proper words" and the "faithful speech."

Although *Notes toward a Supreme Fiction* was published in a limited edition by the Cummington Press in October of 1942, the month after *Parts of a World* appeared, it was not available in a trade volume until it was included in *Transport to Summer* in 1947. There its placement at the end of that volume is somewhat misleading as to the chronology of the writing, but significant in that it emphasizes the absolute centrality of *Notes toward a Supreme Fiction* in the later poetry of Wallace Stevens. Stevens himself recognized its crucial place in his poetry and saw in it the governing idea of his life as a poet: the idea of a fiction that takes on the power to compel belief from the power of the poet's words in expressing it. But *Notes toward a Supreme Fiction* was not intended as a definitive statement of that idea. Stevens wrote to Henry Church, to whom the poem is dedicated: "It is only when you try to systematize the poems in *Notes* that you conclude that it is not the statement of a philosophic theory. A philosopher is never at rest unless he is systematizing; constructing a theory. But these are Notes; the nucleus of the matter is contained in the title. It is implicit in the title that there can be such a thing as a supreme fiction." All of Stevens's poems written after 1942 can be seen as

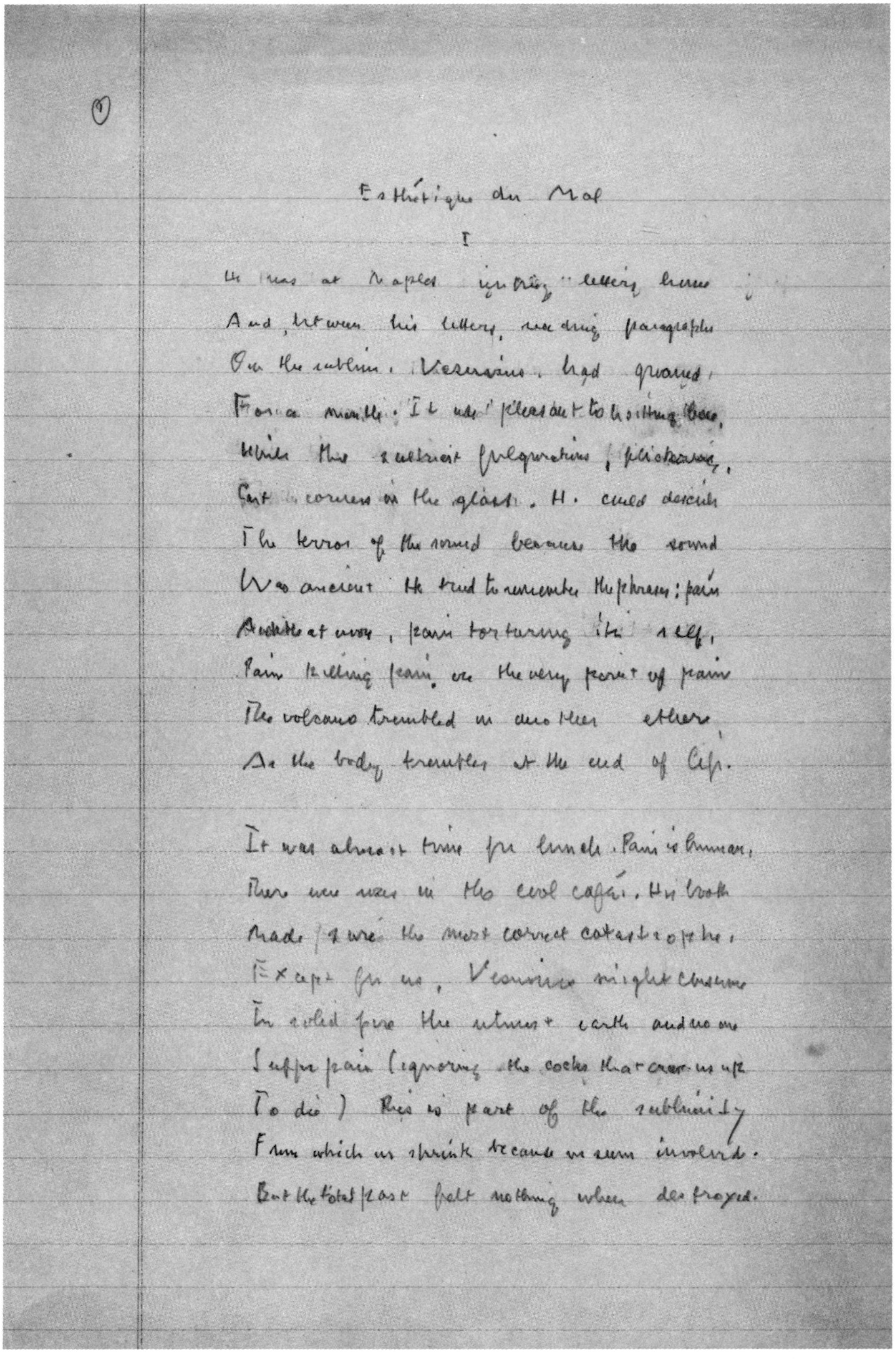

Esthétique du Mal

I

He was at Naples writing letters home
And, between his letters, reading paragraphs
On the sublime. Vesuvius had groaned
For a month. It was pleasant to be sitting there,
While the sultriest fulgurations, flickering,
Cast corners in the glass. He could describe
The terror of the sound because the sound
Was ancient. He tried to remember the phrases: pain
Audible at noon, pain torturing itself,
Pain killing pain on the very point of pain
The volcano trembled in another ether,
As the body trembles at the end of life.

It was almost time for lunch. Pain is human.
There were roses in the cool café. His book
Made sure of the most correct catastrophe.
Except for us, Vesuvius might consume
In solid fire the utmost earth and know
No pain (ignoring the cocks that crow us up
To die) This is a part of the sublimity
From which we shrink. Because we seem involved.
But the total past felt nothing when destroyed.

First page of an early draft for a long poem first published in 1945 (by permission of the Henry E. Huntington Library and Art Gallery)

Clarity in poetry is a precious characteristic but it should be a characteristic of the diction.

Poetic Exercises of 1948

Das Leben Als Glockenspiel. The world is a clock
The fire-flies are in the air, above the tree-tops,
On the night of June twelfth
In spite of a month of vicious weather.
It will thunder in July.
There is a continuing explosive g chimes

Reality is a cliché
From which we escape by metaphor
It is only au pays de la métaphore
Qu'in est poète.

The degrees of metaphor
The absolute object slightly turned
To a metaphor of the object.

Some objects are less susceptible to metaphor than
others. The whole world is less susceptible to
metaphor than a tea-cup is.

First page from a notebook Stevens kept in 1948 (by permission of the Henry E. Huntington Library and Art Gallery) further notes toward the same one supreme fiction, which contains diversity in its unity. There were to be no new themes, only new notes. To another friend Stevens wrote: "As I see the subject, it could occupy a school of rabbis for the next few generations. In trying to create something as valid as the idea of God has been, and for that matter remains, the first necessity seems to be breadth." The idea of a supreme fiction has the advantage of breadth, enough breadth that it could embrace every subject and every form of his subsequent poetry. In the same letter to Church Stevens said: "I have no idea of the form that a supreme fiction would take. The *Notes* start out with the idea that it would not take any form: that it would be abstract. Of course, in the long run, poetry would be the supreme fiction; the essence of poetry is change and the essence of change is that it gives pleasure." While Stevens recognized the firm foundation that *Notes toward a Supreme Fiction* provided him, he could not rest upon his achievement in that poem, because it is of the nature of the supreme fiction to require more notes, more poetry, more change, more pleasure. Far from resting on his laurels, Stevens as an old man produced an enormous amount of poetry of the highest quality, with a remarkable energy and consistency, with a new clarity and sense of urgency, at a time of life when most poets have long since concluded their major work.

Always a poet of the weather, Stevens now found new force in the symbolism of the seasons, as the titles of his next two volumes testify: *Transport to Summer* (1947) and *The Auroras of Autumn* (1950). The slow and beautiful transition from the lush ripeness of summer to the cold glory of autumn in New England is an apt description of this late poetry, in which Stevens is more than ever the anti-mythologizing, anti-autobiographical poet of the absolute, of the perfect idea, and of the marriage of the imagination and reality. He embraced the overwhelming movement of nature, which included his own inevitable death. His language was gradually stripped of its finery to a plainness that is virtually transparent. Of "An Ordinary Evening in New Haven," the major long poem in *The Auroras of Autumn,* Stevens wrote to a friend: "Here my interest is to try to get as close to the ordinary, the commonplace and the ugly as it is possible for a poet to get. It is not a question of grim reality but of plain reality. The object is of course to purge oneself of anything false." His purpose was to find in the most ordinary material the possibility of the sublime: section thirty of "An Ordinary Evening in New Haven" says, "The barrenness that appears is

an exposing." If the poetry became less ornate, it also became more abstract; yet the mode of this abstraction is not one of flat categorical statement, but one of endless qualification and hesitation. A man of profound intellectual humility, Stevens never abandoned his habit of resolute tentativeness. In section twenty-eight he writes:

> This endlessly elaborating poem
> Displays the theory of poetry,
> As the life of poetry. A more severe,
>
> More harassing master would extemporize
> Subtler, more urgent proof that the theory
> Of poetry is the theory of life,
>
> As it is, in the intricate evasions of as,
> In things seen and unseen, created from nothingness,
> The heavens, the hells, the worlds, the longed-for lands.

Wallace Stevens is no severe or harassing master. "An Ordinary Evening in New Haven" is also not held up as a definitive statement, but only as further "notes." He renounces any inclination toward finality and remains true to his idea of the changefulness of the supreme fiction, celebrating again the "ambiguous undulations" and the "fluttering things [that] have so distinct a shade." "An Ordinary Evening in New Haven" concludes with these lines:

> These are the edgings and inchings of final form,
> The swarming activities of the formulae
> Of statement, directly and indirectly getting at,
>
> Like an evening evoking the spectrum of violet,
> A philosopher practicing scales on his piano,
> A woman writing a note and tearing it up.
>
> It is not in the premise that reality
> Is a solid. It may be a shade that traverses
> A dust, a force that traverses a shade.

Of his *Notes toward a Supreme Fiction* Stevens wrote to Church: "The truth is that this ought to be one of only a number of books and that, if I had nothing else in the world to do except to sit on a fence and think about things, it would in fact be only one of a number of books. You have only to think about this a moment to see how extensible the idea is." The number of further books Stevens did produce on the theme of *Notes toward a Supreme Fiction* is remarkable, considering that he never came anywhere near having nothing else in the world to do but to sit on a fence and think about

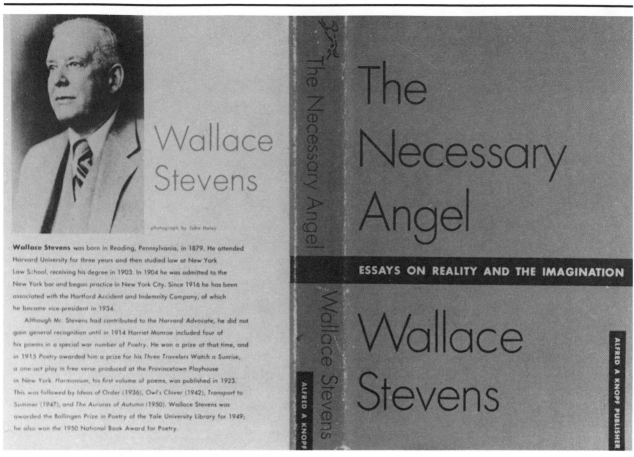

Wallace Stevens was born in Reading, Pennsylvania, in 1879. He attended Harvard University for three years and then studied law at New York Law School, receiving his degree in 1903. In 1904 he was admitted to the New York bar and began practice in New York City. Since 1916 he has been associated with the Hartford Accident and Indemnity Company, of which he became vice-president in 1934.

Although Mr. Stevens had contributed to the *Harvard Advocate*, he did not gain general recognition until in 1914 Harriet Monroe included four of his poems in a special war number of *Poetry*. He won a prize at that time, and in 1915 *Poetry* awarded him a prize for his *Three Travelers Watch a Sunrise*, a one-act play in free verse produced at the Provincetown Playhouse in New York. *Harmonium*, his first volume of poems, was published in 1923. This was followed by *Ideas of Order* (1936), *Owl's Clover* (1942), *Transport to Summer* (1947), and *The Auroras of Autumn* (1950). Wallace Stevens was awarded the Bollingen Prize in Poetry of the Yale University Library for 1949; he also won the 1950 National Book Award for Poetry.

The Necessary Angel

ESSAYS ON REALITY AND THE IMAGINATION

Wallace Stevens

Dust jacket for the essay collection that serves as Stevens's definitive statement of his poetic theory

things. On the contrary, he was a busy executive in a large insurance company, a position that he clung to jealously, even after he reached the mandatory retirement age of seventy. He welcomed the routine of the office, and he dreaded the isolation from the ordinary world of work that he envisaged in being forced to retire. He refused the invitation from Harvard to occupy the Charles Eliot Norton Chair in 1955 for fear that such a move would "precipitate the retirement that I want so much to put off." That such a prestigious position would be offered to him is indicative of the great esteem that his poetry had won for him in his last years. The literary prizes and honorary degrees flooded in, and yet Stevens walked across Elizabeth Park in Hartford to the office every day up to the time of his final illness, to the office where his colleagues, if they knew he was a poet at all, regarded his poetry as a hobby of no more importance than Winston Churchill's painting. One suspects that Stevens treasured the anonymity. He was a man capable to an unusual degree of enjoying the solitary interior life of the imagination to the exclusion

of action and society. One curious fact of his life is that Stevens, the supreme Francophile, never traveled to Europe. When young he was either too busy or too poor, and later, after wars and revolutions in Europe, he preferred the Europe of his imagination. For him France meant books and paintings (which he bought from his Paris bookseller sight unseen) and news from friends abroad and picture postcards and cherished scraps of recherché information. He wrote his bookseller: "I am one of the many people around the world who live from time to time in a Paris that has never existed and that is composed of the things that other people, primarily Parisians themselves, have said about Paris. That particular Paris communicates an interest in life that may be wholly fiction, but, if so, it is a precious fiction." One is reminded of the aesthete and Anglophile Des Esseintes, in Joris Karl Huysmans's *A Rebours* (1884), who says of his decision not to visit England: "I would be mad indeed to go and, by an awkward trip, lose those imperishable sensations." To a friend summering in France Stevens wrote in 1954: "We remain quietly at home, engaged in meditation and prayer and thoughts of Paris."

Only in 1954, on the occasion of his seventy-fifth birthday, did Wallace Stevens agree to the publication of *The Collected Poems of Wallace Stevens*. He included the twenty-five poems he had written since *The Auroras of Autumn* at the end of this book in a section titled "The Rock" because they were not enough to constitute a whole new volume. Among them are some of his most beautiful poems. In "To an Old Philosopher in Rome" Stevens pays his final homage to George Santayana. The figure of Ulysses in "The World as Meditation" is a symbol of the eternal return, Ulysses and not Ulysses, perhaps only the warmth of the sun, and Penelope "would talk a little to herself as she combed her hair,/Repeating his name with its patient syllables,/Never forgetting him that kept coming constantly so near." In "St. Armorer's Church from the Outside" the poet celebrates in his own "chapel of breath" that element of newness among the ruins, "In an air of freshness, clearness, greenness, blue-

ness,/That which is always beginning because it is part/Of that which is always beginning, over and over." In this poem and in "The Planet on the Table" Stevens takes the uncanny stance of looking at his own life as if from the outside. "Prologues to What is Possible" presents the image of a vivid dreamlike voyage in a boat at sea, toward something unknown and mysterious, perhaps frightening, but greatly to be desired. The feeling of all these poems is one of a rare tranquillity, resolution, and fulfillment.

Keeping in mind certain qualifications of the term, the most apt description of Stevens's late poetry is that it is religious. He wrote in a letter of 1951: "I am not an atheist although I do not believe today in the same God in whom I believed when I was a boy"; and to another correspondent the following year he wrote: "At my age it would be nice to be able to read more and think more and be myself more and to make up my mind about God, say, before it is too late, or at least before he makes up his mind about me." In his essay "A Collect of

Edward Weeks, Wallace Stevens, Newton Arvin, Brendan Gill, and Saxe Commins at the 1951 National Book Award ceremonies (courtesy of Publishers Weekly). *Stevens received the poetry award for* The Auroras of Autumn.

Philosophy" (written in 1951) he wrote: "The number of ways of passing between the traditional two fixed points of man's life, that is to say, of passing from the self to God, is fixed only by the limitations of space, which is limitless. . . . In the one poem that is unimpeachably divine, the poem of the ascent into heaven, it is possible to say that there can be no faults, since it is precisely the faults of life that this poem enables us to leave behind. If the idea of God is the ultimate poetic idea, then the idea of the ascent into heaven is only a little below it. . . . The poets of that theme find things on the way and what they find on the way very often interest as much as what they find in the end." Here Stevens is talking of the true belief in the one supreme fiction, and of true poetry as the many interesting things one finds along the way, expressed with the greatest possible exactness. He concludes that essay by praising the poetry, the fictive imagination, and the existential faith of the most abstract philosophers and theoretical physicists: "It is as if in a study of modern man we predicated the greatness of poetry as the final measure of his stature, as if his willingness to believe beyond belief was what had made him modern and was always certain to keep him so."

What Stevens hoped to achieve was "to believe beyond belief." He was a skeptical poet writing in a skeptical age but always with the purpose of finding a release from the bind of skepticism and a deliverance from the poverty and sadness of life. Stevens had come a long way from "Sunday Morning," but there was no sudden reversal or change of mind. It was rather a slow steady path determined by a steadfastness of purpose and a definite goal. This progress from *Harmonium* to "The Rock," from sensibility to meditation, is charted by Louis L. Martz in his essay "Wallace Stevens: The World as Meditation." In her book *Wallace Stevens: Imagination and Faith* Adalaide Kirby Morris argues that "as the Supreme Fiction overthrew the Supreme Being, it assumed many of the accoutrements of traditional religion," and these she traces in Stevens's family heritage, in his language and thought, in his "sacramental symbology," and in his ethics. But to call the "what is possible" of "Prologues to What is Possible" the God of Christianity would be misleading in the extreme, because it sidesteps the whole problem of belief beyond belief. To the end of his life Stevens trod a fine line between stating a metaphysical position and lapsing into romantic solipsism. He rejected vehemently the materialism and nihilism of the modern world and believed in the existence of an absolute, the

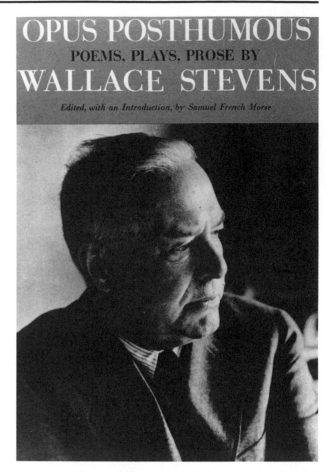

Dust jacket for the volume published two years after Stevens's death. Commenting on Stevens's prose, Elder Olson concluded that Stevens "was not a man who thought consecutively."

rock, the irreducible base of external reality, and in the power of man to know something of that reality through the operation of the creative imagination. What he knows in this way amounts to an intuition of the One, the Good, the True, and the Beautiful, at once immanent and transcendent, and the merest intimations of immortality and of a divine intelligence. In "Long and Sluggish Lines" Stevens says, "The life of the poem in the mind has not yet begun./You were not born yet when the trees were crystal/Nor are you now, in this wakefulness inside a sleep." In "Final Soliloquy of the Interior Paramour," perhaps Stevens's most straightforward statement of his final position, he says, "We feel the obscurity of an order, a whole,/ A knowledge, that which arranged the rendez-vous./Within its vital boundary, in the mind./We say God and the imagination are one. . . ." In this last line it is important not to ignore the "We say" and the final ellipses, which are Stevens's. For Stevens poetry could never be a vehicle for categorical statement, but always, by the nature of metaphorical language itself, only a vehicle for exploration and approximation. What goes beyond that simply goes beyond poetry, what Stevens finally decided when he came to make up his mind about God, before it was too late, is extraneous to his work as a poet. Although Holly Stevens denies that her father was received into the Roman Catholic church on his deathbed, there is a firsthand witness to that effect in Peter Brazeau's oral biography and several other statements by people who knew Stevens in his last days that serve to mitigate the seeming improbability of such a conversion.

After several months of illness, in and out of hospital, Wallace Stevens died of cancer on 2 August 1955. He is buried in the Cedar Hill Cemetery in Hartford. Since the time of his death the esteem in which Stevens is held by readers of poetry on both sides of the Atlantic has never ceased to increase. He was introduced late to the British, only with the first *Selected Poems* in 1952, but one of the first books on Stevens, that by British writer Frank Kermode in 1960, did much to redress the balance and remains a useful introduction to Stevens's life and work. Another very fine survey of Stevens's entire career, also from England, is Lucy Beckett's *Wallace Stevens* (1974). There can be little doubt now of the great success Stevens achieved as a poet for the modern world, in "finding what will suffice," to "help us live our lives."

Letters:
Letters of Wallace Stevens, edited by Holly Stevens (New York: Knopf, 1966).

Bibliographies:
Samuel French Morse, Jackson R. Bryer, and Joseph N. Riddel, *Wallace Stevens Checklist and Bibliography of Stevens Criticism* (Denver: Swallow, 1963);
Theodore L. Huguelet, *The Merrill Checklist of Wallace Stevens* (Columbus: Merrill, 1970);
J. M. Edelstein, *Wallace Stevens: A Descriptive Bibliography* (Pittsburgh: University of Pittsburgh Press, 1973);
"Current Bibliography," *Wallace Stevens Journal*, 1 (1977);
Louis L. Martz, "Manuscripts of Wallace Stevens," *Yale University Library Gazette*, 54 (October 1979): 51-67.

Biographies:
Samuel French Morse, *Wallace Stevens: Poetry as Life* (New York: Pegasus, 1970);

Holly Stevens, *Souvenirs and Prophecies: The Young Wallace Stevens* (New York: Knopf, 1977);
Peter Brazeau, *Parts of A World: Wallace Stevens Remembered: An Oral Biography* (New York: Random House, 1983);
Milton J. Bates, *Wallace Stevens: A Mythology of Self* (Berkeley: University of California Press, 1985);
Joan Richardson, *Wallace Stevens: The Early Years* (New York: Morrow, 1986).

References:
James Baird, *The Dome and the Rock: Structure in the Poetry of Wallace Stevens* (Baltimore: Johns Hopkins University Press, 1968);
Milton J. Bates, "Selecting One's Parents: Wallace Stevens and Some Early Influences," *Journal of Modern Literature*, 9 (May 1982): 183-208;
Bates, "Stevens in Love: The Woman Won, the Woman Lost," *ELH*, 48 (Spring 1981): 231-255;
Lucy Beckett, *Wallace Stevens* (Cambridge: Cambridge University Press, 1974);
Michel Benamou, "Beyond Emerald or Amethyst: Wallace Stevens and the French Tradition," *Dartmouth College Library Bulletin*, new series 4 (December 1961): 60-66;
Benamou, *Wallace Stevens and the Symbolist Imagination* (Princeton: Princeton University Press, 1972);
Richard Allen Blessing, *Wallace Stevens' "Whole Harmonium"* (Syracuse: Syracuse University Press, 1970);
Harold Bloom, "Wallace Stevens: Reduction to the First Idea," *Diacritics*, 6, no. 3 (1976): 48-57;
Bloom, *Wallace Stevens: The Poems of Our Climate* (Ithaca: Cornell University Press, 1977);
Marie Borroff, ed., *Wallace Stevens: A Collection of Critical Essays* (Englewood Cliffs, N.J.: Prentice-Hall, 1963);
Ashley Brown and Robert S. Haller, eds., *The Achievement of Wallace Stevens* (Philadelphia: Lippincott, 1962);
Merle E. Brown, *Wallace Stevens: The Poem as Act* (Detroit: Wayne State University Press, 1970);
William Burney, *Wallace Stevens* (New York: Twayne, 1968);
Robert Buttel, *Wallace Stevens: The Making of Harmonium* (Princeton: Princeton University Press, 1967);
Sharon Cameron, " 'The Sense against Calamity': Ideas of a Self in Three Poems by Wallace Stevens," *ELH*, 43 (Winter 1976): 584-603;

Beverly Coyle, *A Thought to be Rehearsed: Aphorism in Wallace Stevens's Poetry* (Ann Arbor, Mich.: UMI Research Press, 1983);

Dartmouth College Library Bulletin, Special Stevens issue, 4 (December 1961);

Frank Doggett, "Abstraction and Wallace Stevens," *Criticism,* 2 (Winter 1960): 23-37;

Doggett, *Stevens' Poetry of Thought* (Baltimore: Johns Hopkins University Press, 1966);

Doggett, *Wallace Stevens: The Making of the Poem* (Baltimore: Johns Hopkins University Press, 1980);

Doggett, "Wallace Stevens and the World We Know," *English Journal,* 48 (October 1959): 365-373;

Doggett, "Wallace Stevens' Later Poetry," *ELH,* 25 (June 1958): 137-154;

Doggett, and Robert Buttel, eds., *Wallace Stevens: A Celebration* (Princeton: Princeton University Press, 1980);

Denis Donoghue, "On *Notes Toward a Supreme Fiction,*" in his *The Ordinary Universe: Soundings in Modern Literature* (London: Faber & Faber, 1968);

Donoghue, "Wallace Stevens," in his *Connoisseurs of Chaos: Ideas of Order in Modern American Poetry* (London: Faber & Faber, 1965);

Richard Eberhart, "Emerson and Wallace Stevens," *Literary Review,* 7 (Autumn 1963): 51-71;

Eberhart, "Reflections on Wallace Stevens in 1976," *Southern Review,* new series 13 (Summer 1977): 417-418;

Irvin Ehrenpreis, ed., *Wallace Stevens: A Critical Anthology* (Harmondsworth, U.K.: Penguin, 1973);

Richard Ellmann, "Wallace Stevens' Ice-Cream," *Kenyon Review,* 19 (Winter 1957): 89-105;

John J. Enck, *Wallace Stevens: Images and Judgments* (Carbondale: Southern Illinois University Press, 1964);

Daniel Fuchs, *The Comic Spirit of Wallace Stevens* (Durham: Duke University Press, 1963);

Fuchs, "Wallace Stevens and Santayana," in *Patterns of Commitment in American Literature,* edited by Marston Lafrance (Toronto: University of Toronto Press, 1976), pp. 135-164;

Philip Furia and Martin Roth, "Stevens' Fusky Alphabet," *PMLA,* 93 (January 1978): 66-77;

Harvard Advocate, Special Stevens issue (December 1940);

Thomas J. Hines, *The Later Poetry of Wallace Stevens: Phenomenological Parallels with Husserl and Heidegger* (Lewisburg: Bucknell University Press, 1976);

J. Dennis Huston, "*Credences of Summer:* An Analysis," *Modern Philology,* 67 (February 1970): 263-272;

Frank Kermode, *Wallace Stevens* (London: Oliver & Boyd, 1960);

Edward Kessler, *Images of Wallace Stevens* (New Brunswick: Rutgers University Press, 1972);

David M. LaGuardia, *Advance on Chaos: The Sanctifying Imagination of Wallace Stevens* (Hanover, N.H.: University Press of New England, 1983);

Louis H. Leiter, "Sense in Nonsense: Wallace Stevens' 'The Bird with the Coppery, Keen Claws,'" *College English,* 26 (April 1965): 551-554;

Frank Lentricchia, *The Gaiety of Language: An Essay on the Radical Poetics of W. B. Yeats and Wallace Stevens* (Berkeley & Los Angeles: University of California Press, 1968);

A. Walton Litz, *Introspective Voyager: The Poetic Development of Wallace Stevens* (New York: Oxford University Press, 1972);

Isabel G. MacCaffrey, "The Other Side of Silence: 'Credences of Summer' as an Example," *Modern Language Quarterly,* 30 (September 1969): 417-438;

Glen G. MacLeod, *Wallace Stevens and Company: The "Harmonium" Years, 1913-1923* (Ann Arbor, Mich.: UMI Research Press, 1983);

Louis L. Martz, "Wallace Stevens: The World as Meditation," *Yale Review,* new series 47 (1958): 517-536; republished in *The Achievement of Wallace Stevens,* edited by Brown and Haller, pp. 211-231; and *Wallace Stevens: A Collection of Critical Essays,* edited by Borroff, pp. 133-150;

Martz, "The World of Wallace Stevens," in *Modern American Poetry: Focus Five,* edited by B. Rajan (London: Dobson, 1950), pp. 94-109;

George McFadden, "Poet, Nature, and Society in Wallace Stevens," *Modern Language Quarterly,* 23 (1962): 263-271;

McFadden, "Probings for an Integration: Color Symbolism in Wallace Stevens," *Modern Philology,* 58 (February 1961): 186-193;

Peter L. McNamara, "The Multi-Faceted Blackbird and Wallace Stevens' Poetic Vision," *College English,* 25 (1964): 446-448;

McNamara, ed., *Critics on Wallace Stevens* (Coral Gables: University of Miami Press, 1972);

Ralph J. Mills, Jr., "Wallace Stevens and the Poem of Earth," *Gemini/Dialogue,* 3 (1960): 20-30;

Adalaide Kirby Morris, *Wallace Stevens: Imagination and Faith* (Princeton: Princeton University Press, 1974);

Eugene Paul Nasser, *Wallace Stevens: An Anatomy of Figuration* (Philadelphia: University of Pennsylvania Press, 1965);

William Van O'Connor, *The Shaping Spirit: A Study of Wallace Stevens* (Chicago: Regnery, 1950);

Robert Pack, "The Abstracting Imagination of Wallace Stevens: Nothingness and the Hero," *Arizona Quarterly,* 11 (Autumn 1955): 197-209;

Pack, *Wallace Stevens: An Approach to His Poetry and Thought* (New Brunswick: Rutgers University Press, 1958);

Pack, "Wallace Stevens: The Secular Mystery and the Comic Spirit," *Western Review,* 20 (Autumn 1955): 51-62;

Pack, "Wallace Stevens' Sufficient Muse," *Southern Review,* new series 11 (Autumn 1975): 766-779;

Roy Harvey Pearce and J. Hillis Miller, eds., *The Act of the Mind: Essays on the Poetry of Wallace Stevens* (Baltimore: Johns Hopkins Press, 1965);

Alan Perlis, *Wallace Stevens: A World of Transforming Shapes* (Lewisburg: Bucknell University Press, 1976);

Perspective, Special Stevens issue (Autumn 1954);

Craig Raine, "Wallace Stevens, 1879-1955: A Centenary Essay," *Encounter,* 53 (November 1979): 59-67;

Joseph N. Riddel, *The Clairvoyant Eye: The Poetry and Poetics of Wallace Stevens* (Baton Rouge: Louisiana State University Press, 1965);

Riddel, "Wallace Stevens' 'Visibility of Thought,'" *PMLA,* 77 (September 1962): 482-498;

Michael Sexson, *The Quest of Self in the Collected Poems of Wallace Stevens* (New York: Edwin Mellen Press, 1981);

Southern Review, Special Stevens issue, new series 7 (July 1971);

Southern Review, Special Stevens centennial issue, new series 15 (Autumn 1979);

Herbert J. Stern, *Wallace Stevens: Art of Uncertainty* (Ann Arbor: University of Michigan Press, 1966);

Ronald Sukenick, *Wallace Stevens: Musing the Obscure* (New York: New York University Press, 1967);

William York Tindall, *Wallace Stevens,* University of Minnesota Pamphlets on American Writers, no. 11 (Minneapolis: University of Minnesota Press, 1961);

Trinity Review, Special Stevens issue (May 1954);

Helen Hennessy Vendler, *On Extended Wings: Wallace Stevens' Longer Poems* (Cambridge: Harvard University Press, 1969);

Thomas F. Walsh, *Concordance to the Poetry of Wallace Stevens* (University Park: Pennsylvania State University Press, 1963);

Theodore Weiss, "Lunching with Hoon," *American Poetry Review,* 7 (September-October 1978): 36-45;

Henry W. Wells, *Introduction to Wallace Stevens* (Bloomington: Indiana University Press, 1964);

Susan B. Weston, *Wallace Stevens: An Introduction to the Poetry* (New York: Columbia University Press, 1977);

Abbie F. Willard, *Wallace Stevens: The Poet and His Critics* (Chicago: American Library Association, 1978);

Leonora Woodman, *Stanza My Stone: Wallace Stevens and the Hermetic Tradition* (West Lafayette, Ind.: Purdue University Press, 1983);

David P. Young, "A Skeptical Muse: Stevens and Santayana," *Criticism,* 7 (Summer 1965): 263-283.

Papers:

The Wallace Stevens archive is at the Henry E. Huntington Library, San Marino, California.

Trumbull Stickney

(20 June 1874-11 October 1904)

Michele J. Leggott
Auckland University

BOOKS: *Dramatic Verses* (Boston: Charles E. Goodspeed, 1902);

*Les Sentences dans la Poésie Grècque d'Homère à Eu-
ripèdes* (Paris: Société Nouvelle de Librairie et
d'Édition, 1903);

De Hermolai Barbari vita atque ingenio dissertationem
(Paris: Société Nouvelle de Librairie et d'Édition, 1903);

The Poems of Trumbull Stickney, edited by George
Cabot Lodge, William Vaughn Moody, and
John Ellerton Lodge (Boston & New York:
Houghton Mifflin, 1905);

Homage to Trumbull Stickney: Poems, edited by James
Reeves and Seán Haldane (London: Heine-
mann, 1968);

The Poems of Trumbull Stickney, edited by Amberys
R. Whittle (New York: Farrar, Straus & Giroux, 1972).

OTHER: *Bhagavad-Gītā,* translated from Sanskrit
into French by Stickney and Sylvain Lévi
(Paris: Libraire d'Amérique et d'Orient, Ad-
rian Maissoneuve, 1938).

PERIODICAL PUBLICATIONS: "Nature Worship, Ancient and Modern: A Dialogue Between Euripides and William Wordsworth,"
Harvard Monthly, 19 (November 1894): 62-67;

"Herakleitos," *Harvard Monthly,* 19 (February
1895): 176-180;

Review of *Captain Craig,* by Edwin Arlington Robinson, *Harvard Monthly,* 37 (December 1903):
99-102.

When Trumbull Stickney died at age thirty
of a brain tumor, one year after he had returned
from doctoral studies at the Sorbonne to teach classics at Harvard University, only one collection of
his poetry, *Dramatic Verses* (1902), had been published, and a second was still in the planning stages.
After his friends published a memorial volume, *The
Poems of Trumbull Stickney* in 1905, "it was discovered," the *Oxford Companion to American Literature*
(1983) observes, "that he was a representative poet

of his period." The estimate is unjust. Although his
reputation faded rapidly, his poetry continued to
earn the admiration of poets such as Conrad Aiken
(who introduced T. S. Eliot to Stickney's poetry in
about 1908), William Rose Benét, Louis Untermeyer, Allen Tate, Mark Van Doren, W. H. Auden,
and Oscar Williams—all of whom included his
work in their anthologies—and of Edmund Wilson,

Trumbull Stickney

506

who wrote an important essay on Stickney in 1940. A revival of interest in Stickney's poetry, which began in the late 1960s, led to the publication of *Homage to Trumbull Stickney* (1968) and *The Poems of Trumbull Stickney* (1972). At its best Stickney's poetry is clear-cut and musically effective, and at times it is arresting in the condensed brilliance of its imagery. Convinced that the language of rhetoric and the language of lyric poetry should not mix, Stickney deserves to be better known than such frequently anthologized contemporaries as William Vaughn Moody or even Edgar Lee Masters.

Joseph Trumbull Stickney was born in Geneva, Switzerland, the son of Austin Stickney, a classics professor who until 1864 had taught at Trinity College in Hartford, Connecticut, and Harriet Champion Trumbull. The family lived in Europe for much of the poet's childhood. Joseph Trumbull, who was called Joe by family and friends and seems to have begun calling himself Trumbull around 1903, was the third of four children and was particularly attached to his eldest sister Lucy, to whom most of his extant correspondence is addressed.

The Stickneys crossed to New York when Joseph Trumbull was five and stayed there just over a year; they returned to the United States when he was nine and stayed a year and a half, moving seasonally along the eastern seaboard. Stickney attended a Somerset prep school for one term when he was twelve, after which the family lived in New York for two years. Late in 1890, when he was sixteen, they returned once again to the United States after another European sojourn, and Stickney continued preparations begun in London for attendance at Harvard University. He passed his final entrance examinations in spring 1891 and arrived at Harvard the following fall, intending to concentrate in classics.

Extensive private tutoring by his father stood Stickney in good stead academically, and his cosmopolitan upbringing gave him the outward appearance of self-assurance and urbanity. These qualities may have helped to win him the election in his freshman year to the editorial board of the *Harvard Monthly;* he was the first freshman ever granted that honor. His first published poem, however, appeared in the 6 January 1892 issue of the rival student literary magazine, the *Harvard Advocate.* Titled "Elizabethan Lyrics: A Villanelle," its "brightness of fancy" reminded the *Harvard Crimson*'s reviewer of Robert Herrick. The 17 February issue printed his less artificial but still undistin-

guished sonnet, "When winter clothes the earth in glistening snow."

During his freshman year Stickney wrote enthusiastically to his sister about Dante, John Keats, and James Thomson and also expressed admiration, with some reservations, for Robert Browning. Yet, he wrote, "my greatest joy is Greek tragedy in which I foresee I shall be lost for the next 2000 years."

Stickney contributed thirteen poems to the *Monthly* in 1892-1893. Of these poems, more than half are sonnets and nearly all are conventional in sentiment. An occasional phrase stands out ("the wave-rolled spiral shell"; an autumn riverbank "Of packed and soaking leaves"), but in general these moments are not sustained. Stickney's undergraduate verse is strongest when he has a clear formal pattern to follow, as in "Evening: A Study in Metre," which begins:

> Summer is sweet,
> In the air of the tepid night,
>   In the drowsy breeze,
>   In the blossoming trees;—
> Summer is sweet
>   With its scented heat
> And the lazy hours that ease
>
>   Every heart
> From the toil of the day's hot light
>   And ceaseless throes,
>   With their pale repose.
>   Every heart
>   Sips of its part
> Of the love that summer bestows.

With the exception of three poems contributed to Philip Henry Savage's short-lived magazine the *Mahogany Tree* in February and March 1892 and his two contributions to the *Advocate,* Stickney published exclusively in the *Monthly* until his death and expressed distaste for the commercial magazines of that time. He wanted to keep his poetry free of contamination by nonliterary pressures, to write poems unlike those published in such magazines, and to avoid being linked or identified with the effete talents which were symptomatic of New England's literary decline. The same amused eye which observed that Cambridge teas were stifling and Boston literati precious also recognized the era's aesthetic confusions.

Although he was a part of the writers' group associated with the *Monthly,* Stickney appears to have seemed too European to some of Harvard's literary set. In *The Middle Span* (1945) George Santayana remembered his attempt to introduce Stickney to a group of undergraduate poets who met in his rooms for informal "poetry bees." Stickney was rejected by the group for having called a sunset "gorgeous." He found more congenial company in George Cabot ("Bay") Lodge and William Vaughn Moody, both of whom he met through the *Monthly*.

At the end of his sophomore year Stickney fell in love with a married woman and wrote her a copious number of poems. This affair was the first of several which fueled his poetic drives and of which the family disapproved. After his death they took care to destroy incriminating letters and to excise passages from others. Also victims of this familial sense of propriety were letters (considered "undignified" by his younger brother Henry) in which Stickney asked his parents for money.

Stickney's third and fourth years at Harvard were academically undistinguished—Stickney appears to have been bored by his classes—but creatively they were most productive. In his *Monthly* contributions for 1894-1895 the images are sharper and more original, and there are fewer apostrophes to conventional ideals. The reader senses the presence of an actual woman in the two sonnets addressed to "F. L. P.," the second of which begins:

> Your image walks not in my common way.
> Rarely I conjure up your face, recall
> Your language, think to hear your footstep fall
> In my lost home or see your eyes' sweet play.
> Rather you share the life that sees not day[.]

Two competent romantic ballads combine simplicity and understated mystery. The speaker in "In the Past" is a boatman looking into incalculable depths:

> I, in my lonely boat,
> A waif on the somnolent lake,
> Watching the colours creep and float
> With the sinuous track of a snake.
>
> Now I lean o'er the side
> And lazy shades in the water see,
> Lapped in the sweep of a sluggish tide
> Crawled in from the living sea[.]

In "Age in Youth" (1895) a mad old woman walks toward the setting sun as the speaker focuses on the small consequences of her movement:

> The daisies shudder at her hem.
> Her dry face laughs with flowery light;
> An aureole lifts her soiled gray hair:

> "I'll on," she says, "to see this sight."
>
> In the rude math her torn shoe mows
> Juices of trod grass and crushed stalk
> Mix with a soiled and earthy dew,
> With smear of petals gray as chalk[.]

These poems, which are among the earliest included in *Dramatic Verses* (1902), represent something of a watershed in Stickney's development.

Three poems published toward the end of his senior year show Stickney's boredom with academe. The net effect of "Lucretius," "The Commentator After Luncheon," and "When you've averaged emotion, found where Nature goes to school . . ." is a warning that giving up "Sunlight-ripple and sea-burst, the winy air, the spumy sea" for what the schoolmen have to offer is a potentially fatal move: "And a hand that grasps not life, is gathering ashes for its urn."

Stickney's vigorous admiration for the classics directly affected his perception of what was good

Trumbull Stickney (courtesy of Harvard University Archives)

poetry. In published undergraduate essays such as "Pliny and Letter-Writing," "Nature Worship, Ancient and Modern: A Dialogue Between Euripides and William Wordsworth," and "Herakleitos," Stickney rejected what he saw as the stasis and repression characteristic of the nineteenth century for the vitality he found in the ancients, whose goal was "the perfection of the individual through his emotions." One of Stickney's lasting enthusiasms was for Plato's *Republic*. As he wrote to Lucy Stickney in December 1895, "It's my religion entire, as far as I have anything to do with it; & I believe that those of us who can profess no creed, will return to Platonism as the only tenable philosophy. I don't say the Republic ought to be realized or that if it were, the individual or educated wld be very admirable. But as an idea it's a thing to live with—that is for me." For him the *Republic* presented "the only tenable artistic faith I believe, & the only tenable artistic morals."

Stickney was writing from Paris, where he had begun studies at the Sorbonne. After earning his A.B. magna cum laude from Harvard the previous June, he had spent the summer in Germany with his family. To judge by the number of poems written in 1895, and by their quality, release from Harvard was exhilarating and stimulating.

The 110-line "Kalypso," a sensual poem about the nymph's apparent seduction of Ulysses, was written in Lausanne during the autumn of 1895. Stickney considered it the best poem he had yet written in terms of simplicity and metrical finish; and in 1902 he placed it first in *Dramatic Verses*. He saw parallels between his own progress and Lucy Stickney's in painting: "Your past work had too much atmosphere to my mind," he wrote to her, "just as mine had too much thought." As these lines from "Cologne Cathedral," a sonnet written in mid 1895, demonstrate, his concentration on aural and visual qualities was increasing:

> Prayer carved the sable flowers; a choral spun
> Rose-windows in the aisle; and music stayed
> So silken-long by arch and colonnade
> That the lines trembled out and followed on[.]

Early in 1896 Stickney was preparing a book of poetry which he hoped to publish in London that spring. "It seems to me good, even now that I've got it together," he wrote to Lucy. "It is certainly careful, & has no overgush; it is highly unfashionable, therefore, & yet why shouldn't it do as a 'revival of self-restraint.' " But nothing further came of the project.

By this time Stickney had tired of the rigorous graduate course work at the Sorbonne, and he found continued financial dependence on his parents galling. His attempts at obtaining a diplomatic post were unsuccessful. Though Stickney was apparently feeling the effect of "a youth behind viciously spent in the society of bookworms," George Cabot Lodge, who was also in Paris during 1895-1896, reported that Stickney was settled in a "mute not cheerful despair," having decided to earn a *doctorat ès lettres* and (in Cabot Lodge's words) to give up "all his 'morning wishes' poetry etc." While Stickney was too much a realist to have ever contemplated making a career of poetry, he did not stop writing poems. Yet his decision to pursue a doctorate was an important, if reluctant, declaration of priorities.

By mid 1896 he had chosen the topics for the two theses required for the degree. The shorter thesis, to be presented in Latin, was a biography of Ermolao Barbaro, a fifteenth-century nobleman, which also included some previously unpublished letters that Stickney had discovered in a library at Lucca. The longer thesis, in French, concerned the use of gnomic elements in Greek poetry from Homer to Euripides. Work on these theses occupied Stickney until late 1902. He applied himself dutifully to research and writing, often playing his violin alone in his room to compensate for the frustrations: " 'restlessly resigned' seems to me one of the most wonderful expressions I know," he told Lucy.

The chief event of his personal life in 1896-1899 is never made explicit in the extant correspondence but seems to indicate that he was involved in a love affair. At the beginning of this period he published three poems that reappeared in *Dramatic Verses* as part of the "Eride" sequence, twenty-seven poems charting the progress of a love affair from euphoria through complication to disillusion and pain. The last poems in "Eride" were written in late 1899, when Stickney, who was putting together what seems to have been an early version of *Dramatic Verses*, wrote to Lucy Stickney that he had composed the final poem of the romantic sequence in such a state of melancholy that he could not bear to keep it near him.

"Eride" is more significant from a biographical than from a literary point of view. Becoming crepuscular and then uniformly autumnal as passion disintegrates ("golden-gray" is the predominant tone), it begins with the brief vernal period of the affair:

I held these tulips first, before
Bringing you them.
I passed the love I bear you o'er
Flower and stem.
And I would leave them at your door,—
If at your heart's door they might stand!
Keeping awhile
The world behind their petals and
Crimson smile,—
Like seas hid by a meadow-land.

And the arrival of despair is powerfully expressed by the opening of the final poem in part two:

I heard a dead leaf run. It crossed
My way. For dark I could not see.
It rattled crisp and thin with frost
Out to the lea[.]

The poem about which Stickney wrote to his sister is a retrospective of the affair, "Now in the palace gardens warm with age. . . ." It endeavors to call a blessing on joy and pain alike, but the poet-lover cannot rid himself of an inner turmoil which thwarts conventional resignation. The woman who the sequence calls Eride has not been identified, but she was an important presence in Stickney's first Parisian years.

In April 1899, or earlier, Stickney again began compiling a collection of his poems, and in November 1899 he sent the typescript to Henry Stickney in New York for submission to publishers. No one would take the book, and by the summer of 1900 Stickney was pessimistic about his publishing prospects in general: "with some resignation," he wrote Lucy, "I put off the hope of my life. Bay Lodge publishes a novel and another volume this year."

He had also hoped to interest a book publisher in his first completed blank-verse drama, "Prometheus Pyrphoros" ("Prometheus the Firebringer"), which was published in the November 1900 issue of the *Harvard Monthly*. His previous attempts at verse drama included "The Cardinal Play," a fragment about incest and intrigue during the renaissance, which he had written in 1897. He had also written the dramatic monologues "Oneiropolos" (published in the January 1897 issue of the *Monthly*), "Lodovico Martelli" (written in 1898), and "Requiescam" (published in the *Monthly* in February 1900). Stickney's one act "Prometheus Pyrphoros" centers on mankind's necessity to assert his independence against the forces of malignant fate. Its best poetic effects derive from the contrast between Pandora's disembodied voice, which sings

out at intervals, and the engulfing blackness in which most of the action takes place.

William Vaughn Moody was also interested in the Prometheus myth, and Stickney directed Moody's research into its classical sources while Moody was in Paris during the summer of 1902. Moody's *The Firebringer* (1904), however, makes different use of the raw material than Stickney's play, emphasizing the symbolic rather than the human elements of the myth.

Around 1900 Stickney became involved with Mrs. Elizabeth Cameron, a close companion of Henry Adams. The exact nature of their relationship has been a matter for speculation by a number of people, including George Cabot Lodge and Bernard Berenson. Adams did not let the affair color his public reminiscences of Stickney, but Lodge's reports of his private reactions suggest that Adams was unhappy about it. Whether any of the love poems Stickney wrote in 1900-1902 refer to his relationship with Elizabeth Cameron or to earlier or other affairs is unknown. It may even be that the prevailing melancholy of Stickney's poetry and correspondence at this time is a result of the demands his theses made on him, considering that he disliked academic scholarship.

The theses were in fact progressing steadily in 1900, and a revived interest in Sanskrit and in Indian philosophy was beginning to affect Stickney's perception of early Western thought and poetic expression (the Mahâbhrâta's use of the gnomic mode is contrasted with Homer's at one point in the French dissertation). He found the movement of Greek poetry from Homer's lyricism to Euripides' attempts at philosophy, blending metaphysics with poetry, to be a "chilling" development and concluded that, in general, "Greece never quite mixed thought and Beauty."

This belief was partly the result of his work in 1899 and 1900, when he and his former Sanskrit teacher, Sylvain Lévi, translated the Bhagavad Gītā (the translation was published in 1938 by Lévi's wife after her husband's death). Stickney was attracted to the antilogical elements in Eastern thought, and his formerly unreserved admiration for the Greek ethos declined accordingly. His new sympathies, in conjunction with a certain nihilism which was in the air, inform the iconoclastic power of, for example, poems such as "And, the last day being come, Man stood alone . . .", which ends:

Page from the setting copy for Dramatic Verses *(by permission of the Houghton Library, Harvard University)*

—As he died,

Low in the East now lighting gorgeously
He saw the last sea-serpent iris-mailed
Which, with a spear transfixèd, yet availed
To pluck the sun down into the dead sea.

A more welcome diversion from thesis work was the preparation of *Dramatic Verses* for publication in an edition of 352 copies by Charles E. Goodspeed of Boston in October 1902. The book is considerably different from the now-lost 1896 and 1899 typescripts, including as it does such more recent work as the exquisitely modulated "Mnemosyne," "In Summer," "Pity," and the sonnets "You say, Columbus with his argosies . . ." and "He said: 'If in his image I was made. . . .' "

The first section of the book arranges lyric with dramatic poems and comes to a climax with the personally dramatic "Eride" sequence. Next are eighteen sonnets, followed by "Lakeward," which expresses Stickney's fascination with the romance of northern Italy. The final poem is "Prometheus Pyrphoros." The whole book seems designed to display Stickney's technical proficiency, and his predilection for writing about the autumnal phases of love is varied enough stylistically to escape monotony.

Critical notice of *Dramatic Verses* was limited. The *New York Times Book Review* (7 March 1903) declared expansively that the verse "clamors for rereading and occupies the mind of the reader with exclusive possession"; the review included the complete text of "Mnemosyne" and called the poem superior even to the work of Dante Gabriel Rossetti. In the *Dial* (16 July 1903) William Morton Payne was more cautious and quoted from "Kalypso" to illustrate both Stickney's strengths ("a certain power to grip the imagination and excite the nobler emotions") and his weaknesses (an "endeavor to be impressive at the cost of clear thinking and verbal restraint").

By early 1903 Stickney's theses were both complete. They were published immediately after Stickney's successful defense of *Les Sentences dans la Poésie Grècque*, which was scheduled for the end of March. An informed review of the French book appeared in the *Nation* (18 July 1903); the reviewer praised the clarity of Stickney's thought and its concise expression in French, at a time when German was the customary language of European classical scholarship. The review included a useful synopsis of the thesis, tracing Stickney's contention that the related fortunes of rhetorical and lyrical features had precise effects on the moral content of Greek poetry.

Stickney was the first American to earn the prestigious Sorbonne degree. After finishing, he spent three months touring Greece "on a sort of bacchanal" interlude intended to bridge the gap between the Paris he had left behind (already beginning to seem a thing of the past, according to one surviving letter) and the Harvard where he was to take up a teaching position in September. The journal he kept on this trip is lost, but he also wrote seven "Sonnets from Greece." The sestet from one of them, "Near Helikon," catches his mood strikingly:

To me my troubled life doth now appear
Like scarce distinguishable summits hung
Around the blue horizon: places where
Not even a traveller purposeth to steer—
Whereof a migrant bird in passing sung,
And the girl closed her window not to hear.

Back in Cambridge in late August 1903 after an absence of eight years, Stickney was soon irritated by Harvard's negativity: "Life is cheap and comfortable and charming," he is reported to have written, "because there is none of it." To Henry Adams, who asked about his health, he wrote: "You refer to the last thing excavated on classic soil, my own torso. It proves not to be an antique at all, but a work of a New England sculptor who was wrecked in a dory off the Peloponnesian Coast. On being presented to Harvard University, it was found the torso had convulsions & couldn't be kept in place. So it is being packed for further travel."

The reference to convulsions was not entirely lighthearted; in the second semester of the 1903-1904 academic year Stickney had begun to suffer from severe headaches and periods of partial blindness. Despite this affliction, he kept up his teaching duties, assisting in the first-year Greek language course and teaching a spring-term course on Greek elegiac and lyric poetry. He was also involved in planning for a production the next year of Aeschylus' *Choephoroe* ("The Libation Bearers"), in which he was to play Orestes, and he was busy writing. His review in the *Monthly* of Edwin Arlington Robinson's *Captain Craig* was one of the first favorable responses to Robinson's poetry.

Stickney's own poetry continued the swing toward verse drama it had begun with "Prometheus." A play about Julian the Apostate, which he started in 1901, remained incomplete, but in 1903-1904, in addition to working on a metrical translation of

Aeschylus' *Persians,* Stickney was contemplating a new book, to be called "Dramatic Scenes." The only completed poem for this book is an untitled episode about the youth of Benvenuto Cellini.

The book was to have included lyrics, and, throughout the summer of 1904 (which he spent with his family in New Hampshire), Stickney continued to work at his poetry as best he could. By August his health had deteriorated further and a brain tumor was diagnosed. He was taken to Boston, where he experienced a brief recovery, during which, Lucy Stickney reported, he went on composing and revising, although he was now blind. Some of the late fragments are compelling, in particular:

> Sir, say no more.
> Within me't is as if
> The green and climbing eyesight of a cat
> Crawled near my mind's poor birds.

Soon after Stickney died on 11 October 1904 his literary executors began to collect his work for a memorial volume, which was published the following year. George Cabot Lodge wrote an emotional and rambling introduction, which was dropped—after prolonged acrimony—at Moody's insistence. In addition to the poems from *Dramatic Verses,* the volume includes the Julian fragments, "Later Lyrics," the Cellini scene, "Juvenilia," and "Unreprinted Poems." It was variously judged to have been excellently edited (the *New York Times*) and tastelessly overinclusive (the *Nation*). Ferris Greenslet of the *Nation* made a reasoned assessment of Stickney's "romantic and wistful temper," quoting "Sir, say no more" as its most arresting product. He regretted, however, that the poet should be represented by so many "unfinished and imperfect pieces." William Morton Payne in the *Dial* considered even the later poems promising rather than mature work.

None of the reviews was more than cursory. Consequently, Moody wrote a long review-article which appeared in the 16 November 1906 issue of the *North American Review.* Moody had the perfect opportunity to write an attentive and judicious assessment of Stickney's whole career, placing the late poems (and even more important, the poetic fragments) in the context of his entire canon, but Moody, in the belief that Stickney's lyric talent had already peaked, concentrated on his dramatic po-

tential. In a sense he was perhaps justified, since most of the "Later Lyrics" are unimpressive, and the book itself includes too many poems which its editors felt piously obliged to include as "the lost lyricized expression of Stickney's genius." There can be no doubt that, had Stickney lived to gather his own "Dramatic Scenes," he would have been as stern and judicious as he had been in the selection of poems for his 1902 book, and much later work would have been weeded out.

Joseph Trumbull Stickney remained typed among the poetic nonentities of fin-de-siècle American literature primarily because he was not widely published in his lifetime and because his literary executors published an indiscriminate collection of his work after his death. His poetry often failed to reach the audience which might have recognized its original quality, and, when it was mentioned at all, it was usually written off as an example of New England melancholy or Franco-American decadence. Poems by Lodge and Moody appeared in the anthologies, but Stickney's poetry did not. In 1929 Conrad Aiken started to retrieve Stickney's work—a task Edmund Wilson took up in 1940. But it was only in the late 1960s and early 1970s, with the upswing of interest in early-twentieth-century romanticism, that his work began to acquire both the recognition and the circulation that it deserves.

Bibliography:

J. William Myers, "A Complete Stickney Bibliography," *Twentieth-Century Literature,* 9 (January 1964): 209-212.

Biography:

Seán Haldane, *The Fright of Time: Joseph Trumbull Stickney, 1874-1904* (Ladysmith, Québec: Ladysmith Press, 1970).

References:

William Vaughn Moody, "The Poems of Trumbull Stickney," *North American Review,* 183 (16 November 1906): 1005-1018;

Amberys R. Whittle, *Trumbull Stickney* (Lewisburg, Pa.: Bucknell University Press, 1973);

Edmund Wilson, " 'The Country I Remember,' " *New Republic,* 103 (14 October 1940): 529-530.

Papers:

There is a collection of Stickney's papers in the Houghton Library at Harvard University.

Eunice Tietjens
(29 July 1884-6 September 1944)

Daniel J. Cahill
University of Northern Iowa

BOOKS: *Profiles from China: Sketches in Free Verse of People and Things Seen in the Interior* (Chicago: Seymour, 1917);

Body and Raiment (New York: Knopf, 1919);

Jake (New York: Boni & Liveright, 1921);

Japan, Korea and Formosa (Chicago: Wheeler, 1924);

Profiles from Home: Sketches in Free Verse of People and Things Seen in the United States (New York: Knopf, 1925);

Boy of the Desert (New York: Coward-McCann, 1928);

Leaves in Windy Weather (New York: Knopf, 1929);

The Romance of Antar (New York: Coward-McCann, 1929);

The Jaw-Breaker's Alphabet, by Eunice and Janet Tietjens (New York: A. & C. Boni, 1930);

China, by Tietjens and Louise Strong Hammond (Chicago: Wheeler, 1930);

Boy of the South Seas (New York: Coward-McCann, 1931);

The Gingerbread Boy (Racine, Wis.: Whitman, 1932);

The World at My Shoulder (New York: Macmillan, 1938).

PLAY PRODUCTION: *Arabesque,* by Tietjens and Cloyd Head, New York, National Theatre, 20 October 1925.

OTHER: *Poetry of the Orient: An Anthology of the Classic Secular Poetry of the Major Eastern Nations,* edited by Tietjens (New York & London: Knopf, 1928).

PERIODICAL PUBLICATIONS: "A Plea for a Revaluation of the Trite," *Poetry,* 22 (August 1923): 322-325;

"The Cuckoo School of Criticism," *Poetry,* 46 (May 1935): 96-99.

Eunice Tietjens, 1938 (photograph by Thora Averi)

Literary artist and trusted associate editor of *Poetry: A Magazine of Verse* during its formative years, Eunice Tietjens is honored among that small band of minor lyric poets, such as Sara Teasdale and Gladys Campbell, whose verse records a small but vital world of clear perception and feeling. Essentially, Eunice Tietjens was an occasional poet whose work does not represent a grand scheme of vision but a more carefully nurtured response to sights and sounds of life as vital and joyous, a poetry romantic in origin—clear, lucid, uncomplicated. With Harriet Monroe, whose taste in poetry and caste of mind she shared, Eunice Tietjens's spirit was confident and enchanted by the gifts of human life.

Born Eunice Hammond in Chicago on 29 July 1884, the poet was the oldest of four children of Idea Louise Strong Hammond and William Andrew Hammond. A prominent banker, her father, known as Sam, moved his family to the suburb of Evanston, where Eunice attended the public schools until her thirteenth year. Her family was an active and talented combination of individuals, a fact confirmed by their later accomplishments. Her sister Louise became an Episcopal Missionary in China and her other sister, Elizabeth, was a concert cellist. Her brother, Laurens, was an inventor, best remembered for his Hammond electronic organ. After the death of Sam Hammond in 1897, Idea Hammond and her children traveled to Europe for an extended stay. A talented painter with an inveterate love of travel, she first moved her family to Paris for a brief time, eventually settling for longer periods in Geneva and Dresden. Eunice was enrolled in courses at the Collége de France and the Sorbonne and graduated from the Froebel Kindergarten Institute of Dresden. She never earned a college degree, but her broad cosmopolitan learning, her lifelong dedication to literature in its many forms, and her fluency in several Roance languages provided a remarkable intellectual background for her many achievements in literature and the arts. Also, from her mother, she inherited an energy and interest for worldwide travel, an aspect of her life which inspired and shaped much of her poetry. In May 1904, while still living in Paris, she married Paul Tietjens, a young American composer, best known for his musical score of the extravaganza *The Wizard of Oz,* which he and L. Frank Baum had produced earlier in Chicago. The young couple soon returned to the United States, living for a brief time in Michigan while Paul Tietjens and Baum worked on a new musical. In the fall of 1904 the family moved to New York to be close to the activities of the theater. For Eunice Tietjens these years were occupied with domesticity and two daughters; her elder daughter, Idea, died at the age of four. In her autobiography, *The World at My Shoulder* (1938), Eunice Tietjens reflected on this period of her life: "it seems to me that I slept through those six years more soundly than through any period of my youth. Although I wrote a little art criticism for some of the magazines I had no real life of the spirit." In the year after the death of her first daughter, the couple separated and were finally divorced in 1914. Tietjens took her daughter Janet to Evanston, where her mother, who had returned from Paris, was again living in the family home. For a brief time, Eunice Tietjens conducted "a kindergarten in French for

Tietjens (second from right) and photographer Harry Lackman (right) with Red Cross workers distributing toys in French territory recaptured from the Germans, Christmas 1917

the scions of the wealthy," but she soon determined that she wanted to be a writer. With the assistance of the novelist Henry Kitchell Webster, she experimented with the short story. Her real aspiration, however, was to write poetry, and she soon found herself immersed in a new set of friends "who finally brought me to full birth. . . . it began in a sudden and definite blaze." Through Margery Currey and her husband, Floyd Dell, whom she visited in their little apartment in Rogers Park, Tietjens was both encouraged and inspired to believe in her own poetic power. She acquired a new inner vital life for poetry and for human experience. A year or two later Edgar Lee Masters gave her a copy of the Bhagavad Gita and changed the whole course of her spiritual existence, in which the main beauty was exemplified by poetry.

Harriet Monroe, the founder and editor of *Poetry* magazine, accepted several of Tietjens's poems, and in 1913 Tietjens became associated with the magazine "as office girl and general nuisance." The first decade after *Poetry*'s founding in-

Eunice Tietjens in her war correspondent's uniform, Paris 1918 (photograph by Orville Peets)

cluded some of its most exciting and controversial years, and Tietjens, who continued throughout her life to be associated with the magazine in various editorial capacities, lived and worked within that aura of excitement. During these early years she formed a particularly close friendship with Harriet Monroe. During various brief periods, Tietjens acted as editor of *Poetry* and she was both a friend to and admired by a large group of the magazine's contributors, including Carl Sandburg, Edgar Lee Masters, Vachel Lindsay, Arthur Davison Ficke, and Sara Teasdale.

In 1916 Tietjens journeyed to the West Coast with her mother; their ultimate destination was China, but they spent several weeks in Carmel and San Francisco, meeting poets such as George Sterling, Edwin Markham, and Ina Coolbrith and seeing the varied landscapes of California. While in San Francisco, they attended the Panama-Pacific Exposition, where they met Jiro Harada, an art expert to the Emperor of Japan and a devout Zen Buddhist. This meeting was fateful for her poetry. Harada possessed the peace of an oriental mystic. As a commissioner of the exposition, it was his duty to explain his country for visitors, and for Tietjens, "He opened a gate which has never closed, the gateway to the East." Edgar Lee Masters had aroused her interest in the Orient when he gave her the Bhagavad Gita, and, as she traveled through Japan and China, she was possessed by the strange and ethereal beauty of these countries and their cultures. She spent six months in Wusih, China, with her sister Louise, who was stationed at this interior mission. In 1916 the old traditions of Oriental culture remained as they had been for centuries. Visitors from the Western world were a rarity. China and Japan were still strange and remote, largely unaffected by the great industrial changes of the West, but their cultures were highly developed. The poverty, suffering, and human misery which Tietjens witnessed in the remote interior of China was shocking and pained her sensibilities greatly. She was, however, a keen observer of the people, their manner, and their elaborate rituals and ceremonies. The collision of beauty and tragedy that she saw there evoked both fascination and sympathy. "The strange blend of sordidness, tragedy, beauty, and humor" profoundly altered her vision; and the sights and sounds of the Orient became the inspiration for her collection of free-verse poems, *Profiles from China,* published in 1917. Chinese poetry became the dominating model for her poetic work. Free verse seemed, for her, the most flexible medium to capture the unique visual

Cloyd Head, the poet's second husband, with Poo-a-Topé, an Otéa dancer, on Moorea

essence of the Orient. The poems are brief descriptions or short narratives, which close with expressions of personal value or concern. *Body and Raiment*, a collection of earlier verse, appeared in 1919, but it was the essence of the Chinese poems which marked all of her subsequent efforts in poetry.

When Tietjens returned to Chicago in 1916, she resumed her editorial post at *Poetry*, and she also wrote various news features for the *Chicago Daily News*. It was apparent that the United States was at last to enter World War I. Always eager for a new venture, Tietjens requested to be sent to Europe as a war correspondent. To her great surprise, her superior, Charles Dennis, conceded, and in October 1917 she sailed on the French line. Her original assignment was to write human interest stories from Paris, but she also saw the war at first hand on trips to the little towns at the front. "I saw terrible things there, fear and agony and death and heartrending grief," she wrote in *The World at My*

Shoulder. Wartime Paris was filled with mercenary people engaged in "their petty little intrigues and their struggle for personal advantage," and, she wrote, "In Paris I often had the feeling of wading through filth."

On her return to the United States in early 1919, she retired to a cottage with her mother and daughter, Janet, in Burlington, Iowa. The war was an ugly memory, and she turned for solace again to her poetry, putting together her second book, *Body and Raiment.* In the spring of 1919 she went to live in a shack on the Indiana dunes with her young daughter. During this time of renewal she wrote her first novel, *Jake* (1921). As she wrote in *The World at My Shoulder*, "it had nothing to do with the war, but none the less I wrote down and thereby to a large extent purged myself of it, all the sense of human pain and futility that the war had aroused in me."

In February 1920 she married the playwright Cloyd Head. They had two children, a son, Marshall, and a daughter who died at birth. Between 1920 and 1925 the family lived in the Chicago area. In this period of domesticity she renewed her bonds with Harriet Monroe and *Poetry* and enlarged her circle of literary acquaintance through the Poetry Club of the University of Chicago, where she met writers such as George Dillon, Glenway Wescott, Elizabeth Madox Roberts, Janet Lewis, and Elder Olson. It was through her enthusiastic support that *Poetry* magazine published the work of some of these new young poets. In 1922 Tietjens and her husband stayed at the MacDowell Colony in Peterboro, New Hampshire, where they lived in close association with Edwin Arlington Robinson, Elinor Wylie, and Padraic and Mary Colum.

In October 1923 the Heads embarked for a year of "adventure and creative work" in Europe. They stayed for six weeks in Paris, where they met Ezra Pound and Ford Madox Ford. From Paris they traveled southward to the Riviera and to Rome, but eventually settled in Hammamet, in Tunisia. They had sailed into a country "which was to turn our interests permanently away from Europe and towards the Orient—and the primitive." As Tietjens explained in *The World at My Shoulder*, "A great peace came to us in Hammamet. Under the trivial happenings of our daily lives it flowed like a silver river. We were no longer at variance with the earth, conquering her, living apart from her. Some force flowed from these people to us, these people who themselves seemed like moving bits of the earth."

Upon their return to the United States in spring 1925, the family settled in Rockland County, New York. They had written *Arabesque,* a play based on Arab life, which Norman Bel Geddes agreed to produce. After conflicts with Geddes over staging and rewrites, the play opened at the National Theatre in New York on 20 October 1925, but it failed badly after twenty-three performances. Financially devastated, the Heads spent a bleak and uneventful winter in New York, but, ever resilient, Tietjens soon conceived of an idea for an anthology, *Poetry of the Orient,* a collection of the classic secular poetry of the Far and Near East. She immersed herself in research at the New York Public Library, and the resulting anthology proved to be a signal success when it was published by Alfred A. Knopf in 1928. In late 1926 the Heads went once again to North Africa, but they returned to Chicago in late 1927 when Cloyd Head was offered the position of business manager of the Goodman Memorial Theatre at the Art Institute of Chicago.

In this new period of stability, Tietjens devoted her efforts to her own creative work and to editorial assistance at *Poetry.* Two books for young readers grew out of her North African travels, *Boy of the Desert* (1928) and *The Romance of Antar* (1929). She also compiled a new collection of her own poetry, *Leaves in Windy Weather,* which also appeared in 1929.

Tietjens's portrait of Teura, her cook on Moorea

In 1930 she helped her friend Robert Lee Eskridge to write his *Manga Reva, The Forgotten Islands* (1931), a travel book about his experiences in the South Seas. These few years were perhaps among the most productive in her writing career.

Because of management conflicts at the Goodman Theatre, Cloyd Head resigned his position in 1930, and the family made immediate plans to go to the South Seas, where they settled on the island of Moorea for ten months. It was a time of recuperation from the busy and hectic years in Chicago. During these months, Cloyd Head worked on a new play which was later produced with great success, and Tietjens wrote a children's book, *Boy of the South Seas* (1931). Their idyllic life on Moorea ended when the family returned. "We got back from Moorea," Tietjens wrote in the final page of her autobiography, "to find a very different city from the one we had left. The depression had dug itself in by this time. People were beginning to realize that it was to be a long pull; reserves were diminished alarmingly; there was a terror in the eyes one passed on the street, and a stark reality swept our South Sea paradise behind us as fast as the wake of a great steamer sweeps into limbo." The family managed to survive, and soon a fresh opportunity appeared, an offer from the University of Miami, where they taught for two years (1933-1935), Tietjens in the English department as a lecturer on poetry and Head in the dramatics department. After they resigned from the university, they continued to live in Coconut Grove. "It was," she wrote, "not quite Moorea, but a second cousin to it at least." Here she wrote her last book, *The World at My Shoulder* (1938). The next year, while traveling in Scandinavia, it was discovered that she had cancer. She died five years later in Chicago and is buried there.

Eunice Tietjens will not be remembered as a major poet or writer, but she was devoted to poetry, and many of her most successful poems capture the vividness of people and places. Like Harriet Monroe, she had an intense faith in human sensibility and moral progress; and her poetry records this confidence. Her life was devoted to the progress of the arts in every form. Among her great services to the art of poetry was her assistance to Harriet Monroe on the staff of *Poetry* magazine from 1913 to her death.

Papers:
The Newberry Library in Chicago has a collection of Tietjens's letters and manuscripts.

Ridgely Torrence

(27 November 1874-25 December 1950)

Alice Hall Petry
Rhode Island School of Design

BOOKS: *The House of A Hundred Lights: A Psalm of Experience after Reading a Couplet of Bidpai* (Boston: Small, Maynard, 1900);
El Dorado: A Tragedy (New York & London: John Lane/Bodley Head, 1903);
Abelard and Heloise (New York: Scribners, 1907);
Granny Maumee, The Rider of Dreams, Simon the Cyrenian: Plays for a Negro Theater (New York: Macmillan, 1917);
Hesperides (New York: Macmillan, 1925);
The Story of Gio From the Heike Monogatari, Retold by Ridgely Torrence (New York: Japan Society, 1935);
Common Sense: Play in One Act, America In Action: A Series of Plays For Young People, Dealing with Freedom and Democracy (New York: Dramatists Play Service, 1941);
Poems (New York: Macmillan, 1941; enlarged, 1952);
The Story of John Hope (New York: Macmillan, 1948).

PLAY PRODUCTIONS: *Granny Maumee*, New York, Lyceum Theatre, 30 March 1914;
Granny Maumee, Simon the Cyrenian, and *The Rider of Dreams*, New York, Garden Theatre, 5 April 1917.

OTHER: *Selected Letters of Edwin Arlington Robinson*, edited, with an introduction, by Torrence (New York: Macmillan, 1940);
Last Poems of Anna Hempstead Branch, edited, with a foreword, by Torrence (New York: Macmillan, 1948).

Ridgely Torrence occupies what must charitably be called a minor position in American literature. He is remembered primarily as a friend of better-known poets such as Edwin Arlington Robinson, William Vaughn Moody, and Robert Frost, with whom he became acquainted less because of his poetic talents than because of his geniality, charisma, and powerful position as poetry editor at the *New Republic* (1920-1933). Yet Torrence was himself a writer of no mean skill: a playwright, essayist, and biographer, he actively pursued a multifaceted literary career for more than half a century, and in the 1920s he was regarded as a promising poet. His lifetime poetic output was slight, a fact noted with something akin to despair by those who had recognized the promise in his 1925 collection, *Hesperides;* and his best-known poems—widely anthologized, republished in magazines, and familiar to readers throughout the United States—often were not among his better efforts. Even so he should be remembered as a poet whose work garnered both popular acclaim and serious critical attention for much of the first half of the twentieth century.

Though the year of his birth has often been reported as 1875, Frederic Ridgely Torrence was born 27 November 1874 in Xenia, Ohio, the eldest child of Findley David Torrence, a lumber dealer, and Mary Ridgely Torrence. Except for two years in Santa Ana, California, Torrence spent his formative years in Xenia. Although not much is known about his home life, apparently his family was less than enthusiastic about his literary endeavors, for his father allegedly saved Ridgely's college writings to serve as evidence that his son was going insane.

After two years at Miami University in Ohio (1893-1895), where he wrote verse for the *Miami Student* magazine, the restless Torrence transferred to Princeton as a junior in 1895. He contributed essays and verse to the *Nassau Literary Magazine,* served on the editorial board of the student newspaper, the *Princeton Tiger,* and acted in Triangle Club productions. As a special student he was not eligible to receive a degree, and he left school in December 1896, after illness had prevented him from attending classes for most of the fall 1896 semester.

For the next few years Torrence lived in New York and earned his living as a librarian, first at the Astor Library (1897-1901) and then at the Lenox (1901-1903). This type of work apparently was congenial to his temperament, for as Dorothea Kingsland noted in the *Princeton University Library Chronicle* (Summer 1954), Torrence was "a born archivist. Records of all sorts fascinated him." While working as a librarian Torrence continued to write, publishing poetry in *New England Magazine* and essays in *Success.* It was during this time that he made the first of his many remarkable literary acquaintances. Torrence met Edmund Clarence Stedman in 1899, and Stedman, duly impressed by the man whom Hermann Hagedorn once characterized as "a faun-like creature, born in the moon-light," furthered his poetic career significantly by including several of his poems in his *An American Anthology: 1787-1900* (1900). Thus encouraged, Torrence declared in 1900 that he wished to write poetry "that above all *says something,* and that gives men something to chew on," but his first volume of verse really accomplishes neither goal.

The House of A Hundred Lights: A Psalm of Experience after Reading a Couplet of Bidpai (1900), published under his full name, is a twenty-seven-page poem, published in a limited edition of 750 copies, with rather gaudy decorations and a cover design in the fashion of so many limited-edition poetry books at the turn of the century. The text consists of one hundred quatrains, which—as May Sinclair noted in her influential review essay titled "Three American Poets of To-day" (published in both the *Fortnightly Review* and the *Atlantic Monthly* in 1906)—are "written in frank imitation of Omar Khayyám." While she found "no note of originality" in Torrence's poem, Sinclair praised his "aptitude in assimilating style." The fact remains that this pseudo-Persian verse is not impressive. For the most part it offers truisms and commentaries, usually of a cryptic or cynical nature. Quite typical is quatrain number fifty: "Fame sets the pace: the more you chase,/the more she'll turn and taunt and flee,/Till you stand breathless at the goal/and read its name, 'Obscurity.' " Generally Torrence deals with predictable topics: spiritual matters, the hotheadedness of youth, aging, fame, love, fortune, friendship. Although occasionally a brief series of quatrains will constitute a short vignette (in fact the poems in Stedman's anthology are actually twenty-three of the quatrains combined into five units and given appropriate titles), for the most part each quatrain stands alone. Even though Jessie B. Rittenhouse in *The Younger American Poets* (1904) indicated that the quatrains "are arranged with a certain logical view," there is little discernible organic structure to the poem as a whole. Rittenhouse asserted that the book's "philosophy" is of a "jocular" sort and that Torrence was "laughing" at those who seek to plumb life's mysteries, but in fact it seems unlikely that Torrence was attempting to lampoon the *Rubáiyát* tradition in verse.

The House of A Hundred Lights is a young man's book. After its appearance Torrence continued to write poems and publish them in such journals as the *Critic,* the *Atlantic Monthly,* and *Current Literature,* but his next volume of lyric poetry would not appear until 1925. In the meantime, he turned his attentions to writing plays and to pursuing a successful career as an editor. In the first decade of

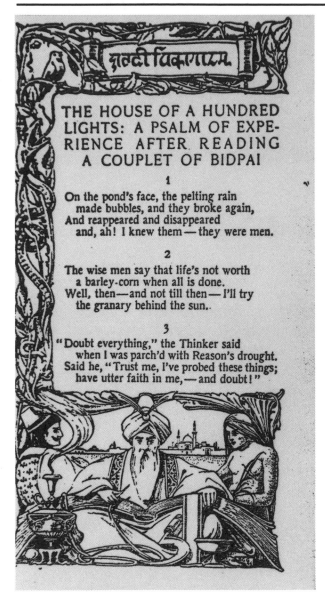

THE HOUSE OF A HUNDRED LIGHTS: A PSALM OF EXPERIENCE AFTER READING A COUPLET OF BIDPAI

1

On the pond's face, the pelting rain
  made bubbles, and they broke again,
And reappeared and disappeared
  and, ah! I knew them—they were men.

2

The wise men say that life's not worth
  a barley-corn when all is done.
Well, then—and not till then—I'll try
  the granary behind the sun..

3

"Doubt everything," the Thinker said
  when I was parch'd with Reason's drought.
Said he, "Trust me, I've probed these things;
  have utter faith in me,—and doubt!"

First page of text in Torrence's first book, a long poem in the style of the Rubáiyát of Omar Khayyám

the twentieth century he wrote two verse plays, *El Dorado: A Tragedy* (1903) and *Abelard and Heloise* (1907), which had a limited critical success but were not produced. Turning to prose drama, Torrence wrote "The Madstone" in 1906-1907 and "The Thunder Pool" in 1907. Neither play was published or produced, though director Henry Miller expressed interest in "The Madstone" as a vehicle for the well-known Russian actress Alla Nazimova. Torrence was not to receive national attention for his dramatic writing until his three one-act prose dramas—*Granny Maumee, The Rider of Dreams, Simon the Cyrenian: Plays for a Negro Theater* (1917)—

opened on Broadway with all-black casts in April 1917. Inspired by his interest in Irish folk drama and based upon the knowledge of black life he had acquired during his childhood in Xenia, the plays were regarded as major achievements in the American theater and milestones in the realistic depiction of blacks.

In 1902, about the same time Torrence was completing *El Dorado*, he met and began an affair with Zona Gale. Their relationship cooled in 1903, and in September of that year he became an assistant editor of the *Critic*, a lively and innovative journal published by Jeannette and Joseph Gilder. He left the *Critic* in March 1905 to become the fiction editor for the *Cosmopolitan*, a position he retained until 1907. But his most significant professional position was that of poetry editor for the *New Republic* (1920-1933). Those thirteen years were important ones for Torrence. He published his verse in such journals as the *Nation* and the *Dial*. He was a visiting professor at Miami of Ohio (1920-1921). He established a professional and personal relationship with Robert Frost (who dedicated his poem "A Passing Glimpse" to Torrence). He brought to light in the pages of the *New Republic* poetry by writers who at the time were relatively unknown, including Wallace Stevens, Elinor Wylie, and Hart Crane; and he published his second volume of poetry, *Hesperides* (1925).

Since the publication of *The House of A Hundred Lights* twenty-five years earlier, Torrence had developed greater maturity and creative self-confidence in his poetry. In thematic and technical complexity the title poem is representative of the collection. The eighty-one-line poem describes the dream vision of a young man disillusioned by the modern, urban world. Recalling the tale of the golden apples, he falls asleep beside a city fountain and fancies himself "in a golden shadow" under a tree that bears "the apples of life, like a ripe world each." He tastes an apple, finds it "bitter," lets "it fall to the ground," and awakens realizing "there was no escape at the world's end stored,/No escape in a sleep or beyond to a sea more vast." But the poem ends on what Torrence evidently had meant to be a positive note: "here where he breathes was the island, glittering-shored"—"a better dream" than that of the golden apples. That one must accept one's position in life and temper it with hope is a Victorian note which may not be expected in a poem published in 1925, and somehow the poem's conclusion does not quite square with the young man's bitter situation or his dream. The overall effect of the poem is melancholy, and the

Times Literary Supplement (16 July 1925) seems justified in noting that in *Hesperides* Torrence "brings much of the stress and hustle which it was his aim to forget."

The notion that one must face the realities of life while nurturing "the fire-like seed" of something better recurs throughout the volume, and often it generates an aura of mysticism, especially in "Eye-Witness." The poem recounts how four tramps, "all homeless reapers of the wind," listen to one of their number sing about his meeting with Jesus during a snowstorm: "I leaned in closer and I saw a face; A light went round me but I kept my place./My heart went open like an apple sliced; I saw my Saviour and I saw my Christ." A hobo himself in the poem, Christ was suffering from "the railroad blues" and yet was able to impart to the tramp a desire to sing Christ's message of love to other unfortunates. As the four tramps merge into "common gold," the poem ends with an image of rebirth: "And earth bore East with all toward the new morning." Although "Eye-Witness" is one of Torrence's best-known poems, it is not typical of his work, for religion was not one of his primary concerns.

Raised a Presbyterian, Torrence came to reject denominational Christianity; but he retained a recognition of man's spiritual needs and an appreciation of the importance of ceremonies in daily existence. One finds both elements in his "Rituals for the Events of Life," a series of poems which are, in effect, secularized versions of such fundamental Christian services as baptism and burial. In "A Ritual for Birth and Naming" (later revised slightly as "Ceremony for Birth and Naming") Torrence's non-Christian ceremony is far more otherworldly than the christening liturgy one finds in the *Book of Common Prayer*. The parents—"gardeners of the precious seed"—are instructed to "Draw honey from the upper hives" and "Make sweet the weather for the flower"; and the child is named "In the three names of Love, Light, and your/Divine Humanity." Torrence's de-Christianized christening, replete with a new trinity, was not the sort of ceremony to capture the popular imagination, especially since some portions of it are as difficult to decipher as the archaic language of the standard service: "you are, through him, of those/ Who leave their colors in the air/When you are dust and he a rose."

The charge most consistently leveled against *Hesperides,* even by reviewers who generally found the volume praiseworthy, was that its thought was "vague and obscure." Some commentators argued that the "music" of the poetry compensated for this obscurity; Carl Magg in the *Literary Review* (27 June 1925) noted that "One may fail at times to get within defining distance of this poet's exact meaning. Still, the exotic tread of his verse echoes in those nooks of reaction where reason never enters." Nonetheless, one may justifiably question the permanent value of poetry which defies rational comprehension.

Not every poem in *Hesperides* is obscure, however; some are almost painfully clear and incisive. The brief "Three O'Clock" (subtitled "Morning") vividly portrays the frustration and waste in the lives of city dwellers by focusing on an early-morning street scene—the "jewel-blue electric flowers/ Are cold upon their iron trees"; as examples of humanity, there are "A drowning one, a reeling one,/And one still loitering after trade"; and "The lights go out in red and gold/But time goes out in gray." The reviewer for the *Dial* (January 1926) singled out "Three O'Clock" as a "nearly perfect poem"; but it is atypical of *Hesperides* in that there is no apparent element of hope or mysticism, and the same may be said of "The Son," one of Torrence's most widely anthologized and best-known poems. It consists of sixteen short lines in four stanzas, and its brevity generates much of its emotional impact. The unidentified speaker repeats what he had heard said by "an old farm-wife,/Selling some barley." From her comments the reader learns that her only child, Charley, "sickened making fence" and died just before his wedding, leaving her alone with her husband. Nowhere does the distraught old woman overtly refer to his death, but her blurring of the two elements which constituted her existence—raising crops and raising her son—makes it clear in the poignant final stanza: " 'It feels like frost was near—/His hair was curly./The spring was late that year,/But the harvest early.' "

Probably the single best-known poem in *Hesperides* is "The Bird and the Tree," first published in the April 1915 issue of *Poetry* and widely republished. The two introductory lines—"Blackbird, blackbird in the cage,/There's something wrong tonight"—sound as if they are the opening of a ballad or Negro spiritual, but Torrence has downplayed the folkloric elements. The poem is a monologue spoken by a black man who knows he will be lynched that night by the Ku Klux Klan ("A white mask to hide the face"). It is evident that the speaker is innocent, a situation which results less in rage or desperation than in resignation: "No use to reek with reddened sweat,/No use to whimper and to sweat./They've got the rope; they've got the guns." The poem is striking for its consistency of tone and immediacy of the emotions, but it is especially notable for Torrence's handling of the central image. It is only in the course of the poem that one comes to realize that the blackbird in the cage which the speaker initially addresses is actually the black man himself in jail. He does find some consolation in his imminent lynching: "Out of a thorny field you go—/For you it may be better so—/And leave the sowers of the ground/To eat the harvest of the fruit." But although this statement is consistent with the poem's tone of resignation, it is neither emotionally nor intellectually satisfying. Perhaps this problem is what Babette Deutsch had in mind when she criticized *Hesperides* in her review for the *New York Tribune* (21 June 1925) for being "occasionally too gentle": "Sometimes one wants a little relieving harshness—the savage gesture that overturned the tables of the money changers in the temple. . . ." The general response to *Hesperides* was favorable, and Torrence's friend Edwin Arlington Robinson reportedly "raged" when the volume failed to receive a Pulitzer Prize. Torrence was widely heralded as one of the most gifted and promising poets of the 1920s. His next volume was eagerly awaited, but it would not appear until 1941.

In the meantime, Torrence continued his career as poetry editor at the *New Republic* and began to receive recognition for his literary endeavors. From his alma mater, Miami of Ohio, he received an honorary doctor of letters degree in 1937, and the following year he served as poet in residence at Antioch College. He prepared *Selected Letters of Edwin Arlington Robinson* (1940) and furthered his career as a playwright by writing *Common Sense* (1941), a one-act drama about Thomas Paine, published by Dramatists Play Service in a series titled America In Action: A Series of Plays For Young People, Dealing with Freedom and Democracy. He also wrote a few poems, which appeared throughout the 1930s in the *Saturday Review of Literature*, the *New Republic,* and *Poetry.*

The paucity of his poetic output during the sixteen years following *Hesperides* became apparent when the long-awaited *Poems* was published in 1941. It includes all the poems from *Hesperides,* with some revisions, and only fourteen new poems. Critics were dismayed. Louis Untermeyer in the *Saturday Review* (19 July 1941) spoke for many in terming Torrence's case "one of the most puzzling in modern poetry." Untermeyer went on to note that *Poems* "presents a continuing problem, a conflict without solution. . . . there is the question of power withheld or diminished, the creative energy

dissipated, the expectation unfulfilled," but he argued nonetheless that Torrence was to be commended for "the discrimination which denies publication to anything meretricious," for the "restraint which limits the expression of a lifetime to thirty-four poems." Several of the new poems are among Torrence's best.

Considering the year the volume was published, one is not surprised to find that the new poems tend to focus on war and inhumanity. "Men and Wheat," for example, employs the same metaphor found in "The Son": the analogy between human death and the harvest of crops. "Men and Wheat" reflects Torrence's despair over World War II: "The sheaves of men lie flat/And are buried where they bleed./But what dread food is that?/And what mouths does it feed?" It would be uncharacteristic of Torrence, however, to be entirely pessimistic in his pacifist poetry. The three-stanza "Prothalamium," parenthetically subtitled "To a bride in war time," is ultimately a statement of faith in the power of love to triumph over destruction: the bride must "Rise above a ruined world/With a more than mortal fire" and "Breed the men with better dreams."

A similar statement of faith in the future is also found in "Lincoln's Dream." One of the longest poems in the book (nine pages), "Lincoln's Dream" is a monologue in which the president broods upon his dream of hearing mourners in the White House and realizing that the corpse is his own. The poem is based on fact; Lincoln did indeed have recurring premonitions about his assassination, a fact that could not have failed to impress a man as mystically inclined as Torrence. But the real point of the poem is Lincoln's hope that the United States would survive as a nation—a hope which seemed threatened in Torrence's day by the worsening situation in Europe.

The new war poems salvaged *Poems* for many readers, and Torrence found himself receiving acclaim for a volume which, for all intents and purposes, had been written a generation earlier. Torrence received the Shelley Memorial Award in 1942, and that same year he was named Poet of the Year by the National Poetry Center. In 1947 he received a $5,000 fellowship from the Academy of American Poets. His last major projects were a biography of black educator John Hope (1948) and an edition of *Last Poems of Anna Hempstead Branch* (1948).

Torrence died of lung cancer on Christmas Day 1950. In 1952 Macmillan published a new edition of *Poems,* which added two minor poems to

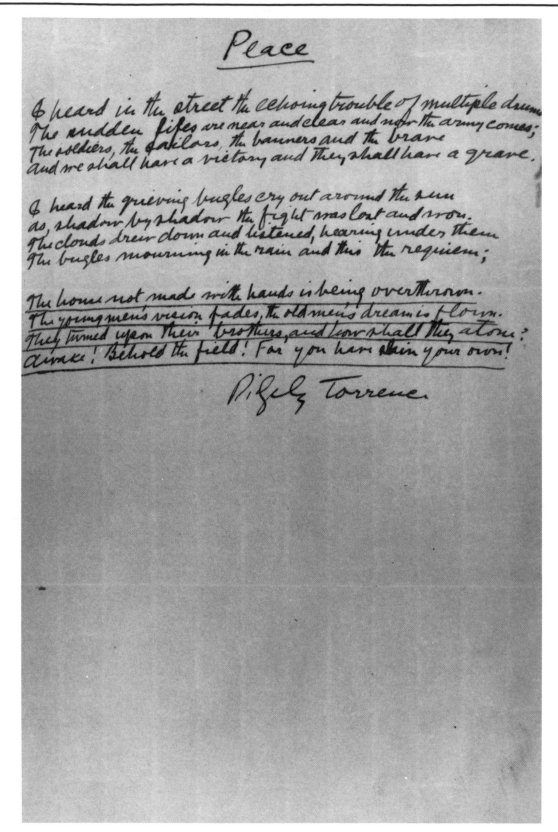

Manuscript for a poem first published in the 23 November 1918 issue of the Boston Evening Transcript *and included in William Stanley Braithwaite's 1919 anthology* Victory! Celebrated by Thirty-eight American Poets *(courtesy of the Lilly Library, Indiana University)*

the 1941 volume. In its review of the 1952 edition, *Time* magazine (1 September 1952) referred to Torrence as a "Poet's Poet," and the label is singularly apt. Evidently only his fellow poets took note of his death, and in the course of more than thirty years his verse has been forgotten. Torrence is regarded now as a fresh poetic voice of the 1920s who somehow never achieved his potential; as the editor responsible for giving exposure to new writers in the *New Republic;* and as the friend of more talented and considerably more productive poets such as Frost. As George Monteiro demonstrates in an article for the *South Carolina Review* (Fall 1982), it seems likely that Torrence's poetry was an unacknowledged (and perhaps unconscious) source of ideas and imagery for Frost; but it is doubtful that Torrence's verse will ever generate interest in its own right. In the final analysis, Ridgely Torrence will be remembered as a tangential figure on the American poetic scene.

Bibliography:
Willard Thorp, "The Achievement of Ridgely Torrence," *Princeton University Library Chronicle,* 12 (Spring 1951): 103-117; "Addenda to Check List," *Princeton University Library Chronicle,* 13 (Spring 1952): 160-161.

References:
John M. Clum, *Ridgely Torrence* (New York: Twayne, 1972);
Hermann Hagedorn, *Edwin Arlington Robinson: A Biography* (New York: Macmillan, 1938);
Dorothea Kingsland, "The Ridgely Torrence Collection," *Princeton University Library Chronicle,* 15 (Summer 1954): 213-214;
George Monteiro, " 'I always Keep Seeing a Light as I Talk With Him': Limning the Robert Frost/Ridgely Torrence Relationship," *South Carolina Review,* 15 (Fall 1982): 32-43;
Austin M. Patterson, "Recollections of Ridgely Torrence," *Princeton University Library Chronicle,* 12 (Spring 1951): 118-120;
Jessie B. Rittenhouse, "Ridgely Torrence," in her *The Younger American Poets* (Boston: Little, Brown, 1904), pp. 299-314.

Papers:
The major depository of Torrence's papers is the Princeton University Library.

George Sylvester Viereck

(31 December 1884-18 March 1962)

James A. Hart
University of British Columbia

BOOKS: *Gedichte* (New York: Progressive Printing, 1904);

A Game at Love and Other Plays (New York: Brentano's, 1906);

Nineveh, and Other Poems (New York: Moffatt, Yard, 1907; London: Brown, Langham, 1907);

The House of the Vampire (New York: Moffatt, Yard, 1907);

Confessions of a Barbarian (New York: Moffatt, Yard, 1910; London: John Lane, 1910);

The Candle and the Flame: Poems (New York: Moffatt, Yard, 1912);

Debate between George Sylvester Viereck . . . and Cecil Chesterton . . . on "Whether the Cause of Germany or that of the Allied Powers Is Just" (New York: Fatherland Corporation, 1915);

Songs of Armageddon and Other Poems (New York: Kennerley, 1916);

Roosevelt: A Study in Ambivalence (New York: Jackson Press, 1919);

Rejuvenation: How Steinach Makes People Young, as George F. Corners (New York: Seltzer, 1923);

The Haunted House, and Other Poems (Girard, Kans.: Haldeman-Julius, 1924);

The Three Sphinxes, and Other Poems (Girard, Kans.: Haldeman-Julius, 1924);

My First Two Thousand Years: The Autobiography of the Wandering Jew, by Viereck and Paul Eldridge (New York: Macaulay, 1928; London: Duckworth, 1929);

Glimpses of the Great (London: Duckworth, 1930; New York: Macaulay, 1930);

Spreading Germs of Hate (New York: Liveright, 1930; London: Duckworth, 1931);

Salome, the Wandering Jewess: My First Two Thousand Years of Love, by Viereck and Eldridge (New York: Liveright, 1930; London: Duckworth, 1930);

My Flesh and Blood: A Lyric Autobiography, with Indiscreet Annotations (New York: Liveright, 1931; London: Jarrolds, 1932);

The Strangest Friendship in History: Woodrow Wilson and Colonel House (New York: Liveright, 1932; London: Duckworth, 1933);

The Invincible Adam, by Viereck and Eldridge (London: Duckworth, 1932; New York: Liveright, 1932);

Prince Pax, by Viereck and Eldridge (London: Duckworth, 1933);

The Kaiser on Trial (New York: Greystone Press, 1937; London: Duckworth, 1938);

The Temptation of Jonathan (Boston: Christopher Publishing House, 1938);

©*Becker & Maass*

526

The Seven against Man (Scotch Plains, N.J.: Flanders Hall, 1941);

All Things Human, as Stuart Benton (New York: Sheridan House, 1949); as George Sylvester Viereck (London: Duckworth, 1951);

Gloria: A Novel (London: Duckworth, 1952);

Men into Beasts (New York: Fawcett, 1952);

The Nude in the Mirror (New York: Woodford Press, 1953);

The Bankrupt (New York: Pyramid Publication, 1955);

[Prison poems], *Wisconsin Poetry Magazine* (July 1958).

OTHER: Dante Gabriel Rossetti, *The House of Life,* edited by Viereck (Girard, Kans.: Haldeman-Julius, 1925);

Oscar Wilde, *Panthea, and Other Poems,* edited by Viereck (Girard, Kans.: Haldeman-Julius, 1925);

Lord Alfred Douglas, *Perkin Warbeck, and Other Poems,* edited by Viereck (Girard, Kans.: Haldeman-Julius, 1925);

Douglas, *The City of the Soul, and Other Sonnets,* edited by Viereck (Girard, Kans.: Haldeman-Julius, 1925);

Algernon Swinburne, *The Triumph of Time and Other Poems,* edited by Viereck (Girard, Kans.: Haldeman-Julius, 1925);

As They Saw Us: Foch, Ludendorff and Other Leaders Write Our War History, edited by Viereck, with the assistance of A. Paul Maerker-Branden (Garden City: Doubleday, Doran, 1929).

Time has worn away the reputations of many poets who, heralded while alive, exist for posterity only in footnotes. George Sylvester Viereck has suffered a worse fate: not only have literary histories paid him scant attention, but at the height of his renown (and notoriety) as a poet he became persona non grata because of his continued vehement defense of Germany after the United States entered World War I. Despite his genuine pro-Americanism, he was expelled from the Poetry Society of America in 1918, dropped from *Who's Who in America,* and saw his poems omitted from anthologies.

Because his political activities distracted potential readers from Viereck's poetry and prevented Viereck himself from writing new poems, his prewar promise was never realized. Yet he deserves more than a footnote. Neither Hyatt H. Waggoner, in his *American Poets from the Puritans to the Present* (1968), nor David Perkins, in his *A History*

of Modern Poetry from the 1890's to the High Modernist Mode (1976), mentions Viereck. Even in 1946 Horace Gregory and Marya Zaturenska, in their *A History of American Poetry, 1900-1940,* dismissed any claim that his poetry was a vehicle for transmitting European culture to the United States, referring to "the now forgotten verse of . . . George Sylvester Viereck with its unconsciously amusing Satanism. . . ." In *The Story of American Literature* (1932) Ludwig Lewisohn had been more laudatory as he confidently pronounced, "Today no one is likely seriously to deny that Viereck was the most conspicuous American poet between 1907 and 1914." To support his judgment, Lewisohn pointed to the chorus of praise which greeted several of Viereck's volumes of poetry and named illustrious critics who believed that Viereck brought "the spirit of modern poetry" to American shores. Lewisohn, however, also undercut such praise by noting that the poetic school and manner that Viereck represented—the French and English decadents—were becoming old-fashioned.

Nevertheless Viereck deserves attention because of his tempestuous blending of careers as a minor and scandalous poet, an indefatigable editor, and a novelist. Furthermore, his persistent support of the German cause is a reminder of the strong pro-German and anti-British feeling of a sizable minority in the United States until 1917 (a feeling that was reborn during the period of isolationism between the two world wars). Though few have defended their pro-German beliefs so ardently, Viereck always maintained that he was a patriotic American, and, despite his admiration for Germany, British and American authors such as Algernon Swinburne and Edgar Allan Poe were the main influence on his work.

Readers were indeed outraged by his verse, not because of revolutionary or modern technique but because of its dwelling upon—some would say obsession with—sensuous description of love, its preaching of a pansexualism or bisexualism in which the sexes fused, and its suggestion of dark vices. When asked, in reference to his poem "The Pilgrim," whether there was such a thing as perversion, he replied, "Perversion is what the other fellow does and what we don't like in the technique of sexual acts. It is not important to anyone except himself and his partner or partners. The sole question is of the effect on the respective nervous and glandular system."

From adolescence Viereck wanted to be the center of attention; yet though he often displayed great confidence and egotism, there were also, as

Phyllis Keller has remarked, "many ambivalences characterizing his intellectual and emotional life." In her psychological analysis, Keller is perhaps overly Freudian in her discussion of the poet's behavior and writings; nonetheless, his parentage and upbringing, particularly in their polarities, often seem to account for George Viereck's activities. Laura Viereck, his mother, was anxious and solicitous; Louis Viereck, his father, born out of wedlock to a beautiful German actress, Edwina Viereck, was impatient and authoritarian. Though Louis von Prillwitz, a Prussian army officer, was Louis Viereck's acknowledged father, many believed that Kaiser Wilhelm I was the child's true father—an idea the poet encouraged. Louis Viereck, who led a checkered social and political career in Germany, married his American-born first cousin, Laura Viereck, in 1881. Their son, George Sylvester Viereck, born in Munich on 31 December 1884, immigrated with his family to the United States in 1896. Having decided early to be a famous poet, Viereck resisted his father's plan to have him take up a trade, lasting only six months as a gardener's apprentice in Baltimore before he rejoined his family in New York and entered public school. In September 1902 he was enrolled at the College of the City of New York, where he was a student in the classical course and earned a B.A. in 1906.

Viereck was an indifferent student, and the most notable event of his college years was probably his meeting William Ellery Leonard and Ludwig Lewisohn, then graduate students at Columbia University, in the early 1900s. Encouraged by his friends, Viereck had his first book, *Gedichte*, a brief collection of poems in German, privately printed in 1904, with financial assistance from Lewisohn, who also supplied an introduction. It gained some favorable comment in a number of American and European newspapers.

Mixed reviews but widespread public attention came two years later with the publication of his first book in English, *A Game at Love and Other Plays* (1906), a group of amoral plays that some thought immoral. In 1907 his first collection of poems in English, *Nineveh, and Other Poems*, brought him great renown as—in the eyes of many readers—a liberating force in a repressed society. Sin and salvation, dressed in sexual imagery, dominate many of the poems; sensuousness and religion are entwined. Several reviewers remarked that Viereck needed to move away from the turbulent sense experiences of adolescence and to develop a more mature poetic style. Yet Viereck's biographer, Elmer Gertz, also the poet's perceptive friend and an

George Sylvester Viereck, circa 1904

admirer of Viereck's poems, has argued with some justification that the title poem, "Nineveh," is more than "the catchpenny shocker played up in the Sunday newspaper supplements of 1907. It was a hymn, rather, to all of the life that swarmed in the metropolis [New York], an inverted apotheosis of the excitement that welled in the city and in the young man's heart." The closing stanzas are apocalyptic:

And when thy body Titan-strong
    Writhes on its great couch of sin,
Yea, though upon the trembling throng
    The very vault of Heaven fall in;

And though the palace of thy feasts
    Sink crumbling in a fiery sea—
I, like the last of Baal's priests,
    Will share thy doom, O Nineveh.

A similar decadent sensuousness dominates many of the poems. There are also poems in which the poet employs images of the flesh in an attempt to arrive at or to convey a mystical meaning. "The Haunted House," for example, closes with these lines:

> With all its beauty and its faultless grace
> Your body, dearest, is a haunted place.
> When I did yield to passion's swift demand,
> One of your lovers touched me with his hand.
> And in the pang of amorous delight
> I hear strange voices calling through the night.

After graduating from City College, Viereck joined the staff of *Current Literature* (which became *Current Opinion* in 1913), maintaining his affiliation with that magazine until 1916. His first novel, *The House of the Vampire*, was published in 1907 to generally unfavorable reviews, and a trip to Europe the following year resulted in *Confessions of a Barbarian* (1910). Most significant, in light of Viereck's later career, are four chapters near the middle of the book in which Viereck compares the American and German systems and betrays what Gertz calls "his instinctive defense and rationalization of things German, notwithstanding their conflict with his own professed beliefs and practices." These same chapters, according to Gertz, were also the basis, during the years immediately preceding World War I, for charges that Viereck was a paid propagandist for the German government. Despite his love for his native country, Viereck chose to remain in the United States when his parents returned to Germany in 1911. Taking over his father's magazine, *Der Deutsche Vor Kämpfer* ("The German Pioneer"), Viereck decided to publish it as a German-language edition of *Current Literature* and renamed it *Rundschau Zweier Welten/Review of Two Worlds* (later published in English as *International: A Review of Two Worlds*). He continued as editor until spring 1918.

In Viereck's second book of poems, *The Candle and the Flame* (1912), the three "gifts" of life—"the belly and the phallus and the grave!"—once more have important roles. The poems, informed by Viereck's reading of works by Sigmund Freud and his followers, convinced some readers that he was possessed by an erotic mania and sang of inflated or unclean passions, and reviews were generally less favorable than those for *Nineveh, and Other Poems*. Once again, however, poems such as the title poem that seem to emphasize the passions also suggest a transcendent meaning:

> Perhaps the passions of mankind
> Are but the torches mystical
> Lit by some spirit hand to find
> The dwelling of the Master-mind
> That knows the secret of it all,
> In the great darkness and the wind.

At times, too, the inflated rhetoric is deflated by what Keller calls a "gentle self-mockery."

In the introduction to *The Candle and the Flame* Viereck spoke of himself and his work in self-congratulatory words that offended several readers. This introduction, like several of his others, offers insight into his poetry and his interests in general. In words that may not be wholly sincere, he spoke of a farewell to poetry; it is true that his interests in fiction, autobiography, and editorial work, especially on behalf of good German-American relations, showed that he was never wholly committed to poetry. More particularly, the outbreak of World War I and the consequent vilification of Germany in much of the American press made him intensify his role as propagandist.

The war broke out in late July 1914, shortly after Viereck had returned to the United States from a two-month visit to his parents in Germany, and in August 1914, while pro-German sentiment was still strong in the United States, Viereck and others founded the *Fatherland,* a weekly magazine dedicated to presenting the German point of view toward the war. The magazine was briefly retitled *New World* in February 1917 before it became *Viereck's: The American Weekly* in the same month. In August 1918 it became *Viereck's American Monthly,* and in October 1920 Viereck dropped his name from the title. He sold the magazine in October 1927.

The sinking of the *Lusitania* in May 1915 solidified anti-German feeling in the United States. Public opinion against Viereck was intensified when the 15 August 1915 issue of the *New York World* published an exchange of letters between Viereck and Dr. Heinrich Albert that suggested Viereck was a paid propagandist for the German government. Viereck denied the charge flatly in an editorial for the *Fatherland* (25 August 1915): "no German official had any control over the policy of my paper." A 1918 U.S. Justice Department investigation of Viereck failed to produce an indictment, but, as Gertz has noted, he "never gave a really satisfactory explanation" of the letters' contents, and his reputation was severely damaged in the eyes of the American public.

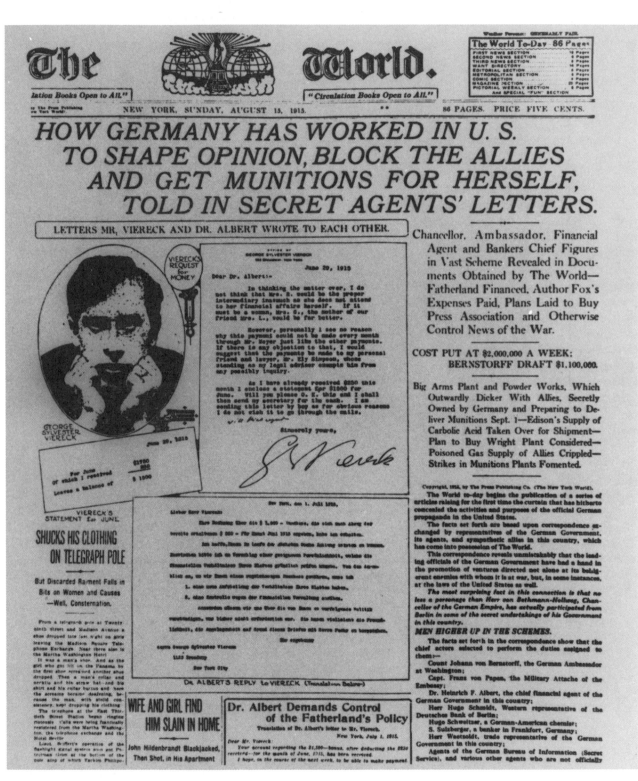

The newspaper story that intensified public opinion against Viereck and led to a U.S. Justice Department investigation of his pro-German activities

At the height of the controversy over his political stance Viereck married Gretchen Hein on 30 September 1915. They had two sons: Peter Robert Edwin (born in 1916) and George Sylvester, Jr. (born in 1918).

Poetry and propaganda were combined in *Songs of Armageddon and Other Poems* (1916). In "William II, Prince of Peace," addressed to the German Kaiser and first published in August 1914, Viereck argued that the Kaiser had to unsheathe his sword in order to maintain the freedom of the Teutonic race in the face of British financial domination, French murders, and Russian pogroms. The poem ends:

> Against the fell Barbarian horde
>   Thy people stand, a living wall
> Now fight for God's peace with thy sword
>   For if thou fail, a world shall fall!

In the dominant pro-Allied atmosphere of 1916 the publication of this eulogy to the Kaiser was imprudent. Some of the poems are self-righteous and inhumane; others, such as "The Neutral" (an appeal to Woodrow Wilson), are poignant, if sentimental. Though the book also contained "Hymn of Armageddon," in praise of Theodore Roosevelt, its reception suffered from the public perception of the poet. The *New York Times*, however, praised the war poems as "the most spirited expressions of the German point of view that have been made in English verse."

Viereck's open pro-Germanism led to ostracism and a decline in both his renown as a poet and his poetic output (though he continued to write prolifically in other genres). He was expelled from both the Poetry Society of America (of which he had been a founding member) and the Author's League.

In 1923, when Viereck's reputation as a writer had reached a low point, E. Haldeman-Julius, publisher of the nickel Little Blue Books, convinced him to edit and write introductions for Little Blue Book collections of verse by the poets he admired. For these books, which included works by poets such as Dante Gabriel Rossetti, Oscar Wilde, and Algernon Swinburne, he wrote introductions that both illuminated those writers' works and exemplified his own ideas about poetry. Haldeman-Julius also published two collections of Viereck's poems, *The Haunted House, and Other Poems* (1924) and *The Three Sphinxes, and Other Poems* (1924), which for the most part contain previously published work. Through systematic mailing and cor-

George Sylvester Viereck, circa 1931

respondence, Viereck was able to make his poetry known once more to a number of well-known literary figures; but he was generally ignored by the poetry-reading public.

In the period between the world wars Viereck devoted much of his time to writing history, psychology, and fiction, but *My Flesh and Blood: A Lyric Autobiography, with Indiscreet Annotations* (1931) contains new poems as well as verse published earlier. His annotations to the poems fuse them with autobiography. Benefiting from the growth in psychological research, he analyzes the sexual themes and complexes in his work:

> Behold the naked ghosts that haunt my soul,
>   Spawn of strange nights, a scarlet brotherhood.
>   Partake of me. This is my flesh and blood.
> Caress my body when you touch this scroll.

Such verses, Gertz believes, are examples of some of Viereck's most striking language and thought.

Viereck's pro-German activities during the 1930s generated more controversy. Though he was not a Nazi and denied charges that he was anti-Semitic, he refused to repudiate his support of Hitler's government, which helped to finance his pro-German publishing activities. In September 1941 he was indicted, under the Foreign Agents Registration Act of 1938, for failing to disclose fully his activities as a paid propagandist for the German government. He was convicted in March 1942, sentenced to a term of two-to-six years, and fined $1,500. The U.S. Supreme Court reversed his conviction in March 1943, after he had served one year in prison, but in July 1943 he was convicted on further charges. The Supreme Court refused to review this case, and he remained incarcerated until May 1947.

After his first conviction his wife tried to convince him to repudiate the Nazis, but Viereck refused, and, after their younger son, George Sylvester Viereck, Jr., was killed while fighting with the U.S. Army in Anzio, Gretchen Viereck became estranged from her husband. Viereck's years in prison led, in Gertz's estimation, to a poetic rebirth. Some of these poems, which appeared as a special issue of the *Wisconsin Poetry Magazine* (July 1958), are effective in their simplicity of feeling ("If You Had Died") or demotic language ("Portrait of an Alley Cat").

After his release from prison, Viereck was largely unable to rehabilitate his literary career, although he had one success, with *Men into Beasts* (1952), a memoir of his prison experiences, which sold nearly 500,000 copies. In 1955 he published *The Bankrupt*, a poem about the decay of Western civilization.

During his last years, plagued by ill health, unable to win back his wife, Gretchen, and still ambivalent about his support of the German Nazi government, he was reconciled to his son, Peter Viereck, now a better-known poet than the father. George Sylvester Viereck died on 18 March 1962, destined to be remembered more for his politics than for his work as a poet.

References:

Elmer Gertz, *Odyssey of a Barbarian: the Biography of George Sylvester Viereck* (Buffalo, N.Y.: Prometheus Books, 1978);

Neil M. Johnson, *George Sylvester Viereck, German American Propagandist* (Urbana, Chicago & London: University of Illinois Press, 1972);

Phyllis Keller, "George Sylvester Viereck . . . The Making of a German-American Militant," in her *States of Being: German Intellectuals and the First World War* (Cambridge & London: Harvard University Press, 1979), pp. 119-188;

Ludwig Lewisohn, *The Story of American Literature* (New York: Harper, 1932), pp. 313, 365-366, 555.

Papers:

The largest collection of Viereck's manuscripts is at the University of Iowa Library.

William Carlos Williams

John Xiros Cooper
Mount Royal College

BIRTH: Rutherford, New Jersey, 17 September 1883, to William George and Raquel Hélène Rose Hoheb Williams.

EDUCATION: M.D., University of Pennsylvania, 1906; University of Leipzig, 1909-1910.

MARRIAGE: 12 December 1912 to Florence Herman; children: William Eric, Paul Herman.

AWARDS AND HONORS: *Dial* Award, 1926; LL.D., University of Buffalo, 1946; Russell Loines Award (National Institute of Arts and Letters), 1948; National Book Award for *Selected Poems* and *Paterson (Book Three)*, 1950; fellow, Library of Congress, 1950; D.Litt., Rutgers University, 1950; D.Litt., Bard College, 1950; appointed Consultant in Poetry, Library of Congress, 1952 (did not serve); Bollingen Prize in Poetry, 1952; Levinson Prize (*Poetry* magazine), 1954; Oscar Blumenthal Prize (*Poetry* magazine), 1955; American Academy of Poets Fellowship, 1956; Brandeis University Creative Arts Medal, 1958; Pulitzer Prize for *Pictures from Brueghel and other poems*, 1963; National Institute and American Academy of Arts and Letters Gold Medal, 1963.

DEATH: Rutherford, New Jersey, 4 March 1963.

BOOKS: *Poems* (Rutherford, N.J.: Privately printed, 1909);
The Tempers (London: Elkin Mathews, 1913);
Al Que Quiere! (Boston: Four Seas, 1917);
Kora in Hell: Improvisations (Boston: Four Seas, 1920);
Sour Grapes (Boston: Four Seas, 1921);
The Great American Novel (Paris: Three Mountains Press, 1923);
Spring and All (Paris: Contact Editions, 1923);
GO GO (New York: Monroe Wheeler, 1923);
In the American Grain (New York: A. & C. Boni, 1925; London: MacGibbon & Kee, 1967);
A Voyage to Pagany (New York: Macaulay, 1928);
A Novelette and Other Prose (1921-1931) (Toulon, France: TO Publishers, 1932);

The Knife of the Times and Other Stories (Ithaca, N.Y.: Dragon Press, 1932);
The Cod Head (San Francisco: Harvest Press, 1932);
Collected Poems 1921-1931 (New York: Objectivist Press, 1934);
An Early Martyr and Other Poems (New York: Alcestis Press, 1935);
Adam & Eve & The City (Peru, Vt.: Alcestis Press, 1936);

Photograph by Charles Sheeler; courtesy of William Eric Williams

White Mule (Norfolk, Conn.: New Directions, 1937; London: MacGibbon & Kee, 1965);

Life along the Passaic River (Norfolk, Conn.: New Directions, 1938);

The Complete Collected Poems (Norfolk, Conn.: New Directions, 1938);

In the Money: White Mule—Part II (Norfolk, Conn.: New Directions, 1940; London: MacGibbon & Kee, 1965);

The Broken Span (Norfolk, Conn.: New Directions, 1941);

The Wedge (Cummington, Mass.: Cummington Press, 1944);

Paterson (Book One) (Norfolk, Conn.: New Directions, 1946);

Paterson (Book Two) (Norfolk, Conn.: New Directions, 1948);

The Clouds, Aigeltinger, Russia, & (Aurora, N.Y.: Wells College Press/Cummington, Mass.: Cummington Press, 1948);

A Dream of Love: A Play in Three Acts and Eight Scenes (Norfolk, Conn.: New Directions, 1948);

Selected Poems (Norfolk, Conn.: New Directions, 1949; enlarged, 1968);

The Pink Church (Columbus, Ohio: Golden Goose Press, 1949);

Paterson (Book Three) (Norfolk, Conn.: New Directions, 1949);

The Collected Later Poems (Norfolk, Conn.: New Directions, 1950; revised, 1963; London: MacGibbon & Kee, 1965);

Make Light of It: Collected Stories (New York: Random House, 1950);

A Beginning on the Short Story [Notes] (Yonkers, N.Y.: Alicat Bookshop Press, 1950);

Paterson (Book Four) (Norfolk, Conn.: New Directions, 1951);

The Autobiography (New York: Random House, 1951; London: MacGibbon & Kee, 1968);

The Collected Earlier Poems (Norfolk, Conn.: New Directions, 1951; London: MacGibbon & Kee, 1967);

The Build-Up: A Novel (New York: Random House, 1952; London: MacGibbon & Kee, 1969);

The Desert Music and Other Poems (New York: Random House, 1954);

Selected Essays (New York: Random House, 1954);

Journey to Love (New York: Random House, 1955);

I Wanted to Write a Poem, reported and edited by Edith Heal (Boston: Beacon Press, 1958; London: Cape, 1967);

Paterson (Book Five) (Norfolk, Conn.: New Directions, 1958);

Yes, Mrs. Williams: A Personal Record of My Mother (New York: McDowell, Obolensky, 1959);

The Farmers' Daughters: The Collected Stories (Norfolk, Conn.: New Directions, 1961);

Many Loves and Other Plays: The Collected Plays (Norfolk, Conn.: New Directions, 1961);

Pictures from Brueghel and other poems (Norfolk, Conn.: New Directions, 1962; London: MacGibbon & Kee, 1963);

Paterson, books 1-5 and notes for book 6 (New York: New Directions, 1963; London: MacGibbon & Kee, 1964);

The William Carlos Williams Reader, edited by M. L. Rosenthal (New York: New Directions, 1966; London: MacGibbon & Kee, 1967);

Imaginations, edited by Webster Schott (New York: New Directions, 1970; London: MacGibbon & Kee, 1970);

The Embodiment of Knowledge, edited by Ron Loewinsohn (New York: New Directions, 1974);

A Recognizable Image: William Carlos Williams on Art and Artists, edited by Bram Dijkstra (New York: New Directions, 1978).

OTHER: "Rome," edited by Steven Ross Loevy, *Iowa Review*, 9 (Spring 1978): 1-65.

TRANSLATIONS: Philippe Soupault, *Last Nights in Paris* (New York: Macaulay, 1929);

Yvan Goll, *Jean sans Terre: Landless John*, translated by Williams, Lionel Abel, Clark Mills, and John Gould Fletcher (San Francisco: Grabhorn Press, 1944);

Pedro Espinosa (Don Francisco de Quevedo), *The Dog & the Fever*, translated by Williams and Raquel Hélène Williams (Hamden, Conn.: Shoestring Press, 1954).

One should perhaps always resist the temptation to sum up a writer's life and work, his "essence," by way of a single revealing anecdote. In the case of William Carlos Williams, however, a story Kenneth Burke has told captures something of that special quality of temper and feeling that pervades Williams's life and work. Some years after Williams had retired from his medical practice he, Burke, and a neighbor's dog were walking slowly along a beach in Florida. The dog was limping. Burke, hoping to help the dog, leaned down clumsily to grasp the injured paw, and the dog, suddenly frightened, nearly bit him. Williams took the paw in his left hand and started to feel around for the problem. "It was a gesture," Burke writes, "at once expert and imaginative, something in which to have

The poet's parents: William George and Raquel Hélène Rose (Elena) Hoheb Williams (courtesy of William Eric Williams)

perfect confidence, as both the cur and I saw in a flash." Probing the dog's padded paw "lightly, quickly, and above all *surely*," Williams found a small burr and removed it without hurting the animal.

This "touch" for handling the body, acquired over many decades as a physician, provides, paradoxically, the best introduction to his writing, for Williams's poetics are uniquely physical. For him reality, perception, and language are materially based, and the knowledge derived from the contact of mind and earth, language and the real, leads to the same sort of awareness that comes from touching and handling, from caressing and probing and cupping the intimately known and loved. One may never be able to "place" the world's body explicitly and smoothly in some supramundane cosmology, either philosophical or religious, but one "knows" it in the same way a mountain climber knows a mountain, not by looking at a map merely, but in his fingers and arms, his feet, his knees, and the twists of his torso, knowing the mountain as a subtly variable network of textures, physical pressures, tolerances, and tastes. The physician cannot avoid this knowledge of each unique human body he touches. Dr. Williams did not, of course, entirely reject conceptual or theoretical knowledge; he merely wanted to acknowledge that the schematizing intelligence was only a small part of a writer's equipment. For him the primary function of the mind was not to classify, analyze, and transcend the world, but to lay it bare and penetrate it. Needing to get one's hands on things, to get one's hands "dirty," distinguished, he felt, the American mind from the European. If there be such a thing as "transcendence," it was got through the acceptance and penetration of things, not by their renunciation.

The philosophical consequences of such an orientation lead in the direction of that quintessential American idea: pragmatism. Had Williams bent his intelligence to philosophy he would no doubt have contributed a superb chapter to pragmatist theory and logic, begun in the last years of the nineteenth century by C. S. Pierce, William James, and John Dewey. His contribution would have surely emphasized the physical dimension of knowing, knowing in the body, not simply in the head. "A thing known passes out of the mind into the muscles . . ." is the perception of a poet, rather than a philosopher. Such a notion of the physicality of knowledge, its material "embodiment," to use one of Williams's favorite words, would have allowed him, Ron Loewinsohn rightly suggests, to appreciate Norman Mailer's perception that Muhammad Ali's combinations of rights and lefts in the boxing ring demonstrate as much intelligence, poise, and humor as anything to be found in the poetry of Alexander Pope or the witty verbal duels of Oscar Wilde's comedies. Although never extensively developed in the abstract, these ideas lie at the heart of Williams's aesthetics and penetrate not only his poetry, but also his thinking about the cultural development of the United States as a whole.

In his thinking about American culture Williams's notion of the concrete particular led him to champion the concrete *and* the particular, to recognize and acknowledge "place" and locality as the "field" in which significant art happens. He early turned a deaf ear to the classical conception of art he heard T. S. Eliot voice in the early years of modernism, an art that upheld the universal over the particular, the abstract over the concrete, the international over the regional, the cosmopolis over "our town."

Yet Williams's position was never a mere unthinking Babbittry; it was not a position minted from fear and ignorance. It was much more positive than that. In his experience of the greatest literature and art, he was struck by the undeniable sense of place and occasion that the great works always seemed to manifest. The best art does not breathe, he believed, an ethereal atmosphere of pure thought and unbodied feeling divorced from necessary contact with the real life of a real place: "every individual, every place, every opportunity of thought is both favored and limited by its emplacement in time and place. Chinese 8th cent., Italian 12th, English 15th, French 18th, African, etc. All sorts of complicated conditions and circumstances of land, climate, blood, surround every deed that is done." In this respect Williams should be grouped with the modernist writers of very similar orientation, poets such as the Scottish modernist Hugh MacDiarmid, or the Nobel laureate from Chile, Pablo Neruda, rather than with cosmopolitan modernists such as T. S. Eliot and Ezra Pound, who were part of the modernism that flourished in the European capitals during the first three decades of the twentieth century. Of course, Williams possessed a cosmopolitan side of his own, derived from his family background, from his English father, from his mother, a woman in whom several distinct cultures joined, from travel, and from his contact with the leading modernist cosmopolites of his time. But when he finally sat down to work out his ideas and beliefs in the 1920s and after, his primary allegiances became visible, and they pointed to the place he called home—the New Jersey of his birth. There, in the intense observation of his place, he made a verbal art as profound and moving as any in modern literature. And beyond his own considerable achievement he would help to make it possible for American writers to feel finally, and finely, at home in their own land, by showing them that the great humane values, the most sophisticated approaches to art, are just as accessible in the vicinity of the Passaic as they are on the Left Bank of the Seine.

He was born on 17 September 1883 in Rutherford, New Jersey, the city in which he would marry, bring up his sons, live, practice his profession, write, and eventually die. Rutherford was still a rural town of about three thousand inhabitants in the 1880s and 1890s. Williams in later years would remember that rural landscape, with its flowering trees, its meadows, and the duck hunters skirting the clumps of trees on crisp fall days. The cold copper mines that had provided the economic backbone of the region in the earlier part of the nineteenth century were already long closed, replaced by small manufacturing concerns and other commercial enterprises.

His father, William George, came from pure British stock, a fact he was never to forget even though he had been taken from England at the age

William Carlos and Edgar Williams (courtesy of William Eric Williams)

ders of the liberal Unitarian Society of Rutherford, at whose services his sons sang in the choir. He understood and promoted the value of the best possible education and insisted that his sons, William Carlos and Edgar, be well-read in the classics and informed about the leading ideas of their time. He was an unbending, dignified man whose ruling passion seemed to be devotion to duty and to the Englishness he never abandoned. He was a man, William Carlos wrote in "Adam" eighteen years after his death, who tasted "the death that duty brings" and who could only be imagined with "a British passport/always in his pocket—."

His mother's family was scattered over a number of Caribbean islands, principally in Martinique and Puerto Rico. Raquel Hélène Rose Hoheb Williams (called Elena at home) was partly French, Dutch, Spanish, and Jewish. She studied art in Paris at l'Ecole des Arts Industrielles from 1876 to 1879. She remembered this happy sojourn in Paris, the "capital of the nineteenth century" as Walter Benjamin called it, her whole life, longing to return there from her exile, first in Puerto Rico, to which she returned at the end of the 1870s, and later in Rutherford. She savored every opportunity to revisit the city of her youthful memories. She was in the charge of her physician brother, Carlos Hoheb, when she met William George Williams. On 29 November 1882 the two young people were married in Brooklyn and went to live in Rutherford, across the Hudson River from New York City.

Elena was an exotic presence in the Williams household. She did not take to the English language very well, preferring to speak her native Spanish at home, and to practice French, the language she most loved, whenever there was anyone about who knew it. She did not mix easily with the citizens of Rutherford and the Williams home received a continual procession of visitors, Elena's relatives and friends from the Caribbean and from Paris, who would arrive for long spells. It was through this contact that she was able to forget the Protestant provincialism of life along the Passaic. She was a profound influence on her eldest son, an influence William Carlos explored explicitly in *Yes, Mrs. Williams: A Personal Record of My Mother* (1959). She provided him with one dimension of the feminine presence that haunts his poetry, and she was a mirror in which he saw reflected something of himself. As he wrote in "Eve,"

I sometimes detect in your face
a puzzled pity for me
your son—

of five. He was to remain a British citizen all his days. He was known as a quiet man whose business, the manufacture and distribution of eau de cologne, often took him from his family for varying lengths of time, including one trip to Latin America that lasted for an entire year. He was in every respect a late-Victorian gentleman, whose regular way of life did not change all through his working years. Perhaps under the influence of George Bernard Shaw's music journalism, he had developed a taste for the music drama of Richard Wagner. His acknowledged favorite among writers was Rudyard Kipling, the apologist and bard of the British imperial presence in what is now called the Third World. William George reflected exactly the culture and temper of liberal progressives in the North Atlantic world of the late nineteenth century. He thought of himself as a socialist, probably having come under the influence of Shaw's Fabianism. Characteristically, he was one of the foun-

I have never been close to you
—mostly your own fault;
in that I am like you.

She seems to have had what is sometimes thought of as the temperament of an artist (that is, she was moody) and a hankering after gentility, insisting all her life that her family respect the canons of good taste and good manners. She longed for the elegance and refinement of Paris, yet she was also something of a puritan, expressing disappointment at the earthiness of some of her son's poetic language. She shared with her husband a love of the opera and would be heard singing arias from *La Traviata* through the house in Rutherford. "Take her to the opera" was William George's suggestion to William Carlos when he left Elena in his son's care for a year.

This exotic, passionate, yet fragile and distant woman was not the only feminine influence on Williams. His grandmother, Emily Dickinson Wellcome, who, living in the Williams home, was primarily responsible for raising him through his early years, played an even more important role. Grandma Wellcome, William George's mother (the name Wellcome came from a second marriage), took little "Willie" under her wing when he was born in 1883. At fifty she was still full of vigor and independence; she had an earthy toughness that contrasted sharply with the delicacy of her vaguely aristocratic daughter-in-law. She taught Williams the English language after it became clear that his mother was not going to make much of an effort to learn the language herself. The two women did not like each other, and occasionally Elena Williams was forced to assert her authority in the Williams household against the encroachments of her mother-in-law. Williams felt closer to his grandmother in many respects than he did to his mother. Certainly the older woman figures more centrally in his work. She became, as Paul Mariani has suggested, "the central mythic presence in Williams' young life." Fierce old Emily Wellcome is remembered in Williams's "Dedication for a Plot of Ground," "Last Words of My English Grandmother," and "The Wanderer," where, Reed Whittemore has argued, she becomes "a strange combination of muse and antimuse." Williams said in *I Wanted to Write a Poem* (1958), that "The Wanderer" "is a story of growing up. The old woman in it is my grandmother, raised to heroic proportions. I endowed her with magic qualities. She had seized me from my mother as her special possession, adopted me, and her purpose in life was to make me her own. But my mother ended all that with a slap in the puss." The tension between Elena Williams and Emily Wellcome ended in 1920 with the older woman's death. Williams romanticized his memory of her; and the feminine principle or spirit she embodied, attaining mythic proportions, was transmuted again and again in many poems and prose pieces. For Williams finally she represented two things, a kind of stubborn independence in the face of constant travail and a great, consuming fecundity, a fruitfulness made richer and more splendid by its contrast with the sterilities of a commercial and conformist America that Williams saw emerging all his life. Later, Florence Herman, Williams's wife, would provide a third dimension in the feminine idea the poet created over his long artistic life.

It is useful for an understanding of Williams's work to emphasize his immediate environment, because, along with the work of most other modernist and post-modernist poets, his art is fundamentally autobiographical. This fact is one of the consequences of an aesthetic based on the local, the concrete, and the particular. One's own life offers itself as the immediate "stuff" of one's art. Immediacy, indeed, came to be one of the great rallying cries of modernism. Any intensive study of Williams's literary output needs to have a firm grasp of the immediate environment, both geographical and domestic, in which he lived, worked, and wrote. Yet one should, of course, avoid narrowly biographical interpretation of works of art. The biographical approach that is most productive for criticism notes the transmutation of immediate materials into the new life of those materials in the poem itself. One should not scrutinize the poem for references to particular people and events, but for what the poet has done with them, what imperative in the poem's idea these materials serve.

With his younger brother Edgar, Williams attended the public schools in his hometown through the early and mid 1890s, was taken to the Unitarian church of which his father was a founder, and indulged in all those pastimes and pleasures which, in semirural Rutherford, he was to remember fondly in *The Autobiography* (1951). In 1897, with her husband off in Argentina on business for a year, Elena Williams took her sons to Europe in order to indulge her longing to revivify the memories of her art-student days in Paris, and to look to the refinement of the boys' education. Williams was fourteen. In Europe the family set up house in Geneva, Switzerland, and the boys attended a private school with an international student body,

William George, William Carlos, Elena, and Edgar Williams, circa 1899 (courtesy of William Eric Williams)

the Chateau de Lancy. Elena Williams's aim was to have the boys acquire fluency in French, but this goal proved almost impossible because the majority of the boys in the school were British and many of the masters spoke English most of the time. By the time the family moved on to Paris for the last few months of their stay in Europe and the two brothers were enrolled in a French school, the Lycée Condorcet, their French was only slightly better than it had been when they first arrived in Geneva. Unable to function in the language of instruction at the Lycée, they were soon floundering in their work and were withdrawn from the school.

Upon the family's return to the United States in 1899, Williams and his brother were sent to private school in New York City, Horace Mann High School, near Columbia University at Morningside Heights. Things went much better for them at Horace Mann, at that time one of the best, and best-known, schools on the eastern seaboard. The two boys commuted from New Jersey to Manhattan's upper West Side every school day for three years. There Williams was introduced for the first time to the systematic study of poetry under the tutelage of William Abbott, who taught Williams something of the English tradition in poetry from Geoffrey

Chaucer to Alfred Tennyson. With Abbott, Williams studied the tradition, but especially John Milton, and the great romantics, William Wordsworth, Samuel Taylor Coleridge, and John Keats. Keats was particularly important, as it was his influence that pervaded Williams's earliest verses. Williams came to love Abbott—"Uncle Billy" as he was affectionately called by his pupils—and dedicated his *Selected Essays* (1954) to his memory, writing that he was "the first English teacher who ever gave me an A." At Horace Mann, however, the *A*'s were few and far between. Williams finished three years at the school with an overall *C* average. It was in this period that he began to write his first imaginative work, keeping a series of copybooks in which he set down free-ranging, Whitmanesque ruminations. Of all the poets he had read, there may have been poets, such as Keats, who exerted specifically literary influences early on, but it was Walt Whitman in whose loose, free-wheeling, passionate idiom Williams filled up his notebooks. For his formal poeticizing, however, the young Williams turned to the lessons of the great English tradition, to the works of Edmund Spenser, Keats, and Tennyson. His early poems are stanzaic and rhymed, with laboriously metered lines in which the massed iambs

Principal cast members for Mr Hamlet of Denmark, *a musical comedy version of Shakespeare's play produced by the Mask and Wig Club at the University of Pennsylvania in 1905 (photograph from* The Record of the Class of Nineteen Hundred and Five). *Williams, who played Polonius, is second from right.*

and trochees are "poetically" phrased. The growing influence of Keats and Tennyson dominated Williams's writing all through his college years. He did not lay aside the Keatsian burden until after the appearance of his first book, *Poems,* which he published privately in 1909.

At Horace Mann, Williams resolved to dedicate his life to writing, having tasted early the intense satisfaction which art can give the practitioner. However, his parents took for granted that an education in a suitable profession lay ahead for him, and their elder son acquiesced in that demand. His artistic ambitions remained his own secret commitment with himself.

From Horace Mann, Williams went on to the school of dentistry at the University of Pennsylvania, in Philadelphia, in 1902. Within a year he had transferred to the medical school, where he bent his energies to the rigors of training in medicine. Meanwhile he kept up with his interest in poetry. During his first semester he met Ezra Pound, who introduced him in the spring of 1905 to another young poet, Hilda Doolittle (H. D.),

whose father was a professor at Penn. The connection with Pound is especially important. Although their friendship had its rocky periods, primarily caused by sometimes violent disagreements over Pound's later socioeconomic and political passions, it lasted for the rest of Williams's life. Pound was a precocious seventeen-year-old sophomore when Williams arrived at Penn as a somewhat shy nineteen-year-old freshman. The younger man, studying languages and humanities, had already developed what often passed in those days as a poet's personality. Given to flamboyance of language, gesture, and dress, Pound was living out the American afterglow of the English fin de siècle, the Yellow Nineties. However, his posturing masked, as Williams could see, a talented young man, whose passionate devotion to poetry was total. He took the young Pound's commitment to writing to heart, and it gave him an immediate contemporary model, more public and showy, that paralleled his own quieter vow.

In his high school and college years Williams was fastidiously working within the formal and thematic bounds of the English poetic tradition, a tradition codified by Francis Turner Palgrave in his widely read anthology, *The Golden Treasury of the Best Songs and Lyrical Poems in the English Language* (1861; revised and enlarged, 1891). But under the influence of Pound, he soon began to grow away from these adolescent attractions and toward something more recognizably modern. Pound's opinions, always forcefully and directly expressed, made Williams aware that the kind of Keatsian and Whitmanesque lyrics he was writing were like those of countless other versifiers, of varying degrees of competence, on both sides of the Atlantic. Pound's importance as an influence on the early Williams was precisely on this point: Pound simply made Williams aware of all the poetic work that did not need doing. Indeed the service Pound rendered Williams in this respect can be seen no more clearly than in a 1909 letter Pound wrote Williams from London responding to the New Jersey poet's first slim volume of Keatsian imitations: "I hope to God you have no feelings. If you have, burn this *before* reading." Lesser writers might have been crushed by the rest of Pound's letter. It is a tribute to Williams's sense of his own vocation that this response firmly closed the door on Palgrave forever and freed Williams to develop his own poetic practice, his own idiom, his own subject matter. Pound's placing comment comes near the end of his letter, when he says that Williams is "out of touch" with the kind of work being produced at the center of the literary world. Stacked up against poems by even writers of the second rank, *Poems* does not measure up. As Pound wrote, "Individual, original it is not. Great art it is not. Poetic it is, but there are innumerable poetic volumes poured out here in Gomorrah [London]. . . . Your book would not attract even passing attention here. There are fine lines in it, but nowhere I think do you add anything to the poets you have used as models."

Putting Williams in touch with what was thought and felt at the heart of the literary world, as London was in the years before World War I, was Pound's greatest service. Pound made Williams aware of the impossibility of pursuing the dead rituals of a moribund poetic tradition, deriving mainly from the decay of English and American romanticism. That past was perceived by the younger generation in 1909 as having made poetry unhealthily sentimental and false to the sources of its original inspiration. It accused the poetry of the nineteenth century of using a poem to ornament a feeling or, worse, to fake it, rather than making

the poem the radiant vehicle for the presentation, as directly and cleanly as possible, of that which, in the world, provokes and stimulates feeling. The younger generation, of course, overstated their condemnations, but there was enough validity to their claims that, when the polemical smoke cleared, the modernist fire could be seen burning with a hard, gemlike flame. If modernism begins anywhere, it begins in this opposition to a tradition clotted with an obsessive dependence on stanzaic regularity, an unnecessarily archaic diction, and intellectual and emotional fuzziness, a kind of bloated profligacy in the spending of the devalued, inflated currencies of the past. What Pound helped Williams learn was the avoidance of "literature," in this degenerated sense of the word, how to avoid it, paradoxically, for the better health of the art. Only one hundred copies of *Poems* were printed, and of that one hundred only the whereabouts of ten are known (nine are in major research libraries). Williams, after he turned from the early sources of his art, did everything he could to discourage readers from looking into this early work. None of the

Photograph of Williams from the 1906 University of Pennsylvania yearbook, The Scope, *for which Williams was art editor*

poems has ever been republished in any of the collections and selections of his work over which Williams had any authority.

The first major modernist attempt to put into practice a positive poetics minted from the aggressive critique of the past was the movement known in London as *imagisme*. Although its principles had begun to be formulated as early as 1908 by T. E. Hulme, an English disciple of the French philosophers Henri Bergson and Georges Sorel, Pound quickly put himself at the center of the group, which flourished in bohemian London from 1911 to 1916. The writers involved preferred to use the French spelling of the name of their movement because the poetry of nineteenth-century France provided one of the literary sources of *imagisme*. The French writer venerated by *les imagistes* as a predecessor was Théophile Gautier, whose *Émaux et Camées* (1852) offered a model of the finely chiselled lyric, built around lucidly presented images, cleanly phrased, and exquisitely musical, a model on which an English poetic practice might be founded, a model, indeed, that not only contrasted with the concurrent Tennysonian norm, but was savored as a superior rebuke to that banal "ideal."

Hulme provided a philosophical justification for *imagisme*, but it was left to Pound to propound a set of operating procedures in an article signed by F. S. Flint, but attributed to Pound (*Poetry*, March 1913):

> 1. Direct treatment of the "thing" whether subjective or objective.
> 2. To use absolutely no word that does not contribute to the presentation.
> 3. As regarding rhythm: to compose in the sequence of the musical phrase, not in the sequence of a metronome.

Many scholars and critics have found it impossible to say exactly what these rules mean within the compass of the larger questions of aesthetics and the history of poetry. However, *les imagistes* knew what they meant, and the poetry produced was recognizably different from the post-romantic gush against which *imagiste* restraint stood firm. Although never a charter member of the movement, Williams was receptive to its doctrines and his poetry was profoundly influenced by it. His verse in this new style was included in the several anthologies that *les imagistes* collected and published in London. In the main, the movement helped reform Williams's rather conventional sense of poetic diction and his heavily rhetorical approach to the

poem. He turned away from the early poetic practice exemplified in "On a Proposed Trip South," which he had included in his first book:

> E'er have I known December in a weave
> Of blanched crystal, when, thrice one short night
> Packed full with magic, and oh blissful sight!
> N'er so warmly doth for April grieve[.]

His new poetic is apparent in "To Mark Antony in Heaven," which appeared in Pound's anthology *Des Imagistes* (1914):

> This quiet morning light
> reflected, how many times
> from grass and trees and clouds
> enters my north room
> touching the walls with
> grass and clouds and trees.

The important change here is not simply the obvious renovations of diction and form; more striking is the change in "voice." In the second excerpt an individual and concretely placeable voice is speaking. It is a voice that, conceivably, might be used in everyday intercourse, under the stress or sway of certain moods or particular circumstances of feeling. The voice of the first excerpt is conventionally "poetic," a voice produced by screwing up one's inwardness into an awkwardly carried conventional poetic posture. This nineteenth-century voice, furthermore, suggests no *particular* speaker, speaking from some concrete context of situation. Instead, we hear a tradition speaking; the young man who has written these lines is merely a field of receptivities in which a poem, entirely impersonal and abstract, is happening. The slightly older man responsible for "To Mark Antony in Heaven" has shifted his ground, and the voice he has created is not simply being produced by the manipulation of certain acceptable literary conventions. It is the voice, the particular, concrete voice, of an experience, finding in the resources of words, word clusters, line breaks, an expressive language which more lucidly embodies the dynamics of things seen, things thought, things felt.

At the University of Pennsylvania Williams undertook that necessary exploration of the tradition, finding in it much to value, much to imitate, but finding finally that a great deal of it needed to be set aside, indeed rejected outright, in order to permit his talent to flower. But Ezra Pound and Hilda Doolittle were not the only influences in those years. While at Penn he met Charles Demuth, an art student, at the boardinghouse where he took

Charles Demuth's 1928 painting I Saw the Figure 5 in Gold, *inspired by Williams's poem "The Great Figure," collected in* Sour Grapes *(by permission of the Metropolitan Museum of Art, Alfred Stieglitz Collection; 1949)*

his meals. This connection would prove to be as fruitful as the connection with Pound. Demuth did not have Pound's irascible and aggressive personality. A bit easier to get along with, he was also tilling a different artistic field, painting, which had the benefit of having been recognized as adjacent to poetry as early as the *Ars Poetica* of Horace in Augustan Rome. Williams and Demuth were fast friends until Demuth's death in 1934. Although his life was short, Demuth exerted an important influence on native American painting in the 1920s. The ten years before World War I, when Williams and Demuth were first getting acquainted, was a very good time to know such a painter. The same renovatory winds which had begun to blow through poetry in movements such as *imagisme* had in fact been reaching hurricane force in painting for a considerable time. Again the impetus and focus of

change in the tradition of representational art had occurred under French leadership. With the impressionists as artistic forefathers, the post-impressionists in the 1890s, Cezanne and Van Gogh principally, had pushed painting to the brink of the breakdown of the representational picture plane toward a more painterly abstractionism. The "materials" of the painter—structure, volume, texture, and, above all, color—instead of doing service in the making of oil replicas of the "real" world, became themselves the overt signs of a new way of seeing.

For Williams contact with Demuth in those years gave him access, through a knowledgeable friend, to the excitement and renovatory energy animating the avant-garde art of that time. Decades later Williams would pinpoint painting as an early and profound influence: "As I look back, I think it was the French painters rather than the writers who influenced us, and their influence was very great. They created an atmosphere of release, color release, release from stereotyped forms, trite subjects." Through his contact with Demuth, Williams learned that the painter's medium is paint, not "stereotyped forms, trite subjects." In the same way the poet's medium is language, words, not the conventional postures, dictions, and rhetorical effects of a thoroughly routine romanticism. Words became material objects that filled the mouth, pushed the mouth in odd shapes and movements, and, moreover, words were of particular places and times, and they had color and tone and accent. When words were embraced by the traditional stanzaic frameworks of nineteenth-century poetry, the prosodic conventions of measure, rhyme, and beat tended to obscure the word's uniqueness, the word's natural rhythms and accents, carried into the poem from everyday life. These rhythms and accents in an American voice were muted by the prosodic and lexical traditions of British practice. By 1913, the date of Williams's second book of poems, *The Tempers,* he had formulated the poetics to which he would devote his art for the rest of his life. He was discovering in that period the grain of the American voice, neither domesticated to the parlor sweetness of the English Georgians nor crushed by Tennyson's more formal grandeur. Instead he was writing poems such as "Della Primavera Transportata Al Morale":

> a green truck
> dragging a concrete mixer
> passes
> in the street—
> the clatter and true sound
> of verse—

He was establishing the primary phonic pigments of a new kind of poetic speech; it would become his signature.

Of course, it would be incorrect to suggest that Williams learned to write by looking at avantgarde pictures. Painting was an important influence that got him pointed in a productive direction, but the work of finding his own approach or style was an entirely verbal one. The influence of the new painting on Williams crystallized in the famous Armory Show in 1913, an exhibition that largely introduced American audiences to post-impressionistic European painting. The general public was outraged and rather obtuse about the new directions. The public taste was very much shaped

by the conventions of three-dimensional space and what was thought to be realistic coloring. Although public reaction to the show was rather negative, the response of the younger generation of artists, writers, architects, and photographers was delight and celebration, a feeling that the massive exhibition that opened on 25th Street in New York represented a profound dilation of visual, plastic, and affective experience, an experience from which American painting and sculpture would never look back. The opening which this exhibition made in 1913 was affirmed and consolidated four years later, in the spring of 1917, in the Society of American Artists show, an event Williams attended and at which he read his futurist poem "Overture to a Dance of Locomotives":

> Porters in red hats run on narrow platforms.
> This way ma'am!
> —important not to take
> the wrong train!

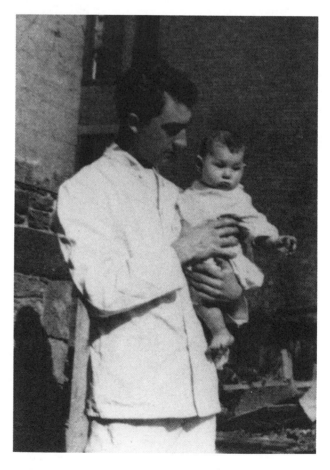

William Carlos Williams in 1908, during his internship at Child's Hospital in New York (courtesy of William Eric Williams)

As far as the development of his own art and the new ideas about writing which Williams began to advance in his prose, he certainly did not take the wrong train. Indeed these developments would transform completely the practice of poetry in America in the twentieth century.

After finishing his medical studies in Philadelphia in 1906, he moved to New York City to intern at the French hospital for two years. From there he went to the small pediatrics unit at Child's Hospital. After six months at this second institution, where he was very unhappy with the administration, he resigned and decided to open a private practice in Rutherford. But before that he wanted to study pediatrics a little more and resolved to spend the better part of the winter of 1909-1910 in Germany in that pursuit. He left for Europe in July for a spot of touring on the Continent before proceeding to Leipzig, where he was to take up a rather lonely residence until March 1910. After taking in as much as he could at the medical college in the German city, he began the long journey back to Rutherford with a visit to his old friend Ezra Pound in London, where he caught up with some of the recent developments in poetics and where he met the important literati in that hub, or so Pound thought it, of the literary world. Through Pound he spent an evening with the great Anglo-Irish poet William Butler Yeats, who was in those years on the threshold of that change of direction that would eventually lead to a Nobel Prize and a seat in the Senate of the Irish Republic.

Back in the United States Williams returned to Rutherford to begin his medical practice, which he did in September 1910. He was promptly appointed physician for the Rutherford public schools as well. Three years before this resettlement in his hometown he had met the daughters of a prosperous German-American Rutherford family by the name of Herman. After an initial interest in the eldest of the Herman girls, Charlotte, Williams had turned his attention to the younger sister, Florence, just before his trip to Europe. Indeed only a few weeks before he left on his trip he had proposed to her and been accepted. On his return their relationship was reestablished and on 12 December 1912, after he put his practice on a sound footing, they were married. In the following year, with the help of Florence's father, they bought the house at 9 Ridge Road in Rutherford where they would live for the rest of their lives. Their two sons were born there in quick succession, William Eric

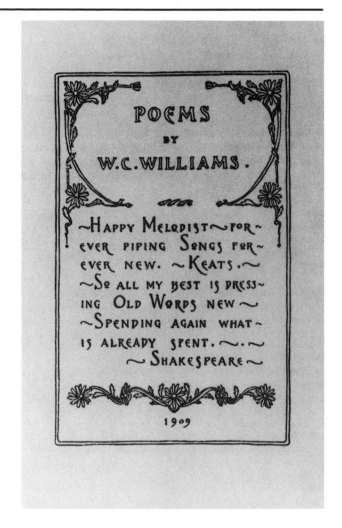

Title page designed by Edgar Williams for his brother's first book, which contains traditional, rhymed poems that betray the influence of Keats and Tennyson (Sotheby Parke Bernet, sale number 3966)

on 7 January 1914 and Paul Herman on 13 September 1916. Williams settled down to a long and fruitful career both as a doctor and as a poet.

In the same year that Williams and his wife moved to 9 Ridge Road an established publisher agreed to publish a Williams manuscript. His first book in 1909 had been printed privately by a local Rutherford printer. *The Tempers* (1913) was accepted, on Pound's recommendation and urging, by Pound's own publisher in London, the small firm run by Elkin Mathews. In 1913 also Williams had four poems accepted by Harriet Monroe's *Poetry,* a small Chicago literary magazine that found itself, occasionally to Monroe's chagrin, sponsoring the new directions poetry was taking. Williams, in a letter thanking her for accepting his work, re-

William Carlos Williams in the Roman amphitheater at Fiesole, Italy, 1910 (photograph by Edgar Williams, courtesy of William Eric Williams)

Having settled in Rutherford and launched his practice and having accepted the rigors and joys of raising a family, Williams, as his work was occasionally being published in London and Chicago, soon came in close contact with the writers and artists living and working in New York and its environs. The focus of this new set of contacts was the small poetry magazine *Others,* founded and edited by Alfred Kreymborg, a friend of Pound's and a New York man of letters, who in 1915 went to live in Grantwood, on the New Jersey Palisades. His small summer retreat became the rendezvous of a large group of writers and artists that included Williams, who first met Kreymborg that year. At Grantwood Williams was introduced to leading poets, artists, and critics of his day: Orrick Johns, Alanson Hartpence, Man Ray, Malcolm Cowley, Walter Arensberg, Mina Loy, Marcel Duchamp, Robert Sanborn, Wallace Stevens, and Maxwell Bodenheim.

In the developing cultural environment of early-twentieth-century America *Others* represented an extension of literary modernism from its original Chicago base at Harriet Monroe's *Poetry.* Founded in 1912, that periodical had sponsored the new poetry, at Pound's transatlantic prodding, virtually alone until the establishment of *Others* in 1915. This growth in avant-garde letters was an inevitable development, although *Others* also represented a rebuke to the Chicago group, and specifically to Harriet Monroe herself, whose commitment to modernism was marked by something less than total enthusiasm. Indeed for Williams she had not lived up to the revolutionary role he felt she was obliged to play in the fostering and promotion of the new American writing—and he told her so.

Others from the beginning saw itself in that role, and it was in its pages that Williams was first featured in his native land. The curious fact is that like a number of other American writers at that time, Pound and H. D. for example, Williams was better known to the London literary scene than to any American equivalent. However, this situation began to change in December 1916, when sixteen of his poems were included in a special number of *Others,* which also featured work by Kreymborg and Bodenheim. In that group of sixteen poems by Williams the technique, approach, orientation, and voice that would characterize his work for a lifetime can be seen fully formed. Most of the poems were quite successful and none more so than "The Young Housewife," an excellent example of the vigorous style which he had developed and a good

minded her of the important role she was playing in bringing into print the work of the American avant-garde—Sandburg, Lindsay, Pound, and himself. He called what was happening a profound revolution. He was referring of course to the revolution in technique, but he meant too an even greater revolution in perception and taste. His work also appeared in London periodicals—the *Egoist,* with which Pound was associated, and the *Poetry Review.* Finally his work was also selected for Pound's *Des Imagistes* (1914). In these venues Williams groped toward that sense of form, idiom, and content which would characterize his poetry thereafter. The poetry of *The Tempers* and his periodical verse represent a positive way of making poetry that is entirely his own. During this time he came out from under the early British influences and also from under Pound's shadow, by which his work in the 1912-1914 period had been obscured.

The house at 9 Ridge Road in Rutherford, New Jersey, where Williams lived from 1913 until his death

example also of the quotidian content, his concentration, beyond the margins of the conventionally "poetical" and "literary," on the forms and substances of the everyday, to which he had turned for good, and that would in fact provide him with the material for his magnum opus, *Paterson.*

> At ten A.M. the young housewife
> moves about in negligee behind
> the wooden walls of her husband's house.
> I pass solitary in my car.
>
> Then again she comes to the curb
> to call the ice-man, fish-man, and stands
> shy, uncorseted, tucking in
> stray ends of hair, and I compare her
> to a fallen leaf.
>
> The noiseless wheels of my car
> rush with a crackling sound over
> dried leaves as I bow and pass smiling.

Here Williams has turned his back on establishing a poem's measure by counting beats or syl-

lables. The verse line has become a rhythmic unit of speech under the control of some affective disposition which the poem generates from line to line. In the old prosody, the verse line was a rhythmic unit whose sound-shape was bent to the requirements of a particular metrical scheme. Of course, within the metrical scheme considerable variation was possible. Williams's ideas about the prosodic requirements of the revolutionary poetry he and his colleagues were writing would develop from the verse practice that began for Williams in the years of World War I. Later in an essay he called "Against the Weather," published in the Spring-Summer 1939 issue of Dorothy Norman's *Twice a Year,* and in a public lecture delivered at the University of Washington in 1948, "The Poem as a Field of Action"—both collected in *Selected Essays* (1954)—he would amplify and attempt to make explicit his own prosodic practice.

With the eschewing of a metrically based prosody Williams also had to turn away from the traditional stanzaic forms and, more important, to develop a different approach to the problem of

Florence Williams, 1928 (courtesy of William Eric Williams)

poetic structure. In metrically disciplined verse the development of the subject of the poem, the dynamics of feeling and thought which make up its internal coherence, are always played rhythmically against the requirements of recurrence in stanza and metrical pulse. Thus structure in such verse arises as a product of the variations in the chosen metrical scheme. Through varying the wavelike monotony of absolute regularity the poet is able to suggest a speaking voice and to isolate thematically important words, word clusters, line breaks, and stanza boundaries. Only through these variations and substitutions (such as the common substitution of a trochaic or spondaic foot at the beginning of an iambic line) in the context of recurrent beats and syllable counts can one talk fruitfully about "rhythm" in a metrical poem. A metrical poem is like a long-term delivery contract which the poet promises to fulfill. The poem's rhythmic interest lies in the poet's nonfulfillment of the promised obligations in the promised way. These variations function to lay bare not the promised sound-shape, but syntax, in whose own phonic structure one hears the sound-shape of a particular human voice.

In "The Young Housewife" Williams develops the internal affective dynamic of the poem in a way that is no longer based on this contrast of metrical recurrence and difference. The poem does not establish metrical expectations independent of the particularities of subject and theme but, as Williams explains in *I Wanted To Write a Poem*, builds the structure more positively on a more open, rhythmically free prosodic field; that is to say that subject and theme more centrally determine the evolved concrete structure of the poem. Thus the position of the word "uncorseted" has been determined neither by the requirements of metrical regularity nor the needs of rhythmical variation, but entirely by thematic considerations. It stands, in midline, gripped, indeed "corseted," by two commas, and its positioning unveils the generative affective conflict in the poem, the tension between the rise, the "uncorseting," of sexual desire in the speaker and the constraints of convention—"the wooden walls of her husband's house" penetrable only in imagination—walls which desire's "noiseless" demand can only "bow and pass smiling." Form here is not separable from content; form embodies theme in the distribution of the words on the page and in the sound-shape of a speaker's voice.

Beyond the verbal structure and sound-shape one can also see clearly the effect of Williams's contact with *les imagistes* in London. The poem achieves a marvelous clarity and hardness of image, which in the context of 1917 served as contrast and rebuke to late-romantic soft-focus effects. Indeed in the combination of voice-centered sound-shape and visual precision one has a lucid example of what Pound meant by an imagiste poem: "an intellectual and emotional complex in an instant of time."

With time Williams worked further and further to explore the compositional possibilities of this new approach. Of course, for him it was not simply a mere technical development, as perhaps it has been appropriated by his later disciples and imitators; for Williams this slowly won sense of the openness of the prosodic field had an ethical emancipatory dimension. It is well to remember that Williams was born into a world sure of its institutions, traditions, and conventional wisdom—a world, however, that with the turn of the century slipped irrevocably into a profound sociohistorical crisis. In that atmosphere of change, with its magnificent possibilities and its anxiety-inducing uncertainties, Williams never wavered in celebrating, through his work, the liberation of art in a new era. The ex-

Pages from the pocket notebook that Williams carried during his rounds as Medical Inspector of Schools for Rutherford, New Jersey, in fall and winter 1914. In addition to entries about ailments and health hazards he jotted down poems and notes for poems (Copyright © 1983 by William Eric Williams and Paul H. Williams. Reprinted by permission of New Directions Publishing Corporation, Agents for the Estate of William Carlos Williams).

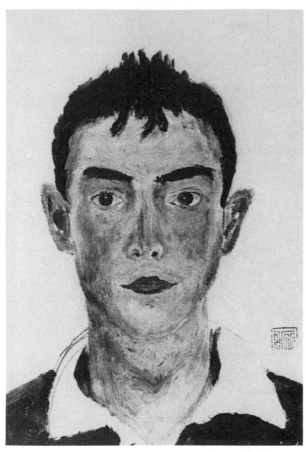

Self-portrait by Williams, 1914 (by permission of the University of Pennsylvania, gift of Mrs. William Carlos Williams, 1965)

plorations in technique, then, were the visible embodiment of a wider commitment.

"The Young Housewife" was republished in Williams's next collection of poems, published in Boston in 1917. With *Al Que Quiere!* Williams entered on a remarkably productive six years of his life. *Kora in Hell: Improvisations* appeared in 1920. *Sour Grapes* followed in 1921. In 1923 his first extended work of prose fiction was published in Paris. *The Great American Novel* is an attempt to write a serious novel. It is an examination of contemporary American life as Williams saw it and as he understood its sources and history. Although glancingly satiric, Williams calling it in *The Autobiography* "a satire on the novel form in which a little (female) Ford car falls more or less in love with a Mack truck," the novel is more or less a commentary on the difficulties of writing a novel within established artistic and social conventions. In 1923 as well Williams published one of his best-known collections of poems, *Spring and All*.

As Williams worked through the consequences and possibilities of his own approach to the writing of poems, he also began to experiment in prose forms. One of the earliest and most successful of such experiments was his series of prose "improvisations" collected in *Kora in Hell*. This work had appeared serially in the *Little Review* (February-June 1919), alongside installments of James Joyce's *Ulysses*. Joyce's modernist novel had two suggestive and encouraging effects on Williams's own practice. One was in the way the Irishman was able to magnify the dim outlines of Greek and Roman myths in the seeming chaos of everyday life. If orderliness in civic, domestic, and personal reality could no longer be sustained on the old basis, then one ought to look more deeply, Joyce seemed to be saying, into the mundane and the banal. There, *Ulysses* seemed to argue with the force of a scientific demonstration, one finds the real mythical patterns and moulds for the social and psychological reality one knows. The second effect of *Ulysses* on Williams was to suggest the possibility of letting go ego-directed meaning, that is, eschewing once and for all the nineteenth-century romantic view that poetry must be self-expression, an expression of personal feeling. Letting go Cartesian concepts of meaning tied to the logic of the ego made available, suddenly, the wider, more encompassing, and more expressive logic of language itself. In this view, language itself becomes a great synthesizer of being and knowledge, in which personal experience finds its necessary and indivisible contact with the wider experience of community and, beyond that, of an entire culture.

In theme and setting *Kora in Hell* leaned obliquely on Dante but rather more heavily on the French symbolist Arthur Rimbaud and especially on his remarkable *Illuminations* (1871). From that work Williams took some procedural lessons, including the adaptation of Rimbaldian stylistic mannerisms. But *Kora in Hell* is not simply Rimbaldian pastiche; Williams was now too close to his own materials, to the sound of American voices, to let the focus and themes of *Kora in Hell* drift entirely into Rimbaud's orbit. Indeed it was his ear that stayed the course and managed to substantiate his work sufficiently, so that Williams himself soon came to establish a verbal body around which others would revolve. One can already hear in passages such as the following the sound, ten years later, of Louis Zukofsky:

> When beldams dig clams their fat hams
> (it's always beldams) balanced near Tellus's

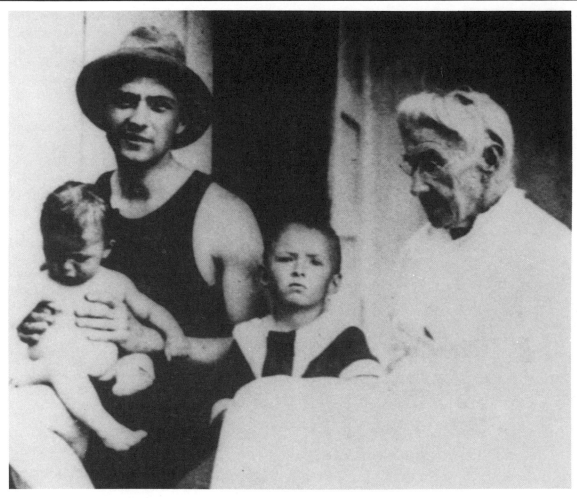

William Carlos Williams with sons, Paul and Bill, and his grandmother, Emily Dickinson Wellcome, 1917 (photograph by Irving B. Wellcome; courtesy of William Eric Williams)

hide, this rhinoceros pelt, these lumped stones—buffoonery of midges on a bull's thigh—invoke,—what you will: birth's glut, awe at God's craft, youth's poverty, evolution of a child's caper, man's poor inconsequence. Eclipse of all things; sun's self turned hen's rump.

Critics have found *Kora in Hell* difficult to interpret, J. E. Slate going so far as to wittily retitle the poem "Kora in Opacity." Of course, the poem is not a philosophical treatise, presenting a coherent body of ideas that can be systematically paraphrased by criticism. The thread that runs through the whole work is Williams's meditation on language and on the act of composing itself. There is no more accurate description of the action of a poem by William Carlos Williams than his own de-

scription of a "dance" in the third strophe of the thirteenth section of *Kora in Hell:*

The words of the thing twang and twitter to the gentle rocking of a high-laced boot and the silk above that. The trick of the dance is in following now the words, *allegro,* now the contrary beat of the glossy leg: Reaching far over as if—But always she draws back and comes down upon the word flatfooted. For a moment we—but the boot's costly and the play's not mine. The pace leads off anew. Again the words break it and we both come down flatfooted. Then—near the knee, jumps to the eyes, catching in the hair's shadow. But the lips take the rhythm again and again we come down flatfooted. By this time boredom takes a hand and the play's ended.

William Carlos Williams (courtesy of William Eric Williams)

up a poem, a novel, a memoir of the period between 1910 and 1930 without soon coming across references to that liveliest of arts, which American artists have taken so readily to heart, especially in its nonballetic forms. Indeed the nonclassical dance in the twentieth century has often been advanced as the true symbol of modernism.

One can see its influence as a metaphor for the creative process again in Williams's next collection, *Sour Grapes* (1921), in poems such as "A Good Night" and in his "futurist" "Overture to a Dance of Locomotives." But more important than simple references to dance in his poems is his intuitive recognition of what the new dance was all about; it was certainly not interested in the established rhetoric of movement one finds in the classical ballet, but in an affirmation of movement in everyday life as itself full of dance, as a potential dance which the dancer makes visible or embodies in the dance proper. This consciousness more and more informs Williams's perception of the natural and gestural movements of the world around him, and more and more he begins to accentuate and bring out the beauty that lies hidden in the simplest and most natural gestures of person and thing. Such a consciousness of life itself, as gesture aspiring to the condition of dance, provides the extraor-

It was not very long after this description was written that the dance became Williams's favorite metaphor for the poetic act.

The fact of such a connection should not be surprising: dance was in a period of great artistic achievement in the 1920s on both sides of the Atlantic. This was certainly true for the classical ballet, but even more so for those forms of dance beyond the margins of the classical tradition. Folk dancing, dance in the music hall and cabaret, and the art dance of the salon and studio explored new expressive directions that influenced not only William Carlos Williams but many writers, painters, and sculptors in that time. From the nonballetic traditions of Jean Avril and Loie Fuller (Yeats's "dancer") there came in the first two or three decades of the new century the dance of Josephine Baker and Isadora Duncan, the *Ballets Russes*, Waslaw Nijinsky, and the great American choreographers and dancers George Balanchine (introduced by Diaghilev) and Martha Graham. One can hardly pick

William Carlos and Edgar Williams, 1917 (courtesy of William Eric Williams)

Front cover for the 1920 volume of experimental prose passages in which Williams worked through his approach to writing poetry

Stroebel, an old friend and assistant to Harriet Monroe at *Poetry*, directed a rather harsh attack on the book that edged on the personally insulting. To challenge this blast, Marjorie Allan Seiffert, another poet and friend of Williams's from his *Others* days, reviewed *Spring and All* again in the April 1924 number of *Poetry*. Her review, although a pointed defense of Williams, did manage to look at the volume coolly enough to recognize its obvious strengths and the maturity of technique and vision which it represented in Williams's development as a poet. The poems, she said, were marked by an extraordinary clarity of image and a lively mobility of language. More important she pointed to Williams's own definition of art in the volume (the first edition of *Spring and All* appeared with a prose commentary, as had *Kora in Hell: Improvisations*) as an objective reality enjoying its own "separate existence," written out of a "condition of imaginative suspense." Although she did not fully understand the implications of what Williams was asserting, she had put her finger on a crucial point. Williams wrote: "Imagination is not to avoid reality,

One of the photographs of William Carlos Williams that Sylvia Beach hung on the wall at her Shakespeare and Company bookshop in Paris (courtesy of the Sylvia Beach Collection, Princeton University Library)

dinary beauty and poignancy of a small poem such as "Arrival" in the *Sour Grapes* collection. The simple movements that accompany the preparations for love—"loosening the hooks of/her dress"—are caught in the moment when they become pure dance:

> The tawdry veined body emerges
> twisted upon itself
> like a winter wind . . . !

In the year of *The Great American Novel* (1923), Williams published a small volume of poems that represents a new plateau in his work and establishes him for the first time as a major American poet. *Spring and All* was not as formally and thematically audacious as *Kora in Hell*, and, indeed, it was neither very widely read in its time nor much appreciated whenever a rare copy of the book fell into a reviewer's line of fire. In November 1923 Marion

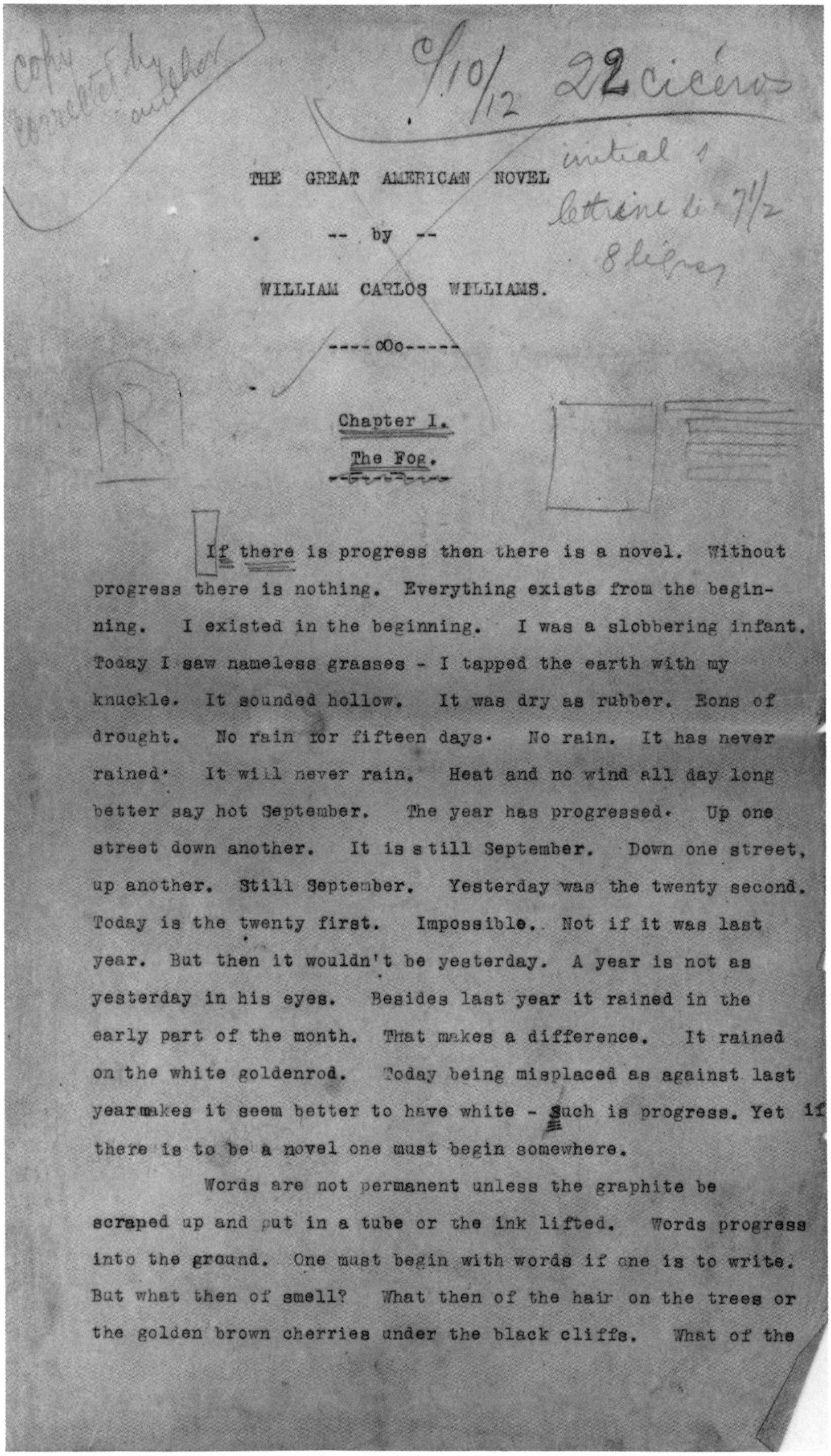

THE GREAT AMERICAN NOVEL

-- by --

WILLIAM CARLOS WILLIAMS.

----oOo----

Chapter I.

The Fog.

If there is progress then there is a novel. Without progress there is nothing. Everything exists from the beginning. I existed in the beginning. I was a slobbering infant. Today I saw nameless grasses - I tapped the earth with my knuckle. It sounded hollow. It was dry as rubber. Eons of drought. No rain for fifteen days. No rain. It has never rained. It will never rain. Heat and no wind all day long better say hot September. The year has progressed. Up one street down another. It is still September. Down one street, up another. Still September. Yesterday was the twenty second. Today is the twenty first. Impossible. Not if it was last year. But then it wouldn't be yesterday. A year is not as yesterday in his eyes. Besides last year it rained in the early part of the month. That makes a difference. It rained on the white goldenrod. Today being misplaced as against last year makes it seem better to have white - such is progress. Yet if there is to be a novel one must begin somewhere.

Words are not permanent unless the graphite be scraped up and put in a tube or the ink lifted. Words progress into the ground. One must begin with words if one is to write. But what then of smell? What then of the hair on the trees or the golden brown cherries under the black cliffs. What of the

First page of the setting copy for Williams's first extended work of prose fiction, published by William Bird's Three Mountains Press in Paris (William Carlos Williams, Imaginations. *Copyright © 1970 by Florence H. Williams. Reprinted by permission of New Directions Publishing Corporation, Agents for the Estate of William Carlos Williams. Courtesy of the Lilly Library, Indiana University)*

William Carlos Williams, 1926 (photograph by Charles Sheeler; courtesy of William Eric Williams)

nor is it description nor an evocation of objects or situations, it is to say that poetry does not tamper with the world but moves it—It affirms reality most powerfully and therefore, since reality needs no personal support but exists free from human action, as proven by science in the indestructibility of matter and of force, it creates a new object, a play, a dance which is not a mirror up to nature. . . ."

Rene Magritte, the French surrealist painter, has painted a rather large picture of a rather large brown pipe on a cream colored background. Under the pipe appear the words "Ceci n'est pas un pipe"—This is not a pipe. And of course it is not a pipe; it is a picture. Williams's best-known poem, "The Red Wheelbarrow," was untitled in the first edition of *Spring and All* and that is perhaps how it should have remained. If a title was thought necessary perhaps something along the lines of Magritte's comment on his picture might have helped generations of readers since 1923 to understand this enigmatic little poem—this is not a red wheelbarrow. "The Red Wheelbarrow" is a poem. Williams's prose comment on the nature of imagination is particularly appropriate. Imagination does not imitate or plagiarize or describe the world, nor does it evoke or put one in the mood to appreciate and gather delight from a nice barn-

yard scene, or a shimmering sunset outside one's window. Reality exists in its own right, is free and independent of human agency. If every human were to suddenly disappear from the earth, reality would remain intact, indestructible. Imagination is not the xerox machine of the psyche. Imagination creates new objects; in Williams's case it creates poems. In reading "The Red Wheelbarrow" one is not being asked to look through the words at some scene which can be located in space and time. First one is dealing with an object made from words, set down in patterns; the words—because they have the capacity to stipulate objects, processes, and events—present an image, not an image *of* the world, but an image *in* the world. The verbal imagination makes separately existing things out of its verbal materials. And not just words in abstract, as one might find them in a dictionary, trailing, kite-like, a long tail of bland denotations, but words as they are shaped by mouths, and as they are cupped and held in one's ears. And not just what the words mean as abstractions, but all their connotations, their latent images and metaphors, their accents, and music. And above all in *Spring and All* one notices how words, like the sails of a yacht, can catch the wind of feeling, fill out, and drive the vessel forward.

"The Pot of Flowers" is not a moment of pure observation; its aesthetic substance is not visual. Certainly the poem presents a visual image, but its beauty lies in its words, rather than in the fidelity with which it depicts some real pot of flowers. Like an object in the world, an object with its own shape, volume, texture, and moving energy, a poem is a unique, unified, and universal object in its own right, instinct with rhythm: "flowers and flowers reversed/take and spill the shaded flame"; sound texture: "red where in whorls/petal lays its glow . . ."; and its own organic form:

> the leaves
> reaching up their modest green
> from the pot's rim
> and there, . . .

form, here, suspensively construed, the word "rim" coinciding with a strophic boundary, a formal "rim."

On a literary sensibility steeped in metaphor and all the subspecies of rhetorical figuration from the poetic tradition, Williams's procedures and effects were almost entirely lost. But such splendors as are to be found in *Spring and All*, although largely indiscernible to the older generation of "versifiers," trope-mongers, and trope-consumers, whose sense of poetic rhythm was limited to the sound palette of the metrical tradition, were heard and recognized by the younger generation in the mid1920s, young poets such as Louis Zukofsky, Charles Reznikoff, and later George Oppen and Lorine Niedecker, among many others. *Spring and All* was a turning point for Williams and for American poetic modernism. At the age of forty, Williams consolidated the accomplishments of fifteen years of experience. He showed in that volume that modernism was not a youthful mania to be abandoned with the passing of life's spring. Unlike T. S. Eliot, for whom "tradition" and conservatism were the final destination for "individual talent," Williams insisted on the efficaciousness of the revolution in art he had helped shape and extend. He was not going to turn his back on it just as it was beginning to produce a rich harvest of poetry. Someone once wrote that middle age is the moment in life when everything seems to hang on the point of being lost. In *Spring and All* nothing is lost, and the promise of a life's spring is fulfilled.

A work in the same mold as *Spring and All*—poetry, prose, fact, aesthetics, social criticism—followed in 1928. *The Descent of Winter*, which appeared in the Autumn 1928 issue of Pound's little magazine the *Exile*, contributes several astonishingly beautiful poems to Williams's oeuvre—"My bed is narrow," "that brilliant field," "To freight cars in the air," "Dahlias." It represents also spring's antagonist, the coming of winter and the darker, more deathly forces of thought, feeling, and history with which one associates the dead time of the year. The book is more clearly than *Spring and All* in journal form, beginning "9/27"—and concluding on 18 December. It explores this chill "descent" in images of pain and death—"In the dead weeds a rubbish heap/in flames"—and of pollution, physical and ethical: "That river will be clean/before ever you will be." The aesthetic point of view so forcefully articulated in the 1923 volume stands undiminished and unchanged in this new work, but there appears, in addition to aesthetics, a much wider and more intense concern with social and political matters:

> and men at the bar
> talking of the strike
> and cash.

"A Morning Imagination of Russia," an encomiastic ode of considerable interest, is placed at the heart of the volume, and halts, for a moment,

the descent. It staunches also the hemorrhage of death imagery, beginning with the stirring of dawn—and social hope—and ending with the possibility of convalescence after sickness and decay. Social transformation is seen not in terms of political action and power, but, characteristically for Williams, in terms of closer, more immediate and tactile contact with reality:

> We have little now but
> we have that. We are convalescents. Very
> feeble. Our hands shake. We need a
> transfusion. No one will give it to us,
> they are afraid of infection. I do not
> blame them. We have paid heavily. But we
> have gotten—touch. The eyes and the ears
> down on it. Close.

Except in the eye-ear pun in the last word—"Close" as nearby, and "Close" as end of the poem—this is not an entirely successful poem qua poem; it strays into the symbolic a little too far, losing touch for a moment with Williams's usual aesthetic. Here the images take on an editorializing function, and although no one can impugn the genuineness of the feeling, the sharpness of his concern, still his usual clarity and intensity in word and rhythm has ebbed. In this regard *The Descent of Winter* is a lesser work than *Spring and All*.

However, what Williams attempts in "A Morning Imagination of Russia" is not a technical and aesthetic dead end. Nor is it new to his work. Williams's first important poem, one he placed at the head of his *The Collected Earlier Poems*, is written to a similar mode and theme. "The Wanderer" (written in 1913) also uses the longer, more prosaic (which is to say, perhaps, more conversational) line as rhythmic base, wanders into symbolic utterance, and engages in social comment. This line of development, after "The Wanderer," continues, in technique at least, with his experiments in dramatic monologue, that is, assimilates Robert Browning's influence through Ezra Pound's example, in such poems as "The Death of Franco of Cologne: His Prophecy of Beethoven" and "Con Brio" (both written by 1913), extends through "History" (written in 1916) and "Tract" (written in 1917), and culminates in the earlier period in the first "Paterson" (written in 1926). This important three-page poem anticipates the *Paterson* to come in the 1940s. In the earlier "Paterson" the idea of seeing a city as a man is first used: "I see myself/in the regularly ordered plateglass of/his thoughts, glimmering. . . ." And the influential notion of poetic objectivity first articulated at length in *Spring and All* is trenchantly formulated in a phrase with which Williams will always be associated: "Say it! No ideas but in things."

The poetic problem which *The Descent of Winter* tackles, but does not adequately solve (the solution would not emerge fully until *Paterson*) is: how does one alloy the vivid intensity and clarity of a lyricism steeled on strict attendance to the image— a technique refined in the school of verbal conciseness, directness of treatment, and musicality— with the need—growing more urgent all through the 1920s—to engage the larger social and historical realities of one's time and place? How could a writer express in the medium of poetry his or her social and political concerns at the center of social life and not turn a poem into a sermon or political harangue or prose tract? If the primary notional vocabulary of poetry was the sensory image as it embodied immediate experience, how could this vocabulary be alloyed to the conceptual thinking the study of society, politics, and economics seemed to necessitate? How could the vivid rhythms of specific perception and concrete contact with things and processes be preserved in a discourse swamped by the general and the abstract?

Ezra Pound's solution in *The Cantos* involved the treatment of concepts as if they were notional images—conceptual ideograms—abstractions rooted in the concrete and real and emerging through time as the accumulated conceptual wisdom of a real people, living a concrete history, in a particular landscape. Turning his back on the theoretical knowledge generated by the experientially alienated analytical logic of Cartesian rationalism, Pound proposed and formulated in his opus an anthropological poetics, which entered a culture at the level of its characterizing concrete experiences where it recovered the knowledge that that culture had derived from meditating on those experiences. Such a knowledge was not systematic in the philosophical sense, but was wholly efficacious nonetheless as concrete knowledge, or what a philosopher might call "recipe" knowledge. Because roots of this knowledge were sunk deep in the actual lived experiences of a people, such knowledge embodied the concrete in a way a philosophical abstraction could not. Thus these conceptual ideograms offered a new way of incarnating the known and, as a result, could be handled as one handled sensory images in a poem. The poetic logic that controlled the unfolding sequence of images in a poem was the logic that made sense of the conceptual ideograms. These two kinds of images mu-

tually vivified and supported each other—the sensory embodying actual experience, and the conceptual embodying the wisdom derived from experience. Clearly here the emphasis is on the concrete, the made, the particular—thus one can know a society better by examining the workmanship of a simple clay bowl than by reading the inflated abstractions on which a national anthem might rest; or one might find the sincerity and beauty of an actual religious ceremony more telling of a culture's values than some abstract conception of deity toward which every member of that society pays a required pro forma respect. This for Pound was the lesson to be learned from four thousand years of Chinese civilization. It was the lesson learned by Williams contemplating the very different life of a people along the banks of the Passaic. For Williams this new orientation would culminate in *Paterson*. Before he thought through to the essentials, in form and content, of that great summative epic, he would immerse himself in a rigorous program of social observation, a program of close attention to the sound and feel of quotidian reality, a celebration, in short, of the ordinary. But he would do this in the medium of prose fiction, both short and long.

There is no time in Williams's life when he did not write poetry, but there is a period from about the mid1920s to about 1950 when he seemed to devote a tremendous amount of his creative power to prose, starting with *The Great American Novel* in 1923. Williams, in 1925, published *In the American Grain,* a series of essays and studies of "American" heroes from Red Eric of Greenland, Columbus, Cortés, and Montezuma, on to Abraham Lincoln. This book, unrecognized in its own time, has finally achieved the status of a classic in the development of a distinctively American prose. Its early impact, light as it was, got Williams labeled an American "primitive" who had finally renounced the deracinated cosmopolitanism of cubist poetics, or so Gorham Munson, writing in the 1920s, thought. Williams's exploration of the "primitive" in America's early history was also praised by D. H. Lawrence. Like Lawrence, Williams celebrates the "beauty of lavish, primitive embrace . . ." glimpsed in certain exemplary lives: Samuel de Champlain, Cotton Mather, Pere Sebastian Rasles, Daniel Boone, George Washington, Aaron Burr, just to mention the subjects of six of the more interesting essays. The label "primitive" was very soon translated as a call for the restoration of "primitivism" in contemporary life. The book, of course, argues for no such thing. It locates and

William Carlos Williams on the roof of Passaic General Hospital, 1936 (courtesy of the Rutherford Public Library)

embodies in these superbly crafted prose essays, sketches, and "characters" the pure essence of American locality. The definitive assessment of this volume's prose style remains to be undertaken. There can be no doubt that when that assessment is done, *In the American Grain* will take its place as one of the decisive moments in the evolution of American prose.

From that work in prose Williams then moved to a novel. *A Voyage to Pagany* (1928), his first in the traditional mode, was based on the five-month trip he and Flossie Williams had taken in 1924 to Europe, where he met, especially in Paris, a great number of the generation of writers and artists whose modernism Williams more or less shared. This novel was not well received in its own time and is not much read today. Its principal interest now lies in the light it throws on that voyage to Europe, where Williams caught up with old friends from his university days (Pound, H. D.) and the New York of the period of World War I (Robert McAlmon) or made the acquaintance of other moving spirits of the new art: James Joyce, Philippe Soupault (whose *Last Nights in Paris* Williams trans-

lated into English in 1929), and Constantin Brancusi. His meeting with McAlmon was particularly important because it instituted again for a few months a fruitful friendship that the two men had shared in New York just after World War I, a period in which they had edited the influential little magazine devoted to modernism, *Contact* (1920-1923). Although the two men would never reestablish the close professional intimacy they had shared in New York, a consequence, largely, of McAlmon's rather dissipated life in the Paris of the "lost generation," Williams would come to McAlmon's aid in subsequent years after the younger writer's return to America a broken and defeated man.

In the 1930s Williams's writings in prose continued in a veritable flood of stories, plays, and novels, including the first part of a trilogy of novels: *White Mule* (1937), which was followed by *In the Money* in 1940, and by *The Build-Up* in 1952. These three novels deal with the spiritual and social growth of a family called Stecher in the early years of the century, as they seek to assimilate themselves to the dominant values of the New World they have chosen for their field of action. Although the trilogy ends "tragically," Williams always saw this long prose work as working out of a tradition of social comedy, a comedy of manners, in which the writer was not the ethical interpreter of a family's rise and fall but someone who simply revealed what he saw without comment. There is here a wish to annihilate the self as the expressive framework of art. This effacement of the "I," one of the major narrative innovations of *White Mule,* was explored and refined in the prose works, where the issue of narrative point of view is of utmost importance in the depiction of the represented world of fiction. *The Great American Novel* of 1923 had begun in the fullness of a personal and electrically expressive ego. The *White Mule* trilogy, however, does not begin with the self as first cause; it begins with society. This attention to the particulars of life along the Passaic, its lived density, helped orient Williams to the thematic materials of *Paterson.*

Williams began publishing collections of short stories in the early 1930s, although his short fiction had been appearing for years in the literary periodicals of his day. *A Novelette and Other Prose* and *The Knife of the Times and Other Stories* were both published in 1932. *Life along the Passaic River* followed in 1938. These stories again and again capture with an unerring eye for the representative, typifying detail the feel of life in twentieth-century America. Williams was particularly adept at embodying the social and psychological tensions that emerge among his characters. As in his poetry, the sharpness with which these conflicts and struggles are depicted is achieved through the telling juxtaposition of episodes and events, and, more important, through the painstaking care for le mot juste in the phrasing. The remarkable prose stylist of *In the American Grain* writes at full stretch in the stories and novels. Concision and directness are the two obvious virtues of his style; an ear attuned to the lift and weight of the voices of real people, a speaking which energizes and focuses the style. Style is obviously the product of discipline and a poet's native inwardness with the entire expressive instrument of language. But a great and good prose style is not merely a technical accomplishment; it is also an ethical one. As Williams explained in "White Mule versus Poetry," an essay published in the August 1937 issue of the *Writer:* "The writing of the language is what interests me. So in writing . . . my greatest concern was to write with attention to marshalling the words into an order which would be free from 'lies.' "

In addition to prose, Williams was interested in the drama, both as an actor and as a playwright. As an actor he engaged in theatricals of all kinds, amateur and professional, at home and on the public stage. At home the Williamses, with their friends and acquaintances, would often sing, dance, and perform skits, sketches, and other light plays by Williams. Williams's interest in the theater, however, extended beyond his own living room. His early association with Alfred Kreymborg led to one memorable engagement as an actor in New York's Greenwich Village in 1916, his stage debut. The play, *Lima Beans,* by Kreymborg, was a dada piece in which Williams played a typical middle-class husband opposite Mina Loy's typical American housewife. Light stuff, compounded of satiric comment on what have come to be known as middle American *mores,* slapstick, and farce, it was enjoyed by the generally bohemian audiences attracted to this sort of avant-garde entertainment. More important than the play was Williams's contact with Mina Loy, a talented, physically attractive, and modish young modernist poet who had already begun to make a reputation for herself in the small magazines— such as *Others, Poetry,* and the *Dial*—in which Williams's own work was also prominent.

From those early experiences with the theater Williams never lost his love for the stage. He went

William Carlos Williams, 1938 (photograph by Charles Sheeler; courtesy of William Eric Williams)

on to write a number of plays, plays generally well-received in their day but now rarely performed or read. His major achievement in dramatic literature is still thought to be *Many Loves,* which was first published in the 1942 volume of *New Directions in Prose and Poetry* and collected in *Many Loves and Other Plays* (1961). *Many Loves* incorporates three one-act plays he had written for a local Rutherford drama group in 1939 and fuses them with a Pirandello-like framework written in verse. The play explores the failure of communication between the sexes and is distinguished by his sympathetic portrayal of his female characters, asserting a forward-looking sensitivity to the position of women in a society dominated by male notions of sexuality and intimacy. A second major drama, *A Dream of Love,* premiered Off-Broadway in 1949 to a warm review in the *New York Times* by playwright William Saroyan. Published in the 1948 *New Directions* annual and collected in *Many Loves and Other Plays,* this play also scrutinizes relationships between the sexes, but this time in the context of a modern marriage, focusing particularly on the problem of fidelity. His third important drama is the nightmarish *Tituba's Children* (written in 1950), a powerful cry of dissent in the midst of the anti-Communist witch hunts that seized American political culture in the late 1940s and 1950s. Also in *Many Loves and Other Plays,* this play represents Williams's final attempt to make overt political and social statements in his art, attempts that characterized much of his work in prose, poetry, and the essay through the 1930s.

His activities in this respect during that decade and after did not entirely displace purely aesthetic and literary concerns. In the early 1930s, in the depths of the Depression, Williams's work was still to be found in the little poetry magazines that managed to hang on to patrons and readers in the socioeconomic maelstrom created by the hard times. Richard Johns's *Pagany* (Boston); Charles Henri Ford and Parker Tyler's *Blues; Hound and Horn,* edited by the neoclassicist critic and poet R. P. Blackmur; the *Miscellany;* Norman MacLeod's *Morada;* and others kept alive the notion of an independent, avant-garde literary culture even in an era when American society and culture were in turmoil.

Important as his contacts with these small magazines and periodicals were, none was more decisive for the middle-aged poet than his contact with Louis Zukofsky and the "objectivism" which Zukofsky began to noise in the early 1930s. The younger Brooklyn poet, a man of great skill and erudition, had already begun work on his vast masterwork, *A,* a twenty-four-part poem that Zukofsky would not finish until the 1970s. Objectivism took the *imagisme* of the first generation of modernists as its point of departure. From that base, Zukofsky developed objectivism as a way of making clearer than *imagisme* ever did the notion of the poem as embodying a radical objectivity. He extended to poetry an optical analogy, namely that a lens brings the rays of an object to a focus. The poem then embodies a mode of ontological being as an object in and for itself. In every word, Zukofsky asserted in his important prose statement "An Objective" (written in 1930), there is a potential for radical objectification based on the axiom that words are "absolute symbols for objects, states, acts, interrelations, thoughts about them." He did not want to call any verbal event "verse" that "did not convey the totality of perfect rest." This emphasis on the materiality and thing-likeness of a poem, a poem, in short, as a verbal artifact in a new and radical sense, was understood as well by *les imagistes.* However, Zukofsky attempted to articulate a more explicit and detailed poetics than the rules-of-thumb that had characterized most *imagiste* theorizing.

In this new development Zukofsky saw Williams as playing a central role. For Williams was one of the old masters of objectivism, a writer who had begun life as an *imagiste* but had worked his way well beyond that starting point and, whether he knew it or not, had intuited objectivism in practice. Trusting to his superb poetic judgment and trusting especially to his eye and ear, he had almost single-handedly devised an aesthetic worthy of capturing America itself in all its diverse, dissonant, shifting reality.

This assessment of Williams was high praise indeed, and Williams was no doubt flattered by the younger poet's attention. Soon after Williams read Zukofsky's assessment of his position in American letters, the two men began a friendship that lasted the rest of Williams's life, a friendship and collaboration still in need of much study. Zukofsky was not, however, the only self-confessed objectivist. There were others, and Zukofsky's To Press helped put these new ideas into circulation. George Oppen, Carl Rakosi, Basil Bunting, Charles Reznikoff constituted this school of poetry revolving first around the To Press and, later, around Rakosi's Objectivist Press. It was this second small press, financed by the contributions from the poets themselves, that first published Williams's *Collected Poems 1921-1931* in January 1934.

It is arguable that contact with this group of writers during the 1930s helped Williams catch his second poetic "breath" after his annus mirabilis of 1922. Their poetry did not transform Williams's own poetic practices. Rather, it was Williams's probable realization that as a practitioner of a certain kind—one who valued sensory alertness, perceptual opportunism, clarity, sharpness of outline in image and tonality—he was now no longer the only poet of talent who adhered to an objectivist poetics, a poetics which this younger generation had named and developed. This perhaps should be emphasized: Zukofsky's adherence to a poetics of objectivism derived from a poetic practice he found in Williams's earlier work. For Williams this theoretical step was not particularly necessary; after all the practitioner qua practitioner does not need to have a theory to explain what he's been doing all along. What this development did do for Williams, however, was to make him acutely aware that the efforts of the 1920s to establish a poetics and a sensibility, divested of its old world costumes, had not been in vain. In the 1930s the objectivists were all the evidence he needed that the moment of clarity at the Armory Show in 1913 had, in fact, given birth to a new sensibility, one that had "taken" on American soil, and found its fittest expression in the energies of the American tongue. Later *Paterson* would establish the poetic efficacy of the native idiom once and for all, bringing to fruition a half-century of American modernism and, beyond that, culminating Walt Whitman's great and daring revolution in technique and theme in mid-nineteenth-century poetry.

As he readied himself and accumulated the thematic and technical materials for his own *Song of Myself* in the 1940s, Williams continued with his busy life at Rutherford, practicing medicine, writing, and keeping up contacts with friends and colleagues all over the North Atlantic world. He took a public part in many of the social and political controversies which dominated the public sphere in the 1930s. Such involvements in the next two decades would come to disappoint Williams and, in the case of the politically motivated withdrawal of his appointment as Poetry Consultant to the Library of Congress in 1952, would hurt him deeply. His medical practice flourished, and he was much loved by his patients, most of them the everyday folk of a thoroughly typical industrial town in what was then the heart of the American economy.

By the late 1930s his children, Bill and Paul, were both heading out into the world. Bill, after an undergraduate career at Williams College, pro-

ceeded to the Cornell Medical School and a distinguished career in medicine. Paul, the younger son, returned to his father's alma mater, the University of Pennsylvania, and from there went on to the Harvard Business School, marriage, and the beginnings of a career with Republic Steel in Canton, Ohio. With the bombing of Pearl Harbor both young men were swept up in the maelstrom of war. Bill Jr. served as a medical officer in the U.S. Navy and shipped off in spring 1942 to the Pacific with an outfit of Seabees. Paul later also shipped out with the U.S. Navy, but drew escort duties on a destroyer, riding shotgun on the Allied shipping lanes across the North Atlantic. Like millions of parents across the country, Williams and his wife had to endure the agony of separation from their sons and to enter that state of anxious hope that became the psychological norm for those back home in a nation at war.

In the late 1930s Pound had put Williams in touch with a wealthy young man from Harvard, James Laughlin, who was interested in modern literature and willing to translate that appreciation into a publishing enterprise that would provide concrete and continuous support for the moderns. Laughlin's New Directions Press, with the publication of *White Mule* in 1937, for all intents and purposes became Williams's permanent publisher, although his relationship with Laughlin and the press was occasionally troubled by the poet's suspicion that Laughlin was a bit too much of a dilettante. Laughlin himself tells the story of how *White Mule* was accidentally allowed to go out of print in 1937 while he was away on a skiing vacation. Williams always knew and acknowledged that Laughlin's heart was in the right place as far as the modernist movement in literature was concerned. Indeed, even with the coming of success in the 1950s and 1960s, Laughlin never diluted the focus of his publishing program by going after potboilers and best-sellers. However, his obvious editorial daring, acumen, and taste in literature were not always complemented by an aggressive program for promotion and distribution of the works he published.

In any case, Laughlin's new press, founded in a rather casual fashion, has been persistently the most important publisher of modernist and avant-garde literature from the late 1930s to the present day. And the press served the important function of keeping in circulation the works of Williams and Pound. After years of seeing their work published by small, poorly financed presses, quickly going out of print, the two senior modernists in American letters could now depend on respectable publishing

Elena and William Carlos Williams, October 1940 (photograph by Irving B. Wellcome; courtesy of William Eric Williams)

runs and a much wider circulation than they ever enjoyed before. In 1938, for example, New Directions published a new volume of Williams's collected poems that was twice as big as the Objectivist Press production of 1934 and published it in an edition of 1,500 copies rather than the much smaller number of the earlier edition.

Williams's association with New Directions could not have come at a more opportune time for he had, by 1937, already made his first substantial commitment toward the composition of *Paterson.* During the 1940s and 1950s, he was gratified to watch New Directions bring out each section of the long poem as it was finished, in handsomely designed editions, on good quality paper, and with a typographical aptness to the content rarely lavished on books by the major commercial publishing houses. In 1963 New Directions would collect all five parts of *Paterson,* as well as the notes for the uncompleted part six, into one volume, which the press has kept continuously in print to the present day. In all, Laughlin would keep fourteen Williams titles on his publishing list after the poet's death in 1963.

In composing *Paterson* Williams realized the epic poem anticipated in his earlier work. "The Wanderer" (written in 1913) provided a poetic initiation into the things of the world, of which the river—"the filthy Passaic"—provided an enduring symbol. This initiatory process is presided over by the feminine principle, variously embodied as muse, fertility goddess, and the young poet's grandmother. This figure would also endure mutatis mutandis in *Paterson.*

Other anticipations were the small imagist poems such as "Proletarian Portrait," which had catalyzed Williams's earlier reputation as a poet of pure vision:

A big young bareheaded woman
in an apron

Her hair slicked back standing
on the street

One stockinged foot toeing
the sidewalk

Her shoe in her hand. Looking
intently into it

She pulls out the paper insole
to find the nail

That has been hurting her[.]

In *Paterson* these pure "lyrics" were made to serve somewhat different poetic ends. He used the image, with a new and deepening authority, as the lexical hoard for a new kind of extended poetic discourse; the image complex provided the essential building block of meaning. A poem like "Proletarian Portrait," capturing an ordinary moment in time, transforming that moment into pure spectacle, when placed in the extended continuities of *Paterson*, accumulated and released a plenitude of resonance and meaning which the naked lyric, gleaming in its denotative skin, has sloughed away. This procedure, the linking together of radiant particulars, permitted the image in its developing contexts to denote more than the thing itself, without abandoning concrete materiality for the general and the abstract:

> That is the poet's business. Not to talk in
> vague categories but to write particularly, as
> a physician works, upon a patient, upon the
> thing before him, in the particular to dis-
> cover the universal. John Dewey had said (I
> discovered it quite by chance), "The local is
> the only universal, upon that all art builds."

This, then, was to be the path to that "Rigor of beauty" which Williams had made his life's quest and which would culminate in *Paterson*.

The clearest anticipation of *Paterson*, however, was written in 1926 in a poem of the same name. "Paterson" won the *Dial* award for poetry in that year and was published in the February 1927 issue. In this poem Williams presents the central image of the later poem, the image of the city as a man, a man lying on his side by the river and peopling the place with his thoughts. But the place is not just a manifestation of his thoughts; the thoughts are also manifestations of the place, hence the poem's key phrase—"Say it! No ideas but in things."—repeated several times:

> Say it! No ideas but in things. Mr.
> Paterson has gone away
> to rest and write. Inside the bus one sees
> his thoughts sitting and standing. His thoughts
> alight and scatter—

> Who are these people? (how complex
> this mathematic) among whom I see myself
> in the regularly ordered plateglass of
> his thoughts, glimmering before shoes and
>   bicycles—?

This whole passage with one minor change was repeated in the opening pages of book one. It was a good place to start indicating the summative character of the books to follow. A whole life of perception, feeling, and thought cascades through the long poem like the water pouring over Passaic Falls, water that "crashes from the edge of the gorge/in a recoil of spray and rainbow mists." From this perspective, *Paterson* can be profitably compared to those summative epics of Williams's contemporary modernists, Pound's *The Pisan Cantos* (1948), Hugh MacDiarmid's *In Memoriam James Joyce*, and T. S. Eliot's *Four Quartets* (1936-1942). Indeed Hugh Kenner has recently argued that *Paterson* represents, partly at least, a response to Eliot's *Four Quartets*, Williams's last word in a feud between the two men that went back to before 1920. The verbal echo to *East Coker* (1940) in the preface to book one is unmistakable:

> For the beginning is assuredly
> the end—since we know nothing, pure
> and simple, beyond
> our own complexities.

This statement was not intended as homage to Eliot, one giant of modern literature saluting another, but as a rebuke. While Eliot's sequence strove to transcend the local and particular, quickening the deeper the poem entered its sacred, otherworldly silences, *Paterson* would be discovered, Williams wrote in his introductory remarks, in "its own idiom," rising "to flutter into life awhile. . . . as itself, locally, and so like every other place in the world." *Paterson* would not begin in philosophical abstractions (*Burnt Norton*) and end in silence, stillness, and annihilation (*Little Gidding*); it would hear and explore the "roar" of the falls "as it crashed upon the rocks at its base"; because, Williams explained, "In the imagination this roar is a speech or a voice, a speech in particular; it is the poem itself that is the answer."

The specifically poetic voice Williams had in the back of his mind in writing *Paterson* was not the voice of one of his immediate contemporaries, but the voice of Walt Whitman, and it is to this precursor that he pays homage at the close of his in-

Passaic Falls in Paterson, New Jersey. Williams's personified Paterson "lies in the valley under the Passaic Falls/its spent waters forming the outline of his back. He/lies on his right side, head near the thunder/of the waters filling his dreams! . . ."

troductory remarks to the poem. Williams sees his own poem as the extension, some would say culmination, of the poetic revolution Whitman announced in the mid-nineteenth century. Whitman, wrote Williams, "always said that his poems, which had broken the dominance of the iambic pentameter in English prosody, had only begun his theme. I agree. It is up to us, in the new dialect, to continue it by a new construction upon the syllables."

Constructing "the new dialect . . . upon the syllables" carried several immediate consequences. First, the final rejection of a specifically poetic diction, the sort of specialized poeticizing language against which the early romantics, Wordsworth especially, had rebelled in the latter part of the eighteenth century. It meant also the forging of a new prosody based on the phrasal patterns of natural speech rhythms rather than the more or less fixed, repetitive pulses of traditional meters, especially the dominant iambic. To this latter task Williams was particularly devoted, going so far as to theorize about prosody and crediting himself with the discovery of a new prosodic sound-shape for Ameri-

can verse based on the notion of the "variable foot." This innovation he felt was not all that new; it was known and practiced by the ancient Greeks in the form of what classicists call their "lame" or "limping" iambics. In a note appended to book one of *Paterson,* he quoted John Addington Symonds on Hipponax: "In order apparently to bring the meter still more within the sphere of prose and common speech, Hipponax ended his iambics with a spondee or a trochee instead of an iambus, doing thus the utmost violence to the rhythmical structure." The quotation accords with Williams's rejection of traditional metrics in favor of a new measure—worked out in practice in the third section of book two—which he called the "relativistic or variable foot," a notion perfectly at home in the Einsteinian universe. Like the earlier *imagistes'* attention to the "musical phrase," the variable foot represents a unit of rhythmical expression determined by the rhythm and density of the poet's own perception, the nature of the subject at hand, and poet and reader's shared knowledge of the common language in which the particular perception, subject, or experience is normatively expressed. The fixed, metronomic foot of traditional metrics apes solidities and certainties that have vanished in our time. Throughout *Paterson,* the search for appropriate form involved the establishment of a new measure, a new "musical pace." Whitman's was the first heave against audition habituated to the drive and beat of the iambus; *Paterson,* Williams seems to be suggesting, would have been impossible without that bit of daring. Free verse is not free, it seems, but variable.

It has been said that writing in general, the placing of graphic symbols on the blank white page, is not simply making visible prior thought processes. Writing itself is a form of thought, and to use writing simply as a recording or reflecting medium ends by denaturing it, by robbing writing of its greatest potential. The development of Williams's poetry can be plotted as a movement toward the apprehension of writing as a uniquely material form of intellection.

The modernist rejection of traditional metrics unveiled this function of writing as thinking more clearly than ever before. The poem's lines were no longer repeatable rhythmical units in need of suitably and tautly impacted fill. Instead each line was conceived as a unique rhythmical event: fragments of necessary syntax, line length, medial pauses, juxtaposed elements, line breaks, the wide variety of possible sound effects, organic stanzaic boundaries make the thought process itself concrete. As Williams wrote in section two of book one,

> There is no direction. Whither? I
> cannot say. I cannot say
> more than how. The how (the howl) only
> is at my disposal (proposal)   : watching—
> colder than stone   .
>
>   a bud forever green,
> tight-curled, upon the pavement, perfect
> in juice and substance but divorced, divorced
> from its fellows, fallen low—
>
>   Divorce is
> the sign of knowledge in our time,
> divorce! divorce!

In the first line the comment about "direction" mutates into a probe of self, "Whither? I." In the second line, simple repetition—"cannot say. I cannot say"—becomes for the speaker a kind of desperate advice to himself: in other words, being unable "to say" is impermissible; he must say. The assonantal repetition in the third line—"more than how. The

how (the howl)) only"—makes audible, which is to say musical, the mind's agony before obstacles to saying. In these movements, some halting, some "tight-curled," words and sounds jostling against each other, the poetry is as fully alive to its own material processes as it is to its topical subjects. He returns to the subject of words in book two, section three:

> She was married with empty words:
>   better to
>   stumble at
>   the edge
>   to fall
>   fall
>   and be
>
>   —divorced
>
> from the insistence of place—
>   from knowledge,
> from learning—the terms
> foreign, conveying no immediacy, pouring down.

This poetry approaches as closely as writing is able to unity of mind and body, to a reassociation of sensibility whereby a thought is grasped not only in the abstract spaces of the mind, but grasped also by the senses. The poet, Williams once suggested to a correspondent, possesses "knowledge in the flesh as opposed to a body of abstract knowledge called science and philosophy." *Paterson* is the embodiment of that principle.

The central topic of *Paterson* is the idea of a city. That such a topic should have suggested itself for his most ambitious work is not surprising, for the city as symbol has had as long and varied a history as has the city as dwelling. The chronicle of Western civilization can, to a large extent, be read as the history of the rise and decline of great cities: Athens, Rome, Jerusalem, Constantinople, Venice. These cities have been the key arenas in the development of Western civilization. To the physical location of these great cities, and to cities in general, a level of symbolic meaning has accumulated over the centuries. Who in Judeo-Christian civilization cannot feel the symbolic pull of the name Jerusalem or Rome? Indeed the most important symbol of paradise in Christianity is the New Jerusalem. For a thousand years the empire centered by Rome was not only a military and administrative center but a focus for all aspects of physical, intellectual, and artistic life. Its secular authority was transformed after the decline of its military power, and it became the spiritual center

Sept 29, 1951

Dear Upton Sinclair:

One of my patients during my office hour today called
my attention to your letter in last weeks issue of New Republic,
in which you asked some questions, very pleasantly I must say,
about the modern poem. Since you quoted from two of my poems it
might be appropriate for me to try to answer you.

If you will try rhythmically to analyse even those
bits of poems, a person of your abilities and experience as a
writer will quickly get to the heart of the matter: it is the
hearing of the poem in modern practise rather than its physical
appearance on the page which is the important thing. And you
know also, where the artist's choice is concerned, that for him
it is important to be free to elect what to
vary from accepted standards. When one line runs over into
another, where no pause in the sequence of words is wanted, he
will terminate his line whereever he pleases. It's a matter of
the sound - which must be allowed to vary as he may desire it.

You see, the measure, the actual measuring, of the
line has been brought into question ever since "free verse"
(which does not exist) came to be seriously practised. But I
don't want to go inot a long progression on the stages of
modern measurement of the line. It wouldn't
help me to get you clear on this one elemental point.

Dropping that, I ought to speak of the materials, the
sort of image that has come into the modern poem : the factory,
the dump heap, anything "ugly" you choose to name. Don't you
see that anything can be used in a poem? It isn't the quality
of the object that makes a picture, for instance, it is the
light we are painting. It doesn't matter what the object is
that we write about, it's what you do with it that counts.
The poem is a device for saying something above or beyond or
in addition to the mere images used. And that something is
carried by the structural amplifications the modern world has
discovered (or wants to discover) as opposed to a world lived
in the past.

Well, that's a beginning at any rate, if you're
interested we might go further with the argument - if we
consider it worth while. In any case the face of the modern
poem has been altered, for better or worse.

Sincerely

9 Ridge Rd, Rutherford, N.J.   William Carlos Williams

Letter to Upton Sinclair in which Williams discusses his theory of prosody (Copyright © 1986 by William Eric Williams and Paul H. Williams. Reprinted by permission of New Directions Publishing Corporation, Agents for the Estate of William Carlos Williams. Courtesy of the Lilly Library, Indiana University)

It doesn't make any difference how you write a poem on the
page, it is merely convenient to follow a certain conventional
manner of doing so. A sonnet would still be a sonnet if
written as prose. It is merely convenient, for certain reasons,
to write it as is usually done. But when, for internal reasons,
the poet finds that is is necessary to vary from a stereotyped
form he is free to do so.

Since you speak specifically of the little Brugel poem I
think I should explain that of all the poems I have written
that one was more a stunt than anything else. If you know the
picture you will remember that it is composed of sperical
masses, the dancers, who go round and round. That is the
structure of the composition. So I was amused to imitate that
spherical structure in the rhythm of the poem. I won't say
it's much of a poem but it at least does what I wanted it to
do.

W.

of Christendom until the Reformation. Even to this day Rome, for Catholics, represents the center of their spiritual world. The Anglo-Welsh poet David Jones has explored the concrete place and mystical-spiritual function of Rome in our civilization in a long poem called *The Anathemata* (1952), which curiously enough he was composing at the same time Williams was working on the central city—Paterson—of his own particular cosmos.

However, mystical insight and sacerdotal celebration of a city whose myth is more powerful than its reality have no part in the idea which Williams embodies in *Paterson*. Indeed the mystical and the otherworldly, in the traditional terms in which such matters are treated in Western culture, have been deliberately avoided; the whole tenor of his work has been toward a grasp of human beings as they are here and now. Interest in the human is paramount in his idea of the city, for *Paterson* is about man; man identified with and personifying the city. In the introductory note Williams briefly sums up this insight: "*Paterson* is a long poem in four parts [later expanded to five]—that a man in himself is a city, beginning, seeking, achieving and concluding his life in ways which the various aspects of a city may embody—if imaginatively conceived—any city, all the details of which may be made to voice his most intimate convictions." This conception encompasses both the poet's vision of reality, the real world, and his idea of man, for it is "an interpenetration both ways." Mr. Paterson is Everyman (but presented in the only way one can directly know him, as an individual—living in time, rooted in history), the sum total of his experiences; he is also the city Paterson, which is the cosmos in miniature, located in specified place.

In book one (1946), "The Delineaments of the Giants," the physical location and topography of Paterson, the city, give rise to its personification as a giant lying on his right side in a bend of the Passaic River, his head near the thunder of the Passaic Falls, his back easily arched with the curve of the river.

> Eternally asleep
> his dreams walk about the city where he persists
> incognito. Butterflies settle on his stone ear.
> Immortal he neither moves nor rouses and is seldom
> seen, though he breathes and the subtleties of his
>   machinations
> drawing their substance from the noise of the pouring
>   river
> animate a thousand automatons. Who because they
> neither know their sources nor the sills of their
> disappointments walk outside their bodies aimlessly

> for the most part,
> locked and forgot in their desires—unroused.

Here are stated some of Williams's most intimate convictions which the city embodies: its aspect as industrial center "locked and forgot" in the permanent depression of economic decline, the closeness of nature and the determining influence of the natural phenomena which form and surround it, the alienation of those who "walk outside their bodies," isolated from their own desires and from the sources of their social and personal beings. From this opening and for the whole of book one, Williams explores what he calls "the elemental character of the place," through reiterated images, through episodic devices, and through the extended and subtle analogical framework of the connection between man and city.

Book two (1948), "Sunday in the Park," comprises what Williams called "the modern replicas" of the elements in book one. Loosely speaking, book two is an interior monologue, and one cannot help but sense James Joyce's Molly Bloom in the background here. A man spends Sunday in the park. He thinks and looks about him; his mind contemplates, describes, comments, associates, stops, stutters, and shifts, bound only by its environment. The mind belongs to a man who is by turns the poet, Mr. Paterson, the American, the masculine principle, Everyman. His monologue is interrupted by blocks of prose: paragraphs from old newspapers, textbooks, and letters, a device Williams uses throughout *Paterson*. The park, on the other hand, is the feminine principle, America, the women of Paterson, Everywoman. In the reiterative symbolism of the whole poem, the water roaring down the falls from the park to Paterson becomes the principle of life, and the feminine and masculine, into which terms everything is translated, strain toward union, a state of "marriage." It never comes off, except in imagination, and there only in transient forms.

Book three (1949), "The Library," Williams notes, seeks "a language to make them [the modern replicas] vocal." The most philosophical of the five books, exploring the relationship between language and reality, this book offers one of the great defenses of language as being most purely itself when used imaginatively. It is also one of the great defenses of the poetics of the languages of everyday life. The great enemies in book three are the technical abstractions of scholars and other academics. Abstraction and generalization are heard as "offense[s] to love, the mind's worm eating/out the core, unappeased."

Book four (1951), "The Run to the Sea," Williams felt, would be "reminiscent of episodes—all that any one man may achieve in a lifetime." The three subjects which this part of the poem introduces in succession are, first, love—of various kinds, each with its own frustrations—in the figure of a triangle involving a New York poet (a homosexual woman), a young nurse (the female Paterson), and the male poet as Paterson; second, science, through the episode of a lecture on atomic fission to which the male Paterson takes his son (as an introduction to his heritage of the disruptive knowledge of his time); and third, money, greed as the cause of the concentration of capital in a few hands and a subsequent social corruption. These three topics all relate to the theme of alienation (divorce, the "sign of knowledge in our time"), first introduced in book one; and they are also intimately related to the problem of language. The question at the start of the third part of book four keeps this overarching theme in the whole poem firmly in sight: "Haven't you forgot your virgin purpose,/the language?"

With the completion of book four in the early 1950s, Williams felt that *Paterson* was finished. However, as the decade passed he began thinking about the ending of book four again; as the aging poet-protagonist of the poem sensed the shifting of attitudes and moods, the closure of 1951 did not fit the situation of 1958. In *I Wanted to Write a Poem* (1958) Williams recalled this shift: "*Paterson* IV ends with the protagonist breaking through the bushes, identifying himself with the land, with America. He finally will die but it can't be categorically stated that death ends *anything*. When you're through with sex, with ambition, what can an old man create? Art, of course, a piece of art that will go beyond him into the lives of young people, the people who haven't had time to create. The old man meets the young people and lives on."

Book five appeared in 1958 without a title and dedicated

> To the Memory
> of
> Henri Toulouse Lautrec,
> *Painter*[.]

This lineation emphasized the topic of Memory as the theme of the book. The poet still calls himself Paterson, and there are significant continuities of image, idea, and metrical form carrying over from

William Carlos Williams in the 1950s (courtesy of the Rare Books and Manuscripts Collection, Van Pelt Library, University of Pennsylvania)

the earlier books, but Mr. Paterson is less bound by his locality and his immediate present. Here the formative idea of place is expanded to encompass time, as is only fitting in a poem written under the sign of memory. Book five is, in essence, Williams's answer to Ezra Pound's meditation on *memoria* in *The Pisan Cantos*. The book opens with a complex image of freedom, playing on the transitivity of the verb phrase "casts off ":

> In old age
>   the mind
>
>
>   casts off
>   rebelliously
>   an eagle
>   from its crag[.]

The reader soon finds that the mind has cast itself off into memory

>   —remember
>   confidently

Paterson, Book V : The River of Heaven

Of asphodel, that greeny flower,

      that is a simple flower

            like a buttercup upon its

branching stem, save

      that it's green and wooden -

         We've had a long life

and many things have happened in it.

      There are flowers also

           in hell. So today I've come

to talk to you about them - of flowers

      that we both love

           even of this poor

colorless thing that no one living

      prizes

           but the dead see

and ask among themselves,

      What do we remember that was shaped

           as this thing

is shaped ? Their eyes fill

with tears.

           Of love, abiding love

it should be

But too weak a wash of crimson

      colors it.

Page from a draft for a section that Williams dropped from Paterson (Book Five) *but later revised as "Asphodel, That Greeny Flower" (William Carlos Williams.* Pictures from Breughel. *Copyright © 1962 by William Carlos Williams. Reprinted by permission of New Directions Publishing Corporation, Agents for the Estate of William Carlos Williams. Courtesy of the Beinecke Rare Book and Manuscript Library, Yale University)*

only a moment, only for a fleeting moment—
with a smile of recognition . .

With time, the poet-protagonist seems to be saying, the cognitive gives way "rebelliously" and "confidently" to the *recognitive*. The great connection that Williams makes is in the linking of recognitive and imaginative processes:

The flower dies down
and rots away   .
But there is a hole
in the bottom of the bag.

It is the imagination
which cannot be fathomed.
It is through this hole
we escape   .   .

When one remembers Williams's earliest "poeticizing," his imitations of John Keats, one realizes that he has come full circle in his old age. This celebration of the imagination rediscovers the inner meaning of Keats's "Ode to a Nightingale." Of course, from that early allegiance he has shucked the romantic poetic diction and the elaborate rhetorical surface. Underneath, at the core,

through art alone, male and female, a field of
flowers, a tapestry, spring flowers unequaled
in loveliness.

In old age comes the marvelous lucidity of vivid remembrance, the pinnacle of an achieved simplicity:

There is a woman in our town
walks rapidly, flat bellied
in worn slacks upon the street
where I saw her.
        neither short
nor tall, nor old nor young
her
        face would attract no
adolescent. Grey eyes looked
straight before her.
                Her
                        hair
was gathered simply behind the
ears under a shapeless hat.

In 1946, the year of the publication of *Paterson (Book One)*, Williams was sixty-three years old. From then until his death in 1963 recognition and public honors began to flow his way. Invitations to speak and read at a variety of venues, literary prizes, even honorary degrees began to accumulate, and Williams lived to experience a sense of satisfaction in seeing the poetry and ideas which he had begun championing before World War I taking root in the American psyche. Indeed several schools of younger poets regarded the Rutherford physician as mentor and one of the first genuine American literary classics. His home at 9 Ridge Road in those latter years of his life was visited by many friends and acquaintances, but, more important for continuity, it was also visited by the young. He also had the satisfaction of seeing his two sons return from the war intact and resume their careers in business and medicine in New York City.

Aging, however, was not all a matter of basking in his new-found celebrity. Growing old also brought death and sickness. His mother, Elena, died in 1949 at what was thought to be the age of 101; her real age (110) was not discovered until 1956 when her baptismal records were consulted. Williams was much amused by his mother's audacity in hiding her age. Problems with his own health also began to multiply, beginning with two hernia operations in 1946. In February 1948 he was struck by a heart attack, which, though slowing him down for a while, did not incapacitate him. In March 1951 he suffered the first of a series of strokes, the effects of which he struggled to overcome to continue writing. The story of this struggle is the stuff of heroism; even as he suffered, his creative impulses never flagged. A very serious stroke threatened his life in August of 1952, and this event was compounded by his difficulties in occupying the Consultancy in Poetry at the Library of Congress. His past involvement in radical politics in the 1930s and during World War II and the publication of *The Pink Church* in 1949, with its unfortunate adjective which by that time had acquired menacing overtones in the vocabulary of American political life, finally blocked his accession to this recognition of his accomplishments and importance in American letters. In early 1953 he was forced, in one of the more dishonorable episodes of American political and cultural history, to relinquish the Library of Congress appointment. From February to April of that year Williams was hospitalized for severe depression. He recovered though and continued to write and publish, harvesting the final and brilliant crop of work which completes his achievement. His third stroke hit in October 1958, shortly after *Paterson (Book Five)* was published. A sixth book was also in the works in the early 1960s but

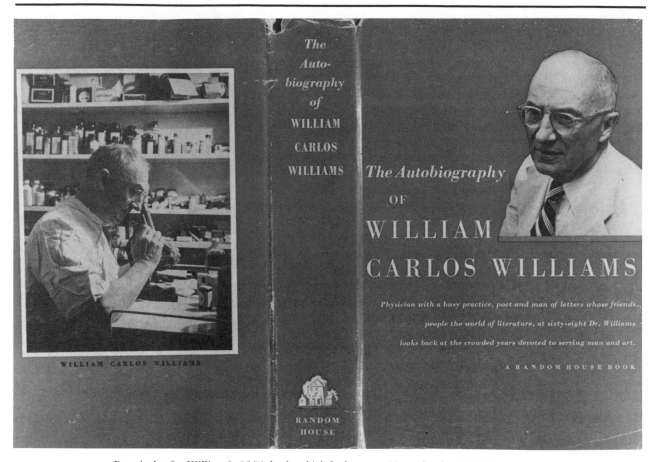

Dust jacket for Williams's 1951 book, which he began writing after his 1948 heart attack

never progressed beyond the note stage. A series of strokes in 1961 finally forced Williams to give up trying to write altogether. His death on 4 March 1963 was commemorated by the posthumous award of a Pulitzer Prize and the Gold Medal for Poetry in that year.

In the last decade or so of his life Williams began to have autobiographical urgings, especially as the physical weakness of his heart became manifest after 1948. His major autobiographical statements in prose were all published in the 1950s. *The Autobiography* (1951) was directly provoked by his heart attack and his sudden awareness of the nearness of mortality. Writing an autobiography might seem an incongruous act in a poet as autobiographical as Williams. Indeed in some ways *The Autobiography* is a bit distant and casual in retailing the narrative of his life. It was always in his art that Williams moved in closer to his own life, communicated with intensity and candor the held intimacies. His courtship of his wife is more vividly and intimately enacted in his novel *The Build-Up* (1952) than in *The Autobiography* of 1951. A second

important autobiographical document is his reminiscence of the composition of some of his major works. *I Wanted to Write a Poem* (1958) was recorded and edited by Edith Heal in a series of conversations and interviews with the Williamses at the poet's home in Rutherford. His tribute to his mother, *Yes, Mrs. Williams: A Personal Record of My Mother* (1959), is a little-known and little-read gem of a book chronicling the life of a fascinating woman. Although the book is focused on Williams's mother, the reader learns much about Williams in an oblique way. The image of the feminine is a constant in all his work, and in this portrait of Elena Williams the reader is given a detailed look at one of the sources of this theme.

Important as these autobiographical writings are for an understanding of Williams's life and work, the last decade of his life should, more aptly for a poet, be remembered for its poetic fertility. Williams continued to progress and to explore new aesthetic territories in his late work, collected in *Pictures from Brueghel and other poems* (1962). Most of the poems in this volume extend and complicate

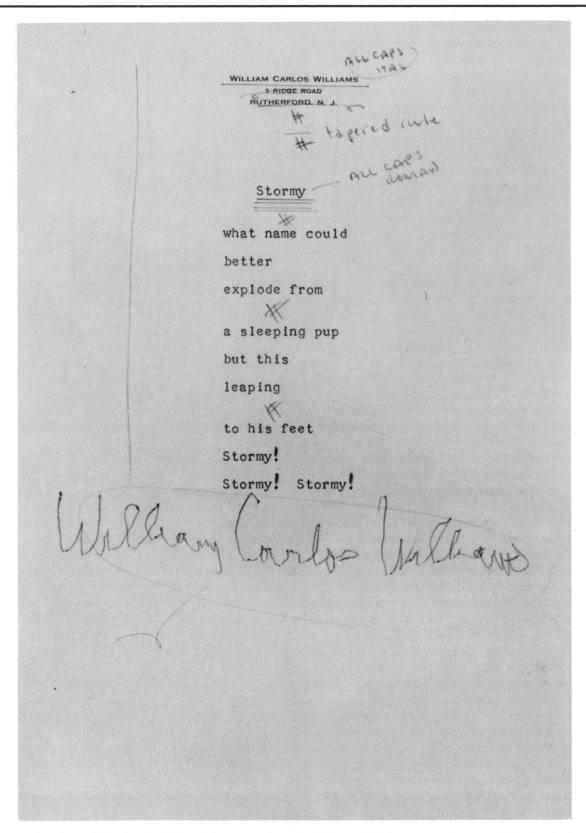

Setting copy for what is believed to be Williams's last poem, about the Williamses' Shetland puppy. It was published in the October-November 1962 issue of Poetry *magazine (Copyright © 1962 by Florence H. Williams. Reprinted by permission of New Directions Publishing Corporation, Agents for the Estate of William Carlos Williams. Courtesy of the Lilly Library, Indiana University).*

the triadic stanza and variable-foot measure which Williams developed in *Paterson (Book Two)* and which in this period he came to call *versos sueltos,* or "loose verses," to distinguish his technique from the vers libre or "free verse" he practiced as an *imagiste* in the 1920s, but from which he eventually turned. In 1953 he told the critic John C. Thirlwall, "The iamb is not the normal measure of American speech. The foot has to be expanded or contracted in terms of actual speech. The key to modern poetry is *measure,* which must reflect the flux of modern life. You should find a variable measure for the fixed measure; for man and the poet must keep pace with this world." Many believe he comes closest to realizing this ideal in his later work. Fellow poet Kenneth Rexroth nearly asserted just such a proposition when he wrote of Williams as the first American "classic," especially in his later work: "his poetic line is organically welded to American speech like muscle to bone, as the choruses of Euripides were welded to the speech of the Athenians in the market place."

Of the many excellencies in *Pictures from Brueghel and other poems* two longer poems stand out. The first, "The Desert Music," originally published in 1954, was first read as the Phi Beta Kappa poem at Harvard University in June 1951. A poem about writing poetry, it celebrates the rediscovery of creative inspiration after a short period in Williams's life when he found himself unable to write. In this rediscovery Williams, near the beginning of the poem, seems to propose that the primary spur to creativity is having something necessary to say: "How shall we get said what must be said?//Only the poem." To embody this theme the poem develops the figure of "the dance":

>   A music
> supersedes his composure, hallooing to us
> across a great distance   . .
>   wakens the dance
> who blows upon his benumbed fingers!

In 1984 this most finely wrought of Williams's later poems was set to music by the young New York composer Steven Reich.

The second notable work in *Pictures from Brueghel and other poems* is "Asphodel, That Greeny Flower," a love poem addressed to the poet's wife. It surveys their years together and recalls in vivid, clear, and distinct images those heightened states of thought and feeling which mark both the progress of their marriage and the poet's artistic development. Both these continuities intertwine in

the poet's mind like the spiralling tendrils of climbing clematis. "Asphodel, That Greeny Flower" has always been associated with the end of Williams's life as a poetic statement that does double duty as a personal credo ("What power has love but forgiveness?") and an artistic manifesto ("Only the imagination is real"). In the poem's "Coda" art and life melt finally into each other and the result is as fitting an epitaph as any poet can hope to earn:

> But love and the imagination
>   are of a piece,
>   swift as the light
> to avoid destruction.

Letters:
The Selected Letters of William Carlos Williams, edited by John C. Thirlwall (New York: McDowell, Obolensky, 1957).

Interviews:
Interviews with William Carlos Williams: "Speaking Straight Ahead," edited by Linda Welshimer Wagner (New York: New Directions, 1976).

Bibliographies:
Emily Wallace, *A Bibliography of William Carlos Williams* (Middletown, Conn.: Wesleyan University Press, 1968); with addenda included in various issues of the *William Carlos Williams Newsletter* and the *William Carlos Williams Review*;

Neil Baldwin and Steven L. Myers, *The Manuscripts and Letters of William Carlos Williams in the Poetry Collection of Lockwood Memorial Library, State University of New York at Buffalo: A Descriptive Catalogue* (Boston: G. K. Hall, 1978).

Biographies:
Mike Weaver, *William Carlos Williams: the American Background* (Cambridge: Cambridge University Press, 1971);

Reed Whittemore, *William Carlos Williams: Poet from Jersey* (Boston: Houghton Mifflin, 1975);

Paul Mariani, *William Carlos Williams: A New World Naked* (New York: McGraw-Hill, 1981).

References:
James E. Breslin, *William Carlos Williams: an American Artist* (New York: Oxford University Press, 1970);

Joel Osborne Conarroe, *William Carlos Williams' 'Paterson': Language and Landscape* (Philadelphia: University of Pennsylvania Press, 1970);

Bram Dijkstra, *The Hieroglyphics of a New Speech: Cubism, Stieglitz, and the Early Poetry of William Carlos Williams* (Princeton: Princeton University Press, 1969);

Charles Doyle, ed., *William Carlos Williams: The Critical Heritage* (London: Routledge & Kegan Paul, 1980);

Kenneth Fields, "The Free Verse of Yvor Winters and William Carlos Williams," *Southern Review*, new series 3 (Summer 1967): 764-767;

James Guimond, *The Art of William Carlos Williams: a Discovery and Possession of America* (Urbana: University of Illinois Press, 1968);

Hugh Kenner, *A Homemade World: the American Modernist Writers* (New York: Knopf, 1975);

Vivienne Koch, *William Carlos Williams* (Norfolk, Conn.: New Directions, 1950);

A. Walton Litz, "William Carlos Williams," in *The Literary Heritage of New Jersey*, edited by Nathaniel Burt, Lawrence B. Holland, and Litz (New Brunswick: Rutgers University Press, 1964), pp. 83-130;

Paul Mariani, *William Carlos Williams: the Poet and his Critics* (Chicago: American Library Association, 1975);

William Marling, *William Carlos Williams and the Painters, 1909-1923* (Athens: Ohio University Press, 1982);

Louis L. Martz, *The Poem of the Mind: Essays on Poetry, English and American* (New York: Oxford University Press, 1966);

Jerome Mazzaro, *William Carlos Williams: the Later Poems* (Ithaca: Cornell University Press, 1973);

J. Hillis Miller, *Poets of Reality: Six Twentieth-Century Writers* (Cambridge: Harvard University Press, 1966);

Miller, ed., *William Carlos Williams: a Collection of Critical Essays* (Englewood Cliffs, N.J.: Prentice-Hall, 1966);

Eric Mottram, "The Making of Paterson," *Stand*, 7, no. 3 (1965): 17-34;

Gorham B. Munson, *Destinations: a Canvass of American Literature Since 1900* (New York: J. H. Sears, 1928);

Alan Ostrom, *The Poetic World of William Carlos Williams* (Carbondale: Southern Illinois University Press, 1966);

Sherman Paul, *The Music of Survival: a Biography of a Poem by William Carlos Williams* (Urbana: University of Illinois Press, 1968);

Walter Scott Peterson, *An Approach to Paterson* (New Haven: Yale University Press, 1967);

Kenneth Rexroth, "The Influence of French Poetry on American" and "A Public Letter for William Carlos Williams's Seventy-fifth Birthday," in his *Assays* (Norfolk, Conn.: New Directions, 1961), pp. 143-174, 202-205;

Benjamin Sankey, *A Companion to William Carlos Williams's 'Paterson'* (Berkeley: University of California Press, 1971);

Joseph Evans Slate, "Kora in Opacity: Williams' Improvisations," *Journal of Modern Literature*, 1 (May 1971): 463-476;

Walter Sutton, *American Free Verse: the Modern Revolution in Poetry* (New York: New Directions, 1973);

Charles Tomlinson, ed., *William Carlos Williams: A Critical Anthology* (Harmondsworth, U.K.: Penguin, 1972);

Rod Townley, *The Early Poetry of William Carlos Williams* (Ithaca: Cornell University Press, 1975);

Linda Welshimer Wagner, *The Poems of William Carlos Williams: a Critical Study* (Middletown, Conn.: Wesleyan University Press, 1964);

Wagner, *The Prose of William Carlos Williams: A Critical Study* (Middletown, Conn.: Wesleyan University Press, 1970);

David R. Weimer, *The City as Metaphor* (New York: Random House, 1966);

Thomas R. Whitaker, *William Carlos Williams* (New York: Twayne, 1968);

Louis Zukofsky, *Prepositions* (London: Rapp & Carroll, 1967).

Papers:

The bulk of Williams's manuscripts and letters is housed in three libraries: the Lockwood Memorial Library, State University of New York, Buffalo; the Beinecke Rare Book and Manuscript Library, Yale University; and the Humanities Research Center, University of Texas, Austin. There are also smaller but important collections of papers at the Alderman Library, University of Virginia; the University of Delaware library; and the Lilly Library, Indiana University.

Appendix: A Survey
of Poetry Anthologies,
1879-1960

A Survey of Poetry Anthologies, 1879-1960

Compiled by Peter Quartermain

"The twentieth century," Conrad Aiken remarked in his 1922 anthology, *Modern American Poets,* "seems to be one of anthologies," and subsequent years have borne him out. Excluding textbooks, the number of anthologies of current verse published in this century runs into the hundreds if not thousands; some of them have aimed at an encyclopedic inclusiveness. Others—such as Yvor Winters's *Twelve Poets of the Pacific* (1937)—have restricted themselves simply to a region, or to an age group: Donald Hall, Robert Pack, and Louis Simpson's *New Poets of England and America* (1957), for instance, confines itself to poets under forty. Some anthologized poems published in a single magazine (Edward J. H. O'Brien's 1918 *The Masque of Poets,* for example, gathering verse which had earlier appeared in the *Bookman*) or written by students (Henry T. Schnittkind's *The Poets of the Future,* published in 1916-1925, for instance). Poets who—like the Fugitives, imagists, and objectivists—belonged to a self-conscious literary group have produced group anthologies. Anthologies, of course, did not spring full-blown into being at the beginning of the century. They are the descendants of identifiable nineteenth-century forebears.

One such ancestor is the series of annual miscellanies and giftbooks—including *The Atlantic Souvenir* (1826-1832), *The Token* (1828-1842), and *The Talisman* (1828-1830)—which, designed for use as Christmas and New Year gifts, were especially popular from 1825 until the end of the Civil War, and left their stamp on the shape of many literary anthologies of the nineteenth century. Lavishly printed, often copiously illustrated, and frequently with ostentatious bindings, they tended toward thematic organization of their contents and—as Augustus White Long remarked in the introduction to his 1905 textbook *American Poems 1776-1900, with Notes and Biographies*—"after decorating the drawing room table a few days at Christmas, [went] to rest under the dust on the top shelf." Best-selling and widely known anthologies such as William Cullen Bryant's *A Library of Poetry and Song, Being Choice Selections from the Best Poets* (1871) followed the English pattern of grouping poems under subject headings and indeed followed precisely the pattern of numerous anthologies designed for the best parlor. Frequently reprinted, it was still popular in the twentieth century, with a final edition of a revised and enlarged version published in 1925.

The nineteenth century saw literally dozens of anthologies such as Elizabeth A. Thurston's *Mosaics of Human Life* (1866) which, grouping its contents under the headings "Betrothal," "Wedded Life," "Babyhood," "Youth," "Single Life," and "Old Age," not only catered to the demands of genteel and sentimental taste but also, providing an apt quotation for every occasion, willy-nilly helped establish a canonical context in which American poets should be read and understood. The major nineteenth-century anthologists who deliberately addressed the canonical matter of *American* poetry were three: William Cullen Bryant (1794-1878), George B. Cheever (1807-1890), and Rufus Wilmot Griswold (1815-1857). William Cullen Bryant's *Selections from the American Poets* (1840) was the first major and successful anthology of American poetry. It remained in print with exactly the same table of contents for much of the nineteenth century, its final edition appearing in 1900.

Somewhat less successful was George B. Cheever's first anthology, designed for the Christmas and New Year market as a giftbook. *The American Common-place Book of Poetry, with Occasional Notes* (1831) was reprinted several times before Cheever published an expanded version of his book: *The Poets of America, with Occasional Notes* (1847), which remained in print into the 1890s. Throughout its career, however, Cheever's anthology remained comfortably in the sentimental giftbook tradition, and Griswold came to dominate the market. "The importance of having books of this nature," said Cheever in the preface to *The Poets of America,* "sweet and chaste in their moral influence, as well as refined in their intellectual and poetical character, is not enough appreciated."

Rufus Wilmot Griswold brought out the first edition of *The Poets and Poetry of America, with an Historical Introduction* in 1842. Griswold made minor corrections for the second printing, and by

1848 the book was in its ninth printing. Griswold then enlarged his survey of American poetry and divided it into two parts: *The Female Poets of America* (1849) and *The Poets and Poetry of America, to the Middle of the Nineteenth Century* (1850). The book was continually revised and brought up to date by Griswold until he died in 1857. R. H. Stoddard considerably enlarged the anthology in 1873, and it remained in print into the 1890s. *The Female Poets of America* was also frequently revised and reprinted into the 1890s, with Stoddard enlarging the 1874 edition. Griswold was more successful than either Bryant or Cheever as a literary nationalist, though his predilection for writers from the eastern seaboard provoked a number of anthologies stirred by regional pride, including William D. Gallagher's *Selections from the Poetical Literature of the West* (1841), a collection of 109 poems written by thirty-eight poets from the Ohio valley.

It was not until the late 1870s that the textbook anthology so familiar to the twentieth-century reader, and so ubiquitous, began to take on its now familiar shape, with the publication of books such as Horace Elisha Scudder's *American Poems: Longfellow: Whittier: Bryant: Holmes: Lowell: Emerson; With Biographical Sketches and Notes* (1879), and it gave rise to a spawn of imitations, culminating in 1900 with the publication of E. C. Stedman's landmark *An American Anthology, 1787-1900: Selections Illustrating the Editor's Critical View of American Poetry in the Nineteenth Century*. Meanwhile, the taste for thematic readings persisted; for example Brander Matthews's *Poems of American Patriotism* was echoed in 1898 by Frederic Lawrence Knowles's *Poems of American Patriotism: 1776-1898*. Clinton Scollard in 1900 edited *Ballads of American Bravery*, and eight years later Burton Egbert Stevenson brought out *Poems of American History*. So, too, the spate of regional anthologies continued unabated, and the long nineteenth-century tradition of coffee-table anthologies of verse came to its final flowering with Thomas W. Herringshaw's leather-bound 1072-page compendium *Local and National Poets of America, With Interesting Biographical Sketches and Choice Selections from Over One Thousand Living American Poets . . .* (1890). As a "biographical dictionary" the book is a forerunner of such reference works as the *Biographical Dictionary of Contemporary Poets: The Who's Who of American Poets* published by Avon House in 1938; in its aim to demonstrate "that America is so rich in Poets and Poesy," it is a descendant of Griswold and Bryant; in its sumptuousness, it is the grandchild of the giftbook; and in its sheer eclecticism, culling its contents from newspaper columns across the continent, and making "no claims whatever . . . for the superiority of its contents; to winnow the chaff from the wheat, and to judge of the merits of these poems, is left entirely to the reader—a task that will undoubtedly prove a source of both profit and pleasure," it has a great deal in common with the productions of the vanity presses of this century, as well as with Alice Roosevelt Longworth and Theodore Roosevelt's *The Desk Drawer Anthology* of 1937.

The following list is arranged chronologically by year of first publication and alphabetically within each year. Although it does not pretend to be exhaustive, it provides a useful brief summary of popular as well as of canonical judgment. It ignores most collections which were not published in the United States. It also excludes most anthologies which were designed as textbooks for use in high school or college, influential though they may have been; later editions of popular anthologies first published before 1879; most exclusively regional anthologies; most anthologies which collect work from one periodical source; and nearly all anthologies of student writing. Brief annotations have been provided for some entries.

1879

Scudder, Horace Elisha. *American Poems: Longfellow: Whittier: Bryant: Holmes: Lowell: Emerson; With Biographical Sketches and Notes*, Boston: Houghton, Osgood; revised edition, Boston & New York: Houghton, Mifflin, 1892.
Important as one of the first textbook anthologies to establish the pattern familiar to the twentieth-century student of poetry, this book was frequently reprinted and still available in the early 1900s.

1882

Matthews, Brander. *Poems of American Patriotism*, New York: Scribners.
Frequently reprinted; the final edition (1922) contains illustrations by N. C. Wyeth.

1892

Repplier, Agnes. *A Book of Famous Verse*, Boston & New York: Houghton, Mifflin.
Frequently reprinted into the twentieth century.

1897

Learned, Walter. *A Treasury of American Verse*, New York: F. A. Stokes.

1898

Knowles, Frederic Lawrence. *The Golden Treasury of American Songs and Lyrics,* Boston: L. C. Page; revised, 1901; London: Routledge, 1906.
Frequently reprinted.

Knowles, as R. L. Paget. *Poems of American Patriotism: 1776-1898,* Boston: L. C. Page; revised as *Poems of American Patriotism from the Time of the Revolution to the Present Day,* Boston: L. C. Page, 1926.
Frequently reprinted until the final, 1926 edition.

1899

Knowles, Frederic Lawrence, as R. L. Paget. *The Poetry of American Wit and Humor,* Boston: L. C. Page.
Reprinted several times until the final, 1918 edition.

1900

Scollard, Clinton. *Ballads of American Bravery,* Boston: Silver, Burdett.

Stedman, Edmund Clarence. *An American Anthology, 1787-1900: Selections Illustrating the Editor's Critical View of American Poetry in the Nineteenth Century,* Boston & New York: Houghton, Mifflin.
The final edition of this anthology appeared unchanged in 1928.

1904

Matthews, Brander. *American Familiar Verse, vers de société,* New York & London: Longmans, Green.

1908

Stevenson, Burton Egbert. *Poems of American History,* Boston & New York: Houghton Mifflin; revised, 1922.
The last edition appeared in 1950.

1910

Humphrey, Lucy H. *The Poetic New World,* New York: Holt.

1912

Earle, Ferdinand. *The Lyric Year: One Hundred Poems,* New York: Mitchell Kennerley.
Representing, says the preface, "one year's work of a hundred American poets" and best known for introducing Edna St. Vincent Millay to American readers with the inclusion of her "Renascence," the

book also includes poems by Zoë Akins, William Rose Benét, Witter Bynner, Bliss Carman, Madison Cawein, Arthur Davison Ficke, Julian Hawthorne, Orrick Johns, Joyce Kilmer, Richard Le Gallienne, Ludwig Lewisohn, Vachel Lindsay, Percy Mac-Kaye, Edwin Markham, George Sterling, Sara Teasdale, Ridgely Torrence, Louis Untermeyer, and George Sylvester Viereck.

Rickert, Edith, and Jessie Paton. *American Lyrics,* Garden City: Doubleday, Page.

Stevenson, Burton Egbert. *The Home Book of Verse, American and English 1580-1912,* New York: Holt; revised and updated, 1918 and 1922.
In 1925, rather than update the anthology further, Stevenson brought out *The Home Book of Modern Verse: An Extension of The Home Book of Verse.* Organized thematically, both anthologies remained in print well into the 1950s.

1913

Braithwaite, William Stanley. *Anthology of Magazine Verse for 1913,* Cambridge: W. S. B.
This is the first volume of this famous and influential annual, which appeared every year through 1929 and had important canonical effects on the poetry of the century.

1914

Pound, Ezra. *Des Imagistes. An Anthology,* New York: A. & C. Boni; London: Poetry Bookshop.
Perhaps the most famous of early modernist anthologies, *Des Imagistes* was first published in February 1914 as volume one, number five, of Alfred Kreymborg's little magazine the *Glebe.* Other imagist anthologies were edited by Amy Lowell in 1915, 1916, 1917, and by Glenn Hughes in 1930.

1915

Lowell, Amy. *Some Imagist Poets,* Boston: Houghton Mifflin.
Lowell edited two more anthologies with the same title in 1916 and 1917.

Pound, Ezra. *Catholic Anthology 1914-1915,* London: Elkin Mathews.
Contains work by T. S. Eliot, Alice Corbin Henderson, Alfred Kreymborg, and other members of the *Others* group, Edgar Lee Masters, Harriet Monroe, and Carl Sandburg, as well as such British or Irish writers as Harold Monro and W. B. Yeats. Published in an edition of 500 copies, the book was not successful. Copies were still available in 1936.

1916

Kreymborg, Alfred. *Others. An Anthology of the New Verse*, New York: Knopf.

The first of three such anthologies, printing work which, generally speaking, was by poets whose work appeared in *Others* magazine, though the poems may have first appeared elsewhere or appear here for the first time. The second and third *Others* anthologies appeared in 1917 and 1920.

Schnittkind, Henry T. *The Poets of the Future: A College Anthology for 1915-1916*, Boston: Stratford, 1916.

Later volumes in this series appeared in 1917, 1918, 1920, 1921, 1922, 1924, and 1925. The 1921 volume is notable for its inclusion of poems by Peter De Vries, Hildegarde Flanner, Ruth Lechlitner, and Louis Zukofsky.

1917

Braithwaite, William Stanley. *The Poetic Year for 1916: A Critical Anthology*, Boston: Small, Maynard.

Eight Harvard Poets, New York: Gomme.

The poets are, as listed on the title page, E. Estlin Cummings, S. Foster Damon, J. R. Dos Passos, Robert Hillyer, R. S. Mitchell, William A. Norris, Dudley Poore, and Cuthbert Wright.

Monroe, Harriet, and Alice Corbin Henderson. *The New Poetry: An Anthology*, New York: Macmillan; revised bibliography, 1919; revised and enlarged as *The New Poetry: An Anthology of Twentieth-Century Verse in English*, 1923; revised and enlarged again, 1932.

The first edition was 404 pages; in 1923 it became 640, and in 1932, 775. The last printing of this important anthology was in 1946.

Teasdale, Sara. *The Answering Voice: One Hundred Love Lyrics by Women*, Boston & New York: Houghton Mifflin; enlarged as *The Answering Voice: Love Lyrics by Women*, New York: Macmillan, 1928.

The first American anthology of poetry exclusively by women poets to be published in the twentieth century.

1918

Braithwaite, William Stanley. *The Golden Treasury of Magazine Verse*, Boston: Small, Maynard.

O'Brien, Edward J. H. *The Masque of Poets: A Collection of New Poems by Contemporary American Poets*, New York: Dodd, Mead.

"I do claim," says O'Brien in his introduction, that this book "is representative." The poems originally appeared anonymously in the *Bookman;* thus, O'Brien claims, this anthology serves "to define the quality of the best contemporary poetry as poetry, rather than as the literary production of writers whose work was sought by the public because of the personalities which produced it." Poetry, he remarks, is always the same: "the circle which begins with the Greek anthology is completed in Imagism, as the circle which begins with Crabbe and Ebenezer Jones is completed in the social poetry of America to-day. What is new in American poetry is fresh experience of life, and I find this as richly expressed in the traditional poetry of Anna Hempstead Branch as in the supposedly radical poetry of Amy Lowell." Among those included, usually with a single poem, are: Conrad Aiken, William Rose Benét, Maxwell Bodenheim, Anna Hempstead Branch, Witter Bynner, Arthur Davison Ficke, John Gould Fletcher, Alfred Kreymborg, Vachel Lindsay, Amy Lowell, Lizette Woodworth Reese, Edwin Arlington Robinson, Carl Sandburg, George Sterling, and Ernest Walsh.

1919

Braithwaite, William Stanley. *Victory! Celebrated by Thirty-eight American Poets*, Boston: Small, Maynard.

Untermeyer, Louis. *Modern American Poetry: An Introduction*, New York: Harcourt, Brace & Howe; revised and enlarged edition, New York: Harcourt, Brace, 1921; revised and enlarged again as *Modern American Poetry: A Critical Anthology*, New York: Harcourt, Brace, 1925; further revised, 1930, 1936, 1942, 1950.

Untermeyer was to become highly influential as a critic, reviewer, and editor. This is the first of the many extraordinarily successful anthologies he put together. In its second revised edition (1925), when it became *Modern American Poetry: A Critical Anthology*, the revisions were so extensive that it became virtually a new book; eventually it rivaled Brooks and Warren's *Understanding Poetry* as a college textbook (as did Oscar Williams's many anthologies of poetry) and had a deep and lasting influence on the shape of the American literary canon during the first half of the twentieth century.

1922

Aiken, Conrad. *Modern American Poets,* London: Secker; revised edition, New York: Modern Library, 1927; enlarged as *Twentieth Century American Poetry,* New York: Modern Library, 1944; revised, 1963.

Designed initially for English readers—who, as Aiken remarked in the preface to the 1963 edition, "made their first annoyed and surprised acquaintance with, among others, Robinson and Stevens"—this important anthology first appeared in the United States in a slightly revised version in 1927. Aiken revised and enlarged it twenty years later, in 1944, when "quite suddenly it appeared that where before there was one poet, now there were fifty." Where the 1927 edition included fifteen American poets (one of them Emily Dickinson), the 1944 edition had fifty-five; after a further twenty years Aiken revised and enlarged the book again, in 1963 including eighty-one poets (one of them, still, Emily Dickinson).

"I find these poets interesting," says Aiken in his preface to the first edition, "because they suggest, taken together, that American poetry, at the moment, is as vigorous and varied as any." He apologizes for the absence of work by Edgar Lee Masters, Ezra Pound, and Carl Sandburg, because "the work of these three poets interests me in the mass, but disappoints me in the item." The fifteen poets in the book are: Emily Dickinson, Edwin Arlington Robinson, Anna Hempstead Branch, Amy Lowell, Robert Frost, Vachel Lindsay, Alfred Kreymborg, Wallace Stevens, William Carlos Williams, John Gould Fletcher, H. D., T. S. Eliot, Conrad Aiken, Edna St. Vincent Millay, and Maxwell Bodenheim.

Johnson, James Weldon. *The Book of American Negro Poetry,* New York: Harcourt, Brace; revised and enlarged edition, 1931.

An anthology of major significance in the history of American poetry as well as in the history of black literature. Johnson's prefaces to both editions are important.

1923

Damon, S. Foster, and Robert Hillyer. *Eight More Harvard Poets,* New York: Brentano's.

The poets, as listed in the table of contents, are Norman Cabot, Grant Code, Malcolm Cowley, Jack Marten, Joel T. Rogers, R. Cameron Rogers, Royall Snow, and John Brooks Wheelwright.

Kerlin, Robert J. *Negro Poets and Their Poems,* Washington, D.C.: Associated Publishers.

1924

Coblentz, Stanton A. *Modern American Lyrics: An Anthology,* New York: Minton, Balch.

Designed for the reader "whose ear has been attuned to graceful rhymes and whose mind has been made ready for exalted thoughts," this anthology avoids "formless effusions . . . filled with the sordid things of everyday," and specifically eschews on the one hand "the raucous crudity of Alfred Kreymborg or of Carl Sandburg" and on the other "the flippant irregularity of Marianne Moore or of William Carlos Williams."

1925

Le Gallienne, Richard. *The Le Gallienne Book of American Poetry,* New York: Boni & Liveright; republished in *The Le Gallienne Book of English & American Poetry,* Garden City: Garden City Publishing, 1935; republished as *The Modern Book of American Verse,* New York: Sun Dial Press, 1939.

Locke, Alain. *The New Negro: An Interpretation,* New York: A. & C. Boni.

The major anthology, based on Locke's special supplement to *Survey Graphic* magazine, announcing and identifying the so-called Harlem Renaissance. It includes poems by Countee Cullen, Claude McKay, Jean Toomer, James Weldon Johnson, Langston Hughes, Georgia Douglas Johnson, Anne Spencer, Angelina Grimké, and Lewis Alexander.

McAlmon, Robert. *Contact Collection of Contemporary Writers,* Paris: Contact Editions.

Though containing much prose as well as verse (some of it by British and Irish writers), and though published in an edition of only three hundred copies, this important anthology is thoroughly representative of expatriate publishing in Paris. The American contributors are Djuna Barnes, Wallace Gould, Ernest Hemingway, Marsden Hartley, H. D. (Hilda Doolittle), John Hermann, Mina Loy, McAlmon, Ezra Pound, Gertrude Stein, and William Carlos Williams.

1927

Brooks, Van Wyck, Alfred Kreymborg, Lewis Mumford, and Paul Rosenfeld. *The American Caravan: A Yearbook of American Literature,* New York: Macaulay.

The first of five such (somewhat irregularly published) annuals, this important and successful anthology (it was a selection of the Literary Guild in 1927) described itself as "a yearbook conducted by literary men in the interests of a growing American literature" and hoped to lead to "the eventual formation of a guild for the cooperative publication of its works. Such a practical enterprise must be the effect of a growing solidarity among American writers, the sense of a common concern, means and object, at the root of these pages." Kreymborg, Mumford, and Rosenfeld went on to edit *The Second American Caravan* (1928), *The New American Caravan* (1929), *American Caravan. IV* (1931), and *The New Caravan* (1936).

Carman, Bliss. *The Oxford Book of American Verse*, New York & London: Oxford University Press.

Cullen, Countee. *Caroling Dusk: An Anthology of Verse by Negro Poets*, New York & London: Harper.
The book is dedicated to William Stanley Braithwaite.

1928
Davidson, Donald. *Fugitives: An Anthology of Verse*, New York: Harcourt, Brace.
A landmark anthology, printing work by contributors to the *Fugitive*, which ceased publication in December 1925. In the words of John Crowe Ransom, "*The Fugitive* flees from nothing faster than from the high-caste Brahmins of the Old South."

1929
Aiken, Conrad. *American Poetry, 1671-1928: A Comprehensive Anthology*, New York: Modern Library, 1929; revised and enlarged as *A Comprehensive Anthology of American Poetry*, New York: Modern Library, 1944.

1930
Imagist Anthology 1930: New Poetry by the Imagists, Richard Aldington, John Cournos, H. D., John Gould Fletcher, F. S. Flint, Ford Madox Ford, James Joyce, D. H. Lawrence, William Carlos Williams. Forewords by Ford Madox Ford and Glenn Hughes, New York: Covici-Friede; London: Chatto & Windus.
Though editorship has been ascribed to Aldington, the volume was probably edited by Hughes, perhaps with Ford's assistance (in his prefatory essay "Those Were the Days" Ford praises "the editor"

for his "jolly good idea"). An unsigned "Note" at the beginning of the book announces that "this volume is not intended as an attempt to revive Imagism as an avant-garde movement. In 1912 certain young and almost unknown authors, who felt friendly towards each other, published their poems together in the 'Imagist' anthology. They have developed along varying lines, but still feel friendly. The present anthology is intended to give specimens of their recent work." In his brief "Foreword" Hughes states that this anthology "is not fighting for anything. It flaunts the Imagist banner not as a challenge, but merely as a symbol. And the Imagists are mustered not for a charge, but for a parade."

Kreymborg, Alfred. *Lyric America: An Anthology of American Poetry (1630-1930)*, New York: Coward-McCann, 1930; revised and enlarged as *An Anthology of American Poetry: Lyric America, 1630-1930 . . . Including Supplement, 1930-1935*, New York: Tudor, 1935; revised and enlarged again as *Lyric America: An Anthology of American Poetry, 1630-1941*, New York: Coward-McCann, 1941.
Including nearly three hundred major and minor poets, the book was designed as a companion to Kreymborg's history of American poetry, *Our Singing Strength: An Outline of American Poetry (1620-1930)* (1929).

Wagner, Charles A. *Prize Poems 1913-1929*, New York: C. Boni.
Modestly successful, the book was reprinted in 1931 and 1936. In the introduction to this anthology of selected prizewinning poems of the period, Mark Van Doren claims that it is "very finely representative" of "the good poetry produced in the United States."

1931
Brown, Robert Carleton. *Readies for Bob Brown's Machine*, Cagnes-sur-Mer: Roving Eye Press.
The preface by Hilaire Hiller explains that the poems in the book, by "experimental modern writers," are expressly designed to be read on Bob Brown's reading machine. Modelled on the ticker-tape machine, Brown's reading machine moved a roll of tape, on which could be printed a whole novel or merely a line of verse, under a magnifying glass. The reader controlled the speed of the tape, thus avoiding wasted time and eye-strain; Brown also wanted the machine to eliminate such "useless words" as articles, prepositions, and other connec-

tives. The "readies" of the title is a word modeled on "movies" and "talkies," and the book itself is a significant forerunner of later experimental writing by such poets as John Cage and the L = A = N = G = U = A = G = E school of the 1970s and 1980s. Among the contributors are Paul Bowles, Kay Boyle, Charles Henri Ford, Eugene Jolas, Alfred Kreymborg, Ezra Pound, Gertrude Stein, and William Carlos Williams.

1932

Braddy, Nella. *The Standard Book of British and American Verse*, Garden City, N.Y.: Garden City Publishing.

Pound, Ezra. *Profile: An Anthology Collected in MCMXXXI*, Milan: Giovanni Scheiwiller.
In a note in his *Active Anthology* (1933) Pound called this book "a critical narrative, that is I attempted to show by excerpt what had occurred during the past quarter century." Like his other anthologies, *Profile* has a pedagogical if not polemical intent; in a note at the beginning of the book Pound calls it "a collection of poems which have stuck in my memory and which may possibly define their epoch, or at least rectify current ideas of it in respect to at least one contour." The poets included are: Arthur Symons, Ezra Pound, Padraic Colum, James Joyce, William Carlos Williams, Ford Madox Ford, Walter de la Mare, T. E. Hulme, H. D. (Hilda Doolittle), Richard Aldington, Allen Upward, W. B. Yeats, Alice Corbin Henderson, T. S. Eliot, Marianne Moore, Mina Loy, Donald Evans, E. E. Cummings, Ernest Hemingway, Robert McAlmon, R. Cheever Dunning, Archibald MacLeish, Louis Zukofsky, Joseph Gordon Macleod, Howard Weeks, Basil Bunting, Emanuel Carnevali, Parker Tyler, and two groups of poems from the New York periodical *New Masses*. The poems are printed in chronological order by date of composition, interspersed with a prose commentary by Pound.

Zukofsky, Louis. *An "Objectivists" Anthology*, Le Beausset, Var, France & New York: To Publishers.
Based on the famous "Objectivists" issue of *Poetry*, Chicago (February, 1932), also edited by Zukofsky.

1933

Benét, William Rose. *Fifty Poets: An American Auto-Anthology*, New York: Duffield & Green.
Benét invited "the best fifty poets in America" to select one brief poem of their own and "add, in a brief paragraph, some of their reasons for choosing their particular poem, as well as something concerning the circumstances under which it was written." Benét also adds a brief commentary on each poem.

Pound, Ezra. *Active Anthology*, London: Faber & Faber.
Designed for an English audience, but nevertheless of great importance in the United States.

1934

Tyler, Parker. *Modern Things*, New York: Galleon Press.
Designed to reach "the large public which is still to be persuaded of the popular virtues of modernist work," the book was only moderately successful.

1935

Grubbs, Verna Elizabeth, as Ann Winslow, *Trial Balances*, New York: Macmillan.
Gathered with "the purpose of picturing all poetic tendencies current among the verse-writers who are from twenty to twenty-five years old," *Trial Balances* includes critical assessments of each poem by "important poets and critics." Thus, Louise Bogan writes an assessment of a poem by Theodore Roethke, Marianne Moore writes about Elizabeth Bishop, Stephen Vincent Benét about Muriel Rukeyser, and Howard Baker about J. V. Cunningham. Among other prose contributors are Witter Bynner, Malcolm Cowley, Hildegarde Flanner, Wallace Stevens, and William Carlos Williams.

1936

Laughlin, James. *New Directions in Prose and Poetry*, Norfolk, Conn.: New Directions.
Dedicated "To the editors [,] the contributors & the readers of *transition* who have begun successfully the revolution of the word," this is the first issue of the most distinguished and influential literary annual to appear in the United States, edited (and published) by the single most important literary publisher in American literary history (he is rivaled only by Jonathan Williams, who as a GI in Europe after World War II founded Jargon Press). Laughlin, a poet in his own right, left Harvard University in the early 1930s to sit at the feet of Ezra Pound at Rapallo, and on his return to the United States founded his own publishing company, New Directions. In the ensuing years the annual failed to appear only three times in 1943, 1945, and 1947.

1937

Del Vecchio, Thomas. *Contemporary American Men Poets: An Anthology of Verse by 459 Living Poets,* New York: Henry Harrison.

Longworth, Alice Roosevelt, and Theodore Roosevelt. *The Desk Drawer Anthology: Poems for the American People,* Garden City: Doubleday, Doran; republished as *The Desk Drawer Anthology: An Anthology that is Different,* London & New York: Hutchinson, 1944.
Reprinted several times. As Theodore Roosevelt explains in his "Foreword," Alexander Woollcott asked his radio audience to send copies of poems they had cut out from whatever source and were keeping; the result, said Roosevelt, is this anthology of "good verses that somehow escaped the accident of fame and were lost in the files of a local newspaper." Poems are arranged alphabetically by author, and include work by Stephen Vincent Benét (two poems), Witter Bynner (one poem), Robert P. Tristram Coffin (five poems), Robert Frost (five poems), Orrick Johns (one poem), Joyce Kilmer (three poems), Vachel Lindsay (one poem), Edwin Markham (two poems), Phyllis McGinley (one poem), Edna St. Vincent Millay (one poem), Dorothy Parker (one poem), Edwin Arlington Robinson (two poems), Carl Sandburg (one poem), and George Sterling (one poem). The book is an interesting and quite useful index of popular taste of the time.

Winters, Yvor. *Twelve Poets of the Pacific,* Norfolk, Conn.: New Directions.
The twelve poets include Winters, Janet Lewis, Howard Baker, Ann Stanford, Clayton Stanford, and Don Stanford.

1938

Brooks, Cleanth, and Robert Penn Warren. *Understanding Poetry: An Anthology for College Students,* New York: Holt; revised, 1950; third edition, 1960; fourth edition, 1976.
Unquestionably the most successful and influential of poetry textbooks, *Understanding Poetry* is a follow-up to the 1936 college textbook, edited by Brooks, John Thibaut Purser, and Warren, *An Approach to Literature,* itself a very successful text which in 1975 was published in its fifth edition. In its various editions *Understanding Poetry* contains sections on "Intention and Meaning," "Ambiguity, Added Dimension, and Submerged Metaphor," and "The Poem Viewed in Wider Perspective." Of great significance in establishing the poetic canon for more

than one generation of students, the book in its third edition (1960) included nine poems by Robert Frost; seven each by A. E. Housman and W. B. Yeats; five by W. H. Auden; four each by Ezra Pound and T. S. Eliot; three each by Hart Crane, Randall Jarrell, and Robinson Jeffers; two each by H. D. (Hilda Doolittle), Richard Eberhart, Marianne Moore, and William Carlos Williams; and one by Wallace Stevens.

Steloff, Frances, and Kay Steele. *We Moderns: Gotham Book Mart 1920-1940: The Life of the Party at Finnegans Wake in Our Garden,* New York: Gotham Book Mart.
We Moderns is not strictly speaking an anthology at all, but a bookseller's catalogue. It is nevertheless one of the most famous and elusive documents produced in the history of American writing in the twentieth century. The contents include brief biographical introductions to contemporary writers by other writers—that on T. S. Eliot, for example, is by Ezra Pound. The foreword is by William Carlos Williams.

1940

MacLeod, Norman. *Calendar: An Anthology of 1940 Poetry,* Prairie City, Ill.: J. A. Decker.
The first of three annual anthologies (1940-1942) with this title sponsored by the YMHA of New York.

Williams, Oscar. *New Poems: 1940: An Anthology of British and American Verse,* New York: Yardstick Press.
Highly influential, this—and the three subsequent volumes of *New Poems* (1942, 1943, 1944) edited by Williams—was of great significance in establishing the popular reputation of many American (and British) poets, such as Richard Eberhart, Delmore Schwartz, Karl Shapiro, and Richard Wilbur.

1941

Brown, Sterling A., Arthur P. Davis, and Ulysses Lee. *The Negro Caravan,* New York: Dryden Press.

1942

Bishop, John Peale, and Allen Tate. *American Harvest: 25 Years of Creative Writing in the United States,* New York: L. B. Fischer.

1945

Benét, William Rose, and Conrad Aiken. *An Anthology of Famous English and American Poetry,* New York: Modern Library.

1946

Williams, Oscar. *A Little Treasury of Modern Poetry, English & American,* New York: Scribners; London: Routledge, 1948; revised and enlarged, 1950.

1947

Laughlin, James. *Spearhead: 10 Years Experimental Writing in America,* New York: New Directions.
Designed to "commemorate, and celebrate, the first ten years' activity of New Directions by reprinting some of the best work that was published in the annual volume *New Directions in Prose & Poetry*" and "to present an impartial historical survey of the significant *experimental* and *advance guard* writing in the United States during the past decade," this landmark anthology also contains previously unpublished work.

1948

Williams, Oscar. *A Little Treasury of American Poetry: The Chief Poets from Colonial Times to the Present Age,* New York: Scribners; revised and enlarged edition, 1952.
Designed for a mass market, this anthology quickly became popular as a high school and college textbook, and served to further establish Williams (who was to become one of the most indefatigable of anthologists) as an establisher of literary canons.

Zukofsky, Louis. *A Test of Poetry,* Brooklyn: Objectivist Press; London: Routledge & Kegan Paul, 1952.
A pedagogical anthology designed for "interested people," this book aims "to suggest standards," to establish "a means for judging the values of poetic writing."

1949

Hughes, Langston, and Arna Bontemps. *The Poetry of the Negro 1746-1949: An Anthology,* Garden City: Doubleday; revised and enlarged as *The Poetry of the Negro 1746-1970,* Garden City: Doubleday, 1970.

Jolas, Eugene. *Transition Workshop,* New York: Vanguard.
Transition was one of the most important of the expatriate magazines of the 1920s and 1930s.

Rodman, Selden. *100 Modern Poems,* New York: Pellegrini & Cudahy.

1950

Auden, W. H., and Norman Holmes Pearson. *Poets of the English Language,* five volumes, New York: Viking.
The contents are arranged historically, from Langland to Yeats; texts in the earlier volumes—notably those of eighteenth-century poetry—are corrupt. The fifth volume covers Tennyson to Yeats (1870-1914). Each volume includes a "calendar" of British and (where relevant) American poetry.

Ciardi, John. *Mid-Century American Poets,* New York: Twayne.
Work by fifteen poets "who have generally been recognized as having done their best work in the last 10 to 15 years, and who were not widely recognized before that time." Each poet, often by answering a questionnaire provided by Ciardi, gives a "statement of writing principles." The poets are: Richard Wilbur, Peter Viereck, Muriel Rukeyser, Theodore Roethke, Karl Shapiro, Winfield Townley Scott, John Frederick Nims, E. L. Mayo, Robert Lowell, Randall Jarrell, John Holmes, Richard Eberhart, John Ciardi, Elizabeth Bishop, and Delmore Schwartz.

Matthiessen, Francis Otto. *The Oxford Book of American Verse,* New York: Oxford University Press.
Like other books in the Oxford series, this anthology rapidly became standard, and—adopted as an alternate selection by the Book-of-the-Month Club—enjoyed fairly wide sales. There is a useful introduction.

1951

Eastman, Max. *The Enjoyment of Poetry,* New York: Scribners.
A critical book by Eastman, first published in 1913, supplemented in this edition by an anthology of poetry that reflects Eastman's conservative taste.

1952

Williams, Oscar. *Immortal Poems of the English Language; British and American Poetry from Chaucer's Time to the Present Day,* New York: Pocket Books, 1952.

1953

Anderson, Margaret. *The Little Review Anthology,* New York: Hermitage House.
A retrospective anthology of works which appeared in the *Little Review.*

Humphries, Rolfe. *New Poems by American Poets,* New York: Ballantine Books.

1954

Williams, Oscar. *The Pocket Book of Modern Verse: English and American Poetry of the Last Hundred Years from Walt Whitman to Dylan Thomas,* New York: Pocket Books; revised edition, New York: Washington Square Press, 1960.

Williams, Oscar. *The New Pocket Anthology of American Verse from Colonial Days to the Present,* Cleveland: World; revised as *An Anthology of American Verse from Colonial Days to the Present,* Cleveland: World, 1966.

1956

Auden, W. H. *The Faber Book of Modern American Verse,* London: Faber & Faber; republished as *The Criterion Book of Modern American Verse,* New York: Criterion, 1956.
Poets from Robinson (born 1869) to Anthony Hecht (born 1922); the book excludes all poets born after 1923, and omits T. S. Eliot because his work is "well-known in England," and Laura Riding Jackson "at her insistence and my regret."

Sitwell, Edith. *The Atlantic Book of British and American Verse,* Boston & New York: Little, Brown/ Atlantic Monthly.
An eclectic selection, with brief essays on select poets.

1957

Hall, Donald, Robert Pack, and Louis Simpson. *New Poets of England and America,* New York: Meridian.

Containing an introduction by Robert Frost, the book includes only work by poets under forty. In their preface the editors comment that "our selection of English poets may not be representative. Though we have read extensively in English books and manuscripts, we cannot claim to be familiar with all the work being done in England today. Nor can we be confident that our judgment of English poetry is as sure as it might be if we were living in England." It rapidly became popular as a text book, was frequently reprinted, and was influential in shaping the canon. A successor, *New Poets of England and America: Second Selection,* edited by Hall and Pack, appeared in 1962; it omitted all those in the earlier volume who in 1962 were over forty and added eighteen new American names.

1959

Carpenter, Margaret Haley. *Anthology of Magazine Verse for 1958 (and Anthology of Poems from the Seventeen Previously Published Braithwaite Anthologies),* New York: Schulte Publishing.

1960

Allen, Donald M. *The New American Poetry, 1945-1960,* New York: Grove Press.
The first—and most important—of the anthologies to include work by a generation of writers whose literary forefathers are Pound and Williams rather than Eliot and Stevens. Though not designed as a textbook, this anthology was widely adopted throughout American colleges and universities, and marks the most significant reformulation of the poetic canon. Among the writers included are Robin Blaser, Robert Creeley, Edward Dorn, Robert Duncan, Allen Ginsberg, Charles Olson, and Jack Spicer.

On the following pages are the introductions and tables of contents for a selection of the most-influential of these anthologies.

An American Anthology, 1787-1900 (1900)
Edited by Edmund Clarence Stedman

INTRODUCTION

The reader will comprehend at once that this book was not designed as a Treasury of imperishable American poems. To make a rigidly eclectic volume would be a diversion, and sometimes I have thought to spend a few evenings in obtaining two thirds of it from pieces named in the critical essays to which the present exhibit is supplementary. In fact, more than one projector of a handbook upon the lines of Palgrave's little classic has adopted the plan suggested, and has paid a like compliment to the texts revised by the editors of "A Library of American Literature."

But no "Treasury," however well conceived, would forestall the purpose of this compilation. It has been made, as indicated upon the title-page, in illustration of my review of the poets and poetry of our own land. It was undertaken after frequent suggestions from readers of "Poets of America," and bears to that volume the relation borne by "A Victorian Anthology" to "Victorian Poets." The companion anthologies, British and American, are meant to contain the choicest and most typical examples of the poetry of the English tongue during the years which they cover. The effective rise of American poetry was coincident with that of the Anglo-Victorian. It has been easy to show a preliminary movement, by fairly representing the modicum of verse, that has more than a traditional value, earlier than Bryant's and not antedating the Republic. Again, as the foreign volume was enlarged by the inclusion of work produced since the "Jubilee Year," so this one extends beyond the course surveyed in 1885, and to the present time. This should make it, in a sense, the breviary of our national poetic legacies from the nineteenth century to the twentieth. Now that it is finished, it seems, to the compiler at least, to afford a view of the successive lyrical motives and results of our first hundred years of song, from which the critic or historian may derive conclusions and possibly extend his lines into the future.

When entering upon my task, I cheerfully assumed that it would be less difficult than the one preceding it; for I had traversed much of this home-field in prose essays, and once again,—aided by the fine judgment of a colleague,—while examining the whole range of American literature before 1890. Many poets, however, then not essential to our purpose, are quoted here. More space has been available in a work devoted to verse alone. Other things being equal, I naturally have endeavored, though repeating lyrics established by beauty or association, to make fresh selections. While verse of late has decreased its vogue as compared with that of imaginative prose, yet never has so much of it, good and bad, been issued here as within the present decade; never before were there so many rhythmical aspirants whose volumes have found publishers willing to bring them out attractively, and never have these tasteful ventures had more assurance of a certain, if limited, distribution. The time required for some acquaintance with them has not seemed to me misspent; yet the work of selection was slight compared with that of obtaining privileges from authors and book-houses, insuring correctness of texts and biographical data, and mastering the countless other details of this presentation. My forbearing publishers have derived little comfort from its successive postponements in consequence of these exigencies and of the editor's ill health. The delay, however, has rounded up more evenly my criticism and illustration of English poetry, carrying to the century's end this last volume of a series so long ago projected.

The anthologist well may follow the worker in mosaic or stained-glass, to better his general effects. Humble bits, low in color, have values of juxtaposition, and often bring out to full advantage his more striking material. The representation of a leading poet is to be considered by itself, and it is a pleasure to obtain for it a prelude and an epilogue, and otherwise to secure a just variety of mood and range. I have allotted many pages to the chiefs reviewed at chapter-length in "Poets of America," yet even as to these space is not a sure indication of the compiler's own feeling. An inclusion of nearly all the effective lyrics of Poe, and of enough of Emerson to show his translunary spirit at full height, still left each of these antipodal bards within smaller confines than are given to Longfellow,—the people's "artist of the beautiful" through half a century of steadfast production, or to Whittier—the born balladist, whose manner and purport could not be set forth compactly. Similar disproportions may appear in citation from poets less known, the effort being to utilize matter best suited to the general design. Time is the test of all traditions, even those of one's own propagating. We still canonize as our truest poets men who rose to eminence when poetry overtopped other literary interests, and whose lives were devoted to its production. Yet there was an innocent tyranny in the extension of the prerogative accorded to the "elder poets" throughout the best days of a worshipful younger generation. The genius of new-comers might have been more compulsive if less overshadowed, and if less subject to the restrictions of an inauspicious period—that of the years immediately before and after the Civil War. Their output I have exhibited somewhat freely, as seemed the due of both the living and the dead. To the latter it may be the last tribute by one of their own kith and kin; to all, a tribute justly theirs whose choice it was to pursue an art upon which they had been bred and from its chiefs had learned beauty, reverence, aspiration,—but which they practised almost to alien ears. Not only their colleagues, but those that should have been their listeners, had perished, North and South. To the older members of this circle,—those born in the twenties, and thus falling within the closing division of the First Period,—even too little space has been allotted: the facts being that not until the Second Period was reached could an estimate be formed of the paging required for the entire book, and that then the selections already in type could not be readjusted.

A veteran author, Dr. English, recalls an assurance to the editor of American compilations famous in the day of Poe and the "Literati," that "his sins," much as he had incurred the wrath of the excluded, "were not of omission but of commission." Dr. Griswold performed an historical if not a critical service; he had a measure of conscience withal, else Poe would not have chosen him for a literary executor. But if this anthology were modelled upon his "Poets and Poetry of America" it would occupy a shelf of volumes. I have not hesitated to use any fortunate poem, howsoever unpromising its source. A ruby is a ruby, on the forehead of a Joss or found in the garment of a pilgrim. Here and there are included verses by masterful personages not writers by profession, and the texts of hymns, patriotic lyrics, and other memorabilia that have quality. As befits an anthology, selections mostly are confined to poems in their entirety, but the aim is to represent a poet variously and at his best; sometimes this cannot be achieved otherwise than by extracts from long poems,—by episodes, or other passages effective in themselves. The reader will find but a few extended Odes other than Lowell's Commemoration Ode and Stoddard's majestic monody on Lincoln, either of which it would be criminal here to truncate. In the foreign compendium there was little to present in the dramatic form, and that not often of a high order; from this volume dramatic dialogue—regretfully in cases like those of Boker and Taylor—is excluded altogether, with the exception of an essential specimen in the prefatory division; but lyrical interludes from dramas are not infrequent. As to sonnets, one often finds them the most serviceable expression of a minor poet. The sonnets of two or three Americans take rank with the best of their time, but I have tried to avoid those of the everyday grade. Finally, whatsoever a poet's standing or the class of selections, my tests are those of merit and anthological value, and the result should be judged accordingly. There is no reception more distrustful, not to say cynical, than that awarded nowadays to a presentment of the artistic effort of one's own time and people. An editor must look upon this as in the nature of things, happy if he can persuade his readers to use their own glasses somewhat objectively. With regard to a foreign field personal and local equations have less force, and to this no doubt I owe the good fortune that thus far little exception has been taken to the selection and range of material used for "A Victorian Anthology."

This brings to mind a departure in the following pages from the divisional arrangement of the last-named compilation. Essaying almost every method of setting forth our own poets, I found it impossible to follow the one which before had worked so aptly. A chronological system proved to be not merely the best, but seemingly the only one, applicable to my new needs.

The ease wherewith the British record permitted a classified arrangement was a pleasure to the orderly mind. It crystallized into groups, each animated by a master, or made distinct by the fraternization of poets with tastes in common. Whether this betokened an advanced or a provincial condition may be debatable, and the test of any "set" doubtless involves the measure of self-consciousness. Surveying the formative portion of the Victorian era it was easy to find the Roisterers, the Poets of Quality, the several flocks of English, Scottish, and Irish minstrels, the Rhapsodists, the Humanitarians, all preceding the composite idyllic school—that with Tennyson at its head. With and after Tennyson came the renaissance of the Preraphaelites, and also new balladists, song-writers, a few dramatists, the makers of verse-a-la-mode, and so on to the time's end. From all this, distinct in the receding past, it was possible to map out a cartograph as logical as the prose survey which it illustrates. But when the latter-day versemakers were reached, an effort to assort them had to be foregone, and not so much from lack of perspective as because, with few exceptions, they revealed more traits in common than in differentiation. It would be too much to expect that subsequent to the Victorian prime and the going out of its chief luminaries there should not be an interval of twilight—with its scattered stars, the Hespers of the past, the Phosphors of a day to come. The earlier groups were discernible, and reviewed by me, in their full activity; at present, when prose fiction, instead of verse, is the characteristic imaginative product, it is not hard to point out its various orders and working-guilds.

A derogatory inference need not be drawn from the failure of attempts to classify the early and later singers of our own land. Poetry led other forms of our literature during at least forty years,—say from 1835 to 1875. Nevertheless, like many observers, I found scarcely a group, except that inspired by the Transcendental movement, of more import than an occasional band such as the little set of "Croakers" when New York was in its 'teens. With the exception of Poe, the *dii majores*, as they have been termed, alike were interpreters of nature, sentiment, patriotism, religion, conviction, though each obtained mark by giving accentuated expression to one or two of these fundamental American notes. With the added exceptions of Whitman and Lanier, and of Lowell in his dialect satire, the leaders' methods and motives have had much in common, and the names excepted were not initiative of "schools." There were a few exemplars, chiefly outside of New England, of the instinct for poetry as an expression of beauty, and of feeling rather than of the convictions which so readily begat didacticism; yet for decades the choir of minor poets have pursued their art in the spirit of the leaders and have availed themselves of the same measures and diction.

Variances of the kind arising from conditions of locality and atmosphere have always been apparent. An approach can be made to a natural arrangement by geographical division somewhat upon the lines of Mr. Piatt's illustrated quarto, in which the lyrics and idylls of the Eastern States, the

Middle, the Southern, the regions of the Middle West and the Pacific Slope, are successively exhibited. Until of late, however, the population and literature of the country were so restricted to the Atlantic seaboard that this method excites a sense of disproportion none the less unpleasing for its fidelity to the record. Thus by a process of exclusion the one satisfactory order proved to be the chronological; this being of the greater value since national evolution is more fully reflected in the poetry of America than in that of countries, further advanced in the arts, wherein lyrical expression has derived importance from its literary worth rather than from its might as the voice of the people. If it is difficult to assort our poets of any one time into classes it chances that they are significantly classified by generations. The arrangement of this volume thus depends upon its time-divisions, of which the sequence can be traced by a glance at the preliminary Table of Contents.

Colonial verse, howsoever witty, learned, and godly, is beyond the purview; and well it may be, if only in obeisance to the distich of that rare old colonist, Nathaniel Ward, who tells us in "The Simple Cobbler of Agawam," that

"Poetry's a gift wherein but few excel;
He doth very ill that doth not passing well."

Those who wish glimpses of life in New England after the forefathers were measurably adjusted to new conditions, may acquaint themselves with the lively eclogues of our first native poet, Ben Tompson. They will find nothing else so clever until—a hundred years later—they come upon the verse of Mistress Warren, the measures grave and gay of Francis Hopkinson, the sturdy humor of Trumbull and his fellow-wits. Barlow's "Columbiad" certainly belonged to neither an Homeric nor an Augustan age. Contemporary with its begetter was a true poet, one of nature's lyrists, who had the temperament of a Landor and was much what the Warwick classicist might have been if bred, afar from Oxford, to the life of a pioneer and revolutionist, spending his vital surplusage in action, bellicose journalism, and new-world verse. A few of Freneau's selecter songs and ballads long have been a part of literature, and with additions constitute my first gleanings of what was genuinely poetic in the years before Bryant earned his title as the father of American song. In that preliminary stage, an acting-drama began with Tyler and Dunlap and should have made better progress in the half-century ensuing. A dialect-ballad of the time, "The

Country-Lovers," by Fessenden of New Hampshire, though unsuited to this Anthology, is a composition from which Lowell seems to have precipitated the native gold of "The Courtin'." Apart from these I think that sufficient, if not all, of what the opening years have to show of poetic value or association may be found in the selections from Freneau and others earlier than the First Lyrical Period,—a period which Pierpont, despite his birth-record, is entitled to lead off, considering the date of his first publications and the relation of his muse to an heroic future.

Accepting the advent of Bryant and Pierpont as the outset of a home minstrelsy which never since has failed of maintenance, our course hitherto divides itself readily into two periods, with the Civil War as a transitional rest between. The First ends with that national metamorphosis of which the impassioned verse of a few writers, giving no uncertain sound, was the prophecy and inspiration. The antecedent struggle was so absorbing that any conception of poetry as an art to be pursued for its own sake was at best not current; yet beauty was not infrequent in the strain of even the anti-slavery bards, and meanwhile one American singer was giving it his entire allegiance. Before reverting to these antebellum conditions, it should be noted that a Second Period began with the war olympiad, lasting to a date that enables a compiler to distinguish its stronger representatives until the beginning of the century's final decade. To complete the survey I add a liberal aftermath of verse produced in these last ten years; for it seems worthwhile to favor a rather inclusive chartage of the tendencies, even the minor currents and eddies, which the poetry of our younger writers reveals to those who care for it. As to omitted names, I reflect that their bearers well may trust to anthologists of the future, rather than to have lines embalmed here for which in later days they may not care to be held to account.

The sub-divisions of each of the lyrical periods,—covering, as to the First Period, three terms of about fifteen years each, and as to the Second, three of ten years each, represent literary generations, some of which so overlap one another as to be in a sense contemporary. Finally, the "Additional Selections" at the end of every sub-division, and succeeding the preliminary and supplementary pages, are for the most part chronologically ordered as concerns any specific group of poems. These addenda have afforded a serviceable means of preserving notable "single poems," and of paying attention to not a few unpretentious writers who, while uttering true notes, have obeyed Wordsworth's injunction to shine in their places and "be content."

Here I wish to set down a few conclusions, not so much in regard to the interest of the whole compilation as to its value in any summary of the later poetry of our English tongue.

When I told a New York publisher—a University man, whose judgment is well entitled to respect—that I had this book in mind as the final number of a series and as a companion to the British volume, he replied off-hand: "You cannot make it half so good as the other: we haven't the material." This I was not ready to dispute, yet was aware of having entertained a feeling, since writing "Poets of America," that if a native anthology must yield to the foreign one in wealth of choice production, it might prove to be, from an equally vital point of view, the more significant of the two. Now having ended my labor, that feeling has become a belief which possibly may be shared by others willing to consider the grounds of its formation.

In demurring to what certainly is a general impression, the first inquiry must be: What then constitutes the significance of a body of rhythmical literature as found in either of these anthologies, each restricted to its own territory, and both cast in the same epoch and language? Undoubtedly, and first of all, the essential quality of its material as poetry; next to this, its quality as an expression and interpretation of the time itself. In many an era the second factor may afford a surer means of estimate than the first, inasmuch as the purely literary result may be nothing rarer than what the world already has possessed, nor greatly differing from it; nevertheless, it may be the voice of a time, of a generation, of a people,—all of extraordinary import to the world's future. A new constructive standard was set by Tennyson, with increase rather than reduction of intellectual power, but shortly before the art of the laureate and his school there was little to choose in technical matters between English and American rhythmists, Landor always excepted. Since the Georgian hey-day, imagination of the creative order scarcely has been dominant, nor is it so in any composite and idyllic era. Our own poetry excels as a recognizable voice in utterance of the emotions of a people. The storm and stress of youth have been upon us, and the nation has not lacked its lyric cry; meanwhile the typical sentiments of piety, domesticity, freedom, have made our less impassioned verse at least sincere. One who underrates the significance of our literature, prose or verse, as both the expression and the stimulant of national feeling, as of import in the past and to the future of America, and therefore of the world, is deficient in that critical insight which can judge even of its own day unwarped by personal taste or deference to public impression. He shuts his eyes to the fact that at times, notably throughout the years resulting in the Civil War, this literature has been a "force." Its verse until the dominance of prose fiction—well into the seventies, let us say—formed the staple of current reading; and fortunate it was—while pirated foreign writings, sold cheaply everywhere, handicapped the evolution of a native prose school—that the books of the "elder American poets" lay on the centre-tables of our households and were read with zest by young and old. They were not the fosterers of new-world liberty and aspiration solely; beyond this, in the case of Longfellow for example, the legends read between the lines made his verse as welcome in Great Britain as among his own country-folk. The criterion of poetry is not its instant vogue with the ill-informed classes; yet when it is the utterance of an ardent people, as in the works of Longfellow, Bryant, Emerson, Lowell, Whittier, it once more assumes its ancient and rightful place as the art originative of belief and deed. Emerson presented such a union of spiritual and civic insight with dithyrambic genius as may not be seen again. His thought is now congenital throughout vast reaches, among new peoples scarcely conscious of its derivation. The transcendentalists, as a whole, for all their lapses into didacticism, made and left an impress. Longfellow and his pupils, for their part, excited for our people the old-world sense of beauty and romance, until they sought for a beauty of their own and developed a new literary manner—touched by that of the motherland, yet with a difference; the counterpart of that "national likeness" so elusive, yet so instantly recognized when chanced upon abroad. In Bryant, often pronounced cold and granitic by readers bred to the copious-worded verse of modern times, is found the large imagination that befits a progenitor. It was stirred, as that of no future American can be, by his observation of primeval nature. He saw her virgin mountains, rivers, forests, prairies, broadly; and his vocabulary, scant and doric as it was, proved sufficient—in fact the best—for nature's elemental bard. His master may have been Wordsworth, but the difference between the two is that of the prairie and the moor, Ontario and Windermere, the Hudson and the Wye. From "Thanatopsis" in his youth to "The Flood of Years" in his hoary age, Bryant

was conscious of the overstress of Nature unmodified by human occupation and training. It is not surprising that Whitman—though it was from Emerson he learned to follow his own genius—so often expressed himself as in sympathy with Bryant, above other American poets, on the imaginative side. The elemental quality of the two is what makes them akin; what differentiates them is not alone their styles, but the advance of Whitman's generation from the homogeneous to the heterogeneous. The younger minstrel, to use his own phrase, also saw things *en masse;* but in his day and vision the synthesis of the new world was that of populous hordes surging here and there in the currents of democracy. Bryant is the poet of the ages, Whitman of the generations. The aesthetic note of poetry was restored by Longfellow, in Vergilian office, and by Edgar Poe with surer magic and endurance. Has any singer of our time more demonstrably affected the rhythmical methods of various lands than Poe with his few but haunting paradigms? He gave a saving grace of melody and illusion to French classicism, to English didactics,—to the romance of Europe from Italy to Scandinavia. It is now pretty clear, notwithstanding the popularity of Longfellow in his day, that Emerson, Poe, and Whitman were those of our poets from whom the old world had most to learn; such is the worth, let the young writer note, of seeking inspiration from within, instead of copying the exquisite achievements of masters to whom we all resort for edification,—that is, for our own delight, which is not the chief end of the artist's throes. Our three most individual minstrels are now the most alive, resembling one another only in having each possessed the genius that originates. Years from now, it will be matter of fact that their influences were as lasting as those of any poets of this century.

The polemic work of Whittier, Lowell, and their allies, illustrates the applied force of lyrical expression. Their poetry of agitation scarcely found a counterpart on the Southern side until the four-years' conflict began; yet any study of the causes and conduct of that war confirms our respect for Fletcher's sage who cared to make the ballads of a nation rather than its laws. His saying never applies more shrewdly than at the stage of a nation's formation when the slightest deflection must needs be the equivalent of a vast arc in the circle of its futurity. It is strange to realize that the young now view the Civil War from a distance almost equal to that between their seniors' childhood and the war of 1812—the veterans of which we watched with kindly humor when their lessening remnant still kept up its musty commemorations. Our youth know the immeasurably larger scope of the mid-century struggle; they cannot understand from the echo of its trumpetings the music of a time when one half of a people fought for a moral sentiment,—the other, for a birthright which pride would not forego. Even the motherland, though gaining a fresh view from that convulsion and its outcome, formed no adequate understanding of her progeny over sea. Years go by, and the oceans are held in common, and the world is learning that our past foretokened a new domain in art, letters, and accomplishment, of which we have barely touched the border. Making every allowance for the *gratia hospitum,* a recent visitor, William Archer, need not fear to stand by what he had the perception to discover and the courage to declare. In his judgment, "the whole world will one day come to hold Vicksburg and Gettysburg names of larger historic import than Waterloo or Sedan." If this be so, the significance of a literature of all kinds that led up to the "sudden making" of those "splendid names" is not to be gainsaid. Mr. Howells aptly has pointed out that war does not often add to great art or poetry, but the white heat of lyric utterance has preceded many a campaign, and never more effectively than in the years before our fight for what Mr. Archer calls "the preservation of the national idea." Therefore an American does not seem to me a laudable reader who does not estimate the following presentation in the full light of all that his country has been, is, and is to be.

Time has not clouded, but cleared, the lenses through which our neophytes regard those distant movements so fully in accord with the modern spirit as Poe's renaissance of art for beauty's sake, and Whitman's revolt against social and literary traditions. The academic vantage no less held its own with Parsons and Holmes as maintainers,—the former our purest classicist, and a translator equalled only by Bayard Taylor. The stately elegance of Parsons limited his audience, yet perfected the strength of his ode "On a Bust of Dante," than which no finer lyric ennobles this collection. Holmes's grace, humor, contemporaneousness, brought him into favor again and again, and the closing days of a sparkling career were the most zestful for the acknowledged master of new "architects of airy rhyme" on each side of the Atlantic. In Lowell, the many-sided, the best equipped, and withal the most spontaneous, of these worthies, their traits were combined. Never was there a singer at once so learned and so unstudied; no other American took the range that lies between

the truth and feeling of his dialect verse and the height of his national odes.

This is not a critical Introduction, and the writer need not dwell upon the shortcomings of our still famous matin choir. These were discussed in commentaries that differ very little from what they would be if written now, though after this farther lapse of time I might not enter upon such judgments with the glow and interest of the earlier years, when those hoar and laurelled heads still shone benignantly above us.

Along the century's midway, a group of somewhat younger poets appeared, whose places of birth or settlement rendered them less subject to the homiletic mood which even Lowell recognized as his own besetting drawback. Taylor, Boker, Stoddard, Read, Story, and their allies, wrote poetry for the sheer love of it. They did much beautiful work, with a cosmopolitan and artistic bent, making it a part of the varied industry of men of letters; in fact, they were creating a civic Arcadia of their own,—but then came the tempest that sent poets and preachers alike to the storm-cellars, and certainly made roundelays seem inapposite as the "pleasing of a lute." Yet my expositions of the then current writers, taken with the sheaf of popular war-songs, Northern and Southern, bound up in a single section, prove that the fury of the fight called forth inspiring strains. Some of these were as quickly caught up by the public as were the best known efforts of the laureate of Anglo-Saxon expansion in a recent day. On the whole, the stern and dreadful war for the Union produced its due share of the lays of heroism and endeavor. But then, as oftentimes, pieces that outrivalled others were wont to have the temporal quality that does not make for an abiding place among the little classics of absolute song.

As the country slowly emerged from the shadow, its elder bards hung up their clarions, and betook themselves to the music of contentment and peace. Their heirs apparent were few and scattered; encouragement was small during years of reconstruction, and without the stimulus of a literary "market;" yet the exhibit in the first division of the post-bellum period shows that song had a share in the awakening of new emotional and aesthetic expression. Fifteen or twenty years more, and a resort to letters as a means of subsistence was well under way,—and like a late spring, vigorous when once it came. Poets, in spite of the proverb, sing best when fed by wage or inheritance. The progress of American journals, magazines, and the book-trade coincided with a wider extension of readers than we had known before. Such a condition may not foster the creative originality that comes at the price of blood and tears, but it has resulted in a hopeful prelude to whatsoever masterwork the next era has in store. The taste, charm, and not infrequent elevation of the verse contained in the three divisions of the second portion of this compilation render that portion, in its own way, a fit companion to the series preceding it. One must forego tradition to recognize this; in the Hall of Letters, as in Congress and wherever a levelling-up movement has prevailed, talent is less conspicuous by isolation than of old. The main distinction between the two Periods is a matter of dynamics; the second has had less to do with public tendencies and events. It has had none the less a force of its own: that of the beauty and enlightenment which shape the ground for larger offices hereafter, by devotees possibly no more gifted than their forbears, yet farther up the altar steps. In its consistency, tested by what went before, it stands comparison as reasonably as the product of the later Victorian artificers, when gauged by that of Tennyson, Arnold, the Brownings, and their colleagues.

It is not my province to specify the chief writers of this Period, so many of whom are still with us. As the country has grown, the Eastern song-belt has widened, and other divisions have found voice. The middle West quickly had poets to depict its broad and plenteous security; and more lately very original notes have come from territory bordering upon the Western Lakes. The Pacific coast and the national steppes and ranges as yet scarcely have found adequate utterance, though not without a few open-air minstrels. Dialect and folk-lore verse represents the new South; its abundant talent has been concerned otherwise with prose romance; yet the song of one woman, in a border State, equals in beauty that of any recent lyrist. American poets still inherit longevity. Since the premature death of the thrice-lamented Taylor—at a moment when he was ready to begin the life of Goethe which none could doubt would be a consummate work—a few others have gone that should have died hereafter. Sill was a sweet and wise diviner, of a type with Clough and Arnold. O'Reilly is zealously remembered, both the poet and the man. In Emma Lazarus a star went out, the western beacon of her oriental race. When Sidney Lanier died, not only the South that bore him, but the country and our English rhythm underwent the loss of a rare being—one who was seeking out the absolute harmony, and whose experiments, incipient as they were, were along the pathways of discovery. Eu-

gene Field's departure lessened our laughter, wit, and tears. In the present year, Hovey, whom the new century seemed just ready to place among its choristers, was forbidden to outlive the completion of the intensely lyrical "Taliesin," his melodious swan-song.

To end this retrospect, it may be said that the imaginative faculty, of which both the metrical and the prose inventions alike were termed poetry by the ancients, has not lain dormant in the century's last quarter; although certain conditions, recognized in the opening chapter of "Victorian Poets" as close at hand, have obtained beyond doubt. The rhythm of verse is less essayed than that of prose—now the vehicle of our most favored craftsmen. Already books are written to show how an evolution of the novel has succeeded to that of the poem, which is true—and in what wise prose fiction is the higher form of literature, which is not yet proved. The novelist has outsped the poet in absorbing a new ideality conditioned by the advance of science; again, he has cleverly adjusted his work to the facilities and drawbacks of modern journalism. It is not strange that there should be a distaste for poetic illusion in an era when economics, no longer the dismal science, becomes a more fascinating study than letters, while its teachers have their fill of undergraduate hero-worship. At last a change is perceptible at the universities, a strengthening in the faculties of English, a literary appetite that grows by what it feeds on. Letters, and that consensus of poetry and science foreseen by Wordsworth, may well be taken into account in any vaticination of the early future. Meanwhile, what do we have? Here as abroad—and even if for the moment there appears no one of those excepted masters who of themselves re-create their age—there continues an exercise of the poet's art by many whose trick of song persists under all conditions. Our afterglow is not discouraging. We have a twilight interval, with minor voices and their tentative modes and tones; still, the dusk is not silent, and rest and shadow with music between the dawns are a part of the liturgy of life, no less than passion and achievement.

The reader will hardly fail to observe special phases of the middle and later portions of this compilation. In my reviews of the home-school a tribute was paid to the high quality of the verse proffered by our countrywomen. This brought out a witticism to the effect that such recognition would savor less of gallantry if more than a page or two, in so large a volume, had been reserved for expatiation upon the tuneful sisterhood. That book was composed of essays upon a group of elder poets, among whom no woman chanced to figure. A single chapter embraced a swift characterization of the choir at large, and in this our female poets obtained proportional attention as aforesaid. The tribute was honest, and must be rendered by any one who knows the field. A succession of rarely endowed women-singers, that began—not to go back to the time of Maria Brooks—near the middle of the century, still continues unbroken. Much of their song has been exquisite, some of it strong as sweet; indeed, a notable portion of our treasure-trove would be missing if their space in the present volume were otherwise filled. Not that by force of numbers and excellence women bear off the chief trophies of poetry, prose fiction, and the other arts; thus far the sex's achievements, in a time half seriously styled "the woman's age," are still more evident elsewhere. It cannot yet be said of the Parnassian temple, as of the Church, that it would have no parishioners, and the service no participants, if it were not for women. The work of their brother poets is not emasculate, and will not be while grace and tenderness fail to make men cowards, and beauty remains the flower of strength. Yet for assurance of the fact that their contribution to the song of America is remarkable, and even more so than it has been— leaving out the work of Elizabeth Browning—to that of Great Britain, one need only examine its representation in this anthology. I am not so adventurous as to mention names, but am confident that none will be ungrateful for my liberal selections from the verse upon the quality of which the foregoing statement must stand or fall.

Poetry being a rhythmical expression of emotion and ideality, its practice as a kind of artistic finesse is rightly deprecated, though even this may be approved in the young composer unconsciously gaining his mastery of technique. Our recent verse has been subjected to criticism as void of true passion, nice but fickle in expression, and having nothing compulsive to express. An international journal declares that "our poets are not thinking of what they shall say, for that lies close at hand, but of how they shall say it." On the whole, I suspect this to be more true abroad than here: our own metrists, if the less dexterous, are not without motive. There was said to be a lack of vigorous lyrics on the occasion of our war with Spain. The world-changing results of the war will find their artistic equivalent at sudden times when the observer, like Keats's watcher of the skies, sees the "new planet swim into his ken"—or at least finds this old planet made anew. Anglo-Saxon expansion or imperialism, call

it as we will, has inspired one British poet, yet he is so much more racial than national that America claims a share in him. As for our poetry of the Spanish war, I think that sufficient will be found in my closing pages to indicate that our quickstep was enlivened by a reasonable measure of prosody. The Civil War was a different matter—preceded by years of excitement, and at last waged with gigantic conflicts and countless tragic interludes, until every home was desolate, North or South. Men and women still survive who—with Brownell, Willson, and others of the dead—made songs and ballads that, as I have said, were known the world over. Why should these veteran celebrants decline upon lesser themes, or not stand aside and let the juniors have their chance? The latter had scarcely tuned their strings when the Spanish fight was over. Still more to the point is the fact that poets of all time have been on the side of revolt. Our own, however patriotic, when there was so little of tragedy and the tug of war to endure, felt no exultation in chanting a feeble enemy's deathsong.

In any intermediary lyrical period its effect upon the listener is apt to be one of experiment and vacillation. It is true that much correct verse is written without inspiration, and as an act of taste. The makers seem artists, rather than poets: they work in the spirit of the graver and decorator; even as idyllists their appeal is to the bodily eye; they are over-careful of the look of words, and not only of their little pictures, but of the frames that contain them,—book-cover, margin, paper, adornment. That lyrical compositions should go forth in attractive guise is delectable, but not the one thing needful for the true poet, whose strength lies in that which distinguishes him from other artists, not in what is common to all. While making a fair presentation of the new modes and tendencies of the now somewhat timorous art of song, a guess at what may come out of them is far more difficult than were the prognostications of thirty years ago. Each phase has its own little grace or effect, like those of the conglomerate modern piano-music. Among those less rational than others I class attempts to introduce values absolutely exotic. The contention for a broad freedom in the chief of arts is sound. It may prove all things, and that which is good will stay. Owing to our farther remove from the European continent, foreign methods are essayed with us less sedulously than by the British minor poets. Both they and we were successful in a passing adoption of the "French forms," which, pertaining to construction chiefly, are common to various literatures. In attempting to follow the Gallic cadences and linguistic effects our kinsmen were bound to fail. Our own craftsmen even less have been able to capture graces quite inseparable from the specific rhythm, color, diction, that constitute the highly sensuous beauty of the modern French school. A painter, sculptor, or architect—his medium of expression being a universal one—can utilize foreign methods, if at a loss for something of his own. But there has not been an English-speaking captive to the bewitchment of the French rhythm and symbolism who has not achieved far less than if he had held fast to the resources of his native tongue. Literatures lend things of worth to one another, but only as auxiliaries and by gradual stages. Between the free carol of the English lyric, from the Elizabethan to the Victorian, and the noble variations of English blank verse in its every age and vogue, our poets have liberties enow, and will rarely go afield except under suspicion of reinforcing barren invention with a novel garniture. The technique of the lyrical Symbolists, for instance, is at best a means rather than an end. Though pertinent to the French language and spirit, it is apt, even in France and Belgium, to substitute poetic material for creative design. That very language is so constituted that we cannot transmute its essential genius; those who think otherwise do not think in French, and even an imperfect appreciation of the tongue, and of its graces and limitations, should better inform them. Titles also are misleading: every poet is a symbolist in the radical sense, but not for the sake of the symbol. The glory of English poetry lies in its imagination and in its strength of thought and feeling. Deliberate artifices chill the force of spontaneity; but at the worst we have the certainty of their automatic correction by repeated failures.

Even as concerns the homely, slighted shepherd's trade, there is a gain in having our escape from provincialism indicated by distrust of inapt models, and through an appeal to our own constituency rather than to the outer world. The intermingling of peoples has qualified Binney Wallace's saying that "a foreign nation is a kind of contemporaneous posterity." The question as to a British or American production now must be, What is the verdict of the English-speaking world? To that vast jury the United States now contributes the largest contingent of intelligent members. Our poets who sing for their own countrymen will not go far wrong, whether or not they bear in mind the quest for "local color,"—as to which it can be averred that our elder group honestly expressed the nature, life, sentiment, of its seacoast habitat,

the oldest and therefore most American portion of this country. Younger settlements have fallen into line, with new and unmistakable qualities of diction, character, atmosphere. Our kinsmen, in their pursuit of local color, more or less deceive themselves; with all its human zest, it is but a secondary value in art, though work surcharged with it is often good of its kind, while higher efforts are likely to fall short. When found, we sometimes fail to recognize it, or care no more for it than for those provincial newspapers which are so racy to native readers and so tedious to the sojourner. What foreigners really long for is something radically new and creative. In any case, praise or dispraise from abroad is now of less import than the judgment of that land in which a work is produced. The method and spirit peculiar to a region make for "an addition to literature," but a work conveying them must have the universal cast to be enduring, though its author waits the longer for recognition. But this was always so; the artist gains his earliest satisfaction from the comprehension of his own guild. Time and his measure of worth may do the rest for him.

A public indifference to the higher forms of poetry is none the less hard to bear. A collective edition of an admired poet's lifework, with not a line in its volumes that is not melodious, or elegant, or imaginative, or all combined, and to which he has applied his mature and fastidious standards, appears without being made the subject of gratulation or extended review. A fresh and noble lyric, of some established order, gains small attention, while fetching trifles are taken up by the press. If a fair equivalent of the "Ode to a Nightingale" were now to come into print, a reviewer of the magazine containing it doubtless might content himself with saying: "There is also a poem by Mr.—." But this, after all, in its stolid fashion may betoken a preference for something revelatory of the infinite unexplored domain of poetic values; a sense that we have a sufficiency of verse which, however fine, is conformed to typical masterpieces; a desire for variants in creative beauty to stimulate us until they each, in turn, shall also pass into an academic grade.

In offering this final volume of a series that has diverted me from projects more in the humor of the hour, I feel a touch of that depression which follows a long task, and almost ask whether it has been worth completion. Would not the labor have been better expended, for example, upon criticism of our prose fiction? The muse sits neglected, if not forspent, in the hemicycle of the arts:—

"Dark Science broods in Fancy's hermitage,
  The rainbow fades,—and hushed they say is Song
With those high bards who lingering charmed the age
Ere one by one they joined the statued throng."

Yet after this verification of my early forecast, why should not the subsidiary prediction—that of poesy's return to dignity and favor—no less prove true? As it is, having gone too far to change for other roads, I followed the course whether lighted by the setting or the rising sun. Concerning the nature and survival of poetry much is said in view of the apparent condition. Song is conceded to be the language of youth, the voice of primitive races,—whence an inference that its service in the English tongue is near an end. But surely poetry is more than the analogue of even those folk-songs to which composers recure in aftertime and out of them frame masterpieces. Its function is continuous with the rhythm to which emotion, age after age, must resort for a supreme delivery,—the vibration that not only delights the soul of infancy, but quavers along the heights of reason and intelligence.

If the word "lost" can be applied to any one of the arts, it is to poetry last of all. Not so long ago it was linked with sculpture, now the crowning triumph of a world's exposition. We must be slow to claim for any century supereminence as the poetic age. Our own country, to return, has not been that of a primitive people, colonial or under the republic; and among all peoples once emerged from childhood modes of expression shift in use and favor, and there are many rounds of youth, prime, and decadence. Spring comes and goes and comes again, while each season has its own invention or restoration. The new enlightenment must be taken above all into account. The world is too interwelded to afford many more examples of a decline like Spain's,—in whose case the comment that a nation of lute-players could never whip a nation of machinists was not a cynicism but a study in ethnology. Her lustration probably was essential to a new departure; while as for America, she has

indeed her brawn and force, but is only entering upon her song, nor does a brood of minor poets imply that she has passed a climacteric. It will be long before our people need fear even the springtime enervation of their instinctive sense of beauty, now more in evidence with every year.

More likely they have not yet completed a single round inasmuch as there has been thus far so little of the indubitably dramatic in our rhythmical production. The poetic drama more than once has marked a culmination of imaginative literature. Constructively, it is the highest form of poetry, because it includes all others metrical or recitative; psychologically, still the highest, going beyond the epic presentment of external life and action: not only rendering deeds, but setting bare the workings of the soul. I believe that, later than Shakespeare's day, the height of utterance in his mode and tongue is not of the past, but still to be attained by us. Thus poetry is indeed the spirit and voice of youth, but the thought of sages, and of every age. Our own will have its speech again, and as much more quickly than after former periods of disuse as the processes of action and reaction speed swiftlier than of old. To one bred to look before and after this talk of atrophy seems childish, when he bears in mind what lifeless stretches preceded the Miltonic and the Georgian outbursts. A pause, a rest, has been indicated, at this time especially innocuous and the safeguard against cloying; meantime our new-fledged genius has not been listless, but testing the wing in fields outside the lyric hedgerows. In the near future the world, and surely its alertest and most aspiring country, will not lack for poets. Whatsoever the prognosis, one thing is to be gained from a compilation of the songs of many: this or that singer may be humble, an everyday personage among his fellows, but in his verse we have that better part of nature which overtops the evil in us all, and by the potency of which a race looks forward that else would straggle to the rear.

—Edmund Clarence Stedman

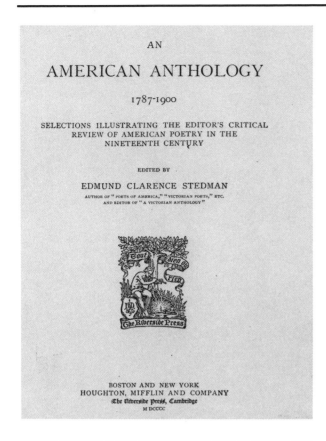

AN

AMERICAN ANTHOLOGY

1787-1900

SELECTIONS ILLUSTRATING THE EDITOR'S CRITICAL
REVIEW OF AMERICAN POETRY IN THE
NINETEENTH CENTURY

EDITED BY

EDMUND CLARENCE STEDMAN

AUTHOR OF "POETS OF AMERICA," "VICTORIAN POETS," ETC.
AND EDITOR OF "A VICTORIAN ANTHOLOGY"

BOSTON AND NEW YORK
HOUGHTON, MIFFLIN AND COMPANY
The Riverside Press, Cambridge
M DCCCC

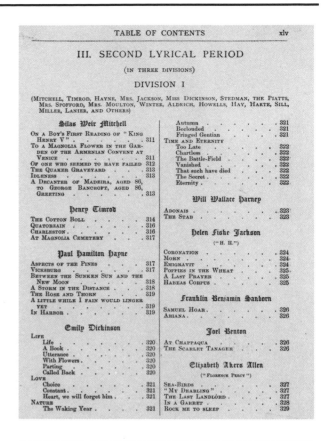

Title page, with the table of contents for the modern section

Contents (cont.) for An American Anthology

Contents (cont.) for An American Anthology

Contents (cont.) for An American Anthology

Anthology of Magazine Verse for 1913 (1913)

Edited by William Stanley Braithwaite

INTRODUCTION

Poetry is one of the realities that persist. The façade and dome of palace and temple, the monuments of heroes and saints, crumble before the ruining breath of time, while the Psalms last. So when another year passes and we sum up our achievements, there is no achievement more vital in registering the soul of a people than its poetry. But in all things that men do, their relationship is objective except those things in which art, religion, love, and nature express their influence through the private thoughts and feelings of men. These four things are the realities, all the others are symbols. And the essence of art, as well as religion and love and nature, is a conscious and mysterious thing, called Poetry. And men will find, if they will only stop to look, that at the bottom of all this poetry, no matter what the theme or the particular artistic shaping, there is something with which they are familiar, because in their own souls there has been an unceasing mystery which they find named in the magic utterance of some lonely and neglected maker of verses.

The poetry in the magazines for this past year has been of a general high standard. The long poems have been well sustained, and there has been a larger quantity of pure lyric pieces than in the past two or three years. The influence of Masefield has shown itself in American verse, notably in the two long poems by Harry Kemp, "The Harvest Hand" and "The Factory." One of the noblest poems of the year is Henry van Dyke's "Daybreak in the Grand Cañon of Arizona," which breathes a fine national spirit, full of reverence for the greatness with which the American destiny is symbolized in the natural grandeur of our country. Mr. Markham has a long narrative in "The Shoes of Happiness," full of his visionary and spiritual promptings. And in "The Vision of Gettysburg" Mr. Robert Underwood Johnson reflects also the national spirit with particular significance.

The poetry of the year in volumes has not been as ample as last year. The three poets who have aroused most discussion are the Bengali poet Tagore, who brought to the Western world in "Gitanjali" a spiritual message full of mystic but exalted idealism; Francis Thompson, the great Catholic poet, because of the publication of his collected works; and Robert Bridges, who, by his appointment to the English laureateship, became known to a large number of readers who had hitherto been unfamiliar with his very perfect and delicate gift of lyric beauty. Of American poets the volumes by Fannie Stearns Davis, William Rose Benét, Josephine Preston Peabody, Margaret Root Garvin, and George Edward Woodberry are the most significant. The most important book of poems of the year by an American poet, however, is that of Nicholas Vachel Lindsay, "General William Booth Enters into Heaven and Other Poems." Here is a man with a big vision, with a fine originality, and an art that is particularly his own. There has been no "Lyric Year" this autumn, but a little volume that serves in some sense its purpose is Miss Jessie B. Rittenhouse's "Little Book of Modern Verse," which is intended to represent the quality of contemporary American verse.

I want to call attention to a poet who has not yet presented himself except through an occasional magazine piece, but who has written two of the finest sonnets in American poetry. Last year I reprinted, in my annual summary, Mr. Mahlon Leonard Fisher's "As an Old Mercer," and pronounced that an achievement which could hardly be surpassed. But in the sonnet "November," which is reprinted in this book, Mr. Fisher has done, I believe, something that is even greater. It must rank with Lizette Woodworth Reese's "Tears" and Longfellow's "Nature" as the best sonnets that have been accomplished by American poets. I have known one competent judge and lover of poetry to declare that not since Keats' "On First Looking into Chapman's Homer" and Miss Reese's "Tears" has there appeared so fine a sonnet in English poetry. The man who has written "November" has added something to American poetry that cannot be too highly estimated.

Another poet who has enriched the magazines this year, after a period of silence, is Mr. Edwin Arlington Robinson, and in "The Field of Glory" we are under the spell once more of that characteristic magic with which he is endowed alone among American poets.

As in former years, in my annual summary in the *Boston Transcript,* I have examined the contents of the leading American monthly magazines. I originally started, nine years ago, when the first summary appeared, with these six: The Atlantic, Harper's, Scribner's, Century, Lippincott's, and McClure's. Later I turned to The Forum. The poetry in McClure's during the two years previous to the beginning of the present year had fallen off; the magazine would reprint occasionally verses from the books of accomplished but little known English and Irish poets, which, with the small amount of space that it devoted to verse, left but little chance of encouragement to native singers. This year I have included The Smart Set, which, under the new editorship of Mr. Willard Huntington Wright, himself a poet of considerable attainment, has been the means of offering the public a high and consistent standard of excellence in the verse it printed.

To the six magazines, namely, Harper's, Scribner's, Century, Forum, Lippincott's, and The Smart Set, I have added this year a weekly, The Bellman. West of New York it is the best edited and most influential periodical published. Indeed, it is widely read in the East. In its pages three of the younger American poets of distinctive achievement have been presented. Though the late Arthur Upson had published some two or three books of verse before The Bellman was established, yet it was practically the first American magazine to print his work. Amelia J. Burr made her first considerable poetic appearance in The Bellman, and the best work, the sonnets that have placed Mr. Mahlon Leonard Fisher in the forefront of contemporary American, or English, sonnet writers, appeared in this same publication. As last year, I have winnowed from other magazines distinctive poems for classification and notice, one each from The Outlook, The Independent, the North American Review, Poetry, A Magazine of Verse; three from the Poetry Journal and three from the Yale Review.

The poems published during the year in the seven representative magazines I have submitted to an impartial critical test, choosing from the total number what I consider the "distinctive" poems of the year. From the distinctive pieces are selected eighty-one poems, to which are added five from the other magazines not represented in the list of seven, making a total of eighty-six, which are intended to represent what I call an "Anthology of Magazine Verse for 1913."

By a further process of elimination, similar to that of previous years, I have made another selection of forty poems which for one reason or another in the purpose of this estimate seem to stand grouped above the others.

The medium of magazine publication, towards which some critics, and some poets too (a fact which can hardly be justified), and a considerable portion of the reading public have a disparaging opinion, is deserving of better repute for the general high quality of poetic art that is published. Not many years ago it was a favorite exercise of the reviewer, when noticing the average book of verse which happened to include selections reprinted from various magazines, to term the work "magazinable," or the poet a "magazine poet." Even poets who detested being called "minor" poets preferred that rather vague and indiscriminate distinction, rather than the unrespectable "magazinable."

Quoting what I have written in previous years, to emphasize the methods which guided my selections, the reader will see how impartial are the tests by which the distinctive and best poems are chosen: "I have not allowed any special sympathy with the subject to influence my choice. I have taken the poet's point of view, and accepted his value of the theme he dealt with. The question was: How vital and compelling did he make it? The first test was the sense of pleasure the poem communicated; then to discover the secret or the meaning of the pleasure felt; and in doing so to realize how much richer one became in a knowledge of the purpose of life by reason of the poem's message."

In one hundred and twenty-one numbers of these seven magazines I find there were published during 1913 a total of 506 poems. The total number of poems printed in each magazine, and the number of the distinctive poems are: Century, total 58, 30 of distinction; Harper's, total 57, 29 of distinction; Scribner's, total 45, 30 of distinction; Forum, total 53, 27 of distinction; Lippincott's, total 66, 21 of distinction; The Bellman, total 53, 25 of distinction; The Smart Set, total 169, 49 of distinction.

Following the text of the poems making the anthology in this volume, I have given the titles and authors of all the poems classified as the distinctive, published in the magazines for the year, only excepting those that are included in the anthology; in addition I give a list of all the poems and their authors in the one hundred and twenty-one numbers of the magazines examined, for the purpose of a record which readers and students of poetry will find useful.

A significant fact which the poetry in this volume must bring to the reader's mind in considering American poetry of today is, that these selections have been published for the first time during the current year. Our poetry needs, more than anything else, encouragement and support, to reveal its qualities. The poets are doing satisfying and vitally excellent work, and it only remains for the American public to do its duty by showing a substantial appreciation.

Lastly, I wish to thank the Boston Transcript for the privilege of reprinting material in this book which originally appeared in the columns of that paper.

—William Stanley Braithwaite.

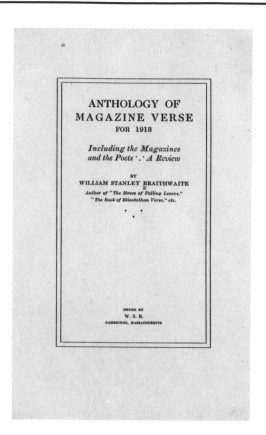

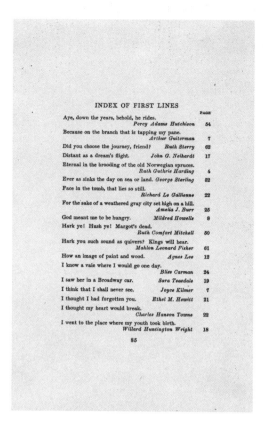

Title page and index of first lines. The volume did not have a table of contents.

Des Imagistes: An Anthology (1914)

Edited by Ezra Pound

[No introduction]

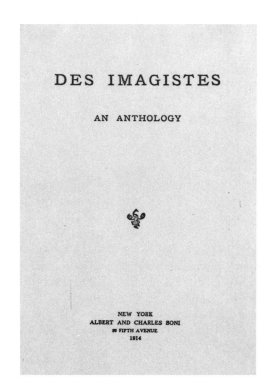

DES IMAGISTES

AN ANTHOLOGY

NEW YORK
ALBERT AND CHARLES BONI
96 FIFTH AVENUE
1914

CONTENTS

5

6

Some Imagist Poets (1915)

Edited by Amy Lowell

PREFACE

In March, 1914, a volume appeared entitled "Des Imagistes." It was a collection of the work of various young poets, presented together as a school. This school has been widely discussed by those interested in new movements in the arts, and has already become a household word. Differences of taste and judgment, however, have arisen among the contributors to that book; growing tendencies are forcing them along different paths. Those of us whose work appears in this volume have therefore decided to publish our collection under a new title, and we have been joined by two or three poets who did not contribute to the first volume, our wider scope making this possible.

In this new book we have followed a slightly different arrangement to that of the former Anthology. Instead of an arbitrary selection by an editor, each poet has been permitted to represent himself by the work he considers his best, the only stipulation being that it should not yet have appeared in book form. A sort of informal committee—consisting of more than half the authors here represented—have arranged the book and decided what should be printed and what omitted, but, as a general rule, the poets have been allowed absolute freedom in this direction, limitations of space only being imposed upon them. Also, to avoid any appearance of precedence, they have been put in alphabetical order.

As it has been suggested that much of the misunderstanding of the former volume was due to the fact that we did not explain ourselves in a preface, we have thought it wise to tell the public what our aims are, and why we are banded together between one set of covers.

The poets in this volume do not represent a clique. Several of them are personally unknown to the others, but they are united by certain common principles, arrived at independently. These principles are not new; they have fallen into desuetude. They are the essentials of all great poetry, indeed of all great literature, and they are simply these:—

1. To use the language of common speech, but to employ always the *exact* word, not the nearly-exact, nor the merely decorative word.

2. To create new rhythms—as the expression of new moods—and not to copy old rhythms, which merely echo old moods. We do not insist upon "free-verse" as the only method of writing poetry. We fight for it as for a principle of liberty. We believe that the individuality of a poet may often be better expressed in free-verse than in conventional forms. In poetry, a new cadence means a new idea.

3. To allow absolute freedom in the choice of subject. It is not good art to write badly about aeroplanes and automobiles; nor is it necessarily bad art to write well about the past. We believe passionately in the artistic value of modern life, but we wish to point out that there is nothing so uninspiring nor so old-fashioned as an aeroplane of the year 1911.

4. To present an image (hence the name: "Imagist"). We are not a school of painters, but we believe that poetry should render particulars exactly and not deal in vague generalities, however magnificent and sonorous. It is for this reason that we oppose the cosmic poet, who seems to us to shirk the real difficulties of his art.

5. To produce poetry that is hard and clear, never blurred nor indefinite.

6. Finally, most of us believe that concentration is of the very essence of poetry.

The subject of free-verse is too complicated to be discussed here. We may say briefly, that we attach the term to all that increasing amount of writing whose cadence is more marked, more definite, and closer knit than that of prose, but which is not so violently nor so obviously accented as the so-called "regular verse." We refer those interested in the question to the Greek Melic poets, and to the many excellent French studies on the subject by such distinguished and well-equipped authors as Remy de Gourmont, Gustave Kahn, Georges Duhamel, Charles Vildrac, Henri Ghéon, Robert de Souza, André Spire, etc.

We wish it to be clearly understood that we do not represent an exclusive artistic sect; we publish our work together because of mutual artistic sympathy, and we propose to bring out our co-öperative volume each year for a short term of years, until we have made a place for ourselves and our principles such as we desire.

—*Amy Lowell*

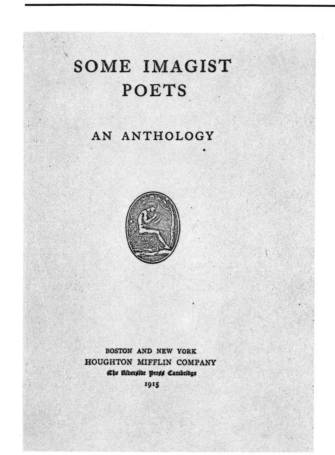

SOME IMAGIST
POETS

AN ANTHOLOGY

BOSTON AND NEW YORK
HOUGHTON MIFFLIN COMPANY
The Riverside Press Cambridge
1915

CONTENTS

[ix]

CONTENTS

Thanks are due to the editors of *Poetry*, *The Smart Set*, *Poetry and Drama*, and *The Egoist* for their courteous permission to reprint certain of these poems which have been copyrighted by them.

Catholic Anthology, 1914-1915 (1915)

Edited by Ezra Pound
[No introduction]

CATHOLIC ANTHOLOGY 1914-1915

LONDON
ELKIN MATHEWS, CORK STREET
1915

Contents

CONTENTS

CONTENTS

Others: An Anthology of the New Verse (1916)

Edited by Alfred Kreymborg
[No introduction]

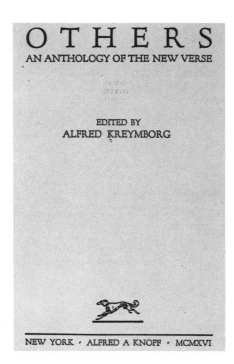

OTHERS

AN ANTHOLOGY OF THE NEW VERSE

EDITED BY
ALFRED KREYMBORG

NEW YORK · ALFRED A KNOPF · MCMXVI

The New Poetry: An Anthology (1917)

Edited by Harriet Monroe and Alice Corbin Henderson

INTRODUCTION

During the last few years there has been a remarkable renascence of poetry in both America and England, and an equally extraordinary revival of public interest in the art.

The editors of this anthology wish to present in convenient form representative work of the poets who are today creating what is commonly called "the new poetry"—a phrase no doubt rash and most imperfectly descriptive, since the new in art is always the elder old, but one difficult to replace with any form of words more exact. Much newspaper controversy, and a number of special magazines, testify to the demand for such a book; also many letters to the editors of *Poetry* asking for information—letters not only from individual lovers of the art, but also from college professors and literary clubs or groups, who have begun to feel that the poetry of today is a vital force no longer to be ignored. Indeed, many critics feel that poetry is coming nearer than either the novel or the drama to the actual life of our time. The magazine *Poetry,* ever since its foundation in October, 1912, has encouraged this new spirit in the art, and the anthology is a further effort on the part of its editors to present the new spirit to the public.

What is the new poetry? and wherein does it differ from the old? The difference is not in mere details of form, for much poetry infused with the new spirit conforms to the old measures and rhyme-schemes. It is not merely in diction, though the truly modern poet rejects the so-called "poetic" shifts of language—the *deems, 'neaths, forsooths,* etc., the inversions and high-sounding rotundities, familiar to his predecessors: all the rhetorical excesses through which most Victorian poetry now seems "over-appareled," as a speaker at a *Poetry* dinner—a lawyer, not a poet—put it in pointing out what the new movement is aiming at. These things are important, but the difference goes deeper than details of form, strikes through them to fundamental integrities.

The new poetry strives for a concrete and immediate realization of life; it would discard the theory, the abstraction, the remoteness, found in all classics not of the first order. It is less vague, less verbose, less eloquent, than most poetry of the Victorian period and much work of earlier periods. It has set before itself an ideal of absolute simplicity and sincerity—an ideal which implies an individual, unstereotyped diction; and an individual, unstereotyped rhythm. Thus inspired, it becomes intensive rather than diffuse. It looks out more eagerly than in; it becomes objective. The term "exteriority" has been applied to it, but this is incomplete. In presenting the concrete object or the concrete environment, whether these be beautiful or ugly, it seeks to give more precisely the emotion arising from them, and thus widens immeasurably the scope of the art.

All this implies no disrespect for tradition. The poets of today did not discard tradition because they follow the speech of today rather than that of Shakespeare's time, or strive for organic rhythm rather than use a mold which has been perfected by others. On the contrary, they follow the great tradition when they seek a vehicle suited to their own epoch and their own creative mood, and resolutely reject all others.

Great poetry has always been written in the language of contemporary speech, and its theme, even when legendary, has always borne a direct relation with contemporary thought, contemporary imaginative and spiritual life. It is this direct relation which the more progressive modern poets are trying to restore. In this effort they discard not only archaic diction but also the shop-worn subjects of past history or legend, which have been through the centuries a treasure-trove for the second-rate.

This effort at modern speech, simplicity of form, and authentic vitality of theme, is leading our poets to question the authority of the accepted laws of English verse, and to study other languages, ancient and modern, in the effort to find out what poetry really is. It is a strange fact that, in the common prejudice of cultivated people during the four centuries from just before 1400 to just before 1800, nothing was accepted as poetry in English that did not walk in the iambic measure. Bits of Elizabethan song and of Dryden's two musical odes, both beating four-time instead of the iambic three, were outlandish intrusions to slight too count. To write English poetry, a man must measure his paces according to the iambic foot-rule; and he must mark off his lines with rhymes, or at least marshal them in the pentameter movement of blank verse.

The first protest against this prejudice, which long usage had hardened into law, came in the persons of four or five great poets—Burns, Coleridge, Keats, Shelley, Byron—who puzzled the ears of their generation with anapaests and other four-time measures, and who carried into their work a certain immediacy of feeling and imagery—a certain modern passion of life—which even Cowper, Thompson and a few others of their time, though they had written of things around them, had scarcely attained. Quarterly critics and London moralists blinked and gasped, but at last the bars had to go down for these great radicals. And before long the extreme virtuosity of Swinburne had widened still further the musical range of the English language.

By the time Whitman appeared, the ear of the average reader—that formidable person—was attuned to anapaests, dactyls, choriambics, sapphics, rhymed or unrhymed. He could not call them by name, but he was docile to all possible intricacies of pattern in any closely woven metrical scheme. But Whitman gave him a new shock. Here was a so-called poet who discarded all traditional patterns, and wove a carpet of his own. Once more the conservatives protested: was this poetry? and, if so, why? If poetry was not founded on the long-accepted metrical laws, then how could they distinguish it from prose, and thus keep the labels and catalogues in order? What was Whitman's alleged poetry but a kind of freakish prose, invented to set forth a dangerous anarchistic philosophy?

It would take too long to analyze the large rhythms of Whitman's free verse; but the mere fact that he wrote free verse and called it poetry, and that other poets—men like Rossetti, Swinburne, Symonds, even the reluctant Emerson—seemed to agree that it was poetry, this fact alone was, in the opinion of the conservatives, a challenge to four centuries of English poets. And this challenge, repeated by later poets, compels us to inquire briefly into the origins of English poetry, in the effort to get behind and underneath the instinctive prejudice that English poetry, to be poetry, must conform to prescribed metres.

Chaucer, great genius that he was, an aristocrat by birth and breeding, and a democrat by feeling and sympathy—Chaucer may have had it in his power to turn the whole stream of English poetry into either the French or the Anglo-Saxon channel. Knowing and loving the old French epics better than the Norse sagas, he naturally chose the French channel, and he was so great and so beloved that his world followed him. Thus there was no longer any question—the iambic measure and rhyme, both dear to the French-trained ears of England's Norman masters, became fixed as the standard type of poetic form.

But it was possibly a toss-up—the scale hung almost even in that formative fourteenth century. If Chaucer's contemporary Langland—the great democrat, revolutionist, mystic—had had Chaucer's authority and universal sympathy, English poetry might have followed his example instead of Chaucer's; and Shakespeare, Milton and the rest might have been impelled by common practice to use—or modify—the curious, heavy, alliterative measure of *Piers Ploughman,* which now sounds so strange to our ears:

In a somer seson,
When softe was the sonne,
I shoop me into shroudes
As I a sheep weere;
In habite as an heremite
Unholy of werkes,
Wente wide in this world
Wondres to here.

Though we must rejoice that Chaucer prevailed with his French forms, Langland reminds us that poetry—even English poetry—is older than rhyme, older than the iambic measure, older than all the metrical patterns which now seem so much a part of it. If our criticism is to have any value, it must insist upon the obvious truth that poetry existed before the English language began to form itself out of the débris of other tongues, and that it now exists in forms of great beauty among many far-away peoples who never heard of our special rules.

Perhaps the first of these disturbing influences from afar to be felt in modern English poetry was the Celtic renascence, the wonderful revival of interest in old Irish song, which became manifest in translations and adaptations of the ancient Gaelic lyrics and epics, made by W. B. Yeats, Lady Gregory, Douglas Hyde and others.

This influence was most powerful because it came to us directly, not at second-hand, through the English work of two poets of genius, Synge and

Yeats. These great men, fortified and inspired by the simplicity and clarity of primitive Celtic song, had little patience with the "over-appareled" art of Tennyson and his imitators. They found it stiffened by rhetoric, by a too conscious morality leading to pulpit eloquence, and by second-hand bookish inspirations; and its movement they found hampered, thwarted of freedom, by a too slavish acceptance of ready-made schemes of metre and rhyme. The surprises and irregularities, found in all great art because they are inherent in human feeling, were being ruled out of English poetry, which consequently was stiffening into forms too fixed and becoming more and more remote from life. As Mr. Yeats said in Chicago:

"We were weary of all this. We wanted to get rid not only of rhetoric but of poetic diction. We tried to strip away everything that was artificial, to get a style like speech, as simple as the simplest prose, like a cry of the heart."

It is scarcely too much to say that "the new poetry"—if we may be allowed the phrase—began with these two great Irish masters. Think what a contrast to even the simplest lyrics of Tennyson the pattern of their songs presents, and what a contrast their direct outright human feeling presents to the somewhat culture-developed optimism of Browning, and the science-inspired pessimism of Arnold. Compared with these Irishmen the best of their predecessors seem literary. This statement does not imply any measure of ultimate values, for it is still too early to estimate them. One may, for example, believe Synge to be the greatest poet-playwright in English since Shakespeare, and one of the great poets of the world; but a few more decades must pass before such ranking can have authority.

At the same time other currents were influencing progressive minds toward even greater freedom of form. Strangely enough, Whitman's influence was felt first in France. It reached England, and finally America, indirectly from Paris, where the poets, stimulated by translations of the great American, especially Bazalgette's, and by the ever-adventurous quality of French scholarship, have been experimenting with free verse ever since Mallarmé. The great Irish poets felt the French influence—it was part of the education which made them realize that English poetry had become narrow, rigid, and insular. Yeats has held usually, though never slavishly, to rhyme and a certain regularity of metrical form—in which, however, he makes his own tunes; but Synge wrote his plays in that wide borderland between prose and verse, in a form which, whatever one calls it, is essentially

poetry, for it has passion, glamour, magic, rhythm, and glorious imaginative life.

This borderland between prose and verse is being explored now as never before in English; except, perhaps in the King James translation of the Bible. The modern "vers-libertines," as they have been wittily called, are doing pioneer work in an heroic effort to get rid of obstacles that have hampered the poet and separated him from his audience. They are trying to make the modern manifestations of poetry less a matter of rules and formulae, and more a thing of the spirit, and of organic as against imposed rhythm. In this enthusiastic labor they are following not only a strong inward impulse, not only the love of freedom which Chaucer followed—and Spenser and Shakespeare, Shelley and Coleridge and all the masters—but they are moved also by influences from afar. They have studied the French *symbolistes* of the 'nineties, and the most recent Parisian *vers-libristes*. Moreover, some of them have listened to the pure lyricism of the Provençal troubadours, have examined the more elaborate mechanism of early Italian sonneteers and canzonists, have read Greek poetry from a new angle of vision; and last, but perhaps most important of all, have bowed to winds from the East.

In the nineteenth century the western world—the western aesthetic world—discovered the orient. Someone has said that when Perry knocked at the gates of Japan, these opened, not to let us in, but to let the Japanese out. Japanese graphic art, especially, began almost at once to kindle progressive minds. Whistler, of course, was the first great creative artist to feel the influence of their instinct for balance and proportion, for subtle harmonies of color and line, for the integrity of beauty in art as opposed to the moralizing and sentimental tendencies which had been intruding more and more.

Poetry was slower than the graphic arts to feel the oriental influence, because of the barrier of language. But European scholarship had long dabbled with Indian, Persian and Sanskrit literatures, and Fitzgerald even won over the crowd to some remote suspicion of their beauty by meeting Omar half-way, and making a great poem out of the marriage, not only of two minds, but of two literary traditions. Then a few airs from Japan blew in—a few translations of *hokku* and other forms—which showed the stark simplicity and crystal clarity of the art among Japanese poets. And of late the search has gone further: we begin to discover a whole royal line of Chinese poets of a thousand or more years ago; and we are trying to search out the secrets of their delicate and beautiful art. The task is difficult, because our poets, ignorant of Chinese, have to get at these masters through the literal translations of scholars. But even by this round-about way, poets like Allen Upward, Ezra Pound, Helen Waddell and a few others, give us something of the rare flavor, the special exquisite perfume, of the original. And of late the Indian influence has been emphasized by the great Bengali poet and sage, Rabindranath Tagore, whose mastery of English makes him a poet in two languages.

This oriental influence is to be welcomed because it flows from deep original streams of poetic art. We should not be afraid to learn from it; and in much of the work of the imagists, and other radical groups, we find a more or less conscious, and more or less effective, yielding to that influence. We find something of the oriental directness of vision and simplicity of diction, also now and then a hint of the unobtrusive oriental perfection of form and delicacy of feeling.

All these influences, which tend to make the art of poetry, especially poetry in English, less provincial, more cosmopolitan, are by no means a defiance of the classic tradition. On the contrary, they are an endeavor to return to it at its great original sources, and to sweep away artifical laws—the *obiter dicta* of secondary minds—which have encumbered it. There is more of the great authentic classic tradition, for example, in the *Spoon River Anthology* than in the *Idylls of the King, Balaustian's Adventure,* and *Sohrab and Rustum* combined. And the free rhythms of Whitman, Mallarmé, Pound, Sandburg and others, in their inspired passages, are more truly in line with the biblical, the Greek, the Anglo-Saxon, and even the Shakespearean tradition, than all the exact iambics of Dryden and Pope, the patterned alexandrines of Racine, or the closely woven metrics of Tennyson and Swinburne.

Whither the new movement is leading no one can tell with exactness, nor which of its present manifestations in England and America will prove permanently valuable. But we may be sure that the movement is toward greater freedom of spirit and form, and a more enlightened recognition of the international scope, the cosmopolitanism, of the great art of poetry, of which the English language, proud as its record is, offers but a single phase. As part of such a movement, even the most extravagant experiments, the most radical innovations, are valuable, for the moment at least, as an assault against prejudice. And some of the radicals of today will be, no doubt, the masters of tomorrow—a phenomenon common in the history of the arts.

It remains only to explain the plan of this anthology, its inclusions and omissions.

It has seemed best to include no poems before 1900, even though, as in a few cases, the poets were moved by the new impulses. For example, those two intensely modern, nobly impassioned, lyric poets, Emily Dickinson and the Shropshire Lad (Alfred Edward Housman)—the one dead, the other fortunately still living—both belong, by date of publication, to the 'nineties. The work of poets already, as it were, enshrined by fame and death has also not been quoted: poets whose works are already, in a certain sense, classics, and whose books are treasured by all lovers of the art—like Synge and Moody and Riley, too early gone from us.

Certain other omissions are more difficult to explain, because they may be thought to imply a lack of consideration which we do not feel. The present Laureate, Robert Bridges, even in the late 'eighties and early 'nineties, was led by his own personal taste, especially in his *Shorter Poems,* toward austere simplicity of subject, diction and style. But his most representative poems were written before 1900. Rudyard Kipling has been inspired at times by the modern muse, but his best poems also antedate 1900. This is true also of Louise Imogen Guiney and Bliss Carman, though most of their work, like that of Arthur Symons and the late Stephen Phillips and Anna Hempstead Branch, belongs, by its affinities, to the earlier period.

On the other hand, we have tried to be hospitable to the adventurous, the experimental, because these are the qualities of pioneers, who look forward, not backward, and who may lead on, further than we can see as yet, to new domains of the ever-conquering spirit of beauty.

—*Harriet Monroe*

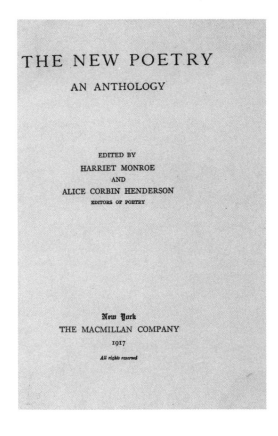

THE NEW POETRY

AN ANTHOLOGY

EDITED BY

HARRIET MONROE

AND

ALICE CORBIN HENDERSON

EDITORS OF POETRY

New York

THE MACMILLAN COMPANY

1917

All rights reserved

TABLE OF CONTENTS

TABLE OF CONTENTS

Contents (cont.) for The New Poetry

Contents (cont.) for The New Poetry

Modern American Poetry: An Introduction (1919)

Edited by Louis Untermeyer

AN INTRODUCTION

"America's poetic renascence" is no longer a phrase; it is a fact. The last few decades have witnessed a sudden and amazing growth in the volume as well as in the quality of the work of our poets. A new spirit, energetic, alert, penetrative, seems to have stirred these states, and a countryful of writers has responded to it. No longer confined to one or two literary centers, the impulse to create is everywhere; there is scarcely a remote corner which has not produced its laureate.

It must be made plain, however, that not even the most ardent admirers of modern American poetry believe that the new poets are the only poets that we have produced, or that they are necessarily greater than the old. What they do believe is this: that the modern poets are different and must be granted their own points of difference. Times change and tastes change with them. The old-fashioned mythological verses and the excellent but too often merely moralizing poems of the immediate past could not be written to-day. Walt Whitman, with his emphasis on the beauty that lurks in familiar things and his insistence on the "divine average," was the greatest of the moderns who showed the grandeur of simplicity, the rich poetry of everyday. "The cow crunching with depressed head surpasses any statue," he wrote; he declared that "a leaf of grass is no less than the journey-work of the stars," and that the common "running blackberry is fit to adorn the parlors of heaven."

Many, though not all of the poets that have succeeded Whitman have found a fresh, living and vigorous poetry in a world of honest and sometimes harsh reality. They respond to the spirit of their times. The singer to-day writes about things unknown to the poet of yesterday. Not only has his view been changed, his vision has widened. He can employ any incident, any subject, instead of being restricted to legendary, classical or traditionally "poetic" themes. In learning to distinguish real beauty from mere prettiness, he is expressing the deepest aspects of life and, in so doing, he is recording not, as has been charged, "more truth than poetry" but more truth *and* poetry.

An editorial in the conservative *New York Times,* which has been none too hospitable to innovators, declared a few months ago, "The so-called society-verse, the didactic rhyme, the musical love-poem that pleased mainly because, in language and sentiment, it was so remote from everyday, prosaic experience, has lost in popularity—superseded, apparently, by a poetry that delights in searching for stronger beauty and in portraying rugged realities."

With the choice of more familiar subjects there has come a further simplification:—the use of a simpler and less stilted language. The rare or rhetorical words have been practically discarded in favor of words that are part of our daily vocabulary; actual speech instead of ornate literary phrasing has become the medium of the modern poet. The "peradventures," "forsooths," "alackadays" and "O thous" have gone. His language, that used to be borrowed almost exclusively from literature, comes now almost entirely out of life. And as his speech has grown less elaborate, so have the forms that embody it. The intricate versification has given way to lines that reflect and suggest the tones of direct talk, even of ordinary conversation. The result of this has been a great gain both in sincerity and intensity; for it has enabled the poet of to-day to put greater emphasis on his emotion than on the shell that covers it—he dwells with richer detail on the *matter* than the manner.

These changes can be easily seen and studied in the work of most of our recent and particularly our contemporary makers of verse. Notice, for instance, in the direct but fully-flavored blank verse of Robert Frost, how the words are so chosen and arranged that the speaker is almost heard on the printed page. Observe how, beneath these native sounds, we hear the accents of his people walking the New England farms and hillsides. Listen to Vachel Lindsay and catch with him the buoyant and even burly music of camp-meetings, negro "revivals" and religious gatherings. Read him aloud, and hear how his words roll with the solemnity of a great prayer or snap, crackle, wink and dance with all the humorous rhythms of a piece of "ragtime." Note how, in the work of E. L. Masters, the author explores the borderland between poetry and prose. Or listen to the quiet but deeply-moving singing of James Oppenheim, music of a biblical quality, like mystical modern psalms. Hear how, without rhyme or a strict rhythm, Carl Sandburg makes little melodies that are sheer music and how, by combining vision with the simplest talk (even with slang), he achieves magic. Examine the delicate verbal designs in the almost carved lines of Emily Dickinson, "H.D.," Adelaide Crapsey.

And, on the other hand, turn to those who, by adapting and sharpening old forms, are no less original. Notice how Edwin Arlington Robinson uses the strictest rhymes and most conventional metres and, by the use of a subtle intellect and even subtler sympathy, makes them more "modern" than the freest free-verse. Examine the homely and mystical verses of Anna Hempstead Branch. Read the outspoken lyrics of Sara Teasdale and see how frank and straightforward these lines are, how different from either the tinkling or over-sentimental love-songs that passed for genuine emotion. Observe how breezy, spirited and full of the tang of native sounds and scenes are the songs of Richard Hovey, Bliss Carman, James Whitcomb Riley, H. H. Knibbs, the two Benéts and a half a dozen others.

Study the highly decorative poetry of Amy Lowell; see how she has responded to Oriental and French influences and how she has incorporated them in her work with a touch entirely her own. Witness how, even in the light verses of Paul Laurence Dunbar and T. A. Daly, there is dignity as well as humor; how in their use of dialect, they have emphasized, paradoxical as it may seem, an

American quality—particularly the fusion of native and foreign tongues and temperaments. Even our deprecated "comic newspaper poetry" has taken on something of a native character; nothing is more remarkable than the rising standards in our satirical and frankly humorous verse.

I will not go into greater detail concerning the growth of an American spirit in our literature nor point out how, in many of the poems in the present collection, the authors have responded to indigenous forces deeper than their backgrounds. I will however, call attention in passing to the fact that, young as this nation is compared to her transatlantic cousins, she is already being supplied with the stuff of legends, ballads and even epics. The modern singer, discarding imported myths, has turned to celebrate his own folk-tales. It is therefore particularly interesting to observe how the figure of Lincoln has been treated by the best of our living poets. I have accordingly included seven poems by seven writers, each differing in manner, technique and angle of vision.

For the rest, I leave the casual reader as well as the student to discover the awakened vigor and energy in this, the most poetic period in native literature. Realizing that this brief gathering is not so much a summary as an introduction, still it is hoped that, in spite of its obvious limitations, this collection will draw the reader on to a closer consideration of the poets here included—even, possibly, to those omitted. The purpose of such an anthology must always be to arouse an interest rather than to satisfy a curiosity. And if it brings its owners nearer the source, it will have fulfilled its prime function. Such, at least, is the hope and aim of the present editor.

—*Louis Untermeyer*

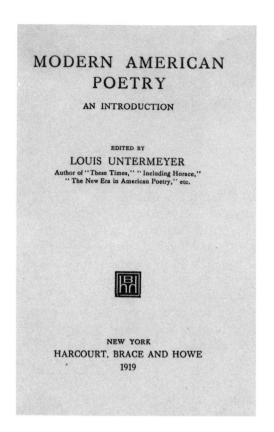

MODERN AMERICAN
POETRY

AN INTRODUCTION

EDITED BY

LOUIS UNTERMEYER

Author of "These Times," "Including Horace,"
"The New Era in American Poetry," etc.

NEW YORK
HARCOURT, BRACE AND HOWE
1919

CONTENTS

The Book of American Negro Poetry
(first edition 1922, revised 1931)
Edited by James Weldon Johnson

PREFACE TO THE FIRST EDITION

There is, perhaps, a better excuse for giving an Anthology of American Negro Poetry to the public than can be offered for many of the anthologies that have recently been issued. The public, generally speaking, does not know that there are American Negro poets—to supply this lack of information is, alone, a work worthy of somebody's effort.

Moreover, the matter of Negro poets and the production of literature by the colored people in this country involves more than supplying information that is lacking. It is a matter which has a direct bearing on the most vital of American problems.

A people may become great through many means, but there is only one measure by which its greatness is recognized and acknowledged. The final measure of the greatness of all peoples is the amount and standard of the literature and art they have produced. The world does not know that a people is great until that people produces great literature and art. No people that has produced great literature and art has ever been looked upon by the world as distinctly inferior.

The status of the Negro in the United States is more a question of national mental attitude toward the race than of actual conditions. And nothing will do more to change that mental attitude and raise his status than a demonstration of intellectual parity by the Negro through the production of literature and art.

Is there likelihood that the American Negro will be able to do this? There is, for the good reason that he possesses the innate powers. He has the emotional endowment, the originality and artistic conception, and, what is more important, the power of creating that which has universal appeal and influence.

I make here what may appear to be a more startling statement by saying that the Negro has already proved the possession of these powers by being the creator of the only things artistic that have yet sprung from American soil and been universally acknowledged as distinctive American products.[1]

These creations by the American Negro may be summed up under four heads. The first two are the Uncle Remus stories, which were collected by Joel Chandler Harris, and the "spirituals" or slave songs, to which the Fisk Jubilee Singers made the public and the musicians of both the United States and Europe listen. The Uncle Remus stories constitute the greatest body of folk lore that America has produced, and the "spirituals" the greatest body of folk song. I shall speak of the "spirituals" later because they are more than folk songs, for in them the Negro sounded the depths, if he did not scale the heights, of music.

The other two creations are the cakewalk and ragtime. We do not need to go very far back to remember when cakewalking was the rage in the United States, Europe and South America. Society in this country and royalty abroad spent time in practicing the intricate steps. Paris pronounced it the "poetry of motion." The popularity of the cakewalk passed away but its influence remained. The influence can be seen today on any American stage where there is dancing.

The influence which the Negro has exercised on the art of dancing in this country has been almost absolute. For generations the "buck and wing" and the "stop-time" dances, which are strictly Negro, have been familiar to American theater audiences. A few years ago the public discovered the "turkey trot," the "eagle rock," "ballin' the jack," and several other varieties that started the modern dance craze. The dances were quickly followed by the "tango," a dance originated by the Negroes of Cuba and later transplanted to South America. (This fact is attested by no less authority than Vicente Blasco Ibañez in his *Four Horsemen of the Apocalypse*.) Half the floor space in the country was then turned over to dancing, and highly paid exponents sprang up everywhere. The most noted, Mr. Vernon Castle, and, by the way, an Englishman, never danced except to the music of a colored band, and he never failed to state to his audiences that most of his dances had long been done by "your colored people," as he put it.

Any one who witnesses a musical production in which there is dancing cannot fail to notice the Negro stamp on all the movements; a stamp which even the great vogue of Russian dances that swept the country about the time of the popular dance craze could not affect. That peculiar swaying of the shoulders which you see done everywhere by the blond girls of the chorus is nothing more than a movement from the Negro dance referred to above, the "eagle rock." Occasionally the movement takes on a suggestion of the now outlawed "shimmy."

As for Ragtime, I go straight to the statement that it is the one artistic production by which America is known the world over. It has been all-conquering. Everywhere it is hailed as "American music."

For a dozen years or so there has been a steady tendency to divorce Ragtime from the Negro; in fact, to take from him the credit of having originated it. Probably the younger people of the present generation do not know that Ragtime is of Negro origin. The change wrought in Ragtime and the way in which it is accepted by the country have been brought about chiefly through the change which has gradually been made in the words and stories accompanying the music. Once the text of all Ragtime songs was written in Negro dialect, and was about Negroes in the cabin or in the cotton field or on the levee or at a jubilee or on Sixth Avenue or at a ball, and about their love affairs. Today, only a small proportion of Ragtime songs relate at all to the Negro. The truth is, Ragtime is now national rather than racial. But that does not abolish in any way the claim of the American Negro as its originator.

Ragtime music was originated by colored piano players in the questionable resorts of St. Louis, Memphis, and other Mississippi River towns. These men did not know any more about the theory of music than they did about the theory of the universe. They were guided by their natural musical instinct and talent, but above all by the Negro's extraordinary sense of rhythm. Any one who is familiar with Ragtime may note that its chief charm is not in melody, but in rhythms. These players often improvised crude and, at times, vulgar words to fit the music. This was the beginning of the Ragtime song.

Ragtime music got its first popular hearing at Chicago during World's Fair in that city. From Chi-

cago it made its way to New York, and then started on its universal triumph.

The earliest Ragtime songs, like Topsy, "jes' grew." Some of these earliest songs were taken down by white men, the words slightly altered or changed, and published under the names of the arrangers. They sprang into immediate popularity and earned small fortunes. The first to become widely known was "The Bully," a levee song which had been long used by roustabouts along the Mississippi. It was introduced in New York by Miss May Irwin, and gained instant popularity. Another one of these "jes' grew" songs was one which for a while disputed for place with Yankee Doodle; perhaps, disputes it even today. That song was " A Hot Time in the Old Town Tonight"; introduced and made popular by the colored regimental bands during the Spanish-American War.

Later there came along a number of colored men who were able to transcribe the old songs and write original ones. I was, about that time, writing words to music for the music show stage in New York. I was collaborating with my brother, J. Rosamond Johnson, and the late Bob Cole. I remember that we appropriated about the last one of the old "jes' grew" songs. It was a song which had been sung for years all through the South. The words were unprintable, but the tune was irresistible, and belonged to nobody. We took it, re-wrote the verses, telling an entirely different story from the original, left the chorus as it was, and published the song, at first under the name of "Will Handy." It became very popular with college boys, especially at football games, and perhaps still is. The song was "Oh, Didn't He Ramble!"

In the beginning, and for quite a while, almost all of the Ragtime songs that were deliberately composed were the work of colored writers. Now, the colored composers, even in this particular field, are greatly outnumbered by the white.

The reader might be curious to know if the "jes' grew" songs have ceased to grow. No, they have not; they are growing all the time. The country has lately been flooded with several varieties of "The Blues." These "Blues," too, had their origin in Memphis, and the towns along the Mississippi. They are a sort of lament of a lover who is feeling "blue" over the loss of his sweetheart. The "Blues" of Memphis have been adulterated so much on Broadway that they have lose their pristine hue. But whenever you hear a piece of music which has a strain like this in it:

you will know you are listening to something which belonged originally to Beale Avenue, Memphis, Tennessee. The original "Memphis Blues," so far as it can be credited to a composer, must be credited to Mr. W. C. Handy, a colored musician of Memphis.

As illustrations of the genuine Ragtime song in the making, I quote the words of two that were popular with the Southern colored soldiers in France. Here is the first:

> Mah mammy's lyin' in her grave,
>   Mah daddy done run away,
> Mah sister's married a gamblin' man,
>   An' I've done gone astray,
> Yes, I've done gone astray, po' boy,
>   An' I've done gone astray,
> Mah sister's married a gamblin' man,
>   An' I've done gone astray, po' boy.

These lines are crude, but they contain something of real poetry, of that elusive thing which nobody can define and that you can only tell is there when you feel it. You cannot read these lines without becoming reflective and feeling sorry for "Po' Boy."

Now, take in this word picture of utter dejection:

> I'm jes' as misabul as I can be,
> I'm unhappy even if I am free,
> I'm feelin' down, I'm feelin' blue;
> I wander 'round, don't know what to do.
> I'm go'n lay mah haid on de railroad line,
> Let de B. & O. come and pacify mah min'.

These lines are, no doubt, one of the many versions of the famous "Blues." They are also crude, but they go straight to the mark. The last two lines move with the swiftness of all great tragedy.

In spite of the bans which musicians and music teachers have placed on it, the people still demand and enjoy Ragtime. In fact, there is not a corner of the civilized world in which it is not known and liked. And this proves its originality, for if it were an imitation, the people of Europe, at least, would not have found it a novelty. And it is proof of a more important thing, it is proof that Ragtime possesses the vital spark, the power to appeal universally, without which any artistic production, no matter how approved its form may be, is dead.

Of course, there are those who will deny that Ragtime is an artistic production. American musicians, especially, instead of investigating Ragtime, dismiss it with a contemptuous word. But this has been the course of scholasticism in every branch of art. Whatever new thing the people like is pooh-poohed; whatever is popular is regarded as not worth while. The fact is, nothing great or enduring in music has ever sprung full-fledged from the brain of any master; the best he gives the world he gathers from the hearts of the people, and runs it through the alembic of his genius.

Ragtime deserves serious attention. There is a lot of colorless and vicious imitation, but there is enough that is genuine. In one composition alone, "The Memphis Blues," the musician will find not only great melodic beauty, but a polyphonic structure that is amazing.

It is obvious that Ragtime has influenced and, in a large measure, become our popular music; but not many would know that it has influenced even our religious music. Those who are familiar with gospel hymns can at once see this influence if they will compare the songs of thirty years ago, such as "In the Sweet Bye and Bye," "The Ninety and Nine," etc., with the up-to-date, syncopated tunes that are sung in Sunday Schools, Christian Endeavor Societies, Y.M.C.A.'s and like gatherings today.

Ragtime has not only influenced American music, it has influenced American life; indeed, it has saturated American life. It has become the popular medium for our national expression musically. And who can say that it does not express the blare and jangle and the surge, too, of our national spirit?

Any one who doubts that there is a peculiar heel-tickling, smile-provoking, joy-awakening, response-compelling charm in Ragtime needs only to hear a skillful performer play the genuine article, needs only to listen to its bizarre harmonies, its audacious resolutions often consisting of an abrupt jump from one key to another, its intricate rhythms in which the accents fall in the most unexpected places but in which the fundamental beat is never lost, in order to be convinced. I believe it has its place as well as the music which draws from us sighs and tears.

Now, these dances which I have referred to and Ragtime music may be lower forms of art, but they are evidence of a power that will some day be applied to the higher forms. And even now we need not stop at the Negro's accomplishment through these lower forms. In the "spirituals," or slave songs, the Negro has given America not only its only folk songs, but a mass of noble music. I never think of this music but I am struck by the wonder, the miracle of its production. How did the men who originated these songs manage to do it? The sentiments are easily accounted for; they are, for the most part, taken from the Bible. But the melodies, where did they come from? Some of them so weirdly sweet, and others so wonderfully strong. Take, for instance, "Go Down, Moses"; I doubt that there is a stronger theme in the whole musical literature of the world.

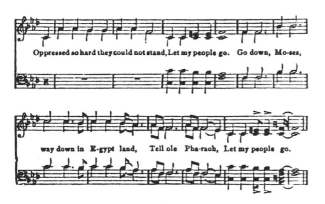

It is to be noted that whereas the chief characteristic of Ragtime is rhythm, the chief characteristic of the "spirituals" is melody. The melodies of "Steal Away to Jesus," "Swing Low Sweet Chariot," "Nobody Knows de Trouble I See," "I Couldn't Hear Nobody Pray," "Deep River," "O, Freedom Over Me," and many others of these songs possess a beauty that is—what shall I say? poignant. In the riotous rhythms of Ragtime the Negro expressed his irrepressible buoyancy, his keen response to the sheer joy of living; in the "spirituals" he voiced his sense of beauty and his deep religious feeling.

Naturally, not as much can be said for the words of these songs as for the music. Most of the songs are religious. Some of them are songs expressing faith and endurance and a longing for freedom. In the religious songs, the sentiments and often the entire lines are taken bodily from the Bible. However, there is no doubt that some of these religious songs have a meaning apart from the Biblical text. It is evident that the opening lines of "Go Down, Moses,"

> Go down, Moses,
>   'Way down in Egypt land;
> Tell old Pharaoh,
>   Let my people go.

have a significance beyond the bondage of Israel in Egypt.

The bulk of the lines to these songs, as is the case in all communal music, is made up of choral iteration and incremental repetition of the leader's lines. If the words are read, this constant iteration and repetition are found to be tiresome; and it must be admitted that the lines themselves are often very trite. And, yet, there is frequently revealed a flash of real primitive poetry. I give the following examples:

> Sometimes I feel like an eagle in de air.

>   You may bury me in de East,
>   You may bury me in de West,
>   But I'll hear de trumpet sound
>   In-a dat mornin'.

> I know de moonlight, I know de starlight;
>   I lay dis body down.
> I walk in de moonlight, I walk in de starlight;
>   I lay dis body down.
> I know de graveyard, I know de graveyard,
>   When I lay dis body down.
> I walk in de graveyard, I walk troo de graveyard
>   To lay dis body down.

> I lay in de grave an' stretch out my arms;
>   I lay dis body down.
> I go to de judgment in de evenin' of de day
>   When I lay dis body down.
> An' my soul an' yo soul will meet in de day
>   When I lay dis body down.

Regarding the line, "I lay in de grave an' stretch out my arms," Col. Thomas Wentworth Higginson of Boston, one of the first to give these slave songs serious study, said: "Never, it seems to me, since man first lived and suffered, was his infinite longing for peace uttered more plaintively than in that line."

These Negro folk songs constitute a vast mine of material that has been neglected almost absolutely. The only white writers who have in recent years given adequate attention and study to this music, that I know of, are Mr. H. E. Krehbiel and Mrs. Natalie Curtis Burlin. We have our native composers denying the worth and importance of this music, and trying to manufacture grand opera out of so-called Indian themes.

But there is a great hope for the development of this music, and that hope is the Negro himself. A worthy beginning has already been made by Burleigh, Cook, Johnson, and Dett. And there will yet come great Negro composers who will take this music and voice through it not only the soul of their race, but the soul of America.

And does it not seem odd that this greatest gift of the Negro has been the most neglected of all he possesses? Money and effort have been expended upon his development in every direction except this. This gift has been regarded as a kind of side show, something for occasional exhibition; wherein it is the touchstone, it is the magic thing, it is that by which the Negro can bridge all chasms. No persons, however hostile, can listen to Negroes singing this wonderful music without having their hostility melted down.

This power of the Negro to suck up the national spirit from the soil and create something artistic and original, which, at the same time, possesses the note of universal appeal, is due to a remarkable racial gift of adaptability; it is more than adaptability, it is a transfusive quality. And the Negro has exercised this transfusive quality not only here in America, where the race lives in large numbers, but in European countries, where the number has been almost infinitesimal.

Is it not curious to know that the greatest poet of Russia is Alexander Pushkin, a man of African descent; that the greatest romancer of France is Alexandre Dumas, a man of African descent; and that one of the greatest musicians of England is Coleridge-Taylor, a man of African descent?

The fact is fairly well known that the father of Dumas was a Negro of the French West Indies, and that the father of Coleridge-Taylor was a native-born African; but the facts concerning Pushkin's African ancestry are not so familiar.

When Peter the Great was Czar of Russia, some potentate presented him with a full-blooded Negro of gigantic size. Peter, the most eccentric ruler of modern times, dressed this Negro up in soldier clothes, christened him Hannibal, and made him a special body-guard.

But Hannibal had more than size, he had brain and ability. He not only looked picturesque and imposing in soldier clothes, he showed that he had in him the making of a real soldier. Peter recognized this, and eventually made him a general. He afterwards ennobled him, and Hannibal, later, married one of the ladies of the Russian court. This same Hannibal was great-grandfather of Pushkin, the national poet of Russia, the man who bears the

same relation to Russian literature that Shakespeare bears to English literature.

I know the question naturally arises: If out of the few Negroes who have lived in France there came a Dumas; and out of the few Negroes who have lived in England there came a Coleridge-Taylor; and if from the man who was at the time, probably, the only Negro in Russia there sprang that country's national poet, why have not the millions of Negroes in the United States with all the emotional and artistic endowment claimed for them produced a Dumas, or a Coleridge-Taylor, or a Pushkin?

The question seems difficult, but there is an answer. The Negro in the United States is consuming all of his intellectual energy in this grueling race-struggle. And the same statement may be made in a general way about the white South. Why does not the white South produce literature and art? The white South, too, is consuming all of its intellectual energy in this lamentable conflict. Nearly all of the mental efforts of the white South run through one narrow channel. The life of every Southern white man and all of his activities are impassably limited by the ever present Negro problem. And that is why, as Mr. H. L. Mencken puts it, in all that vast region, with its thirty or forty million people and its territory as large as a half dozen Frances or Germanys, there is not a single poet, not a serious historian, not a creditable composer, not a critic good or bad, not a dramatist dead or alive.[2]

But, even so, the American Negro has accomplished something in pure literature. The list of those who have done so would be surprising both by its length and the excellence of the achievements. One of the great books written in this country since the Civil War is the work of a colored man, *The Souls of Black Folk*, by W. E. B. Du Bois.

Such a list begins with Phillis Wheatley. In 1761 a slave ship landed a cargo of slaves in Boston. Among them was a little girl seven or eight years of age. She attracted the attention of John Wheatley, a wealthy gentleman of Boston, who purchased her as a servant for his wife. Mrs. Wheatley was a benevolent woman. She noticed the girl's quick mind and determined to give her opportunity for its development. Twelve years later Phillis published a volume of poems. The book was brought out in London, where Phillis was for several months an object of great curiosity and attention.

Phillis Wheatley has never been given her rightful place in American literature. By some sort of conspiracy she is kept out of most of the books, especially the text-books on literature used in the schools. Of course, she is not a *great* American poet—and in her day there were no great American poets—but she is an important American poet. Her importance, if for no other reason, rests on the fact that, save one, she is the first in order of time of all the women poets of America. And she is among the first of all American poets to issue a volume.

It seems strange that the books generally give space to a mention of Urian Oakes, President of Harvard College, and to quotations from the crude and lengthy elegy which he published in 1667; and print examples from the execrable versified version of the Psalms made by the New England divines, and yet deny a place to Phillis Wheatley.

Here are the opening lines from the elegy by Oakes, which is quoted from in most of the books on American literature:

> Reader, I am no poet, but I grieve.
> Behold here what that passion can do,
> That forced a verse without Apollo's leave,
> And whether the learned sisters would or no.

There was no need for Urian to admit what his handiwork declared. But this from the versified Psalms is still worse, yet it is found in the books:

> The Lord's song sing can we? being
> in stranger's land, then let
> lose her skill my right hand if I
> Jerusalem forget.

Anne Bradstreet preceded Phillis Wheatley by a little over one hundred and twenty years. She published her volume of poems, *The Tenth Muse*, in 1650. Let us strike a comparison between the two. Anne Bradstreet was a wealthy, cultivated Puritan girl, the daughter of Thomas Dudley, Governor of Bay Colony. Phillis, as we know, was a Negro slave girl born in Africa. Let us take them both at their best and in the same vein. The following stanza is from Anne's poem entitled "Contemplation":

> While musing thus with contemplation fed,
> And thousand fancies buzzing in my brain,
> The sweet tongued Philomel percht o'er my head,
> And chanted forth a most melodious strain,
> Which rapt me so with wonder and delight,
> I judged my hearing better than my sight,
> And wisht me wings with her awhile to take my flight.

And the following is from Phillis' poem entitled "Imagination":

> Imagination! who can sing thy force?
> Or who describe the swiftness of thy course?
> Soaring through air to find the bright abode,
> Th' empyreal palace of the thundering God,
> We on thy pinions can surpass the wind,
> And leave the rolling universe behind.
> From star to star the mental optics rove,
> Measure the skies, and range the realms above;
> There in one view we grasp the mighty whole,
> Or with new worlds amaze th' unbounded soul.

We do not think the black woman suffers much by comparison with the white. Thomas Jefferson said of Phillis: "Religion has produced a Phillis Wheatley, but it could not produce a poet; her poems are beneath contempt." It is quite likely that Jefferson's criticism was directed more against religion than against Phillis' poetry. On the other hand, General George Washington wrote her with his own hand a letter in which he thanked her for a poem which she had dedicated to him. He later received her with marked courtesy at his camp at Cambridge.

It appears certain that Phillis was the first person to apply to George Washington the phrase, "First in peace." The phrase occurs in her poem addressed to "His Excellency, General George Washington," written in 1775. The encomium, "First in war, first in peace, first in the hearts of his countrymen," was originally used in the resolutions presented to Congress on the death of Washington, December, 1799.

Phillis Wheatley's poetry is the poetry of the Eighteenth Century. She wrote when Pope and Gray were supreme; it is easy to see that Pope was her model. Had she come under the influence of Wordsworth, Byron or Keats or Shelley, she would have done greater work. As it is, her work must not be judged by the work and standards of a later day, but by the work and standards of her own day and her own contemporaries. By this method of criticism she stands out as one of the important characters in the making of American literature, without any allowances for her sex or her antecedents.

According to *A Bibliographical Checklist of American Negro Poetry*, compiled by Mr. Arthur A. Schomburg, more than one hundred Negroes in the United States have published volumes of poetry ranging in size from pamphlets to books of from one hundred to three hundred pages. About thirty of these writers fill in the gap between Phillis Wheatley and Paul Laurence Dunbar. Just here it is of interest to note that a Negro wrote and published a poem before Phillis Wheatley arrived in this country from Africa. He was Jupiter Hammon, a slave belonging to Mr. Lloyd of Queens-Village, Long Island. In 1760 Hammon published a poem, eighty-eight lines in length, entitled "An Evening Thought, Salvation by Christ, with Penettential Cries." In 1788 he published "An Address to Miss Phillis Wheatley, Ethiopian Poetess in Boston, who came from Africa at eight years of age, and soon became acquainted with the Gospel of Jesus Christ." These two poems do not include all that Hammon wrote.

The poets between Phillis Wheatley and Dunbar must be considered more in the light of what they attempted than of what they accomplished. Many of them showed marked talent, but barely a half dozen of them demonstrated even mediocre mastery of technique in the use of poetic material and forms. And yet there are several names that deserve mention. George M. Horton, Frances E. Harper, James M. Bell and Alberry A. Whitman, all merit consideration when due allowances are made for their limitations in education, training and general culture. The limitations of Horton were greater than those of either of the others; he was born a slave in North Carolina in 1797, and as a young man began to compose poetry without being able to write it down. Later he received some instruction from professors of the University of North Carolina, at which institution he was employed as a janitor. He published a volume of poems, *The Hope of Liberty,* in 1829.

Mrs. Harper, Bell and Whitman would stand out if only for the reason that each of them attempted sustained work. Mrs. Harper published her first volume of poems in 1854, but later she published "Moses, a Story of the Nile," a poem which ran to 52 closely printed pages. Bell in 1864 published a poem of 28 pages in celebration of President Lincoln's Emancipation Proclamation. In 1870 he published a poem of 32 pages in celebration of the ratification of the Fifteenth Amendment to the Constitution. Whitman published his first volume of poems, a book of 253 pages, in 1877; but in 1884 he published "The Rape of Florida," an epic poem written in four cantos and done in the Spenserian stanza, and which ran to 97 closely printed pages. The poetry of both Mrs. Harper and of Whitman had a large degree of popularity; one of Mrs. Harper's books went through more than twenty editions.

Of these four poets, it is Whitman who reveals not only the greatest imagination but also the more skillful workmanship. His lyric power at its best may be judged from the following stanza from the "Rape of Florida":

"Come now, my love, the moon is on the lake;
Upon the waters is my light canoe;
Come with me, love, and gladsome oars shall make
A music on the parting wave for you.
Come o'er the waters deep and dark and blue;
Come where the lilies in the marge have sprung,
Come with me, love, for Oh, my love is true!"
This is the song that on the lake was sung,
The boatman sang it when his heart was young.

Some idea of Whitman's capacity for dramatic narration may be gained from the following lines taken from "Not a Man, and Yet a Man," a poem of even greater length than "The Rape of Florida."

A flash of steely lightning from his hand,
Strikes down the groaning leader of the band;
Divides his startled comrades, and again
Descending, leaves fair Dora's captors slain.
Her, seizing then within a strong embrace,
Out in the dark he wheels his flying pace;
. . . .
He speaks not, but with stalwart tenderness
Her swelling bosom firm to his doth press;
Springs like a stag that flees the eager hound,
And like a whirlwind rustles o'er the ground.
Her locks swim in disheveled wildness o'er
His shoulders, streaming to his waist and more;
While on and on, strong as a rolling flood,
His sweeping footsteps part the silent wood.

It is curious and interesting to trace the growth of individuality and race consciousness in this group of poets. Jupiter Hammon's verses were almost entirely religious exhortations. Only very seldom does Phillis Wheatley sound a native note. Four times in single lines she refers to herself as "Afric's muse." In a poem of admonition addressed to the students at the "University of Cambridge in New England" she refers to herself as follows:

Ye blooming plants of human race divine,
An Ethiop tells you 'tis your greatest foe.

But one looks in vain for some outburst or even complaint against the bondage of her people, for some agonizing cry about her native land. In two poems she refers definitely to Africa as her home, but in each instance there seems to be under the sentiment of the lines a feeling of almost smug contentment at her own escape therefrom. In the poem, "On Being Brought from Africa to America," she says:

'Twas mercy brought me from my pagan land,
Taught my benighted soul to understand
That there's a God and there's a Saviour too;
Once I redemption neither sought nor knew.
Some view our sable race with scornful eye—
"Their color is a diabolic dye."
Remember, Christians, Negroes black as Cain,
May be refined, and join th' angelic train.

In the poem addressed to the Earl of Dartmouth, she speaks of freedom and makes a reference to the parents from whom she was taken as a child, a reference which cannot but strike the reader as rather unimpassioned:

Should you, my lord, while you peruse my song,
Wonder from whence my love of Freedom sprung,
Whence flow these wishes for the common good,
By feeling hearts alone best understood;
I, young in life, by seeming cruel fate
Was snatch'd from Afric's fancy'd happy seat;
What pangs excruciating must molest,
What sorrows labor in my parents' breast?
Steel'd was that soul and by no misery mov'd
That from a father seiz'd his babe belov'd;
Such, such my case. And can I then but pray
Others may never feel tyrannic sway?

The bulk of Phillis Wheatley's work consists of poems addressed to people of prominence. Her book was dedicated to the Countess of Huntington, at whose house she spent the greater part of her time while in England. On his repeal of the Stamp Act, she wrote a poem to King George III, whom she saw later; another poem she wrote to the Earl of Dartmouth, whom she knew. A number of her verses were addressed to other persons of distinction. Indeed, it is apparent that Phillis was far from being a democrat. She was far from being a democrat not only in her social ideas but also in her political ideas; unless a religious meaning is given to the closing lines of her ode to General Washington, she was a decided royalist:

A crown, a mansion, and a throne that shine
With gold unfading, Washington! be thine.

Nevertheless, she was an ardent patriot. Her ode to General Washington (1775), her spirited poem, "On Major General Lee" (1776), and her poem, "Liberty and Peace," written in celebration of the close of the war, reveal not only patriotic feeling but an understanding of the issues at stake. In her poem, "On Major General Lee," she makes her hero reply thus to the taunts of the British commander into whose hands he has been delivered through treachery:

O arrogance of tongue!
And wild ambition, ever prone to wrong!
Believ'st thou, chief, that armies such as thine
Can stretch in dust that heaven-defended line?
In vain allies may swarm from distant lands,
And demons aid in formidable bands.
Great as thou art, thou shun'st the field of fame,
Disgrace to Britain and the British name!
When offer'd combat by the noble foe
(Foe to misrule) why did the sword forego
The easy conquest of the rebel-land?
Perhaps TOO easy for thy martial hand.
What various causes to the field invite!
For plunder YOU, and we for freedom fight;
Her cause divine with generous ardor fires,
And every blossom glows as she inspires!
Already thousands of your troops have fled
To the drear mansions of the silent dead:
Columbia, too, beholds with streaming eyes
Her heroes fall—'tis freedom's sacrifice!
So wills the power who with convulsive storms
Shakes impious realms, and nature's face deforms;
Yet those brave troops, innum'rous as the sands,
One soul inspires, one General Chief commands;
Find in your train of boasted heroes, one
To match the praise of Godlike Washington.
Thrice happy Chief in whom the virtues join,
And heaven taught prudence speaks the man divine.

What Phillis Wheatley failed to achieve is due in no small degree to her education and environment. Her mind was steeped in the classics; her verses are filled with classical and mythological allusions. She knew Ovid thoroughly and was familiar with other Latin authors. She must have known Alexander Pope by heart. And, too, she was reared and sheltered in a wealthy and cultured family,—a wealthy and cultured Boston family; she never had the opportunity to learn life; she never found out her own true relation to life and to her surroundings. And it should not be forgotten that she was only about thirty years old when she died. The impulsion or the compulsion that might have driven her genius off the worn paths, out on a journey of exploration, Phillis Wheatley never received. But, whatever her limitations, she merits more than America has accorded her.

Horton, who was born three years after Phillis Wheatley's death, expressed in all of his poetry strong complaint at his condition of slavery and a deep longing for freedom. The following verses are typical of his style and his ability:

> Alas! and am I born for this,
>   To wear this slavish chain?
> Deprived of all created bliss,
>   Through hardship, toil, and pain?
> . . . .
> Come, Liberty! thou cheerful sound,
>   Roll through my ravished ears;
> Come, let my grief in joys be drowned,
>   And drive away my fears.

In Mrs. Harper we find something more than the complaint and the longing of Horton. We find an expression of a sense of wrong and injustice. The following stanzas are from a poem addressed to the white women of America:

> You can sight o'er the sad-eyed Armenian
>   Who weeps in her desolate home.
> You can mourn o'er the exile of Russia
>   From kindred and friends doomed to roam.
> . . . .
> But hark! from our Southland are floating
>   Sobs of anguish, murmurs of pain;
> And women heart-stricken are weeping
>   O'er their tortured and slain.
> . . . .
> Have ye not, oh, my favored sisters,
>   Just a plea, a prayer or a tear
> For mothers who dwell 'neath the shadows
>   Of agony, hatred and fear?
> . . . .
> Weep not, oh, my well sheltered sisters,
>   Weep not for the Negro alone,
> But weep for your sons who must gather
>   The crops which their fathers have sown.

Whitman, in the midst of "The Rape of Florida," a poem in which he related the taking of the State of Florida from the Seminoles, stops and discusses the race question. He discusses it in many other poems; and he discusses it from many different angles. In Whitman we find not only an expression of a sense of wrong and injustice, but we hear a note of faith and a note also of defiance. For example, in the opening to Canto II of "The Rape of Florida":

> Greatness by nature cannot be entailed;
> It is an office ending with the man,—
> Sage, hero, Saviour, tho' the Sire be hailed,

> The son may reach obscurity in the van:
> Sublime achievements know no patent plan,
> Man's immortality's a book with seals,
> And none but God shall open—none else can—
> But opened, it the mystery reveals,—
> Manhood's conquest of man to heaven's respect appeals.
>
> Is manhood less because man's face is black?
> Let thunders of the loosened seals reply!
> Who shall the rider's restive steed turn back?
> Or who withstand the arrows he lets fly
> Between the mountains of eternity?
> Genius ride forth! Thou gift and torch of heav'n!
> The mastery is kindled in thine eye;
> To conquest ride! thy bow of strength is giv'n—
> The trampled hordes of caste before thee shall be driv'n!
> . . . .
> 'Tis hard to judge if hatred of one's race,
> By those who deem themselves superior-born,
> Be worse than that quiescence in disgrace,
> Which only merits—and should only—scorn.
> Oh, let me see the Negro night and morn,
> Pressing and fighting in, for place and power!
> All earth is place—all time th' auspicious hour,
> While heaven leans forth to look, oh, will he quail or cower?
>
> Ah! I abhor his protest and complaint!
> His pious looks and patience I despise!
> He can't evade the test, disguised as saint;
> The manly voice of freedom bids him rise,
> And shake himself before Philistine eyes!
> And, like a lion roused, no sooner than
> A foe dare come, play all his energies,
> And court the fray with fury if he can;
> For hell itself respects a fearless, manly man.

It may be said that none of these poets strike a deep native strain or sound a distinctly original note, either in matter or form. That is true; but the same thing may be said of all the American poets down to the writers of the present generation, with the exception of Poe and Walt Whitman. The thing in which these black poets are mostly excelled by their contemporaries is mere technique.

Paul Laurence Dunbar stands out as the first poet from the Negro race in the United States to show a combined mastery over poetic material and poetic technique, to reveal innate literary distinction in what he wrote, and to maintain a high level of performance. He was the first to rise to a height from which he could take a perspective view of his own race. He was the first to see objectively its humor, its superstitions, its shortcomings; the first to feel sympathetically its heart-wounds, its yearnings, its aspirations, and to voice them all in a purely literary form.

Dunbar's fame rests chiefly on his poems in Negro dialect. This appraisal of him is, no doubt, fair; for in these dialect poems he not only carried his art to the highest point of perfection, but he made a contribution to American literature unlike what any one else had made, a contribution which, perhaps, no one else could have made. Of course, Negro dialect poetry was written before Dunbar wrote, most of it by white writers; but the fact stands out that Dunbar was the first to use it as a medium for the true interpretation of Negro character and psychology. And yet, dialect poetry does not constitute the whole or even the bulk of Dunbar's work. In addition to a large number of poems of a very high order done in literary English, he was the author of four novels and several volumes of short stories.

Indeed, Dunbar did not begin his career as a writer of dialect. I may be pardoned for introducing here a bit of reminiscence. My personal friendship with Paul Dunbar began before he had achieved recognition, and continued to be close until his death. When I first met him he had published a thin volume, *Oak and Ivy*, which was being sold chiefly through his own efforts. *Oak and Ivy* showed no distinctive Negro influence, but rather the influence of James Whitcomb Riley. At this time Paul and I were together every day for several months. He talked to me a great deal about his hopes and ambitions. In these talks he revealed that he had reached a realization of the possibilities of poetry in the dialect, together with a recognition of the fact that it offered the surest way by which he could get a hearing. Often he said to me: "I've got to write dialect poetry; it's the only way I can get them to listen to me." I was with Dunbar at the beginning of what proved to be his last illness. He said to me then: "I have not grown. I am writing the same things I wrote ten years ago, and am writing them no better." His self-accusation was not fully true; he had grown, and he had gained a surer control of his art, but he had not accomplished the greater things of which he was constantly dreaming; the public had held him to the things for which it had accorded him recognition. If Dunbar had lived he would have achieved some of those dreams, but even while he talked so dejectedly to me he seemed to feel that he was not to live. He died when he was only thirty-three.

It has a bearing on this entire subject to note that Dunbar was of unmixed Negro blood; so, as the greatest figure in literature which the colored race in the United States has produced, he stands as an example at once refuting and confounding those who wish to believe that whatever extraordinary ability an Aframerican shows is due to an admixture of white blood.

As a man, Dunbar was kind and tender. In conversation he was brilliant and polished. His voice was his chief charm, and was a great element in his success as a reader of his own works. In his actions he was impulsive as a child, sometimes even erratic; indeed, his intimate friends almost looked upon him as a spoiled boy. He was always delicate in health. Temperamentally, he belonged to that class of poets who Taine says are vessels too weak to contain the spirit of poetry, the poets whom poetry kills, the Byrons, the Burnses, the De Mussets, the Poes.

To whom may he be compared, this boy who scribbled his early verses while he ran an elevator, whose youth was a battle against poverty, and who, in spite of almost insurmountable obstacles, rose to success? A comparison between him and Burns is not unfitting. The similarity between many phases of their lives is remarkable, and their works are not incommensurable. Burns took the strong dialect of his people and made it classic; Dunbar took the humble speech of his people and in it wrought music.

Mention of Dunbar brings up for consideration the fact that, although he is the most outstanding figure in literature among the Aframericans of the United States, he does not stand alone among the Aframericans of the whole Western world. There are Plácido and Manzano in Cuba; Vieux and Durand in Haiti; Machado de Assis in Brazil, and others still that might be mentioned, who stand on a plane with or even above Dunbar. Plácido and Machado de Assis rank as great in the literatures of their respective countries without any qualifications whatever. They are world figures in the literature of the Latin languages. Machado de Assis is somewhat handicapped in this respect by having as his tongue and medium the lesser known Portuguese, but Plácido, writing in the language of Spain, Mexico, Cuba and of almost the whole of South America, is universally known. His works have been republished in the original in Spain, Mexico and in most of the Latin-American countries; several editions have been published in the United States; translations of his works have been made into French and German.

Plácido is in some respects the greatest of all the Cuban poets. In sheer genius and the fire of inspiration he surpasses his famous compatriot,

Heredia. Then, too, his birth, his life and his death ideally contained the tragic elements that go into the making of a halo about a poet's head. Plácido was born in Habana in 1809. The first months of his life were passed in a foundling asylum; indeed, his real name, Gabriel de la Concepcion Valdés, was in honor of its founder. His father took him out of the asylum, but shortly afterwards went to Mexico and died there. His early life was a struggle against poverty; his youth and manhood was a struggle for Cuban independence. His death placed him in the list of Cuban martyrs. On the twenty-seventh of June, 1844, he was lined up against a wall with ten others and shot by order of the Spanish authorities on a charge of conspiracy. In his short but eventful life he turned out work which bulks more than six hundred pages. During the few hours preceding his execution he wrote three of his best-known poems, among them his famous sonnet, "Mother, Farewell!"

Plácido's sonnet to his mother has been translated into every important language; William Cullen Bryant did it in English, but in spite of its wide popularity, it is, perhaps, outside of Cuba the least understood of all Plácido's poems. It is curious to note how Bryant's translation totally misses the intimate sense of the delicate subtlety of the poem. The American poet makes it a tender and loving farewell of a son who is about to die to a heart-broken mother; but that is not the kind of a farewell that Plácido intended to write or did write.

The key to the poem is in the first word, and the first word is the Spanish conjunction *Si* (if). The central idea, then, of the sonnet is, "If the sad fate which now overwhelms me should bring a pang to your heart, do not weep, for I die a glorious death and sound the last note of my lyre to you." Bryant either failed to understand or ignored the opening word, "If," because he was not familiar with the poet's history.

While Plácido's father was a Negro, his mother was a Spanish white woman, a dancer in one of the Habana theaters. At his birth she abandoned him to a foundling asylum, and perhaps never saw him again, although it is known that she outlived her son. When the poet came down to his last hours he remembered that somewhere there lived a woman who was his mother; that although she had heartlessly abandoned him; that although he owed her no filial duty, still she might, perhaps, on hearing of his sad end feel some pang of grief or sadness; so he tells her in his last words that he dies happy and bids her not to weep. This he does with nobility and dignity, but absolutely without

affection. Taking into account these facts, and especially their humiliating and embittering effect upon a soul so sensitive as Plácido's, this sonnet, in spite of the obvious weakness of the sestet as compared with the octave, is a remarkable piece of work.[3]

In considering the Aframerican poets of the Latin languages I am impelled to think that, as up to this time the colored poets of great universality have come out of the Latin-American countries rather than out of the United States, they will continue to do so for a good many years. The reason for this I hinted at in the first part of this preface. The colored poet in the United States labors within limitations which he cannot easily pass over. He is always on the defensive or the offensive. The pressure upon him to be propagandic is well nigh irresistible. These conditions are suffocating to breadth and to real art in poetry. In addition he labors under the handicap of finding culture not entirely colorless in the United States. On the other hand, the colored poet of Latin America can voice the national spirit without any reservations. And he will be rewarded without any reservations, whether it be to place him among the great or declare him the greatest.

So I think it probable that the first world-acknowledged Aframerican poet will come out of Latin America. Over against this probability, of course, is the great advantage possessed by the colored poet in the United States of writing in the world-conquering English language.

This preface has gone far beyond what I had in mind when I started. It was my intention to gather together the best verses I could find by Negro poets and present them with a bare word of introduction. It was not my plan to make this collection inclusive nor to make the book in any sense a book of criticism. I planned to present only verses by contemporary writers; but, perhaps, because this is the first collection of its kind, I realized the absence of a starting-point and was led to provide one and to fill in with historical data what I felt to be a gap.

It may be surprising to many to see how little of the poetry being written by Negro poets today is being written in Negro dialect. The newer Negro poets show a tendency to discard dialect; much of the subject-matter which went into the making of traditional dialect poetry, 'possums, watermelons, etc., they have discarded altogether, at least, as poetic material. This tendency will, no doubt, be regretted by the majority of white readers; and, indeed, it would be a distinct loss if the American

Negro poets threw away this quaint and musical folk speech as a medium of expression. And yet, after all, these poets are working through a problem not realized by the reader, and, perhaps, by many of these poets themselves not realized consciously. They are trying to break away from, not Negro dialect itself, but the limitations on Negro dialect imposed by the fixing effects of long convention.

The Negro in the United States has achieved or been placed in a certain artistic niche. When he is thought of artistically, it is as a happy-go-lucky, singing, shuffling, banjo-picking being or as a more or less pathetic figure. The picture of him is in a log cabin amid fields of cotton or along the levees. Negro dialect is naturally and by long association the exact instrument for voicing this phase of Negro life; and by that very exactness it is an instrument with but two full stops, humor and pathos. So even when he confines himself to purely racial themes, the Aframerican poet realizes that there are phases of Negro life in the United States which cannot be treated in the dialect either adequately or artistically. Take, for example, the phases rising out of life in Harlem, that most wonderful Negro city in the world. I do not deny that a Negro in a log cabin is more picturesque than a Negro in a Harlem flat, but the Negro in the Harlem flat is here, and he is but part of a group growing everywhere in the country, a group whose ideals are becoming increasingly more vital than those of the traditionally artistic group, even if its members are less picturesque.

What the colored poet in the United States needs to do is something like what Synge did for the Irish; he needs to find a form that will express the racial spirit by symbols from within rather than by symbols from without, such as the mere mutilation of English spelling and pronunciation. He needs a form that is freer and larger than dialect, but which will still hold the racial flavor; a form expressing the imagery, the idioms, the peculiar turns of thought, and the distinctive humor and pathos, too, of the Negro, but which will also be capable of voicing the deepest and highest emotions and aspirations, and allow of the widest range of subjects and the widest scope of treatment.

Negro dialect is at present a medium that is not capable of giving expression to the varied conditions of Negro life in America, and much less is it capable of giving the fullest interpretation of Negro character and psychology. This is no indictment against the dialect as dialect, but against the mold of convention in which Negro dialect in the United States has been set. In time these conventions may become lost, and the colored poet in the United States may sit down to write in dialect without feeling that his first line will put the general reader in a frame of mind which demands that the poem be humorous or pathetic. In the meantime, there is no reason why these poets should not continue to do the beautiful things that can be done, and done best, in the dialect.

In stating the need for Aframerican poets in the United States to work out a new and distinctive form of expression I do not wish to be understood to hold any theory that they should limit themselves to Negro poetry, to racial themes; the sooner they are able to write *American* poetry spontaneously, the better. Nevertheless, I believe that the richest contribution the Negro poet can make to the American literature of the future will be the fusion into it of his own individual artistic gifts.

Not many of the writers here included, except Dunbar, are known at all to the general reading public; and there is only one of these who has a widely recognized position in the American literary world, William Stanley Braithwaite. Mr. Braithwaite is not only unique in this respect, but he stands unique among all the Aframerican writers the United States has yet produced. He has gained his place, taking as the standard and measure for his work the identical standard and measure applied to American writers and American literature. He has asked for no allowances or rewards, either directly or indirectly, on account of his race.

Mr. Braithwaite is the author of two volumes of verses, lyrics of delicate and tenuous beauty. In his more recent and uncollected poems he shows himself more and more decidedly the mystic. But his place in American literature is due more to his work as a critic and anthologist than to his work as a poet. There is still another rôle he has played, that of friend of poetry and poets. It is a recognized fact that in the work which preceded the present revival of poetry in the United States, no one rendered more unremitting and valuable service than Mr. Braithwaite. And it can be said that no future study of American poetry of this age can be made without reference to Braithwaite.

Two authors included in the book are better known for their work in prose than in poetry; W. E. B. Du Bois whose well-known prose at its best is, however, impassioned and rhythmical; and Benjamin Brawley who is the author, among other works, of one of the best handbooks on the English drama that has yet appeared in America.

But the group of the new Negro poets, whose work makes up the bulk of this anthology, contains names destined to be known. Claude McKay, although still quite a young man, has already demonstrated his power, breadth and skill as a poet. Mr. McKay's breadth is as essential a part of his equipment as his power and skill. He demonstrates mastery of the three when as a Negro poet he pours out the bitterness and rebellion in his heart in those two sonnet-tragedies, "If We Must Die" and "To the White Fiends," in a manner that strikes terror; and when as a cosmic poet he creates the atmosphere and mood of poetic beauty in the absolute, as he does in "Spring in New Hampshire" and "The Harlem Dancer." Mr. McKay gives evidence that he has passed beyond the danger which threatens many of the new Negro poets—the danger of allowing the purely polemical phases of the race problem to choke their sense of artistry.

Mr. McKay's earliest work is unknown in this country. It consists of poems written and published in his native Jamaica. I was fortunate enough to run across his first volume, and I could not refrain from reproducing here one of the poems written in the West Indian Negro dialect. I have done this not only to illustrate the widest range of the poet's talent and to offer a comparison between the American and the West Indian dialects, but on account of the intrinsic worth of the poem itself. I was much tempted to introduce several more, in spite of the fact that they might require a glossary, because however greater work Mrs. McKay may do he can never do anything more touching and charming than these poems in the Jamaica dialect.

Fenton Johnson is a young poet of the ultra-modern school who gives promise of greater work than he has yet done. Jessie Fauset shows that she possesses the lyric gift, and she works with care and finish. Miss Fauset is especially adept in her translations from the French. Georgia Douglas Johnson is a poet neither afraid nor ashamed of her emotions. She limits herself to the purely conventional forms, rhythms and rhymes, but through them she achieves striking effects. The principal theme of Mrs. Johnson's poems is the secret dread down in every woman's heart, the dread of the passing of youth and beauty, and with them love. An old theme, one which poets themselves have often wearied of, but which, like death, remains one of the imperishable themes on which is made the poetry that has moved men's hearts through all ages. In her ingenuously wrought verses, through sheer simplicity and spontaneousness, Mrs. Johnson often sounds a note of pathos or passion that will not fail to waken a response, except in those too sophisticated or cynical to respond to natural impulses. Of the half dozen or so colored women writing creditable verse, Anne Spencer is the most modern and least obvious in her methods. Her lines are at times involved and turgid and almost cryptic, but she shows an originality which does not depend upon eccentricities. In her "Before the Feast of Shushan" she displays an opulence, the love of which has long been charged against the Negro as one of his naive and childish traits, but which in art may infuse a much needed color, warmth and spirit of abandon into American poetry.

John W. Holloway, more than any Negro poet writing in the dialect today, summons to his work the lilt, the spontaneity and charm of which Dunbar was the supreme master whenever he employed that medium. It is well to say a word here about the dialect poems of James Edwin Campbell. In dialect, Campbell was a precursor of Dunbar. A comparison of his idioms and phonetics with those of Dunbar reveals great differences. Dunbar is a shade or two more sophisticated and his phonetics approach nearer to a mean standard of the dialects spoken in the different sections. Campbell is more primitive and his phonetics are those of the dialect as spoken by the Negroes of the sea islands off the coasts of South Carolina and Georgia, which to this day remains comparatively close to its African roots, and is strikingly similar to the speech of the uneducated Negroes of the West Indies. An error that confuses many persons in reading or understanding Negro dialect is the idea that it is uniform. An ignorant Negro of the uplands of Georgia would have almost as much difficulty in understanding an ignorant sea island Negro as an Englishman would have. Not even in the dialect of any particular section is a given word always pronounced in precisely the same way. Its pronunciation depends upon the preceding and following sounds. Sometimes the combination permits of a liaison so close that to the uninitiated the sound of the word is almost completely lost.

The constant effort in Negro dialect is to elide all troublesome consonants and sounds. This negative effort may be after all only positive laziness of the vocal organs, but the result is a softening and smoothing which makes Negro dialect so delightfully easy for singers.

Daniel Webster Davis wrote dialect poetry at the time when Dunbar was writing. He gained great popularity, but it did not spread beyond his own race. Davis had unctuous humor, but he was crude. For illustration, note the vast stretch between his

"Hog Meat" and Dunbar's "When de Co'n Pone's Hot," both of them poems on the traditional ecstasy of the Negro in contemplation of "good things" to eat.

It is regrettable that two of the most gifted writers included were cut off so early in life. R. C. Jamison and Joseph S. Cotter, Jr., died several years ago, both of them in their youth. Jamison was barely thirty at the time of his death, but among his poems there is one, at least, which stamps him as a poet of superior talent and lofty inspiration. "The Negro Soldiers" is a poem with the race problem as its theme, yet it transcends the limits of race and rises to a spiritual height that makes it one of the noblest poems of the Great War. Cotter died a mere boy of twenty, and the latter part of that brief period he passed in an invalid state. Some months before his death he published a thin volume of verses which were for the most part written on a sick bed. In this little volume Cotter showed fine poetic sense and a free and bold mastery over his material. A reading of Cotter's poems is certain to induce that mood in which one will regretfully speculate on what the young poet might have accomplished had he not been cut off so soon.

As intimated above, my original idea for this book underwent a change in the writing of the introductions. I first planned to select twenty-five to thirty poems which I judged to be up to a certain standard, and offer them with a few words of introduction and without comment. In the collection, as it grew to be, that "certain standard" has been broadened if not lowered; but I believe that this is offset by the advantage of the wider range given the reader and the student of the subject.

I offer this collection without making apology or asking allowance. I feel confident that the reader will find not only an earnest for the future, but actual achievement. The reader cannot but be impressed by the distance already covered. It is a long way from the plaints of George Horton to the invectives of Claude McKay, from the obviousness of Frances Harper to the complexness of Anne Spencer. Much ground has been covered, but more will yet be covered. It is this side of prophecy to declare that the undeniable creative genius of the Negro is destined to make a distinctive and valuable contribution to American poetry.

—*James Weldon Johnson*

1. This statement should probably be modified by the inclusion of American skyscraper architecture. (*Editor, 1931*.)

2. This statement was quoted in 1921. The reader may consider for himself the changes wrought in the decade. (*Editor, 1931*.)

3. Plácido's sonnet and two English versions will be found in the Appendix.

PREFACE TO THE REVISED EDITION

When this book was compiled, only ten years ago, the conception of the Negro as a creator of art was so new, indeed so unformed, that I felt it was necessary to make a rather extended introduction in presenting to the public an anthology of poetry by Negro writers. And so, forty-eight pages were devoted to calling attention to the main contributions which the Negro had already made to our common cultural store, and to setting forth a modest claim for his powers of artistic creation and expression.

Within this brief period the introduction to the original edition of the book has become primarily a matter of historical data. Its statements, claims, and forecasts are today, for the most part, accepted facts. Within the past decade there has grown a general recognition that the Negro is a contributor to American life not only of material but of artistic, cultural, and spiritual values; that in the making and shaping of American civilization he is an active force, a giver as well as a receiver, a creator as well as a creature.

The statement made in the original preface regarding the limitations of Negro dialect as a poetic medium has, it may be said, come to be regarded as more or less canonical. It is as sound today as when it was written ten years ago; and its implications are more apparent. It calls for no modifications, but it can well be amplified here. The passing of traditional dialect as a medium for Negro poets is complete. The passing of traditional dialect as poetry is almost complete. Today even the reader is conscious that almost all poetry in the conventionalized dialect is either based upon the minstrel traditions of Negro life, traditions that had but slight relation—often no relation at all—to actual Negro life, or is permeated with artificial sentiment. It is now realized both by the poets and by their public that as an instrument for poetry the dialect has only two main stops, humor and pathos.

That this is not a shortcoming inherent in the dialect as dialect is demonstrated by the wide compass it displays in its use in the folk creations. The limitation is due to conventions that have been fixed upon the dialect and the conformity to them by individual writers. Negro dialect poetry had its origin in the minstrel traditions, and a persisting pattern was set. When the individual writer attempted to get away from that pattern, the fixed conventions allowed him only to slip over into a slough of sentimentality. These conventions were not broken for the simple reason that the individual writers wrote chiefly to entertain an outside audience, and in concord with its stereotyped ideas about the Negro. And herein lies the vital distinction between them and the folk creators, who wrote solely to please and express themselves.

Several of the poets of the younger group, notably Langston Hughes and Sterling A. Brown, *do* use a dialect; but it is not the dialect of the comic minstrel tradition or of the sentimental plantation tradition; it is the common, racy, living, authentic speech of the Negro in certain phases of real life.

It is not out of place to say that it is more than regretable that the traditional dialect was forced into the narrow and unnatural literary mold it occupies. If Negro poets, writing sincerely to express their race and for their race, had been the first to develop and fix it, they might have been able to make of it something comparable to the literary medium that Burns made of the Scottish dialect. If he addressed himself to the task, the Aframerican poet might in time break the old conventional mold; but I don't think he will do it, because I don't think he considers it now worth the effort.

The original preface also gives a summarized account of the miscellaneous group of Negro poets from Phillis Wheatley, who published a volume of poems in 1773, down to Paul Laurence Dunbar (1872-1906). The selections in the main section of the first edition of the book represented two periods: the first embracing the poets of the Dunbar school and other writers down to the outbreak of the World War; the second embracing the group that emerged during the war. Since the original publication of the book a third group has arisen. The preëminent figures in this younger group are Countee Cullen, who published his first volume, *Color,* in 1925, and Langston Hughes, who published his first volume, *The Weary Blues,* in 1926.

The rise of the World War group involved a revolt against the traditions of Negro dialect poetry, against stereotyped humorous-pathetic patterns, against sentimental and supplicatory moods; it involved an attempt to express the feelings of disillusionment and bitterness the American Negro was then experiencing, and out of it there came poetry of protest, rebellion, and despair. The rise of the younger group involved a revolt against

"propaganda," an effort to get away from "race problem" poetry, an attempt to break through racial barriers that hedge in even art in the United States, a desire to be simply poets.

The poets of the younger group have not succeeded fundamentally in what they undertook to do; in the main they, too, are writing race-conscious poetry, poetry that is, perhaps, more highly charged with race than that of the World War group. But the best of them have found an approach to "race" that is different. Their approach is less direct, less obvious than that of their predecessors, and thereby they have secured a gain in subtlety of power and, probably, in ultimate effectiveness. Some of the younger poets made a futile effort to ignore "race" and all it implies in the United States, to deny intellectually its existence, with the result that they either produced race-conscious poetry of the worst sort—poetry of bombast and braggadocio—or failed to produce anything vital. It is interesting to note how Countee Cullen, Langston Hughes, Sterling A. Brown, Helene Johnson, Arna Bontemps, Frank Horne, Waring Cuney, Gwendolyn Bennett, and others of the group react to this matter of "race." While they have not written exclusively poetry rising out of race-consciousness, it is manifest that their best efforts spring from that source.

Several of the group have dug down into the genuine folk stuff—I mention genuine folk stuff in contradistinction to the artificial folk stuff of the dialect school—to get their material; for example, Langston Hughes has gone to such folk sources as the blues and the work songs; Sterling A. Brown has gone to Negro folk epics and ballads like "Stagolee," "John Henry," "Casey Jones," and "Long Gone John." These are unfailing sources of material for authentic poetry. I myself did a similar thing in writing *God's Trombones.* I went back to the genuine folk stuff that clings around the old-time Negro preacher, material which had many times been worked into something both artificial and false.

I have no intention of depreciating the poetry not stimulated by a sense of race that Aframerican poets have written; much of it is as high as the average standard of American poetry and some of it higher; but not in all of it do I find a single poem possessing the power and artistic finality found in the best of the poems rising out of racial conflict and contact. All of which is merely a confirmation of the axiom that an artist accomplishes his best when working at his best with the material he knows best. And up to this time, at least, "race" is perforce the thing the American Negro poet knows best. Assuredly, the time will come when he will know other things as well as he now knows "race," and will, perhaps, feel them as deeply; or, to state this in another way, the time should come when he will not have to know "race" so well and feel it so deeply. But even now he can escape the sense of being hampered if, standing on his racial foundation, he strives to fashion something that rises above mere race and reaches out to the universal in truth and beauty.

The writers of the younger group are developing. The greater part of their work still lies within the compass of the old circle, but they possess a greater self-sufficiency than any generation before them and are freer from sensitiveness to the approbation or deprecation of their white environment. It is for the purpose of including the writers of this group that this enlarged edition of *The Book of American Negro Poetry* is published. (In this book the term, "American Negro Poetry," is used solely because it is more concise—even if less expository—than the expression, "poetry written by American Negroes.")

The book now contains selections from the work of forty writers, with a summary in the original preface of the work of the more important ones prior to Paul Laurence Dunbar. The sketches of the poets included have been made critical as well as biographical, and a list of references for supplementary reading has been added. An Outline of Study, published separately, for the use of teachers and students, has been prepared by Sterling A. Brown, Professor of English at Howard University. He is also the writer of the included sketch of James Weldon Johnson.

The work of revision has been done during the fellowship granted me by the Julius Rosenwald Fund.

—*James Weldon Johnson*

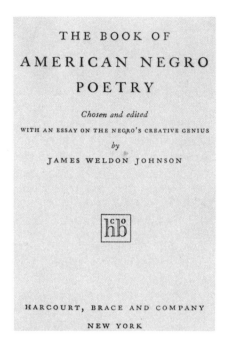

THE BOOK OF
AMERICAN NEGRO
POETRY

Chosen and edited

WITH AN ESSAY ON THE NEGRO'S CREATIVE GENIUS

by

JAMES WELDON JOHNSON

hb

HARCOURT, BRACE AND COMPANY

NEW YORK

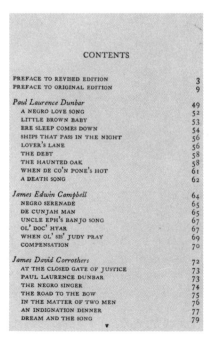

CONTENTS

Title page and table of contents for the 1931 edition

Caroling Dusk: An Anthology of Verse by Negro Poets (1927)
Edited by Countee Cullen

FOREWORD

It is now five years since James Weldon Johnson edited with a brilliant essay on "The Negro's Creative Genius" *The Book of American Negro Poetry*, four years since the publication of Robert T. Kerlin's *Negro Poets and Their Poems*, and three years since from the Trinity College Press in Durham, North Carolina, came *An Anthology of Verse by American Negroes,* edited by Newman Ivey White and Walter Clinton Jackson. The student of verse by American Negro poets will find in these three anthologies comprehensive treatment of the work of Negro poets from Phillis Wheatley, the first American Negro known to have composed verses, to writers of the present day. With Mr. Johnson's scholarly and painstaking survey, from both a historical and a critical standpoint, of the entire range of verse by American Negroes, and with Professor Kerlin's inclusions of excerpts from the work of most of those Negro poets whose poems were extant at the time of his compilation, there would be scant reason for the assembling and publication of another such collection were it not for the new voices that within the past three to five years have sung so significantly as to make imperative an anthology recording some snatches of their songs. To those intelligently familiar with what is popularly termed the renaissance in art and literature by Negroes, it will not be taken as a sentimentally risky observation to contend that the recent yearly contests conducted by Negro magazines, such as *Opportunity* and *The Crisis,* as well as a growing tendency on the part of white editors to give impartial consideration to the work of Negro writers, have awakened to a happy articulation many young Negro poets who had thitherto lisped only in isolated places in solitary numbers. It is primarily to give them a concerted hearing that this collection has been published. For most of these poets the publication of individual volumes of their poems is not an immediate issue. However, many of their poems during these four or five years of accentuated interest in the artistic development of the race have become familiar to a large and ever-widening circle of readers who, we feel, will welcome a volume marshaling what would otherwise remain for some time a miscellany of deeply appreciated but scattered verse.

The place of poetry in the cultural development of a race or people has always been one of importance; indeed, poets are prone, with many good reasons for their conceit, to hold their art the most important. Thus while essentially wishing to draw the public ear to the work of the younger Negro poets, there have been included with their poems those of modern Negro poets already established and acknowledged, by virtue of their seniority and published books, as worthy practitioners of their art. There were Negro poets before Paul Laurence Dunbar, but his uniquity as the first Negro to attain to and maintain a distinguished place among American poets, a place fairly merited by the most acceptable standards of criticism, makes him the pivotal poet of this volume.

I have called this collection an anthology of verse by Negro poets rather than an anthology of Negro verse, since this latter designation would be more confusing than accurate. Negro poetry, it seems to me, in the sense that we speak of Russian, French, or Chinese poetry, must emanate from some country other than this in some language other than our own. Moreover, the attempt to corral the outbursts of the ebony muse into some definite mold to which all poetry by Negroes will conform seems altogether futile and aside from the facts. This country's Negro writers may here and there turn some singular facet toward the literary sun, but in the main, since theirs is also the heritage of the English language, their work will not present any serious aberration from the poetic tendencies of their times. The conservatives, the middlers, and the arch heretics will be found among them as among the white poets; and to say that the pulse beat of their verse shows generally such a fever, or the symptoms of such an ague, will prove on closer examination merely the moment's exaggeration of a physician anxious to establish a new literary ailment. As heretical as it may sound, there is the probability that Negro poets, dependent as they are on the English language, may have more to gain from the rich background of English and American poetry than from any nebulous atavistic yearnings toward an African inheritance. Some of the poets herein represented will eventually find inclusion in any discriminatingly ordered anthology of American verse, and there will be no reason for giving such selections the needless distinction of a separate section marked Negro verse.

While I do not feel that the work of these writers conforms to anything that can be called the Negro school of poetry, neither do I feel that their work is varied to the point of being sensational; rather is theirs a variety within a uniformity that is trying to maintain the higher traditions of English verse. I trust the selections here presented bear out this contention. The poet writes out of his experience, whether it be personal or vicarious, and as these experiences differ among other poets, so do they differ among Negro poets; for the double obligation of being both Negro and American is not so unified as we are often led to believe. A survey of the work of Negro poets will show that the individual diversifying ego transcends the synthesizing hue. From the roots of varied experiences have flowered the dialect of Dunbar, the recent sermon poems of James Weldon Johnson, and some of Helene Johnson's more colloquial verse, which, differing essentially only in a few expressions peculiar to Negro slang, are worthy counterparts of verses done by John V. A. Weaver "in American." Attempt to hedge all these in with a name, and your imagination must deny the facts. Langston Hughes, poetizing the blues in his zeal to represent the Negro masses, and Sterling Brown, combining a similar interest in such poems as "Long Gone" and "The Odyssey of Big Boy" with a capacity for turning a neat sonnet according to the rules, represent differences as unique as those between Burns and Whitman. Jessie Fauset with Cornell University and training at the Sorbonne as her intellectual equipment surely justifies the very subjects and forms of her poems: "Touché," "La Vie C'est la Vie," "Noblesse Oblige," etc.; while Lewis Alexander, with no known degree from the University of Tokyo, is equally within the province of his creative prerogatives in compositing Japanese *hokkus* and *tankas*. Although Anne Spencer lives in Lynchburg, Virginia, and in her biographical note recognizes the Negro as the great American taboo, I have seen but two poems by her which are even remotely concerned with this subject;

rather does she write with a cool precision that calls forth comparison with Amy Lowell and the influence of a rock-bound seacoast. And Lula Lowe Weeden, the youngest poet in the volume, living in the same Southern city, is too young to realize that she is colored in an environment calculated to impress her daily with the knowledge of this pigmentary anomaly.

There are lights and shades of difference even in their methods of decrying race injustices, where these peculiar experiences of Negro life cannot be overlooked. Claude McKay is most exercised, rebellious, and vituperative to a degree that clouds his lyricism in many instances, but silhouettes most forcibly his high dudgeon; while neither Arna Bontemps, at all times cool, calm, and intensely religious, nor Georgia Douglas Johnson, in many instances bearing up bravely under comparison with Sara Teasdale, takes advantage of the numerous opportunities offered them for rhymed polemics.

If dialect is missed in this collection, it is enough to state that the day of dialect as far as Negro poets are concerned is in the decline. Added to the fact that these poets are out of contact with this fast-dying medium, certain sociological considerations and the natural limitations of dialect for poetic expression militate against its use even as a *tour de force*. In a day when artificiality is so vigorously condemned, the Negro poet would be foolish indeed to turn to dialect. The majority of present-day poems in dialect are the efforts of white poets.

This anthology, by no means offered as *the* anthology of verse by Negro poets, is but a prelude, we hope, to that fuller symphony which Negro poets will in time contribute to the national literature, and we shall be sadly disappointed if the next few years do not find this collection entirely outmoded.

....

The biographical notices carried with these poems have been written by the poets themselves save in three cases (Dunbar's having been written by his wife, the younger Cotter's by his father, and Lula Weeden's by her mother), and if they do not reveal to a curious public all it might wish to know about the poets, they at least reveal all that the poets deem necessary and discreet for the public to know.

—*Countee Cullen*

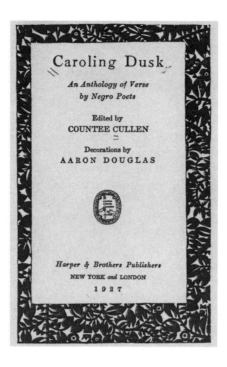

Caroling Dusk

An Anthology of Verse by Negro Poets

Edited by
COUNTEE CULLEN

Decorations by
AARON DOUGLAS

Harper & Brothers Publishers
NEW YORK and LONDON
1927

CONTENTS

CONTENTS

Fugitives: An Anthology of Verse (1928)

Edited by Donald Davidson

FOREWORD

This book represents eleven poets who for four years issued most of their verse in a journal of poetry called *The Fugitive*. It was published in Nashville, Tennessee. The history of *The Fugitive* is as follows:

Originally there were seven friends—Donald Davidson, James Marshall Frank, Sidney Mttron-Hirsch, Stanley Johnson, John Crowe Ransom, Alec B. Stevenson, and Allen Tate. These men, or most of them, had been meeting often for some years at the home of James Marshall Frank and Sidney Mttron-Hirsch, where they talked about poetry and philosophy. In the autumn of 1921 they became interested in the writing of poetry, and after a while their poems and the criticism of them became the chief object of their meetings, which were now held regularly. Manuscripts piled up so rapidly that upon the suggestion of Sidney Mttron-Hirsch, which everybody else naturally fell in with, the group decided to start a poetry magazine as a coöperative undertaking. The first issue came out in April, 1922. There was no editor. Poems were chosen by ballot. The authors hid themselves under pen-names.

After the first issue and a second like it, the poets dropped their pen-names, which were a little fancy and exciting at the time, "Roger Prim," "Henry Feathertop," "Robin Gallivant," being typical of the disguises they used, and they arranged a scheme for regular publication. They devised an administration which at different times included both editorial committees and rotating editorships. Always the coöperative principle was preserved, and although the publishers of *The Fugitive* printed a few outside contributions, they held to the view that the magazine was their own. Wisely or unwisely they gave most of the limited space to their own poetry.

Meanwhile the number of poets who owed direct allegiance to the undertaking had been greatly increased. Within the first few months of publication, Walter Clyde Curry, Merrill Moore, William Yandell Elliott, and William Frierson were taken in. And later Jesse Wills, Ridley Wills, Robert Penn Warren, Laura Riding (Gottschalk), and Alfred Starr appeared successively on the roster of "Fugitives."

Although the magazine carried a few critical editorials, signed by individual members of the staff, the "Fugitives," because they never quite cared to define what they fled from, issued no manifestoes whatever. Their only program at any time was to offer to a small but widely scattered public the best of their own verses and a very few others that had to be at least as good. They disagreed among themselves on the literary principles which they persistently argued. In their public aspect they must have been a little mysterious, at least locally, because they didn't have a "cause." So far as they could see, all they had in common was a certain belief in their poetry and a desire to write more of it. Negatively they avoided public harangues, self-advertising, and social optimism—heresies that seemed to them to have been dropped by the tide of the so-called Reconstruction into the society where they lived.

Matters went on, until in December, 1925, they discontinued publication after having issued nineteen numbers of the magazine. The reasons for this were simple. The poets began to feel that writing poetry was more interesting than publishing a magazine. There wasn't time for both. When administrative tasks had absorbed the time of various members in turn, and no one any longer felt inclined to give his energies to office, the magazine was stopped. But the men in Nashville still meet to talk things over, and they still write; they correspond with the "absent members," men who have gone away.

At no time was *The Fugitive* bothered with financial troubles. In the first days, when the magazine was kept up by subscriptions alone, H. S. Coil came into the group as a friend and business manager. In a later period the business affairs were administered, generously and indeed philanthropically, by Jacques Back, a Nashville business man. Later still, when a simple plan of endowment was used, various persons and organizations made substantial contributions. Among these were the Associated Retailers of Nashville, Joel Cheek, Ward-Belmont College, and other generous friends whose names are recorded more fully in the files of the magazine.

This volume is a survey of the past; it may also be taken as a prospectus. It looks back to some of the earliest work of the poets who ran *The Fugitive,* and it contains poetry that is now published for the first time. Each contributor is responsible for the selection of his own poems. There has been no editing, except in the mechanical sense of collecting manuscripts and fitting them to the limitations of space. Some of those who at one time or another were joined in the Fugitive enterprise have chosen not to be represented by poems. They have nevertheless contributed largely to the group activities, in ways poetical and otherwise, and the poets who appear in this collection wish to pay tribute to the energy and fine spirit of their absent friends.

—Donald Davidson

FUGITIVES

An Anthology of Verse

New York
HARCOURT, BRACE & COMPANY

Contents

Active Anthology (1933)

Edited by Ezra Pound

PRAEFATIO
aut tumulus cimicium

Mr F. V. Morley, with a misplaced sense of humour, has suggested that I write a fifty page preface to two hundred pages of contemporary poesy. This to me, who have for a quarter of a century contended that critics should know more and write less. No two hundred pages of contemporary poetry would sustain the demands I could make in half such a preface. I am moreover confining my selection to poems Britain has not accepted and in the main that the British literary bureaucracy does NOT want to have printed in England.

I shall therefore write a preface mainly about something else.

Mr Eliot and I are in agreement, or "belong to the same school of critics," in so far as we both believe that existing works form a complete order which is changed by the introduction of the "really new" work.

His contempt for his readers has always been much greater than mine, by which I would indicate that I quite often write as if I expected my reader to use his intelligence, and count on its being fairly strong, whereas Mr Eliot after enduring decennial fogs in Britain practically always writes as if for very very feeble and brittle mentalities, from whom he can expect neither resilience nor any faculty for seeing the main import instead of the details or surfaces.

When he talks of "commentation and elucidation" and of the "correction of taste," I go into opposition, or rather, having been there first, I note that if I was in any sense the revolution I have been followed by the counter-revolution. Damn your taste, I would like if possible to sharpen your perceptions, after which your taste can take care of itself.

"Commentation" be damned. "Elucidation" can stand if it means "turn a searchlight on" something or preferably some work or author lying in shadow.

2

Mr Eliot's flattering obeisance to "exponents of criticism," wherein he says that he supposes they have not assumed that criticism is an "autotelic activity," seems to me so much apple-sauce. In so far as the bureaucracy of letters has considered their writing as anything more than a short cut to the feeding trough or a means of puffing up their personal importances, they have done little else for the past thirty years than boost the production of writing about writing, not only as autotelic, but as something which ought to receive more attention from the reading victim than the great books themselves.

Granted that nobody ought to be such a presumptuous imbecile as to hold up the autotelic false horizon, Mr Eliot describes a terrestrial paradise and not the de facto world, in which more immediate locus we observe a perpetual exchange of civilities between pulex, cimex, vermiformis, etc., each holding up his candle before the shrines of his similars.

A process having no conceivable final limit and illustratable by my present activity: I mean on this very page, engaging your attention while I talk about Mr Eliot's essay about other essayists' essays. In the course of his eminently professorial volume he must have mentioned at least forty-five essayists whom tomorrow's readers will be most happy not to hear mentioned, but mention of whom must have contributed enormously to Mr Eliot's rise to his deserved position as arbiter of British opinion.

KRINO

"Existing monuments form an ideal order among themselves." It would be healthier to use a zoological term rather than the word monument. It is much easier to think of the Odyssey or Le Testament or Catullus' Epithalamium as something living than as a series of cenotaphs. After all, Homer, Villon, Propertius, speak of the world as I know it, whereas Mr Tennyson and Dr Bridges did not. Even Dante and Guido with their so highly specialized culture speak of a part of life as I know it. ATHANATOS.

However, accepting for the moment Mr Eliot's monumental or architectural simile: the KRINO, "to pick out for oneself, choose, prefer" (page 381 my edition of Liddel and Scott) which seems to me the major job, is to determine, first, the main form and main proportions of that order of extant letters, to locate, first the greater pyramids and then, possibly, and with a decently proportioned emphasis, to consider the exact measurements of the stone-courses, layers, etc.

Dryden gives T. S. E. a good club wherewith to smack Milton. But with a modicum of familiarity or even a passing acquaintance with Dante, the club would hardly be needed.

A volume of quite sound statistical essays on poesy may quite easily drive a man to the movies, it may express nothing save the most perfect judgements and the utmost refinements of descriptivity and whet, nevertheless, no appetite for the unknown best, or for the best still unread by the neophyte.

A book 66% concerned with manipulating and with rehandling the errors of seventy contemporary pestilential describers and rehashers of opinion, and only 34% concerned with focusing the reader's attention on the *virtu* of books worth reading is, at least to the present victim, more an annoyance than a source of jocundity.

And if I am to put myself vicariously in the place of the younger reader or if I am to exercise parental protectiveness over some imagined offspring, I can find myself too angry for those mincing politenesses demanded by secondary editorial orders.

My opinion of critics is that:

The best are those who actually cause an amelioration in the art which they criticize.

The next best are those who most focus attention on the best that is written (or painted or composed or cut in stone).

And the pestilential vermin are those who distract attention *from* the best, either to the second rate, or to hokum, or to their own critical writings.

Mr Eliot probably ranks very high in the first of these three groups, and deserves badly of us for his entrance into the last.

He uses Dryden legitimately in reducing exaggerated adulation of Milton, but the fact of his resurrecting Dryden poisons Professor Taupin,

and so on *and* so on, thence further proceeding.

3

I don't at this point mean to criticize Taupin's Quatres Essais, but they offer me a fine chance to make an addendum.

Taupin is interesting while writing of Frobenius and Dante. In the latter case I suspect a Flamand ancestry has saved him from the n.r.f dither and wish-wash. There is (naturally?) a let down in the pages following. I suppose this is due to Taupin's respect for his elders. Prof. Eliot in a fit of misanthropy dug up Dryden and Taupin was lured into reading him. The citation from Dryden may have been cleverly inserted by Taupin, at any rate it acts as a foil for his own somewhat contorted style to which one returns with relief from Dryden's platitude and verbosity. I am unable to determine whether Taupin is being superlatively astute and counting on the reader "seeing for himself," or whether he was simply in a hurry, but 30 pages furnish a magnificent *basis* for deduction. Which he refrains from making. He may have expected the reader to see it for himself.

I know from longer experience than Dr René's that there is no use in expecting the reader to do anything of the sort. (No one has, for example, ever noticed the ground-plan of my "Instigations".)

On page 161 Taupin quotes Condillac: "Il y a deux espèces: le talent et le génie. Celui-là continue les idées d'un art ou d'une science connue, d'une manière propre á produire les effets qu'on en doit naturellement attendre . . . Celui-ci ajoute au talent l'idée d'esprit, en quelque sort créateur."

Talent "continues the ideas of a known art or science to produce naturally expectable results".

On page 164 he quotes Milton: "and twilight gray had in her sober livery all things clad."

No one can be so ignorant as to suppose this manner of expression is anything save that of an art *known* and applied by several dozen dramatists. The Shakespearian original or model will instantly spring to the mind of almost any literate reader.

But the known process is vilely used. It is disgustingly used.

The Shakespearian line contains, I admit, one word not absolutely essential to the meaning. It is a monosyllable and three of its four letters serve to concentrate and fulfil the double alliteration preceding.

Anybody but a botcher would have omitted the two useless words from the Milton. He not only derives but dilutes.

However, Taupin continues (still without heaving rocks at the victim): on the next page we find:

"the setting sun. . . ."

Gentlemen, ah wubb-wubb, what did the setting sun do?

"the setting sun. . . .

DESCENDED."

The abject and utter nullity of British criticism in general for over two centuries is nowhere so squalid and naked as in the fact that generations of Britons and humble Americans have gone on swallowing this kind of rubbish. (Despite what Landor had shown them in his notes on Catullus.)

The only camouflage used to put over this idiocy is a gross and uninteresting rhythm.

The clodhoppers needed only one adverb between the subject and predicate to hide the underlying stupidity.

Chateaubriand, in a passage subsequently cited, was not, as Taupin seems to imply, supinely imitating the passage, but possibly trying to correct it, everything in his description is in place. His paragraph, like most so called prose poetry, lacks adequate rhythmic vitality and has, consequently, the dulness germane to its category.

MR ELIOT'S GRIEF

Mr Eliot's misfortune was to find himself surrounded by a horrible and microcephalous bureaucracy which disliked poetry, it might be too much to say "loathed" it. But the emotion was as strong as any in the bureaucratic bosom. Bureaucracy has no loves and is composed mainly of varied minor dislikes. The members of this bureaucracy, sick with inferiority complex, had just enough wits to perceive that Eliot was their superior, but no means of detecting his limits or measuring him from the outside, and no experience that would enable them to know the poisons wherewith he had been injected. For that diagnosis perhaps only a fellow American is qualified, one having suffered an American University. The American University is or was aware of the existence of both German and English institutions, being younger and in a barbarous country, *its* inferiority complex impelled it to comparison and to a wish to equal and surpass, but gave it no immunity from the academical bacilli,

inferiority complex directed against creative activity in the arts.

That there is a percentage of bunk in the "Selected Essays" Mr Eliot will possibly be the last to deny, but that he had performed a self-analysis is still doubtful.

This kind of essay assumes the existence of a culture that no longer subsists and does nothing to prepare a better culture that must or ought to come into being. I say "better", for the new paideuma will at least be a live paideuma not a dead one.

Such essays are prepared NOT for editors who care about a living literature or a live tradition, or who even want the best of Eliot's perception applied to an author of second or third or fourth category (per ex. Seneca), they want to maintain a system wherein it is possible to receive fifteen guineas for an article of approximately 3000-4000 words, in a series to which Mr Eliot's sensitivity and patience will give lustre and wherein his occasional eminence will shed respectability on a great mass of inferior writing.

Their mentality is not far from that of a publisher of cheap editions who occasionally puts in a good book, so that the serious German will think that the miscellany is intellectual (ipse dicebat). Given the two or three real books in his series he believes the German highbrow will buy the rest thinking it the right thing to do.

The study of latin authors was alive a century and a quarter, perhaps hardly more than a century ago.

Young men are now lured into colleges and universities largely on false pretences.

We live in a vile age when it is impossible to get reprints of the few dozen books that are practically essential to a competent knowledge of poetry. When Alexander Moring and Prof. Rouse set out to republish the books that had been good enough for Shakespeare, the enterprise went on the rocks. You can't get a current edition of Golding's Metamorphoses, or of Gavin Douglas, or of Salel; the British grocer will break a contract for printing Cavalcanti when he would not dream of breaking a contract for prunes.

In the matter of education, if the young are not to profit by our sweats, if they are not to pluck the fruits of our experience in the form of better curricula, it might be well to give it up altogether. At any rate the critic not aiming at a better curriculum for the serious study of literature is a critic half-baked, swinging in a vacuum. It would be hypocrisy to pretend that Eliot's essays are not aimed at professors and students.

The student is best aided by being able to read and to own conveniently the best that has been created.

Yeats, who has always been against the gang and the bureaucracy, now muddled, now profound, now merely celtic or erroneously believing that a free Ireland, or at least a more Oirish Ireland, would help the matter, long ago prayed for a new sacred book.

Every age has tried to compound such a volume. Every great culture has had such a major anthology. Pisistratus, Li Po, the Japanese Emperor who reduced the number of Noh dramas to about 450; the hackneyed Hebrew example; in less degree the middle ages, with the matter of Britain, of France, and of Rome le Grant.

The time to be interested in Seneca may possibly have been before Mr Shakespeare had written his plays. But assuming that Mr Eliot's plenum exists, the relations of its different components have been changed in our time; there are most distinctly the movies which bear on all dramatic construction and there are Max Ernst's few volumes of engravings which have distinctly said their word about the freudian novel.

If the past 30 years have a meaning, that meaning is not very apparent in Mr Eliot's condescensions to the demands of British serial publication. If it means anything it means a distinct reduction in the BULK of past literature that the future will carry.

I should have no right to attack England's most accurate critic were it not in the hope of something better, if not in England, at least somewhere in space and time.

There is a habit or practice of attacking the lists in "How to Read". Young academes who have not read the works listed say my choice is capricious, most of them do not stop to see what my lists are lists OF.

I have catalogued the towns in Dorset without mentioning Durham. I have listed the cities in England and Scotland and omitted Berwick-on-Tweed. Therefore the assistant professor or the weekly reviewer is educated, superlatively educated, and I am still impetuus juventus, sipping with the bally bee and wholly unscientific in my methods.

Mr Aldington was perhaps the most vociferous, he vociferized about forty contradictions of things that I hadn't said, perhaps out of kindness, thinking it the only way his paper would give the booklet two columns, perhaps because he fawncied

himself as the fine olde northern rough-haired St Bernard defending the kittens of Alexandria. He has always tended to lose his shirt and breeches if one made any restrictive remarks about Greeks, even though it were only to suggest that some Greeks wrote better than others.

Ut moveat, ut doceat, ut delectet.

There are at least three kinds of inaccurate statement which might with advantage be dissociated.

1. The somewhat violent statement conveying a perception (quia perception it is something perceived by the writer), the inaccuracy of such statement is often more apparent than real, and as every reader resists an opinion diverse from his own, such statement is often, one might say is usually, corrected or more than corrected in transit.

2. There is the apparently careful statement containing all the possible, or at least so many, modifications of the main proposition that the main meaning is either lost in transit or so dampened down that it has no effect on the reader.

Both these kinds of statement can be justified in various ways depending on where and why they are used.

3. There is the inaccurate statement that is just simply vague, either because the writer doesn't KNOW or because he is incompetent in expression.

Such ignorance in successful vendors of their wares to current publications very often disguises itself as verity No. 2.

Camouflage might be further subdivided:
A. "Sound opinion," i.e., restating accepted opinion without direct or personal knowledge.
B. Covering this ignorance either with restrictive clauses, or scintillating with paradox.

There is gongorism in critical writing as well as in bad poetry. You might say that discussion of books ceases to be critical writing and becomes just the functioning of bureaucracy when the MAIN END (telos) is forgotten.

As we cannot educate our grandfathers, one supposes that critical writing is committed for the purpose of educating our offspring, our contemporaries, or ourselves, and that the least a critic can do is be aware of the present even if he be too swinish to consider the future.

The critic is either a parasite or he is concerned with the growth of the next paideuma.

Marinetti is thoroughly simpatico. Writing and orating *ut moveat,* he has made demands that no one considers in their strict literal sense, but which have, and have had, a definite scope.

"An early play of no merit whatever," "the brain of a fourth-rate playwright" as matters of an highly specialized clinic may conceivably have something to do with critical standards. The first impression is that their importance must be limited to some very minor philological field. Their import for tomorrow's paideuma is probably slight.

As specialist and practising writer one might want to know whether Seneca wrote any other lines as effective as

Per alta vada spatia sublimi aethere
testare nullos esse, qua veheris, deos.

Mr Eliot can think of no other play which reserves such a shock for the last word. (ref. or cf. O. Henry's stories, bell in the last pp.)

The only trouble with the citation is that it is a bit ambiguous: Mr E. and Prof. Miller disagreeing as to its theological import, Mr Eliot inclining to the christian interpretation, or what Seneca ought to have meant. No, I mustn't exaggerate. Seneca is not being Christian. Mr E. votes against a sweeping atheistical meaning. I can't personally see that the old half-bore goes further than asserting that the gods are not in that particular district of the aether. If there is anything about justice, it must be in the context, not in the two lines quoted.

In the present decomposition and under the yoke of the present bureaucracy, it would probably be too much to demand that before discussing an author a reviewer answer the following questions:

1. Have you read the original text of the author under discussion? or how much of it have you read?

2. Is it worth reading? or how much of it is worth reading? and by whom?

As for Elizabethan dramedy, Lamb and Hazlitt are supposed to have set the fad, but Lamb at any rate did pick out a volume of selections; showing what he thought might be the basis of an interest.

The proportion between discussion and the exhibits the discusser dares show his reader is possibly a good, and probably a necessary, test of his purpose. In a matter of degree, I am for say 80% exhibit and 20% yatter.

Mr Eliot and Miss Moore are definitely fighting against an impoverishment of culture, against a paucity of reading program. Neither they nor anyone else is likely to claim that they have as much interest in life as I have, or that I have their patience in reading.

That does not make it any less necessary to distinguish between Eliot registering his belief re a value, and Eliot ceding to the bad, not to say putrid habits of the bureaucracy which has surrounded him.

As alarmist, as capricious, perverse, etc., etc., I repeat that you cannot get the whole cargo of a sinking paideuma onto the life-boat. If you propose to have any live literature of the past kept in circulation, available (flat materialism) in print at prices the eager reader can pay, there has got to be more attention to the best and to the basic. Once that is established you can divagate into marginalia, but the challenge will be more incisive and the criteria will be more rigorous.

In citing the Miltonic burble I am merely on my way towards a further assertion.

The critical sense shows more in composition than in a critical essay.

The unwelcome and disparate authors whom I have gathered in this volume have mostly accepted certain criteria which duller wits have avoided.

They have mostly, if not accepted, at any rate faced the demands, and considered the works, made and noted in my "How to Read". That in itself is not a certificate of creative ability, but it does imply a freedom from certain forms of gross error and from certain kinds of bungling which will indubitably consign many other contemporary writings to the ash-bin, with more than expected celerity.

Mr Bunting probably seems reactionary to most of the other contributors. I think the apparent reaction is a definite endeavor to emphasize certain necessary elements which the less considering American experimentors tend to omit. At any rate Mr B. asserted that ambition some years ago, but was driven still further into the American ambience the moment he looked back upon British composition of, let us say, 1927-8.

I believe that Britain, in rejecting certain facts, (facts, not opinions) in 1912-15 entered a sterile decade.

Willingness to experiment is not enough, but unwillingness to experiment is mere death.

If ten pages out of its two hundred and fifty go into a Corpus Poetarum of a.d. 2033, the present volume will amply be justified. (Yes, I know I have split the future of that verb. Var. will, and amply.)

I have not attempted to represent all the new poets, I am leaving the youngest, possibly some of the brightest, to someone else or to future effort, not so much from malice or objection to perfect justice, as from inability to do everything all at once.

There are probably fifty very bright poems that are not here assembled. I suspect Mr S. Putnam has written two or three. Mr Bridson is champing on the bit. Someone more in touch with the younger Americans ought to issue an anthology or a special number of some periodical, selected with *criteria,* either his or mine.

The assertion implicit in this volume is that after ten or twenty years of serious effort you can consider a writer uninteresting, but the charges of flightiness and dilettantism are less likely to be valid. In fact they are unlikely to be valid if a consistent direction can be discovered.

Other things being equal, the results of processes, even of secondary processes, application, patience, etc., are more pertinent from living writers than from dead ones, or are more pertinent when demonstrably IN RELATION with the living present than with the classified past.

Classic in current publishers' ads seems to have attained its meaning via classé, rangé.

The history of literature as taught in many institutions (? all) is nothing more (hardly more) than a stratified record of snobisms in which chronology sometimes counts for more than the casual relation and is also often wholly ignored, I mean ignored usually when it conflicts with prejudice and when chronological fact destroys a supposed causal relation.

I have resisted several temptations to reply to attacks on "How to Read," because on examination the stricture was usually answered in my own text, and the attacker, had he been serious, could have found the correction where he assumed the fault. Several objectors (ut ante) simply have not taken the trouble to consider what my lists are lists of.

Others ignorant of the nature of some of the texts cited have assumed that they are not what they are.

Others have assumed that where, for sake of brevity, I have not given reasons for the inclusion of certain items, no reasons exist or can possibly.

Madox Ford made a serious charge, but not against what is on the pages of the booklet. He indicated that a section of what would be a more nearly complete treatise on the whole art of composition was not included. You can't get everything into 45 pages. Nor did the author of H.T.R. claim universal knowledge and competence. Neither in the title nor anywhere in the text did the booklet claim to be a treatise on the major structure of novels and epics, nor even a guide to creative composition.

As for experiment: the claim is that without constant experiment literature dies. Experiment is ONE of the elements necessary to its life. Experiment aims at writing that will have a relation to the present analogous to the relation which past masterwork had to the life of its time.

>Eliot applying what he has learned from
>>Morire.
>>>Cupio.
>>>>Profugo.
>>>>>Paenitiunt fugae.
>>Medea.
>>>Fiam.
>>>>Mater es.
>>>>>Cui sim vides.

applying what he has learned by being bored with as much of the rest of Seneca as he has bothered to read, is a vastly more vital Eliot, and a much more intensively critical Eliot than when complying with the exigencies of the present and verminous system for the excernment of book-reviews.

I might also assert that Eliot going back to the original has derived a vastly more vivid power than was possible to the century and more of Elizafiers who were content to lap the cream off Lamb and Hazlitt or to assume a smattering of Elizabethan bumbast from Elizabethan derivers. Quod erat demonstrandum. Quod erat indicatum, even by the present disturber of repose anno 1917 and thereabouts. And herein lies also the confutation of that horrible turba parasitorum paedagogorumque volgus which Mr Eliot tolerates in his vicinage.

—Ezra Pound

ACTIVE
ANTHOLOGY

EDITED BY

EZRA
POUND

LONDON
FABER AND FABER LTD
24 RUSSELL SQUARE

List of Authors

New Directions in Prose and Poetry (1936)

Edited by James Laughlin IV

PREFACE: NEW DIRECTIONS

A considerable part of the material included in this volume was first printed in the literary section of the Social Credit magazine, *New Democracy*. When, in October, 1935, I chose for the title of that section the name "New Directions" I composed in explanation an editorial in which I proposed that the department would attempt to collect in its pages all the most technically-advanced prose and poetry of American writers, all the work which exhibited a desire on the part of its author to set out in a new philological direction, collect it *because* it, and the fact that it existed at all, reflected the change in the state of the world mind whose spearhead was the New Economics of Major Douglas.

The emphasis of leadership was then upon the economist rather than the poet.

But since that time, nearly a year of hard experience in the propagation of Social Credit has led me to feel that the emphasis should be reversed: it is the poet—the word-worker—who must lead.

The economist (at least *one* economist!) has the right answer to the paradox of poverty amid plenty, but he is confronted by such a solid wall of static thinking that he cannot force his ideas across.

Society has a highly trained incapacity to think along other than familiar lines.

Because poverty has always existed your average educated citizen cannot believe that a system which would do away with it could function. We are faced, finally, by a mass lack of imagination. And the key to that deficiency is language. Only the writer is in a position to fit the key in the lock and turn it.

We think with words. We are entirely dependent upon them for communal action. The amount of thinking that even an isolated individual could do without words to conceptualize his perceptions would be almost negligible—limited in fact to what a horse or dog can do. Pavlov's dogs could handle two feeling-concepts at once: the hunger-feeding concept and the bell-hearing concept; man, with his system of signs, can work with half a dozen and have any number more on his shelves. No won-

der that the words for soul and breath-speech are cognate in almost all languages.

We think with words. And the clarity of our thought (and consequently our actions) depends on the clarity of our language. If we have only a hazy notion of what our words mean we will not be persons of luminous character. If the community allows one word to mean two things mistakes will be made by its members in their social actions. And if we allow many words to mean, in effect, nothing at all we shall be eligible for the presidency of a large university, a national trust, or a legislative body. That sentence is not meant to be funny; it is too tragically true.

Only the word Babel can render the state of the common knowledge in the social sciences today. Only the Pillar of Salt can signify the adaptability of our "intellectual leaders" for tearing down the Tower.

A few days ago at the Harvard Tercentenary Gilson, the great Medievalist, appealed for a hierarchy of universally accepted logical values to save the "civilized" world from chaos. How right he was! But will his plan be feasible? Not unless there is a housecleaning in every European language. Not unless there is a hacking away of dead wood . . . a polishing of terms . . . a scraping off of barnacles and associational verdigris.

It is the word worker who must show the way.

The world is in crisis, and language is at once the cause and the cure. New social concepts could stop the waste and the destruction. But they can only be introduced into minds ready to receive them, minds *able* to think along new lines, minds capable of imagination.

Language controls thought. It is not the other way around, as most people think, flattering their human vanity. There is at first, of course, in the development of any culture a vernal period in which thought does dominate. But it doesn't last long in a non-ideographic language. Almost at once, as soon as the culture has advanced to a fairly general literacy, the process of ossification sets in and language, becoming, in its state of sclerosis, a force in itself, impeding by its sclerosis the free flow of ideas, having an obstinate life of its own, begins to condition and then to control the modes of thought.

Language controls thought—as the Church Fathers knew when they insisted on continual care of terminology—as Ogden and Richards knew when they wrote "The Meaning of Meaning"—and the fluidity and flexibility of thought depends upon the fluidity and flexibility of language.

Without the unsubtle lubrication of fresh blood it is hard to conceive of a new social order except by revision of verbal orientation. And it is the writer alone who can accomplish that reorientation. But it will not be the slick paper writers who cater to inferiority complexes, or the editor who will print nothing "unfamiliar to his readers" or the commercial publishers' hair-oil boys. It will be men like Cummings or Carlos Williams who know their business well enough to realize the pass to which language has come and are willing to endure obscurity and poverty to carry on their experiments.

Always, in every age the best writers have understood and resisted ossification. The fertile periods of literature are those of philological innovation. And, as Fenollosa has pointed out, "all nations have written their strongest and most vivid literature before they invented a grammar." Shakspere did not hesitate to invent words. Neither did Rabelais.

Language I conceive as the kinetic sum of two opposing forces—the will of the individual to express his ego in his own way & the will of the community to get things done efficiently by standardizing the system of communication as much as possible. As long as the two opposites are in proper balance a healthy social body can be expected—a reasonable rate of evolution.

But when standardization goes too far, because the resistance of individualism lags, when habits of language are formed which prevent the individual from thinking (and acting) as an individual, then the social cancer begins to proliferate. And nothing but a purification of language can check its spread. Bentham knew this but he couldn't break through the hedge.

The problem, the danger, is the subtlety of the disease. You cannot put your finger on any single word or type of word and say, "Here, look at this chancre!" For ossification operates through groupings, through usage-fixed associations, which are ultimately, in the back of the brain, controlled, I think, by sound. You can picture the whole process of educative assimilation as the building up of sound tracks in the under mind. We can derail ourselves by attention. It is the general inattention through innocence which is responsible for the condition.

Bentham's remedy was simply redefinition. "Phraseoplerosis," he called it. Trace every fictional entity to its material basis, he said, and abuse becomes impossible. But Bentham didn't have to deal with the universal diffusion of print. The groupings were not then indelibly engraved in every mentality by constant repetition. Today the situation is worse and the physic must be proportionately more drastic.

If every grade school teacher could suddenly, like Saul on the road to Damascus, be struck with the light. . . . If at the same time each could be implemented with enough intelligence and invention to teach language as it has never been taught before, to teach the children every subject from a linguistic axis. . . . If every horse wore gold shoes which were cast before every doorstep. . . .

But in the realm of possibility—what we can do now is to support Basic English and experimental writing and practise as much personal verbal chastity as possible (in which I am afraid I set a very bad example!).

Basic English has a distinct national as well as an international value, of which I am sure its backers are aware. Its method of word selection stems from Bentham, and although it cannot turn English into an ideographic language where the material-metaphorical origin of every sign is *visible* in its structure, it can, by its limitation of the vocabulary and simplified syntax, shatter the old sound tracks to pieces. As Ezra Pound has already said, you can be reasonably sure that a "philosopher" is really a philosopher and not another unwitting logodaedalist if he can make his ideas substantial in Basic.

Experimental writing—supposing some circulation for it—is of even greater value in that it attacks more radically the visual and conceptual fronts of the congealed associations as well as the oral one. In this light, it becomes a patriotic duty to read a little Stein now and again, much as it may bore you, simply to physic your sluggish mental intestine. I have made some interesting experiments with Stein texts as verbal cathartics on disinterested subjects. Ten average individuals were asked to write a short paragraph on some such nonmaterial subject as "Religion and the State"; they were then asked to read Stein for ten minutes; then asked to write on the same subject again without consulting their previous effort. The results were all alike—a marked decrease in the use of stereotyped and stock phrases, a greater directness of style.

I believe then, that experimental writing has a real social value, apart from any other. And it is with this in mind that this collection is published at this time. For however my contributors may see themselves I see them as agents of social reform as well as artists. Their propaganda is implicit in their style and in probably every case (originally, at least) unconscious. For their protection I must make it very clear that in this preface I am speaking for myself alone. I hope that they will find themselves in sympathy with my views, but it was not on this basis that the selection of material was made. If I have *used* them I hope it has not been to a degree which transcends the critic's accepted privilege. Their points of departure and immediate objectives are various, but all have a similar ultimate aim—the perfection of a clearer, richer, more meaningful verbal expression.

The Cocteau "Mystère Laic" (in the brilliant translation by the violinist Olga Rudge) is republished because it did not attract at the time of first American publication in "Pagany" the attention which it deserved and because nothing has since appeared from any other hand to supersede its method as the most significant new direction in the technique of criticism of our time. Cocteau's Indirect Criticism is the gravestone of the Polite Paragraph of the preceding century. Pound has adjusted the technique to the requirements of criticism in the social sciences. The impact is that of a short jab to the chin.

Montagu O'Reilly is in close touch with "orthodox" Parisian Surrealism, but Lorine Niedecker is not. She lives in Wisconsin and her ideas are all her own. Among her most interesting experiments were the poems written on three levels of consciousness which appeared about a year ago in the Wilson-Drummond "Westminster" Anthology. Henry Miller, who is extremely versatile, uses Surrealism as part of his repertoire. He is the author of the book which a number of competent judges think the best and an equal number the worst of the past few years: "Tropic of Cancer" is published by the Obelisk Press in Paris and cannot be imported into the United States. In my estimation Miller is the most vivid of living American writers.

Miss Stein is probably more alive to sclerosis of language than any other writer in this collection. Language decay, and not Cubist painting, was the catalyst to her lonely and valourous career. It is to her, through my analyses of her work, that I owe the inception of the train of thought which culminates in this preface, which is, in turn, a partial sketch of the chapter on language in my book *Understanding Gertrude Stein* which is now in progress. "A Waterfall And A Piano" represents a new "period" in Miss Stein's anabasis.

The prototype of Kay Boyle's short-short form is, of course, that of Hemingway's interludes in *In Our Time*, which were published alone under that title by the Three Mountains Press. I have it on second hand that Dr. Hemingstein had great profit of its exercise, and on first hand that Miss Boyle found it very unsatisfactory to write in any other once it was mastered. It is by the kindness of Mr. Charles Pearce that the stories from *365 Days* are reprinted.

It remains only to be said that I consider the metric of my own verse tentative, and that it is always a delight to quote to embattled Georgians who protest the novelty of Mr. Cummings' typography the line of Father Ennius written ca. 200 B.C.:

"saxo cere comminuit brum."

I expect that *all* of my contributors would like to do the same to me!

—*James Laughlin IV*

NEW DIRECTIONS

in

Prose and Poetry

———

Edited by
James Laughlin IV

NEW DIRECTIONS
NORFOLK, CT.
1936

CONTENTS

A Little Treasury of Modern Poetry (1946)

Edited by Oscar Williams

INTRODUCTION

I

I think England has had more good poets from 1900 to the present day than during any period of the same length since the early seventeenth century.

W. B. Yeats

If we include in the list of good poets both the American and the English, the modern period shows itself resplendent in its wealth of poetry. So I have decided to call this collection of modern poetry a *treasury*, although that word connotes such riches that it has been applied before only to anthologies that draw their selections from centuries. I have taken the poems here included mostly from the time between 1896, the year of the publication of A. E. Housman's *Shropshire Lad,* and the present, a short fifty years, yet so abundant, not only in the number of its poetic techniques and subject matters, that it rivals any preceding century.

Perhaps variety is exactly its chief characteristic. Former periods have had a discernible prevailing poetic attitude and a permissible kind of poetic subject matter. We have achieved limitless freedom of choice as to subject matter: anything that can be thought or talked about is acceptable as material for poems. And the range of what educated and sensitive persons do think and talk about would not too long ago have seemed incredible. Awareness has been sharpened by knowledge of all geographical *loci,* has been broadened by the study of the literatures and customs of all nations, has been intensified by knowledge of depth psychology and kept sensitized by the incessant impact of those emotions inevitable when life is uncertain and tragic through war and the nature-disturbing activities of the scientists. We have not only been taught by the cultures of all past societies, in which sense we are great inheritors, but we have also had forced upon our vision innumerable vistas of possible new environments, choosing among which coerces us into being the arbiters of the future.

Certainly this extension of influences, material, and conflicts, has been a stimulus to the development of good poets.

Also, the desuetude of nineteenth century materialism, with its obverse of belief in "progress," a philosophy so narrow that it imposed a mental stricture upon imagination which even poets could not escape, has brought about a freer and more truthful manipulation of ideas. The central attitude of science has, ever since its rise to power, positively affected all contemporary attitudes, even of those who deny scientific values. So that, when science itself swung round to at least an oblique recognition of the non-material mysteries of life, the essentially spiritual art of poetry could flourish less self-consciously. It is now possible for a truth-respecting poet to admit the validity of much scientific discovery without denying the mysterious realities.

In fact, certain scientific data have become material which the poet can comfortably use. Devices which have evolved from an understanding of the new psychology are part of modern poetic equipment, and may, in some measure, add to the effectiveness of a poem which, if written by a poet of like calibre in the nineteenth century, would have been of little interest. And, whatever we may think of the end results of science, we must admit that scientific method, both logical and empirical, has contributed to literary craftsmanship by way of its influence upon recent literary criticism. Extraordinary advances in critical method make the inspection of a poem today by a first-class critic as close and careful as a chemical analysis. Poets read, practice, and write in the light of this severe and agile examination, with the result that contemporary minor poetry, at least, has reached an unprecedented high of quality.

Of course this observation upon the general production of verse does not hold for the work of major poets. In any age the major poet acts as though by revelation, in strict conformance to the truth of life, which is his base, no matter how his form may depend upon tradition. He does not have to wait for any formulation of the fundamentals of depth psychology in order to use its reality in his work. It is not by accident that the Œdipus Complex derives its name from the work of an ancient poet. The vital perception of a major poet makes all his discoveries of the future with an urgent immediacy and contrives from them the theme of his poems, which he produces as by an act of nature. An insight which the poet considers only structural material incidental to the integral whole of his poem is, for the scientist, a discovery upon the exposition of which he may expend the energies of a lifetime.

In our time, all that is extrovert is worshipped; therefore the scientist has a numerous following; the poet is revealed to a diminishing few. Nevertheless, though the audience diminishes, this century has had, and now has living, an astonishing number of good poets. Of major poets it may have produced no more than has any other like number of years. But all good poetry is not the work of major poets alone. A fair percentage of the finest English poetry has sprung from minor poets. When I say "minor" I mean neither impostors nor poetasters; I mean good poets who have either not managed to produce in quantity or who have not had great individual influence upon the main stream of English literature.

The major poet is almost always a technical innovator, the minor poet utilizes devices already evolved but, in their use, creates poems distinctly his own and thus distinctly valuable. I have included many such poems by minor poets because they seem to me to represent their period, as well as being in themselves, as poems, effective.

II

. . . people are exasperated by poetry which they do not understand, and contemptuous of poetry which they understand without effort . . .
                                                    T. S. Eliot

Readers' objections to verse are various. Not long ago the use of "unpoetic" subject matter was decried; I doubt if many people are left who raise this particular objection. But there is still a rather considerable, and especially vociferous, group who are angered by texturally loaded and technically or semantically complex poetry. They impugn it on the ground of obscurity, *i.e.*, their own inability to understand it. It would not be important to take notice of these objectors were it not that they have, firstly, gotten the bulk of the attention which the popular press gives to poetry, and, secondly, that many of them, if they could be persuaded to do some attentive reading of good verse and good crit-

icism, would quickly lose their hasty prejudice and discover the exhilaration that competently read complex poetry might give them.

Poetry is an art that yields its effects to those who are educated in reading it. Skill is almost as essential in reading as in writing. I have often noticed that the loudest in declaiming against the best of our contemporary poets are those who have, in the main, confined their reading of Shakespeare to the Sonnets, of the great English lyric poetry to *The Golden Treasury* and the Victorians, while their inspection of American poetry has been limited to Whitman (and his many imitators) and the Imagists (minus Pound). As to any kind of analysis of poems, they are ignorant. They have never heard of the excellent criticism available which might make them aware of what values to look for in a poem. I have included in this collection several poems sure to irritate this group, but I can assure them that their irritation will give way to pleasure if they will gather up their tolerance and courage and undergo a course of reading of the best poets, old and new, and of the modern critics. They will discover, for instance, that a poet such as Dylan Thomas is not writing obscure private nonsense any more than did John Donne.

Readers who have already made the initial discoveries and are alert to the subtleties and bits of puzzle that a good poem has to offer, will, I am sure, find much in this *Little Treasury* to please them. Nevertheless, I have some fears that readers most eager to play the kind of game that Empson has to offer will not take kindly to certain of my choices. For I have also included poems very simple in meaning and treatment. Much as I respect the admirable jugglery of several components spun into perfect integration by a poem-maker alive at all points of the intellect as well as of the senses, my principal criterion for the choice of individual poems was such as admitted many different kinds of verse, whether from the point of view of content or form.

III

And I think that to transfuse emotion—not to transmit thought but to set up in the reader's sense a vibration corresponding to what was felt by the writer—is the peculiar function of poetry.
                                                    A. E. Housman

Whatever the magic of poetry, it exists in the realm of feeling. In that realm each poem has its own organic unity, obeying the laws of its own nature.

The natural laws of one poem may vary a good deal from those of another, just as the natural laws of the bee's organism are quite different from those of the cat's. Yet both move about in the same universe, each admirable and complete in its own way. One poem may have a higher kind of being than another, it may have more organs and thus function through a larger body of sensations. But, simple or complex, so long as it is not maimed by the lack of its own peculiar emotional unity, it is a poem.

So I made my basic rule for the choice of poems very simple: if a poem gave me that experience which I have learned comes as a reaction to reading a true poem, I included it, provided it conformed to my space limitation. In other words, I *felt* the poem. My limitations as to length were that most poems must be short, under seventy-five lines if possible, none more than one hundred-and-fifty lines long (with two exceptions to which I refer in the editorial note that follows this Introduction).

I am sorry that I cannot be explicit in expository terms as to what I mean when I say that I felt or experienced a certain work as a poem. In so far as I know, though many definitions have been offered, no one has ever made a definition of a poem that has been satisfactory to all of the best poets and critics. Some have spoken of their physiological reactions, such as a chill, a sensation in the chest or the pit of the stomach, *etc.*, others have used the term "aesthetic emotion" which, to my mind, is just calling the reaction by another name, others have gone very thoroughly into every detail of the poem's construction. But the mystery remains. Something beyond superior craftsmanship enters into the structure of a good poem, and in that something the magic is contained.

Also, opinions differ as to the meaning of "pure" poetry, or as to whether such an expression should be used at all. T. S. Eliot has written, ". . . indeed it might be said in our time, that the man who cannot enjoy Pope as poetry probably understands no poetry." On the other hand, Housman, while a great admirer of Pope, would not concede Pope's work or most of the work written in the eighteenth century to be "pure" poetry in the sense that Blake's is.

No two persons are likely to be equally stirred by all of any one list of poems. Every human being has a different complex of associations and will react more or less strongly to the vocabulary or imagery of a particular poet, in accordance with his own psychological nature. If he has critical acumen, he is likely to come pretty close to choosing, as genuine poetry, a majority of the poems that would be chosen by someone else of like acumen, but his rating of individual poems would be different. Some poems are more richly embellished as to vocabulary, images, phonetic cadences, and the like, while others may be salted with ideas, or ironical, or witty, undecorated and even "dry." One reader may prefer those poems which are romantic and rich in texture, another may look especially for excellences of form. The value of one poem may be predominantly that of its content, that of another of its form or its embellishment. The best poems are those in which form, texture and theme are all in perfect harmony. It is from these last that the reader is most likely to receive the emotional experience closest to that of the poet, or to what the poet intended.

IV

When we read Kipling we can usually say, "That is just how I feel." Of course there is nothing "wrong" with that, but, when we read a great poet, we say, "I never realized before what I felt. From now on, thanks to this poem, I shall feel differently."

W. H. Auden

Most of us are not given to accuracy when we formulate our thoughts about what we perceive or feel, and we perceive only a small fraction of the world about us, so intent are we upon the business of existence. But the poet is, by the peculiar usefulness of his nature, under a compulsion to be fully accurate in his medium of words when he puts into form his response to a concept or percept. This drive to accuracy causes him to explore the details of his theme and feel it completely as a whole. In the process, if he is a good poet, he clarifies in his poem something that has not been fully expressed before. This compelling need for precision also causes a condensation of thought and feeling which loads the poem with its emotional charge. The irrelevant and the expository are not to be found in poetry. The display of the poet is not an explanation or a description of a thing, it is the thing itself. He exhibits the tiger or the dove; he does not tell its habitat, its usefulness or its history, he allows the reader to see for himself what it is.

A poem which shows us a feeling that we have had before may be valuable in that it keeps the emotional faculty alive. As we learn to look for something better, we may outgrow poems like this, but they are a necessary state in our growth and their value for others is not impaired as we pass on to other poetic experiences. There are a few poems of this kind in this book. Since they at one time gave me enjoyment and enlightenment, and as I still realize them as emotional wholes, I have included them.

But the majority of the poems herein present their themes in such fashion as to show fresh ways of feeling or knowing, so they function as nourishment for the *growth* of emotional, or perceptual capacity. Some of them as, for example, The Waste Land, have had this effect not only upon readers as individuals, but upon our literary generation as a whole, thus affecting, and developing, the tradition of English poetry itself.

A poem of such magnitude is not quite the result of "inspiration," which is considered by some to be the only authentic source of poetry. Without the "divine fire" no man would be a poet; but without intellect no man would be a great poet. Nor can such a poem be read without the use of an intelligence to some degree comparable with that of the author. Some people object to the notion that the intellect should be called into operation at all during the reading of a poem. They have somehow acquired the idea that feeling and intellect are opposites. A little reflection will show that, on the contrary, emotion deepens when the intellect is aroused to action simultaneously with the feeling. You cannot feel anything unless your mind is brought to attention upon the idea of it, and the more definitely you think about it, the stronger your emotion is likely to be. For instance, if you hear of the death of a friend, you think of him; the clearer your concept of him, the more strongly you are likely to feel. If you at the same time begin to ask "Why did he die?" "How did he die?" "What did his life signify?" *etc.*, this very use of analytical thought will deepen your emotion. Thus it is with poetry. It has many devices for producing a clear emotional experience and those of the intellect are not the least significant.

V

The pleasure is the pleasure of powers that create a truth that cannot be arrived at by the reason alone, a truth that the poet recognizes by sensation. The morality of the poet's radiant and productive atmosphere is the morality of the right sensation.
                                                    Wallace Stevens

Most of what we may call "educated" humanity, while imbued with respect for science, neglects poetry, considering it not compatible with, or, at least, not directed by reality. Now reason is worthy of all respect, and is nowhere more respected than among poets. But any one avenue of reason may well become a rut. No one is more reasonable than the scientist, yet is he not a man who travels an undeviating road with such intentness on his direction that he loses the faculty of turning his head about to see the countryside? The poet knows that life is a whole commingled of reason, instinct and the objective world of *all* phenomena. He keeps it knit together by a spiritual understanding which is above reason, which it supervises through virtue of its ability to comprehend all, rather than one segment or function of life. Reason is a tool and not an accomplishment, a tool that the poet can on occasion use as well as the scientist. Because he is aware of life as a totality, the poet is closer to truth than the scientist and, above all, does surely the right thing at the same time.

The scientist discovers, reveals, invents, but is his invention ever produced at the right time in so far as humanity is concerned? If so, it is only by accident and not by insight of the scientist. Did radio appear at the exact moment when it would answer a need in the enrichment of the human mind? Or did atomic power? The one came before public taste was educated in the values of music, or was so trained in psychology that it could resist advertising, the other just in time to improve killing instead of leisure. No poet would so mistake his timing. The poet perceives, he has the right sensation for his hour and he articulates this sensation. Moreover, it is only when he is right for his time and communicates the essentials of his time that he is a true poet who will communicate to the ages.

Occasionally a poet seems to come too early; he represents not his own time but a later one. This might be said of Gerard Manley Hopkins, who is included in this anthology because he was first published in 1918, and has had a profound influence upon poets since that year. Hopkins was born in 1844, as was Robert Bridges, who outlived him by more than forty years. It is to the latter that we owe the miraculous fortune of Hopkins' publication.

From Hopkins' concentrated style we receive a terrific charge of emotion fused with a religious content which had long been lacking in poetry. The advent of this major poetry has, in its effect upon younger poets, extended the resources of poetic technique. But its impetus to new directions in English poetry has been greater than that: the younger poets have learned a lesson in the admixture of intelligence with fully expressed emotion, a lesson badly needed. And no less was Hopkins' kind of feeling needed by mankind at that time, and all through the twentieth century. The pity is that mankind rarely has an appetite for what it needs. I doubt if Hopkins really wrote ahead of his time. It was at the precise moment when he was writing his poetry that, had it been accepted by its proper audience, it would have produced the fullest effect. The almost blank period between 1900 and 1910 would have been a little fuller, and the stance of the Georgians would have been less titwillowy.

There is a relation between the state of society and the poet's poem, there is a relationship between the contemporary poet and the contemporary reader, which is exactly right. If people had learned earlier to expose themselves to poetry undoubtedly we should not now be accustomed to contemplating the end of the world as imminent. (Thanks to the atomic bomb today's poets may end the tradition, so they had better be read now.) For the poet is always on the side of life; consistent readers of poetry are also on the side of life. When a poet promulgates the sensuous pleasures he is no less moral than when he paints the hope of heaven, or reveals the truth of tragedy. To be on the side of life is to be moral.

VI

Poetry . . . is the supreme form of EMOTIVE *language.*

I. A. Richards

The direct intensity of Hopkins' passion was set into verse before most of the other poems in this anthology were written. Such utterance as his was impossible to poets who wrote between his time and the nineteen-thirties. Feeling was not rushed forth in such a way as to take us by storm. Hardy's realism, Bridges' deliberation, Edith Sitwell's artifacts (in America, Marianne Moore's syllabic patterns and Wallace Stevens' colorful irony) had not this kind of direct expression. Both the Georgians with their claim of writing from pure feeling and the Imagists with theirs of recording pure percepts, seem to us now not to have expressed emotion at all. The poetry of Wilfred Owen, another innovator of major importance, releases the impact of its feeling with a kind of delayed action. It is not until the advent in the middle 'thirties of such poets as George Barker and Dylan Thomas that we find emotion again released immediately and directly.

In Hart Crane there is, however, a rising curve of such release.

We can now clearly see the mounting graph of intensity as it passed through the poetry of the first half of the twentieth century, nourished by increments of the intelligence, which presents the issues of reality, and of the creative imagination, which expands the sensibility. This increase and this clarification are exemplified in the work of a single poet, W. B. Yeats, who was born in 1865 and lived to 1939. Yeats' verse began with the weakly esotericism of the 'nineties and developed to a full expression of the poetic strength of his period, a period when poetry took cognizance, for the first time in the history of that period, of the whole situation of mankind as well as of individual experience.

Oddly enough the round outflow of direct passion seems to have become again possible to poets in general only after the development of the other, and greater, new impetus given to poetry in our time. This new direction was, of course, that given by T. S. Eliot, to whom twentieth-century literature is so greatly indebted, not only for poetry of the very first order, but also for criticism without which we cannot help feeling we should be as though blind. Mr. Eliot made poets and readers alike aware of the fundamental importance of intelligence in both the making and appraisal of poems. Ezra Pound helped to sharpen the wits and scholarship of talented poets. But, except upon the highly gifted few, the knowledge of Eliot's and Pound's complexity might well have had the stultifying effect of drying up the juices of feeling by an overdose of erudition. Hopkins' influence has balanced this tendency without reducing respect for intelligence. It would be almost impossible for minor verse so devoid of real values as that of the Georgians to "get by" today.

My belief that the motional unity of a poem is of primary importance determined the arrangement of this anthology. I might have put the poems in chronological order, which might be called an historical arrangement. Instead I have placed them according to theme, such as Mortality, Love, War, *etc.* Readers interested in placing each poet in time will find his dates listed in the Index of Authors, those wanting to see at a glance any particular poet's representation will find it in the same index. Any one poet may have several poems scattered throughout the book, but I believe that in a volume designed as this one is, for easy carrying about and use at odd moments, it is more convenient to have the poems divided in such a way that the reader can quickly find a poem to fit his mood or the pleasure of the moment, than to have them arranged more matter-of-factly.

The intention behind using the running-heads, with their classification into emotional divisions, was not to bundle individual poems together as if they were chapters of a story about the theme, but simply to place them in proximity. It is, of course, impossible to pass from one poem to the next as if each continued the same thought as the one preceding it. Every poem makes its own entity of its own internal factors, without relation to any other poem. To read along instantaneously from one to the next would be to amputate the magic of the first and be blunt to the magic of the second.

VII

The rhetorician would deceive his neighbors,
The sentimentalist himself; while art
Is but a vision of reality.

                              W. B. Yeats

Without doubt some readers will miss some poems which they like, or have been taught to admire, and object to their omission. I may say bluntly that there are some poets whom I consider spurious in spite of their having achieved a full measure of popularity or of acceptance by the schools. Sham poems do not deserve to lie alongside the pages graced by the real thing. If any such have slipped past my guard I do not know it.

The poetasters and the sentimentalists are always with us; serious readers are not likely to be deceived by them. But even competent critics are occasionally taken in by the skilful rhetorician. The term "academic" is generally applied to work easy to spot from its very dullness. However, the true academic is that literary figure who confuses his contemporaries by displaying a mock talent wrapped in the cellophane of rhetoric that obeys all the rules, even to the simulation of the faults of the best poets. But a watchful eye can spy the academic no matter how quick his leap into the devices of the great. Even if he is as fast as Superman there are a few simple characteristics of the careerist that cannot be hidden. He absorbs the most talked about traits of a model. Then he adds characteristics from this great poet and that (provided always that the poets he imitates are those most recently lauded), patches out a style for himself and achieves a career by the same strategy that men in other fields achieve careers by. This academic is the most subtle and dangerous of the enemies of art.

He penetrates everywhere, since he is an accomplished salesman of his personality; his line is almost erudite and his morals lacking in the one essential morality of the real poet: the kind of honesty that can understand its own heart. The academic is likely to know everything there is to know about poetry except its essence; his critical acumen consists in waiting until he hears another voice recommending.

Good poets have their influences and models, true, but of these they make a distinctive integer; the academic borrows without respecting. Appropriating someone else's possession is not the same thing as endeavoring to model oneself after another man's admired character. Nor does the rhetorician present us with simple pastiche; he flourishes something slicker than that: it shines but has no heat, the dress is stolen but worn with such effrontery you might think it is his own. I have done my best to keep this imposter out of good company.

Other omissions I have made upon the ground that certain writings look like poetry, have passed as poetry, but are demonstrably not so; among their authors are certain members of past "schools," the Imagists, *etc.* A few poets, whom I willingly concede to be genuine since they have had the right effect upon people whose sensitivity I respect, I myself have been unable to "feel" and so could not persuade myself to include.

As I have said above, many long poems of importance are not in the collection. If the design of this anthology were to represent the stature and range of the most significant modern poets, an altogether different kind of book would have resulted. In order to fully represent Eliot and Yeats, for instance, I should have had to include Eliot's later work (some of *The Four Quartets*) as well as his earlier, and Yeats' earlier work along with his later. Many of the excellent short pieces by minor figures would have had to be dropped, and relatively few names would make up the contents.

So this *Little Treasury* is not a means of expressing my opinion upon the comparative statures of the poets of the twentieth century. The stricture of shortness in number of lines would, of itself, prevent the amount of page representation of any one poet from being an indication of my evaluation of his rank. And even if I should have the temerity to make such an evaluation, it would remain one man's opinion. A perfect judge would have to be a keen and unprejudiced critic with pre-knowledge of the standards of posterity. I am not so prophetic, and never unprejudiced; my judgments are always arrived at through the medium of my own taste, *i.e.*, what I am activated into liking.

VIII

It is a fact that both an epic and a limerick are poems . . . You can only distinguish in them differences of effect and quality.

Geoffrey Grigson

Now I like high and serious poetry to such a degree that I cannot imagine life worth living without it, but for that very reason I like light verse also: it is poetry at play. It is significant that so important a poet as Auden should have found it well within his concept of poetry to write light verse. Indeed, a considerable body of his writing has been in this category. No one can completely understand the character of poetry unless he sees it in all its aspects, just as he cannot understand a friend unless he sees him having fun as often as he sees him serious. Our century has not been an easy one and its hard circumstances are reflected in the fact that the percentage of light verse of quality which it has produced is small, and the percentage of serious verse, large. Yet we have had enough of it, I believe, to warrant my inclusion of a section of this poetry at play.

Exactly what makes a poem "light" is hard to define, but I shall give some of my own thoughts about the matter. Light verse might be defined quite as, in drama, comedy is defined, as a form which takes the accepted social *mores* for granted, a means of expression that gives a sense of security because it never lets in the notion of that outer chaos and questionability of fundamental axioms which tragedy presents.

Light verse is not necessarily funny or entertaining; it can have a serious content and purpose. It is play partly because it is very consciously constructed, but play is not always laughter-provoking, witness the football game. But it can be very funny indeed. It utilizes, to produce its effects, pun and satire, meter and nonsense, and other effective devices. Some light verse is farce and we enjoy it as such.

It is interesting to try and trace the methods which recur as a kind of principle in the making of such poetry. Light verse is written in a familiar, everyday kind of speech. It often makes outrageous statements in the off-hand tone of a housewife discussing the most commonplace details of daily life. For instance,

Billy, in one of his nice new sashes,
*   Fell in the fire and was burned to ashes;*
Now, although the room grows chilly,
*   I haven't the heart to poke poor Billy.*

In "Billy," the announcement is made that the child met a horrible death and the poet goes on with the most matter-of-fact, everyday air to comment on this tragedy as if not poking Billy's ashes were on the same level as giving him a piece of candy. "I haven't the heart to refuse him." But this quatrain is "light" also because it shows, by the very point it makes in showing that it is nonsense, complete agreement with our social *mores*, in this instance that it is so bad a crime to kill or be callous to children that even to think of such a thing is funny. The ancients who exposed unwanted babies to die would not have considered this thought nonsense.

The same principle is behind the funniness of Miss Twye (page 607). If our women were accustomed to taking their baths in mixed company, which they say is a Japanese custom, the point of the situation would not exist, even if the matter-of-fact tone were present.

We are also amused by over-emphasis of the trivial or by under-emphasis of the large. I have included curses, tirades, satires and other poems that illustrate this principle. When we hear Pound curse out the rain, we enjoy having the weather get the attention that it wouldn't get if we really were the noble creatures we sometimes like to think ourselves. So much rage at a little discomfort makes us smile over the fallibility of humans. When we hear ANON. discuss the merits of being either a rooster or a crow with the absolute assumption that he might become either with the seriousness of a man choosing a career, it is the attitude more than the homely speech that furnishes the fun.

IX

To maintain gaiety at a definite level of taste is as difficult and requires as much composed unity of approach and as mature an attitude towards the material as is required to maintain fury or disgust . . . Gaiety, and especially gaiety in finished form, is the last thing to be caught in a formula of facility . . .

R. P. Blackmur

But, even in light verse, not every attempt that follows the rules is poetry. Light verse may be written more by wit and cynicism than by inspiration, yet the point it makes and the style it dons must be in agreement, the joke or flavor sharp enough to retain its freshness and please a quick mind. Children are fond of puns, no matter what, but adults will not tolerate bad ones.

There is a certain kind of ostensibly funny rhyming which is generally referred to as "society" verse. It is favored by newspapers and the lay public that likes to try its hand at stanzaic humor. Some of its prototypes have been good, Gilbert is an example. I have avoided most of this material because it exercises neither the mind nor the funny bone. One imperative of humor is to engage the mind. In Ogden Nash's

> *Candy*
> *Is dandy*
> *But liquor*
> *Is quicker*

the reader must complete the thought for himself. So too in *Head and Heart* by C. D. B. Ellis. It is not enough for the rhymes themselves to be funny. Neither does the use of dialect or slang constitute genuinely humorous poetry.

A few readers may object to my placing certain poems in the light, instead of the serious, verse section. But a little thought about each will give them the clue as to why I did so. The poems which comment upon the social scene may especially seem to them not of proper content for this classification. But it is the poet's rôle to speak for the issues of the day in whatever tone he finds fitting; the greater the range of tones, the more fully will poetry perform this one of its functions.

X

> *. . . no one comes so near the invisible world as the sage and the poet, unless it be the saint—who is but one spirit with God, and so infinitely closer to Him than anyone. I also point out the benefits men receive from poetry. Though in themselves of no help to the attainment of eternal life, art and poetry are more necessary than bread to the human race. They fit it for the life of the spirit.*
>
> Jacques Maritain

The majority of mankind today knows nothing of poetry, the name for them means hifalutin doggerel. The educated minority is, during school days, exposed to poetry instead of being inoculated with it. For this art is neither an extraneous growth upon the pragmatic activity which has become so universally synonymous with existence, nor an obsolete organ like the appendix. On the contrary, it is the ichor which man's spiritual nature secretes

for the purpose of healing the kind of wounds from which we today suffer. Just as medical science used to make the mistake of draining off the very blood needed to restore health, modern society is ever busy trying to dry up the real essence of the arts, because their usefulness has been forgotten and not rediscovered.

The poet has a high and responsible position to fill in the complex of society. Humanity's ignorance of this necessity, and some others, has directly led to the terrible distortion of the whole social mechanism, which is so misdirected that its energies rush to the end of universal murder instead of maintaining the precise balance of natural and enjoyable living for all. Almost perfunctory statements of alarm over the use of the atomic bomb barely conceal a fundamental indifference to its threat, or what must follow from the fulfillment of that threat. All the elaborate inventiveness of man has been turned to manipulation of the inanimate; human emotions would have responded as miraculously to a like well-developed technique of expansion and control.

Poetry explores the possibilities of emotion, couples its niceties with thought, and thereby creates a kind of discipline for the whole man, not neglecting his physical nature. And poetry is made by the poet, much more definitively made by an individual man than any other product, except those of the other arts. Presidents and scientists are honored although they function only as part of a group, and their product is ephemeral in that it is sure to be quickly replaced by a better. This is probably because the apparent benefits received from politicians and scientists need only be accepted, the salutary delights of poetry must be worked for if the reader is to have them. The poet is doing enough to prepare the way for the millennium. He mitigates none of his own suffering, as he refuses no labor, to bring up, from what today is an abyss not pleasant to enter, the poems that would nourish man back to fullness of health.

XI

> *The world grown wiser is its wisdom gone. The machines are working but we have lost the arts. Our degradation spreads along the winds. There is no corner of the world that is not sullied with our news.*
>
> Sacheverell Sitwell

But, unless the human heart can cleanse itself faster than the laboratory can manufacture its hell-fire, it is now too late. Eyes trained to mere spectacle are not attracted by the sunny landscape of the spirit but find the sun more dazzling in the absolute of an atomic explosion. Almost no rôles except those of Jeremiah and Cassandra are left to saint and poet, and even they must be played in the wings. The audience insists upon chief actors who are senseless enough to perform a cataclysm.

However we must continue to set life into form. Readers of poetry, no less than its makers, have an urgent task: to create a focus of understanding. Since with God all things are possible, poets and readers in unison may still work their own miracle by which the human heart may yet so enlarge that it outweighs the atomic bomb.

—Oscar Williams

Contents

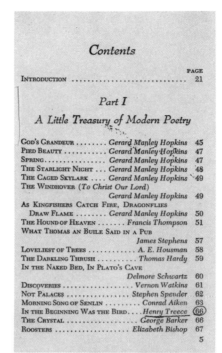

Contents

Contents

Contents

Contents

Contents (cont.) for A Little Treasury of Modern Poetry, English and American

Contents

Contents

Contents

Contents

Contents

Part II

*A Little Treasury of
Modern Light Verse*

Contents (cont.) for A Little Treasury of Modern Poetry, English and American

Books for Further Reading

Ackroyd, Peter. *Notes for a New Culture: An Essay on Modernism.* New York: Barnes & Noble, 1976.

Aiken, Conrad. *A Reviewer's ABC: Collected Criticism of Conrad Aiken from 1916 to the Present.* New York: Meridian Books, 1958.

Aiken. *Scepticisms: Notes on Contemporary Poetry.* New York: Knopf, 1919.

Aiken. *Ushant: An Essay.* New York: Duell, Sloan & Pearce/Boston: Little, Brown, 1952.

Aldington, Richard. *Life for life's Sake: A Book of Reminiscences.* New York: Viking, 1941.

Alvarez, A. *The Shaping Spirit: Studies in Modern English and American Poets.* London: Chatto & Windus, 1958.

Anderson, Margaret. *My Thirty Years' War: the Autobiography: Beginnings and Battles to 1930.* New York: Covici-Friede, 1930.

Antheil, George. *Bad Boy of Music.* Garden City: Doubleday, Doran, 1945.

Baker, Houston A., Jr. *Blues, Ideology, and Afro-American Literature: A Vernacular Theory.* Chicago: University of Chicago Press, 1984.

Bardolph, Richard. *The Negro Vanguard.* New York: Rinehart, 1959.

Barnard, Mary. *Assault on Mount Helicon: A Literary Memoir.* Berkeley: University of California Press, 1984.

Beach, Sylvia. *Shakespeare and Company.* New York: Harcourt, Brace, 1959.

Beer, Thomas. *The Mauve Decade: American Life at the End of the Nineteenth Century.* New York: Knopf, 1926.

Berman, Marshall. *All That is Solid Melts into Air: The Experience of Modernity.* New York: Simon & Schuster, 1982.

Bigsby, C. W. E., ed. *The Black American Writer,* volume 2, *Poetry and Drama.* De Land, Fla.: Everett Edwards, 1969.

Blackmur, R. P. *Anni Mirabiles, 1921-1925: Reason in the Madness of Letters.* Washington, D.C.: Library of Congress, 1956.

Blackmur. *Language as Gesture: Essays in Poetry.* New York: Harcourt, Brace, 1952.

Bogan, Louise. *Achievement in American Poetry, 1900-1950.* Chicago: Regnery, 1951.

Bogan. *Selected Criticism: Prose, Poetry.* New York: Noonday, 1955.

Bontemps, Arna, ed. *The Harlem Renaissance Remembered.* New York: Dodd, Mead, 1972.

Bornstein, George. *Transformations of Romanticism in Yeats, Eliot and Stevens.* Chicago: Chicago University Press, 1976.

Borroff, Marie. *Language and the Poet: Verbal Artistry in Frost, Stevens, and Moore.* Chicago: University of Chicago Press, 1979.

Bradbury, John M. *The Fugitives: A Critical Account.* Chapel Hill: University of North Carolina Press, 1958.

Bradbury. *Renaissance in the South: A Critical History of the Literature.* Chapel Hill: University of North Carolina Press, 1963.

Bradbury, Malcolm, and James McFarlane, eds. *Modernism.* Harmondsworth, U.K.: Penguin, 1976.

Brawley, Benjamin G. *The Negro in Literature and Art,* second revised edition. New York: Duffield, 1929.

Bronz, Stephen H. *Roots of Negro Racial Consciousness: The 1920's. Three Harlem Renaissance Authors.* New York: Libra, 1964.

Brooks, Cleanth. *Modern Poetry and the Tradition.* Chapel Hill: University of North Carolina Press, 1939.

Brooks, Gladys. *If Strangers Meet: A Memory.* New York: Harcourt, Brace & World, 1967.

Brooks, Van Wyck. *Scenes and Portraits: Memories of Childhood and Youth.* New York: Dutton, 1954.

Brown, Sterling A. *Negro Poetry and Drama.* Washington, D.C.: Associates in Negro Folk Education, 1937.

Bruns, Gerald L. *Modern Poetry and the Idea of Language. A Critical and Historical Study.* New Haven: Yale University Press, 1974.

Bryher (Winifred Ellerman). *The Heart to Artemis: A Writer's Memoirs.* New York: Harcourt, Brace & World, 1962.

Burke, Kenneth. *Counterstatement.* Berkeley: University of California Press, 1968.

Butcher, Margaret Just. *The Negro in American Culture: Based on Materials Left by Alain Locke.* New York: Knopf, 1956.

Butterfield, R. W., ed. *Modern American Poetry.* Totowa, N.J.: Barnes & Noble, 1984.

Cambon, Glauco. *The Inclusive Flame: Studies in Modern American Poetry.* Bloomington: Indiana University Press, 1963.

Christ, Carol T. *Victorian & Modern Poetics.* Chicago: University of Chicago Press, 1984.

Clearfield, Andrew M. *These Fragments I Have Shored: Collage and Montage in Early Modernist Poetry.* Ann Arbor: UMI Research Press, 1984.

Coffman, Stanley K., Jr. *Imagism: A Chapter for the History of Modern Poetry.* Norman: University of Oklahoma Press, 1951.

Cook, Albert. *Prisms: Studies in Modern Literature.* Bloomington: Indiana University Press, 1967.

Cork, Richard. *Vorticism and Abstract Art in the First Machine Age,* 2 volumes. Berkeley: University of California Press, 1976.

Cowan, Louise. *The Fugitive Group: A Literary History.* Baton Rouge: Louisiana State University Press, 1959.

Cowley, Malcolm. *The Dream of the Golden Mountains: Remembering the 1930s.* New York: Viking, 1980.

Cowley. *Exile's Return: A Literary Odyssey of the 1920's,* revised edition. New York: Viking, 1951.

Cowley, ed. *Writers at Work: The Paris Review Interviews,* series 1. New York: Viking, 1958.

Crosby, Caresse. *The Passionate Years.* New York: Dial, 1953.

Cunard, Nancy. *These Were the Hours: Memories of My Hours Press, Réanville and Paris, 1928-1931,* edited by Hugh Ford. Carbondale & Edwardsville: Southern Illinois University Press, 1969.

Davenport, Guy. *The Geography of the Imagination: Forty Essays.* San Francisco: North Point Press, 1981.

Davidson, Donald, ed. *Fugitives: An Anthology of Verse.* New York: Harcourt, Brace, 1928.

Davie, Donald. *The Poet in the Imaginary Museum. Essays of Two Decades.* Manchester: Carcanet Press, 1977.

Davis, Arthur P. *From the Dark Tower: Afro-American Writers 1900-1960.* Washington, D.C.: Howard University Press, 1974.

Dembo, L. S. *Conceptions of Reality in Modern American Poetry.* Berkeley: University of California Press, 1966.

Deutsch, Babette. *Poetry in our Time: A Critical Survey of Poetry in the English-Speaking World 1900 to 1960,* revised and enlarged edition. Garden City: Doubleday, 1963.

Deutsch. *This Modern Poetry.* New York: Norton, 1935.

Donoghue, Denis. *Connoisseurs of Chaos: Ideas of Order in Modern American Poetry.* New York: Macmillan, 1965.

Donoghue. *Seven American Poets from MacLeish to Nemerov. An Introduction.* Minneapolis: University of Minnesota Press, 1975.

Duffey, Bernard. *The Chicago Renaissance in American Letters: A Critical History.* East Lansing: Michigan State College Press, 1954.

Ehrenpreis, Irwin, ed. *American Poetry.* Stratford-Upon-Avon Studies, no. 7. London: Arnold, 1973.

Eliot, T. S. *The Sacred Wood: Essays on Poetry and Criticism.* London: Methuen, 1920.

Eliot. *Selected Essays, 1917-1932.* London: Faber & Faber, 1932.

Ellman, Richard. *Eminent Domain: Yeats among Wilde, Joyce, Pound, Eliot and Auden.* New York: Oxford University Press, 1967.

Ellman, and Charles Feidelson, Jr., eds. *The Modern Tradition: Backgrounds of Modern Literature.* New York: Oxford University Press, 1965.

Emanuel, James A., and Theodore L. Gross, eds. *Dark Symphony: Negro Literature in America.* New York: Free Press, 1968.

Feder, Lillian. *Ancient Myth in Modern Poetry.* Princeton: Princeton University Press, 1971.

Fender, Stephen. *The American Long Poem: An Annotated Selection.* London: Arnold, 1977.

Fitch, Noel Riley. *Sylvia Beach and the Lost Generation: A History of Literary Paris in the Twenties and Thirties.* New York: Norton, 1983.

Fletcher, John Gould. *Life Is My Song: The Autobiography of John Gould Fletcher.* New York & Toronto: Farrar & Rinehart, 1937.

Ford, Hugh. *Published in Paris: American and British Writers, Printers, and Publishers in Paris, 1920-1939.* New York: Macmillan, 1975.

Ford, ed. *The Left Bank Revisited. Selections from the Paris Tribune, 1917-1934.* University Park & London: Pennsylvania State University Press, 1972.

Forrest-Thomson, Veronica. *Poetic Artifice: A Theory of Twentieth-Century Poetry.* Manchester: Manchester University Press, 1978.

Foster, Richard. *The New Romantics: A Reappraisal of the New Criticism.* Bloomington: Indiana University Press, 1962.

Fowlie, Wallace. *The Clown's Grail: a Study of Love in its Literary Expression.* London: Dobson, 1948; republished as *Love in Literature: Studies in Symbolic Expression.* Bloomington: Indiana University Press, 1965.

Frank, Joseph. *The Widening Gyre: Crisis and Mastery in Modern Literature.* New Brunswick: Rutgers University Press, 1963.

Frankenberg, Lloyd. *Pleasure Dome: On Reading Modern Poetry.* Boston: Houghton Mifflin, 1949.

Fredman, Stephen. *Poet's Prose: The Crisis in American Verse.* Cambridge: Cambridge University Press, 1983.

French, Warren, ed. *The Thirties: Fiction, Poetry, Drama.* De Land, Fla.: Everett Edwards, 1967.

Frohock, W. M. *Strangers to This Ground: Cultural Diversity in Contemporary American Writing.* Dallas: Southern Methodist University Press, 1961.

Frye, Northrop. *The Modern Century.* Toronto: Oxford University Press, 1967.

Fussell, Edwin. *Lucifer in Harness: American Meter, Metaphor and Diction.* Princeton: Princeton University Press, 1973.

Gaines, James R. *Wit's End: Days and Nights of the Algonquin Round Table.* New York & London: Harcourt Brace Jovanovich, 1977.

Gayle, Addison, ed. *The Black Aesthetic.* Garden City: Doubleday, 1971.

Gayle, ed. *Black Expression: Essays by and about Black Americans in the Creative Arts.* New York: Weybright & Talley, 1969.

Gefin, Laszlo K. *Ideogram: History of a Poetic Method.* Austin: University of Texas Press, 1982.

Gibson, Donald B., ed. *Five Black Writers: Essays on Wright, Ellison, Baldwin, Hughes, and LeRoi Jones.* New York: New York University Press, 1970.

Gould, Jean. *American Women Poets: Pioneers of Modern Poetry.* New York: Dodd, Mead, 1980.

Greenbaum, Leonard. *The Hound and Horn: The History of a Literary Quarterly.* The Hague: Mouton, 1966.

Gregory, Horace, and Marya Zaturenska. *A History of American Poetry, 1900-1940.* New York: Harcourt, Brace, 1946.

Gross, Harvey, ed. *Sound and Form in Modern Poetry: A Study of Prosody from Thomas Hardy to Robert Lowell.* Ann Arbor: University of Michigan Press, 1964.

Guggenheim, Peggy. *Out of this Century: Confessions of an Art Addict.* New York: Universe Books, 1979.

Hall, Donald. *Remembering Poets: Reminiscences and Opinions.* New York, Hagerstown, San Francisco & London: Harper & Row, 1978.

Halpert, Stephen, and Richard Johns. *A Return to Pagany: The History, Correspondence, and Selections from a Little Magazine 1929-1932.* Boston: Beacon Press, 1969.

Hamburger, Michael. *The Truth of Poetry: Tensions in Modern Poetry from Baudelaire to the 1960s.* New York: Harcourt, Brace & World, 1970.

Hamovitch, Mitzi Berger, ed. *The Hound & Horn Letters.* Athens: University of Georgia Press, 1982.

Hansen, Harry. *Midwest Portraits: A Book of Memories and Friendships.* New York: Harcourt, Brace, 1923.

Harriman, Margaret. *The Vicious Circle: the Story of the Algonquin Round Table.* New York: Rinehart, 1951.

Hartman, Charles O. *Free Verse: An Essay on Prosody.* Princeton: Princeton University Press, 1980.

Hill, Herbert, ed. *Anger and Beyond: The Negro Writer in the United States.* New York: Harper & Row, 1966.

Hoffman, Frederick J. *The Twenties: American Writing in the Postwar Decade,* revised edition. New York: Collier, 1962.

Hoffman, Charles Allen, and Carolyn F. Ulrich. *The Little Magazine: A History and a Bibliography.* Princeton: Princeton University Press, 1946.

Hollander, John, ed. *Modern Poetry: Essays in Criticism.* London, Oxford & New York: Oxford University Press, 1968.

Huggins, Nathan. *Harlem Renaissance.* New York: Oxford University Press, 1971.

Hughes, Glenn. *Imagism and the Imagists: A Study in Modern Poetry.* Stanford: Stanford University Press, 1931.

Isaacs, J. *The Background of Modern Poetry.* London: Bell, 1951.

Jackson, Blyden, and Louis Rubin. *Black Poetry in America: Two Essays in Historical Interpretation.* Baton Rouge: Louisiana State University Press, 1974.

Jackson, Lears. *No Place of Grace: Antimodernism and the Transformation of American Culture, 1880-1920.* New York: Pantheon, 1981.

Janssens, G. A. M. *The American Literary Review: A Critical History, 1920-1950.* The Hague: Mouton, 1968.

Jarrell, Randall. *Poetry and the Age.* New York: Knopf, 1953.

Jarrell. *The Third Book of Criticism.* New York: Farrar, Straus & Giroux, 1969.

Johnson, Carol. *The Disappearance of Literature.* Amsterdam: Rodopi, 1980.

Johnson, W. R. *The Idea of Lyric: Lyric Modes in Ancient and Modern Poetry.* Berkeley: University of California Press, 1982.

Jones, Peter, ed. *Imagist Poetry.* Harmondsworth, U.K.: Penguin, 1972.

Joost, Nicholas. *Scofield Thayer and The Dial: An Illustrated History.* Carbondale & Edwardsville: Southern Illinois University Press, 1964.

Josephson, Matthew. *Life Among The Surrealists. A Memoir.* New York: Holt, Rinehart & Winston, 1962.

Juhasz, Suzanne. *Metaphor and the Poetry of Williams, Pound, and Stevens.* Lewisburg: Bucknell University Press, 1974.

Kenner, Hugh. *Gnomon: Essays on Contemporary Literature.* New York: McDowell Obolensky, 1958.

Kenner. *A Homemade World: The American Modernist Writers.* New York: Knopf, 1974.

Kenner. *The Pound Era.* Berkeley: University of California Press, 1971.

Kermode, Frank. *Continuities.* London: Routledge & Kegan Paul, 1968.

Kermode. *Puzzles and Epiphanies: Essays and Reviews, 1958-1961.* London: Routledge & Kegan Paul, 1962.

Kermode. *Romantic Image.* London: Routledge & Kegan Paul, 1957.

Kindilien, Carlin T. *American Poetry in the Eighteen Nineties: A Study of American Verse, 1890-1899.* Providence: Brown University Press, 1956.

Kramer, Dale. *Chicago Renaissance: the Literary Life in the Midwest, 1900-1930.* New York: Appleton-Century, 1966.

Kreymborg, Alfred. *Our Singing Strength: An Outline of American Poetry.* New York: Coward-McCann, 1929.

Kreymborg. *Troubadour: An Autobiography.* New York: Boni & Liveright, 1925.

Krieger, Murray. *The New Apologists for Poetry.* Bloomington: Indiana University Press, 1963.

Kronick, Joseph G. *American Poetics of History: From Emerson to the Moderns.* Baton Rouge: Louisiana State University Press, 1984.

Langbaum, Robert. *The Mysteries of Identity: A Theme in Modern Literature.* New York: Oxford University Press, 1977.

Langbaum. *The Poetry of Experience: The Dramatic Monologue in Modern Literary Tradition.* New York: Random House, 1957.

Langford, Richard E., and William E. Taylor, eds. *The Twenties: Poetry and Prose. 20 Critical Essays*. De Land, Fla.: Everett Edwards, 1966.

Locke, Alain. *Four Negro Poets*. New York: Simon & Schuster, 1927.

Loeb, Harold. *The Way It Was*. New York: Criterion, 1959.

Lowell, Amy. *Tendencies in Modern American Poetry*. New York: Macmillan, 1917.

Lutyens, David Bulwer. *The Creative Encounter*. London: Secker & Warburg, 1960.

MacLeish, Archibald. *Poetry and Experience*. Boston: Houghton Mifflin, 1960.

Mariani, Paul. *A Usable Past: Essays on Modern and Contemporary Poetry*. Amherst: University of Massachusetts Press, 1984.

Martz, Louis L. *The Poem of the Mind: Essays on Poetry, English and American*. New York: Oxford University Press, 1966.

Mazzaro, Jerome, ed. *Modern American Poetry: Essays in Criticism*. New York: McKay, 1970.

McAlmon, Robert. *Being Geniuses Together 1920-1930*, revised edition, with additional material by Kay Boyle. Garden City: Doubleday, 1968.

McMillan, Dougald. *Transition: The History of a Literary Era, 1927-1938*. New York: Braziller, 1976.

Mellow, James R. *Charmed Circle: Gertrude Stein & Company*. New York & Washington, D.C.: Praeger, 1974.

Miles, Josephine. *The Primary Language of Poetry in the 1940s*, University of California Publications in English, volume 19, no. 3. Berkeley: University of California Press, 1951.

Miller, James E., Jr. *The American Quest for a Supreme Fiction: Whitman's Legacy in the Personal Epic*. Chicago: University of Chicago Press, 1979.

Miller, J. Hillis. *Poets of Reality: Six Twentieth-Century Writers*. Cambridge: Harvard University Press, 1965.

Miller, R. Baxter, ed. *Black American Literature and Humanism*. Lexington: University Press of Kentucky, 1981.

Monroe, Harriet. *A Poet's Life: Seventy Years in a Changing World*. New York: Macmillan, 1938.

Moore, Marianne. *Predilections*. New York: Viking, 1955.

Morgan, A. E. *The Beginnings of Modern American Poetry*. London: Longmans, Green, 1946.

Morton, Lena Beatrice. *Negro Poetry in America*. Boston: Stratford, 1925.

Mumford, Lewis. *The Brown Decades: A Study of the Arts in America, 1865-1895*, revised edition. New York: Dover, 1955.

Munson, Gorham B. *Destinations: A Canvass of American Literature Since 1900*. New York: Sears, 1928.

O'Connor, William Van. *Sense and Sensibility in Modern Poetry*. Chicago: Chicago University Press, 1948.

Parry, Albert. *Garrets and Pretenders: A History of Bohemianism in America,* revised edition, with a new chapter by Harry T. Moore. New York: Dover, 1960.

Paz, Octavio. *The Bow and the Lyre,* translated by Ruth L. C. Simms. Austin: University of Texas Press, 1973.

Paz. *Children of the Mire; Modern Poetry from Romanticism to the Avant-Garde,* translated by Rachel Phillips. Cambridge: Harvard University Press, 1974.

Pearce, Roy Harvey. *The Continuity of American Poetry.* Princeton: Princeton University Press, 1961.

Perkins, David. *A History of Modern Poetry from the 1890's to the High Modernist Mode.* Cambridge: Harvard University Press, 1976.

Perloff, Marjorie. *The Poetics of Indeterminacy: Rimbaud to Cage.* Princeton: Princeton University Press, 1981.

Pinsky, Robert. *The Situation of Poetry: Contemporary Poetry and its Tradition.* Princeton: Princeton University Press, 1976.

Plimpton, George, ed. *Writers at Work: The Paris Review Interviews,* series 2-5. New York: Viking, 1963-1981.

Poggioli, Renato. *The Theory of the Avant-Garde,* translated by Gerald Fitzgerald. Cambridge: Harvard University Press, 1968.

Pound, Ezra. *Literary Essays of Ezra Pound,* edited, with an introduction, by T. S. Eliot. London: Faber & Faber, 1954.

Pound. *Make It New: Essays.* London: Faber & Faber, 1934.

Pound. *Selected Prose, 1909-1965,* edited by William Cookson. New York: New Directions, 1973.

Pratt, John Clark. *The Meaning of Modern Poetry.* Garden City: Doubleday, 1962.

Pratt, William, ed. *The Imagist Poem: Modern Poetry in Miniature.* New York: Dutton, 1963.

Press, John. *The Chequer'd Shade. Reflections on Obscurity in Poetry.* London: Oxford University Press, 1958.

Pritchard, William H. *Lives of the Modern Poets.* New York: Oxford University Press, 1980.

Putnam, Samuel. *Paris Was Our Mistress.* New York: Viking, 1947.

Quinn, Sister M. Bernetta. *The Metamorphic Tradition in Modern Poetry: Essays on the Work of Ezra Pound, Wallace Stevens, William Carlos Williams, T. S. Eliot, Hart Crane, Randall Jarrell and William Butler Yeats.* New Brunswick: Rutgers University Press, 1955.

Raban, Jonathan. *The Society of the Poem.* London: Harrap, 1971.

Raiziss, Sona. *The Metaphysical Passion: Seven Modern American Poets and the Seventeenth Century Tradition.* Philadelphia: University of Pennsylvania Press, 1952.

Rajan, B., ed. *Modern American Poetry,* Focus 5. London: Dobson, 1950.

Ransom, John Crowe. *Beating the Bushes; Selected Essays, 1941-1970.* New York: New Directions, 1972.

Ransom. *The New Criticism.* Norfolk, Conn.: New Directions, 1941.

Ransom. *The World's Body,* revised edition. Baton Rouge: Louisiana State University Press, 1968.

Ransom, Allen Tate, Donald Davidson, and others. *I'll Take My Stand: The South and the Agrarian Tradition, By Twelve Southerners.* New York & London: Harper, 1930.

Redding, Jay Saunders. *To Make a Poet Black.* Chapel Hill: University of North Carolina Press, 1939.

Reid, B. L. *The Man from New York: John Quinn and His Friends.* New York: Oxford University Press, 1968.

Revell, Peter. *Quest in Modern American Poetry.* Totowa, N.J.: Barnes & Noble, 1981.

Rexroth, Kenneth. *American Poetry in the Twentieth Century.* New York: Herder & Herder, 1971.

Rexroth. *Bird in the Bush: Obvious Essays.* New York: New Directions, 1959.

Rittenhouse, Jessie B. *My House of Life: An Autobiography.* Boston & New York: Houghton Mifflin, 1934.

Rittenhouse, *The Younger American Poets.* Boston: Little, Brown, 1904.

Rollins, Charlemae. *Famous American Negro Poets.* New York: Dodd, Mead, 1965.

Rosenfeld, Paul. *Port of New York: Essays on Fourteen American Moderns.* New York: Harcourt, Brace, 1924.

Rosenthal, M. L. *The Modern Poets: A Critical Introduction.* New York: Oxford University Press, 1960.

Rubin, Louis D. *The Wary Fugitives: Four Poets and the South.* Baton Rouge: Louisiana State University Press, 1978.

Rukeyser, Muriel. *The Life of Poetry.* New York: Current Books, 1949.

Schauch, Margaret. *Modern English and American Poetry: Techniques and Ideologies.* London: Watts, 1956.

Schwartz, Delmore. *Selected Essays,* edited by Donald A. Dike and David H. Zucker. Chicago: University of Chicago Press, 1970.

Scully, James, ed. *Modern Poetics.* New York: McGraw-Hill, 1965.

Sergeant, Howard. *Tradition in the Making of Modern Poetry,* volume 1. London: Britannicus Liber, 1951.

Shapiro, Karl. *In Defense of Ignorance.* New York: Random House, 1960.

Shapiro, ed. *Prose Keys to Modern Poetry.* New York & London: Harper & Row, 1962.

Smoller, Sanford. *Adrift Among Geniuses: Robert McAlmon, Writer and Publisher of the Twenties.* University Park & London: Pennsylvania State University Press, 1975.

Spears, Monroe K. *Dionysus and the City: Modernism in Twentieth-Century Poetry.* New York: Oxford University Press, 1970.

Stanford, Donald E. *Revolution and Convention in Modern Poetry: Studies in Ezra Pound, T. S. Eliot, Wallace Stevens, Edwin Arlington Robinson and Yvor Winters.* Newark: University of Delaware Press, 1983.

Stauffer, Donald. *A Short History of American Poetry.* New York: Dutton, 1974.

Stead, C. K. *The New Poetic: Yeats to Eliot.* London: Hutchinson, 1964.

Stepanchev, Stephen. *American Poetry Since 1945: A Critical Survey.* New York: Harper & Row, 1965.

Stewart, John L. *The Burden of Time: The Fugitives and Agrarians; the Nashville Groups of the 1920's and 1930's, and the Writing of John Crowe Ransom, Allen Tate, and Robert Penn Warren.* Princeton: Princeton University Press, 1965.

Straumann, Heinrich. *American Literature in the Twentieth Century,* second revised edition. New York: Harper & Row, 1965.

Sutton, Walter. *American Free Verse: The Modern Revolution of Poetry.* New York: New Directions, 1973.

Sypher, Wylie. *Loss of Self in Modern Literature and Art.* New York: Random House, 1962.

Sypher. *Rococo to Cubism in Art and Literature.* New York: Random House, 1960.

Tashjian, Dickran. *Skyscraper Primitives: Dada and the American Avant-Garde, 1920-1925.* Middletown, Conn.: Wesleyan University Press, 1975.

Tate, Allen. *Essays of Four Decades.* Chicago: Swallow, 1968.

Tate. *The Man of Letters in the Modern World, Selected Essays: 1928-1955.* New York: Meridian/London: Thames & Hudson, 1955.

Tate. *Memoirs and Opinions, 1926-1974.* Chicago: Swallow, 1975.

Tate. *Reactionary Essays on Poetry and Ideas.* New York & London: Scribners, 1936.

Tate. *Reason in Madness: Critical Essays.* New York: Putnam's, 1941.

Taupin, René. *L'Influence du symbolisme français sur la poésie americaine (1890-1920).* Paris: Champion, 1929.

Taylor, Carole A. *A Poetics of Seeing: The Implications of Visual Form in Modern Poetry.* New York & London: Garland, 1985.

Tietjens, Eunice. *The World at My Shoulder.* New York: Macmillan, 1938.

Turner, Darwin. *In a Minor Chord: Three Afro-American Writers and Their Search for Identity.* Carbondale & Edwardsville: Southern Illinois University Press, 1971.

Unger, Leonard. *The Man in the Name: Essays on the Experience of Poetry.* Minneapolis: University of Minnesota Press, 1956.

Untermeyer, Louis. *American Poetry Since 1900.* New York: Holt, 1923.

Untermeyer. *From Another World: The Autobiography of Louis Untermeyer.* New York: Harcourt, Brace, 1939.

Van Doren, Mark. *Autobiography.* New York: Harcourt, Brace, 1958.

Vendler, Helen. *Part of Nature, Part of Us: Modern American Poets.* Cambridge: Harvard University Press, 1979.

Vickery, John. *The Literary Impact of the Golden Bough.* Princeton: Princeton University Press, 1973.

Waggoner, Hyatt H. *American Poets, from the Puritans to the Present.* Boston: Houghton Mifflin, 1968.

Waggoner. *The Heel of Elohim: Science and Values in Modern American Poetry.* Norman: University of Oklahoma Press, 1950.

Wagner, Jean. *Black Poets of the United States from Paul Laurence Dunbar to Langston Hughes,* translated by Kenneth Douglas. Urbana: University of Illinois Press, 1973.

Walker, Robert H. *The Poet and the Gilded Age: Social Themes in Late Nineteenth Century Verse.* Philadelphia: University of Pennsylvania Press, 1963.

Warren, Robert Penn. *A Plea in Mitigation: Modern Poetry and the End of an Era.* Macon, Ga.: Wesleyan College, 1966.

Wasserstrom, William. *The Time of "The Dial."* Syracuse: Syracuse University Press, 1963.

Weatherhead, A. Kingsley. *The Edge of the Image: Marianne Moore, William Carlos Williams, and Some Other Poets.* Seattle: University of Washington Press, 1967.

Weaver, Mike. *William Carlos Williams: The American Background.* Cambridge: Cambridge University Press, 1971.

Wees, William C. *Vorticism and the English Avant-Garde.* Toronto: University of Toronto Press, 1972.

Weirick, Bruce. *From Whitman to Sandburg in American Poetry.* New York: Macmillan, 1924.

Wells, Henry W. *The American Way of Poetry.* New York: Columbia University Press, 1943.

Welsh, Andrew. *Roots of Lyric: Primitive Poetry and Modern Poetics.* Princeton: Princeton University Press, 1978.

Wertheim, Arthur Frank. *The New York Little Renaissance: Iconoclasm, Modernism, and Nationalism in American Culture, 1908-1917.* New York: New York University Press, 1976.

Wheelwright, Philip. *Metaphor & Reality.* Bloomington: Indiana University Press, 1962.

Wickes, George. *Americans in Paris.* Garden City: Doubleday, 1969.

Williams, Ellen. *Harriet Monroe and the Poetry Renaissance: The First Ten Years of* Poetry *1912-1922.* Urbana: University of Illinois Press, 1977.

Williams, Jonathan. *The Magpie's Bagpipe. Selected Essays.* San Francisco: North Point Press, 1982.

Williams, William Carlos. *The Autobiography of William Carlos Williams.* New York: Random House, 1951.

Williams. *The Embodiment of Knowledge,* edited by Ron Loewinson. New York: New Directions, 1974.

Williams. *Selected Essays.* New York: Random House, 1954.

Wilson, Edmund. *Axel's Castle: A Study in the Imaginative Literature of 1870-1930.* New York & London: Scribners, 1931.

Winters, Yvor. *In Defense of Reason.* Denver: University of Denver Press, 1947.

Winters. *On Modern Poets.* Cleveland & New York: Meridian/World, 1959.

Wright, George T. *The Poet in the Poem: The Personae of Eliot, Yeats, and Pound.* Berkeley: University of California Press, 1960.

Yatron, Michael. *America's Literary Revolt.* New York: Philosophical Library, 1959.

Young, James O. *Black Writers of the Thirties.* Baton Rouge: Louisiana State University Press, 1973.

Zukofsky, Louis. *Prepositions: The Collected Critical Essays,* enlarged edition. Berkeley: University of California Press, 1981.

Contributors

Shelley Armitage ....*West Texas State University*

Harriette Cuttino Buchanan ....*Appalachian State University*

Daniel J. Cahill ....*University of Northern Iowa*

Dennis Camp ....*Sangamon State University*

John Xiros Cooper ....*Mount Royal College*

Sharon G. Dean ....*Indiana University*

Alexander Globe ....*University of British Columbia*

Donald J. Greiner ....*University of South Carolina*

Dalton Gross...*Southwest Texas State University*

William Harmon...........................*University of North Carolina at Chapel Hill*

James A. Hart ....*University of British Columbia*

Paula L. Hart ....*University of British Columbia*

E. Claire Healey ....*Montclair State College*

William G. Holzberger...*Bucknell University*

Laura Ingram...*Columbia, South Carolina*

Philip K. Jason.......................................*United States Naval Academy*

Nancy Carol Joyner ....*Western Carolina University*

Virginia M. Kouidis ....*Auburn University*

JoAnna Lathrop.....................................*University of Nebraska at Lincoln*

Michele J. Leggott...*Auckland University*

Robert K. Martin..*Concordia University*

Jeanne-Marie A. Miller ....*Howard University*

Joseph Miller ....*Vancouver, British Columbia*

Russell Murphy......................................*University of Arkansas at Little Rock*

Penelope Niven..*Earlham College*

Colin Partridge ....*University of Victoria*

Alice Hall Petry.....................................*Rhode Island School of Design*

Peter Quartermain ....*University of British Columbia*

Peter Revell ....*Westfield College, London*

William H. Robinson...*Rhode Island College*

Anne E. Rowe ....*Florida State University*

Herbert K. Russell ....*John A. Logan College*

Alfred W. Satterthwaite..*Haverford College*

Joseph W. Slade ....*Long Island University*

Susan Sutton Smith ....*State University of New York College at Oneonta*

Anne H. Tayler ....*Yukon College*

Marshall Van Deusen ....*University of California, Riverside*

Meredith Yearsley...*Vancouver, British Columbia*

Cumulative Index

Dictionary of Literary Biography, Volumes 1-54
Dictionary of Literary Biography Yearbook, 1980-1985
Dictionary of Literary Biography Documentary Series, Volumes 1-4

Cumulative Index

DLB before number: *Dictionary of Literary Biography*, Volumes 1-54
Y before number: *Dictionary of Literary Biography Yearbook*, 1980-1985
DS before number: *Dictionary of Literary Biography Documentary Series*, Volumes 1-4

C

E

H

Cumulative Index

I

K

L

Cumulative Index

Cumulative Index

N

P

Cumulative Index

Q

R

Y

Z